CONCISE ENCYCLOPEDIA OF
INDUSTRIAL RELATIONS

Concise Encyclopedia of Industrial Relations

with Bibliography

ARTHUR MARSH

Gower Press

Published by
Gower Press, Teakfield Limited,
Westmead, Farnborough, Hants., England

ISBN 0 566 02095 5

Typeset by Inforum Limited, Portsmouth
Printed in Great Britain by Biddles Limited, Guildford, Surrey

Preface

This *Concise Encyclopedia* originated in 1973 as the *Dictionary of Industrial Relations*. For the present version the text has been completely revised, up-dated, enlarged and reset. The number of entries has been increased by almost one-fifth and the number of references to books and articles to almost 1,200.

The notion of compiling a work of this kind was conceived more than ten years ago when I was engaged in research for the Donovan Royal Commission on Trade Unions and Employers' Associations. Evidence submitted to the Commission seemed to provide a wealth of information which could readily be used as a basis for a book of reference. The very existence of the Commission suggested a growing importance of industrial relations in the life of the nation which has been confirmed by the ill-fated Industrial Relations Act and its more traditional successors the Trade Union and Labour Relations Act 1974 and the Employment Protection Act 1975 with their attendant legislation covering so many aspects of industrial practice.

The plan and method of the *Encyclopedia* do not differ materially from those of its predecessor. Finding one's way about in industrial relations demands a knowledge of terms, expressions, practices and institutions. New terms are being coined day by day, trade unions and employers' associations and their joint bodies change their names at less frequent intervals. This volume embodies them as they might be found to exist in the late Spring of 1978. Reissues of the *Encyclopedia* will attempt to bring them up-to-date from time to time.

Each entry contains cross-references in **bold type** and each includes, wherever possible, a written source from which the term or expression or institution involved can be illustrated, its origin examined and its meaning and significance further investigated. The coverage of books and articles is not intended to be comprehensive, but it will be found to be a useful guide and a source from which other information can often be obtained. The sources used are those which are likely to be the most readily available to the reader. Alas! there are all too few specialised collections on industrial relations in this country. Those interested in developing such might do worse than take this volume as their basis if they wish to relate principally to Britain or the United Kingdom. International entries have been included from the United States of America, from the Federal Republic of Germany, from France, Sweden and elsewhere, only when these appear to have a direct relation to the British scene.

The *Encyclopedia* owes a debt of gratitude to those, too numerous to mention, who have so freely given the information on which it is based. As Dr Johnson implied in a compilation infinitely more distinguished, what can be said of a lexicographer other than that he is 'a writer of dictionaries, a harmless drudge'? The habit of reading helps, insatiable curiosity is useful and devoted assistance essential. In this latter requirement the burden of the day has rested with Jess, my wife, who so carefully ordered the material, and with Jenni Atkinson, whose patience in checking references seems, happily, to be inexhaustible. Faults and omissions are my own. Like the worthy Doctor I must plead, if found in error, one excuse only — 'Ignorance, pure ignorance'.

St Edmund Hall,   AIM
    Oxford.
September 1978

A

AAOCST. Amalgamated Association of Operative Cotton Spinners and Twiners; see **Spinners and Twiners, Amalgamated Association of Operative Cotton.**

ABS. Association of Broadcasting Staff; see **Broadcasting Staff, Association of.**

ABT. Association of Building Technicians; see **Building Technicians, Association of.**

ABSENCE; also **absence from work** and **absenteeism.** The failure of workers to report for work. Terms susceptible to many different definitions involving, *inter alia,* problems of defining **lateness** (q.v.). The British Institute of Management (*Absence from Work: Recording and Analysis,* BIM, 1955) defines **absence** as 'lost time, whatever the cause or reason given, of over one-hour's duration' (thus limiting lateness to absence of less than one hour), and **absenteeism** as 'the kind of absence which a reasonable person, having regard to all the existing circumstances, may regard as avoidable'. Difficulties of definition and measurement also lie in distinguishing different reasons for absence and the degree of responsibility to be attributed to the absentee. Hence it can, as in the BIM definition above, be assumed to include substantially any failure to attend work; others think it proper to exclude certain agreed or inevitable absences, e.g. holidays, **sickness absence** or absences with reasons given, or may make other conditions designed to separate voluntary from involuntary absence, or avoidable from unavoidable absence. Frederick J. Gaudet, *Solving the Problems of Employees' Absence,* American Management Association, Research Study 57, 1963, lists 41 formulae for measuring absence, including the **Blue Monday Index** (q.v.). Concern over absenteeism became acute during the 1939-45 War, and employers in Britain frequently express concern that it is rising, especially it is alleged as a result of current levels of social security benefits. In 1970 a Confederation of British Industry study (*Absenteeism,* CBI, 1970) concluded that benefits might have a significant effect at the lower end of the wage scale, but that employers might be wise to diagnose and treat their own individual factory problems; see also: Hilde Behrend, *Absence under Full Employment,* University of Birmingham, 1951, R.B. Buzzard, 'Attendance and Absence in Industry; the Nature of Evidence', *British Journal of Sociology,* Vol. 5, No. 3, 1954; J.P.W. Hughes, 'Sickness Absence Recording in Industry', *British Journal of Industrial Medicine,* Vol. 9, No. 4, 1952 and L.J. Handy, 'Absenteeism and Attendance in the British Coalmining Industry', *British Journal of Industrial Relations,* Vol. 6, No. 1, March 1968, pp. 27-50, and R.M. Jones, *Absenteeism in Britain,* Manpower Papers No. 4, HMSO, 1971.

ABSENCE FROM WORK; see **absence.**

ABSENTEEISM. Persistent or intermittent absence conforming to a pattern suggesting either that absence was avoidable (see **absence** above), or more frequently, that it constituted behaviour lacking in appreciation of the work situation, patriotic duty, etc.

ABUSIVE DISMISSAL. The termination of a contract of employment by an employer in circumstances which are lawful, but in which dismissal may be socially unwarranted or for which insufficient reasons have been adduced. Some legal systems make dismissals unlawful, even when the provisions as to notice have been complied with, if an abuse of managerial power is involved; see C.D.Drake, *Labour Law,* Sweet and Maxwell, 1973, 2nd ed. The **Industrial Relations Act 1971** introduced the concept of abusive dismissal into English law by providing legal redress for **unfair dismissal** (q.v.) in circumstances not previously covered by the concept of **wrongful dismissal.**

ACAS. Advisory, Conciliation and Arbitration Service (q.v.).

ACCESSION RATE; see **labour turnover.**

ACCIDENT. Commonly defined as an event without apparent cause, an unintentional act, resulting in injury or mishap; among those investigating or seeking to reduce industrial or other accidents, defined as involving more than uncontrollable chance: 'an unplanned event, being the result of some non-adjustive act on the part of the individual [which] may or may not result in injury', A.G. Arbous and J.E. Kerrich 'Accident Statistics and the Concept of Accident Proneness', *Biometrics,* Vol. 7, No. 4, 1951, p. 340); an event involving indications, many or fewer, that it is 'accidental', e.g. expectedness or unexpectedness, avoidability or unavoidability, intention or unintention etc. (see E.A. Suchman, 'On Accident Behaviour', in *Behavioural Approaches to Accident Research*, Association for the Aid of Crippled Children, New York, 1961 and 'A Conceptual Analysis of the Accident Phenomenon', *Social Problems*, Vol. 8, No. 3, 1961, p. 241). Among the available definitions some exclude and some include industrial diseases, e.g. dermatitis, pneumoconiosis, asbestosis, scrotal cancer etc., the latter therefore tacitly accepting the familiar association of 'health and safety' and the problem of duration, i.e. that such diseases may originally have been caused by exposures which, like those involved in cuts and bruises, may have been 'accidental'. For a study of the available statistics on both these subjects; see P.J. Shipp and A.S. Sutton, *A Study of the Statistics relating to Safety and Health at Work*, Committee on Safety and Health at Work, Research Paper, HMSO, 1972. The most influential theory in accident research has been that of **accident proneness**, i.e. the theory that some people are more liable to accidents than others due to innate personal characteristics (see, for example, C.A. Drake 'Accident Proneness: a hypothesis', *Character and Personality*, Vol. 8, 1942, W.L. Cresswell and P. Froggatt, *The Causation of Bus Driver Accidents*, OUP, 1963 and M.S.Shulzinger, 'A Closer Look at Accident Proneness', *National Safety News*, Vol. 69, No. 6, 1954), but other theories lay emphasis on adjustment and stress, unconscious motivation and situations (see A.R. Hale and M. Hale, *A Review of the Industrial Accident Research Literature*, Committee on Safety and Health at Work Research Paper, HMSO, 1972); also **Robens Report** (*Committee on Safety and Health at Work*, 1970-72, Cmnd. 5034, July 1972), **notifiable accident**, and International Labour Office, *Encyclopaedia of Occupational Health and Safety*, ILO, Geneva, 2 vols, 1972; also **Health and Safety at Work Act 1974**.

ACCIDENT BENEFIT; see **sickness and accident benefit, injury benefit.**

ACCIDENT BOOK. A book required to be kept by every owner (being an employer) of any mine or quarry, or of any premises to which the Factories Act 1961 applies and every employer of ten or more persons on the same premises under the Social Security (Claims and Payments) Regulations 1975, S.I. 1975, No. 560. The order requires that the particulars of any accident, and the name, address and occupation of injured persons and other details shall be entered, and the book preserved for three years after the last entry is made; see also **notifiable accident.**

ACCIDENT PRONENESS; see **accident.**

ACROSS-THE-BOARD INCREASE; see **across-the-board settlement.**

ACROSS-THE-BOARD SETTLEMENT. A settlement on wages or conditions of work affecting all workers involved in the **bargaining unit** concerned in the agreement; hence **across-the-board increase,** an increase in pay giving a fixed and common monetary or percentage increase to all workers, as distinct from a **tapered increase, stepped increase** or **pro-tanto increase** (q.v.). Across-the-board increases giving the same monetary increase to all grades have the effect of maintaining **differentials;** percentage increases widen them. Attempts at wage structuring within an industry or plant sometimes seek to adjust the effects of such increases to give special attention to some groups rather than to others, e.g. to lower paid workers; see for example, **Engineering Package Deal Agreements,** and **low pay.**

ACTION CENTRED LEADERSHIP. An approach to leadership training associated with the name of John Adair of the **Industrial Society** and derived from military practice. It lays emphasis on the positive responsibilities of the leader towards the needs of his subordinates, dividing these into three overlapping groups: 'task needs' (the need to achieve results by establishing clear tasks and objectives); 'group maintenance needs' (the need to achieve cohesion by setting appropriate standards, e.g. of quality and safety); and 'individual needs' (the need to meet the requirements of the individuals in respect of training, lines of authority, grievance handling, etc.).

ACTION RESEARCH. A type of applied research. Definitions of action research differ, though all include the notion that although it may use scientific method as far as possible, it is not primarily concerned to establish theoretical propositions or scientific principles, these being subordinate to more immediate and practical considerations of social change. This may be expressed more or less neutrally, and more or less narrowly, e.g. Michael Argyle (*The Scientific Study of Social Behaviour*, Methuen, 1957, p. 13) '... any investigation in which social change is the prior object and the discovery of scientific results a subordinate one'; Social Science Research Council, 1970, 'Research commissioned to monitor and evaluate the operations of specifically implemented policy schemes so as to enable policy makers and administrators to assess the effectiveness of such schemes'; more broadly, Duncan Mitchell, *A Dictionary of Sociology*, Routledge and Kegan Paul, 1968, ' ... investigation of a kind oriented to the ends of altering and improving a social situation or helping people in need'; and Wendell L. French and Cecil H. Bell, *Organisation Development*. Prentice-Hall, 1973, pp. 84-95, research attempting to 'bring together in a single Co-operative Venture the skills and resources of both men of science and action; see **organisation research.**

ACTIVITY RATE, sometimes known as **participation rate,** the percentage of the total population in a given age group which is in the **working population** (q.v.); or sometimes the proportion of the civilian employees including registered unemployed (e.g. in National Economic Development Council, *Conditions Favourable to Faster Growth*, HMSO, 1963, p. 15). Most recent activity rates for Great Britain and projections to 1986 are given in 'New projections of future labour force', *Department of Employment Gazette*, June 1977, pp. 587-92. These suggest that the activity rates of males and non-married females will be much the same in 1986 as in 1976 but that those for all females will rise from 46.3 per cent to 48.0 per cent. The National Economic Development Council, op. cit., has noted that low activity rates may, to some extent, be regarded as an indication of **concealed unemployment.**

ACTIVITY SAMPLING. A work study technique in which a large number of instantaneous observations are made over a period of time of a group of machines, processes or workers. Each observation records what is happening at that instant and the percentage of observations recorded for a particular activity or delay is a measure of the percentage of the time during which that activity occurs (British Standards Institution, *Glossary of Terms Used in Work Study*, BS 3138, 1969, No. 31007). Also known as **ratio-delay study,**

random observation method, observation ratio study, snap-reading method and **work sampling.** Also **rated activity sampling,** an extension of activity sampling in which a rating is applied to each work element so that the work content may be established in addition to the proportion of time occupied by other activities and delays; see International Labour Office, *Introduction to Work Study*, 1969, Ch. 21, and B.L.Hansen, *Work Sampling for Modern Management*, Prentice-Hall, 1960.

ACTORS' EQUITY ASSOCIATION, BRITISH (EQUITY). A trade union for actors formed by leading members of the profession in December 1929 following the collapse of two previous organisations, the Actors' Association and the Stage Guild. Equity has based its policy upon the **Equity Shop Clause** and the **Casting Agreement,** the former requiring the employer to accept that 'the Artist shall be required to work only with members of the British Actors' Equity Association', and the latter (the first of which came into operation in the West End in 1964 and extended since to films, ITV, the provincial theatre etc.) designed to establish control over newcomers to the business. The union absorbed the Variety Artistes' Federation in 1966. *Address*: 8 Harley Street, London W1N 2AB. *Tel*: 01-636 6367. *TUC Affiliated Membership, 1977*: 24,263.

ACTSS. Association of Clerical, Technical and Supervisory Staffs; see **Transport and General Workers' Union.**

ACTT. Association of Cinematograph, Television and Allied Technicians; see **Cinematograph, Television and Allied Technicians, Association of.**

ADDED HOURS. The notional numbers of additional hours worked as a result of payment for overtime at premium rates, e.g. six hours overtime at time-and-one-half attracts pay for nine hours, three of them 'added hours'.

ADDED VALUE. A measure of productivity expressed in financial terms; the extent to which the saleable value of raw materials can be enhanced by the manufacturing process, as in the following formula: $AV = a - b \pm c$; where AV = Added Value, a = value of sales, b = value of productive materials and c = changes in the level of finished stocks and work-in-progress. The concept is used in such payment schemes as the **Rucker Plan** (q.v.).

ADDITIONAL DAYS. A term used in the engineering industry and introduced in 1965 to distinguish between Bank and other paid holidays and the two additional days' paid holiday provided for in the terms of the agreement of 22 December 1964. Additional days are, under the agreement, to be arranged by mutual consent according to the practice of each district, carry no premium payment for work done on them, and are not subject to qualifying conditions; see **qualifying days,** Engineering Handbook of National Agreements, 2.41.

ADMINISTRATION OF ESTATES (SMALL PAYMENTS) ACT 1965; see **nomination procedure.**

ADMINISTRATIVE MANAGEMENT, INSTITUTE OF (IAM) formerly the Office Management Association and the Institute of Office Management. An organisation claiming to be the only British organisation specialising in problems of management in the office and the study of office organisation and practice. It had divisions dealing with **O and M** (q.v.), with Electronic Data Processing and with Office Supervisors, and is notable for its contributions on the grading of office work and for its **Clerical Salaries Analysis,** first undertaken in 1942 and repeated since on alternative years. *Address*: Ironstore House, 205 High Street, Beckenham, Kent. *Tel*: 01-658 0171.

ADMINISTRATIVE, TECHNICAL AND CLERICAL STAFF or **ATC employees.** A group of staff workers for purposes of remuneration in the public sector, and especially in local government. For the purposes of earnings surveys in the public and private sectors (see **earnings**) defined by the Department of Employment as including managers, superintendents and works' foremen; research, experimental, development, technical and design employees (other than operatives); draughtsmen and tracers; and office (including works' office) employees and salesmen and representatives, but excluding directors paid by fee, working proprietors and managers remunerated predominantly by a share of profits.

ADMISSION TO A TRADE UNION; see **membership of a trade union.**

ADVERSARY SITUATION; see **negotiation.**

ADVERSARY TRADE UNIONS. Defined by J.Bergman, O.Jacobi and W.Muller-Jentsch (*Gewerkschaften in der Bundesrepublik*, Frankfurt am Main, 1975) as those which attempt to realise their objectives by immediate wage demands and strategies, ignore the needs o the national economy and make demands based upon market conditions and their own current strength; contrasted with 'co-operative trade unions' which try to protect the interests of their members by tailoring both wage demands and strategy to the state and the economy and the needs of growth: see also **negotiation.**

ADVISORY COMMITTEE ON WOMEN'S EMPLOYMENT; see **Women's Employment, Advisory Committee on.**

ADVISORY, CONCILIATION AND ARBITRATION SERVICE (ACAS). An agency established by Royal Warrant on 2 September 1974 and made statutory under s. 1 of the **Employment Protection Act 1975** on 1 January 1976. The Service is charged with the general duty of promoting the improvement of industrial relations (and in particular the extension of collective bargaining) and with the reform of collective bargaining machinery. It is operated by a Council consisting of a Chairman and nine members, three of whom are independent, three representatives of employers and three representatives of trade unions. The work of ACAS falls broadly into five areas, none of them wholly new, but now for the first time brought together into a single agency independent of ministerial control. First, the Service carries on the **conciliation, mediation** and **arbitration** functions previously exercised in collective disputes by the Department of Employment, leaving only **Courts of Inquiry** under the Industrial Courts Act 1919 as the formal province of the Secretary of State for Employment, and adding to these functions the former **Industrial Arbitration Board** under the title **Central Arbitration Committee** (q.v. also **collective conciliation**). Second, it assumes the role of **individual conciliation** in cases of alleged **unfair dismissal** (q.v.), on equal pay complaints by individuals under the **Equal Pay Act 1970,** on complaints of **discrimination** under the **Sex Discrimination Act 1975** (s. 64) and the **Race Relations Act 1976** (s. 55) and, from 1 June 1976, issues arising from the

Employment Protection Act: payment during **medical suspension, maternity leave** and trade union membership and activities, time off in the event of redundancy to look for work or arrange training, and written statements of reasons for dismissal. Third, ACAS has taken over the short-term advisory work previously done by the **Manpower and Productivity Service** between 1969 and 1972 and subsequently by the **Conciliation and Advisory Service** and the longer term inquiry functions originally developed by the **Commission on Industrial Relations** established as a result of the **Donovan Royal Commission on Trade Unions and Employers' Associations 1965-1968**, and now disbanded. Finally, and most controversially, the Service is responsible, under ss. 11-16 of the Employment Protection Act (see **Section 11 Reference**) for handling recognition references lodged by independent trade unions, first by conciliation, then by inquiry and subsequently by discussions with the parties and by final report. The Service's collective conciliation and arbitration has greatly increased since 1974 and it is also responsible for **Codes of Practice** in industrial relations (q.v.); see also **ACAS**, *Annual Report 1976. Address*: Cleland House, Page Street, London SW1P 4ND. *Tel*: 01-222 4383.

AEF. Amalgamated Union of Engineering and Foundry Workers; see **Engineering and Foundry Workers, Amalgamated Union of.**

AEU; see **Amalgamated Engineering Union.**

AFL (or AF of L); see **American Federation of Labor.**

AFL-CIO; see **American Federation of Labor-Congress of Industrial Organisations.**

AFTERNOON SHIFT or backshift. The second shift in a **three shift** or **continuous shift system,** falling in the afternoon, and followed by the **night shift**, third shift, or **graveyard** or **lobster shift.**

AGENCY SHOP. A provision of a collective agreement originating in the United States and designed to eliminate **free-riders** (q.v.), non-union members in a **bargaining unit** being required to pay the union a sum equal to the union's fees and dues as a condition of remaining in employment. The US Supreme Court, in the case of

Retail Clerks, Local 1625 v. Schermerhorn No. 368, June 1963, decided that the agency shop was legal under Section 8(a)(3) of the **Taft-Hartley Act**, but that it was within the authority of states to outlaw it under Section 14(b). The agency shop has not traditionally been a British practice, although there have been instances in which it has been informally agreed between trade unions and managements that to deal with the free-rider situation non-members should donate the equivalent of union dues to agreed charitable purposes. In making **pre-entry closed shop** agreements and arrangements void, and in establishing the legal right of individuals not to be members of trade unions or organisations of workers (see **closed shop**), the **Industrial Relations Act 1971** (s. 11) provided that employers and registered **trade unions** might make agency shop agreements (if necessary after a successful ballot conducted by the **Commission on Industrial Relations**). These provisions were repeated in the **Trade Union and Labour Relations Act 1974** (q.v.).

AGENCY SHOP AGREEMENT; see **agency shop.**

AGGRO. Action in industrial relations designed by one party to put pressure on the other; trouble thought by one party in collective bargaining to have been engineered or stirred up by the other to obtain a negotiating advantage; abbreviation of 'aggravation'.

AGRICULTURAL AND ALLIED WORKERS, NATIONAL UNION OF (NUAAW). A trade union for agricultural workers taking its present title as a result of a decision of 1968 and in recognition of its interests in industries ancillary to agriculture. The union was founded by George Edwards as the Eastern Counties Agricultural Labourers' and Small Holders' Union in 1906 and followed many unsuccessful attempts to form permanent organisations for agricultural workers, including Joseph Arch's National Agricultural Labourers' Union founded in 1872, none of which survived. It changed its name to the National Agricultural Labourers' and Rurual Workers' Union in 1909 and to National Union of Agricultural Workers in 1920; see Reg Groves, *Sharpen the Sickle!*, The Porcupine Press, 1949, *Address*: Headland House, 308 Gray's Inn Road, London WC1X 8DS. *Tel*: 01-278

7801. *TUC Affiliated Membership, 1977*: 85,000.

AGRICULTURAL WAGES ACT 1948. An Act currently in force which consolidated without amendment, previous legislation on the subject of agricultural wages in England and Wales. A Wages Board to fix a minimum wage in agriculture was first established under the Corn Production Act 1917. This remained until 1921, when the Corn Production Act was repealed, and was replaced in 1924 by an Agricultural Wages (Regulation) Act which set up County Wages Committees and an Agricultural Wages Board for England and Wales. From 1924 to 1940 the former fixed the minimum rates of wages, overtime rates etc., and the latter acted in an advisory capacity and made the necessary Orders. During the war the Wages Board became responsible for fixing a national minimum wage and county committees settled county rates, the transfer of wage fixing machinery from the counties to the Agricultural Wages Board being made permanent in 1947. These arrangements, and that of the Agricultural (Miscellaneous Provisions) Act 1944, which empowered the Board to fix a time rate basis for piecework and to apply the **Holidays With Pay Act 1938** to farmworkers included in it, were incorporated in the 1948 Act. Subsequently the definition of 'London' in the Act has been altered (London Government Order 1965, s. 3(12)), the Board empowered to introduce a sick pay scheme for agricultural workers (Agricultural Act 1967, s. 67), and the Minister empowered to extend the function of agricultural wages committees to deal with matters arising from a wages structure in the industry (Agricultural (Miscellaneous Provisions) Act 1968, s. 46). A new wage structure in which premium rates are applied for certain qualifications, skill and positions of responsibility came into force in May 1972. There are forty-six County Agricultural Wages Committees, and the Agricultural Wages Board consists of five independent members appointed by the Minister of Agriculture, Fisheries and Food, eight members nominated by the National Farmers' Union, and eight representatives of workers (five NUAAW and three TGWU).

AGRICULTURAL WAGES BOARD; see **Agricultural Wages Act 1948.**

AGRICULTURAL WAGES (SCOTLAND) ACT 1949. An Act similar to the **Agricultural Wages Act 1948** and applying to Scotland.

AGSRO. Association of Government Supervisors and Radio Officers; see **Government Supervisors and Radio Officers, Association of.**

ALDINGTON-JONES REPORT. The report of the Joint Special Committee on the Ports' Industry under the joint chairmanship of the Rt Hon. The Lord Aldington and Mr J.L.Jones, General Secretary of the Transport and General Workers' Union. An interim report was published on 25 July 1972, two further statements on 15 August 1972 and 7 November 1973 and a final report in April 1974. The Committee was established by the National Joint Council of the Port Transport Industry in May 1972 to deal with the dockworker employment situation which had arisen as a result of the run-down of the ports and developments in container handling facilities. The Committee initially abolished the **Temporarily Unattached Register,** i.e. the pool of dockworkers for whom there was no regular work and began a Special Voluntary Severance scheme of limited duration. It then attempted to secure job opportunities for registered dockworkers and to minimise the risk of a further imbalance between numbers of dockworkers and work available. The original issue gave rise to a number of cases of blacking of container ports by dockers, with consequent action by the Industrial Court on complaints from container and transport firms; see **Heaton Transport (St Helen's) Ltd v. Transport and General Workers' Union;** see also **decasualisation, Dock Labour Scheme, National Modernisation Committee.**

ALIENATION. A concept central to Marxist thought and since developed by other writers, especially Robert Blauner (*Alienation and Freedom*, University of Chicago Press, 1964). Marx regarded alienation as a characteristic of capitalist society which denied the worker a meaningful and creative existence by making work (by contrast with leisure) a deprivation, by imposing it upon him, and by conditioning him to labour for others. (Karl Marx, *Selected Writings In Sociology and Social Philosophy*, ed. Bottomore and Rubel, Penguin, 1970). Other writers including non-Marxists have used the concept to summarise the supposed effects of industrialisation on the worker, whether through capitalism, large scale organisation, bureaucracy, or other causes, in estranging him from his work. Blauner (op. cit.) distinguishes four dimensions of alienation: powerlessness, meaninglessness, isolation, and self-estrangement, and considers it to exist (p. 15), 'when workers are unable to control their immediate work processes, to develop a sense of purpose and function which connects their jobs with the overall organisation of production, to belong to integrated industrial communities, and when they fail to become involved in the activity of work as a mode of personal expression'; see also **trust relations**, and Frank Johnson (ed.), *Alienation, Concept, Term and Meanings*, Seminar Press, 1973.

ALL-CARD JOB; see card.

ALL-IN CONTRIBUTION or **all-purpose contribution.** A contribution made by a trade union member to his union, usually weekly, which entitles him to all the services provided; contrasted with the situation in which the member pays a basic contribution and additional payments for additional services or benefits. Alternatively, a contribution to a trade union which is paid inclusive of political levy; (see **political fund**), sometimes known as a 'combined' or 'standard' contribution. The Trade Union Act 1913, s. 6, allows for both a separate levy for the political fund or for an all-in arrangement, provided that in the latter case contracting-out members are relieved of payment by one method or another; see M.A. Hickling *Citrine's Trade Union Law*, Stevens, 1967 p. 450 et seq.

ALL-IN RATE. An hourly time rate paid within an establishment which includes items which, in other establishments, might be shown separately, e.g. various **make-up payments, merit pay;** the hourly equivalent of an **upstanding wage.** The object of an all-in rate is often to ensure that overtime premia and holiday pay are made on the basis of take-home pay rather than on a much lower basic rate.

ALL-OR-NONE EMBARGO. An **embargo** in which workers refuse to work overtime unless this is offered to a whole department or section: Shipbuilding Employers' Federation, *Evidence to the Royal Commission on Trade Unions and Employers' Associations.* WE/311, Appx E, p. 3.

ALLOWABLE LATENESS; see lateness.

ALLOWANCES. (1) Payments made in addition to basic rates of wages or salary to compensate the worker for exceptional conditions or for out-of-pocket expenses considered legitimately to be involved in his day-to-day work or to occur from time to time, e.g. **height money, dirty money,** stagger allowance (see **stagger**), **shift allowance, outworking allowance, travelling time,** lodging allowance, clothing allowance, **tool allowance** etc.
(2) (work study). Time added to the **basic time** for a job, task or operation to compensate for fatigue, personal requirements, unavoidable delays etc., basic time plus allowances being commonly known as **allowed time** or **standard time** (q.v.). Examples are: **relaxation allowances, changeover allowances, interference allowances,** etc.; see International Labour Office. *Introduction to Work Study*, revised edition, 1969, p. 317 *et seq.*, and for criticisms of the application of allowances, R. Marriott, *Incentive Payment Systems*, Staples Press, 3rd (revised) edition, 1968, p. 111 *et seq.*, and H. Pornschlegel and R. Birkwald, *Handbuch der Erholungszeitermittlung*, Cologne, Bund-Verlag, 1968. The British Standards Institution, *Glossary of Terms Used in Work Study*, BS 3138, 1969, lists nine allowances: relaxation, excess work, contingency, changeover, interference, policy, learner, unoccupied time, and bonus increment.

ALLOWED TIME or **standard time.** The total time in which a job should be completed at **standard performance,** inclusive of allowances for fatigue, rest, personal needs and contingencies. Hence, in the engineering industry, sometimes thought of as **floor-to-floor time** (i.e. the time allowed to do the job, assessed by work measurement or **demonstration**), plus such additions. Alternatively, 'allowed time' is sometimes used to describe the time for allowances added to basic time to arrive at **standard time.**

ALL-PURPOSE CONTRIBUTION; see all-in contribution.

ALL-UNION SHOP. An establishment or shop in which all employees are trade union members; more commonly referred to as a **closed shop** or **100 per cent shop.**

ALTERNATE STANDARD. A standard time for alternative method due to changes in tools, equipment or machinery; EPA, *Glossary of Work Study Terms.*

ALTERNATING SHIFT. Usually employed to describe a shift arrangement in which the employee works alternatively for weekly or for longer periods on dayshift and nightshift but sometimes also to shift systems in which he alternates every two or three days; see **three shift system.**

AMALGAMATED ASSOCIATION OF BEAMERS, TWISTERS AND DRAWERS (HAND AND MACHINE); see **Beamers, Twisters and Drawers (Hand and Machine), Amalgamated Association of.**

AMALGAMATED ASSOCIATION OF FELT HAT TRIMMERS AND WOOL FORMERS;; see **Felt Hat Trimmers and Wool Formers, Amalgamated Association of.**

AMALGAMATED ASSOCIATION OF OPERATIVE COTTON SPINNERS AND TWINERS (AAOCST); see **Spinners and Twiners, Amalgamated Association of Operative.**

AMALGAMATED ENGINEERING UNION (AEU). A trade union which amalgamated with the **Amalgamated Union of Foundry Workers (AUFW)** in January 1968 to form the **Amalgamated Union of Engineering and Foundry Workers (AEF)** and which has, since April 1970, made up the Engineering Section of the **Amalgamated Union of Engineering Workers** (AUEW). The Amalgamated Society of Engineers (1851), which became the AEU on amalgamation with nine other societies in 1920, was the prototype and most successful product of the **New Unionism** (or **New Model Unionism**) of the mid-nineteenth century. Its reputation during this period was generally that of an aristocratic, conservative and wealthy association of time-served craftsmen, as much concerned with **friendly benefits** as with wages and conditions. In the last decade of the century AEU members such as John Burns and Tom Mann, leaders of the Great Dock Strike of 1889, were also concerned to develop trade unionsim among the unskilled, and the first decade of the twentieth century witnessed a struggle between the Society's Delegate Meeting and the Executive over decisions to open the ranks of the union to semiskilled workers and to make the Executive more responsible to the rank and file. The subsequent growth of the union, from 88,000 members of 1900 to 460,000 in 1920 was principally the result of the first world

war and relaxation of membership qualifications, and the highly democratic constitution of the union also dates from this period. A women's section was instituted in 1943. The union showed a tendency to right wing labour leadership after the second world war, but in the years preceding the 1968 amalgamation with the AUFW a reaction had appeared. In 1967 it had rather more than 1.1 million members and was the second largest trade union in Britain; see J.B. Jefferys, *The Story of the Engineers,* Lawrence and Wishart, 1945 and E.P. 1971 and *Trade Unions and the Contemporary Scene* (Evidence to the Royal Commission on Trade Unions and Employers' Associations), AEU, November 1965.

AMALGAMATED SOCIETY OF BOILERMAKERS, SHIPWRIGHTS, BLACKSMITHS AND STRUCTURAL WORKERS (ASB); see **Boilermakers, Shipwrights, Blacksmiths and Structural Workers, Amalgamated Society of.**

AMALGAMATED SOCIETY OF JOURNEYMEN FELT HATTERS AND ALLIED WORKERS; see **Felt Hatters and Allied Workers, Amalgamated Society of Journeymen.**

AMALGAMATED SOCIETY OF LACE MAKERS AND TEXTILE WORKERS; see **Lace Makers and Textile Workers, Amalgamated Society of.**

AMALGAMATED SOCIETY OF TEXTILE WORKERS AND KINDRED TRADES (ASTWKT); see **Textile Workers and Kindred Trades, Amalgamated Society of.**

AMALGAMATED SOCIETY OF WIRE DRAWERS AND KINDRED TRADES; see **Wire Drawers and Kindred Trades, Amalgamated Society of.**

AMALGAMATED SOCIETY OF WOODCUTTING MACHINISTS (ASWM); see **Woodcutting Machinists, Amalgamated Society of.**

AMALGAMATED SOCIETY OF WOODWORKERS (ASW); see **Woodworkers, Amalgamated Society of.**

AMALGAMATED TEXTILE WAREHOUSE OPERATIVES; see **Textile Warehouse Operatives Amalgamated.**

AMALGAMATED TEXTILE WORK-

ERS' UNION (ATWU); see **Textile Work-ers' Union Amalgamated.**

AMALGAMATED TRANSPORT AND GENERAL WORKERS' UNION (ATGWU); see **Transport and General Workers' Union, Amalgamated.**

AMALGAMATED UNION OF ASPHALT WORKERS (AUAW); see **Asphalt Workers, Amalgamated Union of.**

AMALGAMATED UNION OF BUILD-ING TRADE WORKERS OF GREAT BRITAIN AND IRELAND (AUBTW); see **Building Trade Workers of Great Britain and Ireland, Amalgamated Union of.**

AMALGAMATED UNION OF ENGINEERING AND FOUNDRY WORKERS (AEF); see **Engineering and Foundry Workers, Amalgamated Union of.**

AMALGAMATED UNION OF ENGINEERING WORKERS; see **Engineering Workers, Amalgamated Union of.**

AMALGAMATED UNION OF FOUN-DRY WORKERS; see **Foundry Workers, Amalgamated Union of.**

AMALGAMATED WEAVERS' ASSO-CIATION (AWA); see **Weavers' Association, Amalgamated.**

AMALGAMATION. The merging of trade unions. Periodic moves towards amalgamation have always been character-istic of British trade unionism. Such a move became especially strong in the 1880s, mostly in order to reduce trade union rivalry. This tendency was rein-forced in the second decade of the twen-tieth century by the development of ideas of **industrial unionism** (q.v.); see Sidney and Beatrice Webb, *History of Trade Unionism*, 1666-1920, 1919 ed. p. 546 *et seq.* The first world war stimulated some major amalgamations, especially the **Amalgamated Engineering Union** (an amalgamation of ten unions in 1920), the **Transport and General Workers' Union** (an amalgamation of eighteen unions in 1921) and the **National Union of General and Municipal Workers** (an amalgama-tion of four unions in 1924). Until 1917 the law demanded that each union amalgamat-ing should secure a two-thirds majority of

the entire membership **(Trade Union Act Amendment Act 1876, s.12).** The **Trade Union (Amalgamation) Act 1917** eased these requirements in order to encourage amalgamations. A vote of 50 per cent of the members of each union was required, and a 20 per cent majority of those voting. These conditions proved too stringent in practice. While maintaining the Act as one method of merger, a second method known as **transfer of engagements** (q.v.) was added in the **Societies (Miscellaneous Provisions) Act 1940** for cases in which one union was content simply to be absorbed by another, and in the **Trade Union (Amalgamations, etc.) Act 1964,** both methods were further simplified by amending the 1917 Act provisions to allow amalgamation on a simple majority of the votes recorded in each union, and transfer of engagements on a simple majority of votes of the transferor union only (see M.A. Hickling, *Citrine's Trade Union Law*, Stevens, 1967, p. 456 *et seq.*, and Cyril Grunfeld, *Modern Trade Union Law*, Sweet and Maxwell, 1970, Chapter 13). Since 1927, the Trades Union Con-gress, in default of the practicability of any general plan for structural change among unions, has encouraged amalgamations within industrial groupings and, especially since the report to the 1964 Congress, met with considerable success (TUC, *Trade Union Structure and Closer Unity*, Final Report, 1947 and *Trade Unionism — Evi-dence to the Royal Commission on Trade Unions and Employers' Associations,* 1966, p. 158 *et seq.*).

AMERICAN FEDERATION OF LABOR (AFL). A national organisation in the United States originally established in 1881 as a federation of craft unions (the Federation of Organised Trade and Labor Unions of the United States of America and Canada) and taking the title Ameri-can Federation of Labor in 1886. The AFL, which merged with the **Congress of Industrial Organisations** (CIO) in 1955 to form the **American Federation of Labor-Congress of Industrial Organisations** (AFL-CIO), was particularly associated with the name of Samuel Gompers who held the office of President from 1886 to his death in 1952, when he was succeeded by George Meany. At the time of the merger, the AFL claimed 10,200,000 dues paying members and comprised 110 national and international unions with 45,000 local unions and 900 local trade and federal labor unions of 165,000 mem-bers directly affiliated with AFL; see

L.L.Lorwin, *The American Federation of Labor*, Brookings Institution, Washington, 1933; Philip Taft, *The AF of L from the Death of Gompers to the Merger*, Harper, 1959; J.O.Morris, *The Conflict within the AFL; A Study of Craft versus Industrial Unionism, 1891-1938*, Cornell University Studies in Industrial and Labor Relations, Vol. X, 1958.

AMERICAN FEDERATION OF LABOR-CONGRESS OF INDUSTRIAL ORGANISATIONS (AFL-CIO). The organisation resulting from the merger of the **American Federation of Labor** and the **Congress of Industrial Organisations,** neither party being willing either to adopt a new title or abandon its own; see A.J.Goldberg, *AFL-CIO: Labor United*, McGraw-Hill, 1956, and John Hutchinson, *The Constitution and Government of the AFL-CIO*, University of California, Berkeley, 1959, and 'The Constitution and Government of the AFL-CIO,' *California Law Review*, December 1968.

AMU. Associated Metalworkers' Union; see **Metalworkers' Union, Associated.**

AMULREE REPORT. The report of the Committee on **Holidays with Pay** (Cmd. 5724, 6 April 1938), under the chairmanship of The Rt Hon. Lord Amulree. The Committee found that out of a total of 18½ million employed workpeople, approximately 10¾ million were not provided with paid holidays. It recommended that all industries without paid holiday agreements giving at least one week's holiday with pay should conclude such an agreement, that **Trade Boards,** County Agricultural Wage Committees and other statutory minimum wage bodies should be empowered to consider and determine the matter, and that an annual holiday with pay statute should not be introduced until the Parliamentary Session 1940-41 in order to encourage voluntary acceptance of the HWP principle. The second recommendation was incorporated into the **Holidays with Pay Act 1938;** see G.C.Cameron 'The Growth of Holidays with Pay in Britain'; in G.L.Reid and D.J.Robertson (eds.) *Fringe Benefits, Labour Costs and Social Security*, George Allen and Unwin, 1965, Ch. 10.

ANALOGUE. An outside job, post or grade, specified in a survey of the **Civil Service Pay Research Unit** (q.v.), with which a grade within the Civil Service can be compared; see Geoffrey Walker, *Pay Research in the Civil Service*, National and Local Government Officers' Association, TUE 6, 1968.

ANALYTICAL ESTIMATING. A work measurement technique, being a development of estimating, whereby the time required to carry out elements of a job at a defined level of performance is estimated from knowledge and practical experience of the elements concerned (BS 3138, 1969, No. 31004). It is claimed to be particularly useful for non-repetitive work on which it has not been possible for basic times to be synthesised for all the elements concerned. R.M.Currie (*Work Study*, Pitman, 4th ed. 1977 and *The Measurement of Work*, British Institute of Management, 1965) describes it as involving elements of longer duration than those used for timing or rating, on which an estimator with knowledge of the job puts a standard time at 100 rating. The ILO (*Introduction to Work Study*, 1969) notes that 'there are practical problems in its application which make it unsafe for use by inexperienced work study men' and Currie advises the development of a data bank of estimates, and the use of synthetic data wherever possible in supplementation.

ANDREW v. NATIONAL UNION OF PUBLIC EMPLOYEES. *The Times*, 9 July 1955. A case in which an injunction was awarded against the **National Union of Public Employees** restraining it from expelling seven new members on the grounds that they had been poached or recruited from another union contrary to the principles of the **Bridlington Agreement** (q.v.). The effect of the case, along with that of **Spring v. National Amalgamated Stevedores and Dockers** (q.v.) was to challenge the view that if a union submitted itself to an agreement contained in the rules of the **Trades Union Congress,** such an agreement would be binding by implication on the members of that union. As a result, the TUC asked unions to include in their rules the provision that 'Notwithstanding anything in these rules, the Executive Committee may by giving six weeks' notice in writing terminate the membership of any member if necessary in order to comply with a decision of the Disputes Committee of the Trades Union Congress'. Most affiliated unions have followed this advice; see also **Bridlington Agreement.**

ANNUAL HOLIDAYS; see **holidays with pay.**

ANNUAL IMPROVEMENT FACTOR. A term which came into prominence in the United States following an agreement between the General Motors Corporation and the Union of Automobile Workers in 1948, which provided for an annual increase in pay during the life of the agreement designed to enable the workers to share the benefits arising from increased productivity. Cost of living adjustments were also provided for in the contract; see Frederick H. Harbison, 'The General Motors-United Auto Workers Agreement of 1950', *Journal of Political Economy*, October 1950.

ANOMIE. A concept originally developed by the French sociologist Emile Durkheim to describe a condition of breakdown of society arising from 'an acute disjunction between cultural norms and goals and the socially structured capacities of members of the group to act in accordance with them'; see R.K.Merton, *Social Theory and Social Structure*, Collier Macmillan, 1968. Sometimes also used to describe the effect on the individual of such a normless and disorderly social situation (see, for example, K.Young, *Personality and Problems of Adjustment*, Appleton-Century-Crofts, New York, 1952), Alan Fox and Allan Flanders ('The Reform of Industrial Relations, Donovan to Durkheim', *British Journal of Industrial Relations*, Vol. VII, No. 2, July 1969, pp. 151-80) have used the term to summarise the normlessness or lack of social regulation in collective bargaining in Britain identified in the Report of the Donovan Royal Commission on Trade Unions and Employers' Associations, 1965-1968, Cmnd. 3623, June 1968, see **Donovan Commission.**

ANTI-PIRATING AGREEMENTS. Agreements between employers, usually in the form of an unwritten code, prohibiting aggressive recruitment tactics and in some cases restraining the hiring of labour by one firm from the workers of another; **no-poaching agreements.** Such agreements are said to be common in the United States of America, but less common in Britain. D.I.Mackay, D.Boddy, J.Brack, J.A. Diack and N.Jones, *Labour Markets under Different Employment Conditions*, George Allen and Unwin, 1971, pp. 88-9. The prevention of **enticement of labour** has, however, been a traditional concern

of **employers' associations;** see also **form of inquiry.**

ANTI-SWEATING LEAGUE; see **sweating.**

APAC. Association of Patternmakers and Allied Craftsmen; see **Patternmakers and Allied Craftsmen, Association of.**

APEX. Association of Professional, Executive, Clerical and Computer Staff; see **Professional, Executive, Clerical and Computer Staff, Association of** (formerly Clerical and Administrative Workers' Union).

APPEALS PROCEDURE. Usually employed to describe a procedure for dealing with workers' grievances (see **grievance**). Appeals procedures appear, in general, to be comparable with **grievance procedures,** but there are those who would claim them to have special features. At Glacier Metal, for example, it has been thought of as a judicial mechanism within an executive system; see Wilfred Brown, *Exploration in Management*, Heinemann, 1960, Chapter XVIII and *Organisation*, Heinemann 1971, Ch. 20. The concept of appeal is used in a similar sense by the **Code of Practice,** *Disciplinary Practice and Procedures in Employment*, para. 16 as a desirable final stage in an individual grievance procedure.

APPREHENDED DISPUTE. A **dispute** or **difference** between workers or a trade union or trade unions and an employer or employers, of which notice has been given or received, e.g. 'If agreement is not achieved (after consultation between the parties) the workers may give notice of an apprehended dispute, in which case the management will not operate the proposed change for seven working days' (*Procedure — Manual Workers* 1972, II(1)(b): engineering industry). The expression seems to have originated in the **Conciliation Act 1896,** s. 2(1): 'Where a difference exists or is apprehended between an employer or any class of employers and workmen ...', and was reiterated in the **Industrial Courts Act 1919,** s. 2(1): 'Any trade dispute as defined in this Act, whether existing or apprehended, may be reported to the Minister by or on behalf of either of the parties to the dispute ...'. The distinction being made here is between a situation in which the parties are already joined in combat (an 'existing dispute'), and one in which they have exhausted available procedures between themselves, but have not yet embarked upon industrial action.

APPRENTICE; see **apprenticeship and indentured apprentice.**

APPRENTICESHIP. Defined by the Ministry of Labour (*Glossary of Training Terms*, HMSO, 1967) as 'any system by which an employer undertakes by contract, written or implied, to employ a young person and to train him or have him trained systematically for a trade or occupation for a period, the duration of which has been fixed in advance and in the course of which the **apprentice** agrees to work in the employer's service'; hence a **craft apprentice**, an apprentice who is being taught a craft or trade (e.g. in the electricity supply industry one of the following; mechanical fitter, electrical fitter, electrician, meter mechanician, instrument mechanic, jointer and linesman, or in engineering as fitters, turners, instrument makers, patternmakers, moulders, coremakers, etc.); **student apprentice**, an apprentice generally possessing superior qualifications on entry and following a course of study up to degree level or its equivalent; **graduate apprentice**, an apprentice undertaking training after obtaining a degree, etc. The tendency in recent years, and especially since the **Industrial Training Act 1964**, has been for apprentice-type training to grow generally, for craft apprenticeships to shorten (usually from five to four years), and for other types of apprenticeships (sometimes under that title and sometimes as traineeships, etc.) to increase in numbers. Training methods have also changed, e.g. in engineering, towards **module training**, i.e. towards building up the skill and knowledge of individuals as needed in packages or modules based on skills or groups of skills, and away from on-the-job training to a combination of this and off-the-job training with day or block release for further educational studies; see also **Carr Report. Contracts of apprenticeship** provide for an undertaking from the master to teach the apprentice and for the apprentice to obey his master and learn his trade. In the absence of express agreement or a wage regulation order, apprentices subject to contracts are not entitled to wages, though these are commonly provided for in collective agreements, and the employer has limited powers to dismiss an apprentice unless such powers are written into the agreement; see Olga Aikin and Judith

Reid, *Labour Law 1, Employment, Welfare and Safety at Work*, Penguin Education, 1971, and B.A.Hepple and Paul O'Higgins, *Employment Law*, Sweet and Maxwell, 1976; see also Gertrude Williams, *Recruitment to Skilled Trades*, Routledge and Kegan Paul, 1957, Kate Liepmann, *Apprenticeship*, Routledge and Kegan Paul, 1960, Gertrude Williams, *Apprenticeship in Europe*, Chapman and Hall, 1963, John Wellens, *The Training Revolution*, Evans Bros, 1963; see also **indentured apprentice.**

APPROVED CLOSED SHOP. A form of closed shop, permitted by the **Industrial Relations Act 1971** (now repealed) in which a worker was required to be a member of a **registered trade union** as a term of contract of his employment. The object of this provision of the Act was to allow the protection of a closed shop to unions which might otherwise find effective organisation, and collective bargaining beyond their capacity. The status no longer exists.

APT. Association of Polytechnic Teachers; see **Polytechnic Teachers, Association of.**

ARBEITSGERICHT; see **labour courts.**

ARBETSDOMSTOLEN; see **labour courts.**

ARBITER; see **arbitration.**

ARBITRABLE GRIEVANCE; see **grievance.**

ARBITRATION. A procedure under which a neutral third party, an **arbitrator**, or in Scotland an **arbiter** (also known as an **umpire, referee** etc.), hears both the trade union and the employer side in a **dispute** or a **difference**, and issues an award binding upon them voluntarily (hence **voluntary arbitration**) or compulsorily (hence **compulsory arbitration**), a procedure contrasted with **conciliation** or **mediation** (q.v.), in which the conciliator or mediator attempts to persuade the parties to settle the issue themselves. The meaning of arbitration seems now to have stabilised; in the last century it was sometimes used to mean **collective bargaining**, e.g. by A.J.Mundella: 'It is well to define what we mean by arbitration. The sense in which we use the word is that of an arrangement for open and friendly bargaining in which masters and men meet and talk over their common affairs openly and freely' (*Arbitration as a Means of Preventing Strikes*, Bradford, 1868); the Devonshire Royal Commission on Labour, 1891-1894, C-7421, HMSO 1894, p. 49 (see **Devonshire Commission**), defined arbitration in its modern sense as 'the settlement by one or more presumably impartial persons of an issue on which the parties have failed to agree'. Voluntary arbitration has been the custom in Britain, both in the sense that the two parties concerned have been expected to agree to reference of an issue to an arbitrator, and in the sense that awards have not been considered to be more than morally binding upon the parties (but see **compulsory arbitration** for the situation under SR and O 1305 and SR and O 1376 between 1940 and 1959). Industrial arbitration legislation in Britain in its modern sense dates from the Cotton Arbitration Act 1800 and is now principally exercised by the **Advisory, Conciliation and Arbitration Service** under the **Employment Protection Act 1975**; voluntary machinery for arbitration in particular industries, e.g. the Pit and District Conciliation Schemes and the National Reference Tribunal in the coal mining industry, the **Railway Staff National Tribunal,** the Civil Service Arbitration Tribunal and in the **terminal arbitration** arrangements of **Joint Industrial Councils** and other bodies; (see Lord Amulree, *Industrial Arbitration*, OUP, 1929; M.T. Rankin, *Arbitration Principles and the Industrial Court*, P.S.King, 1931; H.A.Turner, *Arbitration*, Fabian Research Series No. 153, 1952; and K.W. Wedderburn and P.L.Davies, *Employment Grievances and Disputes Procedures in Britain*, University of California Press, 1969); see also **Boards of Arbitration, Boards of Conciliation and Arbitration, contract arbitration, Committee of Inquiry, Committee of Investigation, Court of Inquiry, grievance arbitration, judiciable arbitration, nonjudiciable arbitration, single arbitration, Central Arbitration Committee, Joint CBI/TUC Conciliation and Arbitration Service, Panel of Investigation.**

ARBITRATOR; see **arbitration.**

ARMED FORCES REVIEW BODY; see **review bodies.**

ARTICULATED BARGAINING. Collective bargaining at three different but inter-related levels, i.e. at national industry level, at sectoral level and at plant level. The practice was introduced in Italy in 1962 in an attempt to 'articulate' a system to take the place of exclusive national bargaining which had, in the 1950s, been progressively broken down by workplace negotiation, by concluding an agreement in engineering to determine bargaining levels and procedures which should give to each level an appropriate negotiating content and function; see G. Giuigni, 'Recent developments in collective bargaining in Italy', *International Labour Review*, Vol. 91, No. 4, April 1965, pp. 273-91.

ARTIFICER. Defined by OED as 'one who makes by art or skill, especially a craftsman' or a 'soldier mechanic'; employed in the Royal Navy to denote a skilled craftsman; e.g. engine room artificer, electrical artificer. As used in the **Truck Act 1831** ss. 1-4 (see **Truck Acts)** the expression evidently means a **workman** as defined in the Employers and Workman Act 1875.

ASB. Amalgamated Society of Boilermakers, Shipwrights, Blacksmiths and Structural Workers; see **Boilermakers, Shipwrights, Blacksmiths and Structural Workers, Amalgamated Society of.**

ASCERTAINMENT SYSTEM. Coal industry; a system whereby the aggregate proceeds of coal obtained at a pit (or more usually in a district), less costs other than wages, was divided in agreed proportions between wages and profits, the sum allocated to wages being paid in the form of a percentage added to basic rates. A detailed description of the system is given in the Green Award of 1942: see National Coal Board, *Memoranda of Agreements*, Part I, 20 March 1940 to 31 July 1946, p. 30 *et seq.* or *Report of a Board of Investigation into the immediate wages issue in the Coal-Mining Industry*, 18 June 1942.

ASEE. Association of Supervisory and Executive Engineers; see **Supervisory and Executive Engineers, Association of.**

ASHFORD v. ASSOCIATION OF SCIENTIFIC, TECHNICAL AND MANAGERIAL STAFFS (1973). ICR 296; 123 L.J. 422; *The Times*, 5 April 1973, NIRC. A case in which two members of the union purported to resign, the one summarily and the other giving seven days' notice. The union required them to submit applications to the union's national executive council for approval, giving their reasons. Both were expelled on refusing to do so. The NIRC held that the rules concerning resignation might have been reasonable under the Industrial Relations Acts; 65(3) but that insufficient notice was given; see **membership of a union.**

ASKING CARD. A card given to a trade union member on being discharged by an employer or on leaving one employment to take up another, the function of the card being to indicate that the member is paid-up and acceptable by the union for work elsewhere. Rules of the **Amalgamated Society of Journeymen Felt Hatters and Allied Workers of Great Britain** 1948.

ASLEF. Associated Society of Locomotive Engineers and Firemen; see **Locomotive Engineers and Firemen, Associated Society of.**

ASPHALT WORKERS, AMALGAMATED UNION OF (AUAW). A trade union formed in 1938 by the amalgamation of the National Union of Asphalt Workers with the Northern Asphalt Workers' Union, and organising workers in the mastic asphalt and felt manufacturing industry. *Address:* Jenkin House, 173A, Queen's Road, Peckham, London SE15 2NF. *Tel:* 01-639 1669. *TUC Affiliated Membership 1977*: 3,014.

ASSESSOR. A person appointed to aid **arbitrators** or chairmen of **Courts of Inquiry** by giving specialist or technical advice. The Secretary of State for Employment has authority, at the request of the arbitrator or of the parties to a dispute, to appoint such assessors where he has been instrumental in setting up the tribunal concerned. This happens infrequently, but has been a regular feature of hearings by the National Reference Tribunal for the Coalmining Industry.

ASSISTED AREAS. A generic name given to **Development Areas, Intermediate Areas** and **Special Development Areas,** all being areas of Great Britain reckoned to require special measures to encourage employment and the growth and proper distribution of industry. Under the Industrial Development Act 1966 most of Scotland, most of Wales, the Northern Region of England, the Furness Peninsula, Merseyside, most of Cornwall and North Devon were designated Development Areas; in the following year areas in which pit closures were expected to cause high and persistent unemployment (Central Scotland, South Wales, the North East and West Cumberland) were given

additional financial assistance and known as 'special development areas'. In 1969 the Hunt Committee (The *Intermediate Areas*, Cmnd. 3998, April 1969) recommended the concentration of assistance in more defined localities within the development regions. The necessary powers were provided in the Local Employment Act 1970 to designate as Intermediate Areas the Yorkshire Coalfield, North Humberside, North East Lancashire, the Notts/Derby Coalfield, Plymouth, part of South East Wales, and Leith in Scotland. In 1971 Special Development Area status, earning the highest rates of financial assistance, was accorded to the older industrial conurbations of West Central Scotland, Tyneside and Wearside and a few other places, and a year later Intermediate Area status was extended to almost the whole of the North West and the Yorkshire and Humberside Planning Regions and to those parts of Wales not already assisted areas. Further extensions were made in 1974. The assisted areas in 1977 cover a considerable area of Great Britain and contain some 43 per cent of all employees.

ASSOCIATED METALWORKERS' UNION (AMU); see **Metalworkers' Union, Associated.**

The Assisted Areas □

ASSOCIATED SOCIETY OF LOCO-
MOTIVE ENGINEERS AND FIRE-
MEN (ASLEF); see Locomotive
Engineers and Firemen, Associated
Society of.

ASSOCIATION BARGAINING; see
multi-employer bargaining.

ASSOCIATION OF BROADCASTING
STAFF (ABS); see Broadcasting Staff,
Association of.

ASSOCIATION OF BUILDING TECH-
NICIANS (ABT); see Construction,
Allied Trades and Technicians, Union of.

ASSOCIATION OF CINEMATO-
GRAPH TELEVISION AND ALLIED
TECHNICIANS (ACTT); see Cinemato-
graph, Television and Allied Technicians,
Association of.

ASSOCIATION OF CLERICAL, TECH-
NICAL AND SUPERVISORY STAFFS
(ACTSS). A section of the Transport and
General Workers' Union (q.v.).

ASSOCIATION OF FIRST DIVISION
CIVIL SERVANTS (FIRST DIVISION
ASSOCIATION). see First Division Civil
Servants, Association of.

ASSOCIATION OF GOVERNMENT
SUPERVISORS AND RADIO OFFI-
CERS; see Government Supervisors and
Radio Officers, Association of.

ASSOCIATION OF HOSPITAL CON-
SULTANTS AND SPECIALISTS; see
Hospital Consultants and Specialists,
Association of.

ASSOCIATION OF PATTERN-
MAKERS AND ALLIED CRAFTS-
MEN; see Patternmakers and Allied
Craftsmen, Association of.

ASSOCIATION OF POLYTECHNIC
TEACHERS; see Polytechnic Teachers,
Association of.

ASSOCIATION OF POST OFFICE
EXECUTIVES (APOE); see Post Office
Executives, Association of.

ASSOCIATION OF PROFESSIONAL,
EXECUTIVE, CLERICAL AND COM-
PUTER STAFF (APEX); see Profes-
sional, Executive, Clerical and Computer
Staff, Association of.

ASSOCIATION OF SCIENTIFIC,
TECHNICAL AND MANAGERIAL
STAFFS (ASTMS); see Scientific, Techni-
cal and Managerial Staffs, Association of.

ASSOCIATION OF SUPERVISORY
AND EXECUTIVE ENGINEERS
(ASEE); see Supervisory and Executive
Engineers, Association of.

ASSOCIATION OF TEACHERS IN
TECHNICAL INSTITUTIONS; see
Teachers in Further and Higher Educa-
tion, National Association of.

ASSOCIATION OF UNIVERSITY
TEACHERS (AUT); see University
Teachers, Association of.

ASTMS. Association of Scientific, Technical and Managerial Staffs; see Scientific,
Technical and Managerial Staffs, Association of.

ASTWKT. Amalgamated Society of Tex-
tile Workers and Kindred Trades; see
Textile Workers and Kindred Trades,
Amalgamated Society of.

ASW. Amalgamated Society of Woodworkers; see Construction, Allied Trades
and Technicians, Union of.

ASWM. Amalgamated Society of Woodcutting Machinists; see Woodcutting
Machinists, Amalgamated Society of.

ATC EMPLOYEES; see Administrative,
Technical and Clerical Staff.

ATGWU. Amalgamated Transport and
General Workers' Union; see Transport
and General Workers' Union, Amalgamated.

ATTACHMENT OF EARNINGS ACT
1971; see Attachment of Earnings Order.

ATTACHMENT OF EARNINGS
ORDER. An order directed to a person
who appears to the court to have a debtor
in his employment and which operates as
an instruction to that person to make periodical deductions from the debtor's earnings and to pay the amounts deducted to
the collecting officer of the court. The law
relating to civil debts was amended and
extended by the Attachment of Earnings
Act 1971 which came into force on 2
August 1971. Priority Orders are concerned with the maintenance of wives and
families and with the payment of fines etc.;

Non-priority Orders are made in other cases; Attachable Earnings in relation to a pay-day are earnings after deduction of income tax, national insurance contributions, and amounts deductible under any enactment or for the purposes of superannuation. An employer may take 5p from the debtor's earnings each time and in respect of each order when making a deduction; see Mark Freedland, *Attachment of Earnings*, Jordan and Sons, 1971.

ATTENDANCE BONUS; see attendance money.

ATTENDANCE MONEY. (1) Sometimes also called **attendance bonus**: a payment for attendance at work or for good-timekeeping, usually in the form of a fixed sum per day or per shift, which is lost if attendance or timekeeping fail to maintain the standards required, e.g. in coalmining, Revision of Wages Structure 1963, C1.15, which allowed for an additional payment if a worker makes more than twenty attendances in four consecutive weeks. Little information is available on the operation of attendance money in Britain; inclusion in the terms of industry-wide agreements is said to have declined and employers are said to be sceptical about its usefulness (Confederation of British Industry, *Absenteeism*, 1970, pp. 12-13). (2) A fall-back payment to a casual worker who attends for work, but for whom no work is available, e.g. in the Dock Labour Scheme; see *Final Report of the Committee of Inquiry under the Rt Hon. Lord Devlin into certain matters concerning the Port Transport Industry*, Cmnd. 2734, August 1965.

ATTI. Association of Teachers in Technical Institutions; see **Teachers in Further and Higher Education, National Association of.**

ATTITUDE. Gordon W. Allport, *Handbook of Social Psychology* (ed.), G.Lindzey, Addison-Wesley, 1968 Vol. 1 pp. 43-5, gives as representative definitions: 'The specific mental disposition towards an incoming (or arising) experience, whereby that experience is modified; or a condition of readiness for a certain type of activity' (Warren, 1934); 'A mental disposition of the human individual to act for or against a definite object' (Droba, 1933), and 'A mental and neutral state of readiness, organised through experience, exerting a directive or dynamic influence upon the individual's response to all objects and situations to which it is

related' (Allport, 1935), G. Duncan Mitchell, *A Dictionary of Sociology*, Routledge and Kegan Paul, 1968, adds further characteristics: 'A term normally used to refer to a learned disposition, evidenced by the behaviour of an individual or group of individuals, to evaluate an object or class of objects in a consistent or characteristic way'; he also notes that 'the term has acquired the connotation of a predisposition to respond in a particular way to an external stimulus'. It is this possibility of using attitudes to predict group acceptability or response which had led to the development of **attitude surveys** in the practice of industrial relations, by consultants attempting to devise relevant and acceptable payment or working systems and as informational and diagnostic guides to various workplace problems in industrial relations, e.g. labour turnover, absenteeism and participation. For the technical problems and practice of such surveys; see A.N.Oppenheim, *Questionnaire Design and Attitude Measurement*, Heinemann, 1968; S.L.Payne, *The Art of Asking Questions*, Princeton University Press, 1951, C.Sellitz *et al.*, *Research Methods in Social Relations*, Methuen, 1959, and D.Mackenzie Davey, D. Rockingham Gill and P. McDonnell, *Attitude Surveys in Industry*, Institute of Personnel Management, 1970; see also **organisation development.**

ATTITUDE SURVEY; see attitude.

ATTITUDINAL STRUCTURING. One of the four models of collective bargaining behaviour advanced by Richard E. Walton and Robert McKersie (*A Behavioral Theory of Labor Negotiations*, McGraw-Hill, 1965) in an attempt to provide predictive hypotheses on how people will tend to behave in varying circumstances and bargaining conditions, the others being **integrative bargaining, distributive bargaining**, and **intraorganisational bargaining**. Attitudinal structuring is described as activities that influence the attitudes of the parties towards each other and affect the basic relationship bonds between the social units involved.

ATWU. Amalgamated Textile Workers' Union; see **Textile Workers' Union, Amalgamated.**

AUAW. Amalgamated Union of Asphalt Workers; see **Asphalt Workers, Amalgamated Union of.**

AUBTW. Amalgamated Union of Building Trade Workers of Great Britain and Ireland; see **Building Trade Workers of Great Britain and Ireland, Amalgamated Union of.**

AUEW. Amalgamated Union of Engineering Workers; see **Engineering Workers, Amalgamated Union of.**

AUEW/TASS. The Technical and Supervisory Section of the **Amalgamated Union of Engineering Workers,** formerly the **Draughtsmen and Allied Technicians' Association** (q.v.).

AUFW. Amalgamated Union of Foundry Workers; see **Foundry Workers, Amalgamated Union of.**

AUT. Association of University Teachers; see **University Teachers, Association of.**

AUTOMATION. An expression, sometimes attributed to John Diebold (*Automation. The Advent of the Automatic Factory,* 1952), used to describe a new wave of technological change taking place in developed countries, particularly in the United States, from the beginning of the 1950s. These changes were associated with the development of automatic control of operations in manufacturing (e.g. in chemicals, oil refining, steel and numerical control of machine tools), the use of computers in data processing (e.g. in banking, accounting and scientific calculations) and in the use of special purpose equipment (e.g. in telephone exchanges, navigation systems etc.): hence automation defined as 'mechanisation of sensory control and thought processes' (C.Killingsworth, Automation, Jobs and Manpower in *Exploring the Dimensions of the Management Revolution,* Government Printing Office, Washington, 1964). Also applied loosely to **Detroit Automation,** an advanced stage of mechanisation in assembly work, and even more loosely, to technical change resulting from any type of mechanisation. Concern about automation in its stricter sense has mainly resulted from its possible effects on the level of employment, occupational structure, levels of skill, and on social structure generally. Very little longer term unemployment appears to be attributable to automation alone (see **technological unemployment**) but there is evidence that it is contributing to reductions in **direct labour** and to the rising proportion of **white collar workers** in the labour force. It seems not to have substantial effect on the level of skills generally. For the results of research on automation; see P. Sadler, *Social Research on Automation, A Social Science Research Council Review,* Heinemann, 1968. Also *Automation, A Report in the Technical Trends and their Impact on Management and Labour,* Department of Scientific and Industrial Research, HMSO, 1956; F. Pollock, *The Economic and Social Consequences of Automation,* Basil Blackwell, 1957; H.A.Rhee, *Office Automation in Social Perspective,* Basil Blackwell and Mott, 1968; Enid Mumford and Olive Banks, *The Computer and the Clerk,* Routledge and Kegan Paul, 1967.

AUTONOMOUS BARGAINING. Defined by the Donovan Royal Commission on Trade Unions and Employers' Associations, 1965-1968, Cmnd, 3623, June 1968, p. 18 (see **Donovan Commission**) as arising in workplace bargaining when 'however the external bargaining procedures respond to its growth, their control has continued to diminish and with it the control of trade unions and employers' associations'; see also **fractional bargaining, fragmented bargaining.**

AUTONOMOUS REGULATION. Defined by J.D.M.Bell, *The System of Industrial Relations in Great Britain,* Allan Flanders and H.A.Clegg (Eds.), Basil Blackwell, 1964, p. 192, as a method of trade unionism which includes 'any way of regulating (or attempting to regulate) working conditions by the enforcement of the union's own rules and administrative arrangements'. He suggests that, in the scheme of trade union methods used by Sidney and Beatrice Webb (*Industrial Democracy,* 1898), it is the element of autonomous regulation which logically distinguishes **mutual insurance** (q.v.) from **collective bargaining** and **legal enactment.**

AWA. Amalgamated Weavers' Association; see **Weavers' Association, Amalgamated.**

AWARD. The findings of an **arbitrator, umpire** or arbitration body; the document embodying such findings, or what is awarded, in terms of money, conditions of work etc.; e.g. the findings of **single arbitrators,** the former **National Arbitration Tribunal, Industrial Disputes Tribunal,** and the present **Industrial Arbitration Board.** More loosely used to describe settlements jointly arrived at by employers and trade unions in standing machinery (e.g. Burnham Awards; see **Burnham Committees**), and by *ad hoc* negotiation, either under official encouragement (see **Bevin Award**), or otherwise.

AWARD 326. National Arbitration Tribunal Award 326 of 20 March 1943 which increased the national bonus (see **piecework supplement**) in the engineering industry, consolidated 20s. of the bonus into basic rates, and altered the basis of the **minimum piecework standard** (q.v.) by raising the piecework percentage from 25 per cent to 27½ per cent.

AWARD 470. National Arbitration Tribunal Award 470, 2 December 1943, which guaranteed a pieceworker in the engineering industry a minimum payment of his time rate; see **pieceworkers' guarantee.**

B

B. Standard output per minute in the Bedeaux wage incentive system; see **Bedeaux System.**

BACK PAY. Payment due to an employee as a result of underpayment in the past arising from the misapplication of a collective agreement or contract of employment, or from other error in wage or salary administration; to be distinguished from **retrospective payment** (q.v.)

BACKSHIFT. An **afternoon shift** (or second shift) in a **three shift** or **continuous shift system**, the first shift being known as morning shift, and the third as night shift, especially in the coalmining industry.

BACM. British Association of Colliery Management; see **Colliery Management, British Association of.**

THE BADGER CASE. A situation in which the International Trade Unions in 1977 brought before the International Investment and Multinational Enterprise Committee of the **Organisation for Economic Co-operation and Development**, the case of Badger Belgium (NV) an affiliate of an American company, in which that company had refused to meet a shortfall in legally obliged **severance pay** and the debts of the Belgian subsidiary when this

was closed down. The Badger Case has been regarded as a test for the OECD's *Guidelines for Multinational Enterprises*, a voluntary code produced by that body in June 1976. Negotiations subsequently led to an agreement in which The Badger Co. Inc. USA agreed to supplement the assets of Badger Belgium by the amount necessary to pay the severance pay; see R. Blanpain, *The Badger Case*, Kluwer, 1978.

BAKERS AND ALLIED WORKERS, SCOTTISH UNION OF. A trade union founded in 1888 for workers in the bakery industry in Scotland, originally for men, but, since 1926, for women also. In 1919 the title of the union was the Scottish National Federal Union of Operative Bakers and Confectioners, and there have been several changes of name since, the current title of the union having been adopted in 1955, before which it was known as the Scottish Union of Bakers, Confectioners, Biscuit Bakers and Bakery Workers. As a result of falling membership the union merged with the Union of Shop, Distributive and Allied Workers in January 1978 as the Scottish Bakers' section. *Address:* 'Baxterlee', 127 Fergus Drive, Glasgow G20 6AU. *Tel:* 041-946 4213. *TUC Affiliated Membership 1977:* 8,693.

BAKERS' FOOD AND ALLIED WORKERS' UNION (BU). A trade union for bakery workers originating in Manchester in 1849. The original society became part of the first Amalgamated Union of Operative Bakers of England which was formed in 1861; this eventually became the Amalgamated Union of Operative Bakers, Confectioners and Allied Workers, a title which was shortened to Bakers' Union in 1964 and later expanded to take into account the widening organisational interests of the union. *Address:* Stanborough House, Gt. North Road Stanborough, Welwyn Garden City, Herts. AL8 7TA. *Tel:* Hatfield 60150. *TUC Affiliated Membership, 1977:* 56,135.

BALANCED TIME; see **balancing time.**

BALANCING TIME. The practice of altering the pattern of working hours while leaving the actual number of working hours unchanged (resulting in **balanced time**), e.g. by starting a working day later and finishing later, leaving the length of the working day unaltered, or, over a period, arranging overtime hours worked to be exactly replaced, hour for hour, by time off in lieu.

BALLOT RIGGING. The falsification of returns, or the improper manipulation or misrepresentation of votes at an election for a trade union official or in relation to other balloting procedures allowed for in trade union rules. The most celebrated case of ballot rigging in modern times occurred in the election for General Secretary of the Electrical Trades Union (see **Electrical, Electronic Telec mmunication and Plumbing Trades Union**) in 1959, as a result of which the ETU was expelled from the **Trades Union Congress** on 1961 (but readmitted in 1962). In the case of **Byrne and Chapple v. Foulkes, Haxell and Others** (1961) the defendants, after a forty-two dey trial, were found guilty of fraudulent conspiracy, Winn J. *inter alia* granting a declaration that the election of Haxell was contrary to the rules of the union and void and that Byrne was duly elected General Secretary; see Trades Union Congress, *Report,* 1961, pp. 471-93 and C. H. Rolph, *All Those in Favour? The ETU Trial,* André Deutsch, 1962. The effect of the case was to break the communist hold of the union's executive council.

BALPA; see **British Airline Pilots' Association.**

BANDING. A method of rationalising pay structures in which jobs judged to be of approximately qual value, either less precisely 'by eye' or more precisely by **job evaluation** (q.v.), are brought to a common rate of basic pay; typically the establishment of a series of bands at appropriate differential differences to replace a large number of separate rates in random patterns developed by *ad hoc* adjutments over time. The number of bands, the spread of job size within a band and the differential step between each band, can vary widely to meet different needs. **Broad banding,** the inclusion of a wide range of jobs on the same pay rate, aids the flexible employment of labour over a range of tasks; narrow bands tend to require greater pay adjustment f workers are transferred from one job to another. For examples of banding see National Board for Prices and Incomes Reports Nos. 18 and 146 on the *Pay of Industrial Civil Servants* (see **Industrial Civil Servant**), and 29, *Manual Workers in Local Authorities, in the National Health Service, Gas and Water Supply,* Cmnd. 3230, March 1967.

BANK EMPLOYEES, NATIONAL UNION OF (NUBE). A trade union formed in 1946 as a result of the amalgamation of the Bank Officers' Guild (1918) and the Scottish Bankers' Association (1919) and catering for managerial, clerical, non-clerical, engineering and maintenance staff of all banks in England, Scotland and Wales. The union also has a membership staff of foreign and overseas banks in the United Kingdom, merchant banks and finance houses. Its history has been a constant struggle for recognition (see R. M. Blackburn, *Union Character and Social Class,* Batsford, 1967). In 1963 its complaint to the **International Labour Office** that, in refusing to recognise NUBE, the banks were acting contrary to Article 98 of the ILO, was subject to an inquiry by Lord Cameron (Cmnd. 2202, HMSO, November 1963). The report found the case unproven, but recommended that the four banks directly concerned - District, Martins, National Provincial and Yorkshire - should receive NUBE representations and urged general talks on national negotiating machinery. In 1967 strike action took place in Wales and Blackpool, Nottingham, Bolton and Doncaster in support of national machinery after two staff associations and other participants had withdrawn from the existing arrangements. In 1968 national negotiating machinery was established in the banking industry for the first time, and in 1970 further national machinery was created at the national level for Scottish banks of issue. The rate of growth of the union between 1967 and 1969 exceeded 50 per cent. *Address:* Sheffield House, Portsmouth Road, Esher, Surrey, KT10 9BH *Tel:* 0372-66624. *TUC Affiliated Membership, 1977:* 111,609.

BANK HOLIDAYS. In *England and Wales:* Easter Monday, 1 May (from 1978 onwards), the last Monday in May (Spring Holiday), the last Monday in August (August Bank Holiday), 26 December (if not a Sunday), 27 December (when 25 or 26 December is a Sunday), New Year's Day; in *Scotland:* New Year's Day (if not a Sunday, otherwise 3 January), 2 January (if not a Sunday, otherwise 3 January). Good Friday, the first Monday in May, the last Monday in May, the first Monday in August, Christmas Day (if not a Sunday, otherwise 26 December); *Northern Ireland:* 17 March (if it is not a Sunday, otherwise 18 March), Easter Monday, 1 May (from 1978 onwards), the last Monday in May, 12 July, the last Monday in August, 26 December (if not a Sunday), 27 December (when 25 or 26 December is a Sunday), New Year's Day; alternative or additional days may be declared by proclamation **(Banking and Financial Dealings Act 1971)**. In England, Wales and Northern Ireland, Good Friday and Christmas Day are **public holidays**, not bank holidays: public and bank holidays are sometimes collectively known as **statutory holidays** or **recognised public holidays**. Bank Holidays were originally instituted by the **Bank Holidays Act 1871**.

BANK HOLIDAYS ACT 1871; see bank holidays.

BANKING. The technique sometimes practised by payment by result workers of delaying the booking of work done (or putting such work 'in the back of the book'), in order to use such banked work to control or stabilise earnings or as a reserve for holiday or other purposes. In the latter use it may be associated with **bull weeks** (q.v.). Banking may sometimes be associated with false booking or overbooking.

BANKING AND FINANCIAL DEALINGS ACT 1971; see bank holidays.

BARGAINING AGENT; see sole bargaining agent.

BARGAINING IN GOOD FAITH; see good-faith bargaining.

BARGAINING THEORY OF WAGES. An attempt to explain **wage determination** (see **wage theories**) in terms of factors concerned with **collective bargaining**, i.e. in terms of degrees of monopoly in the **labour market**, or of labour market institutions, **coercive comparisons** etc., each being concerned with the relative bargaining power of trade unions and employers; see A.M. Ross, *Trade Union Wage Policy*, University of California Press, 1948; J.T. Dunlop (ed.), *The Theory of Wage Determination*, Macmillan 1964; R. Perlman (ed.), *Wage Determination, Market or Power Forces?* D.C. Heath and Co., 1964, D.J. Robertson, *Factory Wage Structures and National Agreements*, CUP, 1960, and S.W. Lerner, J.R. Cable and S. Gupta (eds), *Workshop Wage Determination*, Pergamon Press, 1969; see also **wage theories, share of wages, marginal productivity theory of wages.**

BARGAINING UNIT. A group of

workers held to be appropriate for collective bargaining purposes. In Britain bargaining units, whether at national (or industry-wide), company, plant, local or domestic levels, have traditionally been those accepted by voluntary agreement or **custom and practice.** The **Industrial Relations Act 1971** (now repealed), attempted to define the term and provided a procedure for determining such units and establishing **sole bargaining agents.** The **Industrial Relations Code of Practice** February 1972 (74-81) advises that (i) bargaining unit arrangements which are found to be working well 'should not be disturbed without good reason'; (ii) a bargaining unit 'should cover as wide a group of employees as practicable'; (iii) the common interests of employees, their own wishes, their training, experience and qualifications, and a number of other matters should be taken into account when defining a bargaining unit. It also advises that bargaining units should be voluntarily agreed, and that differences about them should first be processed through voluntary machinery and conciliation; see also **sole bargaining rights.**

BARGER v. TRANSPORT AND GENERAL WORKERS' UNION (1974) ITR 80; (1974) IRLR 57, NIRC A case in which, *inter alia*, it was ruled that the plaintiff was entitled to resign from the union with reasonable notice, see **membership of a union.**

BARTH PREMIUM PLAN. A premium payment plan or incentive payment scheme in use in the United States of America but little employed in Britain. It differs from other such schemes (see **Halsey System, Rowan System** and **Bedeaux System**) in its method of calculating earnings, the formula being

$$\text{rate per hour} \sqrt{\frac{\text{standard hours produced}}{\text{x actual hours worked.}}}$$

BASE RATE or **basic rate.** The pay of a worker for a fixed unit of time, e.g. an hour, a day etc., apart from the payment of overtime or other premiums; usually the basis on which such premiums are paid, e.g. time-and-one-quarter, time-and-a-half etc. (see **overtime**), and usually guaranteed as minimum take home pay; sometimes known as the **datal rate**. In some circumstances, the basic rate may differ from this definition; e.g. formerly in engineering, where the **basic rate** for the calculation of piecework earnings was lower than the guaranteed **minimum time rate** by the amount of the **piecework supplement** (q.v.) or where the basic rate may differ by domestic agreement, from one establishment to another. Sometimes called the **bonus rate** (see **bonus**).

BASIC MOTION TIME (BMT). A predetermined motion time system developed by P. Presgrave and G. B. Bailey in Canada in 1950. A basic motion is defined as a single complete movement of a body member, and BMT takes into account distance moved, visual attention necessary to complete the motion, degree of precision required, the amount of force used, and other factors.

BASIC PAY. The element of a wage or salary packet, or of earnings, which pay structures or arrangements ensure is guaranteed from one pay period to another; hence usually the **basic rate,** or basic salary, however defined, net of overtime and piecework earnings, or casual payments, **perks, tips, allowances** etc. A number of reports in the 1960s identified the tendency for the gap between basic pay, and **take-home pay,** or **earnings** to widen in many British industries and thought it undesirable e.g. the National Board for Prices and Incomes (Report No. 17, *Wages in the Bakery Industry,* Final Report, Cmnd. 3019, June 1966, paras 41 and 42), considered a large disparity between basic pay and earnings to be both uneconomic and unfair; 'uneconomic in that the worker is dependent on a large number of supplements to his basic rate which are uncertain in their nature and which can therefore make him resistant to change . . . and unfair in that the employer reaps the benefit of the employees' willingness to work more than the standard 40 hours without any obligation to maintain the workers' incomes beyond the guaranteed basic wage for these hours'.

BASIC RATE; see **base rate.**

BASIC TIME or **basis time. A work study** term defined as the time for carrying out an element of work at **standard rating,** i.e.

$$\frac{\text{Observed Time x Observed Rating}}{\text{Standard Rating}}$$

Basic time, with the addition of **relaxation allowance** and any allowance for additional work becomes, in work study parlance, a definition of the work content of a job or operation, to which is added other allowances to obtain **standard time.** International Labour Office, *Introduction to Work Study,* Geneva, 1969, Chapter 17.

BASIS TIME, see **basic time.**

BASKET, CANE, WICKER, AND FIBRE FURNITURE MAKERS OF GREAT BRITAIN AND IRELAND, NATIONAL UNION OF (NUB). A trade union founded in 1896, which changed to the above title in 1946, being previously the Basket, Skip and Hamper Makers' Association. The original members of this amalgamation were the British Amalgamated Union of Journeymen Basket, Cane and Wicker Furniture Makers, The London Union of Journeymen Basketmakers (1876), the Lancashire and Cheshire Union of Skip and Basket Makers, the Yorkshire United Skip, Basket and Hamper Makers' .Society, and the Scottish Union of Journeymen Basket Makers and Northern Ireland (1868). Membership of the union had declined to 48 by the 1970s and in 1973 the union was disbanded.

BDA. British Dental Association; see **Dental Association, British.**

BEAMERS, TWISTERS AND DRAWERS' (HAND AND MACHINE), AMALGAMATED ASSOCIATION OF. A trade union organising workers concerned in the weaving of cotton, linen and man-made fibres in Lancashire, Cheshire and Cumberland, first established in 1866 and reconstituted as an 'amalgamation' of semi-autonomous district societies in 1889. It has currently 20 such district unions or branches. *Address:* 27 Every Street, Nelson, Lancs, BB9 7NE. *Tel:* 0282 64181. *TUC Affiliated Membership 1977:* 1,215.

BEC; see **British Employers' Confederation.**

BEDEAUX SYSTEM or 'Bedeaux Plan'. A wage incentive payment system popular in the 1920s, and named after Charles Bedeaux, a French engineer and industrialist. The aim of the Bedeaux system was to increase the incentive to individual workers by providing a bonus on time saved on **standard time** set for a job, and to reduce the bonus payment as output increased beyond a certain level, the worker thus sharing 'with the employer the gains or losses resulting from changes in output'. Though other schemes (see **Halsey,**

Rowan and Barth) have similar characteristics, the Bedeaux System has been particularly the object of trade union suspicion as involving unjustifiable means of reducing labour costs (see N. C. Hunt, *Methods of Wage Payment in British Industry*, Pitman, 1951, pp. 81-4). Bedeaux engineers used the letter 'B' to designate the unit of measurement, each B being the equivalent of one minute and 60 Bs the standard task to be performed in one hour. In one form or another the Bedeaux System is still widely used, especially in medium and small size firms. Under the original scheme only 75 per cent of the bonus earned was paid to the worker, the remaining 25 per cent being placed in a pool to provide bonus for **indirects** and supervisors. This characteristic still persists in some factories, though some firms now pay full bonus. The scheme is said, because of the points system used, to be of the greatest value in production planning, but to be costly and complicated to install and maintain, and for workers to understand; R. Marriott, *Incentive Payment Systems*, 3rd (revised) ed. Staples Press, 1968, p. 56 *et seq.*

BEDSTEAD ALLIANCES. Alliances between combinations of employers and workers which took practical shape for a time in the 1890s, but did not survive the nineteenth century, in which employers undertook to sell only at prices which would yield them a profit and enable them to pay adequate wages, and workers undertook to strike the works of any employer who failed to do this; so called because a leading case of the system was the metal bedstead trade, but other Alliances were also formed in china electrical fittings, china door furniture, fenders etc.; see E. J. Smith, *The New Trades Combination Movement*, 1899 and E. H. Phelps Brown, *The Growth of British Industrial Relations*, Macmillan, 1959, p. 137 *et seq.*

BEGINNER'S RATE. Starting rate, or **trainee rate**. A rate of pay for an inexperienced employee, paid for a limited period, at the end of which the worker is given the full rate for the job.

BELL-HORSES; see **pacers.**

BELLRINGER DISPUTE. A name sometimes given to the strike at Briggs Motor Bodies in 1957 which resulted from the ringing of a bell by the chairman of the shop committee, Mr McLoughlin. The dispute gave rise to the **Cameron Report**

(q.v.) which identified the extent of unrest at Fords, Dagenham and the existence of an uncontrolled shop stewards' organisation; see H. A. Turner, Garfield Clack and Geoffrey Roberts, *Labour Relations in the Motor Industry*, Allen and Unwin, 1967, p. 275 *et seq.*

BENCH MARKS. Jobs which are precisely described and measured so that they may be used as standards against which other less well defined jobs may be compared; see **comparative estimating.**

BENEFITS. Assistance, usually, but not invariably of a pecuniary kind, made to workers by statute (for example under the National Insurance and Health Service Acts), by trade unions under their rules, by collective agreement or management policy (see **fringe benefits**). Benefits to members were a permissive statutory object of trade unions under the Trade Union Acts and registered unions were required (Trade Union Acts 1871 and 1876) to include rules laying down the conditions under which a member might become entitled to benefit, though the courts would not entertain proceedings by a union member against his union or officials for specific performance of a benefit rule: **accident** or **disablement benefit (Shanks v. United Operative Masons' Association** (1874) 1R.823, **Sayer v. Amalgamated Society of Carpenters and Joiners** (1902) 19TLR 122, **Burns v. Cunningham** (1885) 1ShCtRep. 318); **sickness benefit (General Union of Operative Carpenters and Joiners v. O'Donnell** (1877) 1 ILTJ 282, **Old v. Robson** (1890) 59 LJMC 41, **Burke v. Amalgamated Society of Dyers** (1906) 2 K.B. 583); **tool benefit (Mudd v. General Union of Operative Carpenters and Joiners** (1910) 26 TLR 518); **superannuation benefit (Cullen v. Elwin** (1904) 90 LT 840, **Russell v. Amalgamated Society of Carpenters and Joiners** (1912) AC421, **Miller v. Amalgamated Engineering Union** (1938) Ch 669, **Cameron v. Associated Society of Locomotive Engineers and Firemen** (1930) 46 ShCtRep. 84); **funeral benefit (Crocker v. Knight** (1892) 1 QB 702); and **strike benefit (Swaine v. Wilson** (1889) 24 QBD 252). The **Trade Union and Labour Relations Act 1974** makes it obligatory for superannuation schemes of unions to be examined by a qualified actuary and submitted to the **Certification Officer**; see also **nomination procedure.**

BETRIEBSRÄTE. Works Councils (q.v.) established by law in the Federal Republic of Germany. As a form of workers' participation in Germany, Betriebsräte date from the late nineteenth century. They were first made generally obligatory during the first world war and embodied in the Works Council Act (Betriebsrätegesetz) 1920, which was followed by a further act on the appointment of Works Council members to supervisory boards (Gesetzüber die Entsendung von Betriebsrätmitgliedern in den Aufsichtsrat) in 1922. For a British account of this period see C. W. Guillebaud, *The Works Council: A German Experiment in Democracy*, CUP, 1922. Works Councils, destroyed by the Nazi régime, were reinstated by the Allied Control Council in 1946, and in the Federal Works Constitution Act (Betriebsverfassungsgesetz) of 1952 (see also **codetermination** (Mitbestimmung)). Under the Act a Works Council representative of all employees has to be set up in all undertakings employing more than five adult workers. Election to Betriebsräte has no direct relationship to trade union organisation; nor are they 'joint' councils, nor negotiating bodies. Their function is to give workers co-determination rights on such subjects as working hours, administration of factory welfare services, the fixing of job and piece rates and principles or remuneration, co-operation rights in influencing management decisions, and **disclosure of information** rights. The Act also provided for one-third of the supervisory boards of companies to be employees' representatives; see H. Neumann-Duesberg *Betriebsverfassungsrecht*, Berlin, 1960, and F. Fürstenberg, 'Workers Participation in Management in the Federal Republic of Germany', *International Institute for Labour Studies Bulletin* No. 6, June 1969. One-third representation now applies to companies with fewer than 2,000 employees. A second Works Constitution Act of 1972 has given extended codetermination rights to Works Councils over short time working, overtime, dismissal and other subjects; see Martin Pelzer and Ralf Boer, *Betriebsverfassungsgesetz (Labour Management Relations Act)* Fritz Knapp Verlag, Frankfurt am Main, 1977, 2nd ed. (in German and English).

BETTER CONDITIONS CLAUSE. A clause in a collective agreement affecting more than one establishment or undertaking and providing that each establishment or undertaking is to continue to observe any practices which are more favourable to the workers concerned than provided for in the agreement itself; see H. A. Clegg, *General Union*, Basil Blackwell, 1954, p. 154.

BETTESHANGER MINERS. An incident arising out of the operation of S.R. and O. 1305, 1940 (see **National Arbitration Tribunal**), which made strikes illegal except in defined circumstances, and under which 1,000 men on strike at Betteshanger Colliery in Kent were prosecuted in 1941. The ineffectiveness of legal proceedings in obtaining a return to work in this case has often been quoted in order to question the utility of legal sanctions in enforcing decisions upon large bodies of workers or in reinforcing collective bargaining. For an account of the dispute see Report of the **Royal Commission on Trade Unions and Employers' Associations, 1965-1968**, Cmnd. 3623, 1968 Appendix 6 (Written Evidence of Sir Harold Emmerson, GCB, KCVO); see also **compulsory arbitration**.

BEVIN AWARD; see **toolroom operatives' agreement**.

BFMF; see **British Footwear Manufacturers' Federation**.

BFMP. British Federation of Master Printers; see **British Printing Industries Federation**.

BFTT. British Federation of Textile Technicians; see **Textile Technicians, British Federation of**.

BIBLIOGRAPHIES AND SOURCES ON INDUSTRIAL RELATIONS. Extensive summaries are to be found in George Sayers Bain and Gillian B. Woolven, 'The Literature of Labour Economics and Industrial Relations, A Guide to its Sources', *Industrial Relations Journal*, Summer 1970 (and in J. Fletcher (ed.), *The Use of Economics Literature*, Butterworths, 1971) and 'The Primary Materials of British Industrial Relations', *British Journal of Industrial Relations*, Vol. IX, No. 3, November 1971. Principal bibliographical sources in and for Great Britain are: *A London Bibliography of the Social Sciences*, London School of Economics and Political Science (1931-   ), V. L. Allen, *International Bibliography of Trade Unionism*, Merlin Press, 1968, Carole Faubert, *Personnel Management, A Bibliography*, Institute of Personnel Management 1968, Waldo Chamberlin, *Industrial Relations in Wartime: Great Britain 1914-1918*, Stanford University

Press, 1940, J. McDougall (ed.), *An Interim Bibliography of the Scottish Working Class Movement*, Scottish Committee for the Study of Labour History, 1965, R. and E. Frow and M. Katanka, *The History of British Trade Unionism: A Select Bibliography*, Historical Association, London, 1969, and A. W. Gottschalk *et al.*, *British Industrial Relations, An Annotated Bibliography*, University of Nottingham, Department of Adult Education, 1969.

BIDLINE SYSTEM. An arrangement between airline pilots and British Airways, Overseas Division, whereby a pilot is allowed, according to seniority, to choose a month's line of work in advance, especially as regards destination and length of trips.

BIM. British Institute of Management (q.v.).

'BIM INDEX'. A formula for measuring **labour turnover** (q.v.) recommended by the **British Institute of Management**; viz.

$$\frac{\text{leavers over a period}}{\text{average number employed over the same period}} \times 100$$

BIRD v. BRITISH CELANESE LTD (1945) KB 336. A case in which it was ruled that a deduction of two days' wages from a spinner employed on terms which included in internal works rules the right of the employer to suspend employees for misconduct or disobedience was not an illegal deduction under the Truck Act 1896. K. W. Wedderburn, *Cases and Materials on Labour Law*, CUP, 1967, p. 130 *et seq.*

BIRMINGHAM AND MIDLAND SHEET METAL WORKERS' SOCIETY; see Sheet Metal Workers' Society, Birmingham and Midland.

BISAKTA. British Iron, Steel and Kindred Trades Association; see **Iron and Steel Trades Confederation.**

BJIR. British Journal of Industrial Relations (q.v.).

'BLACK CIRCULAR'. The name given to Circular 16 of the General Council of the **Trades Union Congress** in 1935, which threatened to withdraw recognition from **trades councils** which accepted delegates 'in any way connected with either communist or fascist organisations or any ancillary

bodies'. The rule against Communists was modified in 1943.

BLACK FRIDAY; see Triple Alliance.

BLACK GOODS; see blacking.

BLACKCOATED WORKER. A synonym for **white collar worker** (q.v.). Of the two expressions, blackcoated worker seems to have been preferred in common usage until after the second world war. David Lockwood (*The Blackcoated Worker*, George Allen and Unwin, 1966), uses the term interchangeably with 'clerical worker' throughout his study.

BLACKING. A form of **boycott** (q.v.) in which trade union members refuse to handle **black** or **tainted goods**, i.e. those used, manufactured, processed or carried by employers with whom their own or other unions are in dispute. Blacking has also been used as a political weapon e.g. in the 'Jolly George' strike of 1919 in which there was a refusal to load arms to be used by the Poles against Soviet Russian troops; see K. G. J. C. Knowles, *Strikes,* Basil Blackwell, 1952, p. 17. Also used to describe the exchange of 'blacks' or proofs between newspaper houses, a practice objected to by journalists as leading to underpayment and staff reductions; see F. J. Mansfield, *Gentleman - the Press!. The Official History of the National Union of Journalists,* W. H. Allen and Co., 1943, p. 407 *et seq.*; see also **Heaton Transport (St Helens) Ltd v. Transport and General Workers' Union;** for the legal position of blacking, see **trade dispute;** also **secondary boycott.**

BLACKLEG. A worker who remains at work while his colleagues are on strike, who accepts work during a strike, or who passes pickets; sometimes used of a worker who accepts work at lower rates and on worse conditions than other workers. In the United States more usually known as a **scab.** Blacklegs are sometimes thought of as involved in **strikebreaking** though the latter activity would seem to be more organised and systematic than blacklegging usually is.

BLACKLEGS' CHARTER. A popular expression used by trade unionists to describe any measure or document which is regarded as anti-union, and hence an encouragement to **blacklegs**; e.g. the **Document, the Trade Disputes and Trade Union Act 1927,** the **Industrial Relations**

Act 1971, especially on **membership of a trade union** (q.v.).

BLACKLISTING. The use of a blacklist of names circulated by employers or their associations in order to prevent the employment of particular workers on grounds of trade union or other activities; the use of similar lists by trade unions, usually to identify **blacklegs** or **scabs** (q.v.), or to influence an employer's customers. The formal use of blacklists by employers may now be considered rare, though informal exchange of information on workers thought to be undesirable as employees may be more common. K.G.J.C. Knowles, *Strikes,* Basil Blackwell, 1952, p. 123 comments that 'allegations of employer-blacklisting are not uncommon, particularly in the engineering and ship-building industries, though one would hardly expect to find precise evidence'. Knowles also quotes a 1948 instance of the **National Union of Mineworkers** threatening to blacklist members of another union from working in the coal mining industry, (p. 124), though formal trade union blacklisting is also rare. Blacklist decisions of the courts are discussed by Cyril Grunfeld, *Modern Trade Union Law,* Sweet and Maxwell, 1970. In **Jenkinson v. Neild** (1892) 8 TLR 640, and **Bulcock v. St Anne's Master Builders' Association** (1902) 19 TLR 27, the legality of employers' blacklists was upheld; it was not upheld in the case of trade union blacklists in **Trollope v. London Building Trades Federation** (1895) 72 LT 342 and **Quinn v. Leatham** (1901) AC 495. The situation is currently affected by several provisions of the Trade Union and Labour Relations Acts 1974 and 1976 and of the Employment Protection Act 1975 (see **freedom of association**); see **City of Birmingham District Council v. Beyer** (1977) IRLR 211 (EAT) for a recent case of blacklisting by an employer.

BLACKMAIL FRIDAY; see **Red Friday.**

BLAKE GRID; see **Managerial Grid.**

BLANKET AGREEMENT. Sometimes used to describe a collective agreement covering an entire industry (i.e. **a national agreement,** or **industry-wide agreement**), or one covering a large group of workers, or a large geographical area.

BLASTFURNACEMEN, ORE MINERS, COKE WORKERS AND KINDRED TRADES, NATIONAL UNION

OF (NUB). A trade union formed in 1921 by the amalgamation of districts of the National Federation of Blastfurnacemen, Ore Miners and Kindred Trades (1892). The union dates its origin from the Cleveland Association of Blastfurnacemen (1878), which registered in 1882. The Federation declined to enter the **Iron and Steel Trades Confederation** (1 January 1917), and the NUB has also remained outside it. Jack Owen, *Ironmen,* NUB, 1953. *Address:* 93 Borough Road West, Middlesbrough, Cleveland, TS1 3AJ. *Tel:* 0642-42961 and 49772. *TUC Affiliated Membership 1977:* 16,777.

BLIND ALLEY JOB; see **dead end job.**

BLIND AND DISABLED, NATIONAL LEAGUE OF THE. A trade union founded in 1899 as the National League of the Blind, changing to its present name in 1968. Members were originally to be found mainly in the basket, brush and matting trades, but are now more widely distributed and to be found in bedding, upholstery, wire work, machine knitwear, cardboard box making, light engineering, weaving, boot repair, braille printing, telephone operating etc. The union has members in Northern Ireland, but those in the Republic seceded before 1923. It had its highest membership in 1945, 7,320 members. *Address:* Tottenham Trades Hall, 7 Bruce Grove, London, N17 6RA. *Tel:* 01-808 6030. *TUC Affiliated Membership 1977:* 4,250.

BLIND, INDUSTRIAL ADVISERS TO; see **Industrial Advisers to the Blind Ltd.**

BLOCK VOTE. A vote for or against a particular resolution case *en bloc,* i.e. by giving each delegation at a conference a single voting card bearing the number of members it represents, and counting the votes for and against on this basis. The block vote is used at the **Trades Union Congress,** the **Confederation of Shipbuilding and Engineering Unions** annual meeting, and at many union conferences. Its use at Labour Party Conferences has led to intermittent conflict between trade unions and Divisional Labour Parties. Martin Harrison, *Trade Unions and the Labour Party,* George Allen and Unwin, 1960, p. 246 *et seq.*

BLOW. A rest from work; a break. Hence **blow times;** breaks from work, whether these are explicitly or tacitly recognised by collective agreement or whether they are not; **blow system;** extension of blow times are regular intervals into a regular pattern, e.g. taking half-an-hour off in every three, or even more; see Economist Intelligence Unit: *Survey of the National Newspaper Industry,* 1966, p. 95, which cites a blow system in which only half a shift is actually worked; see also **welting** and **spelling.**

BLOW SYSTEM; see **blow.**

BLOW TIMES; see **blow.**

BLUE BOOK. A name traditionally given to official reports of Parliament and the Privy Council, issued in a blue paper cover; also, and for the same reason, used of the text of the productivity bargain offered by the ESSO management at the Fawley Refinery to the unions in February 1960, and subsequently agreed after negotiation; see Allan Flanders, *The Fawley Productivity Agreements,* Faber and Faber, 1964. The use of the term on this occasion has led to other similar agreements being referred to by the colour of their covers, e.g. the **Orange Book** (a subsequent offer of a productivity deal at Fawley), the **Red Book** (Mobil Oil at Coryton Refinery; see F. E. Oldfield, *New Look Industrial Relations,* Mason Reed, 1966), the **Magenta Book** (Stewarts and Lloyds, Corby) etc.

BLUE COLLAR UNION; see **blue-collar workers.**

BLUE-COLLAR WORKERS. A term used, especially in the United States, to describe manual workers, i.e. workers who are not **white-collar workers** (q.v.), and are concerned either with traditional craft skills, with wholly unskilled work, or with semi-skilled production operations; hence **blue-collar union,** a union catering for such manual workers. R. Blauner (*Alienation and Freedom,* University of Chicago Press, 1964, p. 169) includes among blue-collar workers those who have 'non-manual' responsibility for continuous process technology, and identifies 'the shift from skill to responsibility as the most important historical trend in the evolution of blue-collar work'.

BLUE-EYED BOYS. Workers or groups of workers especially favoured by employers; in particular **regulars,** men in the labour pool of the Dock Labour Board who are the favourites of particular fore-men and whom he will always select if they are available at the **free call,** i.e. the procedure by which foremen in some ports pick the gangs they want before allocation by the Board itself. *Final Report of the Committee of Inquiry under the Rt. Hon. Lord Devlin into certain matters concerning the Port Transport Industry,* Cmnd. 2734, August 1965, p. 6.

BLUE MONDAY. The first day of the working week on which **absenteeism** (q.v.) tends to be higher than subsequent days, and lowest of all on Friday in a five-day week. Hence **Blue Monday Index,** a measure of voluntary absenteeism devised by Hilde Behrend (*Absence under Full-Employment,* University of Birmingham, 1951), and calculated by taking the difference between Friday and Monday attendances per hundred workers.

BLUE MONDAY INDEX; see **Blue Monday.**

BLUE SKY BARGAINING. Unrealistic and unreasonable demands by either trade unions or managements in negotiation, especially in the United States. Harold S. Roberts, *Dictionary of Industrial Relations,* BNA, 1966.

BLUE UNION. The **National Amalgamated Stevedores and Dockers** (blue tickets), as distinct from the **Transport and General Workers' Union,** the union with the largest membership among dockers (white tickets). The NASD originated in the National Amalgamated Stevedores Protection League which was derived from the Labour Protection League of 1872. The failure to incorporate the Stevedores' Union into the amalgamation of 1922 which produced the Transport and General Workers' Union has led to intermittent warfare between the two organisations (see John Lovell, *Stevedores and Dockers, A Study of Trade Unionism in the Port of London, 1870-1914,* Macmillan, 1969). A dispute between them in 1954 resulted in the TUC Disputes Committee, under the **Bridlington Agreement,** calling on the NASD to restore membership recruited from the TGWU. Though this was done, the legal position of the Bridlington Agreement was challenged in 1956 in the case of **Spring v. National Amalgamated Stevedores and Dockers** (q.v.) and the blue union, having failed to satisfy the requirements of the Committee on Membership and Accounts, was expelled from the TUC in 1959: *Final Report of the Com-*

*mittee of Inquiry under the Rt. Hon. Lord
Devlin into certain matters concerning the
Port Transport Industry,* Cmnd. 2734,
August 1965, pp. 33-40.

BMA. British Medical Association; see
Medical Association, British.

BMT. Basic Motion Time (q.v.).

BOARDS OF ARBITRATION. Arbitration bodies set up by the Secretary of State
for Employment under the **Industrial
Courts Act, 1919** s. 2(2)(c), consisting of
'one or more persons nominated by or on
behalf of the employers concerned and an
equal number of persons nominated by or
on behalf of the workmen concerned, and
an independent chairman appointed by
the Minister'. Forty-five such Boards
sat between 1946 and 1970, and rarely
more than two in any particular year,
single arbitrators being more frequently
used. The awards of Boards were not normally published and the parties were
required by the Department to agree in
advance that should a Board be unable to
reach a unanimous decision, the chairman
should be authorised to make an award
with the full powers of an umpire (Ministry of Labour, *Evidence to the Royal Commission on Trade Unions and Employers'
Associations,* 1965, p. 103). The powers of
the Secretary of State to set up Boards of
Arbitration have been repealed by the
Employment Protection Act 1975; see also
arbitration.

**BOARDS OF CONCILIATION AND
ARBITRATION** or **Joint Boards of Conciliation and Arbitration.** Joint Committees of workers and employers, providing
for **conciliation** through an independent
chairman or by a chairman elected by the
parties, sometimes alternately, sometimes
with a casting vote and sometimes with
provision for **arbitration.** The device of
the Board of Conciliation was a conspicu-
ous form of organised industrial relations
in Britain from the 1860s to the 1890s, and
owed much to the work of A. J. Mundella,
Rupert Kettle and David Dale, lasting
longest of all in the iron industry. Provision was made in the **Conciliation Act
1896** (now repealed) for the registration of
Boards of Conciliation and Arbitration,
but this measure seems to have been ineffective, and Boards were mostly overtaken
by direct negotiation and other developments in industrial relations machinery,
particularly **Joint Industrial Councils**
(q.v.); see E. H. Phelps Brown, *The*

Growth of British Industrial Relations,
Macmillan, 1965.

BOARDS OF MEDIATION; see **mediation.**

**BOILERMAKERS, SHIPWRIGHTS,
BLACKSMITHS AND STRUCTU-
RAL WORKERS, AMALGAMATED
SOCIETY OF (ASB).** A trade union
formed by the merger in January 1963 of
the Associated Blacksmiths, Forge and
Smithy Workers Society, the United
Society of Boilermakers, Shipbuilders and
Structural Workers and the Shipconstructors and Shipwrights Association. The full
integration of the Society was achieved in
April 1969, each union working for some
time after amalgamation as a separate section for trade purposes. The union was
reckoned in 1971 to have some 30,000
members in shipbuilding and shiprepairing, the bulk of its membership being in
the engineering industry. It is nevertheless
best known as a shipbuilding union, where
it organises a variety of crafts, mainly in
the steel trades - welders, platers, shipwrights, boilermakers, caulkers, burners,
drillers, riveters, blacksmiths, loftsmen
and riggers; it also generally organises
supervisors up to foreman level; see Commission on Industrial Relations, *Shipbuilding and Shiprepairing,* Cmnd. 4756,
August 1971. A forerunner of the present
Society, the Boilermakers' and Iron and
Steel Ship Builders' Society (see D. C.
Cummings, *A Historical Survey of the
Boiler Makers' and Iron and Steel Ship
Builders' Society,* R. Robinson, Newcastle-
upon-Tyne, 1905) played a prominent part
in the foundation of the Federation of
Engineering and Shipbuilding Trades (see
**Shipbuilding and Engineering Unions,
Confederation of**). J. E. Mortimer, *A His-
tory of the Boilermakers' Society,* Allen
and Unwin, 1973. *Address:* Lifton House,
Eslington Road, Newcastle-upon-Tyne,
NE2 4SB. *Tel:* 0632 81-3205/6. *TUC Affil-
iated Membership 1977:* 128,403.

BONA-FIDE TRADE UNION. An
imprecise expression used to describe
workers' organisations in good standing in
the trade union movement. Good standing
may be judged on acceptability for membership of **Trade Union Congress** (see
TUC, *Report,* 1946, p. 255), or other
representative body, such as the **Confederation of Shipbuilding and Engineering
Unions,** or the **General Federation of
Trade Unions,** which would normally
exclude **breakaways** and **company** or

house unions (q.v.), as well as those without established negotiating rights in any section of industry with which they happened to be concerned. Unions may in some cases be 'bona-fide' in some circumstances but not in others; see **wrong unions, independent union, independent trade union.**

BONSOR v. MUSICIANS' UNION (1955) All ER 518; (1956) AC 104. A leading case in which it was established that the wrongfully expelled trade union member may recover damages from his union for breach of contract. This overruled the decision in **Kelly v. Natsopa** (1915), 31, TLR 632, in which the Court of Appeal held that damages could not be awarded for wrongful expulsion on the grounds that the officials concerned were acting as agents for the entire union membership including the expelled member, who could not sue for his own agents' acts. Bonsor was fifty-two weeks in arrears with his dues and was expelled on the decision of the Branch Secretary, an act which the rules required could only be made by the Branch Committee; see K. W. Wedderburn, *Cases and Materials on Labour Law,* CUP, 1967, p. 643 *et seq.*

BONUS. A broad term applied to any payment above the regular basic rate or standard payment. It may be applied to **premium payments** for overtime or shift work ('overtime bonus' or 'shift bonus'), to payments for attendance ('attendance bonus' or **attendance money**) for good timekeeping (see **clocking**), for work under exceptional conditions etc., as well as to incentive payments made under **payment by results** or an **incentive payment system** or as **production bonuses**, all of which may be known as **bonus schemes. Ex gratia payments,** may also be known as bonuses, e.g. Christmas bonus. When used in PBR schemes, the rate on which earnings from time saved by the pieceworker, i.e. the **basic rate**, is sometimes known as the **bonus rate.**

BONUS HOURS; see **shift differential.**

BONUS INCREMENT (work study); see **allowances.** 'An addition, other than **policy allowance** (q.v.) to **standard time** (or some constituent part of it, e.g. work content) as a basis for an incentive scheme'. British Standards Institution, *Glossary of Terms Used in Work Study,* BS 3138: 1969, A 1016.

BONUS RATE; see **bonus.**

BONUS SCHEMES; see **bonus.**

BOOSTER PAYMENT; see **compensatory payment.**

BOOT, SHOE AND SLIPPER OPERATIVES, ROSSENDALE UNION OF. A trade union, formed in 1895, with membership formerly confined to the Rossendale Valley, but now to be found in East Lancashire and the Fylde Coast. It declined to join the newly formed **National Union of Footwear, Leather and Allied Trades** (1971), but has with it a **spheres of influence agreement.** *Address:* 7 Tenterfield Street, Waterfoot, Rossendale BB4 7BA *Tel:* 070 62 5657. *TUC Affiliated Membership, 1977:* 6,107.

BOOT AND SHOE OPERATIVES, NATIONAL UNION OF (NUBSO); see **Footwear, Leather and Allied Trades, National Union of.**

BOULTING v. ASSOCIATED CINEMATOGRAPH, TELEVISION AND ALLIED TECHNICIANS. (1963) 2 QB 606. A case in which the plaintiffs sought an injunction to restrain the defendants from taking any action to compel them to join a union according to the provision of Rule 7(a) of ACTAT. The court found for the defendants, but the case was also notable for the interpretation placed upon the use of injunctions under the **Trades Disputes Act 1906** s.4 (see **injunction**).

BOULWARISM. A collective bargaining approach followed by the General Electric Company (USA) and named after a former Vice-President for Employee and Public Relations, Lemuel Boulware, the main feature of which is that, after hearing the union's case, the company, on the basis of research and study, makes an offer which it considers to be 'right' and only alters this if new information can be produced which will convince it that this is not so. The approach has brought the company into conflict with the National Labor Relations Board which has held that the method violates the good faith bargaining duty provided for by the **Taft-Hartley Act;** see Herbert R. Northrup, *Boulwarism,* University of Michigan, Ann Arbor, Michigan, 1964.

BOX STEWARD; see **shop steward.**

BOYCOTT. A form of industrial action in

which workers and/or their unions attempt to put economic pressure upon an employer to recognise the union or to make bargaining concessions to it by refusal to handle, use or purchase his products or services, or by causing others to do the same. Where the refusal is directed against the employer immediately concerned, it is often known as a **primary boycott**, and where it is operated by third parties, a **secondary boycott**. Boycotts have been less widely used in Britain than in some other countries, and have rarely gone to extremes, being confined to milder forms of **blacking** (q.v.). Secondary boycotts, which frequently aim at cutting off supplies to, or from, the employer in dispute, have involved possible breaches of **commercial contracts**, and the union official or officials concerned in the possibility of using unlawful means, either of indirectly procuring such a breach (e.g. by a **sympathetic strike**), or by directly inducing a third party to break his contract with the employer in dispute. The Donovan **Royal Commission on Trade Unions and Employers' Associations 1965-1968** (Cmnd. 3623, June 1968) commented on the uncertainties of the legal position and recommended that breaches of all contracts should be protected against actions in tort where a **trade dispute** was concerned. This is now substantially the position under the Trade Union and Labour Relations Act 1974, as amended in 1976 (see **trade dispute**).

BPC. British Productivity Council (q.v.).

BPIF. British Printing Industries Federation (q.v.).

BRANCHING. The act involving a trade union member being summoned to appear at his branch, or other constitutional authority, to explain his conduct in a trade union activity, or to face a charge involving a breach of trade union rule; also, 'to be branched'.

BREAKAWAY UNION. A trade union, sometimes known as a **splinter union**, formed by dissident members seceding from an existing union. Examples of breakaways in recent times are the United Clothing Workers' Union (which appeared in 1929 as a breakaway from the Tailors' and Garment Workers' Union), the National Passenger Workers' Union (formed in 1937 when for a time the London busmen seceded from the **Transport and General Workers' Union**), and the

Engineering Officers' (Telecommunication) Association (a splinter from the **Post Office Engineering Union**). None of these organisations have survived. A more recently active breakaway, the National News Guild which had as its slogan 'Newsmen, elected by newsmen, to negotiate all conditions relative to newsmen's affairs' is said still to exist, though as an effective force it collapsed some seventeen years ago. Breakaways are discussed by Shirley W. Lerner (*Breakaway Unions and the Small Trade Union*, George Allen and Unwin 1961), who attributes them to increasing centralisation of decision making in trade unions. Breakaways have become increasingly uncommon in recent years. Difficulties in obtaining negotiating rights against the hostility of established unions, as well as the growth of **workplace bargaining** (q.v.), and the readier access of existing organisations to legislative support, may account for this; see also, **wrong union, bona-fide trade union**.

BREEN v. AMALGAMATED UNION OF ENGINEERING AND FOUNDRY WORKERS AND OTHERS. Times Law Report, 28 January 1971 (Court of Appeal). A case in which it was maintained by Lord Denning, Master of the Rolls, that decisions of trade union district committee, though made in the exercise of a discretion conferred by the union rules, may be declared invalid if the committee has not acted fairly and, where necessary, given the member affected by its decision an opportunity to be heard. The case arose out of the refusal of an AEF district committee to approve the appointment of a shop steward elected by trade union members at the place of work.

BRIDLINGTON AGREEMENT. A set of 'principles for the avoidance of disputes' in inter-union relations first laid down for TUC affiliated unions in 1924 (the **Hull Main Principles**) and revised at the Bridlington Congress in 1939. The Agreement advises that unions in frequent contact with each other should reach agreement on **spheres of influence, recognition of cards**, transfer of members and machinery for composing differences, and provides that no union should accept a member of another union into membership without inquiry. If the reply shows that he is under discipline, in arrears, or engaged in a trade dispute, the application should not be accepted; nor should a union begin recruitment among a grade of workpeople in an establishment where another union already has a majority of such workpeople and negotiates for them, except with that union's consent. (TUC, *Relations Between Unions*, p. 12, 1964). The Disputes Committee of the TUC is authorised to act in applying the Bridlington principles only when the unions concerned have made an effort to resolve the issue between themselves, or where industry machinery has been tried and failed (see **inter-union disputes**). The Agreement is strictly limited in its operation (John Hughes, *Trade Union Structure and Government*, Royal Commission on Trade Unions and Employers' Associations, Research Paper s.5 (Part I), 1967 pp. 27-30), and is thought by some to have weakened what they consider to be the right of trade union members to join the union of their choice (S. W. Lerner, 'The TUC Jurisdictional Dispute Settlement, 1924-1957', *Manchester School*, September 1968 and Chapter 2 of *Breakaway Unions and the Small Trade Union*, Allen and Unwin, 1961). The Bridlington principles have been called a 'morally binding code of conduct made between persons of similar views' without legal force. As a result of actions in the courts contesting the application by unions of the rulings of the TUC Disputes Committee in the 1950s (see **Spring v. National Amalgamated Stevedores and Dockers** and **Andrew v. National Union of Public Employees**) the TUC asked affiliated unions to include within their rules the provision that: 'notwithstanding anything in these rules the Executive Committee may by giving six weeks' notice in writing terminate the membership of any member if necessary to comply with a decision of the Disputes Committee of the Trades Union Congress'. Most have done so but legal judgements have continued to affect the operation of the Agreement, the most recent being **Rothwell v. APEX and the TUC** (q.v.). The TUC recodified the Bridlington Principles in 1973 and reissued the booklet *Relations Between Unions* under the title *TUC Disputes Procedure* in that year. Congress in 1976 endorsed a number of further changes consequential on the Rothwell judgement. Rule 12(h) now provides that Disputes Committee awards are binding on unions when issued; Rules 11(c), 12(f) and 13(b) have been revised to ensure the observance of principles of natural justice during the investigation of disputes; Rule 12 now explicitly provides that the General Secretary may intervene in disputes; and Rule 12(c) now affirms that procedural regulations have the same force as

the Rules themselves. The full use of the Bridlington Procedure is recommended in the Industrial Relations Code of Practice 1972; see **Codes of Practice.**

BRIEFING GROUPS. A system of communication advocated by the **Industrial Society** in which managers hold face-to-face meetings with their subordinates and **supervisors** with their work groups in order to keep them informed of management decisions, views and attitudes. It is claimed that systematic use of briefing groups acts both as an adjunct and encouragement to joint consultation and negotiation and as a means of counteracting informational distortions resulting from the operation of the **grapevine** and from elected union representatives passing selective reports from meetings at higher management levels to the shop floor. In particular its object is to re-establish the authority of supervision.

BRITISH ACTORS' EQUITY ASSOCIATION (EQUITY); see **Actors' Equity Association, British.**

BRITISH AIRLINE PILOTS' ASSOCIATION (BALPA). A trade union formed in 1937 and claiming to represent over 90 per cent of pilots in the civil air transport industry in the United Kingdom. An earlier commercial pilots' union, the Federation of British Civilian Air Pilots was formed in 1924, but later collapsed, a professional association of a non-trade union character, the Guild of Airline Pilots and Navigators (GAPAN) being formed in 1929. The formation of BALPA eight years later was, in part, a criticism of GAPAN, but it was not until 1943 that the Association conclusively affiliated with the **Trades Union Congress,** and it did not become a registered trade union under the Trade Union Act 1871, until 1946. It still regards itself as a **professional association** as well as a trade union; see British Airline Pilots' Association, *History of Balpa,* BALPA, 1957. Acrimony and mistrust surrounded the early relations between the Federation of British Civilian Air Pilots and Imperial Airways, and something of this has remained between BALPA and present day corporations and companies in civil aviation and between the Association and the National Joint Council for Civil Air Transport; see *Report of a Court of Inquiry under Mr A. J. Scamp into the Dispute between the British Airline Pilots' Association and the National Joint Council for Civil Air Transport,* Cmnd. 3428,

October 1967 and A. N. J. Blain, *Pilots and Management; Industrial Relations in the U.K. Airlines,* Allen and Unwin, 1972. *Address:* 81 New Road, Harlington, Middx. *Tel:* 01-759 9331. *TUC Affiliated Membership 1977:* 4,536.

BRITISH ASSOCIATION OF COL-LIERY MANAGEMENT; see **Colliery Management, British Association of.**

BRITISH DENTAL ASSOCIATION; see **Dental Association, British.**

BRITISH EMPLOYERS' CONFEDER-ATION (BEC). A national organisation of employers confining its membership to national employers' organisations dealing with industrial relations and promoting the interests of employers generally on matters of common concern in their relations with workpeople. The BEC originated as the **National Confederation of Employers' Organisations** (NCEO) which changed its title in 1939. In 1965 the BEC came together with the Federation of British Industries, and the National Association of British Manufacturers to form the **Confederation of British Industry** (CBI), following proposals made by Sir Henry Benson and Sir Sam Brown (*Report on the Formation of a National Industrial Organisation,* April 1964). Before the merger the BEC had in membership 53 employers' federations.

BRITISH FEDERATION OF MASTER PRINTERS (BFMP); see **Master Printers, British Federation of.**

BRITISH FEDERATION OF TEXTILE TECHNICIANS (BFTT); see **Textile Technicians, British Federation of.**

BRITISH FOOTWEAR MANUFAC-TURERS' ASSOCIATION (BFMA). An employers' organisation dating from 1895 and known until 1960 as the Incorporated Federated Associations of Boot and Shoe Manufacturers of Great Britain and Northern Ireland. The Federation now comprises 17 local associations in the United Kingdom and represents some 300 firms employing some 60,000 operatives and 15,000 other workers, smaller firms being principally located in Leicester, NE London, Northampton and Norwich, and larger firms in Bristol, East Tilbury, Kendal, SW England and Stafford. The majority of firms in Lancashire, primarily in the Rossendale Valley, are separately represented by the Lancashire Footwear Manu-

facturers' Association. The Federation's functions have always related mainly to labour matters, though overseas trade and its organisation have become important interests in the past decade. Following the first and only major strike in the industry, it reached an agreement with the **National Union of Boot and Shoe Operatives** (q.v.) in the 1895 Terms of Settlement which laid down procedures which have, with minor changes, been in force ever since that time, and the present system of biennial negotiations dates from the end of the 1914-18 war, with the addition in 1956 of a separate agreement on incentives based on time study. For non-operative workers, a procedure agreement was signed between the Federation and the National Association of Footwear Supervisory Staffs in 1968. *Address:* Royalty House, 72 Dean Street, London W1V 5HB. *Tel:* 01-437 5573/5.

BRITISH INSTITUTE OF MANAGE-MENT (BIM). An independent body, founded in 1947 on the recommendation of the Baillieu Committee set up by the Board of Trade, and concerned with the raising of standards of management in Britain. The Institute consists of some 10,000 collective subscribers (private firms, nationalised industries, trade unions, employers' associations, trade associations, etc.) and 20,000 individual members in three grades - Associate, Member and Fellow. It provides management services, has an information service, and runs courses and conferences, some of them in the field of industrial relations. *Address:* Management House, Parker Street, London WC2. *Tel:* 01-405 3456.

BRITISH IRON, STEEL AND KIN-DRED TRADES ASSOCIATION (BISAKTA); see **Iron and Steel Trades Confederation.**

BRITISH JOURNAL OF INDUS-TRIAL RELATIONS (BJIR). A primary journal of industrial relations in the United Kingdom covering every aspect of the subject (1963-   ) and published three times a year. In addition to articles and book reviews, the British Journal publishes in each issue a chronicle of the main events in British industrial relations in the previous four months. It is published by the London School of Economics and Political Science, Houghton Street, Aldwych, London WC2. For notes on industrial relations journals in general, see George Sayers Bain and Gillian B. Woolven, 'The Literature of Labour Economics and Industrial Relations, A Guide to its Sources', *Industrial Relations Journal,* Summer 1970 and in J. Fletcher (ed.), *The Uses of Economic Literature,* Butterworths 1971.

BRITISH JOURNAL OF SOCIOLOGY. The leading sociological journal in Britain frequently containing articles of interest in the industrial field, and published from the London School of Economics and Political Science, Houghton Street, Aldwych, London WC2.

BRITISH MEDICAL ASSOCIATION (BMA); see Medical Association, British.

BRITISH PAPER AND BOARD INDUSTRY FEDERATION. An employers' association open to firms engaged in the making, coating or impregnating of paper and board, formerly, for industrial relations only, the Employers' Federation of Papermakers and Boardmakers. The industrial relations side of the Federation began as a small association of mills in Lancashire in 1913, followed in 1915 by the formation of similar associations in Scotland and the South of England, these associations coming together four years later to represent the whole industry; see Arthur Baker, *The Employers' Federation of Papermakers and Boardmakers, A Brief History,* March 1953. Between 1941 and 1943 it adopted with the unions procedure agreements similar to those in the engineering industry (A. I. Marsh and W. E. J. McCarthy, *Disputes Procedures in Britain,* Royal Commission on Trade Unions and Employers' Associations Research Papers 2(2), 1968, Chapter Three). *Address:* 3 Plough Place, Fetter Lane, London EC4. *Tel:* 01-353 5222.

BRITISH PRINTING INDUSTRIES FEDERATION (BPIF), formerly the **British Federation of Master Printers.** An organisation formed in 1900 to co-ordinate the work of a large number of local associations of printing employers, now consisting of ten autonomous alliances covering the whole of England and Wales, the **Society of Master Printers of Scotland** and three associations in Ireland, the latter four bodies being responsible for their own wage negotiations. Federation membership of almost 4,000 firms represents approximately 80 per cent of the general printing and bookbinding industry, newspaper production being covered by the **Newspaper Publishers' Association** and the **Newspaper Society** (q.v.). The BPIF is primarily concerned with industrial relations. It also provides a service to its members on management accounting, technical development, as well as on legislation, education and training, public relations and through the Young Master Printer movement; see Mary Sessions, *The BFMP: How it Began,* William Sessions Ltd 1950 and Ellic Howe, *The British Federation of Master Printers, 1900-1950,* BFMP, 1950; and annually, *The Printing Industries' Annual,* BPIF. *Address:* 11 Bedford Row, London WC1R 4DX. *Tel:* 01-242 6904.

BRITISH PRODUCTIVITY COUNCIL (BPC). An autonomous organisation formed in 1952 as the successor to the United Kingdom Section of the Anglo-American Council on Productivity and concerned, particularly through conferences, seminars and visual aids, to create a wider appreciation of the need for higher productivity and the methods that lead to it. The Council has paid particular attention to the development of **work study** (q.v.) and operates both nationally and through local productivity associations. The BPC ceased to be government grant aided after March 1973. *Address:* Goschen Buildings, 12-13 Henrietta Street, Covent Garden, London WC2. *Tel:* 01-836 0723.

BRITISH ROLL TURNERS' TRADE SOCIETY (BRTTS); see Roll Turners' Trade Society, British.

BRITISH SEAFARERS' JOINT COUNCIL. A joint council of trade unions represented on the **National Maritime Board,** formed in 1917 to 'promote a closer relationship between seafarers' organisations and to sponsor co-ordinated action on matters of common interest'. The objects of the Council were approved in the **Rochdale Report** (q.v.).

BRITISH SHIPPING FEDERATION LIMITED; now the **General Council of British Shipping** (q.v.).

BROAD BANDING; see banding.

BROADCASTING STAFF, ASSOCIATION OF (ABS). A trade union representing those who work in television, radio and associated fields as permanent staff, on a temporary or short-term contract, or as freelances. The union had its origin in the BBC Staff (Wartime) Association established in May 1940 by programme and engineering staff, and recognised for negotiating purposes by the BBC in September of the same year. In 1946 the (Wartime) Association merged with the Association of BBC Engineers, which had been similarly recognised and became the BBC Staff Association, taking its present title in February 1956. It was recognised by the Independent Television Authority in May 1956, and, together with the **Musicians' Union, British Actors' Equity Association, the National Union of Journalists, the Association of Cinematograph, Television and Allied Technicians, the National Association of Theatrical, Television and Kinematograph Employees, the Writers Guild of Great Britain** and the **Electrical, Electronic, Telecommunication and Plumbing Union,** makes up the **Federation of Broadcasting Unions.** The membership of the union voted in favour of amalgamation with the **Association of Cinematograph, Television and Allied Technicians** in 1978. *Address:* Kings Court, 2 Goodge Street, London W1P 2AE. *Tel:* 01-637 1261. *TUC Affiliated Membership 1977:* 14,159.

BROADCASTING UNIONS, FEDERATION OF; see **Broadcasting Staff, Association of.**

BROKEN TIME. A situation occurring where there are **split shifts** (q.v.), i.e. where the working day does not consist of a continuous period of work, but in which the worker works for a certain period, is then off duty, and later returns to complete the shift; see also **spreadover.**

BROOK MOTORS LTD AND TRANSPORT AND GENERAL WORKERS' UNION. Industrial Court Award 3168, 7 May 1968. A reference to the Industrial Court (now Central Arbitration Committee) under the Terms and Conditions of Employment Act 1959, s. 8 (see **claims procedure**) in which it was ruled that the **Guaranteed Week** Agreement of 1964 between the Engineering Employers' Federation and the Confederation of Shipbuilding and Engineering Unions was not applicable to a non-federated firm; see also **Dawes Cycle Co. Ltd and National Society of Metal Mechanics.**

BROOME v. DPP (HL) (1974) ICR 84; (1974) All ER 314. A case in which it was reaffirmed that pickets (see **picketing**) only have the right to attend for the purpose of communicating information and persuading people to work or not to work and that once these objectives are exceeded, they are subject to normal legal liabilities.

BROWN v. AMALGAMATED UNION OF ENGINEERING WORKERS (1976) ICR 147. The plaintiff was elected Divisional Organiser in a postal ballot in which by an administrative error one union branch had received no ballot papers and others had their papers held up in the post. He was prevented from taking office by the Executive Council, which held another ballot at which another member was elected. The court held that the election of officials was not invalidated by the fact that some members had not received ballot papers, provided that the election had been conducted substantially in accordance with the rules of the union, as in this case; see **membership of a union.**

BROWN BOOK AGREEMENT; see **Melters' Brown Book Agreement.**

BROWN BOOKLET AGREEMENT. An agreement of April 1921 between the Steel Ingot Makers' Association, the Board of Conciliation and Arbitration for the Manufactured Iron and Steel Trade of the North of England, the Scottish Steel Makers' Wages Association and the **Iron and Steel Trades Confederation** transferring lower-paid workers on flat war bonuses to the **melters' sliding scale.** The principle of such a transfer became known as the **stepping scheme** arrangement and was subsequently applied to other workers, Sir Arthur Pugh, *Men of Steel,* Iron and Steel Trades Confederation, 1951, p. 357.

BRTTS. British Roll Turners' Trade Society; see **Roll Turners' Trade Society, British.**

BRUSHMAKERS AND GENERAL WORKERS, NATIONAL SOCIETY OF (NSBGW). A trade union tracing its origin to 1747 and claiming to be the union with the longest continuous existence in the world. A Brushmakers' Benevolent Institute was established in 1828 to act for all the local societies of the day, those for which records still exist including Manchester (formed 1747), Bristol (1782), Lyme Regis (1786), Leeds (1791) and London (1806), which, from the early 1800s acted as Head Society, making the whole into a form of national union. A United Society of Brushmakers issued a member-

ship certificate in 1839, though local societies continued to enjoy a great deal of
autonomy, and early in the present century the National Society of Brushmakers
was formed, as a genuinely national
union, 'General Workers' being added to
the title in 1971. William Kiddier, *The Old
Trade Unions - from unprinted records of
the Brushmakers,* London 1930. *Address:*
20 The Parade, Watford WD1 2AA. *Tel:*
Watford 21950. *TUC Affiliated Membership 1977:* 1,547.

**BU. Bakers' Food and Allied Workers'
Union** (q.v.).

BUDDY LISTS; see FOC lists.

**BUILDING AND CIVIL ENGINEER-
ING HOLIDAYS SCHEME MANAGE-
MENT LIMITED; see holidays with pay.**

**BUILDING INDUSTRY, NATIONAL
JOINT COUNCIL FOR THE (NJCBI).**
A national joint council between building
trade unions and employers' associations
(particularly the **National Federation of
Building Trades Employers**) which provides joint machinery for national negotiations on wages and conditions of work
resulting in National Working Rules, for
procedures for dispute and grievance handling, for **apprenticeships** (in the National
Joint Apprenticeship Scheme), and for
training, safety, health and welfare. The
NJC was established in 1926 after a number of attempts covering about thirty years
to create national machinery for the industry. Late nineteenth century essays in this
direction were followed, after the dispute
of 1904, by a network of conciliation
boards, including in 1908, a National
Board of Conciliation. This continued to
operate during the short-lived Industrial
Council for the Building Industry, 1918-24
(see Rodger Charles, *The Development of
Industrial Relations in Britain 1911-1939,*
Hutchinson, 1973), and under a further
attempt to create workable national negotiating arrangements, the National Wages
and Conditions Council (1921-26). The
present NJC produced a substantially integrated machinery by 1932, including the
Green Book Procedure for emergency disputes (q.v.) which operated from 1927 to
1970. It has been marked by a high level of
co-operation between trade unions and
employers; see I. G. Sharp, *Industrial Conciliation and Arbitration in Great Britain,*
Allen and Unwin, 1950, Chapter VI. W. S.
Hilton, *Industrial Relations in Construction,* Pergamon Press, 1968 and R. Post-

gate, *The Builders' History, 1923.
Address:* 11 Weymouth Street, Portland
Place, London W1N 3FG. *Tel:* 01-580
1740.

**BUILDING TECHNICIANS, ASSO-
CIATION OF (ABT).** A trade union
formed in 1919, which was absorbed by
the Amalgamated Society of Woodwork-
ers in 1970, which now forms part of the
**Union of Construction, Allied Trades and
Technicians** (q.v.) and is known as the
Supervisory, Technical, Administrative,
Managerial and Professional (STAMP)
Section.

**BUILDING TRADES EMPLOYERS,
NATIONAL FEDERATION OF
(NFBTE).** A national employers' association in the building industry first formed
in 1878 as the National Association of
Master Builders of Great Britain and Ireland, changing its name to the National
Federation of Building Trades Employers
of Great Britain and Ireland in 1901 and to
is present title in 1928. The Federation
claims to be the central organisation of
building trades employers in the country.
It comprises ten Regional Federations and
over 260 Local Associations, and has a
number of affiliated organisations - the
Scottish National Federation of Building
Trades (Employers), the Joinery and
Woodwork Employers' Federation, the
Federation of Registered House-Builders,
the National Federation of Plastering Contractors, the National Association of Shopfitters and the National Association of
Scaffolding Contractors. Its full trade
membership is over 16,000, comprising
members who operate as subcontractors
as well as those who are main contractors,
and it is claimed that this membership
covers some 80 per cent of the employment capacity of the country. In addition
the NFBTE has a number of members affiliated indirectly through the Joinery and
Woodwork Employers' Federation, and
the National Association of Shopfitters.
Substantially all the larger firms in the
building industry, a majority of medium-
sized firms and a considerable number of
small firms are claimed among the
NFBTE's membership; many larger ones
also being affiliated to the Federation of
Civil Engineering Contractors (see **Civil
Engineering Contractors, Federation of**),
Agreements made between the NFBTE,
other smaller specialist associations, and
building trades unions, meeting together
as the National Joint Council for the Building Industry apply generally throughout

the industry, and are followed both by non-federated employers and by those in membership of the Federation of Master Builders, comprising some 18,000 small firms. The NFBTE is notable for its close relations with organisations representative of employees and for its initiatives in many directions, including the provision of an Advisory Service for the Building Industry (established 1954), which provides management consultancy and courses for directors, executives and managers of building firms. *Address:* 82 New Cavendish Street, London W1M 8AD. *Tel:* 01-580 4041.

BUILDING TRADES OPERATIVES, NATIONAL FEDERATION OF; see **Construction Unions, National Federation of.**

BUILDING TRADE WORKERS OF GREAT BRITAIN AND IRELAND, AMALGAMATED UNION OF (AUBTW). A trade union formed in 1921 by amalgamation of the Manchester Order of Bricklayers (founded in 1829), the Operative Stone Masons (founded 1831) and the London Order of Bricklayers (founded as a result of the insolvency of the London Division of the Friendly Society of Bricklayers in 1848). After the second world war the AUBTW, like other building unions, was affected by sharply declining membership and from the 1950s became concerned in a number of amalgamations (with the National Builders' Labourers' and Construction Workers' Society in 1952, the National Society of Street Masons, Paviours and Roadmakers in 1966 and the Amalgamated Slaters, Tilers and Roofing Operatives in 1969). In 1971 the union merged with the **Amalgamated Society of Woodworkers** to form a new amalgamation known in 1972 as the **Union of Construction, Allied Trades and Technicians** (q.v.) Before amalgamation the TUC affiliated membership of the AUBTW was 61,097; see W. S. Hilton, *Foes to Tyranny,* AUBTW, 1963.

BULCOCK v. ST ANNE'S MASTER BUILDERS' ASSOCIATION; see **blacklisting.**

BULL PERIOD; see **bull weeks.**

BULL WEEKS. Weeks of low absenteeism and high overtime, output and earnings which tend to precede the weeks in which holidays fall, especially in the coalmining industry (see George B. Bald-win, *Beyond Nationalisation,* Harvard University Press, 1955; pp. 210-11). In some industries the Bull Period before the Christmas holiday may be as long as two or three weeks; bull weeks may sometimes be associated with **banking** (q.v.).

BULLETIN OF COMPARATIVE LABOUR RELATIONS. A journal of comparative labour relations published once or twice a year and dealing with developments in different countries as well as topics of international interest (1970-). The bulletin was initiated by the Institute for Labour Relations of the University of Leuven, and is published by the Kluwer Law Publishing Division, PO Box 23, Deventer, The Netherlands.

BULLOCK REPORT. The Report of the *Committee of Inquiry on Industrial Democracy* under the chairmanship of Lord Bullock (Cmnd. 6706, January 1977). The terms of reference of the Committee required it to report on how the representation of trade unions on boards of directors of companies could best be achieved, bearing in mind the 50 per cent proposal of the Trades Union Congress on supervisory boards (TUC, *Industrial Democracy,* 1974, paras 88-91), the draft **Fifth Directive** of the European Economic Commission (q.v.) and such proposals as those of the Confederation of British Industry for flexible participation arrangements and **participation agreements** (q.v.). The Committee was opposed to a two-tier board system (i.e. one consisting of both a supervisory, or 'policy' board and a management or executive board for each company) and proposed a 2X + Y formula on reconstituted unitary boards, i.e. that there should be an equal representation of employees and shareholders (2X), plus a third group of directors (Y), co-opted with the agreement of each of the other two groups, given that this third group was made up of an uneven number greater than 1 and less than one-third of the total board, nominations being left to the trade unions concerned. The three employer members of the Committee dissented from this proposal in a minority report. They laid emphasis on 'substructures' of representation to underpin board level representation in each company and supported the idea of one-third representation of employees on supervisory boards, with nominations either by employees or by recognised trade unions; see **Betriebsräte, co-determination, workers' participation.** The Report was envisaged as a stage in the implementation of the Labour Party's commitment to **industrial democracy** following the repeal of the Industrial Relations Act 1971 (see **Trade Union and Labour Relations Acts 1974 and 1976**), and the **Employment Protection Act 1975.** A White Paper on Industrial Democracy issued by the Callaghan government in May 1978 suggested considerable amendments to the Bullock approach as a basis for future legislation.

BUMMAREE. The name given to self-employed porters in London wholesale markets. They were closely concerned in the events leading to the *Committee of Inquiry into the causes of industrial unrest arising from the present arrangements for the delivery, handling of meat at Smithfield Market,* Chairman Mr (later Sir) Roy Wilson, HMSO, 1958; see also National Board for Prices and Incomes, Report No. 126. *Smithfield Market,* October 1969, Cmnd. 4171.

BUMPER STRIKE. A form of strike in which trade unions call out their members factory by factory, strikes being supported by the contributions of the members in work. Much more commonly used in the nineteenth century than today (K. G. J. C. Knowles, *Strikes,* Blackwell, 1952, p. 12), though the tactics of DATA in the 1960s may have had something in common with it; see also **bumping.**

BUMPING; see **seniority.**

BUNDESARBEITSGERICHT;   see **Labour Courts.**

BUREAUCRACY. A term variously used to describe (a) the tasks and procedures of administration, (b) a body of administrative officials, and (c) a situation tending towards centralisation and improper use of power. Also **bureaucratisation,** a feature of bureaucratic administration with emphasis on the office rather than on the individual office-holder, with consequent depersonalisation of relationships, especially in large organisations (see **size-effect**). 'Bureaucracy' was first used as a sociological term in its modern sense by Max Weber and has developed as one component of organisational theory. Bureaucratisation has been particularly associated with the growth of **white-collar unionism** (q.v.); see David Lockwood, *The Blackcoated Worker,* George Allen and Unwin, 1966; A. Sturmthal (ed.), *White Collar Trade Unions,* Urbana, University of Illinois Press, 1968; R. M. Blackburn and K. Prandy, 'White-Collar Unionism: A Conceptual Framework', *British Journal of Sociology,* xvi, June 1965. For a critical commentary, see G. S. Bain, *The Growth of White-Collar Unionism,* OUP, 1970, Ch. VI; Elliott Jaques, *A General Theory of Bureaucracy,* Heinemann, 1976.

BUREAUCRATISATION; see **bureaucracy.**

BURKE   v.   AMALGAMATED SOCIETY OF DYERS (1906) 2 KB 583; see **benefits.**

BURNHAM COMMITTEES. Standing joint committees appointed by the Secretary of State for Education and Science to review the remuneration of teachers and to make recommendations. The first Burnham Committee was established in 1919 under the chairmanship of Lord Burnham 'to secure the orderly and progressive solution of the salary problem in public elementary schools by agreement · on a national basis and its correlation with the solution of the salary problem in secondary schools'. Three committees were developed, one for elementary, one for secondary and one for technical schools. These committees were chosen as the approved committees under s. 89 of the Education Act 1944. At present one committee exists for primary and secondary schools and one for teachers in colleges of further education under the **Remuneration of Teachers Act 1965.** Each committee comprises a management and a teachers' panel with an independent chairman. The Secretary of State is represented directly on the management panel of each committee and must implement any agreements which the committees make. There is provision for arbitration if agreement is not reached and awards are binding on the Secretary of State unless each House of Parliament resolves that national economic circumstances are such that the awards should not be made effective. There is separate machinery for Scotland in the form of a **Scottish Committee for Teachers' Salaries.** (Remuneration of Teachers (Scotland) Act 1967); see National Board for Prices and Incomes, *Scottish Teachers' Salaries,* Report No. 15, Cmnd. 3005, May 1966; see also **Wood Report.**

BURNS v. CUNNINGHAM (1885) 1 Sh Ct Rep. 318; see **benefits.**

BUSINESS UNIONISM. An expression used to describe trade unions, especially in the United States, which are considered to be non-idealistic and which have as their primary objective improvements in wages and working conditions; see Philip Taft, 'On the Origins of Business Unionism', *Industrial and Labor Relations Review,* October 1963.

BUSMEN'S CHARTER. A policy document drawn up by the National Passenger Trade Group Officers and Committee of the Transport and General Workers' Union advocating a basic minimum wage rate of *15 per week, a standard working week based on 40 hours and five days, with a daily ceiling of 8 hours and a reduction in spells in charge of a vehicle, three weeks' paid annual holiday, a closed shop, a greater share of savings from the operation of one-man buses, an overtime agreement and limitation of **spreadovers** (q.v.). *Transport and General Workers' Union Record,* June 1967. National Board for Prices and Incomes, *Productivity Agreements in the Bus Industry,* and *Pay and Municipal Busmen. Reports* No. 50, Cmnd. 3498 and No. 63, Cmnd. 3605, April 1968.

BUTTERWORTH REPORT. The report of the *Inquiry into the Work and Pay of Probation Officers and Social Workers,* Cmnd. 5076, August 1972. The terms of reference of the inquiry were to establish the facts and to advise on the appropriate pay relationships between probation officers, local authority social workers and social workers in hospitals at all levels of these three services. It recommended that the pay of probation officers and hospital social workers should be related to the existing salary structure in the local authority service, that there should be a common starting point for pay for all newly qualified entrants and *inter alia* that there should be a reappraisal of manpower needs and staff deployment.

BUTTY. Also known as a **puffler.** A **labour-only sub-contractor** (q.v.) formerly found in coalmining, who supplied labour for contract work in the pits; also in other places of work such as brickyards and shipyards. George B. Baldwin (*Beyond Nationalisation,* Harvard University Press, 1955, p. 162) comments that the control of the butty over pay 'made many butties into working-class robber barons, and led to much inequality of treatment among different men and much petty racketeering'; see also **contract system.** Some butties were owners or part-owners of public houses, leading to abuses which were legislated against in the Mines Regulation Act 1842 and the Payment of Wages in Public-Houses Prohibition Act 1883 which still remains on the statute book.

BYE-TURNMAN. A workman who is not in regular employment but attends a works in the expectation of being employed there temporarily to take the place of any regular workman who happens not to come to work; a **casual worker.** Manufactured Iron Trade, Scotland; Board of Trade (Labour Department), *Report on Collective Agreements.* Cd. 5366, HMSO, 1910.

BYRNE AND CHAPPLE v. FOULKES, HAXELL AND OTHERS (1961); see **ballot rigging.**

C

CAC. Central Arbitration Committee (q.v.)

CA'CANNY. Go-slow methods or restrictions by workers, either in relation to some particular claim or grievance, or in order to limit output for purposes of controlling the labour market or some aspect of it. In both cases outright withdrawal of labour is avoided, but the object in the first instance is more tactical and in the second more strategic. **Go-slow, slow-gear strike, lazy strike, folded arms strike, stay-in strike, working without enthusiasm** (q.v.) or in some forms **work-to-rule** (q.v.) are expressions used mainly to describe its tactical use. The word 'ca'canny' itself is usually (but not invariably) employed to indicate strategic use, e.g. to describe a unilaterally imposed method of **work sharing** (q.v.) to maintain employment, limitation of output to maintain piecework prices, etc.; see **restrictive practices, protective practices, craft control, quota restriction, gold bricking.**

CADET. A term used since about 1865 in the merchant navy to describe an officer in training; an **officer cadet.** Cadets in the merchant navy were formerly known as **apprentices.** The word has, however, been used to describe officer trainees in military and other naval circumstances for a much longer period, and at least from the end of the eighteenth century; see *Oxford English Dictionary.*

CAFETERIA WAGE PLAN. A system in which the worker is given a choice of the benefits he can enjoy arising out of a total sum of money available for wage or salary increase, principally with the aim of maximising **job satisfaction.** Th system has been recommended in the United States, particularly for managers (Edward E. Lawler, 'The Mythology of Management Compensation', *California Management Review* 1966). At least one case of manual workers being given a 'cafeteria' choice exists in Britain.

CALL-BACK PAY; see **call out.**

CALLING-IN; see **call-out.**

CALLING-OUT PAYMENT; see **call-out.**

CALL-OUT also **calling in, calling-out payment, workers recalled to work.** When an operative is called upon to return to work after his normal finishing time and before his next normal starting time; usually ranks for **premium payment;** see, for example, *National Working Rules and Industrial Determinations for the Electrical Contracting Industry,* Section II, 9 (c); **calling-in;** see chemical industry agreements. **Calling-out payment,** Papermaking & Boardmaking, National Agreement No. 10; **workers recalled to work** (Engineering Industry Handbook of National Agreements 2.23); also **call-back pay.**

CAMERON v. ASSOCIATED SOCIETY OF LOCOMOTIVE ENGINEERS AND FIREMEN (1930) 46 Sh. Ct. Rep. 84; see **benefits.**

CAMERON REPORT. The name given to the numerous inquiries chaired by the Hon. Lord Cameron, DSC, QC including; *Complaints made by the National Union of Bank Employees to the Committee on Freedom of Association of the International Labour Organisation* (Cmnd. 2202, November 1963); *National Federated Electrical Association and the Electrical Trades Union* (Cmd. 8968, 1953); *Briggs Motor Bodies* (**Bellringer Dispute,** Cmnd. 131, March 1957); *Webber Offset* (Cmnd. 3184, 1967); *British Transport Commission and National Union of Railwaymen* (Interim, Cmd. 9352, Jan. 1955, Final,

Cmd. 9372, January 1955); *Port Transport Industry* (Cmnd. 510, 1958).

CAPITAL-SHARING SCHEMES. A generic term used to describe a variety of schemes whereby workers receive *future* benefits in the form of monetary lump-sum payments or ownership of wealth assets from their employer in place of *present* wage and salary increases etc. or of some part of these. Such schemes have grown up in France, the Netherlands, in the Federal Republic of Germany, in Denmark, Italy and Switzerland. They are usually understood to exclude arrangements which encourage workers voluntarily to increase their savings out of existing income and have been thought of as offering some benefit to trade unions in return for restraint in money wages incomes as well as redistributing wealth without leading to an increase in consumption or a reduction in investment, i.e. as combining the twin goals of a reduction in inflationary pressure and maintenance of investment while encouraging greater equality. Such schemes have attracted little trade union interest in the United Kingdom; see Derek Robinson, *Incomes Policy and Capital Sharing in Europe,* Croom Helm, 1973.

CARD. A trade union membership card; hence **card steward,** a trade union official whose job it is to collect contributions and see that memebrs are **paid-up members; card check,** a check to see which workers are trade union members and, if so, whether they are **in compliance** (see also **non-compliance men**), or a **card inspection; all-card job,** a job which is open to trade union members only (see **closed shop**); **card carrying member,** a trade union member who has evidence of his membership in the form of a membership card - also one who is in compliance; **card-holder,** a trade union member who plays no active part in the activities of the union, a passive member, one duty of shop stewards often being defined as 'to turn cardholders into active trade unionists'; **card vote,** a vote at a conference on the basis of the number of members represented by a trade union (see **block vote**), so called because each delegation at a conference is given a single voting card bearing the number of members it represents.

CARD CARRYING MEMBER; see **card.**

CARD CHECK; see **card.**

CARDHOLDER; see **card.**

CARD INSPECTION; see **card.**

CARD SETTING MACHINE TEN-TERS' SOCIETY. A craft union formed in 1872 and concerned with the preparation of card clothing used in the processing of fibre to yarn, an industry now confined almost exclusively to a few firms in the West Riding of Yorkshire. M. Speirs, *One Hundred Years of a Small Trade Union; A History of the Card Setting Machine Tenters' Society,* CSMTS, 1972. *Address:* 36 Greenton Avenue, Scholes, Cleckheaton. Yorks, BD19 6DT. *Tel:* 0277 670022. *TUC Affiliated Membership 1977:* 140.

CARD STEWARD; see **card.**

CARD VOTE; see **card.**

CAREERS SERVICE. An employment service for young people resulting from a reorganisation of the **Youth Employment Service** which took effect on 1 April 1974 following the **Employment and Training Act 1973.** Under that Act (ss. 8-10) each local education authority was required to provide such a service, thus bringing to an end the previous arrangement whereby the Department of Employment made provision in some areas and local education authorities in others, although young people can also obtain career guidance at Employment Offices or **Jobcentres** run by the **Employment Service Agency** (now a Division of the **Manpower Services Commission).** The Act also removed the age limit of 18 which had previously applied, making it possible for all young people, rather than school leavers alone, to obtain advice from their local careers office. There are some 2,250 Careers Officers in Great Britain.

CARETAKERS' ASSOCIATION, MANCHESTER AND DISTRICT. Once a separate union of caretakers, cleaners and school meal service employees within Manchester, it is now a section of the **National Union of Public Employees.** It had some 950 members when it transferred its engagements to NUPE in 1971. It is still affiliated to the **General Federation of Trade Unions** under the rule which allows separate sections of non-affiliated unions to retain membership. *Address:* School House, Wendover Road, Wythenshaw, Manchester 23. *Membership 1977:* 1,680.

CARLISLE AGREEMENT. The name given to a number of agreements between trade unions and employers made at Carlisle; notably the agreement of August 1902 in which the Amalgamated Society of Engineers accepted the **premium bonus system** in federated engineering firms, and that of October 1907 in which the Engineering Employers' Federation, the ASE, the Steam Engine Makers' Society and the United Machine Workers' Association agreed to make procedural changes in the Terms of Settlement of 1898; see A. I. Marsh, *Industrial Relations in Engineering,* Pergamon Press, 1965.

CARPET TRADE UNION, NORTHERN. A textile trade union, formerly the Northern Counties Carpet Trades Association, founded in 1892. *Address:* 22 Clare Road, Halifax, HX1 2HX. *Tel:* 0422 60492. *TUC Affiliated Membership 1977:* 2,119.

CARR REPORT. The report, in 1958, of a sub-committee of the Ministry of Labour's National Joint Advisory Council under the chairmanship of Mr Robert Carr, now Lord Carr and then Parliamentary Secretary to the Ministry, to look at industrial training and in particular to examine the adequacy of existing institutions to cope with the so-called 'bulge' of school leavers expected to come on to the labour market in the early 1960s. The Committee recommended that training should be developed on its existing foundations with assistance from an Industrial Training Council and was successful in increasing the number of apprenticeships for school leavers. Its view on the adequacy of the industrial training system was, however, rapidly superseded in the **Industrial Training Act 1964** (q.v.); see also **apprenticeship.**

CARTLEDGE AND OTHERS v. E. JOPLING AND SONS LTD. (1963) 1 All ER 341. A case involving seven steel dressers who, in 1956, issued writs against their employer as a result of contracting pneumoconiosis. It is of interest in that they were statute barred from receiving damages through no fault of their own, and that this led ultimately to the Limitation Act 1963 which deprives defendants of the right of relying on the three-year limitation provided by the Law Reform (Limitation of Actions etc.) Act 1954 in personal injury actions to which the Act applies; see A. D. Wolff, *The Time Barrier to Personal*

Injuries Claims, Butterworth, 1969, pp. 6-12.

CARUS v. EASTWOOD; see works rules.

CAS. Conciliation and Advisory Service (q.v.).

CASH BOOK STEWARD or cash steward. A trade union branch official responsible for receiving and paying out moneys and keeping correct records of transactions.

CASSIDY v. MINISTER OF HEALTH (1951) 2 KB 343; see **contract of service.**

CASTELLION METHOD. A method of **job evaluation** associated with the name of Dr Lucien Cortis, each job being analysed according to the kinds of decision made, the frequency of decision-making, the kinds of computations, comprehension and vigilance required etc., points being given to each factor. The method is described in T. T. Paterson, *Job Evaluation: Vol. 1, A New Method,* Business Books, 1972.

CASTING AGREEMENT; see Actors' Equity Association, British.

CASUAL; see casual worker.

CASUAL WORK; see casual worker.

CASUAL WORKER, sometimes abbreviated to **casual.** A worker employed on **casual work,** i.e. work which is intermittent in character, as in the docks (see **decasualisation**), exhibition contracting (National Board for Prices and Incomes, *Pay and Conditions of Workers in the Exhibition Contracting Industry,* Report No. 117, Cmnd. 4088, June 1969), or on seasonal work e.g. in catering, seaside occupations etc. (see **seasonal unemployment**). Also a worker who may be employed on irregular work on a full-time basis, e.g. in the national newspaper industry, where casuals may be part-time (i.e. available for work irregularly as required depending, for example, on the varying page length of a newspaper), or full-time (i.e. required regularly to attend work, but only when the newspaper is published, e.g. at week-ends). Casual work has often been identified as unskilled work, with irregular and low earnings, with poor relationships between management and workers and

with other problems, though none of these assertions is universally applicable.

CATHOLIC INDUSTRIAL RELATIONS TEACHING. Authoritative teaching is to be found in five major papal documents: **Rerum Novarum** *(On the Condition of the Working Classes),* Pope Leo XIII (1891); **Quadragesimo Anno** *(On Reconstructing the Social Order),* Pope Pius XI (1931); **La solennità della Pentecoste** (broadcast commemorating the 50th anniversary of Rerum Novarum) Pope Pius XII, 1941; **Mater et Magistra** *(On Christianising contemporary advances in the organisation of society)* Pope John XXIII (1961); and **Populorum Progressio** *(On the development of Nations),* Pope Paul VI (1967). On industrial relations the main heads of teaching are: that wages must suffice for the maintenance of wage earners' families at decent levels (see **just wage**); that wage contracts ought to be modified to provide some element of partnership so that workers can share in ownership and profits with management (see **co-partnership**); that workers have the right freely to form and join trade unions; that workers have the right to strike wherever the grievance is serious and other remedies have failed; see J.-Y. Calvez and J. Perrin, *The Church and Social Justice,* Burns Oates, 1961, J. Messner, *Social Ethics,* Herder, 1965.

CATU. Ceramics and Allied Trades Union (q.v.).

CAWU. Clerical and Administrative Workers' Union; see **Professional, Executive, Clerical and Computer Staff Association of.**

CBI. Confederation of British Industry (q.v.).

CCOA. County Court Officers' Association; later **Court Officers' Association** (q.v.).

CEASE AND DESIST ORDER. An order issued by the National Labor Relations Board, or state agency, in the United States of America to a trade union or to an employer to stop an **unfair labor practice** held to be in violation of the law. An order specifies the action which the union or employer is to cease, and the action which is to be taken to remedy the situation.

CELLULAR GROUP PRODUCTION; see **group technology.**

CELLULAR MANUFACTURE; see **group technology.**

CENTRAL ARBITRATION COMMITTEE (CAC). A permanent arbitration tribunal set up under the **Employment Protection Act 1975** s. 10 and replacing the **Industrial Arbitration Board** (before 1971 known as the Industrial Court). The CAC was brought into operation on 1 February 1976, assuming the role of the IAB, with added jurisdictions from the 1975 Act. After the passing of the Industrial Courts Act 1919 (now repealed) the primary role of the Industrial Court was to provide standing facilities for arbitration with the consent of both parties when their own procedures had been exhausted. To this was added after 1919 a number of special arbitral functions. After 1946 cases arising out of the Fair Wages Resolution of the House of Commons (see **fair wage principle**) which remained unresolved were referred to it for decision by the Minister of Labour (later the Secretary of State for Employment); a similar procedure came to be applied under the concept of '**statutory fair wages**') to a number of industries under the Civil Aviation Acts 1946 and 1949, the Road Traffic Acts 1930 and 1933 (now 1960), the Films Act 1960, the Road Haulage Wages Act 1938 and others in which an award of the Court became an **implied term of contract** (q.v.) of the workers concerned. Later other cases involving implied terms were referred to the Court under s. 8 of the Terms and Conditions of Employment Act 1959 (now embodied in Schedule 11 of the Employment Protection Act 1975; see **Schedule 11**), and in 1970 the Equal Pay Act (ss. 3, 4 and 5) gave the Court statutory authority after 29 December 1975, to amend collective agreements, pay structures, wage regulation orders and agricultural wages orders which were judged to be discriminatory. All these functions were passed on from the Industrial Court to its successor the Industrial Arbitration Board, and have now been assumed by the Central Arbitration Committee. New jurisdictions under the Employment Protection Act 1975 deal with cases in which, under a **Code of Practice** (q.v.) it is alleged that an employer has failed to disclose information (see **Disclosure of Information**) or to provide time off (see **Facilities for Trade Unions**) etc.; s. 16 of the Act enables an independent trade union to complain to the Committee that an employer is not complying with a current recommendation of the **Advisory,**

Conciliation and Arbitration Service (ACAS) to recognise that trade union and to claim improved terms and conditions of employment and, if necessary, to make an award determining new terms and conditions of employment (see **trade union recognition**). In the circumstances of the 1970s the original arbitration function of the CAC has much declined; between 1958 and 1970 the Industrial Court dealt on average with 30 cases a year; the case load of the CAC (references received) in 1977 was as follows

Type of case	Number of cases
Arbitration	10
Section 8 (now Schedule 11)	742
Section 16 Recognition	7
Section 19 Disclosure	13
Fair Wages Resolution	230
Equal Pay	21
Independent Broadcasting Act 1973	1
Road Traffic Act 1960	4
Road Haulage Wages Act 1938	2
	1030

During 1977 the CAC made 308 awards; see **First Annual Report, 1977.**

CENTRAL TRAINING COUNCIL; see **Industrial Training Act 1964.**

CEO. Confederation of Employee Organisations; see **Employee Organisations, Confederation of.**

CERAMIC AND ALLIED TRADES UNION (CATU). A trade union organising workers in the pottery industry, principally based in North Staffordshire, but national in coverage, and taking its present title in January 1970. Trade unionism in the pottery industry has a long history, and the National Union of Operative Potters was in 1833 one of the 'big five' of British trade unions. The present union dates from the National Amalgamated Society of Male and Female Pottery Workers formed in 1906 by the merger of the Hallow Ware Pressers' Union, the China Potters' Federation and the Printers' and Transferers' Society. This became the National Society of Pottery Workers in 1919 which absorbed in 1921 the Packers' Society and the United Ovenmen's Society. W. H. Warburton, *History of Trade Union Organisations in the Potteries,* Unwin Brothers Ltd., 1931 and D. L.

Gregory and R. L. Smyth, *The Worker and the Pottery Industry,* Department of Economics, University of Keele, 1971. *Address:* 5 Hillcrest Street, Hanley, Stoke-on-Trent, ST1 2AB *Tel:* 0782 24201-3. *TUC Affiliated Membership, 1977:* 46,559.

CERTIFICATION. The use by employers of **the document** (q.v.) or certificate to ensure that they are only employing non-unionists; see John Child, *Industrial Relations in the British Printing Industry,* Allen and Unwin, 1967, p. 82; 'In 1846 ... the master printers of Edinburgh forced a show-down by introducing a system of 'certification' under which they agreed to give preference to non-unionists and to blacklist all strikers'; also certification under the Trade Union and Labour Relations Act 1974; see **certification officer.**

CERTIFICATION OFFICER. An official with the title Certification Officer for Trade Union and Employers' Associations, appointed by the Secretary of State for Employment under the Employment Protection Act 1975, s. 7, as an independent statutory authority to determine the independence of trade unions under a procedure laid down in s. 8 of that Act; see **independent trade union.** The Act also transferred to the Certification Officer certain functions previously carried out by the Chief Registrar of Friendly Societies, viz. maintaining a list of trade unions and employers' associations (see **listed trade union**); supervising the statutory procedures for **transfer of engagements** (q.v.), **amalgamations** (q.v.) and changes of trade union name (see **Trade Union (Amalgamations etc.) Act 1964**); and supervising the administration of **political funds** (q.v.) under the **Trade Union Act 1913.** *Address:* Vincent House Annexe, Hide Place, London SW1P 4NG. *Tel:* 01-828 7603. There is also an Assistant Certification Officer for Scotland. *Address:* 19 Heriot Row, Edinburgh EH3 6HT.

CERTIFIED SICKNESS ABSENCE; see **sickness absence.**

CERTIFIED TRADE UNION. An unregistered trade union granted a certificate that it was a trade union under the **Trade Union Act 1913** s. 2(3). The relevant sections of this Act were repealed in the **Industrial Relations Act 1971,** and the status of certified trade union no longer exists. Other than confirming an organisation's trade union objects, the status carried with

it no other privileges or obligations. Between 1913 and 1965, 102 certificates were issued by the Registrar of Friendly Societies and not withdrawn, the great majority to **employers' associations; 29** certificates were withdrawn during the same period.

CHAIN MAKERS' AND STRIKERS' ASSOCIATION. A trade union founded in 1899 and formerly known as the United Chain Makers and Chain Strikers Association (1902). *Address:* Unity Villa, Sidney Road, Cradley Heath, Warley, Worcs. B64 5BA. *Tel:* 0384 66482. The union was suspended from membership of the TUC by decision of the 1972 Congress for failure to comply with Congress policy of non-registration under the **Industrial Relations Act 1971,** and has not reaffiliated. The union signified its intention of winding up in 1978.

CHANGE OF PRACTICE PRINCIPLE. The principle that there shall be no change in agreed rates of wages or agreed prices for jobs unless there has been a change in machinery, plant, equipment, working conditions, or other modification of circumstances sufficiently notable to justify it. The principle aims at protecting employers from continuous claims and employees from **rate cutting** or **dilution;** see Engineering *Handbook of National Agreements* 2.51 (a): 'No piecework prices, bonus or basis times once established may be altered except for the following reasons: (1) A mistake in the calculation on either side, or (2) the material, means or method of production or the quantities are changed, or (3) a mutual arrangement has been come to between the employer and the worker in the same way as a new price is arranged'; also in the steel industry: 'there was to be no alteration in the agreed rates of wages unless there was a definite alteration in the machinery, plant or equipment' (Frederick Scopes, *The Development of the Corby Works,* Stewarts and Lloyds Ltd, 1968, p. 237), a works example of the principle established in the **Melters' Sliding Scale Agreement** of 1905, Clause 8. On dilution aspects, see for example, *Engineering, Manual Workers Procedure,* 1922, II(1)(b).

CHANGEOVER ALLOWANCE. (work study) see **allowances.** 'An allowance to compensate workers for the time spent on necessary activities or waiting time, at the start and/or end of a job or batch ...

denoted as Job Changeover Allowance or Batch Changeover Allowance', British Standards Institution, *Glossary of Terms Used in Work Study,* BS 3138, 1969, No. A1019.

CHANNEL MONEY. Payment made to the crew of a merchant ship at a paying off port before they receive the balance of their wages; usually made if the ship is not paying off on the day of arrival and enables the crew to pay customs duty, etc.

CHAPEL. A collective expression for all printing workers in a department and the name given to the unit of organisation of a trade union at workshop level; hence **father of the chapel** (FOC), the elected chairman of the chapel and the substantial equivalent in other industries of the **shop steward** (q.v.); **imperial chapel,** a chapel representative of a number of chapels of the same union in a house or office, and **federated chapel,** a chapel representative of all the chapels in a house or office, irrespective of union. Chapels were first described and stated as being of some antiquity by Joseph Moxon, *Mechanick Exercises,* 1683, Martin Robertson, 3rd ed., 1970). He suggested that the name derives from the books of divinity they first produced; others have proposed an origin in the nearness of Caxton's press to Westminster Abbey or in the 'chapelles' or caps worn by French journeymen working in London in the sixteenth century (Ellic Howe and Harold E. Waite, *The London Society of Compositors,* Cassell and Co., 1948, p. 32). Chapels were at first representative of both masters and journeymen, but subsequently became confined to the latter, and in the late eighteenth and early nineteenth centuries became the basis of the local societies which preceded the national unions of today. The chapel combines its original functions as a self-governing and disciplining workshop organisation and its later role as a unit of trade union organisation (A. J. M. Sykes, 'Trade Union Workshop Organisation in the Printing Industry - the Chapel', *Human Relations,* Vol. 13, No. 1, 1960, pp. 49-65). For a comment on the current role of the FOC and Chapel in the national newspaper industry, see Economist Intelligence Unit, *The National Newspaper Industry,* 1966, p. 224, *et seq.;* **clerk of the chapel,** see **collecting steward.**

CHARGEHAND. An employee working to some extent with tools or on production, but also concerned to some degree with supervision **(working chargehand, leading hand, leading toolsetter,** etc.), or in some cases working entirely as a supervisor, and hence the equivalent of **foreman;** see **supervisor.** The situation varies from one establishment and one working situation to another.

CHECK-OFF. The arrangement whereby employers deduct trade union contributions or dues from the wages of trade union members in their employment and pay them over to the union or unions concerned. Also known as **payroll deduction schemes** (a **Treasury Deduction Scheme** offered check-off to recognised staff associations in July 1965, q.v.), **contribution deduction schemes, deduction schemes,** and the **list system** (for merchant seamen on foreign-going ships operating under the **National Maritime Board,** q.v.). There is no reason to believe that check-off deductions constitute a violation of the **Truck Acts** (q.v.) where workers covered by these Acts are concerned. It was laid down by the House of Lords in **Hewlett v. Allen** (1894, A.C. 383) that the payment by an employer of an employee's wages to a third party acting as the employee's agent was not a 'deduction' within the meaning of s. 3 of the 1831 Act. Authority is normally given in writing, but 'all that is required from employees is simply their agreement, expressed or implied, to the deduction' (C. Grunfeld, *Modern Trade Union Law,* Sweet and Maxwell, 1970). A collective agreement may be a legal authority to deduct (see **Williams v. Butlers Ltd**). Some regard check-off as an alternative to the **closed shop** (q.v.). The practice of the check-off grew rapidly in Britain in the 1960s. Few unions now oppose it in principle, and the Treasury Deduction Scheme led to particularly rapid growth in the public sector. Early in 1966 about one in five trade union members had check-off facilities (see A. I. Marsh and J. W. Staples, *Check-off Agreements in Britain,* Royal Commission on Trade Unions and Employers' Associations, Research Papers 8, 1968, pp. 45-64). A TUC survey published in January 1972 suggested that by 1971 the proportion had increased to one in three.

CHECK STEWARD or check-book keeper. A trade union branch official whose task it is to enter members' contributions into the contribution book.

CHECKWEIGHER, in the coalmining industry more popularly known as a **check-**

weighman. An official appointed by workers to check the accuracy of weights as taken by the employer, when their earnings are related to the weight of the output produced. The statutory right of coal miners to appoint their own checkweighers is provided for in the Coal Mines Regulation Acts 1887 to 1908. The Checkweighing in Various Industries Act 1919, extends the principle to a number of industries mentioned in the Act (iron and steel manufacture, loading or unloading of goods into and from vessels, manufacture of cement and lime) and to any other industry by regulation made by the Secretary of State; see Ian Fife and E. A. Machin, **Redgrave's Health and Safety in Factories,** Butterworth 1976, p. 1758, *et seq.* For the early history of checkweighmen in coalmining, and their first statutory recognition in 1860, see R. Page Arnot, *The Miners: A History of the Miners' Federation of Great Britain,* Allen and Unwin, 1949. Some writers regard the checkweighman as incorporating some of the functions of a **shop steward** (q.v.).

CHECKWEIGHMAN; see **checkweigher.**

CHEMICAL INDUSTRIES ASSOCIATION LIMITED (CIA). An employers' organisation formed in 1966 by the merger of a trade association, the Association of British Chemical Manufacturers, with an organisation of employers for industrial relations purposes, the Association of Chemical and Allied Employers (1941), first formed in 1918 as the Chemical Employers' Federation. The Association's representatives make up the employers' side of the Chemical and Allied Industries Industrial Council (composed of the Chemical, Fertiliser, and Plastics JICs) and of the Drug and Fine Chemical Joint Conference, Collective agreements (including those made in Gelatine and Glue) directly affect about 90,0000 hourly paid workers. The CIA became notable for its Joint Standing Committee with the unions set up in 1968 to oversee the operation of the industry's framework agreement on **productivity bargaining;** see A. I. Marsh and W. E. J. McCarthy, *Disputes Procedures in Britain,* Royal Commission on Trade Unions and Employers' Associations, Research Papers, 2 (Part 2), 1968, Chapter Four. *Address:* Alembic House, 93 Albert Embankment, London SE1 7TU. *Tel:* 01-735 3001-8.

CHEMICAL WORKERS' UNION
(CWU). A trade union which took this title in 1936 after developing as the National Union of Drug and Chemical Workers (1920), from the Amalgamated Society of Pharmacists, Drug and Chemical Workers (1918), itself derived from the Retail Chemists' Association (1912). The union's history was dominated by the fact that the impetus for development of the Society of Pharmacists came from seceding members of the Cripplegate Branch of the Shop Assistants' Union, leading to charges of breakaway and poaching which led to its withdrawal from the Trades Union Congress in 1924 (which it did not rejoin until 1943), and to its continuing exclusion from national negotiations in the chemical industry; see S. W. Lerner, *Breakaway Unions and the Small Trade Union,* Allen and Unwin, 1961. The union merged with the **Transport and General Workers' Union** in 1971.

CHEQUERS AND DOWNING STREET TALKS. Talks on the economic situation between the Heath administration, the **Confederation of British Industry** and the **Trades Union Congress** between July and November 1972, with which the National Economic Development Council was also associated. The talks ranged widely over incomes, prices and economic growth in an attempt to find a voluntary basis for a **prices and incomes policy;** they broke down on 2 November, and were followed by an interim statutory standstill on prices and incomes of 90 days (**A Programme for Controlling Inflation: The First Stage,** Cmnd. 5125, November 1972, and the **Counter Inflation (Temporary Provision) Act 1972);** see also Trades Union Congress, *The Chequers and Downing Street Talks,* TUC, November 1972.

CHIEF REGISTRAR OF FRIENDLY SOCIETIES. The official charged by the **Trade Union Act 1871,** with the registration of trade unions both of employees and employers see **trade union, employers' association, registered trade union** and **certified trade union**). The Registrar's powers on registering a trade union were, on all but political fund rules (see **political fund**), minimal, and members had the right of appeal to him on two instances only, alleged breaches of political fund rules (**Trade Union Act 1913**) and alleged breaches in the statutory procedure regulating the merger of unions (Trade Union (Amalgamations, etc.) Act 1964; see **amalgamation**). The Registrar, under the terms of the **Industrial Relations Act 1971** (now repealed), gave up his office in respect of trade unions on 30 September 1971 and was replaced by the **Chief Registrar of Trade Unions and Employers' Associations** (q.v.). His final Report for 1970 (Part 4, Trade Unions) contained an account of the Registrar's work since 1871. The Registrar's functions are now carried out by the **Certification Officer** (q.v.).

CHIEF REGISTRAR OF TRADE UNIONS AND EMPLOYERS' ASSOCIATIONS.

An official appointed by the Crown under the terms of the **Industrial Relations Act 1971** (ss. 63 and 64) from 1 October 1971 with substantially greater powers over registration than his predecessor, the **Chief Registrar of Friendly Societies** (q.v.). The Registrar was required to register eligible organisations and might require their rules to be altered to conform to Schedule 4 of the Act (see **registered trade union**), and might apply to the **Industrial Court** for cancellation of registration, as well as investigating complaints of members (on subjects other than the **political fund** (q.v.)) (s. 81), or breach of rules on his own initiative; he was also responsible for the **special register** (q.v.). Following the repeal of the Industrial Relations Act, the office of the Chief Registrar was replaced from 1 February 1976 by that of the Certification Officer for Trade Unions and Employers' Associations (see **Certification Officer**).

CHILDREN AND YOUNG PERSONS.

Statutorily defined, for the purposes of the prohibition or regulation of their employment as, in the case of a child, 'any person who is not over school age' (Education Act 1944, s. 58 and Education (Scotland) Act 1946, s. 138 (1)) and in the case of a young person, 'a person who has ceased to be a child and who is under the age of eighteen years' (Employment of Women, Young Persons and Children Act 1920). A number of Acts of Parliament restrict the employment of children and young persons, especially the Children and Young Persons Act 1933 (no employment of children under 13, except by parental permission on light agricultural work; no employment of children during school hours, before 6 a.m. or after 8 p.m. on any day, or for more than 2 hours on any school day or on a Sunday, with powers to local authorities to make byelaws on the employment of young persons), Young Persons (Employment) Act 1938 etc.: see Ian Fife and E. A. Machin, *Redgrave's*

Health and Safety in Factories, Butterworth 1976, p. 1600 *et seq.*

CIGARETTE MACHINE OPERATORS' SOCIETY (CMOS); see Tobacco Mechanics' Association.

CINEMATOGRAPH, TELEVISION AND ALLIED TECHNICIANS, ASSOCIATION OF (ACTT). A trade union originally formed in 1933 as the Association of Cine Technicians and having a spheres of influence agreement with the **Electrical, Electronic Telecommunication and Plumbing Union** (EETPU) and the **National Association of Theatrical, Television and Kine Employees** (NATKE) in entertainment and communications dating from 1946. Its members are mainly in Independent Television, film production and professional film processing and it is a signatory to four major trade union agreements covering production and technical staff in these areas. Its first industrial agreement was signed with the Gaumont-British Picture Corporation in 1936; a national agreement covering film processing workers followed in 1938, and recognition and agreements in short film, newsreel and feature film production followed during the war. The union's name was changed in 1956 to include reference to television technicians, and following the establishment of Independent Television in 1954, it signed its first agreement with the Programme Contractors' Association in 1957. *Address:* 2 Soho Square, London W1V 6DD. *Tel:* 01-437 8506. *TUC Affiliated Membership 1977:* 18,682.

CIO. Congress of Industrial Organisations (q.v.).

CIR. Commission on Industrial Relations (q.v.).

CISO. Confederation of Independent Staff Associations; see **Independent Staff Associations, Confederation of.**

CITU. Confederation of Insurance Trade Unions; see **Insurance Trade Unions, Confederation of.**

CITY OF BIRMINGHAM DISTRICT COUNCIL v. BEYER (1977) ILIR 211 (EAT). A case in which it was found by the Employment Appeal Tribunal that a bricklayer dismissed after giving a false name and a bogus reference in order to obtain employment because he knew that his record as a trade unionist would prevent him from getting a job if he did not do so was not unfairly dismissed; see **blacklisting** and **freedom of association.**

CIVIL AIR TRANSPORT EMPLOYERS' SECRETARIAT. An organisation established in 1947 to secure liaison between all airline operators, whether private or public, in membership of the National Joint Council for Civil Air Transport established as a result of the Civil Aviation Act 1946. The Head of the Secretariat acts both as secretary of the Employers' Executive Committee and of the Employers' Side of all national consultative and negotiating bodies. *Address:* 200 Buckingham Palace Road, London SW1W 9TJ. *Tel:* 01-834 2323.

CIVIL AVIATION ACT 1949. An Act principally known in industrial relations for s. 15(1) which requires that the terms and conditions of employment of persons employed by any independent enterprise providing air transport services must not be less favourable than those observed by the British Airways Board for persons employed on comparable work, disputes arising which are not otherwise disposed of being referred by the Advisory, Conciliation and Arbitration Service to the **Central Arbitration Committee,** (see **Schedule 11 Claims).**

CIVIL AND PUBLIC SERVANTS (Executive and Directing Grades) SOCIETY OF (SCPS). A society whose origins go back to 1893 with the formation of the Association of Clerks of the Second Division and 1918 with the 'old' Society of Civil Servants which subsequently amalgamated (the former under the title of Association of Executive Officers of the Civil Service), together with other Executive Grade Unions, to form the Society of Civil Servants (Executive, Directing and Analogous Grades). The union adopted its present title in 1976 after amalgamation with the Association of Officers of the Ministry of Labour and the Customs and Excise Group to take into account the fact that much of its membership worked outside the Civil Service proper. *Address:* 124-126 Southwark Street, London SE1 0TU *Tel:* 01-928 9671. *TUC Affiliated Membership 1977:* 104,910.

CIVIL AND PUBLIC SERVICES ASSOCIATION (CPSA). The **recognised association** (q.v.) for the clerical, secretarial, typing and allied grades of the Civil Service, of the Post Office Corporation and of a number of other quasi-Civil Service departments. The union had its origins in the Assistant Clerks Association formed in 1903, which in 1920 became the Clerical Officers Association, and two years later merged with two other clerical unions to form the Civil Service Clerical Association. The union took its present title in 1969 in recognition of its growing membership in public employment outside the Civil Service proper. In 1970 it had recourse to strike action for the first time in its history, having adopted a strike policy in the previous year as a result of difficulties in Civil Service pay negotiations arising in 1968. In 1973 the union merged with the Ministry of Labour Staff Association and in 1974 with the Court Officers' Association. Bernard Newman, *Yours for Action,* Civil Service Clerical Association, 1953; B. V. Humphreys, *Clerical Unions in the Civil Service,* Blackwell and Mott, 1958. Address: 215 Balham High Road, London SW17 7BQ. *Tel:* 01-672 1299. *TUC Affiliated Membership 1977:* 230,572.

CIVIL CONSPIRACY; see **conspiracy.**

CIVIL EMPLOYMENT; see **working population.**

CIVIL ENGINEERING CONSTRUCTION CONCILIATION BOARD FOR GREAT BRITAIN. A national joint negotiating body founded in December 1919, originally between the **Federation of Civil Engineering Contractors** (q.v.) and a single trade union, the National Amalgamated Union of Enginemen, Firemen, Mechanics, Motormen and Electrical Workers, which was later joined by other operatives' organisations representing labourers. The Board was originally established despite the hostility of craft unions associated with the **National Joint Council for the Building Industry** and contained no representatives of craft unions until 1952. In that year when its constitution was revised to provide for four representatives of the **General and Municipal Workers' Union,** four of the **Transport and General Workers' Union,** one of the National Union of Enginemen, Firemen, Mechanics and Electrical Workers (now incorporated in the TGWU) and four representatives of the craftsmen, of which two are representative of woodworkers and one of bricklayers (now represented by the **Union of Construction, Allied Trades and Technicians).** The Conciliation Board made its first Working Rule

Agreement in 1921 and in 1952 adopted Rules of Procedure for the Speedy Settlement of Disputes in which in addition to regular meetings of the Board disputes unresolved locally could be handled by an *ad hoc* Disputes Sub-Committee; see W. S. Hilton, *Industrial Relations in Construction,* Pergamon Press, 1968, Ch. 8.

CIVIL ENGINEERING CONTRACTORS, FEDERATION OF. An employers' organisation formed in June 1919 and forming the employers' side of the **Civil Engineering Construction Conciliation Board for Great Britain** established in December of the same year. It represents the vast majority of civil engineering contractors in Britain and has as its main functions collective bargaining with construction unions, conditions of contract and liaison and negotiation with government. General Conditions of Contract for works of civil engineering construction were agreed between the Federation, the Institution of Civil Engineers and the Association of Consulting Engineers in 1950, and their use has been steadily growing. *Address:* Romney House, Tufton Street, London SW1P 3DU. *Tel:* 01-222 2544.

CIVIL SERVANTS, SOCIETY OF. see **Civil and Public Servants, (Executive and Directing Grades) Society of.**

CIVIL SERVICE ALLIANCE. A group of staff associations in the Civil Service represented on the Staff Side of the **Civil Service National Whitley Council.** In its later form it was set up in 1939 and consisted of the Civil and Public Services Association, the Inland Revenue Staff Federation, the Ministry of Labour Staff Association and the County Court Officers' Association. It has now ceased to function; see B. V. Humphreys, *Clerical Unions in the Civil Service,* Blackwell and Mott, 1958.

CIVIL SERVICE ARBITRATION TRIBUNAL. A special tribunal established in 1936 to arbitrate on differences between the Staff and Official Sides of the Civil Service National and Departmental Whitley Councils. The jurisdiction of the Tribunal is confined to non-industrial civil servants with an upper salary limit and claims are required to relate to a **class** (q.v.). Individual cases are therefore excluded from arbitration. Also excluded are superannuation, the granting or refusal of established status, numbers of staff and actual times of attendance at

work, though the Tribunal is free to rule on questions of pay and allowances, weekly hours of work and annual leave. Its jurisdiction over some subjects remains in question between the parties. Appeals to the Tribunal reached their peak in 1952 and have declined in numbers since that time, partly because of the diminishing popularity of arbitration in the service and partly because of the activity of the **Civil Service Pay Research Unit** (q.v.) and the operation of **incomes policies;** see H.M. Treasury, *Staff Relations in the Civil Service,* HMSO, 1965, pp. 20-5; S. J. Frankel, 'Arbitration in the British Civil Service', *Public Administration,* Vol. XXXVIII, 1960, p. 29 and H. Parris, *Staff Relations in the Civil Service,* George Allen and Unwin, 1973.

CIVIL SERVICE CLERICAL ASSOCIATION (CSCA). A former title of the **Civil and Public Services Association,** (q.v.).

CIVIL SERVICE COMMISSION; see **Civil Service Department.**

CIVIL SERVICE DEPARTMENT (CSD). The department of the Civil Service, established in November 1968 and, *inter alia,* responsible for recruitment, manpower planning, management techniques and organisation and pay in the Civil Service. Its establishment was recommended by the Committee on *The Civil Service* (Fulton Committee) *1966-1968,* Cmnd. 3638, June 1968, Chapter 7, to replace and supplement the functions of the 'Pay and Management' group of the Treasury on the grounds that the role of central management in the Civil Service required enlargement, that conventional Treasury arrangements gave rise to a lack of professionalism and that a single-minded approach from a single department was needed to remove these defects. On the role of the CSD in reforming the Civil Service: R. W. L. Wilding, 'The Post-Fulton Programme, Strategy and Tactics', *Public Administration,* Vol. 48, Winter 1970, pp. 391-403; Sir William Armstrong, 'The Civil Service Department and its Tasks', Ch. 23 in R. A. Chapman and A. Dunsire (eds). *Style in Administration; Readings in British Public Administration,* George Allen and Unwin, 1971, Civil Service Department, *First Report of the Civil Service Department,* HMSO, 1970, and *Second Report of the Civil Service Department, 1971.* The **Civil Service Commission,** first constituted by Order in

Council in 1855, forms part of the Department, but retains its independence in selecting recruits for the Civil Service.

CIVIL SERVICE NATIONAL WHITLEY COUNCIL; see Whitleyism.

CIVIL SERVICE PAY RESEARCH UNIT (PRU). An independent fact-finding organisation proposed by the Priestley Royal Commission in the Civil Service, which reported in 1955, and brought into existence by a joint statement by the Official and Staff Sides of the National Whitley Council issued in April 1956. The purpose of the PRU is to provide the facts against which to implement the Commission's principle that Civil Service Pay should be determined by 'fair comparison with the current remuneration of outside staffs employed on broadly comparable work, taking into account differences in other conditions of service'. It describes and defines the similarities and differences in the grades with which comparison is being made, and discovers the pay and conditions of service of such comparable jobs; see **analogue.** It has no function beyond fact-finding, negotiations being conducted by the parties themselves. The operations of the PRU were suspended when Phase 1 of the Wilson government's pay policy came into effect on 1 August 1975. The PRU was reactivated in November 1977 to provide information for the pay award of April 1979. The new agreement provides for the establishment of a board composed of a Chairman and nine members, including four voting members from outside the Civil Service, which will submit an annual report to the Prime Minister.

CIVIL SERVICE UNION (CSU). A trade union formed in 1917 as the Minor Grades Association by messengers employed in the Ministry of Education and reorganised under its present title in 1944. It aims to organise all non-industrial civil servants in categories other than administrative, executive, clerical and scientific grades, and has membership, some industrial, in a number of autonomous public bodies outside the civil service, e.g. the Agricultural Research Council, the United Kingdom Atomic Energy Authority, the British Airports Authority, the Forestry Commission, etc. The union also organises and represents the domestic staff of the Royal Household. A government decision in January 1968 to cut numbers of messengers and office cleaners led

the union to set up a defence fund and since that date strikes and other forms of industrial action have been undertaken. *Address:* 17-21 Hatton Wall, London EC1N 8JP. *Tel:* 01-242 2991-5. *TUC Affiliated Membership 1977:* 46,758.

CIVILIAN LABOUR FORCE; see working population.

CLAIM. A demand for improved terms or conditions in **collective bargaining;** an assertion of a right to something, whether arising out of a collective agreement or not, e.g. to **recognition** of a trade union, or to a **benefit;** see also **Schedule 11 Claims.**

CLAIMS PROCEDURE; see Schedule 11 Claims.

CLASS. A group of workpeople distinguished from other groups of workpeople in a workplace or industry on grounds of sex, job classification, method of payment or other accepted criterion, e.g. as in the 1922 *Procedure - Manual Workers, Engineering Industry,* Clause I(b): '. . . it is not the intention to create any specially favoured class of workpeople'. In the non-industrial Civil Service, in which arbitration claims must relate to a class, this has been defined as 'any well-defined category of civil servants who for the purpose of a particular claim occupy the same position or have a common interest in a claim', which is now accepted to exclude groups which are part of a larger category unless any already-existing differential in conditions of service exists between them and other groups; see H.M. Treasury, *Staff Relations in the Civil Service,* HMSO, 1965, p. 21.

CLASSIFICATION OF OCCUPATIONS AND DIRECTORY OF OCCUPATIONAL TITLES (CODOT). A comprehensive method of classifying jobs published by the Department of Employment in October 1972 (Department of Employment, *Classification of Occupations and Directory of Occupational Titles,* HMSO, 1972, in three volumes). CODOT replaces an earlier unpublished classification system in use within the Department, and is compatible with other national and international classifications. Its main purposes are claimed to lie in improving the matching of vacancies and applications in the Department's employment and career guidance services, in assisting employers in identifying and classifying occupations and codifying those in which their workers have had experience, and as a reference document for a new system of occupational statistics. It came into general use in local Employment Offices in November 1972 and is expected to last at least ten years.

CLASS UNIONISM. Trade union structure based upon the notion of one big union of all workers. TUC, *Trade Union Structure and Closer Unity,* 1947, p. 6, describing the results of the inquiry into trade union structure emerging from the Hull Congress of 1924: '. . . . it was shown in regard to class unionism that one big union, however theoretically perfect, was a long way from being realised . . . and that one big union could not be regarded as a practical possibility at that time'. The idea has recently been revived in the United States as a counter to the **multi-national corporation.**

CLAUSE (j). A clause of the Overtime on Dayshift Agreement in the engineering industry (*Handbook of National Agreements* 2.21(j)) which provides that **systematic overtime** is deprecated as a method of production, that union workmen shall not be required to work more than 30 hours' overtime in any four weeks after full shop hours have been worked, that overtime is not to be restricted where breakdowns, repairs, replacements, alterations, trial trips or completion of work against delivery dates are involved, and that 'the employers have the right to decide when overtime is necessary, the workpeople or their representatives being entitled to bring forward . . . any cases of overtime they desire discussed. Meantime, the overtime required shall be proceeded with'. The implication of these provisions for **managerial prerogatives** was the immediate cause of the engineering lock-out of 1922; see **Mackenzie Report** and A. I. Marsh, *Industrial Relations in Engineering,* Pergamon Press, 1965, p. 155 *et seq.*

CLEAN-UP PERIOD. A part of the working day, before meal breaks or at the end of the shift, allowed for workers to wash and change their clothes (also known as **wash-up period** or **wash-up time**) and/or to clean up the workplace so that this is left in good working condition for the next shift; may also refer to an allowance made during the course of calculating the **standard time** for a job to allow time for washing up or cleaning up.

CLEARING NIGHT. A night, provided

for in trade union rule, on which members are required to become clear by paying their contributions up to date.

CLERICAL AND ADMINISTRATIVE WORKERS' UNION (CAWU) now known as the Association of Professional, Executive, Clerical and Computer Staff; see **Professional, Executive, Clerical and Computer Staff, Association of.**

CLERICAL SALARIES ANALYSIS; see **Administrative Management, Institute of.**

CLERICAL, TECHNICAL AND SUPERVISORY STAFFS, ASSOCIATION OF (ACTSS); see **Transport and General Workers' Union.**

CLERICAL WORK EVALUATION (CWE). A technique employed by P-E Consulting Group Ltd. for indirect work measurement which is claimed to show savings as high as 25 per cent. It uses a Booking and Sampling for Indirect Standards (BASIS) method which is said to be simpler and cheaper to operate than more complex systems of measuring work; see also **Clerical Work Improvement Programme** (CWIP), **Group Capacity Assessment** (GCA), and **Variable Factor Programming** VFP).

CLERICAL WORK IMPROVEMENT PROGRAMME (CWIP). A technique of work measurement for application especially in offices, other white collar and indirect areas, used by W. D. Scott and Company using Predetermined Time Systems as developed by Paul B. Mulligan and Co. Inc. of the United States. The technique involves initial work simplification and 'work measurement . . . if accuracy sufficient to enable management to manage'; see J. E. Bayhylle, *Productivity Improvement in the Office,* Engineering Employers' Federation, Research Paper 2, December 1968; also **Group Capacity Assessment** (GCA), **Variable Factor Programming** (VFP) and **Clerical Work Evaluation** (CWE).

CLERICAL WORK MEASUREMENT; see **Clerical Work Improvement Programme** (CWIP), **Group Capacity Assessment** (GCA), **Variable Factor Programming** (VFP) and **Clerical Work Evaluation** (CWE).

CLERK OF THE CHAPEL; see **collecting steward.**

CLICKER. The foreman of a **companionship** of compositors who distributes the copy etc.; a foreman shoemaker who cuts the leather and gives out the work. OED gives the latter as the original sense.

CLOCK CARD or **time card;** see **clocking.**

CLOCKED HOURS. The number of hours per day or per week actually worked, especially in the steel industry, in which **overtime, shift premiums** etc. are paid as **gift hours** (q.v.) i.e. as hours paid for over and above those actually worked.

CLOCKING. The practice of recording on clocks the time at which employees attend for work, or, most frequently, attend for work and leave work; hence **clock cards, time cards, clocking on** (or **clocking-in**), **clocking-off** (or **clocking-out**). The most common way of recording attendance in British industry, especially in manufacturing, sometimes accompanied by **timekeeping bonuses** and/or the practice of **quartering** (q.v.), both designed to discourage **lateness,** the one by means of a monetary reward and the other by a type of fine. Some companies regard clocking as an out-of-date form of discipline; see Wilfred Brown, *Piecework Abandoned,* Heinemann, 1962, Ch. 7, and BIM Information Note 11, *Abolition of Time Clocks,* January 1961. Some such companies have expressed themselves pleased with the abolition of clocks. Others have adopted a system of **honour cards,** i.e. cards on which employees enter their times of arrival and departure themselves, with varying results. A survey by the Institute of Personnel Management showed 64 per cent of manual workers clocking in 1970 compared with 93 per cent in 1966.

CLOCKING-OFF or **clocking-out.** Recording the time of departure from the workplace by means of a time clock; see **clocking.**

CLOCKING-ON or **clocking-in.** Recording the time of arrival at the workplace by means of a time clock; see **clocking.**

CLOSED SHOP. In the United States an arrangement whereby an employer can hire and employ only workers who are already members of the union and continue to be so. Thus defined, the closed shop is illegal in federal labour statutes. In Britain the expression has been used to describe a number of situations. The **Trades Union Congress** (1946 Report, p. 255) interpreted it 'as trade unionists generally understand the term', to imply exclusive membership and bargaining rights given to a single union and this it condemned as 'alien to British trade union practice'. V. L. Allen, 'Economic effects of compulsory trade unionism,' *Oxford Economic Papers,* Vol. 6, No. 1, February 1954, pp. 70-1) has adopted a slightly less limited definition including the possibility of more than one union with bargaining rights, and situations in which workers must agree to *become* members of appropriate trade unions and obey their regulations before they commence work. W. E. J. McCarthy, *The Closed Shop in Britain,* Blackwell, 1964, p. 3, adopted a much broader definition; 'a situation in which employees come to realise that a particular job is only to be obtained and maintained if they become and remain members of one of a specified number of trade unions'. This leaves the question open whether the situation involves a **pre-entry closed shop** or a **post-entry closed shop** (i.e. whether trade union membership is required before or after hiring) and whether it involves more or less formal means of enforcement (whether, for example, it is done by making trade union membership a condition of employment with the agreement of the employer, or whether trade union members enforce it informally by refusing to work with 'nons', or non-trade union workers). The approach of the Ministry of Labour, in its evidence to the Donovan **Royal Commission on Trade Unions and Employers' Associations** (p. 86) was similar, recognising that trade union membership might be either formally or in practice a condition of employment, that it might include situations in which the employer would recruit only trade union members and thus give the union control over the supply of labour and situations in which recruits, if not already members of trade unions would have to join them after engagement (sometimes known as the **union shop,** q.v.), and that maintenance of a closed shop might be either by formal agreement with the employer or by tacit understanding backed by the possibility of strikes or threat of strikes to obtain and preserve 100 per cent membership. Some observers have regarded '100 per cent membership' and the closed shop as synonymous terms. Thus Charles Dukes, President of the TUC (1946 Report, p. 13): 'The closed shop is nothing new in British practice. It means for us the well founded claim that workers in an industry should be in their appropriate unions. The 100 per cent union shop is a recognised objective of trade union policy and organisation'. Others have considered that there is a vital distinction of method between the two; see John Darragh; *The Closed Shop*, p. 6: 'The TUC has never officially adopted the closed shop policy, preferring the 100 per cent principle under which, where possible, employment is restricted to trade union members, not by agreement, but by their own refusal to work with non-unionists'. One reason for the distinction may have been the unpopularity of the expression 'closed shop'. There was a tendency after the last war to assume that the closed shop had become undesirable, unnecessary and unimportant as an instrument of trade union action (see Noah Barou, *British Trade Unions*, Gollancz, 1947 and V. L. Allen, *Power in Trade Unions*, Longmans Green, 1954). In 1964 W. E. J. McCarthy (*op. cit.*) calculated that almost 40 per cent of Britain's trade unionists were in closed shops of one kind or another, and therefore roughly one worker in six of those employed in the country. This suggested that the closed shop was more normal than it was commonly believed to be at the time. Objections to it have mainly centred around the argument either that it reduces the individual worker's freedom or that its economic effects are damaging. Both the Ministry of Labour and the Royal Commission on Trade Unions and Employers' Association (Evidence 1965, p. 88, and Report p. 163) pointed to the possible advantages of the closed shop in stabilising industrial relationships and in contributing towards the efficiency of negotiating and consultative machinery, and to the difficulty of legal prohibition. In the United States it is usually considered that the effect has been small in those states which prohibit both closed and union shops. 'Employers who want good relations with their unions have usually winked at the law just as good employers in traditional closed shop industries have winked at Taft-Hartley'. Frederick Meyers, *'Right to Work' in Practice*, New York Fund for The Republic, 1959). Both the Ministry and the Donovan Commission suggested means of safeguarding the individual while retaining the legality of the closed shop and this approach was accepted by the Labour Government in 1969 (*In Place of Strife*, Cmnd. 3888, p. 34). The Conservative Party in 1968 proposed that 'strikes to enforce a closed shop should no longer be "protected trade

disputes"' (*Fair Deal at Work,* April 1968, p. 30, referring to the effect of **The Trades Disputes Acts 1906 and 1965**, q.v.) and that there should be a statutory right for every employee to join a trade union and equally a statutory right not to do so (Conservative Party Conference, 8 October 1969). The **Industrial Relations Act 1971** (now repealed) gave legislative form to these intentions by: (a) making **pre-entry closed shop** agreements or arrangements void (s. 7); (b) providing that the worker, as between himself and his employer, should have the right to belong to the **registered trade union** of his choice, and, if he was a member, to participate in its activities, or to be a member of no registered trade union or **organisation of workers** (s. 5); (c) making it an **unfair industrial practice** for an employer to prevent a worker from exercising his rights under s. 5 or to dismiss, penalise or otherwise discriminate against him, unless an **agency shop** or an **approved closed shop** (q.v.) was in existence; (d) making it an unfair industrial practice for any person (including a trade union or organisation of workers, or an official of either) to call, organise, procure or finance or threaten a **strike** or an **irregular industrial action short of a strike** to induce an employer to comply with a pre-entry closed shop agreement or to commit an unfair industrial practice under s. 5 (ss. 33(3), 7(1)). The Industrial Relations Act 1971 thus sought to end the closed shop outside the limited area of approved closed shops and agency shops. Since its repeal, the Trade Union and Labour Relations Acts 1974 and 1976 have provided, for the first time in Britain, statutory support for closed shops by removing the right of individuals *not* to belong to trade unions (while retaining their right to belong) and by providing for the *fair* dismissal of employees who refuse to join trade unions which have union membership agreements or arrangements with their employers except on grounds of genuine 'religious belief to being a member of any trade union whatsoever' (see **union membership agreement**). These provisions have undoubtedly increased the extent of formal closed shop arrangements in Britain, some of them including (like the Post Office) their own internal appeal machinery to which, for its own affiliated unions, the Trades Union Congress has added an **Independent Review Committee** (q.v.). Opinions differ on the severity with which these arrangements are likely to impinge on individuals in practice; see Brian Weekes, 'The Law and Practice of the

Closed Shop', *Industrial Law Journal,* Vol. 5, No. 4, December 1976, pp. 211-22. For a study of the closed shop situation during the period of the Industrial Relations Act 1971 see Brian Weekes, Michael Mellish, Linda Dickens and John Lloyd, *Industrial Relations and the Limits of Law,* Basil Blackwell, 1975.

CLOSED UNION; see **open union.**

CLOTH PRESSERS' SOCIETY. A trade union founded in 1872 as the Huddersfield Cloth Pressers' Society, to which the Leeds Society of Cloth Pressers (1860) transferred its engagements in 1934. It is now a unitary organisation, having no branches, with members mostly in the Huddersfield area and staffed entirely by part-time officers. *Address:* 34 Southgate, Honley, nr. Huddersfield, HD7 2NT. *Tel:* 0484 61175. *TUC Affiliated Membership 1977:* 70.

CM. corresponding member (q.v.).

CMC WAGE SYSTEM. Cotton Manufacturing Commission Weaving Wage System; a partly job evaluated (see **job evaluation)** system designed to replace the weavers' **uniform list** (q.v.). The system was agreed between the Cotton Spinners' and Manufacturers' Association and the Weavers' Amalgamation in 1949 and employed a point rating scheme to assess the relative difficulty of different types of loom, as well as an incentive payment arrangement.

CMOS. Cigarette Machine Operators' Society: see **Tobacco Mechanics' Association.**

COA. Court Officers' Association (q.v.).

COALITION BARGAINING. Defined by William N. Chernish (*Coalition Bargaining. A Study of Union Tactics and Public Policy,* University of Pennsylvania Press and OUP, 1969, p. 5) as '... the joining together of a number of local unions, having different international affiliations, for the purpose of bargaining with a company or an industry as a single unit ... a form of joint bargaining which seeks to increase union bargaining power in dealing with a firm which has several locations which are represented by different unions ...'. Dr Chernish prefers the term coalition bargaining to a possible alternative term, **co-ordinated bargaining.**

COCKBURN COMMISSION. The **Royal Commission on Labour Laws** appointed in 1874 to consider the question of common law conspiracy in trade disputes arising principally out of the Criminal Law Amendment Act 1871, which reported in February 1875. The report of the Commission was followed by the **Conspiracy and Protection of Property Act 1875,** which repealed the Criminal Law Amendment Act 1871 and the Master and Servant Act 1867. It removed the application of the doctrine of criminal conspiracy to acts done in contemplation or furtherance of a trade dispute, and remained on the Statute Book until repealed by the **Industrial Relations Act 1971.** For other Royal Commissions on industrial relations generally, see **Erle Commission, Devonshire Commission, Dunedin Commission, Donovan Commission.**

CODES ˋ OF PRACTICE. Practical guides for the purpose of improving industrial relations drafted by the Advisory, Conciliation and Arbitration Service under s.6 of the Employment Protection Act 1975 and, subject to approval by both Houses of Parliament, coming into effect on such dates as the Secretary of State for Employment may by Order appoint. Codes are not legally enforceable but are admissible in evidence before industrial tribunals and before the **Central Arbitration Committee** (q.v.). They may therefore, in setting standards in the areas to which they refer, affect the outcome of the deliberations of these bodies. The notion of a general Industrial Relations Code of Practice seems to have originated in April 1968 in the Conservative Party's policy statement on industrial relations, *Fair Deal at Work* (q.v.). The resultant Code came into existence in February 1972 under ss. 2-4 of the Industrial Relations Act 1971 and, after the repeal of that Act, was retained in Schedule I, Part I, paras. 1-3 of the Trade Union and Labour Relations Act 1974. The Employment Protection Act 1975, in amplification of that Schedule, enacted that Codes should also be produced on Disclosure of Information (see **Information, Disclosure of)** and on time off For Trade Union Duties and Activities (see **Facilities for Trade Unions).** The former Code came into effect in 1977 and the latter is scheduled to do so on 1 April 1978. In addition a Code of Practice on Disciplinary Practice and Procedures in replacement of paras 130-3 of the 1972 Industrial Relations Code of Practice also came into effect in 1977; (see

Disciplinary Procedure). The **Sex Discrimination Act 1975** provides for Codes of Practice to be drawn up by the Equal Opportunities Commission; codes are also provided for in the **Health and Safety at Work Act 1974.**

CO-DETERMINATION. (Federal Republic of Germany). An expression used to describe one or other, or both, of the sets of rights given to workers under (1) the Works Constitution Acts 1952 and 1972 (Betriebsverfassungsgesetz), and (2) the Co-determination Acts 1951 and 1976 (Mitbestimmungsrecht), to participate in managerial decision making. The type and the effect of participation rights varies. Under (1) the right of the Works Council (see **Betriebsräte**) is to information and prior consultation on some matters; on others to 'co-decision', and one-third employee representative membership of Supervisory Boards of companies (Aufsichtsräte) is also legally mandatory in companies employing fewer than 2,000; under (2) two sets of provisions now apply. In the iron and steel and coal mining industries only (1951 Act), 'co-management' is legally established in the sense of numerical parity between shareholders' and employees' representatives on Supervisory Boards, moderated by the election to the Board of an additional 'neutral member' representing neither interest, most employees' representatives being in practice appointed by the relevant trade unions. In addition, the Act makes provision for a labour director on the Management Boards of companies who is appointed by a majority of employees' representatives on the appropriate Supervisory Boards and enjoys the same legal standing as the commercial and technical directors. The 1976 Act, applying to some 600-700 firms outside iron and steel which employ more than 2,000 workers, gives parity to shareholder and employee representation on supervisory boards, with a 'tie-breaking' vote in favour of the former, and without a final employee say on the appointment of a labour director. To the Deutscher Gewerkschaftsbund (the Federal German Trades Union Congress) co-determination 'represents a comprehensive system of social, political and economic thought aimed at transforming society' (Abraham Shuchman, *Co-determination,* Public Affairs Press, Washington DC, 1957, p. 1). The second Works Constitution Act represented the result of trade union pressure; also the 1976 Act, a compromise resulting from DGB demands for the extension of the steel and coal Act to other industries, which was more strongly resisted by the employers (see Gisbert Kley, *Co-determination in Coal and Steel, Replies to the DGB's Demands;* Siegfried Balke, *Expansion of Co-determination in the Federal Republic of Germany,* and Ernst-Gerhard Erdmann, *The Myth of Co-determination,* Bundesvereinigung der Deutschen Arbeitgeberverbände, Köln 1970). One-third representation of employees' representatives has also been pressed by the Federal Republic for the Supervisory Boards of the proposed European Company; see also W. M. Blumenthal, *Co-determination in the German Steel Industry,* Princeton 1956, F. Fürstenberg, 'Workers' Participation in Management in the Federal Republic of Germany', *International Institute for Labour Studies Bulletin 6,* June 1969, and W. Kolvenbach, *Workers' Participation in Europe,* Kluwer/Metzner, 1977. Co-determination in its German form has found little favour with either trade unions or managements in Britain up to the present. In Germany the pressure for the 1951 Act to be more widely applied still continues; see also **industrial democracy, workers' participation, Bullock Report.**

CODOT. Classification of Occupations and Directory of Occupational Titles (q.v.)

COERCIVE COMPARISON. A term used by Arthur M. Ross (*Trade Union Wage Policy,* University of California Press, 1948, p. 53 *et seq.*) to describe the way in which the dynamic of trade union wage policies is principally to be explained. Ross sees equitable comparisons as an important element in this dynamic, such comparisons becoming 'coercive' in wage determination in specific circumstances, e.g. when several locals of a union centralise their wage policies and consolidate their strategies, when separate industrial establishments are brought together in common ownership, when the state plays an increasingly active part in setting rates of pay, when rival unions compete for jurisdiction etc., noting that 'under these circumstances, small differences become large, and equal treatment becomes the *sine qua non* of industrial peace', p. 74.

COHEN COUNCIL. The **Council on Prices, Productivity and Incomes** (q.v.) (after its first Chairman, Lord Cohen).

COHSE. Confederation of Health Service Employees; see **Health Service Employees, Confederation of.**

COLLECTING STEWARD. A trade union lay official, usually appointed by the branch, to be responsible for the workplace collection of contributions and for paying these to the union; often known as **collectors,** or **card stewards,** in the printing industry as **clerks of the chapel,** by the Amalgamated Engineering Union as **contribution collectors** (Rule 5, Clause 3, first introduced, March 1968). Collectors are frequently paid commission on contributions collected; see for example, the rules of the **Transport and General Workers' Union** and the **General and Municipal Workers' Union.** In most cases collectors are formally distinct from **shop stewards** (q.v.) but the same individual may in practice double the two functions.

COLLECTIVE AGREEMENT. An agreement arrived at by **collective bargaining** (q.v.), as contrasted with an agreement arrived at by **individual bargaining,** at whatever level in the industrial hierarchy **(industry-wide agreement, national agreement, company agreement, local agreement, plant or works agreement, domestic agreement, workshop agreement,** etc.), about procedural or substantive terms (hence **procedure agreements** and **substantive agreements)** and whether a **fixed-term agreement** or an **open-ended agreement.** In Britain the degree of formality (see **formalisation)** involved in the making or acceptance by the parties of the obligations of a collective agreement can vary widely from one situation to another, ranging from formal written **comprehensive agreements** to **custom-and-practice,** notes or minutes of joint meetings, or simply action by one party which is assumed to be agreed because it is not questioned by the other party (see, for example, A. I. Marsh, E. O. Evans and P. Garcia; *Workplace Industrial Relations in Engineering,* Engineering Employers' Federation and Kogan Page, November 1971, Ch. 4). The trend of informed opinion has recently favoured more written and comprehensive agreements, particularly at company and plant level (see Donovan **Royal Commission on Trade Unions and Employers' Associations 1965-1968,** Cmnd. 3623, June 1968, para. 162 *et seq., P. A. L.* Parker, W. R. Hawes and A. L. Lumb, *The Reform of Collective Bargaining at Plant and Company Level,* Department of Employment, Manpower Papers No. 5,

HMSO, 1971), though movement in this direction may be slow. Until the **Industrial Relations Act 1971** no agreement between a trade union and an employer's association could be directly legally enforced **(Trade Union Act 1871,** s. 4(4)) and it was widely understood (and confirmed in **Ford v. Amalgamated Engineering and Foundry Workers' Union)** that to secure legal enforceability in other cases (i.e. to be binding in more than honour), the parties to an agreement would require to show intention to create legal relations (see for example, O. Kahn-Freund (ed.). *Labour Relations and the Law,* Stevens and Sons, 1965 p. 25 *et seq.).* The 1971 Act sought to reverse this situation making legally enforceable (a) any collective agreement made *in writing* after the commencement of the Act unless it contained a provision, however expressed (see **disclaimer clause** or **rebuttal clause)** that it was not intended to be a legally enforceable contract (s. 34) and (b) any agreement made by a joint negotiating body, if recorded in writing. Cyril Crabtree, *The Industrial Relations Act,* Charles Knight and Co., 1971, Chapter 6. The intention was to encourage the making of legally enforceable agreements. This, like many aspects of the Industrial Relations Act, was not effective in practice. With the repeal of the 1971 Act by the **Trade Union and Labour Relations Act 1974** the legal situation returned substantially to its pre-1971 position. Now, as before 1971, a collective agreement may become an **implied term** (q.v.) of an individual worker's contract of employment.

COLLECTIVE BARGAINING. A method, or process, of conducting negotiations about wages and working conditions and other terms of employment between an employer, or group of employers, or employers' association on the one hand, and representatives of workers and their organisations on the other, with a view to arriving at **collective agreements;** often distinguished from **joint consultation** (q.v.) in which the element of bargaining or negotiation is assumed to be absent. Collective bargaining is generally recognised as a central feature of democratic industrial relations systems and the most desirable and normal means of regulating contracts of employment; see ILO Convention 84 (1947) on the Right of Association and the Settlement of Labour Disputes in Non-Metropolitan Territories ('all practical measures shall be taken to assure to trade unions which are representative of the workers concerned the right to conclude collective agreements with employers and employers' organisations'), the general undertaking of a similar kind in Convention 98, Article 4 (1949), and in Recommendation 91 (1951). Beatrice Potter (later Mrs Sidney Webb) claimed to have originated the expression 'collective bargaining' in her book *The Co-operative Movement of Great Britain*, in 1891, and she and her husband later developed it in *Industrial Democracy*, 1897, where it was regarded as an alternative to **individual bargaining** (in individual bargaining 'the employer makes a series of separate contracts with isolated individuals', in collective bargaining 'he meets with a collective will and settles, in single agreement, the principles on which, for the time being, all workmen of a particular group, or class, or grade, will be engaged', 1902 ed. p. 173), and as one of three trade union methods, the others being **mutual insurance** and **legal enactment**. The Webbs acknowledged that the area of collective bargaining might be wider than that of trade unionism, but that trade unions were necessary for continuity and elasticity (pp. 178-9); they also outlined the need for forms of collective bargaining machinery, and saw the process as a compromise between the claims of employers and unions to exercise unilateral control over the work situation (pp. 217-18). The concept of collective bargaining was little developed until W. M. Leiserson, *Constitutional Government in American Industries*, American Economic Review, Supplement, 1922, and then almost ignored until N. W. Chamberlain, *Collective Bargaining*, McGraw-Hill, 1951 (2nd edition, 1965, with J. W. Kuhn). Chamberlain reduced theories of the nature of the bargaining process to three: the marketing theory (a means of contracting for the sale of labour); the governmental theory (a form of industrial government), and the managerial theory (a method of management), F. H. Harbison (*Goals and Strategy in Collective Bargaining*, Harper, 1951) emphasises collective bargaining as a conflict resolving process ('a process of accommodation between two institutions which have both common and conflicting interests') and for its social values ('the core function of collective bargaining is to generate pressure for the enhancement of the dignity, worth and freedom of individuals in their capacity as workers'). For a critique of the Webbs, Chamberlain, Harbison and others, see Allan Flanders, 'Collective Bargaining: A Theoretical Analysis', *British Journal of Industrial Rela-*

tions, March 1968 and *Management and Unions*, Faber, 1975. Flanders considers collective bargaining to be a political rather than an economic process, involving rule making and power relationships as well as making social contributions to the dignity of workers. In *A Behavioral Theory of Labor Negotiations*, McGraw-Hill, 1965, Richard E. Walton and Robert B. McKersie adopt four models of collective bargaining, **distributive bargaining, integrative bargaining, attitudinal structuring** and **intra-organisational bargaining** in an attempt to provide predictive hypotheses about how people will behave in bargaining situations; see also **coalition bargaining, co-ordinated bargaining, co-operative bargaining, conjunctive bargaining, practical bargaining, fragmented bargaining, work-group bargaining, industry-wide bargaining, national bargaining, district bargaining, company bargaining** and Allan Flanders (ed.), *Collective Bargaining*, Penguin Modern Management Readings, 1969.

COLLECTIVE BARGAINING COMMITTEE. A committee established by the **Trades Union Congress** in 1970 to keep developments in collective bargaining under review, to follow up the TUC's **Post-Donovan Conferences** between unions on developments in bargaining needed in different sectors of industry, and to take the initiative in discussing with unions particular problems such as low pay, minimum earnings guarantees, holidays, long hours, incremental scales and payment systems. The Collective Bargaining Committee was the successor to the **Incomes Policy Committee** established in October 1965 and wound up in February 1970. In 1974 its role was taken over by the TUC's Economic Committee.

COLLECTIVE BARGAINING SIT-IN: see **sit-in strike**.

COLLECTIVE CONCILIATION. Conciliation (q.v.) in disputes or differences arising between employers and trade unions in collective bargaining, representation or grievance handling, as contrasted with **individual conciliation** (q.v.).

COLLECTIVE CONTRACT. A device considered by Guild Socialists (see **Guild Socialism**) to encourage workers' control and defined by G. D. H. Cole (*Workshop Organisation*, OUP, 1923 and Hutchinson, ed. A. I. Marsh, 1973, p. 133 *et seq.*) as 'a plan under which the workers in each shop, under the auspices of their unions, would enter into a collective contract with their employer to produce for an agreed price the required output and would themselves undertake the organisation of the shop and necessary discipline and supervision'. Collective contract was not a practical success. H. A. Clegg (*A New Approach to Industrial Democracy,* Basil Blackwell, 1960, pp. 121-8) identifies more recent collective arrangements for sharing work and wages akin to the guild socialist conception and rejects some, such as **labour-only-sub-contracting** (q.v.) as unacceptable to trade unions, and others as limited in application or running counter to modern trends of organisation.

COLLECTIVE REDUNDANCY; see **Collective Redundancy Directive** and **redundancy.**

COLLECTIVE REDUNDANCY DIRECTIVE. A Directive of the Council of Ministers of the European Economic Community of 17 February 1975 (*Official Journal of the EEC,* 1975, L48/29) requiring prior consultation with workers' representatives on collective redundancies, i.e. in those involving at least 10 workers in establishments with 21-99 workers, 10 per cent in those employing 100-299 workers and at least 30 per cent in those employing more than 300 workers, and to make it obligatory on members to comply with the Directive within two years. In Britain, the necessary changes to statutory redundancy practice (see **Redundancy Payments Act 1965**) were made in the Employment Protection Act 1975 ss. 99-107, though there appear to be differences. The EEC concept of 'collective redundancies' appears to be broader and not to be restricted to situations in which there is (as in the Redundancy Payments Act) a cessation or reduction of business or a decline in demand for work of a particular kind; the Directive also requires the employer to consult workers' representatives 'with a view to reaching agreement' and to 'ways and means of avoiding collective redundancies', neither provided for in the Employment Protection Act; finally, the Directive refers to 'workers' representatives' and not, as in the Employment Protection Act, 'recognised trade unions'.

COLLECTOR; see **collecting steward.**

COLLIERY MANAGEMENT, BRITISH ASSOCIATION OF (BACM). A trade union formed after coal industry nationalisation in 1947 to organise and represent all managerial, technical, professional and administrative staff in the mining industry and its associated ancillary undertakings. The union was not at first welcomed by other unions, but it was eventually recognised as the management union in the industry by the National Union of Mineworkers and the National Association of Colliery Overmen, Deputies and Shotfirers, with whom it now holds demarcation agreements. BACM became affiliated to the Trades Union Congress in 1977. *Address:* BACM House, 317 Nottingham Road, Old Basford, Nottingham NG7 7DP. *Tel:* Nottingham 76949/75819. *TUC Affiliated Membership, 1977:* 15,769.

COLLIERY OVERMEN, DEPUTIES AND SHOTFIRERS, NATIONAL ASSOCIATION OF (NACODS). A trade union consisting of thirteen Area Associations having in membership 'underofficials' in the coal industry, i.e. overmen, deputies, shotfirers and certain other officials below the grade of Under-Manager. Before 1910, when it was first established as a national association, the union existed as a federation of autonomous areas. It adopted its present title when the coal industry was nationalised in 1947. *Address:* Argyle House, 29-31 Euston Road, London NW1 2SP. *Tel:* 01-837 0908. *TUC Affiliated Membership, 1977:* 20,141.

COMBINE COMMITTEE. Abbr. for **joint shop stewards combine committee;** a committee of shop stewards organised to represent the interests of trade union members, usually irrespective of union, employed in a combine or multi-establishment company. Such committees are normally unofficial, i.e. formally unsanctioned by official trade union organisation, and have been a matter of controversy in the trade union movement; see Trades Union Congress, *Report on Disputes and Workshop Representation,* TUC Report, 1960. For an inquiry into their possible effects on earnings see S. W. Lerner and J. Marquand, 'Regional Variations in Earnings, Demand for Labour and Shop Stewards Combine Committees in the British Engineering Industry', *Manchester School,* September 1963; also S. W. Lerner and J. Bescoby, 'Shop Steward Committees in the British Engineering Industry', *British Journal of Industrial Relations,* July 1966 and A. I. Marsh, E. O. Evans and P. Garcia, *Workplace Indus-*

trial Relations in Engineering, EEF and Kogan Page, 1971.

COMMERCIAL CONTRACTS, breaches of; see **boycott.**

COMMERCIAL MOTORMEN'S UNION, SCOTTISH (SCMU). A trade union tracing its origin from the Scottish Carters' Association founded in 1898. The union later became the Scottish Horse and Motormen's Association, which changed to its present name in 1964; see Hugh Lyon, *The History of the Scottish Horse and Motormen's Association,* 1898-1919, Civic Press Ltd, Glasgow, 1919; Angela Tuckett, *The Scottish Carter,* Allen and Unwin, 1967. The union merged with the **Transport and General Workers' Union** in 1971.

COMMISSION ON INDUSTRIAL RELATIONS (CIR). A Commission established by Royal Warrant in March 1969 and reconstituted as a statutory body under the **Industrial Relations Act 1971** on 1 November 1971. The establishment of the CIR was recommended by the Donovan **Royal Commission on Trade Unions and Employers' Associations, 1965-1968** (Cmnd. 3623, June 1968, para. 198 *et seq.*) to act as a third party in developing and improving collective bargaining and the general conduct of industrial relations. During the period 1969-71, when there was no provision on any issue for the legal enforcement of the Commission's recommendations, it reported on nine references involving trade union recognition alone and nine dealing with the improvement of procedures at company and/or plant level, a further two references dealing with both issues; in addition, two references were concerned with the industrial relations situation in particular industries (*Report 22,* Shipbuilding and Shiprepairing and *Report 23,* The Hotels and Catering Industry, Part I, Hotels and Restaurants), and one (*Report 17*) with Shop Stewards Facilities, making 23 reports in all. Under the Industrial Relations Act, the CIR became a statutory body and investigated and reported on matters referred to it by the Secretary of State for Employment and by the **Industrial Court,** advised the Secretary of State on revisions to the **Code of Industrial Relations Practice** and performed the functions of commissions of inquiry required by the **Wages Councils Act 1959** to examine proposals to set up, vary, or abolish **wages councils.** Though the CIR could still, under s. 121 of the 1971 Act, handle references made by the Secretary of State in much the same way as it formerly did before November of that year, its role differed from its previous role especially in that (a) the CIR was now required to include in its annual report a general review of the development of collective bargaining in the previous year (s. 123); (b) applications for procedural references could formally be made by employers and registered trade unions, through the **Industrial Court** (as well as by the Secretary of State) and, failing voluntary settlement, the findings of the Commission could be made legally binding (s.41); (c) in recognition and similar issues the Commission operated within the framework provided for dealing with **sole bargaining rights** (s.45), **agency shops** (s.12) and **approved closed shops** (s.17 and Schedule 1), its functions including the arranging of necessary ballots, and its role falling within the aegis of the Industrial Court; (d) the terms of the Act (s.121 (1) (d) and (e)) specifically included **disclosure of information** by employers to their employees or unions with negotiating rights and facilities for training in industrial relations as proper subjects of reference to the CIR (references concerning both were before the Commission before the passing of the Act); and (e) the functions already referred to in relation to the Code of Industrial Relations Practice and wages council legislation; see also Commission on Industrial Relations, *First General Report* (No. 9, Cmnd. 4417, July 1970), *Second General Report* (No. 25, Cmnd. 4803, November 1971). *Annual Report for 1972,* and *Annual Report for 1973.* The first chairman of the CIR during its first, non-statutory, phase was George Woodcock, former General Secretary of the **Trades Union Congress;** during its latter, statutory phase L. F. (now Sir Leonard) Neal. The Commission was abolished on 16 September 1974 as a result of the Trade Union and Labour Relations Act of that year. In its final Report (No. 90, August 1974) it described and assessed its work since 1969, concluding that it had not fulfilled the high hopes originally placed in it, partly because of under-use and partly because of its political unacceptability to the Trades Union Congress after 1971.

COMMISSION FOR RACIAL EQUALITY; see **Race Relations Acts.**

COMMITTEE OF INQUIRY. A committee, similar to a **Committee of**

Investigation, set up by the Secretary of State for Employment or other minister to inquire into an industrial relations matter of public concern. On industrial relations such Committees are, according to the Ministry of Labour, *Written Evidence to the Royal Commission on Trade Unions and Employers' Associations* (HMSO, 1965, p. 107), set up under the 'general powers' of the Secretary of State, i.e. those which he enjoys by virtue of his ministerial position. Of nineteen such Committees which delivered twenty-one reports between 1946 and 1966, seven were, however, expressly appointed under the **Conciliation Act 1896** now repealed. (K. W. Wedderburn and P. L. Davies, *Employment Grievances and Disputes Procedures in Britain,* University of California Press, 1969 p. 233). Examples of Committees of Inquiry are the Committees of Inquiry into the Pay of London Busman, into Labour-only Subcontracting (see **Phelps Brown Report**), into the **Fine Tubes Dispute,** and into labour problems in the port transport industry (see **Devlin Report**). Inquiries of a similar nature are now conducted by the **Advisory Conciliation and Arbitration Service** (q.v.), e.g. in 1976 into *The Electrical Supply Industry (negotiating and representative arrangements for managerial and higher executive grades),* ACAS Report No. 4, and into *Industrial Relations in the National Newspaper Industry,* ACAS Report No. 5; see **Panel of Investigation.**

COMMITTEE OF INVESTIGATION. An *ad hoc* committee set up by the Secretary of State for Employment under the **Conciliation Act 1896,** s. 22, to 'inquire into the causes and circumstances of a difference' between employers and workmen is usually known as a Committee of Investigation, being less formal than a **Court of Inquiry** (q.v.) and having no obligation to lay its report before Parliament. Such Committees were usually of the three-man kind, and were used when the public interest in an issue was less wide than would be appropriate for a Court of Inquiry (Ministry of Labour, *Written Evidence to the Royal Commission on Trade Unions and Employers' Associations,* HMSO, 1965, p. 107). The **Committee of Inquiry** (q.v.) formed an alternative to the Committee of Investigation, where the inquiries concerned were of a more 'general' nature; see K. W. Wedderburn and P. L. Davies, *Employment Grievances and Disputes Procedures in Britain,* University of California Press, 1969, p. 232 *et seq.* Following

the repeal of the Conciliation Act 1896 in 1975, investigations of this kind now rest with the **Advisory, Conciliation and Arbitration Service** (q.v.); see **Panel of Investigation.**

COMMITTEE ON RELATIONS BETWEEN EMPLOYERS AND EMPLOYED; see **Whitleyism.**

COMMON EMPLOYMENT doctrine of; see **employers' liability.**

COMMON RULE. A device ascribed to trade unions by the Webbs (S. and B. Webb, *Industrial Democracy,* 1898, 1913 ed. p. 560 *et seq.*). '. . . the Standard Rate, the Normal Day, and Sanitation and Safety, are but different forms of one principle - the settlement, whether by **Mutual Insurance** (q.v.), **Collective Bargaining** (q.v.) or **Legal Enactment,** of minimum conditions of employment, by Common Rules applicable to whole bodies of workers. All these Regulations are based on the assumption that when, in the absence of any Common rule, the conditions of employment are left to "free competition" this always means that they are arrived at by **individual bargaining** between contracting parties of unequal economic strength. Such a settlement, it is asserted, invariably tends, for the mass of the workers, towards the worst possible conditions of labor - ultimately, indeed, to the barest subsistence level . . . We find accordingly that the Device of the Common Rule is a universal feature of Trade Unionism . . .'.

COMMUNICATION; see **communications.**

COMMUNICATIONS. While there would be no general agreement about the precise usage of the word, either in its plural or in its singular form **communication,** it seems logical and widely acceptable to distinguish as follows. 'Communication': the process by which information is imparted or exchanged between individuals and groups, whether this be in the form of facts, orders, grievances, ideas or emotions; hence also to the means or system by which communication takes place - by written or spoken word, by personal contact or committee etc. - and the merits or demerits of different types of information (see International Labour Office, *Examination of Grievances and Communications within the Undertaking,* 1965, pp. 56-7). 'Communications': the social system or systems associated with communication, or more often the control system or systems involved; hence the function of communications in regulating or co-ordinating behaviour. Management thought has usually tended to pay most attention to the 'communications' aspect of the problem, though 'communication' is usually also present, e.g. 'To achieve the objects of communication it is essential that management should devise and implement a systematic and comprehensive chain of communications groups from top management to shop floor' - Confederation of British Industry, *Communication and Consultation, Report of a Working Party*, Sept. 1966, p. 4. Loosely used, the expression 'communications' has come to be thought of in some circles as a successor to **human relations** (q.v.) as a popular cure-all for industrial relations ills; see Cecil Chisholm (ed.), *Communications in Industry*, Business Publications in collaboration with B. T. Batsford Ltd, 1955. For a number of views; see J. K. L. Taylor, *Attitudes and Methods of Communication and Consultation between Employers and Workers at Individual Firm Level*, Organisation for Economic Co-operation and Development, 1962 and Raymond Williams, *Communications*, Chatto and Windus, 1966, Penguin Books 1968; see also **disclosure of information**.

COMMUNITY INDUSTRY. A scheme proposed and run by the National Association of Youth Clubs in co-operation with local authorities and others for employing young people who find it difficult to obtain or keep a job on work of social value in development and intermediate areas with high youth unemployment. The scheme has operated since 1972. Originally it was financed by the Department of Employment with material support from local authorities; the cost to the former in 1976 was over £3 million: the **European Social Fund** contributed £1.2 million in 1975. From 1 August 1977 administrative responsibility for the scheme was transferred from the Department to the **Manpower Services Commission.**

COMPANIONSHIP (or **'ship**). A group of men, usually compositors, working together, traditionally paid by the piece, and organised by a **clicker** - printing industry.

COMPANY AGREEMENT. A collective agreement negotiated at company level; see **company bargaining.**

COMPANY BARGAINING. Collective bargaining at company-wide level as distinct from **industry-wide bargaining, district bargaining, plant bargaining,** etc., and determining terms and conditions of work for a substantial part of the employees of that company. Company bargaining, as thus defined, is limited in Britain; its extension was advocated by the Donovan **Royal Commission on Trade Unions and Employers' Associations, 1965-1968,** Cmnd. 3623, June 1968, as representing the development of a more orderly system from that arising from traditional **national bargaining** and fragmented workplace bargaining (see **domestic bargaining**). Developments in the direction of company bargaining occasioned by **incomes policy, productivity bargaining** and other pressures and the extent of developments are discussed in B. C. Roberts and John Gennard, 'Trends in Plant and Company Bargaining', *Scottish Journal of Political Economy*, Vol. XVII No. 2, June 1970; Department of Employment, *The Reform of Collective Bargaining at Plant and Company Level*, Manpower Series No. 5, 1971 and A. I. Marsh, E. O. Evans and P. Garcia, *Workplace Industrial Relations in Engineering*, EEF and Kogan Page 1971.

COMPANY UNION or **house union.** Most rigorously defined, a union existing within a single company and dominated or strongly influenced by the company, and therefore not a **bona-fide trade union** or an **independent trade union** (q.v.). The classic case of such an organisation in Britain was that established by Mr G. A. Spencer (hence **Spencer Union**) mainly in the Nottinghamshire coalfield, after the General Strike of 1926, as the Notts and District Miners' Industrial Union, which was financially assisted for pension purposes by colliery owners and devoted most of its expenditure to superannuation benefit. But also applied by some observers to more or less borderline cases, many of which would pass the statutory test of independence laid down in the current Trade Union and Labour Relations Act, e.g. to **staff associations** (q.v.) in British banks, to non-TUC unions or to unions with special restrictions on striking; see K. G. J. C. Knowles, *Strikes,* Basil Blackwell, 1952, pp. 83-8.

COMPARABILITY. An argument used in **collective bargaining** to justify an improvement in wages, salaries or working conditions on the grounds that this is necessary to bring these into line with comparable workers or situations elsewhere. Comparability has played a considerable part in wage and salary determination in the public sector - see **fair comparisons, Priestley Formula, Guillebaud Formula** - and in reinforcing collective bargaining generally; see **claims procedure.** Its force in contributing to inflation was recognised by the **National Board for Prices and Incomes** which argued that formulae for linking pay increases to other increases elsewhere would spread increases in rates, regardless of the reasons originally given for them, and frustrate the case for special treatment (*First General Report,* Cmnd. 3087, August 1966). It therefore opposed the use of comparisons, both in the public and private sector. Its views were reflected in the criteria for wage increases in White Papers during the period of the **Prices and Incomes Policy** 1965-70 except where pay had fallen seriously out of line with the level of remuneration in similar work; see H. A. Clegg, *The System of Industrial Relations in Great Britain,* Basil Blackwell, 3rd ed. 1976, see also **coercive comparison, differentials, relativities.**

COMPARATIVE ESTIMATING. A work measurement technique said to be particularly useful in jobbing work, in which the time for a job is evaluated by comparing the work in it with the work in a series of similar jobs (known as **bench marks**), the work content of which has been measured. The method involves selecting a number of bench mark jobs which are measured and set out on a spread sheet; bench mark jobs are then compared with unmeasured jobs, and these jobs inserted in the same work group as the bench mark job containing a similar amount of work. It is claimed to give a degree of accuracy of job times between those offered by **time study** and **PMTS** on the one side and **analytical estimating** on the other. It is said to have originated in the United States in the 1950s and been later developed by the London Methods Engineering Council and Imperial Chemical Industries.

COMPENSATING REST; see relaxation allowance.

COMPENSATION. Usually employed to mean recompense for loss or damage, e.g. as in **Workmen's Compensation** or in cases involving **unfair dismissal** (q.v.). Also used, especially in the United States, and occasionally in Britain, in the sense of 'payment' or **remuneration,** and often defined to include 'total compensation', i.e. to include pensions, **fringe benefits,** etc.

COMPENSATORY PAYMENT also **booster payment,** and **make-up payment.** A sum paid to a worker in order to increase his wage or earnings to an acceptable figure and unrelated to his performance or hours worked, for example in the docks industry; see *Report of a Court of Inquiry into a dispute between the parties represented on the National Joint Council for the Port Transport Industry,* Cmnd. 4429, July 1970, p. 17. Also **session money,** sums paid by **turn** or session for the same purpose (Royal Albert Docks, Port of London).

COMPENSATORY TIME OFF. Special time off, especially in the form of days holiday or leave, allowed to employees in lieu of overtime pay, or for extra time put in by employees for which no overtime can be paid, e.g. in certain sections of public employment, or among certain grades of staff employee for whom no provision for overtime payment exists.

COMPLAINTS PROCEDURE. A form of **grievance procedure** (q.v.) adopted in 1963 for the Merchant Navy by the **National Maritime Board** (q.v.). The procedure allows for a seaman to take a complaint to the head of his section (e.g. his bosun), failing satisfaction to the head of his department (e.g. the Chief Officer), to the Master of his ship, and if still not satisfied, to the management of the shipping company in writing. **Shipboard liaison representatives** (q.v.) have no function in the scheme (other than an obligation to encourage its use) and cannot accompany or represent their members without consent; see D. H. Moreby, *Personnel Management in Merchant Ships,* Pergamon Press, 1968, pp. 115-16.

COMPLETENESS. An expression used by R. M. Blackburn (*Union Character and Social Class,* Batsford, 1967) to indicate the proportion of potential members of an organisation who are actual members; hence 'level of completeness', the percentage of potential members who have joined a trade union. Blackburn acknowledges G. Simmel (*The Sociology of Georg Simmel,* ed. K. H. Wolff, Collier-Macmillan 1964), as the source of the term, while noting that Simmel's use of it differs from his own, and regards the term **density** as incorrect.

COMPREHENSIVE AGREEMENT. A collective agreement incorporating in a single document, usually at company or plant level, all, or a substantial number of, the procedures and conditions of work applying to that company or establishment, and therefore an agreement which is not 'partial' (i.e. does not apply only to one practice or to a single group of workers), and which is not liable to **fragmented bargaining** (q.v.). The notion of comprehensive agreements has been closely associated with the development of **productivity bargaining**; hence the term 'comprehensive productivity agreements' (National Board for Prices and Incomes, *Productivity Agreements,* Report No. 36, Cmnd. 3311, June 1967, para. 6 *et seq.*), examples being those concluded by Esso, Alcan, British Oxygen, Electricity Supply and other companies and corporations after 1960. The Donovan **Royal Commission on Trade Unions and Employers' Associations 1965-1968,** Cmnd. 3623, June 1968, laid emphasis on the comprehensive agreement in preventing fragmented bargaining by and disorder in the workplace by resolving conflict between the formal and informal systems (paras 162 and 203 (8)). In the national newspaper industry the term 'comprehensive agreement' is used to describe **chapel** (and hence 'partial') agreements designed to achieve more realistic manning levels, etc. (almost invariably on a sharing of cost savings basis; National Board for Prices and Incomes, *Costs and Revenue of National Newspapers,* Report No. 141, Cmnd. 4277, February 1970, para. 41), and sometimes applied in a specialised, and fragmented, fashion, e.g. on 'comprehensive' staffing levels, for instance, agreed staffing levels to cover all sizes of newspapers, on tidying up payment extras, or on the provision of a 'comprehensive service' for an equated or **upstanding wage.**

COMPULSORY ARBITRATION. (1) An arrangement by which the parties to an industrial dispute are required by law to submit it to arbitration by a third party and to receive an award, by contrast with **voluntary arbitration** (q.v.). Compulsory arbitration laws usually, but not invariably, provide for binding awards; they may be applied to industry generally, or confined to particular industries (e.g. public utilities), whose interruption would cause inconvenience or loss to the community; see J. H. Richardson, *Introduction to the Study of Industrial Relations,* Allen and Unwin, 1954, pp. 367-71. Britain had compulsory arbitration in this sense during two world wars (see **Treasury Agreement,** 1915 and **National Arbitration Tribunal,** 1940-51). **Courts of Inquiry** are thought by some to incorporate some features of compulsory arbitration (Richardson *op. cit.* p. 371). (2) Arbitration at the instance of one party only, as under the **National Arbitration Tribunal,** the **Industrial Disputes Tribunal** 1951-59 and the current **Schedule 11 Claims** procedure (q.v.) in Britain. Arguments for restoring the IDT position were put by the **Trades Union Congress** to the Donovan **Royal Commission on Trade Unions and Employers' Associations 1965-1968;** see W. E. J. McCarthy, *Compulsory Arbitration in Britain; the Work of the Industrial Disputes Tribunal,* Royal Commission on Trade Unions and Employers' Associations, Research Papers No. 8, 1968, pp. 31-44; see also **terminal arbitration.** For a comparative study in five countries see J. J. Doewenburg, W. J. Gershenfeld, H. J. Glasbeck, B. A. Hepple and K. F. Walker, *Compulsory Arbitration,* Lexington Books, 1976.

COMPULSORY TRADE UNIONISM. A generic expression used by some writers to describe under a single heading different forms of the **closed shop** (q.v.); see V. L. Allen, *Power in Trade Unions,* Longmans Green, 1954, p. 56 and 'Some Economic Aspects of Compulsory Trade Unionism', *Oxford Economic Papers,* Vol. 6, No. 1, February 1954, pp. 69-81. W. E. J. McCarthy regards the term as a euphemism of questionable acceptability and usefulness (*The Closed Shop in Britain,* Blackwell, 1964, p. 7 *et seq.*); see B. Weekes, 'Law and the Practice of the Closed Shop', *Industrial Law Journal* Vol. 5, No. 4, December 1976 for the view that closed shops in Britain may often be so loosely administered as not to constitute compulsory trade unionism.

CON (abbreviation for **consideration**). A type of allowance for conditions of work formerly made in the South Wales coalfield. A County Court ruling that **con** was an **ex gratia payment,** and a subsequent reduced allowance on a new hard seam were the immediate causes of the Cambrian dispute of 1910. E. H. Phelps Brown, *The Growth of British Industrial Relations,* Macmillan, 1965, p. 319.

CONCEALED UNEMPLOYMENT or **disguised unemployment.** A name given to various situations in which the labour force is being underemployed without this being reflected in the number of workers out of work: (1) where **activity rates** are low, indicating that the labour force could be enlarged if suitable work were available; (2) where workers at work are underemployed (see **underemployment**); (3) where there is **short-time working.** The effect of all these situations is to suggest that Department of Employment statistics of **registered unemployed** may, especially in circumstances of rising **unemployment**, be in some respects too low, partly because of hidden labour reserves (particularly married women), and partly because of those currently employed who are not working full weeks or are being employed on tasks which do not use their skills fully; see David Metcalf and Ray Richardson, 'The Nature and Measurement of Unemployment in the U.K.', *Three Banks Review*, No. 93, March 1972.

CONCESSIONARY COAL or **miners' coal.** A form of **payment in kind** in the coal mining industry. '. . . part of the wage structure of every district except Lancashire and Cumberland. In the latter districts this privilege was won in 1950 after a major unofficial strike in 1949'. George B. Baldwin, *Beyond Nationalisation*, Harvard University Press, 1955, p. 28.

CONCILIATION. A term commonly used in Britain as synonymous with **mediation,** i.e. the procedure under which a neutral third party attempts to persuade the parties concerned to settle their dispute without seeking to impose his own terms of settlement upon them; a process defined by the **Royal Commission on Labour, 1891-1894** as 'the exercise of good offices by some outside agency with a view to avert an impending rupture between the parties, or, if the rupture has taken place, to bring them together as soon as possible, without acting as arbitrator or making an award, though it might sometimes make, or even publish, recommendations as to the course which should be followed'. Sometimes, however, currently used to cover all three principal methods of settling disputes, **negotiation, mediation and arbitration** (see, for example, H. A. Turner, *Arbitration: A Study in Industrial Experience,* Fabian Research Series 153, 1952, p. 2). This appears to be a reversion to older nineteenth century usage. S. and B. Webb, *Industrial Democracy,* 1913 ed. p. 223 notes that '. . . there has been until recently no clear distinction between **collective bargaining,** conciliation and arbitration' and quote Henry Crompton,

Industrial Conciliation, London 1876, who described typical cases of representative employers and workmen meeting to bargain as 'conciliation' (also the use of **Boards of Conciliation,** and the current use of the 'Conciliation Schemes' in the coal mining industry, derived from earlier usage); see G. B. Baldwin, *Beyond Nationalisation, The Labor Problems of British Coal,* Harvard University Press, 1955, for a surprised reaction to this) and A. J. Mundella, *Arbitration as a Means of Preventing Strikes,* Bradford, 1868 as saying: 'It is well to define what we mean by arbitration. The sense on which we use the word is that of an arrangement for open and friendly bargaining in which masters and men meet together and talk over their common affairs freely and openly'. Until 1975 the main conciliation powers of government in Britain derived from the **Conciliation Act 1896** and the **Industrial Courts Act 1919** (see Ministry of Labour, *Written Evidence to the Royal Commission on Trade Unions and Employers' Associations,* 1965, p. 94 *et seq.*), the policy of government being to provide 'a continuation of the process of collective bargaining with outside assistance . . . the intention of conciliation [being] to help the parties concerned to find a mutually acceptable basis for a settlement of the difference which has arisen between them' (*op. cit.,* p. 95). For this purpose the Ministry of Labour and its successors provided facilities for conciliation and conciliation officers, latterly organised under a **Manpower and Productivity Service** and a **Conciliation and Advisory Service** (q.v.). Following the repeal of the Conciliation Act 1896 and the partial repeal of the Industrial Courts Act 1919, the Employment Protection Act 1975 now places conciliation and the functions previously performed by the Services among the responsibilities of the **Advisory, Conciliation and Arbitration Service** (ACAS), q.v. ACAS now distinguishes between cases of 'individual conciliation', i.e. those arising out of individual cases received from **industrial tribunal** (q.v.) and those of a type arising from industrial disputes or differences between employers and trade unions. Of the latter 2,891 were completed in 1977 compared with 2,851 in 1975. It also distinguishes **'mediation'** (q.v.) as a separate process from 'conciliation' in some cases; see also K. W. Wedderburn and P. L. Davies, *Employment Grievances and Disputes Procedures in Britain,* University of California Press, 1969, Part III Ch. 10, and **Joint CBI/TUC Conciliation and Arbitrative Service.** For a study of conciliation cases involving Department of Employment conciliators during the first six months of 1972, see J. F. B. Goodman and J. Krislov 'Conciliation in industrial disputes in great Britain: A survey of the attitudes of the parties', *British Journal of Industrial Relations*, Vol. XII, No. 3, November 1974 pp. 327-51.

CONCILIATION ACT 1896. An Act which followed the report of the Devonshire **Royal Commission on Labour, 1891-1894** (C.-7421, HMSO, 1894), now repealed by the **Employment Protection Act 1975.** It made provision for the registration of **Boards of Conciliation and Arbitration** and provided that the Board of Trade might inquire into the causes and circumstances of a **difference**, or nominate a person to do so, or might appoint **conciliators** or arbitrators. The Act was normally regarded as the basis for the broad conciliation powers of the Department of Employment before the establishment of the **Advisory, Conciliation and Arbitration Service** (q.v.); see K. W. Wedderburn and P. L. Davies, *Employment Grievances and Disputes Procedures in Britain,* University of California Press, 1969, Ch. 10 and **conciliation**.

CONCILIATION AND ADVISORY SERVICE (CAS). A service provided by the **Department of Employment** from 1 March 1972 and performing the functions previously undertaken by the **Manpower and Productivity Service** (q.v.). The Service sought to locate and remove obstacles to the effective use of manpower, to promote improved ·industrial relations and to encourage the development of modern personnel practice. In addition it carried responsibility for the Department of Employment's function of conciliation in industrial disputes and in respect of complaints of alleged infringement of individual rights under the **Industrial Relations Act 1971** (e.g. **unfair dismissal**), as well as offering advice about the implications for management of the **Industrial Relations Code of Practice.** With the repeal of the Industrial Relations Act, the duties of the Service have merged with those of the **Advisory, Conciliation and Arbitration Service** (q.v.).

CONCILIATION AND ARBITRATION SERVICE, JOINT CBI/TUC; see **Joint CBI/TUC Conciliation and Arbitration Service.**

CONCILIATION GRADES. Non-salaried workers employed by the British Railways Board whose rates of pay and conditions of service are determined under the Machinery for Negotiation for Railway Staff between the BRB and the railway unions; the workers covered by the term are generally described in other industries as **manual workers** and include station porters, ticket collectors, signalmen, guards and shunters, permanent way staff, footplate and locomotive shed staff. Excluded are workshop grades falling under the **Railway Shopmen's National Council** and since 1969 some 26,000 staff now employed by National Carriers Limited and Freightliners Limited. Charles McLeod, *All Change; Railway Industrial Relations in the Sixties,* Gower Press, 1970; National Board for Prices and Incomes, *Pay and Conditions of Service of British Railway Staff,* Cmnd. 2873, January 1966.

CONCILIATION PAUSE. A discretionary reserve power in strikes proposed in the Labour government's White Paper *In Place of Strife* (Cmnd. 3888, 1969, pp. 28-9) and later abandoned after trade union opposition. The proposed power was to apply in cases of unconstitutional strikes or those in which there was no effective procedure or negotiation, and to take the form of an Order requiring a return to work without industrial action for 28 days, normally on *status quo* terms, after normal conciliation methods had failed, a financial penalty being imposed for non-compliance. The notion of a conciliation pause had something in common with that of a **cooling-off period** (q.v.) but was intended to apply to unofficial rather than official strikes and to constitute a final addition to, rather than an imposed opportunity for, normal conciliation methods.

CONCILIATOR; see **conciliation.**

CONDITIONS OF EMPLOYMENT AND NATIONAL ARBITRATION ORDER 1305 (1940); see **National Arbitration Tribunal** and **compulsory arbitration.**

CONFEDERATION; see **federation.**

CONFEDERATION OF BRITISH INDUSTRY (CBI). A national employers' organisation formed in July 1965 as a result of the merger of the Federation of British Industries, the **British Employers' Confederation** and the National Association of British Manufacturers. The CBI's membership includes individual firms, nationalised industries, trade associations and employers' associations and **employers' organisations**. It claims that there are one hundred or more national employers' organisations in membership and that it represents firms employing more than three-quarters of the labour force in the private sector of industry and transport. Like its trade union counterpart, the **Trades Union Congress**, the CBI, in its labour and social affairs functions, is not a negotiating organisation, but rather formulates general employer policy for implementation by its members and for expression to the government and the public. Unlike its predecessor in the labour and industrial relations field, the BEC, the CBI deals also with trade questions. *Address:* 21 Tothill Street, London SW1H 9LP. *Tel:* 01-930 6711.

CONFEDERATION OF EMPLOYEE ORGANISATIONS; see **Employee Organisations, Confederation of.**

CONFEDERATION OF HEALTH SERVICE EMPLOYEES (COHSE); see **Health Service Employees, Confederation of.**

CONFEDERATION OF INDEPENDENT STAFF ORGANISATIONS (CISO); see **Independent Staff Organisations, Confederation of.**

CONFEDERATION OF INSURANCE TRADE UNIONS. see **Insurance Trade Unions, Confederation of.**

CONFEDERATION OF SHIPBUILDING AND ENGINEERING UNIONS (CSEU); see **Shipbuilding and Engineering Unions, Confederation of.**

CONFERENCE ON INDUSTRIAL REORGANISATION AND INDUSTRIAL RELATIONS; see **Mond Turner Conferences.**

CONFLICT; see **industrial conflict.**

CONFLICTS OF INTEREST; see **interest disputes.**

CONFLICTS OF RIGHTS; see **rights disputes.**

CONGRESS OF INDUSTRIAL ORGANISATIONS (CIO). An organisation of trade unions in the United States origi-

nally formed as the Committee for Industrial Organisation in November 1935 to help to develop organisation in mass production industries along industrial lines, and known as the Congress of Industrial Organisations after its expulsion from the **American Federation of Labor** in 1937. John L. Lewis became its first President and remained its head until 1942 when he was succeeded by Philip Murray. In 1955 the CIO merged with the AFL into the **AFL-CIO** (see **American Federation of Labor-Congress of Industrial Organisations**).

CONJUNCTIVE BARGAINING. A state of collective bargaining seen by Neil W. Chamberlain and James W. Kuhn (*Collective Bargaining,* 2nd ed. McGraw-Hill, 1965) as one in which union and management regard their relationship as involving minimum coercion and commitment only without admission of mutual dependence. Chamberlain and Kuhn claim that conjunctive bargaining, for all its limitations, may have produced benefits for employers and for the public, but that a more fruitful relationship can emerge from **co-operative bargaining,** in which each party recognises that it is more likely to secure its objectives if it appreciates the objectives of the other, and obtains its support. The concept of co-operative bargaining appears to have something in common with those of **integrative bargaining** and **productivity bargaining** (q.v.).

CONSEILS DE PRUD'HOMMES. **Labour courts** in France dating from the revival by Napoleon in 1806 of courts of the same name said to be of fourteenth-century origin, and now operating under an Ordinance and Decree of 22 December 1958. Conseils de prud'hommes are notable for their lay membership representative of employers and employees ('judgement by peers'). Their jurisdiction relates to 'differences which may arise in connection with the contract of employment or the contract of apprenticeship between employers or their representatives and employees, workers or apprentices of either sex whom they employ'; they have no jurisdiction, therefore, over disputes arising from collective agreements as such. Their form and operation has general approval in France, criticism being mainly directed at the fact that not all areas of the country have access to courts, that the jurisdiction of some is too limited and that the courts to which appeals are taken are not specialised in labour matters; see Xavier Blanc-Jouvan, 'The Settlement of Labour Disputes in France', in Benjamin Aaron (ed.), *Labour Courts and Grievance Settlement in Western Europe*, University of California Press, 1971 and W. H. McPherson and F. Myers, *The French Labor Courts: Judgment by Peers*, University of Illinois, 1966.

CONSIDERATION; see con.

CONSOLIDATED PRODUCTION BONUS; see **production bonus**.

CONSOLIDATED TIME RATE (CTR). Minimum times rates for fitters and labourers in the engineering industry introduced in the 1950 national wage settlement in which the timeworkers' national bonus was consolidated with the basic rate. CTRs, expressed as hourly rates, formed minimum rates for both timeworkers and for payment by results workers (see **pieceworkers' guarantee**), and rates to which overtime and other premia and holiday payments were applied. Some districts and some firms had differential payments over and above CTRs, the resulting minimum rates also being known as CTRs in most cases. Consolidated Time Rates disappeared at the final stage of the Package Deal Agreement of 22 December 1964 and were converted on 1 January 1968 into **minimum time rates** (q.v.) A. I. Marsh: *Industrial Relations in Engineering*, Pergamon Press, 1965 and Engineering *Handbook of National Agreements*, 3.1; see also **standard consolidated time rate**.

CONSOLIDATION. A term applied to a process through which all, or significant component parts, of the earnings or take-home pay of workers are brought together into a single rate (see **consolidated time rate**, **minimum time rate** and **standard consolidated time rate** for examples of consolidation in the engineering and steel industries). The object of consolidation is usually to simplify or rationalise pay structure by merging fixed (or sometimes variable) components within it, and to increase the amount of take-home pay attributable to the standard or basic rate in relation to other factors.

CONSPIRACY. An agreement or combination to do something which is unlawful or to do something which is lawful by unlawful means. **Criminal conspiracy** was of importance in hampering trade union activity before the **Trade Union Act 1871**, it being held that agreements in unreason-

able restraint of trade, the trade union itself (**Hilton v. Eckersley (1855)** 6 E and B 47; **Hornby v. Close** (1867) 2 QB 153) or a concerted action to interfere with trade, e.g. a combination to strike, were criminal conspiracies. **The Trade Union Act 1871** provided (s. 2) that the purpose of a trade union was not criminal merely because it was in restraint of trade and the **Conspiracy and Protection of Property Act 1875** (also **Trade Disputes Act 1906**, s. 5(3)), that acts done in contemplation or furtherance of a trade dispute by two or more persons should not, merely because they were done or agreed to be done as part of collective action, constitute an indictable offence. Criminal conspiracy raised few serious problems in industrial relations thereafter, by the **Criminal Law Act 1977** (q.v.) has recently amended the law to take account of some difficulties arising in the 1970s. The tort of **civil conspiracy** has had greater importance, and includes situations in which two or more persons combine to inflict damage on a third party either in general form, i.e. with a predominant purpose other than that of forwarding their own legitimate interests, or in the narrower form of using means which would be unlawful whatever their motive. In **Quinn v. Leatham** (1901), AC 495, the House of Lords found that a case of actionable conspiracy had been made in both forms; this and the **Taff Vale** decision (also 1901) implied that in calling a strike a union's funds could be taken to compensate an employer for the loss which the strike inevitably caused him. The **Trade Disputes Act 1906** (q.v.) gave immunity to trade unions in actions for tort or conspiracy in contemplation or furtherance of a trade dispute (s. 1), and also against actions for tort in general (s. 4). The provisions of this Act are now incorporated into the Trade Union and Labour Relations Act 1974 and include immunity from actions relating to *any* breach of contract arising from a trade dispute (i.e. including commercial contracts as well as contracts of employment).

CONSPIRACY AND PROTECTION OF PROPERTY ACT 1875. An Act repealing the Criminal Law Amendment Act 1871, permitting peaceful picketing and providing that acts done in contemplation or furtherance of a **trade dispute** should no longer be a **criminal conspiracy** unless such an action done by an individual would have been punishable as a crime (s. 3). S. 7 of the Act, however, defines a number of intimidatory and related activities which are criminal offences that might be committed by pickets (see **picketing**), and s. 5 makes it a criminal offence to break one's contract of service or contract for service, either alone or in combination, knowing that the probable consequence will be to endanger human life, cause serious bodily injury or expose valuable property to destruction or serious injury. (S. 4 of the Act, which formerly, as extended by the Electricity (Supply) Act 1919, s. 31, made it a criminal offence for gas, water and electricity workers to break their contracts knowing that the probable consequence would be to deprive persons supplied by such undertakings of their supply, was repealed by the **Industrial Relations Act 1971** and has not been re-enacted.) Arising in part from the case of **R. v. Jones** (q.v.) on the **Shrewsbury Pickets**, s. 3 of the Act was repealed and the range of penalties which might be imposed under ss. 5 and 7 restricted by the **Criminal Law Act 1977** (q.v.).

CONSTANT WAGE PLAN. A payment arrangement designed to give employees a regular weekly income even though there are wide fluctuations in the working week; see A. D. H. Kaplan, *The Guarantee of Annual Wages*, Brookings Institution, 1947.

CONSTITUTIONAL STRIKE. A strike which takes place after the relevant disputes procedure or the provisions for the avoidance of disputes between the trade union and the employer or employers' association have been exhausted; the opposite of an **unconstitutional strike** which takes place in violation of such a **no-strike clause**. A constitutional strike need not necessarily be an **official strike** (q.v.) since the union or unions concerned may not necessarily give it their formal approval according to the provisions of their rule books. Such a situation has frequently occurred in the engineering industry (see A. I. Marsh, *Industrial Relations in Engineering*, Pergamon Press, 1965).

CONSTRUCTION, ALLIED TRADES AND TECHNICIANS, UNION OF (UCATT). The title adopted in 1971 by an amalgamation of construction unions consisting of the **Amalgamated Society of Woodworkers**, which absorbed in January 1970 the Amalgamated Society of Painters and Decorators, and the **Association of Building Technicians**, and in 1971 merged with the **Amalgamated Union of Building Trade Workers** and the Amal-

gamated Union of Sailmakers. The largest union in the amalgamation, the Amalgamated Society of Woodworkers, was formed in 1860 as the Amalgamated Society of Carpenters and Joiners. In 1918, on merger with the Amalgamated Union of Cabinet Makers (formed in 1833), it became the Amalgamated Society of Carpenters, Cabinet Makers and Joiners, and changed its name to Amalgamated Society of Woodworkers after a further amalgamation in 1921 with the General Union of Carpenters and Joiners (1827). The ASW was traditionally associated with a craft outlook, and it resisted for many years proposals for a single union in the building industry including less skilled societies of the kind substantially secured by the formation of UCATT. The Association of Building Technicians has now become the Supervisory, Technical, Administrative, Managerial (STAMP) section of the union, see S. Higenbottam, *Our Society's History*, ASW, 1939 and T. J. Connelly, *The Woodworkers, 1860-1960*, ASW, 1960. *Address:* Ucatt House, 177 Abbeville Road, Clapham, SW4 9RL. *Tel:* 01-622 2442. *TUC Affiliated Membership 1977:* 293,521.

CONSTRUCTION UNIONS, NATIONAL FEDERATION OF (NFCU). A federation of trade unions in the construction industry, known until 1 January 1970 as the **National Federation of Building Trades Operatives** (NFBTO). In its time it was reckoned by many to be the most effective trade union federation in Britain; see W. S. Hilton, *Industrial Relations in Construction*, Pergamon Press, 1968. It was dissolved following the formation of the **Union of Construction Allied Trades and Technicians** (q.v.).

CONSTRUCTIONAL ENGINEERING UNION (CEU). A trade union representing all grades of workers in engineering construction - steel erectors, riggers, crane drivers, scaffolders, fitters, welders, etc. - formed in 1924 by agreement with the **British Iron, Steel and Kindred Trades Association** (q.v.) from a section of that union. In April 1970, the CEU became the Construction Section of the newly formed **Amalgamated Union of Engineering Workers** (q.v.). It is party to national agreements with the **Engineering Employers Federation** on Outside Steelwork Erection and Steam Generating Plant Erection (Handbook of National Agreements, 6.2 and 6.3) and along with other unions to site agreements in the erection of chemical plants, gas plants, power stations etc. *Address:* 190 Cedars Road, Clapham, London SW4 0PP. *Tel:* 01-622 4451. *TUC Affiliated Membership, 1977:* 25,000.

CONSTRUCTIVE CONFLICT. A concept developed by Mary Parker Follett *(Dynamic Administration,* ed. H. C. Metcalf and L. Urwick, Pitman 1973, Ch. I) and based upon the notion that conflict in industry can be used constructively to increase integration and to resolve problems by a process of uncovering the real situation, breaking up the 'whole-demand' by revealing the complexities beneath, and by intelligent anticipation and response. Arguments relating to this and other concepts of Mary Parker Follett have sometimes been used to distinguish **consultation** from **negotiation** (q.v.); see National Institute of Industrial Psychology, *Joint Consultation in British Industry,* Staples Press, 1952, pp. 27-8. There appears to be nothing in her writings to justify this view, though she was undoubtedly concerned to emphasise the common purpose underlying industrial relationships.

CONSTRUCTIVE DISMISSAL. A situation in which an employee terminates his contract of employment in circumstances in which his employer's conduct has been such as to entitle him to do so. The concept became one of particular importance as a result of the **Redundancy Payments Act 1965** (s. 3(1)(c)) since, in its absence, 'by making conditions of employment unbearable, the unscrupulous employer could ensure that the employee left of his own accord', thus avoiding his obligations as an employer under the Act (Cyril Grunfeld, *The Law of Redundancy,* Sweet and Maxwell, 1971 p. 57). No specific provision of this kind was written into the Industrial Relations Act 1971 in providing for statutory compensation for **unfair dismissal** (see S. D. Anderman, *Voluntary Dismissal Procedures and the Industrial Relations Act,* PEP Broadsheet No. 538, September 1972), but this was taken care of in the Trade Union and Labour Relations Act 1974 (Schedule 1, para 5 (2)(c)), which includes in the statutory definition of 'dismissal' the situation in which 'the employee terminates [his] contract [of employment], with or without notice, in circumstances such that he is entitled to terminate it without notice by reason of the employer's conduct'. In **Western Excavating (ECC) Ltd. v. Sharp (1977)** it was ruled by the Court of Appeal that whether or not this provision applied should be determined according to contractual principles and *not* by applying a test of unreasonable conduct by the employer. This appears to restrict its interpretation to a narrower area than previously supposed by some **industrial tribunals.**

CONSULTATION; see **joint consultation.**

CONSUMER PICKETING; see **picketing.**

CONTINENTAL SHIFT SYSTEM; see **three shift system.**

CONTINGENCY ALLOWANCE (work study); see **allowances.** 'A small allowance which may be included in **standard time** to meet legitimate and expected items of work or delays, the precise measurement of which may be uneconomical because of their infrequent or irregular occurrence'. British Standards Institution, *Glossary of Terms Used in Work Study,* BS 3138, 1969, No. 35007.

CONTINUITY RULE. A practice in the docks noted by the Devlin Committee (*Final Report of the Committee of Inquiry under the Rt. Hon. Lord Devlin into certain matters concerning the Port Transport Industry,* Cmnd. 2734, HMSO, August 1965) and known in Hull as **shaving** whereby casual workers employed for the **turn,** and hence liable to be put off at the end of the half day, claimed to be entitled to complete the job which they had begun, although it might last for several days. The object of the practice was either to secure the prolongation of jobs and hence earnings, or to secure a fairer distribution of available jobs. In London an agreement of 1944 governed its use; it was considered by the Committee to result in waste of money, time and inefficiency; see **restrictive practices.**

CONTINUOUS THREE SHIFT SYSTEM; see **three shift system.**

CONTRACT OF APPRENTICESHIP; see **apprenticeship.**

CONTRACT ARBITRATION. Arbitration designed to operate in **conflicts of interest** issues in the conclusion of new collective agreements or contracts on terms and conditions of work, as distinct from **grievance arbitration** (q.v.). The term is an American one (see, for example, Irving Bernstein, 'Arbitration', Ch. 23 in Arthur

Kornhauser, Robert Dubin and Arthur M. Ross (eds.): *Industrial Conflict*, McGraw-Hill, 1954, who admits that the usage is vague, but considers the distinction analytically important); and has so far had little application in Britain; sometimes known in the United States as **nonjudiciable arbitration**.

CONTRACT PIECEWORK. A form of **group piecework** in which a contract price is agreed between a gang or squad and an employer for a particular job, irrespective of the time taken to complete it, distribution of the contract price being made by the squad-leader; a **job price contract,** or variation on the **contract system** (q.v.); see N. C. Hunt, *Methods of Wage Payment in British Industry,* Pitman, 1951, p. 102.

CONTRACT OF SERVICE. A contract in which the **servant,** or person employed to do work for him, is subject to the control and direction of the employer in respect of the manner in which the work is to be done; i.e. a contract involving a **master and servant** relationship as contrasted with a **contract for service,** in which the person employed is known as an independent contractor. There is no clear text in law which would determine such a distinction (see B. A. Hepple and Paul O'Higgins, *Employment Law,* Sweet and Maxwell, 1976, pp. 54-7). The courts have not restricted themselves to cases in which there is an ordinary contract of service, but have often stated that the right to control is the ultimate test, e.g. in **Performing Rights Society Ltd. v. Mitchell and Booker Ltd.** (1924) 1 KB 762, in which it was held that the defendants, who employed a dance band on written contract for one year, were liable for breaches of copyright by the band, on grounds that they controlled it at every point, including the music to be played. More recent cases have tended to accept broader definitions, allowing for the fact that in modern conditions all employers of labour may not be able to exercise detailed control over specialised labour, e.g. in **Cassidy v. Minister of Health** (1951), 2 KB 343 (in which the defendant was held liable for the negligence of medical staff), that the contract may be a 'mixed' one determinable by asking whether the work done is an integral part of the business (**Stevenson, Jordan and Harrison Ltd. v. Macdonald and Evans** (1952), 1 TLR 101), or such that all aspects of the employment relationship have to be considered (**Ready Mixed Concrete v. Minister of Pensions** (1968), 2

WLR 775; (1968) 1 All ER 433); see K. W. Wedderburn, *Cases and Materials on Labour Law,* 1967. Express power to dismiss may be evidence that the contract is one of service, though not conclusively (see **Dogget v. Waterloo Taxicab Co. Ltd.** (1910) 2 KB 336); see D. J. Keenan and L. Crabtree, *Essentials of Industrial Law,* Pitman, 1972.

CONTRACT SYSTEM. A **butty** or **labour-only sub-contracting** system in the iron and steel industry said to have been derived from the early years of the iron trade when the master puddler or forgeman engaged and paid the labour used by family enterprises; also in the shipbuilding trade (especially platers' helpers) and in textiles (piecers employed and paid by cotton-spinners). In iron and steel the system had lost much ground by the 1890s and is said to have become substantially extinct after the Hawarden Bridge Dispute of 1909-10; see Sir Arthur Pugh, *Men of Steel,* Iron and Steel Trades Confederation, 1951, p. 154 *et seq.* The contract system was subject to abuse by exploitation of workers by leading hands: '. . . the practice for a small minority of highly skilled leading hands to exploit the main body of workers by employing them at day wages, while they themselves appropriated the piecework balances accruing under their contracts with the employers' (G. D. H. Cole, *A Short History of the Working Class Movement, 1787-1947,* George Allen and Unwin, 1948 ed., p. 239); see also **job price contract** and **contract piecework**.

CONTRACTING-IN; see **contracting-out**.

CONTRACTING-OUT. An expression used to describe any arrangement in which it is assumed that individuals will act according to the general will, unless they signify that they intend to do otherwise; the opposite of **contracting-in,** an arrangement in which each individual has separately to signify his willingness to act, even if the act is generally agreed. In industrial relations the most celebrated example of contracting-out and of its opposite, contracting-in, has arisen in relation to trade union **political funds** (q.v.). **The Trade Union Act 1913,** which established a statutory basis for such funds, provided that trade union members might contract out; this was reversed in the **Trade Disputes and Trade Unions Act 1927,** and the 1913 situation restored by the **Trade Disputes**

and Trade Unions Act 1946. Contracting-out is reckoned to produce a higher yield for trade union political funds than contracting-in, and hence to be more financially favourable to the Labour Party, to which such funds are principally made available. Contracting-in still applies in Northern Ireland.

CONTRACTS OF EMPLOYMENT ACT 1972. An enactment originating in 1963 giving both employers and employees rights to minimum periods of notice to terminate employment and laying upon the former the duty of giving their employees written particulars of their main terms of employment not later than 13 weeks after employment commences (i.e. of giving employees **Statements of Particulars**). The 1963 Act as amended by the **Trade Union and Labour Relations Act 1974**, now requires the following periods of notice and particulars to be given: by an employee who has been continuously employed for more than four weeks, not less than one week's notice; by an employer to an employee who has been continuously employed for more than four weeks, one week's notice if his period of continuous employment is less than two years, thereafter, not less than one week's notice for each year of continuous employment up to twelve years and over twelve years, not less than twelve weeks' notice; written particulars; a. the scale or rate of remuneration, or method of calculating remuneration; b. the intervals at which remuneration is paid (e.g. weekly, monthly, etc.); c. any terms and conditions relating to hours of work; d. any terms and conditions relating to holiday entitlement (including any entitlement to accrued holiday pay on termination of employment to be precisely calculated), sick pay and pension schemes; d. the length of notice which the employee is required to give and entitled to receive; e. any disciplinary rules applicable to the employee; f. a person to whom the employee can apply if he is dissatisfied with any disciplinary decision relating to him and from whom he can seek redress of any grievance relating to his employment. The requirement to note also the employee's rights to belong or not to belong to a trade union and to state where an **agency shop** is in operation has now disappeared with the repeal of the **Industrial Relations Act 1971** which gave rise to them. Statements of Particulars are not required for part-time employees working less than sixteen hours weekly. It is sufficient on any item in such a State-

ment for an employee to be referred to some other document for the information required, provided that this is accessible to him, e.g. to a collective agreement, to a notice board, or to any such place where the information can readily be found. See B.A. Hepple and Paul O'Higgins, *Employment Law,* Sweet and Maxwell, 1976, Department of Employment, *Contracts of Employment Act, 1972, Notes for Guidance of Employers,* D. Knight Dix Waddy, *Dix on Contracts of Employment,* 5th ed. 1976.

CONTRIBUTION DEDUCTION SCHEMES; see **check-off.**

CONTRIBUTIONS; see **trade union contributions.**

CONTRIBUTIONS COLLECTOR; see **collecting steward.**

CONTRIBUTORY NEGLIGENCE; see **Law Reform (Contributory Negligence) Act 1945** and **employers' liability.**

CONTROLLED DAYWORK; see **measured daywork.**

CONVENER or CONVENOR. A lay officer of the Amalgamated Engineering Union (now the Engineering Section of the **Amalgamated Union of Engineering Workers**) appointed from among their own number by shop stewards or the shop committee in a works or department under Rule 13 of the union. Conveners were first authorised in rule on the formation of the AEU in 1920, and their role is formally defined as being synonymous with that of shop stewards and shop committees generally. In practice their experience and senior status tend to give them a special role in grievance procedure and in negotiations, especially in federated engineering establishments. The AEU has more than 2,000 conveners, none formally recognised by the **Engineering Employers' Federation,** but usually formally or informally accepted by their managements, and many of a full-time character. The expression convener is sometimes used to describe lay officers of other unions performing similar functions but outside the AEU the term **senior shop steward** or some variation on this is usually preferred; in 1969, 77.1 per cent of 432 federated engineering establishments had conveners or senior stewards, 19.2 per cent having both; 30.6 per cent had conveners only and

27.3 per cent senior stewards only, to a total of 893 (A. I. Marsh, E. O. Evans and Paul Garcia, *Workplace Industrial Relations in Engineering,* EEF and Kogan Page, 1971); see H. A. Clegg, A. J. Killick and Rex Adams, *Trade Union Officers,* Basil Blackwell, 1961, W. E. J. McCarthy, *The Role of Shop Stewards in British Industrial Relations,* Royal Commission on Trade Unions and Employers' Associations, Research Papers 1, 1966; J. F. B. Goodman and T. G. Whittingham, *Shop Stewards in British Industry,* McGraw-Hill, 1969. Following the trade union repudiation of the 1922 **Engineering Procedure Agreement** by manual workers in 1971 a new agreement of March 1976 (clause 9) acknowledged the existence of 'chief shop stewards' in domestic procedures.

CONVENTIONAL BARGAINING. Collective bargaining about pay and conditions which makes no provision for any concession or compensatory action by trade union members, or with no *quid pro quo;* bargaining which increases labour costs without necessarily obtaining any changes of practice on the part of the employee which would lead to higher labour productivity. Ken Jones and John Golding, *Productivity Bargaining,* Fabian Research Series 257, November 1966.

CONVENTION NO. 1; see International Labour Convention No. 1, 1919.

CONVENTIONS NOS 11, 84, 87 AND 98. Conventions of the **International Labour Organisation** on **Freedom of Association** and the Right to Organise.

CONVENTION NO. 14; see International Labour Convention No. 14, 1921.

CONVENTIONS NOS 89 AND 90. Conventions of the **International Labour Organisation** (q.v.) restricting the employment of women and young persons in industrial undertakings during the night (see **night work**). The United Kingdom has not ratified these conventions, on the grounds that the **Factories Act 1961** permits male young persons of 16 years and over to be employed at night in certain industries, and that the Secretary of State for Employment may allow exemptions for women in certain circumstances.

CONVENTION NO. 100; see International Labour Convention No. 100, 1951.

CONVENTION NO. 111; see discrimination.

CONVERSION FACTOR. In general, any factor used in converting payments, wages or salaries from one level to another, or from one scale to another. In engineering, normally used to refer to the money factor used to convert work into wages, e.g. to the multiplication of the time saved by a time-pieceworker by the **basic** (or **bonus**) **rate** to produce the amount of bonus earnings payable in addition to payment for hours worked; also used to describe the factor to be applied to **allowed times** when the basic rate is to be increased without increasing earnings for unchanged effort, e.g. in the application of the new basic rates laid down in the **Package Deal Agreement** and applied from 1 January 1968 (see *Handbook of National Agreements* 3.115(i)).

COOLING-OFF PERIOD. A legal device aimed at encouraging industrial peace either by delaying strike action for a specific period of time in industries generally, or by similarly requiring delay or return to work in particular industries or circumstances so that tempers may be allowed to cool and mediation or conciliation processes resumed. Both types of cooling-off period are to be found in the United States, the latter under the national emergency provisions of the **Taft-Hartley Act** through which the President can, in appropriate cases involving national health or safety, seek an injunction from the federal courts imposing an 80 day cooling off period. The Donovan **Royal Commission on Trade Unions and Employers' Associations 1965-1968** (Cmnd. 3623, 1968, paras. 418-25) considered the proposal that similar arrangements might be applied to Britain and rejected it on the grounds that few British strikes would lend themselves to the Taft-Hartley methods and that the current more flexible arrangements offered better prospects of peaceful settlements. The Conservative Party in its policy statement *Fair Deal at Work* (1968, pp. 40-1) advocated the adoption of a Taft-Hartley type procedure in Britain, and the **Industrial Relations Act 1971** contained provisions for a cooling-off period and **strike ballots** in national emergency disputes (see **national emergency procedures**). The **conciliation pause,** proposed by the Wilson government in *In Place of Strife* (Cmnd. 3888, 1969) and later abandoned, bore some relation to a cooling-off period, though not one in any sense similar to that provided for in the 1971 Act.

COOPERS' AND ALLIED WORKERS' FEDERATION OF GREAT BRITAIN.

A federation of trade unions of coopers comprising two larger societies, the Amalgamated Society of Coopers, and the National Trade Union of Coopers (originally the Edinburgh and London Societies which merged in 1947, to which were added in 1965 the Liverpool Coopers and in 1968 the Sheffield and District Coopers), and some smaller local sections - the Manchester and Salford Society of Coopers and the Burton-on-Trent Society of Coopers. Work in the trade has fallen off dramatically in the past decade resulting in a marked loss of membership of the union. *Address:* 121 West Regent Street, Glasgow G2 25D. *Tel:* 041-248 3709. *TUC Affiliated Membership 1977:* 1,066.

CO-OPERATIVE BARGAINING.

A concept of collective bargaining used by Neil W. Chamberlain and James W. Kuhn (*Collective Bargaining,* 2nd ed. McGraw-Hill, 1965) in contrast to **conjunctive bargaining** (q.v.).

CO-OPERATIVE CONTRACTING.

A method of payment and organising work in construction, mining, sawmilling and timber described by A. E. C. Hare, *Industrial Relations in New Zealand,* London 1946, and akin to self-employed labour-only sub-contracting (see **labour-only subcontracting**). Workers are paid according to the output of the group, 'but, unlike a group piece wage, each contract is negotiated separately, no standard piece rate being possible ... discipline being left to the members [of the group] ... who select their own leader who negotiates the contract ... the employer providing the necessary tools and equipment', pp. 123-4.

CO-OPERATIVE INSURANCE SOCIETY EMPLOYEES, NATIONAL UNION OF (NUCISE).

A trade union formed in 1923 by district managers and assistant managers of the Co-operative Insurance Society. It was recognised by the Society but not accepted into affiliation by the Trades Union Congress, and later affiliated to the Transport and General Workers' Union in 1933. It retains its own General Secretary and contribution scales. All of its affiliations are through the TGWU and the majority of its activities are conducted through the staff section of that union, the Association of Clerical, Technical and Supervisory Staffs.

CO-OPERATIVE OFFICIALS, NATIONAL ASSOCIATION OF.

A trade union affiliated to the Trades Union Congress consisting of the National Co-operative Managers' Association and the Co-operative Secretaries' Association, and founded in 1917. *Address:* Saxone House, 56 Market Street, Manchester M1 1PW. *Tel:* 061-834 6029. *TUC Affiliated Membership, 1977:* 5,461.

CO-OPERATIVE TRADE UNIONS; see **adversary trade unions.**

CO-ORDINATED BARGAINING; see **coalition bargaining.**

CO-OWNERSHIP; see **co-partnership.**

CO-PARTNERSHIP.

Defined in a memorandum on *Co-partnership and Industrial Unrest,* 1911 as, in its simplest form, involving a worker in receiving, in addition to wages, a share in the final profit of the business, and his accumulation of this share, or some part of it, in the capital of the business, thus gaining him the ordinary rights of and responsibilities of a shareholder. (Board of Trade Labour Department, *Report on Profit-Sharing and Labour Co-partnership,* Cd. 6496, 1912). Exponents of co-partnership regard it as going beyond **profit-sharing** in the latter sense, i.e. as involving an element of ownership or **co-ownership,** though not of **workers' control** (see Ernest Wall, *Progressive Co-partnership,* Nisbet, 1921), and as a variant on **employees shareholding** (George Copeman, *The Challenge of Employee Shareholding,* Business Publications, 1958); see also **Scott Bader Commonwealth Ltd, John Lewis Partnership,** and P. Derrick and J.-F. Phipps, *Co-ownership, Co-operation and Control,* Longmans, 1969: Acton Society Trust and Guy Naylor, *Sharing the Profits,* Garnstone Press, 1968; and **Industrial Participation Association.** The early history of co-partnership schemes were often associated with the desire of employers to provide an alternative to trade unionism, and though this is less frequently the case today, their influence appears to have declined.

COPOU. Council of Post Office Unions; see **Post Office Union, Council of.**

CORNELL REVIEW. The **Industrial and Labour Relations Review** (q.v.).

CORONATION STRIKE. A strike of busmen beginning in Kent on 14 April 1937, spreading to London on 1 May and finally ending on 28 May, thus coinciding with the coronation of King George VI. It was inspired by the busmen's Rank and File Movement which opposed the leadership of Ernest Bevin in the Transport and General Workers' Union, and was the subject of a Court of Inquiry (Cmd. 5454 and 5464, 1937); see H. A. Clegg, *Labour Relations in London Transport,* Basil Blackwell, 1950.

CORRESPONDING MEMBER (CM). The secretary of an office committee in the **Draughtsmen's and Allied Technicians' Association** (now AUEW/TASS). CMs act as collectors of subscriptions and distributors of information to union members, as well as taking responsibility for liaison between their office and the Association. J. E. Mortimer, *A History of the Association of Engineering and Shipbuilding Draughtsmen,* AESD, 1960. CMs are often thought of as the equivalent of **shop stewards** (q.v.), though they are not formally responsible for negotiation, nor are they nationally recognised by the **Engineering Employers' Federation.**

COST CURVE; see **learning curve.**

COST OF LIVING INDEX; see **retail prices index.**

COST-OF-LIVING SLIDING SCALE. An arrangement whereby rates of wages are moved automatically upwards or downwards on a predetermined scale according to the movement of an agreed cost-of-living index, or index of retail prices (see **retail prices index**), a practice more recently known as **wage indexation** or simply as **indexation,** though this term is also applied to other factors than wages, e.g. to pensions (**index-linked pensions**), to long-term contracts, loans, mortgages etc., as a means of offsetting inflation; see T. Leisner and M. King (eds.), *Indexing for Inflation,* Heinemann, 1975. Cost-of-living sliding scales have been intermittently popular at industry-wide level as devices for keeping real wages constant, thereby reducing wrangling about adjustments. Some originated in the aftermath of the first world war (e.g. building, 1921) and a few in the second world war (e.g. iron and steel, 1940). In 1960 some two million workers were covered by such sliding scale arrangements, 95 per cent of them in building, civil engineering, iron and steel,

printing, furniture manufacture, boots and shoes and hosiery. By 1970 this was reduced to 160,000, less than 1 per cent of the total working population. Their growing unpopularity has been shared by both trade unions and employers, the former becoming convinced that they tend to take the edge off wage demands designed to increase real wages and the latter that they constitute a commitment to wage inflation which ought to be avoided; see Ministry of Labour, *Industrial Relations Handbook,* 1961, pp. 188-9 and J. F. B. Goodman and G. M. Thomson, '"Cost of Living" Indexation Agreements in Post-war Collective Bargaining', *British Journal of Industrial Relations,* Vol. XI, No. 2, July 1973, pp. 181-210, also **escalator clauses** and **selling price sliding scale,** and for a latter-day development **threshold agreement.**

COST-REDUCTION PLANS. A term used by Robert B. McKersie (Changing Methods of Wage Payment, in John T. Dunlop and Neil W. Chamberlain (eds.), *Frontiers of Collective Bargaining,* Harper and Row, 1968) to describe systems of wage payment in which savings in costs below specified norms are divided between workers and management in a predetermined way, e.g. the Long Range Sharing Plan negotiated in 1962 between Kaiser Steel and the Steelworkers' Union in the USA. McKersie also classifies **Scanlon** and **Rucker Plans** as cost-reduction plans.

COT. Conciliation Officer (Tribunal); see **conciliation.**

COTTON MANUFACTURING COMMISSION WEAVING WAGE SYSTEM; see **CMC Wage System.**

COTTON MANUFACTURING INDUSTRY (TEMPORARY PROVISIONS) ACT 1934. An Act providing that rates of wages (in practice in the form of a **Uniform Price List** (q.v.)) agreed between employers and unions in the cotton industry could be given statutory effect by an Order of the Minister of Labour after a laid-down procedure had been followed. The effect of the Act was similar to that intended more generally by the **Terms and Conditions of Employment Act 1959** s. 8, though under its provisions the failure of an employer to pay might lead, not only to an employee suing for the amount payable, but also constituted a criminal offence. The Act was continued in operation by successive Expiring Laws Continuance Acts until 1957.

COUNCIL OF POST OFFICE UNIONS (COPOU); see **Post Office Unions, Council of.**

COUNCIL ON PRICES, PRODUCTIVITY AND INCOMES also known as the **Cohen Council** and the **Three Wise Men.** A national council of three members set up in 1957, initially with Lord Cohen as Chairman, other members being from time to time Sir Harold Howitt, Sir Dennis Robertson, Professor E. H. Phelps Brown, Sir Harold Emmerson and Lord Heyworth (later chairman), 'to keep under review changes in prices, productivity and the level of incomes (including wages, salaries, and profits) and to report thereon from time to time'. The Council issued four reports (two in 1958, one in August 1959 and one in July 1961) before being formally abolished in March 1962. They were principally of a descriptive-analytical nature, commenting on the state of the economy and upon current government policy and future possibilities.

COUNSELLING. The practice of giving guidance to individual workers on their personal problems and future prospects and development. Counselling within the firm is more highly developed in the United States than in Britain; see John F. McGowan and Lyle D. Schmidt, *Counseling: Readings in Theory and Practice,* Holt, Rinehart and Winston, 1962, and James F. Adams, *Problems in Counselling, A Case Study Approach,* Collier Macmillan, 1962. In this country 'personal counselling is now mainly related to training and promotion programmes and is likely to be biased towards knowledge of the needs of the organisation rather than of the individual' and help on private affairs is most likely to be provided outside the workplace: Anne Crichton, *Personnel Management in Context,* Batsford, 1968, p. 121 *et seq.* Counselling is sometimes used to mean 'employment counselling' see **vocational guidance.**

COUNTER-INFLATION ACT 1973. An Act providing for the control of prices, pay and dividends following the expiry of the **Counter-Inflation (Temporary Provisions) Act 1972.** Part I of the Act provided for the establishment of two Agencies, the Price Commission and the **Pay Board** authorising the Treasury to prepare a code for these Agencies in the restriction of prices, pay, dividends and rents under powers provided under Part II; see also **incomes policy.** The Pay Board and the powers under the Act to control pay (but not the Price Commission) were abolished in July 1974 after the return of a Labour government to office and followed by the development of the **Social Contract** (q.v.)

COUNTER-INFLATION (TEMPORARY PROVISIONS) ACT 1972. An Act of November 1972 bringing into operation a 90-day standstill on pay, prices, rents and dividends, with an option to extend the standstill for a further 60 days. The Act followed the failure of the Heath government to obtain a voluntary **incomes policy;** see **Chequers and Downing Street Talks.**

COUPLING-UP. A situation giving rise to **premium payment** in the engineering industry (*Handbook of National Agreements,* 2.26) Coupling-up applies where workers on one shift are required to work after the end of that shift in order to meet workers on the following shift to pass on directions or information necessary for operational continuity; it is not applied where continuity of operation only is involved; see **hand-over pay.**

COURT OF INQUIRY. An *ad hoc* body, usually but not invariably consisting of three persons (an independent chairman and a nominee from each side of industry), appointed by the Secretary of State for Employment under the **Industrial Courts Act 1919,** s. 4, to inquire into the causes and circumstances of a dispute. The formal intention of the Court of Inquiry is to report to Parliament as a last resort when no agreed settlement of a dispute seems possible, and when an unbiased independent examination of the facts is considered to be in the public interest (Ministry of Labour, *Written Evidence to the Royal Commission on Trade Unions and Employers' Associations,* HMSO, 1965, p. 106); it is not formally concerned with **conciliation** or **arbitration.** Observers in the early 1960s detected a change of attitude in the use of Court of Inquiry machinery in which 'the [Ministry of Labour] views it as one more technique for facilitating voluntary settlements, after the exhaustion of customary procedures - much as [it] regards the other procedures [it] provides for this purpose - such as the conciliation service' (W. E. J. McCarthy and B. A. Clifford, 'The Work of Industrial Courts of Inquiry', *British Journal of*

Industrial Relations, Vol. IV, March 1966); later in the 1960s some courts, while having no formal status as such, appeared to verge upon the function of arbitration; see also K. W. Wedderburn and P. L. Davies, *Employment Grievances and Disputes Procedures in Britain,* University of California Press, 1969. Courts of Inquiry have fallen almost entirely into disuse in the 1970s. Though they may be convened from time to time, and though the sections of the Industrial Courts Act authorising the Secretary of State to set them up were not repealed by the **Employment Protection Act 1975,** the kind of activity with which they are concerned is now effectively in the hands of the **Advisory, Conciliation and Arbitration Service** (q.v.); see **Panel of Investigation.**

COURT OFFICERS' ASSOCIATION (CCOA), formerly the County Court Officers' Association. An association negotiating on behalf of the staff employed in County Courts - Ushers, Bailiffs, Typists, Clerical Officers and executive clerical grades with salary scales above a given level. Clerks employed in the Metropolitan Courts formed an association in 1882; this became national, and the present union established, in 1924. The Association affiliated to the TUC in 1966 and was granted direct representation on the Staff Side of the Civil Service National Whitley Council in 1969. In January 1974 it amalgamated with the **Civil and Public Service Association.**

COVENTRY TOOLROOM AGREEMENT. An agreement between the Coventry and District Engineering Employers' Association and the Amalgamated Engineering Union (Coventry District) and dated 7 January 1941, providing that the district basis for payment of skilled toolroom operatives should be the weighted average of the inclusive earnings of skilled production workers in federated engineering establishments in Coventry. The agreement was a variation on the national **Toolroom Operatives' Agreement** of 1940 (q.v.) which related the earnings of skilled toolroom operatives to those of skilled production workers in the same establishment and, like the Coventry Toolroom Agreement, was continued after the war (see A. I. Marsh, *Industrial Relations in Engineering,* Pergamon Press, 1965). The Agreement was replaced on 25 November 1971 after the Coventry Association had withdrawn from it earlier in the year. The new agreement provides

for a formal continuation of the 1941 Agreement until February 1972 and thereafter a system of plant bargaining, under certain guarantees, and subject to six monthly examination by a Joint AUEW Association Skilled Toolroom Operatives Committee.

COWBOY or **high-flier** or **ratebuster** (q.v.); a worker whose main object is maximum earnings rather than security of employment; Innis MacBeath, *The Times Guide to the Industrial Relations Act,* 1971, p. 15.

CPM. Critical Path Method; see **Network Analysis.**

CPSA; see **Civil and Public Services Association.**

CRAFT. A manual occupation requiring extensive training and a high degree of skill, as possessed by a **craftsman,** and usually judged by his having served an apprenticeship (see **apprentice**). The precise amount of skill and competence required of a craftsman has never been easy to define with precision, and this has frequently been associated with his training (qualifying him to receive the **craft rate**), and also with his capacity, within his own trade, to handle a variety of jobs and materials with a minimum of direction and supervision. It has recently been suggested that three levels of skill have begun to emerge with the area of craft generally; the traditional level where jobs have been unaffected by technological change, a less complex level where job content has been devalued by technological change, and a super-craftsman level where technology has made jobs increasingly complex and demanding (see National Board for Prices and Incomes, *Job Evaluation,* Report No. 83, Cmnd. 3772, September 1968; see also **craft control, dilution, craft union.**

CRAFT APPRENTICE; see **apprenticeship.**

CRAFT CONTROL. The control of craft societies over the working conditions of their members by the unilateral assertion of craft rights, rules and privileges. The assertion that such control was being attempted has been the occasion for clashes between trade unions and managements on a number of occasions, especially in the engineering industry, and led to the counter assertion of **managerial prerogative** (q.v.) see A. I. Marsh, *Industrial*

Relations in Engineering, Pergamon Press, 1965 and R. O. Clarke, 'The Dispute in the British Engineering Industry 1897 - 1898, An Evaluation', *Economica,* May 1957, pp. 128-37 and for observations from a politically left-wing standpoint, J. Hinton, *The First Shop Stewards' Movement,* George Allen and Unwin, 1973. Sometimes regarded as a form of **workers' participation** (q.v.); see also **machine question, restrictive practices.**

CRAFT DIFFERENTIAL; see **differential.**

CRAFT GILDS also known as **trade gilds.** Associations of masters within mediaeval society to regulate trade and to protect the common interests of their members, especially in controlling entry to their craft. Gilds usually included journeymen as well as masters, though their government rested with the latter, it being assumed that all good journeymen would become masters. The craft gild system is reckoned to have fallen into decay by the seventeenth century and now only survives ritualistically in such bodies as the London Livery Companies; see G. D. H. Cole, *A Short History of the British Working Class,* Allen and Unwin, 1948 ed. pp. 10-13. At one time, perhaps in part as a misreading of Luigi Brentano (*The History and Development of Gilds and the Origins of Trades Unions,* Trübner 1870) it was popularly believed that trade unions were in direct line of descent from craft gilds. Such an idea of continuity was not held by Brentano himself, nor by most other scholarly authorities, and was specifically refuted by Sidney and Beatrice Webb (*History of Trade Unionism, 1666-1920,* 1920 ed. p. 11 *et seq.*) both on grounds of lack of evidence and of dissimilarities of purpose, the gild being designed to perpetuate customary regulation and the trade union to put other regulation in its place.

CRAFT RATE or **skilled rate.** The **time rate** of pay appropriate to a time-served **craftsman** who has been apprenticed to his trade, payable to him by reason of the type of work which he has been trained to do, rather than because of the work which he is doing; hence the **machine question,** the resistance of craftsmen to **dilution** (q.v.); see **craft.**

CRAFTSMAN; see **craft.**

CRAFT UNION. A term conventionally used to describe a trade union which limits its membership to workers possessing certain trade skills; sometimes, therefore, considered to be a **horizontal union** since these skills may be common to a number of industries. **Craft unionism;** a type of trade unionism using the technique and organisation of craft unions, e.g regulation of entry, especially by **apprenticeship** (q.v.), **demarcation,** or the reservation of jobs for organised workers with particular trade skills, and, associated particularly with the past; see **trade movements, craft control, mutual insurance.** Craft unions have historically been **closed unions** (q.v.); many, however, have relaxed their conditions to allow for more open entry, thus creating, in the terminology of H. A. Clegg, A. J. Killick and Rex Adams (*Trade Union Officers,* Basil Blackwell, 1961, p. 17) **ex-craft unions;** see also John Hughes, *Trade Union Structure and Government,* Royal Commission on Trade Unions and Employers' Associations, Research Papers 5 (Part 1), 1967; also **typology of unions.**

CRICKET BALL MAKERS, TESTON INDEPENDENT SOCIETY OF. A trade union originally organising craftsmen manufacturing sports equipment (mainly cricket and hockey balls), in a firm at Teston, near Maidstone. It was formed in 1919 as a breakaway from the Amalgamated Society of Cricket Ball Makers, and has survived this organisation to be the only cricket ball union in existence. In recent years it has extended to cover plastic made sports goods and sports equipment distribution. *Address:* 2 Invicta Villas, Malling Road, Teston, Nr. Maidstone, Kent ME18 5AP. *Tel:* 0622 812994 (home) 812230 (works). *Current Membership, 1977:* 43.

CRIMINAL CONSPIRACY; see **conspiracy.**

CRIMINAL LAW ACT 1977. An Act largely derived from the Report of the Law Commission on Conspiracy and Criminal Law Reform (Law Com., No. 76) which criticised the existing law on criminal conspiracy. The Act abolishes the offence of conspiracy at common law and replaces this by a statutory offence. One effect of this is that the penalty for criminal conspiracy arising from successful prosecutions under the Conspiracy and Protection of Property Act 1875, ss. 5 and 7, formerly unlimited if the option of trial by jury was accepted rather than by a magistrates' court, is now limited not to exceed that laid down for the substantive offence committed, see P. T. Wallington, 'The Criminal Law Act 1977', *Industrial Law Journal,* Vol. 7 No. 1, March 1978. See also **Conspiracy and Protection of Property Act 1875** and **Shrewsbury Pickets.**

CRIMINAL LAW AMENDMENT ACT 1871. An Act which amended the law relating to threats, violence, molestation and obstruction making it an offence to use such means with a view to coercing an employer or workman to act in certain ways, e.g. to become a member of a trade union, to quit work, etc. Under the Act a mere threat of strike was no longer a statutory offence, and except in the case of certain specified conduct, no person was liable for punishment for doing, or conspiring to do, any act, on the ground that it restrained, or tended to restrain the free course of trade. As a result of the case of **R. v. Bunn** (1872) 12 Cox 316, it appeared that although a strike was no longer a criminal conspiracy in restraint of trade, it could generally be indicted as a conspiracy to coerce, and the Act, following a **Royal Commission of Labour Laws** appointed in 1874, was repealed by the **Conspiracy and Protection of Property Act 1875;** see also **conspiracy.**

CRITERIA. Standards, or characteristics, by which the worth, rightness or public interest involved in a proposal or an action may be judged, e.g. criteria for exceptional pay increases (i.e. those over the **norm,** q.v.) laid down in government White Papers in connection with **incomes policy,** or for the application of **productivity agreements** by the **National Board for Prices and Incomes** (*Reports No. 36* and *123,* Cmnd. 3311, and 4136, June 1967 and August 1969) or the use of **Payment by Results** (*Report No. 65,* Cmnd. 3627, May 1968). Sometimes the alternative word **guidelines** is used.

CRITICAL PATH METHOD (CPM); see **network analysis.**

CROCKER v. KNIGHT (1892) QB 702; see **benefits.**

CROSS-BOOKING. A unofficial system which may be operated by workers on payment by results schemes of making false returns on loosely-priced jobs to compensate for poor times on other jobs. H. A.

Clegg, *A New Approach to Industrial Democracy,* Basil Blackwell, 1960, p. 121.

CROWN EMPLOYMENT. Employment in the military or civil service of the Crown. In practice most civil employees of the Crown are **industrial civil servants** and **non-industrial civil servants** in government departments. Members of the Home Civil Service are bound by regulations and instructions issued by the Civil Service Department, by statutes applying specially to Crown employment (e.g. on the appointment of aliens), and by the common law. The current view appears to be that civil servants have **contracts of employment,** subject to the implied term that civil servants can be dismissed at any time at the will of the Crown, with or without notice, though they are under the Trade Union and Labour Relations Act 1974 given a right of appeal against **unfair dismissal,** and most of the rights under the **Employment Protection Act 1975** apply to those in Crown employment. The **Contracts of Employment Act 1972,** the **Redundancy Payments Act 1965** and much other labour legislation does not, however, bind the Crown.

CSD. Civil Service Department (q.v.).

CSEU. Confederation of Shipbuilding and Engineering Unions; see **Shipbuilding and Engineering Unions, Confederation of.**

CSMTS. Card Setting Machine Tenters' Society (q.v.).

CSU. Civil Service Union (q.v.).

CTR. consolidated time rate (q.v.).

CULLEN v. ELWIN (1904) 90 LT 840; see **benefits.**

CUMULATIVE EXTRAS; see **gift hours.**

CUSTOM AND PRACTICE. A generic term used to describe unwritten and informal rules in the workplace which regulate work and employment; custom and practice may consist of joint unwritten understandings between workers and various levels of management or, more loosely, of precedents to be argued by either side for application to the solution of conflicts about new rules or the application of rules to new situations. Some writers appear to limit the use of the term to unilateral union or **work group** rules only, i.e. to 'informal rules which management has no say in making, but tacitly has to accept', e.g. on job demarcation, regulation of output, manning etc.; see Allan Flanders, *Collective Bargaining: Prescription for Change,* Faber and Faber, 1967, and *Management and Unions: The Theory and Practice of Industrial Relations,* Faber and Faber 1975, and William Brown, 'A Consideration of Custom and Practice', *British Journal of Industrial Relations,* Vol. X, No. 1, March 1972.

CUSTOMS AND EXCISE FEDERATION. A trade union formed in 1917 by amalgamation of the National Customs and Excise Federation and the Customs and Excise Officers' Association. The history of the union is given in P. S. Keyte, *The Customs and Excise Federation, 1917-1967,* Customs and Excise Federation, 1967. It subsequently formed part of the Customs and Excise Group and was dissolved in 1975 on amalgamation of that Group with the Society of Civil Servants in 1975 to form the **Society of Civil and Public Servants** (q.v.).

CWE. Clerical Work Evaluation (q.v.)

CWIP. Clerical Work Improvement Programme (q.v.).

CWU. Chemical Workers' Union (q.v.).

CYBERNETICS. A term attributed to N. Weiner, *Cybernetics or Control and Communication in the Animal and the Machine,* Massachusetts Institute of Technology Press, 1961 and defined by H. Frank (*Kybernetik und Philosophie,* Dunker and Humbolt, 1966) as 'the calculative theory and the constructional technique of information, of information processing and of information processing systems'. In industrial relations, cybernetics have mainly been considered as an aspect of **automation** (q.v.).

CYCLICAL UNEMPLOYMENT. Mass unemployment or reduction in work resulting from periodic fluctuations in the level of activity in the economy, and associated with the international trade cycle. The reduction of cyclical unemployment was a major preoccupation of economists during the period between the wars of 1914-18 and of 1939-45; see J. A. Hobson, *The Economics of Unemployment,* Macmillan, 1931, A. C. Pigou, *The Theory of Unemployment,* Frank Cass, 1968, Mac-

millan 1933, and the work of J. M. Keynes (especially *The General Theory of Employment, Interest and Money,* Macmillan 1936 (new ed. 1974), which challenged the classical theory of employment in a form more acceptable than that of Hobson, and gave rise to the development of **full-employment** policies; see W. H. Beveridge, *Full Employment in a Free Society,* Allen and Unwin, 1944 (new ed. 1960).

D

DANGER MONEY. An **allowance** for working in abnormally hazardous conditions; see also **differentials.**

DARG. A day's work, or a quota of work, or **stint**; e.g. as in John Child, *Industrial Relations in the British Printing Industry,* Allen and Unwin, 1967, p. 140: [In the nineteenth century] '. . . the printing unions did not explicitly fix a "stint" or "darg", but over the years there developed some standard of work effort which was considered "fair".' Formerly also the words 'darger' or 'dargsman', a day labourer.

DATA. Draughtsmen's and Allied Technicians' Association (q.v.).

DATAL RATE. A synonym for **day rate** or **time rate** used in some industries, particularly iron and steel, where it usually represents the shift time rate, i.e. the rate payable for an eight-hour working shift, including a meal break.

DAWES CYCLE CO. LTD AND NATIONAL SOCIETY OF METAL MECHANICS. Industrial Court Award 3110, 3 August 1966. A reference to the Industrial Court (now **Central Arbitration Committee**) under the Terms and Conditions of Employment Act 1959, s. 8 (see **Schedule 11 Claims**) in which it was ruled that the **Guaranteed Week** Agreement of 1964, between the **Engineering Employers' Federation** and the **Confederation of Shipbuilding and Engineering Unions** was not applicable to a non-federated firm; see also **Brook Motors Ltd and Transport and General Workers' Union.**

DAY NURSERIES. Nurseries for children under the age of five, and therefore not attending school, usually with the aim of enabling young married women to take up gainful employment. The object of such nurseries is not primarily educational. Where public provision is concerned, nursery schools with educational objectives are provided for under the Education Act 1944, s. 9, and day nurseries under the National Health Service Act 1946, s. 22. Both have been slow to develop. Industrial day nurseries organised by companies are, like other private day nurseries, subject to the **Nurseries and Child Minders' Regulation Act 1948;** see Roger and Mary Kingsley, *An Industrial Day Nursery: The Personnel Manager's Guide,* Institute of Personnel Management, 1969, and IPM Information Note, *Company Day Nurseries,* 1975.

DAY RATE. A rate of payment for the day (or **day wage**) or by the hour over the working day; sometimes (**daywork**) contrasted with the rate for **shiftworking** (or **shift rate**) and sometimes with the incentive rate, or piece rate; hence 'to work day rate', to work at **timework stroke,** rather than **piecework stroke,** or to **go slow.**

DAY SHIFT. Either normal working hours (say 8.30 a.m. - 4.30 p.m.) or if an establishment is operating a **double day shift** or **three shift system,** the first shift, usually 6 a.m. to 2 p.m.

DAY WAGE; see **day rate.**

DAYWORK. Work done during the day, i.e. not at night, or according to a system involving **shiftworking.** In some usages, the opposite of **piecework,** e.g. to work daywork; to work at a dayworker's (or timeworker's) fixed rate of pay, and hence at a timeworker's pace rather than an incentive pace; **daywork stroke;** see also **measured daywork, controlled daywork.**

DAYWORK STROKE: see **timework stroke.**

DE. Department of Employment; see **Employment, Department of.**

DEAD END JOB or **blind-alley job.** A job without prospects of promotion or increased pay, or both; hence also jobs without prestige or job satisfaction.

DEAD HORSE. Defined by Alan Gilpin (*Dictionary of Economic Terms,* Butterworths, 4th ed. 1977) as 'work which has been paid for but has yet to be completed; a procedure observed in some factories, where workers are paid in advance for work which they have yet to complete'. In the United States' printing industry **dead horse rule;** a **make-work practice** or type of **featherbedding** in which type set up for advertising is required to be melted down and reset before being used in another newspaper; a form of **fat** (q.v.); see Paul Jacobs, *Dead Horse and the Featherbird; the Specter of Useless Work,* University of California, Berkeley, Reprint 190, 1962.

DEAD HORSE RULE; see **dead horse.**

DEAD MAN'S MONEY; see **split shift.**

DEAD TIME, waiting time or **standing time.** Period in which a payment by results worker is unable to continue working because of factors beyond his control, e.g. material shortage, machine breakdown; hence payment for dead time or waiting time.

DEATH BENEFIT or **funeral benefit.** A benefit paid to the beneficiary of a deceased worker. Death benefit is the most universal of all trade union monetary benefits (Arthur Marsh and Peter Cope, 'The Anatomy of Trade Union Benefits in the 1960s', *Industrial Relations Journal,* Summer 1970); it may also be paid from private, or employer organised, insurance, and, where related to industrial accidents or prescribed diseases, under the **Industrial Injuries Acts** (Department of Health and Social Security Leaflet NI 10). Death grant is also payable under the National Insurance Acts (Leaflet NI 49).

DECASUALISATION. The policy, as usually understood, of reducing or eliminating from an industry or from an economic activity, the use of casual labour (see **casual worker**); the provision of methods or procedures for ensuring regular employment. Casual labour is to be found in many industries (e.g. agriculture, construction, printing); the word 'decasualisation' has especially been applied to the port transport industry, both as socially desirable, and as contributing towards greater efficiency in the docks; see **Dock Labour Scheme** and **National Modernisation Committee** and the Devlin Report (*Final Report of the Committee of Inquiry into certain matters concerning the Port Transport Industry,* Cmnd. 2734, 1965) in which decasualisation is understood to mean the elimination of the casual employer as well as of the casual employee, p. 10.

DECLARATION OF INTENT. The **Joint Statement of Intent on Productivity, Prices and Incomes;** a document signed by representatives of the Government, the Trades Union Congress, and of management organisations on 15 December 1964, pledging themselves to raise productivity throughout industry and commerce, to keep total money increases in line with increases in real national output, and to maintain a stable price level. The Declaration formed the basis of the **prices and incomes policy** pursued by the Wilson administration between 1964 and 1970 (see also **incomes policy**) and was particularly associated with the name of Mr George (now Lord George) Brown, then First Secretary of State for Economic Affairs.

DECLARATION OF PHILADELPHIA; see **Philadelphia, Declaration of.**

DEDUCTIONS. Sums deducted from wages before these are received by the worker in the pay packet. The Truck Act 1831 (see **Truck Acts**) makes it illegal for an employer to make a deduction from wages unless such a deduction is expressly authorised by Act of Parliament (e.g. the **National Insurance (Industrial Injuries) Act 1965** in the case of insurance contributions and the **Attachment of Earnings Act 1971**), and that of 1896 makes it illegal to deduct money for fines for misconduct, bad workmanship or materials, unless the workman has previously signed a contract agreeing to submit to such deductions, such a contract also being subject to the conditions of the Act. For a detailed account of the law on deductions and fines; see Ian Fife and E. A. Machin, *Redgrave's Health and Safety in Factories,* Butterworths, 1976, p. 1740 *et seq.;* also **check-off.**

DEDUCTION SCHEMES; see **check-off.**

DEFENSE OR DEFENSIVE STRIKE; see **negative strike.**

DEMARCATION. The existence of a boundary between the work appropriate to one craft or skill and that appropriate to another, and hence a device to preserve the value and status of trades or jobs by preventing interchange (see **interchangeability**) or overlapping between them (see **flexibility**). Hence **demarcation dispute,** a dispute over 'who does what?', or conflict between occupational groups concerning the establishment or maintenance of job rights as these groups perceive them; see John Hilton (ed.) *Are Trade Unions Obstructive?* Gollancz, 1935, p. 328, and J. E. T. Eldridge, *Industrial Disputes,* Routledge and Kegan Paul, 1968, p. 92. Demarcation disputes may occur between different groups in the same union, but are most commonly thought of as taking place between unions organising different crafts, trades or jobs, and hence as **inter-union disputes** of a type which involve more than conflicts about membership alone, e.g. **poaching,** or **membership disputes,** or in S. W. Lerner's terminology, **jurisdictional disputes** (q.v.) of a kind which would fall within the competence of the Disputes Committee of the Trades Union Congress under the **Bridlington Agreement.** Some collective agreements include provisions for dealing with demarcation disputes, e.g. shipbuilding and marine engineering (see Eldridge, op. cit. p. 104 *et seq.* and *Engineering Handbook of National Agreements,* Ref. 2.74) and so do the rules of some trade union federations, though not the Confederation of Shipbuilding and Engineering Unions. Kate Liepmann (*Apprenticeship,* Routledge and Kegan Paul, 1960, p. 158) distinguishes **vertical demarcation,** i.e. the defence of craftsmen's jobs against dilution, from other types which may be thought of as **horizontal demarcation;** see also **restrictive practices, spheres of influence,** and **national demarcation procedure agreement** (shipbuilding).

DEMARCATION DISPUTE; see **demarcation.**

DEMONSTRATION. The performance of a task by a nominee of management in order to demonstrate to the worker or workers concerned that the piecework price, bonus or basis time proposed by the management for that task is a reasonable one: engineering industry, for particular unions; see A. I. Marsh, *Industrial Relations in Engineering,* Pergamon Press, 1965; also **Manchester Piecework Regulations.**

DEMOTION PAYMENT. A payment made to a worker displaced from a more skilled or better paid job as a result of technical or other change of a permanent character as an alternative to **redundancy** (q.v.), especially in the steel industry.

DENSITY OF UNIONISATION; see **union density.**

DENTAL ASSOCIATION, BRITISH (BDA). An association of dentists formed in 1880 which in 1952 took over the functions of the incorporated Dental Society and the Public Dental Services Association. It negotiates conditions of service and remuneration for all dental practitioners in the National Health Service, in the Armed Forces and in Dental Teaching Schools. *Address:* 64 Wimpole Street, London WIM 8AL. *Tel:* 01-935 0875. *Membership, 1977:* 13,000.

DEP. Department of Employment and Productivity; now the Department of Employment; see **Employment, Department of.**

DEPARTMENT OF EMPLOYMENT (DE); see **Employment, Department of.**

DEPARTMENT OF EMPLOYMENT GAZETTE. The official journal of the Department of Employment, containing articles and labour statistics and published monthly. It dates from 1893 and was formerly known as the *Ministry of Labour Gazette* and the *Employment and Productivity Gazette.*

DEPARTMENT OF EMPLOYMENT AND PRODUCTIVITY (DEP) now the Department of Employment; see **Employment, Department of.**

DESIGNATED AREA ALLOWANCE. An allowance paid to doctors working in the National Health Service with practices in the most 'undoctored areas', see **Kindersley Committee,** *Twelfth Report* (Review Body on Doctors' and Dentists' Remuneration, Cmnd. 4352, May 1970) paras 148-50.

DETROIT AUTOMATION; see **automation.**

DEVELOPMENT AREA; see **assisted areas.**

DEVLIN REPORT. Name given to the reports of a number of Courts and Committees of Inquiry under the chairmanship of Lord Devlin, especially in the port transport industry; Operation of the Dock Workers (Regulation of Employment) Scheme (Cmd. 9813, August 1958), Port Transport (Cmnd. 2523 and Cmnd. 2734, October 1964), Wages Structure for Dock Workers (Cmnd. 3104, August 1966); see also **Devlin Stage I and II.**

DEVLIN STAGE I AND II; see **National Modernisation Committee.**

DEVONSHIRE COMMISSION. The **Royal Commission on Labour 1891-1894,** set up with the Duke of Devonshire in the chair, as a result of a wave of strikes in 1889, including the London Dock Strike. The Commission produced five reports and made no agreed recommendations about the legal status of trade unions. It did, however, result in the **Conciliation Act 1896** which provided that the Board of Trade might inquire into the causes and circumstances of disputes, and make provision for conciliation and arbitration; see Lord Amulree, *Industrial Arbitration,* OUP, 1929, p. 105 *et seq.* For other Royal Commissions on industrial relations generally; see **Erle Commission, Cockburn Commission, Dunedin Commission, Donovan Commission.**

DIFFERENCE. '... a distinction between the expressions difference and **dispute** was also drawn in the official publications of the Board of Trade [about 1895], the expression dispute being confined to those cases in which the difference between the parties resulted in a stoppage of work': Lord Amulree, *Industrial Arbitration,* OUP, 1929, p. 112. The distinction has been substantially maintained to this day. The **Conciliation Act 1896,** while proclaiming its intention to 'make better provision for the prevention and settlement of disputes', confined the powers of intervention of the Board of Trade to 'differences' (s. 2) a word which it did not define, though perhaps with the same distinction in mind, since the object of the Act lay primarily in conciliation. The **Industrial Courts Act 1919** referred not to differences, but to **trade disputes** (q.v.), the meaning of the term now being identical with that given in the **Trade Union and Labour Relations Act 1974.**

DIFFERENTIALS. Differences, whether planned, negotiated or arising *de facto,* between the wage rates, salaries, earnings or conditions of individual workers or groups of workers. Differentials may in some cases be thought of as arising out of effort (e.g. the higher payment usually made to payment by results workers compared with timeworkers), or skill (hence **skill differential,** or **craft differential** - a higher payment made to workers with greater skill compared with those of lesser skill, or to **major trades,** e.g. fitting, turning, compared with **minor trades,** bricklaying etc.); or they may arise out of sex differences (see **equal pay**), or for inconvenience, dirt or danger (hence **shift differential,** paid for working inconvenient or socially abnormal hours; **dirty money** or **dirt money,** paid for handling dirty cargo, or working in dirty conditions; **danger money,** paid for working in abnormally hazardous conditions, **height money** for working at abnormal heights etc.); or they may arise from age (see, for example, **wage-for-age scales**); or from responsibilities accepted (see **Paterson Method, time-span** etc.); or from considerations of location (see, for example, **London weighting**); see also **wage structure,** and the role of differentials in **wage drift** and **earnings drift.** Guy Routh (*Occupation and Pay in Great Britain, 1906-1960*, CUP, 1965) has drawn attention to the rigidity of inter-class and inter-occupational differentials over time, semi-skilled men earning 86 per cent of the all-class average in 1913 and 85 per cent in 1960, unskilled the same percentage in both years, and women 63 per cent of the all-class average in 1913 and 64 per cent in 1960. On the distribution and dispersion of employment incomes; see Harold Lydall, *The Structure of Earnings*, OUP, 1968; also E. H. Phelps Brown and Margareth Browne, *A Century of Pay: The Course of Pay and Production in France, Germany, Sweden, the United Kingdom and the United States of America, 1860-1960*, Macmillan, 1968.

DIFFERENTIAL PIECE-RATE PLAN. An **incentive payment** or **premium bonus system** particularly advocated by F. W. Taylor (1856-1915) and sometimes therefore known as the **Taylor Differential Piece-rate Plan.** The system allows for no guaranteed mimimum wage and provides for a low differential rate for output below standard and a substantially higher differential rate (50 per cent higher) above standard. Taylor's maxim being that the former 'should be fixed at a figure which will allow a workman to earn scarcely an ordinary day's pay when he falls off from his maximum pace, so as to give him every inducement to work hard and well'. The rigour of this system was relaxed by an associate of Taylor's, H. L. Gantt (hence **Gantt Task and Bonus Plan**) which allowed for a **pieceworker's guarantee,** thus allowing a time rate system for workers of less than standard efficiency and a piece-rate system for workers of standard or more than standard efficiency. It was further adapted by D. V. Merrick in the Winchester Repeating Arms Company

(hence **Merrick Differential Piece-rate Plan**) which allows for higher piece-rates in three steps, 10 per cent being paid at 83 per cent of standard, and a further 10 per cent at standard. **Multiple piece-rates, multiple time plans** or **stepped bonus plans** of this kind have been approved by some experimenters; see C. A. Mace, *Incentives-Some Experimental Studies*, Industrial Health Research Board Report, HMSO, 1935; also N. C. Hunt, *Methods of Wage Payment in British Industry*, Pitman, 1951, p. 87 *et seq.*, and R. Marriott, *Incentive Payment Systems*, Staples Press, 3rd (revised) ed. 1968.

DILUTEE; see dilution.

DILUTION. A term used to describe two separate, but often closely related processes: (1) the dilution of *work*, i.e. the gradual 'de-skilling' of work by increased mechanisation, or by the breaking down of jobs into parts, some of which can be performed by less skilled, or unskilled labour; and (2) the dilution of *craft*, e.g. by the upgrading of less skilled men to do the job of, for example, time-served craftsmen. Both processes are implied in the definition given by G. D. H. Cole (*Workshop Organisation*, OUP, 1923 and Hutchinson, ed. A. I. Marsh, 1973, p. 48n.): '...the introduction of less skilled workers to undertake the whole or part of the work previously done by workers of greater skill or experience, often, but not always accompanied by simplification of machinery, or the breaking up of the job into a number of simpler operations.' Process (2) may occur as a result of **Relaxation** (or Dilution) **Agreements** (q.v.), those upgraded without having served an acceptable and full form of apprenticeship or training being known as **dilutees;** see also **Skillcentres** (and on attitudes of those trained there, K. Hall and I. Miller, 'Industrial Attitudes to Skills Dilution', *British Journal of Industrial Relations*, Vol. IX, Number 1, March 1971, pp. 1-20), **restrictive labour practices** and **vertical demarcation.**

DIMENSIONAL MOTION TIMES (DMT); see **Predetermined Motion Time Systems.**

DIRECT LABOUR or directs; see **production workers.** Also a building labour force employed by a local authority, a public corporation, or a private company to do construction and maintenance work which might otherwise be done by outside contractors; hence 'to build houses, etc., by direct labour', a subject of controversy especially in local government circles; see *Building by Direct Labour,* Federal Employers' Press, 1960.

DIRT MONEY or **dirty money.** An **allowance** paid for handling dirty cargo, or for working in dirty conditions; see also **differentials.**

DISABLED PERSONS. Persons handicapped by injury, disease or congenital deformity, especially those eligible to be registered under the **Disabled Persons (Employment) Acts 1944** and **1958.** The Acts cover disablement of all kinds and their object is to enable disabled persons to find work by providing a specialist placing service through **Disablement Resettlement Officers** attached to **Job Centres** or **Employment Offices** by holding special courses, by providing sheltered employment and by requiring employers of 20 or more workers to employ a quota of disabled persons (currently 3 per cent of total employees) and to reserve vacancies for registered disabled persons in 'designated' employments. In April 1977 532,402 persons were registered under the Disabled Persons Acts compared with 620,691 in April 1971. Of these, 14.1 per cent were unemployed. In the 1970s there was a considerable increase in the percentage of firms failing to employ their quota. This and the high unemployment rate among registered disabled people led in May 1977 to a Manpower Services Commission guide on *Positive Policies* for the disabled, urging companies to enlarge their conceptions of the work which could be done by such persons. In 1973 consideration was given to the unsatisfactory nature of the quota system, but this was ultimately retained without change (10 December 1975). See also **Employment Service, Remploy Ltd** and **Industrial Rehabilitation Unit;** and D. Lees and S. Shaw (eds.), *Impairment, Disability and Handicap,* Heinemann, 1974.

DISABLED PERSONS (EMPLOYMENT) ACTS; see **disabled persons.**

DISABLED PERSONS' EMPLOYMENT CORPORATION. More commonly known as **Remploy Ltd** (q.v.).

DISABLEMENT BENEFIT. One of three main types of benefit provided by the **Industrial Injuries Acts** for insured persons injured by accident at work or suffering from prescribed industrial diseases, the others being **injury benefit** and **death benefit.** Payment may take the form either of a weekly pension, or in certain cases, a gratuity, the amount paid varying according to the degree of disablement suffered; see Department of Health and Social Security *Leaflet* NI 6; C. D. Drake, *Labour Law,* Sweet and Maxwell, 2nd ed. 1973.

DISABLEMENT   RESETTLEMENT OFFICER (DRO); see **disabled persons.**

DISCHARGE. To dismiss from employment; sometimes used to describe a dismissal for whatever cause; sometimes (especially in analysis of **labour turnover** (q.v.), distinguished from other non-voluntary terminations of employment, e.g. those arising from **redundancy,** and confined to those in which the worker is being dismissed for unsuitability, misconduct etc.

DISCIPLINARY   PROCEDURE. A procedure established at industry, company or plant level, for dealing with instances in which employees are alleged to have been involved in behaviour of a kind which might be expected to result in **suspension,** or, in extreme cases, dismissal (see **dismissal procedure, summary dismissal, industrial misconduct**) e.g. bad timekeeping,   absenteeism,   negligence, drunkenness, theft from the employer, insubordination, safety violation, fighting, falsifying clock cards, gambling, etc., especially, but not necessarily when these types of behaviour are regarded as subject to discipline in **works rules,** or works custom. Special disciplinary procedures have traditionally been used in the public sector, but have been less common in private industry (see K. W. Wedderburn and P. L. Davies, *Employment Grievances and Disputes Procedures in Britain,* University of California Press, 1969, Ch. 7, and Ministry of Labour, *Dismissal Procedures, A Report,* HMSO, 1967). The Report of the Donovan **Royal Commission on Trade Unions and Employers' Associations 1965-1968** (Cmnd. 3623, June 1968, para. 182), recommended the general adoption of 'effective rules and procedures governing disciplinary matters, including dismissal, with provision for appeals'; the **Industrial Relations Act 1971** (now repealed) provided for remedies in cases of **unfair dismissal** and for an **Industrial Relations Code of Practice,** February 1972 (130-3) advised that   formal   disciplinary   procedures should exist in all but very small establishments. In 1977, under the Trade Union and Labour Relations Act 1974 and the Employment Protection Act 1975 (see **Codes of Practice**) the advice was replaced by a separate Code on *Disciplinary Practice and Procedures in Employment.* This emphasised that procedures should be in writing, should give the employee an opportunity to state his case with a representative, to appeal if necessary, and that a system of warnings should be followed before suspension without pay or dismissal. The Code also advises that no disciplinary action should be taken against a **shop steward** until the circumstances of the cases have been discussed with the full-time official of the union concerned: see also Orme W. Phelps, *Discipline and Discharge in the Unionised Firm,* University of California Press, 1959 and S. D. Anderman, *Voluntary Dismissals Procedure and the Industrial Relations Act,* Political and Economic Planning, Broadsheet 538, September 1972, and R. T. Ashdown and K. H. Baker, *In Working Order, A Study of Industrial Discipline,* Department of Employment, Manpower Papers No. 6, HMSO, 1973.

DISCIPLINE OF TRADE UNION MEMBERS; see membership of a trade union.

DISCLAIMER CLAUSE. A clause inserted in a written collective agreement during the currency of the **Industrial Relations Act 1971** (now repealed) stating that the agreement, or part of it, was not intended by the parties to be legally enforceable. Under the Act such agreements were enforceable at law unless such a disclaimer was made. This was almost invariably insisted upon by trade unions; sometimes known as a **rebuttal clause, exclusion clause, or 'tina lea' clause** (standing for the initials of the words, This Is Not A Legally Enforceable Agreement).

DISCLOSURE AGREEMENT; see information, disclosure of.

DISCLOSURE OF INFORMATION; see information, disclosure of.

DISCONTINUOUS THREE SHIFT SYSTEM; see three shift system.

DISCRIMINATION. An unfair act or an unfair or unequal application of a policy to an individual or a group; in trade union terms, usually synonymous with **victimisation,** i.e. any such act taken by an employer against a trade union member because of his trade union activity, whether by dismissal, refusal to promote, allocation to unfavourable or poorly paid work, etc. In a more general sense 'any distinction, exclusion or preference made on the basis of race, colour, sex, religion, political opinion or social origin, which had the effect of nullifying or impairing equality of opportunity or treatment in employment or occupation' (ILO Convention No. 111, *Discrimination in Respect of Employment,* 1958). This Convention has not yet been ratified by the UK government, but legislation has in the last decade gone some way towards meeting international and European standards, e.g. in the **Race Relations Acts 1968** and **1976,** the **Equal Pay Act 1970** and the **Sex Discrimination Act 1975.** The first and third of these Acts recognise three forms of discrimination, 'direct discrimination' (i.e. less favourable treatment on grounds of sex, marital status, or race), 'indirect discrimination' (i.e. conduct which has a discriminatory effect, although the discriminator had no intention to discriminate, e.g. as a result of historical attitudes), and 'discrimination by way of victimisation' (i.e. cases in which the person victimised is treated less favourably by the discriminator than he would treat other persons in the same circumstances); see B. A. Hepple, *Race, Jobs and the Law in Britain,* Harmonsworth, 2nd ed. 1970 and for a summary, B. A. Hepple and P. O'Higgins, *Employment Law,* Sweet and Maxwell, 2nd ed., 1976, Ch. 11.

DISGUISED UNEMPLOYMENT or **concealed unemployment** (q.v.).

DISMISSAL. The termination of a contract of employment; see also **abusive dismissal, unfair dismissal, dismissal procedure, dismissal with notice, lay-off, redundancy, summary dismissal.**

DISMISSAL PAY; severance pay, or **redundancy pay** (q.v.).

DISMISSAL PROCEDURE. A procedure, at industry, company or plant level, to be followed in dismissing an employee for **redundancy** (q.v.), for sickness, for unsuitability, for **industrial misconduct,** etc. The coverage of a dismissal procedure may in some aspects be broader than that of a **disciplinary procedure** (in including, for example, dismissals for unsuitability, which may suggest no disciplinary penalty), and in some aspects narrower (in that it may deal with dismissal only and not with other penalties against workers for misconduct). Outside the public sector it has principally been dealt with through **disputes procedures** (Ministry of Labour, *Dismissal Procedures - A Report,* HMSO, 1967). The **Trade Union and Labour Relations Act 1974** now provides for compensation for employees in the event of **unfair dismissal**, and a Code of Practice advises on **disciplinary procedures** (q.v.) including those dealing with dismissal.

DISMISSAL WITH NOTICE. The termination of a **contract of employment** by the giving of the amount of notice or payment in lieu of notice, the length of notice being expressly contained in the contract, implied in it, or fixed in terms of the minimum periods of notice laid down in the **Contracts of Employment Act 1972;** see B. A. Hepple and P. O'Higgins, *Employment Law,* Sweet and Maxwell, 1976, Ch. 15; also **summary dismissal, wrongful dismissal, unfair dismissal.**

DISPUTE. A word used both narrowly to mean a **difference** (q.v.) between the parties in collective bargaining which has resulted in a stoppage of work, and more loosely to describe any situation in which there has been a failure of voluntary negotiation at any stage to reach a settlement, whether this has resulted in a strike or not, i.e. as the equivalent of the phrase 'a question or issue in dispute'. It appears in its narrower sense in the engineering expression 'Provisions for Avoiding Disputes'. Also **apprehended dispute;** a dispute which has been notified to the proper authorities, especially one in which a stoppage has not taken place; **emergency disputes procedure** (in the building industry) q.v., **trade dispute, disputes of rights, disputes of interest, industrial dispute.**

DISPUTE BENEFIT. Benefit paid to trade union members in the form of monetary payments while on strike (**strike pay,** or **strike benefit**), when locked out (**lockout pay**), when victimised (**victim** or **victimisation benefit** or **sacrifice**). Substantially all principal trade unions in Britain provide for dispute benefit, the exceptions being a small number of organisations in the public sector. Substantially all provide in their rules that authorisation of dispute benefit (see **official strike**) is a national function; Arthur Marsh and Peter Cope, 'The Anatomy of Trade Union Benefits in the 1960s', *Industrial Relations Journal* Summer 1970. After the 1939-45 war,

expenditure on dispute benefit was for some years low, never, until the late 1960s, exceeding 10p per head in any one year; in 1969, however, it rose to 19p per head and in 1970, to 40p per head; *Report of the Chief Registrar of Friendly Societies For the Year 1970,* Part 4, Trade Unions, HMSO, 1971; by 1974 it had fallen to 35p per head, and in 1977 to 17p (*First Annual Report of the Certification Officer,* 1976).

DISPUTE PROCEDURE. Broadly defined, any procedure designed to resolve disagreement between workers and their employers or between trade unions and employers, on either principal definition of the term **dispute** (q.v.), i.e. any set of procedural rules, incorporating all, or any of the following; a **grievance procedure, a disciplinary procedure,** a **dismissal procedure, a redundancy procedure, a negotiating procedure,** etc. (see A. I. Marsh, *Disputes Procedures in Britain,* Research Papers 2 (Part 1), Royal Commission on Trade Unions and Employers' Associations, HMSO, 1966), and N. Singleton, *Industrial Relations Procedures,* Department of Employment Paper No. 14, HMSO, 1976. Narrower definitions of the term are also found, e.g. the **Industrial Relations Code of Practice,** February 1972 (124-8), distinguishes disputes procedures as dealing with collective disputes, whether **disputes of rights** or disputes of interest, from individual grievance procedures.

DISPUTES OF INTEREST; see **interest disputes.**

DISPUTES OF RIGHTS; see **rights disputes.**

DISTRIBUTIVE BARGAINING. One of four models of collective bargaining behaviour advanced by Richard E. Walton and Robert B. McKersie *(A Behavioral Theory of Labor Negotiations,* McGraw-Hill, 1965) in an attempt to provide predictive hypotheses on how people will tend to behave in varying circumstances and bargaining conditions, the others being **integrative bargaining, attitudinal structuring** and **intraorganisational bargaining.** Distributive bargaining comprises competitive behaviours that are intended to influence the division of limited resources.

DISTRIBUTIVE SHARES; see **share of wages.**

DISTRICT AGREEMENT. A collective agreement arrived at in a locality by **district bargaining** between a trade union or trade unions and employers on wages or conditions of work, often with the involvement of **district committees**. District agreements in Britain probably reached their highest point of development before the first world war, being gradually superseded thereafter by **national** (or **industry-wide**) **agreements**. Relatively few important district agreements now exist (see **Manchester Piecework Regulations, Coventry Toolroom Agreement**). The **district rate**, though it has sometimes survived as a negotiated rate, was in many cases as an historical development a commonly accepted (rather than agreed) rate, plus agreed additions. It now tends to be loosely used to describe the national agreed rate applied in a district, or even a craftsman's rate accepted in a works or establishment, whether negotiated at district level or not.

DISTRICT BARGAINING; see **district agreement.**

DISTRICT COMMITTEE. A lay committee of elected trade union members, serviced by a full-time or part-time **district secretary**, with responsibility for the affairs of a trade union, or sometimes of a confederation of trade unions, in a particular locality. District Committees of individual unions are particularly associated with **craft unionism** in which regulation of the interests of the craftsman was particularly a local matter, and in which district committees sought to initiate and take part in **trade movements**. Unions with a background of this kind commonly retain their local negotiating authority, e.g. those of the Amalgamated Union of Engineering Workers, Engineering Section; see Rule 13. The expression may, in the case of some unions, refer to district committees of a different kind.

DISTRICT RATE; see **district agreement.**

DISTRICT REFEREE. (1) A person appointed to act as an **arbitrator** at district level in the coal mining industry (see G. B. Baldwin: *Beyond Nationalisation,* Harvard University Press, 1953 p. 67). (2) A person appointed by a trade union district committee to whom reference can be made in case of any neglect (e.g. Rules of the Amalgamated Union of Engineering Workers, Engineering Section, Rule 13 (20)).

DISTRICT SECRETARY. A part-time, or more usually nowadays, full-time trade union official with responsibility for a district. In some situations his responsibility may be exercised in serving a **district committee** (q.v.) and in this case he is usually elected by ballot in his particular locality; but he may also be appointed in some cases, e.g. in the case of the Transport and General Workers' Union. District Secretaries of confederations of unions (e.g. the **Confederation of Shipbuilding and Engineering Union**) are usually part-time and nominated from among the officials of affiliated organisations.

DIVISION OF LABOUR. A phrase attributed to Adam Smith (*Wealth of Nations,* 1776, Everyman ed. 1910, Book 1, Ch. I) to describe the breaking down of a process into its component operations and the allocation of each operation or group of operations to separate workers or groups of workers. For an extended discussion, see A. Marshall, *Principles of Economics,* Macmillan and Co. 8th ed. 1920, pp. 208-21. The notions of production simplification and work specialisation have been carried on in **scientific management** and **work study** (q.v.).

DMT. Dimensional Motion Times (q.v.).

DOCKING. To make a deduction from pay as a fine or penalty, or for other purposes; see **deductions, Truck Acts, Attachment of Earnings Act 1971.**

DOCK LABOUR SCHEME. A permanent national scheme for the registration and employment of dock workers which was developed from wartime arrangements and established in 1947 by an order made under the Dock Workers (Regulation and Employment) Act 1946. The **National Dock Labour Board,** consisting of representatives of management and of trade unions with an independent chairman, is, under the scheme, responsible for the management of the labour force of the whole industry, maintaining registers of dock workers and therefore, through local boards, control of labour supply in the industry. The Scheme's policy of joint control has not always been popular with employers in the industry; nor has its underlying objective of **decasualisation** of dock labour been easy to attain. As a result of the Devlin inquiry (*Final Report* *of the Committee of Inquiry into certain matters concerning the Port Transport Industry,* Cmnd. 2734 August 1965) some details of the scheme have been tightened up and further progress made with decasualisation: *Report of a Court of Inquiry on the National Joint Council for the Port Transport Industry,* Cmnd. 4429, July 1970, David F. Wilson, *Dockers,* Fontana /Collins, 1972 and S. Hill, *The Dockers,* Heinemann, 1976; see also **National Modernisation Committee,** and **Aldington-Jones Report.** In 1976 a new Dock Work Regulation Act reconstituted the National Dock Labour Board on a wider representative basis, laid down the basis of a new Dock Labour Scheme for definable dock areas within half a mile of harbours or harbour land and charged the Board with securing stability of employment for dock workers in a permanent labour force. The Act came into force on 1 August 1977.

DOCKS NATIONAL MODERNISATION COMMITTEE; see **National Modernisation Committee.**

DOCK WORKERS EMPLOYMENT SCHEME. The formally correct title for the **Dock Labour Scheme** (q.v.).

DOCTORS' AND DENTISTS' REMUNERATION, REVIEW BODY ON; see **Kindersley Committee.**

DOCTORS' AND DENTISTS' REMUNERATION, ROYAL COMMISSION ON; see **Pilkington Commission.**

DOCTORS' AND DENTISTS' REVIEW BODY; see **Kindersley Committee** and **review bodies.**

THE DOCUMENT. A signed undertaking in which the worker is required, as a condition of employment, to leave, or not to join a trade union; a device used by employers to resist trade union organisation and recognition. The term is said to have originated in 1834 when, in the course of the rapid organisation of the Grand National Consolidated Trade Union, many employers insisted on non-union undertakings from workers in the form of a document (W. Milne-Bailey, *Trade Union Documents,* G. Bell and Sons, 1929, p. 17). For other nineteenth-century references to The Document; see Sidney and Beatrice Webb, *History of Trade Unionism, 1666-1920* and H. A. Clegg, A. Fox and P. Thompson, *A History of British Trade Unions since 1889,*

Vol I, OUP, 1964, *inter alia;* also for a modern instance see D. C. Thomson. In the United States both written and oral agreements incorporating provisions of The Document are known as **yellow dog contracts,** are contrary to public policy and unenforceable in the courts (Norris-La-Guardia Act 1932, s. 3); see also **certification.**

DOGGETT v. WATERLOO TAXICAB CO. LTD (1910) 2 KB 336; see **contract of service.**

DOMESTIC AGREEMENT. A collective agreement made at sub-**plant agreement** or **works agreement** level, and more or less informal according to tradition and circumstances. Hence domestic agreements might be considered to include both the effects of **custom and practice** and of managerial decisions not questioned by trade union representatives, agreed notes of joint or *ad hoc* management union committees, and formal written agreements at departmental and other similar levels; see **domestic bargaining.**

DOMESTIC APPLIANCE AND GENERAL METAL WORKERS, NATIONAL UNION OF (NUDAGMW). A trade union originating in a stoppage in the stove grate industry in Rotherham and district in 1890 and originally known as the National Union of Stove Grate, Fender and General Light Metal Workers. It continues to be a predominantly Northern based union, but has members in Birmingham, London and Wales all working in the domestic appliance industry. The union adopted its present title in the middle 1960s to take account of the broader nature of the work of its members outside the traditional 'Yorkshire range'. *Address:* Imperial Buildings, High Street, Rotherham S60 1PB. *Tel:* 0709 2820. *TUC Affiliated Membership, 1977:* 5,400.

DOMESTIC BARGAINING. Collective bargaining by managers and supervisors and workers and their representatives, at a sub-plant level and hence, in the main, informal bargaining in the plant, works or establishment over piecework prices, allowances, rates, conditions, etc.; bargaining at the workplace less formal and comprehensive than **plant bargaining,** and hence often associated with **fractional bargaining,** or **fragmented bargaining.** The expression is particularly associated with the engineering industry; see A. I. Marsh,

Industrial Relations in Engineering, Pergamon Press, 1965; but it is also employed elsewhere, and is generally similar in usage to **workshop bargaining** or **workplace bargaining**.

DONATION or donation benefit; unemployment benefit, particularly that provided in trade union rules, e.g. Card Setting Machine Tenters' Society, Rules, 1948, Rule 19. Sometimes known as **out-of-work donation**, a name also given to payments for the unemployed made by the Lloyd George Coalition government in 1918-19; see, for example, Wal Hannington, *Never on Our Knees,* Lawrence and Wishart, 1967, p. 77 *et seq.*

DONOVAN COMMISSION. The **Royal Commission on Trade Unions and Employers' Associations 1965-1968**, under the Chairmanship of the Rt Hon. Lord Donovan, the most recent of five Royal Commissions concerned with British trade unions, industrial relations and the law relating to them since 1867 (see **Erle Commission, Cockburn Commission, Devonshire Commission, Dunedin Commission**). The Donovan Commission was occasioned principally by the postwar growth of short **unconstitutional** and **unofficial strikes** at workplace level and by uncertainties about the law following **Rookes v. Barnard** and other cases. It reported in June 1968 (Cmnd. 3623), on the following terms of reference: 'to consider relations between managements and employees and the role of trade unions and employers' associations in promoting the interests of their members and in accelerating the social and economic advance of the nation, with particular reference to the Law affecting the activities of these bodies'. The Commission diagnosed the ills of British industrial relations as arising out of the undermining of the traditional formal industry-wide system of collective bargaining by the development of informal, fragmented and often disorderly styles of negotiation on pay and conditions adopted by, or acceded to, by trade unions, employers' associations, managers and shop stewards at workplace level (paras 46-74). It was in general pessimistic about the possibilities of improving this situation by legalistic means (though it did not rule out this approach if all else failed), preferring to advocate voluntary reform by the encouragement of properly constructed plant and company agreements, both procedural and substantive, adequate attention to pay structures and a pos-

itive approach to industrial relations policies by managements. To advance such an objective the Commission proposed the review of industrial relations by companies, supported by the registration of agreements, and the establishment of an Industrial Relations Commission (later known as a **Commission on Industrial Relations**), to investigate problems arising from this registration and to deal with issues of trade union recognition and with questions on the general state of relations in a factory or industry. It believed that with this assistance to **voluntarism,** workplace stoppages would fall in number and that greater formality would also serve as a basis for improving the approach to manpower utilisation in British factories. Other recommendations proposed increased protection for workers against **unfair dismissal,** the encouragement of collective bargaining by making void any stipulation in a contract of employment that an employee should not belong to a trade union, confirmation of the legality of the **closed shop,** the establishment of standards of trade union rules through registration, and the setting up of a review body of two trade unionists with a lawyer as chairman to deal with issues arising out of rule registration, with complaints against disciplinary actions by unions and against election malpractices. The Wilson administration's White Paper *In Place of Strife,* (Cmnd. 3888, January 1969) adopted broadly the lines of the Donovan Commission in its primary concern for the encouragement and reform of collective bargaining and the maintenance of voluntarism, but also proposed a **'conciliation pause'** (q.v.) in unconstitutional and other strikes where, because of the absence of agreed procedure or for other reasons, adequate joint discussions had not taken place and, where the effect of strike action was likely to be serious, with ultimate possibility of financial penalties for non-compliance (paras 93-6); it also proposed discretionary powers for the Secretary of State to impose a compulsory strike ballot in threatened major official strikes which appeared not to have the support of trade union members (paras 97-8), and for the Secretary also to be able to impose settlements in inter-union disputes under pain of fines after failure by the Trades Union Congress and the Commission on Industrial Relations to promote voluntary agreement (para. 60). In April 1969 a short Bill introduced urgently to put these additional proposals into effect met strong opposition from trade unions and from

Labour Members of Parliament, and were dropped on a 'solemn and binding undertaking' being made by the Trades Union Congress that it would take measures to deal with unconstitutional strikes. A subsequent Industrial Relations Bill omitting these provisions was overtaken by the fall of the Wilson administration in June 1970, following which the Heath government introduced its own measure, later passed as the **Industrial Relations Act 1971;** see H. A. Clegg, *The System of Industrial Relations in Great Britain,* Basil Blackwell, 3rd ed. 1976 and Peter Jenkins, *The Battle of Downing Street,* Charles Knight, 1970. The Donovan Commission produced eleven Research Papers: 1, W. E. J. McCarthy, *The Role of Shop Stewards in British Industrial Relations;* 2, (Part 1) A. I. Marsh, *Disputes Procedures in British Industry,* (Part 2) A. I. Marsh and W. E. J. McCarthy, *Disputes Procedures in Britain;* 3, Alan Fox, *Industrial Sociology and Industrial Relations;* 4, 1-*Productivity Bargaining,* 2-*Restrictive Labour Practices;* 5, John Hughes (Part 1) *Trade Union Structure and Government,* (Part 2) *Membership Participation and Trade Union Government;* 6, George Sayers Bain, *Trade Union Growth and Recognition;* 7, V. G. Munns and W. E. J. McCarthy, *Employers' Associations: The Results of Two Studies;* 8, *Three Studies in Collective Bargaining,* 1-Jack Steiber, *Grievance Arbitration in the United States,* 2-W. E. J. McCarthy, *Compulsory Arbitration in Britain,* 3-A. I. Marsh and J. W. Staples, *Check-off Agreements in Britain;* 9, E. G. Whybrew, *Overtime Working in Britain;* 10, W. E. J. McCarthy and S. R. Parker, *Shop Stewards and Workshop Relations;* 11, *Two Studies in Industrial Relations,* 1-Nancy Seear, *The Position of Women in Industry,* 2-Robert B. McKersie, *Changing Wage Payment Systems.*

DOUBLE DAY SHIFT. A shift system, most frequently applied to manufacturing processes employing women, which involves two shifts, usually 6 a.m. to 2 p.m. and 2 p.m. to 10 p.m.; sometimes combined with a **night shift** for men to provide continuous working. In the engineering industry (*Handbook of National Agreements,* 2.3) the normal shift week consists of five shifts of 7½ hours, Monday to Friday, with ½ hour meal break without pay, timeworkers being paid for 44 hours at the time rate of the worker concerned and payment by results workers at PBR earnings, plus 37½ hours at the appropriate national **piecework supplement,** plus a

shift bonus of 6½ hours at the time rate of the worker concerned; see **shift working; two shift system.** Under the **Factories Act 1961** s. 97 (provisions formerly contained in the Employment of Women and Young Persons Act 1936 s. 1 and the Factories Act 1937, s. 157(2)) the Secretary of State for Employment may authorise the employment of women and young persons over 16 years of age to work double day shifts, under conditions laid down in the Act and under such conditions as he may impose under it; but he is required not to grant authorisation unless a secret ballot of all the workpeople concerned has been held under Statutory Rule and Order No. 1367, 1936, except in the case of new factories; see Ian Fife and E. A. Machin, *Redgrave's Health and Safety in Factories,* Butterworths, 1976, p. 312 *et seq.*

DOUBLE EMPLOYMENT. The practice of holding two jobs at the same time, see **moonlighting.**

DOUBLE-JOBBING;   moonlighting, (q.v.).

DOUBLE-TIME. Premium payment (q.v.) for work performed at twice the standard rate for the job, e.g. on **overtime,** for **shiftworking,** or for work done on holidays.

DOWN TIME or **machine down time.** Brief periods of idleness while waiting for repair, set-up or adjustment of machinery which may occasion payment of **waiting time** (q.v.). Down time is usually distinguished from **idle time** (or **machine idle time**) in which machines cannot be worked for other reasons than breakdown, etc., e.g. shortage of materials.

DOWNER. A short unconstitutional **strike** (q.v.) characteristic of some stoppages in the motor industry. G. Clack, *Industrial Relations in a British Car Factory,* CUP, 1967, p. 61, describes downers generally as being stoppages on narrow issues, quickly begun and quickly called off, 'attention getters' rather than actions to obtain general economic concessions and as a form of 'brinkmanship' to which both shop stewards and managers responded quickly to obtain a return to work.

DOWRY GRANT or **marriage grant.** A sum of money paid to a female member by a trade union on her marriage; dowry grants are not commonly provided for in trade union rules and in 1965 they existed in such unions as the **Confederation of Health Service Employees,** the **Bakers' Union,** the **Iron and Steel Trades Confederation,** the **National Union of Brushmakers** and the **Tobacco Workers' Union;** see Arthur Marsh and Peter Cope, 'The Anatomy of Trade Union Benefits in the 1960s', *Industrial Relations Journal,* Summer 1970.

DRAUGHTSMEN'S AND ALLIED TECHNICIANS' ASSOCIATION (DATA). A trade union first formed on the Clyde in 1913 as an Association of Engineering and Shipbuilding Draughtsmen (AESD) which subsequently became national in its scope, and took the above title in 1960 in recognition of the fact that it organised not only draughtsmen and tracers, but also designers, calculators, estimators and planning engineers. The AESD secured a national procedure agreement with the Engineering and Allied Employers' National Federation (now the **Engineering Employers' Federation**) in 1924 and with the Shipbuilding Employers' Federation (now the **Shipbuilders and Repairers National Association**) in 1941. It was notable in the 1960s for the aggressiveness of its policy of selective strikes in raising salaries, and obtained the first national wage-for-age scale for draughtsmen and tracers in engineering in 1968. On amalgamation with the **Amalgamated Union of Engineering and Foundry Workers** and the **Constructional Engineering Union** in April 1970, the Association became the Technical and Supervisory Section of the **Amalgamated Union of Engineering Workers** (AUEW/TASS); see J. E. Mortimer, *A History of the Association of Engineering and Shipbuilding Draughtsmen,* AESD, 1960; Graham Wootton, 'Parties in Union Government: the AESD', *Political Studies,* Vol. IX, No. 2, June 1961. *Address:* Onslow Hall, Little Green, Richmond TW9 1QN Surrey. *Tel:* 01-948 2271. *TUC Affiliated Membership 1977:* 161,607.

DRIFTER. A casual worker in the **Dock Labour Scheme** pool who was not regularly in demand, and who obtained work mainly by being allocated to a foreman to make up his gang: *Final Report of the Committee of Inquiry under the Rt Hon. Lord Devlin into certain matters concerning the Port Transport Industry,* Cmnd. 2734, August 1965.

DRIVING. Attempts to obtain more out-

put from workers by methods regarded by them, or by their trade union, as unacceptable, especially by using the **slate system** (q.v.) and by various forms of pressure and implied or actual victimisation; sometimes identified with **humbugging;** (nineteenth century); E. Hopwood, *A History of the Lancashire Cotton Industry and the Amalgamated Weavers' Association,* AWA, 1969, pp. 61-2; see **pacers, whips, rate busters.**

DRO. Disablement Resettlement Officer; see **disabled persons.**

DUAL MEMBERSHIP AGREEMENT. An agreement between two unions whereby the membership of the one is, for certain purposes, included as part of the membership of the other, e.g. in the coalmining industry, as a result of an agreement of 1946, in which members of the **Amalgamated Engineering Union** in the industry also became, for representation purposes, members of the **National Union of Mineworkers,** a variation on this agreement being also made with members of the **Transport and General Workers' Union** and of the **General and Municipal Workers' Union** in the industry; see George B. Baldwin, *Beyond Nationalisation,* Harvard University Press, 1955 p. 55.

DUAL-PURPOSE MANNING. An arrangement on shipboard that traditional deck and engine-room labour groups become interchangeable, with the result that men can be employed in both areas (see also **general-purpose manning**). Dual-purpose manning is said to have passed the experimental stage in tankers and bulk carriers, and is now an accepted manning system. Hence **dual-purpose ratings** and **dual-purpose officers;** see D. H. Moreby, *Personnel Management in Merchant Ships,* Pergamon Press, 1968, pp. 181-2.

DUAL-PURPOSE OFFICERS; see **dual-purpose manning.**

DUAL-PURPOSE RATINGS; see **dual-purpose manning.**

DUAL UNIONISM. A term used, especially in the United States, to describe a situation in which two or more unions which organise the same or similar groups of workers co-exist in the same bargaining unit; see Walter Galenson, *Rival Unionism in the US,* American Council on Public Affairs, 1940. Galenson regards dual unionism as a non-competitive situation, and reserves the term **rival unionism** (q.v.) for the situation in which competition for membership develops. Others regard dual unionism and rival unionism as synonymous activities giving rise to **inter-union disputes;** see also S. W. Lerner, *Breakaway Unions and the Small Trade Union,* Allen and Unwin, 1961, p. 71.

DUAL WORKING. Circumstances in which the same printing workers are employed by a newspaper publisher to produce more than one title of newspaper, a practice contrasted with the situation in which workers in a publishing house are assigned to one title only.

DUES; trade union dues (q.v.).

DUNEDIN COMMISSION. A **Royal Commission on Trade Disputes and Trade Combinations** set up in June 1903 as a result of the **Taff Vale Case** and reporting in January 1906, (Cd. 2825). The Commission reported in favour of trade unions accepting full legal responsibility for their actions, subject to some amendments of the law. The **Trades Disputes Act 1906** which followed gave greater immunity to unions from legal proceedings than the Commission proposed; see Sidney and Beatrice Webb, *History of Trade Unionism 1666-1920,* 1919, p. 605 *et seq.* For other Royal Commissions on industrial relations generally; see **Erle Commission, Cockburn Commission, Devonshire Commission, Donovan Commission.**

DYERS' AND BLEACHERS' ASSOCIATION, NOTTINGHAM AND DISTRICT. A trade union formed in 1962 by the amalgamation of the Basford Bleachers' Society and the Basford Dyers' Association, and having (June 1977), some 800 members recruited from the 'wet' side of the textile finishing industry. It is affiliated to the **General Federation of Trade Unions.** *Address:* 59 Bannerman Road, Bulwell, Nottingham. *Tel:* 0602 273007.

DYERS, BLEACHERS AND TEXTILE WORKERS, NATIONAL UNION OF (NUDB AND TW). A union formed in 1936 by the amalgamation of three unions in dyeing, bleaching and wool textiles based on Bradford and Bolton and now covering the whole of the wool textile industry in the North West and Yorkshire, and the finishing end of the cotton indus-

try in Lancashire; also with membership in carpets, dry cleaning, silk, hosiery, jute, flax and hemp and other ancillary industries. Prospects for the woollen industry in the 1960s encouraged talks on amalgamation with the Hosiery Workers' Union and the Lancashire textile unions. The Saddleworth and District Weavers' Association (1,333 members) amalgamated with the union in April 1973. Ben Turner, *A Short History of the General Union of Textile Workers,* General Union of Textile Workers, 1920; Walter Bateson, *The Way We Came,* Thornton and Pearsons, 1928. *Address:* National House, Sunbridge Road, Bradford BD1 2QB. *Tel:* 0274 25642. *TUC Affiliated Membership 1977:* 58,756.

E

EARLY WARNING SYSTEM. A system for giving prior warning of some threat of development, e.g. in military or defence matters, or in economic affairs. In **incomes policy** in Britain, a notification system enabling the government to examine pay and price proposals before they were put into effect. A voluntary early warning system was introduced by the Wilson administration in November 1965. This was given legal force in Part II of the **Prices and Incomes Act 1966;** (see **prices and incomes policy**), the government being given powers, in the case of terms and conditions of employment, to delay the implementation of a notified claim for thirty days, or, if a reference was made to the **National Board for Prices and Incomes** until that Board reported. The **Trades Union Congress,** through its **Incomes Policy Committee,** also set up its own early warning system for the vetting of claims which it retained after the activation of Part II of the **Prices and Incomes Act 1966.** Both fell out of use before the defeat of the Wilson administration at the polls in June 1970.

EARNINGS. Defined by the Department of Employment as the total remuneration which employees receive from their employers in the form of money, either as wages or as salaries, including overtime and other premium payments, bonuses, commission or other payments of any kind, and before deduction of income tax or of the employee's contribution to national insurance or superannuation funds. Thus defined, earnings do not include income in kind or employers' contributions to national insurance, holiday funds or superannuation benefits. **Earnings surveys** were begun by the Ministry of Labour in 1940, inquiries being made into the average weekly earnings and working hours of manual workers in manufacturing and a number of non-manufacturing industries in the United Kingdom each April and October, and published in the Gazette, normally in the following August and February. An **Occupational Earnings Survey** for manual workers in Great Britain, held under the Statistics of Trade Act 1947 each January and June was begun in January 1963, and published for most industries in the May and October issues of the Gazette (reports on construction appearing in June and November) on a sample basis (except for construction) to all firms with 500 or more employees, to a 50 per cent sample of firms with between 100 and 499 employees and to a 10 per cent sample of those with between 25 and 99 employees. In 1955 the Ministry of Labour began an annual inquiry into the earnings of **administrative technical and clerical** (ATC) employees in the public sector, and in 1959 this was extended to the production industries; it has been carried out in October and covers the United Kingdom. (For an account of these three surveys; see Department of Employment, *British Labour Statistics, Year Book, 1969,* 1971, p. 8 *et seq.*). In 1966 the House of Commons Estimates Committee commented unfavourably on information about earnings, and especially information about the distribution of the earnings of individuals about the average (see **low pay**). The first **New Earnings Survey** for 1968 was published in six instalments in the Gazette in 1969, and in one volume in 1970, giving a more detailed analysis of earnings, and has been repeated since that time on a sample survey basis; other earnings surveys have been reduced or discontinued; the April and October surveys are to be confined to October only, the administrative, technical and clerical surveys were ended after October 1970, and the Occupational Earnings Surveys substantially discontinued (*Employment and Productivity Gazette,* February 1970, and *Statistical News,* August 1970).

EARNINGS DRIFT; see **wage drift.**

EARNINGS GAP. The difference between gross earnings and basic rates of pay for a standard working week, usually consisting of three main elements; earnings resulting from **payment by results, overtime,** and **allowances** or other rates settled at plant or domestic level over and above industry-wide agreements; see **wage drift** and **income policy.**

EARNINGS-RELATED SUPPLEMENTS; see **sickness benefit, unemployment benefit.**

EARNINGS SURVEYS; see **earnings.**

EASTHAM v. NEWCASTLE UNITED FOOTBALL CLUB; see **retain and transfer.**

ECFTU. European Confederation of Free Trade Unions; see **International Labour Movement.**

ECONOMIC STRIKE. A stoppage of work arising out of the inability of the employer or his association to agree with the union or unions with which he negotiates about wages, hours, or other conditions of work. The expression is more commonly used in the United States of America than in Britain; in the USA the National Labour Relations Board makes a distinction between economic strikes and **unfair labor practices** strikes, the latter being 'protected' in the sense that the Board will order reinstatement of workers after the strike is concluded, and the former not so 'protected'; see Bureau of National Affairs, *Labour Relations Expediter:* also **strike.**

EDUCATION ACT, 1918; see **Youth Employment Service.**

EDUCATION (CHOICE OF EMPLOYMENT) ACT 1910; see **Youth Employment Service.**

EDUCATIONAL INSTITUTE OF SCOTLAND. A trade union organising teachers and lecturers in schools and colleges in Scotland and holding more than two-thirds of the seats on the teachers' side of the main negotiating bodies for Scottish teachers, The Scottish Teachers' Salaries Committee and the Scottish Teachers' Service Conditions Committee. It affiliated to the Trades Union Congress in July 1977. *Address:* 46 Moray Place, Edinburgh EH3 6BH. *Tel:* 031-225 6244. *TUC Affiliated Membership, 1977:* 45,357.

EDWARDS v. SOCIETY OF GRAPHI-

CAL AND ALLIED TRADES. (1970) 3 All ER. A case in which a trade union member, dismissed from his job as a result of an admitted mistake by the union in withdrawing his membership, was subsequently readmitted, first as a temporary and later as a full member, but was unable to be found suitable employment by the union, and was awarded substantial damages against it. The case was notable for the reported statement by Lord Denning MR that the **right to work** (q.v.(1)) was legally recognised and that the union existed to protect it; see R.W.Rideout, 'Edwards v. Sogat', *Federation News*, Vol. 20, No. 4, October 1970.

EEC FIFTH DIRECTIVE; see **Fifth Directive.**

EEF. Engineering Employers' Federation (q.v.).

EETPU. Electrical Electronic Telecommunication and Plumbing Union (q.v.).

EFFICIENCY AGREEMENT. A term used by the National Board for Prices and Incomes (*Productivity Agreements*, Report No. 123, Cmnd. 4136, August 1969) to extend the definition of 'productivity agreement' (see **productivity bargaining**) to cover periodic pay or salary reviews involved in adapting working methods to changing technology. The Board suggested that the expression 'productivity agreement' might be confined to those situations in which specific changes in working practices might be agreed in return for directly related improvements in pay and conditions, while 'efficiency agreement' might cover those situations in which these improvements could be linked to forecasted and costed gains resulting from co-operation in technical change and technological innovation. The Board did not exempt efficiency agreements from the **criteria** proposed for productivity agreements as more narrowly conceived.

EFFICIENCY BAR; see **incremental scale.**

EFFICIENCY CURVE; see **learning curve.**

EFFICIENCY PAY. A payment made to workers on the grounds that they have contributed to the efficiency of the enterprise, e.g. in London Transport, where busmen have received a payment relating to bus seating capacity and cash takings: National Board for Prices and Incomes, *Pay and Conditions of Busmen*, Cmnd. 3012, May 1966, p. 10.

EFFICIENCY RATING; see **performance appraisal** and **merit rating.**

EFFORT BARGAIN (EFFORT BARGAINING). A term introduced by Hilde Behrend ('The Effort Bargain', *Industrial and Labor Relations Review*, July 1957, pp. 503-15) to describe the kind of individual and collective bargaining involved in the operation of **incentive payment** or **payment-by-results systems** (q.v.). Effort is considered to be a subjective notion, variable within certain limits, views on which are held by particular managements or managers and working groups or workers themselves, making it necessary for a bargain to be struck between the upper limit of effort which workers are willing to expend, and the lower limit which managements are willing to accept. Dr Behrend argues that friction results from workers and managements failing to share the same conceptions of the 'right' standard of effort and the 'correct' rate of pay for it (see **ca'canny, restrictive practices, goldbricking, quota restrictions** *inter alia*) and that the successful operation of incentive payment systems depends on skill in effort bargaining. Successful **effort rating** and **rate fixing** (q.v.) depend less on scientific technique than on the skill of the time-study expert in estimating the worker's norms of effort, and systems of payments by results not acceptable to the worker may result in decreased rather than increased output. Effort bargaining has come to be used not only of the process of arriving at particular effort/earnings bargains, but also, in contradistinction to **productivity bargaining** (q.v.), to the agreed introduction of payment by results systems, though it is sometimes suggested that one can run into the other (Royal Commission on Trade Unions and Employers' Associations, Research Papers 4, I, *Productivity Bargaining*, pp. 7-8); see also **fair day's work,** and **wage-work bargaining.**

EFFORT RATING; see **rating.**

EIGHT HOURS DAY MOVEMENT. A movement for a statutory eight hour day designed to relieve unemployment by work sharing and to increase leisure advocated by the Social Democratic Federation as part of a socialist programme during the period of the **new unionism**

(q.v.). The eight hour day as a general aspiration has a much longer history; see Gösta Langenfelt, *The Historic Origin of the Eight Hours Day*, Stockholm, 1954. It was revived by the SDF as a demand for restriction of the working day of public servants in 1884 and followed by Tom Mann's celebrated pamphlet *What a Compulsory Eight Hours Working Day Means to the Workers in 1886* (Dent/Pluto Press 1972); see Sidney Webb and Harold Cox, *The Eight Hours Day*, Walter Scott, 1891. The TUC adopted legislative enforcement in 1891, after the publication of the Webb and Cox study which came out in favour of this method, and agitation by individual trades persisted over the turn of the century more as an article of faith than a serious aspiration; see A.E.P.Duffy, 'The Eight Hours Day Movement, in Britain', *Manchester School*, Sept. 1968. The forty-hour five-day week did not become general in Britain until the second half of the 1960s.

EIU REPORT. The Report of the Economist Intelligence Unit on *The National Newspaper Industry*, 1966; see **Newspaper Industry, National Joint Board for.**

ELECTRICAL CONTRACTING INDUSTRY, JOINT INDUSTRY BOARD FOR: see **Electrical Contractors' Association.**

ELECTRICAL CONTRACTORS' ASSOCIATION. An employers' association originating in a body of the same title founded in 1901. In its original form the association was debarred from commercial or industrial relations matters and in 1916 two further associations were formed for these purposes, the former being dealt with by the National Electrical Contractors Trade Association, and the latter by the National Federated Electrical Association (NFEA), which was registered as a trade union. The present Association, formed in January 1970, now combines all these functions in a single organisation. National agreements between the Electrical Trades Union (now the **Electrical, Electronic, Telecommunication and Plumbing Union**) and the Association date from the formation of the National Joint Industrial Council for the Electrical Contracting Industry in 1919. In 1968, as part of the 1966/1969 Industrial Agreement, this was redesignated the **Joint Industry Board for the Electrical Contracting Industry**. At the same time, the old semi-skilled category of 'electrician's mate' was abolished and a

grading system introduced, workers being graded electrician, approved electrician or technician according to qualifications, practical skill and length of service. *Address:* 55 Catherine Place, Westminster, London SW1E 6ET. *Tel:* 01-828 2932. *Joint Industry Board. Address:* Kingswood House, 47/51 Sidcup Hill, Sidcup, Kent DA1 6HJ. *Tel:* 01-302 0031.

ELECTRICAL ELECTRONIC TELECOMMUNICATION AND PLUMBING UNION (EETPU). A trade union formed as the Electrical Trades Union in 1890 as a result of an amalgamation between the Amalgamated Society of Telegraph and Telephone Construction Men and the Union of Electrical Operatives agreed in principle in 1889. Early members of the union were mostly contracting electricians, telegraph and telephone wiremen and labourers, but growth in the use of electricity has brought membership in addition in electricity generation and supply, in engineering and most other industries. The union changed its name after merger with the Plumbing Trades Union on 1 July 1968. The ETU has been particularly known for the vigour of its negotiations, for the sometimes turbulent nature of its internal affairs (including the case of Byrne and Chapple v. Foulkes and others; see **ballot rigging**) and for its development of residential education at its training colleges; see *Fifty Years of the Electrical Trades Union*, ETU, 1939; Gordon Schaffer, *Light and Liberty; Sixty Years with the Electrical Trades Union*, ETU, 1949; *The Story of the ETU*, ETU, 1952. *Address:* Hayes Court, West Common Road, Hayes, Bromley, Kent, BR2 7AU. *Tel:* 01-462 7755. *TUC Affiliated Membership 1977:* 420,000.

ELECTRICAL POWER ENGINEERS' ASSOCIATION (EPEA); see **Engineers' and Managers' Association.**

ELECTRICAL TRADES UNION; see **Electrical Electronic Telecommunication and Plumbing Union.**

ELECTRICITY (SUPPLY) ACT 1919; see **Conspiracy and Protection of Property Act 1875.**

EMAS. Employment Medical Advisory Service; see **Employment Medical Advisory Service Act 1972.**

EMA. Engineers' and Managers' Association (q.v.).

EMAS. Employment Medical Advisory Service; see **Employment Medical Advisory Service Act 1972.**

EMBARGO. A ban or prohibition operated by a trade union or its members. May be the same as a **boycott** or **secondary boycott** (q.v.), or a complete or conditional refusal to co-operate with an employer in connection with some particular practice, e.g. an embargo on overtime, a refusal to work overtime generally, or agreement to work only on certain circumstances (see **all-or-none embargo**), to undertake weekend work, etc.

EMBOURGEOISEMENT. A concept defined by J.H.Goldthorpe, D. Lockwood, F. Bechofer and J.Platt (*The Affluent Worker: Industrial Attitudes and Behaviour*, CUP, 1968 p. 1) as 'the thesis that, as manual workers and their families achieve relatively high incomes and living standards, they assume a way of life which is more characteristically "middle class" and become in fact progressively assimilated into middle class society'. For an analysis of the thesis see; J.H.Goldthorpe and D.Lockwood, 'Affluence and the British Class Structure', *Sociological Review*, Vol. 11, No. 2, July 1963, and for an empirical study, op. cit., and subsequent volumes in the same plan of inquiry.

EMERALD CONSTRUCTION CO. LTD v. LOWTHIAN. (1966) 1 WLR 691. A case in which an injunction was obtained by the plaintiff company against Amalgamated Union of Building Trade Workers officials in circumstances involving **labour-only sub-contracting** (q.v.). The union did all in its power to oppose the sub-contracting arrangement, eventually declaring the job black and picketing the premises. It was held that the sub-contract was not one of employment and that the union officials concerned had acted wrongly in trying to procure the main contractor wrongfully to repudiate or terminate it. K.W.Wedderburn, *Cases and Materials on Labour Law*, CUP, 1967 pp. 492-5.

EMERGENCY DISPUTES PROCEDURE; see **Green Book Procedure.**

EMERGENCY PROCEDURES; see **national emergency procedures.**

EMERSON WAGE PAYMENT PLAN or Emerson Efficiency Plan. A **premium payment** or **gain sharing plan** developed by Harrington Emerson in the United States, said to have been adopted by a number of British firms. Bonus becomes payable at 67 per cent efficiency and this is increased rapidly to 10 per cent of time rate at an efficiency of 90 per cent; thereafter a bonus of 1 per cent is paid for every additional 1 per cent gain in efficiency, so that at 100 per cent efficiency (standard performance) a bonus is 20 per cent. Beyond standard performance the worker is paid the wages of time taken, plus the wages of time saved, plus a certain bonus percentage of wages of time taken; see N.C.Hunt, *Methods of Wage Payment in British Industry*, Pitman, 1951 p. 84 and R. Marriott, *Incentive Payment Systems*, 3rd (revised) ed., Staples Press, 1968 p. 59.

EMOLUMENT. Defined in the *Oxford English Dictionary* as profit or gain from station, office or employment; dues, remuneration or salary. In current usage 'emoluments' are usually used in the sense of 'pay and emoluments', i.e. payments or benefits arising out of work performed which are not basic pay; e.g. as in **quantifiable emoluments** (q.v.), and have to be added to arrive at gross pay, or **true money rate.** These may include bonuses, pensions, merit pay, etc.

EMPLOYEE. In general usage, anyone who is employed for wages or salary and not, therefore, a person who is self-employed, or who receives commission, royalties or fees, but has no contract of employment of a normally understood kind. In the **Trade Union and Labour Relations Act 1974** (s. 30), an individual who has entered into or works under a contract of employment otherwise than in police service; the definition is narrower than that for **worker** (q.v.).

EMPLOYEE APPRAISAL. The technique of estimating systematically the performance of workers, particularly those who are salaried or on staff conditions. Appraisal methods may vary from simple verbal or written judgements (poor-adequate-good), to more elaborate methods of ranking, simple or by paired comparisons, and linear scale methods of various kinds. These methods are summarised in G. McBeath and D.N. Rands, *Salary Administration*, Business Books Ltd, 3rd edition, 1976 and E. Anstey, C.Fletcher and J.Walker, *Staff Appraisal and Development* George Allen and Unwin, 1976; see also **performance appraisal.**

EMPLOYEE BENEFITS; see **fringe benefits.**

EMPLOYEE DIRECTORS; see **worker directors.**

EMPLOYEE ORGANISATIONS, CONFEDERATION OF (CEO). A confederation of organisations of employees not in membership of the Trades Union Congress formed in June 1973 in succession to the **Confederation of Independent Staff Associations.** The CEO consisted originally of 21 such organisations registered as independent unions under the Industrial Relations Act 1971. At present (January 1978) it has 42 affiliated organisations, with a total membership of about 75,000; 10 of these have certificates of independence under the Trade Union and Labour Relations Act 1974 (see **independent trade union**). It provides advice, training and other assistance to these affiliates, its main emphasis being on political and financial independence in relationships with government, and on constructive rather than militant collective bargaining with employers. *Address*: 39 High Street, Wheathampstead, St. Albans, Herts. AL4 8DG. *Tel*: Wheathampstead (058 283) 3481.

EMPLOYEE RELATIONS. A new journal designed to provide up-to-date information on personnel management, health and safety, collective bargaining, communications and industrial legislation, launched in 1978 by MCB Publications Ltd, 198/200 Keighley Road, Bradford, West Yorkshire, England BD9 4JO.

EMPLOYEE REPORTS. Printed reports, usually annual, in which companies provide information to their employees showing their financial position, trading activities, manpower situation etc., frequently in a form judged to be readily assimilable and understood. While some companies have produced such reports for many years, others were stimulated to do so by s. 57 of the Industrial Relations Act 1971 which required undertakings employing more than 350 employees to make annual financial statements to their employees. The repeal of this provision in 1974 has not led to a diminution of the practice and an Accountancy Age Award is given each year to the UK company which is judged to have produced the most effective report for its employees; see L.D.Parker, *The Reporting of Company Financial Results*, Institute of Chartered Accountants of England and Wales, 1977; also **information, disclosure of,** and *The Future of Company Reports*, Cmnd. 6888, HMSO July 1977, a government green paper in which it is proposed that, in addition to an extended requirement on financial information, companies above a certain size should also be obliged to provide under the Companies Act an **employment statement** giving information on employment and training, unions recognised, participation arrangements, pensions and sick pay provisions, numbers of man-days lost through industrial disputes, numbers of disabled people employed etc.

EMPLOYEE SHAREHOLDING; see **co-partnership.**

EMPLOYEE SOCIETY. An expression introduced by Peter F. Drucker (*American Journal of Sociology*, January 1953) to describe a society based on the relationship of people to impersonal organisations and characterised by a strict system of rank and status, such as that which, he contends, has been developing in the United States.

EMPLOYER CONCILIATION. An expression coined by A.I.Marsh and R.S.Jones ('Engineering Procedure and Central Conference at York in 1959', *British Journal of Industrial Relations*, June 1964) to describe a procedural situation in which trade unions are required to take matters arising, not to joint bodies or mutually agreed conciliators or arbitrators (**joint conciliation**) but to panels of employers, who therefore act in the dual capacity of employers and conciliators. Employer conciliation was characteristic of the approach to industrial relations under the **Engineering Procedure Agreement** derived from the **Terms of Settlement** of 1898; see A.I.Marsh and W.E.J.McCarthy, *Disputes Procedures in Britain*, Royal Commission on Trade Unions and Employers' Associations, Research Papers 2 (Part 2), p. 1 and Chs. 2 and 3, HMSO, 1968. **External Conferences** held under the 1976 National Engineering Procedure Agreement. Manual Workers are commonly conducted on similar lines.

EMPLOYER REFERENCE. A question or issue in a **grievance procedure** or **disputes procedure** initiated by an employer, as contrasted with a **union reference,** i.e. a question or issue taken up by a trade union on behalf of its member or members.

Employer references tend to be less common than **union references;** see, for example, A.I.Marsh, *Industrial Relations in Engineering*, Pergamon Press, 1965 (some 9 per cent of all references to engineering Central Conference at York in 1959). Among the reasons for this are the considerations that the union and its members have more possibilities of substantive gains from procedure than employers, and that employers may find it no easier to establish the terms which they would like to see after procedure has been exhausted than by obtaining settlements at lower levels.

EMPLOYER STRIKE INSURANCE; see **mutual strike aid.**

EMPLOYERS, INTERNATIONAL ORGANISATION OF (IOE). An organisation of employers founded in 1920 and claiming to be the only world organisation authoritatively representing the interests of employers of the free world in all social labour matters at the international level. Its objects are to promote private enterprise and to defend the international interests of employers. Its current membership covers 85 central employer federations in 81 countries. It encourages the formation of independent employer organisations in developing countries. The IOE has special observer status at the United Nations and co-ordinates employers' views on the purpose and content of guidelines for the industrial relations activities of multinational companies. It also has close contact with the **Organisation for Economic Cooperation and Development** (OECD) where its Business and Industry Advisory Committees (BIAC) are balanced by Trade Union Advisory Committees (TUAC). Its role in the **International Labour Organisation,** where it is responsible for the secretariat of the employers' group, has increased since the withdrawal of the United States of America from that body. *Address:* 28 Chemin de Joinville, PO Box 68, CH-1216 Cointrin - Geneva.

EMPLOYERS' ASSOCIATION. In general usage, an organisation of employers which exists for the purposes of negotiation with trade unions or with the object of assisting, influencing or controlling the industrial relations decisions of member firms; currently preferred for most purposes to **employers' organisation** (q.v.) and usually contrasted with 'trade association', i.e. an organisation of employers

which represents the trading interests of a group of producers or providers of a particular commodity or service, though some (indeed an increasing number) of employers' associations may provide both functions. Under the **Trade Union and Labour Relations Act 1974** the **Certification Officer** is required to maintain a list of both trade unions and employers' associations. Listing has, however, none of the advantage for the latter which it has for the former (see **listed trade union**). 168 were listed on 31 December 1977. Unlisted employers' associations, operating as companies limited by guarantee or with no incorporated status, greatly exceed this figure. Some 900 employers' associations of all these descriptions are known to the Department of Employment. The Donovan **Royal Commission on Trade Unions and Employers' Associations** (Cmnd. 3623, June 1968) criticised employers' associations for their lack of initiative and assigned to them the role of promoting and supporting effective and comprehensive agreements in company, and factory; see A.I.Marsh, 'The Contribution of Employers' Associations', in B.Towers, T.G.Whittingham and A.W.Gottschalk, *Bargaining for Change*, Allen and Unwin, 1972, also V.G.Munns and W.E.J.McCarthy, *Employers' Associations*, Royal Commission on Trade Unions and Employers' Associations, Research Papers 7, HMSO, 1967.

EMPLOYERS' FEDERATION OF PAPERMAKERS AND BOARDMAKERS; see **British Paper and Board Industry Federation.**

EMPLOYER'S FINAL OFFER or **Final Offer Arbitration.** A procedure for handling industrial disputes in which it is assumed that, if employees are informed of the employer's last offer and have an opportunity of voting by secret ballot in an election conducted by an impartial public agency, they are likely to accept that offer. An assumption of this kind was involved in the **National Emergency Procedures** which formed part of the **Industrial Relations Act 1971** but the idea seems to have originated in the United States of America in the Smith-Connally (War and Labour Disputes) Act 1943 and in the **Taff-Hartley Act 1947.** In neither country does it seem to have fulfilled the expectations of the legislators; see J.L.Stern, C.M.Rehmus, J.J.Loewenberg, H. Kasper and B.D. Dennis, *Final Offer Arbitration*, Lexington Books, 1975.

EMPLOYERS' LIABILITY. The liability of the employer to pay damages to his servants (or employees), and sometimes to other workers occupied on his factory or site, for personal injuries which they have sustained in the course of their work, or to other workmen not in his employment. The notion at common law includes the employer's **personal liability** (i.e. for accidents due to his own act or default), and also his **vicarious liability** (i.e. his liability for the acts of his servants in the course of their employment, as where one workman injures another by careless handling of a lifting device), both as a rule requiring proof of negligence. It also includes liability for breach of statutory duty, e.g. of the obligation, under ss. 12-16 of the **Factories Act 1961**, to fence dangerous machinery. The evolution of the present legal situation dates from 1837 (**Priestley v. Fowler**, 3 M and W 1) which erected the doctrine of **common employment**, i.e. that an employer is not liable to his own servants for the negligence of their fellow servants. The Employers' Liability Act 1880 gave partial protection to workmen, but proved inadequate and the Workmen's Compensation Acts (1897, 1906 and a consolidating Act in 1925) - see **workmen's compensation** - were based on a new principle, that compensation became automatically payable whenever a workman met with an accident in the course of his employment, leaving the workman to sue at common law as an alternative, and by 1898 (**Groves v. Wimborne (Lord)** 2 QB 402) it had been firmly established that the workman had a remedy whenever his injuries resulted from a breach of statutory duty in relation to the Factories Acts and similar legislation. By the **Law Reform (Contributory Negligence) Act 1945**, contributory negligence lost much of its force, and the **Law Reform (Personal Injuries) Act 1948** abolished the doctrine of common employment after a series of notable cases (**John v. Lindsay and Co.** (1891), AC 371, **Radcliffe v. Ribble Motor Services Ltd** (1939) AC 215; (1939) 1 All ER 637 and **Lancaster v. London Passenger Transport Board** (1948) 2 All ER 796, *inter alia*). The Workmen's Compensation Acts were replaced by a state insurance scheme under the National Insurance (Industrial Injuries) Act 1965 (see **Industrial Injuries Acts**). Recent additions to legislation are the **Employers' Liability (Defective Equipment) Act 1969** and the **Employers' Liability (Compulsory Insurance) Act 1969** (q.v.); see also **Health and Safety at Work Act 1974**, K.W. Wedderburn, *Cases and Materials on Labour Law*, CUP, 1967 Ch. 6 and J.Munkman, *Employers' Liability at Common Law*, 8th ed. Butterworths 1975.

EMPLOYERS' LIABILITY (COMPULSORY INSURANCE) ACT 1969. An Act coming into force on 1 January 1972 requiring all employers carrying on business in Great Britain, unless qualifying for exemption, to insure and maintain insurance under approved policies with authorised insurers against their liability for bodily injury or disease sustained by their employees arising out of and in the course of their employment in Great Britain. From 1 January 1973 all employers have been required to display a certificate of insurance, or copies of it, at each of their premises or sites for the information of their employees.

EMPLOYERS' LIABILITY (DEFECTIVE EQUIPMENT) ACT 1969. An Act coming into force on 25 October 1969 and providing that where an employee suffers personal injury in the course of his employment as a result of a defect in equipment provided by his employer for the purposes of his employer's business, and the defect is attributable to a third party, the injury shall be deemed to be also attributable to negligence on the part of the employer, but without prejudice to the law relating to **contributory negligence.**

EMPLOYERS' ORGANISATION. A term sometimes used to describe an organisation of employers which negotiates with trade unions as contrasted with a 'trade association', the latter being an organisation of employers which represents the commercial and trading interests of a group of producers or providers of a particular commodity or service. There are, however, organisations which perform both functions (e.g. the **Chemical Industries Association,** the **National Farmers' Union,** etc.), and **employers' association** (q.v.) is generally thought to be a better term to describe an employers' organisation for industrial relations, though this term also has its difficulties.

EMPLOYMENT AGENCIES. Private, fee paying agencies through which employment may be obtained. Such agencies are unimportant in the placing of workers in skilled or unskilled manual work in Britain (see **employment offices** and **job shops**) but were reckoned in 1966 to handle 12 per cent of clerical and commercial, and 3 per cent of managerial, executive and technical engagements. Until the Employment Agencies Act 1973 employment agencies were not subject to control by any general legislation, but local authorities could apply to the Home Secretary for powers to make by-laws under s. 85 of the Public Health Acts (Amendment) Act 1907 where female domestic servants were concerned and about 50 local authorities had obtained powers to prohibit the operation of an agency without a licence, including the Greater London Council; see National Board for Prices and Incomes, *Office Staff Employment Agencies, Charges and Salaries*, HMSO, Cmnd, 3828, November 1968. Since 1 November 1976 it has been an offence for an Employment Agency to operate without a licence from the Secretary of State for Employment. It is also an offence for both employment agencies and **employment businesses** (q.v.) to charge workers fees for finding or attempting to get them jobs.

EMPLOYMENT APPEAL TRIBUNAL. An appellate body to which all appeals from **industrial tribunals** have been referred since its establishment on 1 February 1976. The Tribunal derives its existence and powers from the Employment Protection Act 1975 s. 87. Originally, appeals from industrial tribunals could be taken to a Divisional Court of the Queen's Bench and in 1972 and 1973 were dealt with by the **National Industrial Relations Court**. They reverted to the Divisional Court after the abolition of the NIRC by the Trade Union and Labour Relations Act 1974. As a result the number of appeals greatly declined and inconsistency tended to appear among tribunals. The Tribunal is a superior court of record and may, with the consent of a judge, punish for contempt. Unlike the NIRC, it has no original jurisdiction of its own. Its proceedings require equal numbers of persons whose experience is as representatives of employers and workers (two or four in total), although with the consent of the parties, proceedings may be heard by a judge and one appointed member.

EMPLOYMENT BUSINESS. An agency employing workers itself and hiring them out to a third party as distinguished from an **employment agency** (q.v.) which provides a service to find workers jobs or which supplies employers with workers; alternatively known as a temporary staff contractor. Under the Employment Agen-

cies Act 1973, employment businesses must be licensed by the Secretary of State for Employment, advertise the nature of their business clearly and have statutory obligations to the hirer and to the worker.

EMPLOYMENT COUNSELLING; see **vocational guidance.**

EMPLOYMENT, DEPARTMENT OF (DE). The government department in Great Britain with historical responsibility for manpower, employment services, industrial training, conciliation and arbitration and other functions affecting labour and industrial relations. Since the early 1970s many of these functions have been hived off to agencies established by statute, e.g. to the **Manpower Services Commission**, and the **Advisory, Conciliation and Arbitration Service** and to local authorities (see **Careers Service**). The department continues to be directly responsible for unemployment benefit and employment statistics. The DE originated from the Labour Department of the Board of Trade, which became the **Ministry of Labour** in 1916, a title which was retained until 1939, when it became the **Ministry of Labour and National Service** on being given the task of administering the Military Training Act of that year (see Sir Godfrey Ince, *The Ministry of Labour and National Service*, Allen and Unwin, 1960). With the ending of National Service, the title Ministry of Labour was resumed until May 1968, when it was changed to **Department of Employment and Productivity** under a Secretary of State, the words 'and Productivity' being later dropped by the Health administration. The Department has its Headquarters at 8 St. James's Square, London SW1Y 4JB. *Tel:* 01-214 6000. *Regional Offices - Eastern and Southern:* Bryan House, 76-80 Whitfield St., London W1P 6AN. *Tel:* 01-636 8616; *London and South Eastern:* Hanway House, Red Lion Square, High Holborn, London WC1 4NH. *Tel:* 01-405 8454; *Midlands:* 2 Duchess Place, Hagley Road, Birmingham B16 8NS. *Tel:* 021-455 7111; *Northern:* Wellbar House, Gallowgate, Newcastle-upon-Tyne, NE1 4TP. *Tel:* 0632-27575; *North Western:* Sunley Building, Piccadilly Plaza, Manchester M60 7JS. *Tel:* 061-832 9111; *South Western:* The Pithay, Bristol BS1 2NQ. *Tel:* 0272 291071; *Yorkshire and Humberside:* City House, City Station, Leeds LS1 4JH. *Tel:* 0532-38232; *Scottish:* 43 Jeffrey St., Edinburgh EH1 1UU. *Tel:* 031-556 8433; *Wales:* Companies House, Crown Way,

Maindy, Cardiff CF4 3UW. *Tel*: 0222-388 588.

EMPLOYMENT EXCHANGES now employment offices and **job centres**; see **Employment Service.**

EMPLOYMENT MEDICAL ADVISORY SERVICE (EMAS); see **Employment Medical Advisory Service Act 1972.**

EMPLOYMENT MEDICAL ADVISORY SERVICE ACT 1972. An Act setting up a new **Employment Medical Advisory Service** (EMAS) which received the Royal Assent in May 1972, and implemented recommendations of a sub-committee of the Secretary of State's Industrial Health Advisory Committee which reported in 1966. The Act abolished the Appointed Factory Doctor Service and provided for a new Service with a staff of full-time and part-time doctors specialising in occupational medicine and based upon the country's main industrial centres. EMAS which came into operation on 1 February 1973, was originally a part of the **Department of Employment** but is now part of the Health and Service Executive (see **Health and Safety at Work Act 1974**). It advises on the medical aspects of the employment of young people and examines and follows up those in need of medical advice, gives medical advice to employers, trade unions and others, studies health hazards in factories, examines people employed on particularly hazardous processes and performs other related duties.

EMPLOYMENT OFFICE; see **Employment Service.**

EMPLOYMENT AND PRODUCTIVITY, DEPARTMENT OF. Now the Department of Employment; see **Employment, Department of.**

EMPLOYMENT PROTECTION ACT 1975. A far reaching extension of the law of industrial relations in Britain constituting a second stage of the 1974 Labour government's legislative programme in the field, the first being the **Trade Union and Labour Relations Act** which, in the previous year, had repealed the **Industrial Relations Act 1971.** A considerable part of the Act is concerned to increase the *individual* rights of employees, e.g. in respect of **guarantee payments, maternity pay** and **unfair dismissal**, but much is devoted to the reinforcement of trade union activity by recog-

nition procedures (see **Section 11 Procedure**), by new procedures for handling **redundancies** (ss. 99-107), by a re-enactment of the 1971 Acts provision for **disclosure of information** for collective bargaining, by protecting employees acting in a trade union capacity (ss. 53-56) and by providing that time off work should be granted for trade union activities (ss. 57-62); see **Facilities for Trade Unions**. The Act also established on a statutory basis the **Advisory, Conciliation and Arbitration Service**, provided *inter alia* for longer periods of notice under the **Contracts of Employment Act 1972**, amended the law on **Wages Councils** and made provision for **Statutory Joint Industrial Councils** and provided for a new form of Section 8 Procedure under its **Schedule 11 Claims**. Its general intention was officially stated to be 'to improve industrial relations by encouraging the development and strengthening of collective bargaining and to provide employees with a series of fundamental new rights and greater job security': *Department of Employment Press Notice* November 1975. Some observers have found the contents of the Act radical in various respects, e.g. on trade union facilities, or on Schedule 11 claims; others have taken a different view, viz. B.A. Hepple and P. O'Higgins, *Encyclopaedia of Labour Relations Law*, 1978; 2-1500: 'Not the Labour government's best friend nor its worst enemy could charge it with enacting a socialist conception of an industrial relations system. Rather, what this Act confirms is the traditional legal perspective on labour relations; one which sees the law as impinging on questions of individual rights of employees and employers and, in its modern trend, tending to maintain the autonomy of the collective parties on either side of the industrial relations system'; see also **Central Arbitration Committee.**

EMPLOYMENT PROTECTION (CONSOLIDATION) ACT 1978. A consolidation Act bringing together, without alteration, the individual employment rights previously contained in the **Redundancy Payments Act 1965**, the **Contracts of Employment Act 1972**, the **Trade Union and Labour Relations Acts 1974 and 1976** and the **Employment Protection Act 1975.** Other provisions of these Acts relating to collective rights, to the **Advisory, Conciliation and Arbitration Service** etc., remain as before.

EMPLOYMENT SERVICE. A public ser-

Proportions of engagements made in 1966

Class of employee	Through the Ministry	Through private fee paying agencies
	per cent	per cent
Unskilled manual	26	negligible
Skilled or semi-skilled manual....................	22	negligible
Clerical and commercial	11	12
Managerial, executive and technical....................	94	3

vice designed to find suitable jobs for people and suitable people for jobs and therefore involving the possession of information about available jobs and applicants, and its advertisement, advisory interviewing, aptitude testing, **occupational guidance**, and the use of such other techniques and facilities as to promote the operation of the labour market. The operation of employment services differs from one country to another; see Richard A. Lester, *Manpower Planning in a Free Society,* Princeton University Press, 1972. In the United Kingdom, **employment exchanges** (now **employment offices** and **jobcentres**) were begun in a small way in 1905 and made general by the Labour Exchanges Act 1909, the system being reinforced by the **Employment and Training Act 1948** which became the legal foundation for the post-war employment service under the Ministry of Labour and of **Youth Employment Service** (q.v.). Specialised employment registers have mostly been discontinued, but special arrangements exist for hotels and catering, for nursing, and for commercial and clerical jobs as well as a **Professional and Executive Register** (q.v.); see also **Employment Transfer Scheme, Key Workers' Scheme** and **Nucleus Labour Force Scheme**. In December 1971 it was announced by the government that the employment service would be modernised (Department of Employment, *People and Jobs, A Modern Employment Service,* December 1971) by being developed as a self-managing **Employment Service Agency** (now **Division**), with separate offices and staff from that administering unemployment benefit, and with improved informational, interviewing and occupational guidance arrangements under the control of a **Manpower Services Commission** (q.v.); see **Employment and Training Act 1973.** Changes were also outlined for the **Profes-**

sional and Executive Register and for the Youth Employment Service. A Ministry of Labour sample survey of the attitudes and practices of employers among firms employing more than 100 workers showed the above proportions of engagements made through the Ministry and private fee paying agencies in 1966; see also **Jobcentres**. From 1 April 1978 the Employment Service Agency ceased to be a separate executive agency and became an operating division of the Manpower Services Commission.

EMPLOYMENT SERVICE AGENCY; see **Employment Service.**

EMPLOYMENT STATEMENT; see **employee reports.**

EMPLOYMENT AND TRAINING ACT 1948; see **Employment Service.**

EMPLOYMENT AND TRAINING ACT 1973. An Act providing for the establishment of the **Manpower Services Commission,** the **Employment Service Agency** and the **Training Services Agency,** amending the **Industrial Training Act 1964** (q.v.), and for the development of a **Careers Service** (q.v.).

EMPLOYMENT TRANSFER SCHEME formerly known as the **Resettlement Transfer Scheme.** A scheme administered by the Employment Service Agency to help unemployed men and women being made redundant in their home areas to transfer to work away from home.

EMPLOYMENT OF WOMEN, YOUNG PERSONS AND CHILDREN ACT 1920. An Act restricting the employment of women, young persons and children in industrial undertakings. It prohibits the employment of children, i.e. persons not over school age, in any industrial undertaking, and the employment of young persons, i.e. those between the age of school leaving and 18 years, at night, with some exceptions (see **night work**); see Ian Fife and E.A. Machin, *Redgrave's Health and Safety in Factories*, Butterworths, 1976, p. 1591 *et seq.*

EMPLOYMENTAL UNIONISM. An expression used by Sidney and Beatrice Webb (*The History of Trade Unionism, 1666-1920*, 1920 ed. p. 531) to describe the form of trade unionism adopted by the **National Union of Railwaymen** (1913) which they regarded as transcending **industrial unionism** 'in that it seeks to enrol in one union, not merely all sections of railway workers, but actually all who are employed by any railway undertaking, thus including not only the engineering and woodworking mechanics in the railway engineering workshops, but also the cooks, waiters and housemaids . . . the sailors and firemen on board the railway companies' fleets of steamers and . . . the compositors, lithographers and bookbinders whom the railways' printing works employ in the production of tickets, timetables, office stationery . . .'.

ENGINEER SURVEYORS' ASSOCIATION (ESA). A trade union founded in 1914 and organising personnel employed in the specialist function of surveying for insurance purposes. It merged with the **Association of Scientific, Technical and Managerial Staffs** in 1975.

ENGINEERING EMPLOYERS' FEDERATION (EEF). A federation of 20 local engineering employers' associations in the United Kingdom in 1976-77, estimated to cover some 6,000 establishments with a labour force of more than 1.1 million manual and some 600,000 staff workers. The EEF was founded in 1896 and is the largest industry-wide employers' organisation for industrial relations purposes in the country. For some years after amalgamation with the Midland Employers' Federation at the end of the first world war, the two organisations were known as the Engineering and National Employers' Federations, and from 1924 to 1961, when the pre-1918 title Engineering Employers' Federation was readopted, the style 'Engineering and Allied Employers' National Federation' was used. About one-quarter of the labour force of federated engineering firms is in general and electrical engineering, one-seventh in vehicles, and one-twentieth in metal manufacture, with smaller numbers in the manufacture of metal goods, marine engineering and in construction. The EEF negotiates industry-wide agreements on **minimum earnings levels** and conditions with the **Confederation of Shipbuilding and Engineering Unions**, from 1964 to 1972 in the form of **Package Deals**, and sectional agreements with unions for Telephone Exchange Equipment Installation, Lift Manufacture, etc. (see *Handbook of National Agreements*). It was notable in the past for its advocacy of **managerial prerogatives** (q.v.), especially in the lockouts of 1897-8 (see R.O. Clarke, 'The Dispute in the British Engineering Industry, 1897-8', *Economica*, May 1957, pp. 128-37), and 1922 (see A. Shadwell, *The Engineering Industry and the Crisis of 1922*, John Murray, 1922 and B. Pribićević, *The Shop Stewards Movement and Workers Control, 1910-1922*, Basil Blackwell, 1959). Its views have moderated and developed, especially in the 1960s, on this and other matters, particularly in the areas of workplace bargaining, training and services to member firms: A.I. Marsh, *Industrial Relations in Engineering*, Pergamon Press, 1965 and Royal Commission on Trade Unions and Employers' Associations, *Employers' Associations*, Research Papers 7, HMSO, 1967, Eric Wigham, *The Power to Manage*, Macmillan, 1972. *Address*: Broadway House, Tothill Street, London SW1H 9HQ. *Tel*: 01-839 1266.

ENGINEERING AND FOUNDRY WORKERS, AMALGAMATED UNION OF. An amalgamation, in January 1968, of the **Amalgamated Engineering Union** and the **Amalgamated Union of Foundry Workers** (q.v.), which was, in April 1970, amalgamated with the **Draughtsmen and Allied Technicians' Association** and the **Constructional Engineering Union** to form the **Amalgamated Union of Engineering Workers** (q.v.), of which it became the Foundry Section.

ENGINEERING JOINT TRADES MOVEMENT. An *ad hoc* organisation for the co-ordination, when necessary, of national claims and negotiations of engineering industry trade unions before the affiliation of the Amalgamated Engineering Union to the **Confederation of Shipbuilding and Engineering Unions** (q.v.) in 1947; see A.I. Marsh, *Industrial Relations in Engineering*, Pergamon Press, 1965.

ENGINEERING LONG-TERM AGREEMENTS; see Engineering Package Deal Agreements.

ENGINEERING PACKAGE DEAL AGREEMENTS or **Engineering Long-Term Agreements.** The name given to two national agreements between the **Engineering Employers' Federation** and the **Confederation of Shipbuilding and Engineering Unions** dated 22 December 1964 and 10 December 1968, the former running to 1 January 1968 and the latter to 31 December 1971. The agreements were the first of their kind in the industry on a national basis, both in respect of their **package deal** and of their long-term character. They provided both for general increases in rates of pay and for the progressive establishment of new **minimum earnings levels**, for improvements in holidays and other working conditions, and for undertakings on productivity. In August 1971, the unions refused to contemplate further package deal agreements, and subsequently broke off national negotiations and relations with the Employers nationally to continue bargaining at a district level, no further national agreement being made until 18 August 1972 and this relating to national minimum rates and holidays only (Reports of Proceedings at *Special Conferences between the Engineering Employers Federation and the Confederation of Shipbuilding and Engineering Unions,* 26 August 1971, 16 November 1971, 15 December 1971 and 14, 15 and 18 August 1972); see also A.I. Marsh, *Industrial Relations in Engineering,* Pergamon Press, 1965, Peter Smith, 'The Engineering Settlement' in K. Coates, Tony Topham and M. Barratt Brown, *Trade Union Register,* Merlin Press, 1969, and National Board for Prices and Incomes, *Pay and Conditions of Service of Engineering Workers,* Report No. 49, Cmnd. 3495, December 1967 and Report No. 104, Cmnd. 3931, February 1969.

ENGINEERING PROCEDURE AGREEMENT. A description usually applied to the **1922 Procedure Agreement, Manual Workers** made between manual worker unions and the Engineering and National Employers' Federations after the lockout of that year; sometimes confused with the **York Memorandum** (q.v.) and sometimes referred to as the **Managerial Functions Agreement** because of clauses in it giving management the formal right to make a wide range of workshop changes before agreement with workpeople or the exhaustion of procedure (see **managerial prerogatives**), leading to a counter demand from trade unions for the application of **status quo** (q.v.) to such situations. The agreement originated in the 1898 Terms of Settlement in the industry, and has been criticised on other counts — for its use of **employer conciliation,** for its failure to recognise **conveners,** for its alleged prolixity, and for its inadequacy in regulating shop floor relations in the industry (see A.I. Marsh and R.S. Jones, 'Engineering Procedure and Central Conference at York in 1959', *British Journal of Industrial Relations,* June 1964, A.I. Marsh, *Industrial Relations in Engineering,* Pergamon Press, 1965, A.I. Marsh and W.E.J. McCarthy, *Disputes Procedures in Britain,* Royal Commission on Trade Unions and Employers' Associations, Research Papers 2 (Part 2), HMSO, 1968, Ch. 2, and A.I. Marsh, 'The Staffing of Industrial Relations Management in Engineering', *Industrial Relations Journal,* Summer 1971. Minor changes were made in the agreement in 1955, and discussions were begun between the EEF and the CSEU on more thoroughgoing revisions in the later 1960s; these broke down, particularly on the status quo issue, and on 23 June 1971, a motion for withdrawal from the Procedure was passed at the annual meeting of the Confederation of Shipbuilding and Engineering Unions and subsequently implemented. The industry had no national procedure agreement between 1971 and April 1976 when a new agreement between the EEF, the CSEU and 16 individual unions came into operation, allowing for status quo and removing the York Central Conference as the last procedural stage.

ENGINEERING TRADES JOINT COUNCIL (ETJC); see Whitleyism.

ENGINEERING WORKERS, AMALGAMATED UNION OF (AUEW). An amalgamation in April 1970 of the Amalgamated Union of Engineering and Foundry Workers (AEF), the **Draughtsmen and Allied Technicians' Association** (DATA) and the **Constructional Engineering Union** (CEU) (q.v.). The Instrument of Amalgamation allowed for four sections, Engineering, Foundry, Technical and Supervisory, and Construction, each section retaining its own organisation, but coming together in a National Conference with a National Executive Council, the ultimate object being to create one union for the engineering industry. On amalgamation, the combined membership of the three unions was almost 1.4 million. A common rule book was drafted in 1972 but has never been implemented. AUEW and Engineering Section *Address*: 110 Peckham Road, London SE15 5EL. *Tel*: 01-703 4231. *TUC Affiliated Membership, 1977*: 1,168,990; Constructional Section. *Address*: 190 Cedars Road, Clapham, London SW4 0PP. *Tel*: 01-622 4451. *TUC Affiliated Membership, 1977*: 25,000; Foundry Section *Address*: 164 Chorlton Road, Brook's Bar, Manchester, M16 7NU. *Tel*: 061-226 1151; *TUC Affiliated Membership, 1977*: 56,479. AUEW/Technical, Administrative and Supervisory Section. *Address*: Onslow Hall, Little Green, Richmond, Surrey TW9 1QN. *Tel*: 01-948 2271. *TUC Affiliated Membership, 1977*: 161,607.

ENGINEERS' AND FIREMEN'S UNION, GRIMSBY STEAM AND DIESEL FISHING VESSELS. A trade union organising engineers and firemen on Grimsby trawlers. It was founded by fourteen engineers in 1896 and at one point in its history had 1,200 members; its membership subsequently declined; see *Federation News*, Vol. 10, No. 4, 1960, pp. N72-73. The union transferred its engagements to the **Transport and General Workers' Union** in 1976.

ENGINEERS' AND MANAGERS' ASSOCIATION (EMA). A trade union known until April 1977 as the **Electrical Power Engineers' Association** (EPEA). The EPEA, originally formed as the Association of Electrical Station Engineers in January 1913 and registered later in the same year as the Association of Electrical Engineers, adopted that title in 1918 and represented technical, scientific and managerial staff in the electricity supply industry only, dating its negotiating role in that industry from an arbitration award of that year which excluded the Electrical Trades Union from that function for grades above switchboard attendants. Following a decision of the Annual Delegate Conference in April 1976 to recruit engineers and managers in other occupations and industries, the present name of the Association was adopted, the title 'EPEA' being retained by members in electricity supply. In January 1977 the union absorbed the **Association of Supervisory and Executive Engineers** and later in the year the Westinghouse Engineering Staff Association, and the Shipbuilding and Allied Industries Management Association (1,600 members). *Address*: Station House, Fox Lane North, Chertsey, Surrey KT16 9HW. *Tel*: Chertsey (093-28)

64131/4. *TUC Affiliated Membership, 1977*: 44,000.

ENGRAVERS, UNITED SOCIETY OF (USE). A trade union formed in 1908 through the amalgamation of the Scottish and English engravers' societies, founded in 1888 and 1889 respectively. The Society was a craft union restricted to 'capable craftsmen, designers or efficient ancillary operatives'. It amalgamated with the **Society of Lithographic Artists, Designers, Engravers and Process Workers** in April 1973.

ENTICEMENT OF LABOUR. The poaching of workers of one employer by another employer analogous to the **poaching** of members of one union by another union (q.v.). Legal action in such cases is confined to an injunction to restrain the poaching employer from employing the individual concerned during his period of notice, or to action for procuring breach of contract, proof of which is usually difficult. Employers have commonly preferred to discourage enticement through their associations, e.g. as in engineering, where until recently a **Form of Inquiry** was used when setting on workpeople (now replaced by more informal methods) and in which public advertisement at grossly enhanced rates or including promises of exceptionally high earnings are regarded as a breach of faith with other federated employers. (A.I. Marsh, *Industrial Relations in Engineering*, Pergamon Press, 1965, p. 68.)

EOC. Equal Opportunities Commission; see **Sex Discrimination Act 1975.**

EPEA. Electrical Power Engineers' Association; see **Engineers' and Managers' Association.**

EPHEMERAL COMBINATIONS; see **ephemeral unions.**

EPHEMERAL UNIONS or **ephemeral combinations.** An expression used by Sidney and Beatrice Webb (*The History of Trade Unionism, 1666-1920*, 1919 ed., p. 22) to describe those short-lived organisations of workers which preceded the period of the Industrial Revolution and which failed to become 'continuous associations of wage-earners for maintaining and improving the conditions of their working lives'.

EQUAL OPPORTUNITIES COMMIS-

SION (EOC); see **Sex Discrimination Act 1975.**

EQUAL PAY. The payment of equal remuneration to all employees in an establishment or work unit who are performing the same kind (and amount) of work, regardless of race, sex, or other characteristic of the individual worker or workers concerned; in Britain usually thought of in terms of equal pay for women; now subject to the **Equal Pay Act 1970** (q.v.). **Trades Union Congress** resolutions on equal pay date from the 1890s, and in 1919 the House of Commons adopted a resolution in favour of equal pay in the Civil Service and in local government. Following the Royal Commission on Equal Pay, 1944-46, the government again accepted the principle, but it was not applied to **non-industrial civil servants** and to teachers until the 1950s (in seven instalments for civil servants from 1 January 1955 and for teachers from 1 May 1955). International Labour Organisation **Equal Remuneration Convention** (No. 100), 1951, lays down 'equal remuneration for men and women for work of equal value', and Article 119 of the Treaty of Rome, supplemented by a resolution of December 1961, appears to support a similar principle. For problems of implementing equal pay for reasons of difficulties of definition, of achieving equal opportunities and on grounds of cost; see G.J. Mepham, *Problems of Equal Pay*, Institute of Personnel Management, 1969; also 'Costs of Equal Pay', *Employment and Productivity Gazette*, Vol. LXXVIII, No. 1, January 1970, and P.J. Sloane and B. Chiplin, 'The Economic Consequences of the Equal Pay Act, 1970', *Industrial Relations Journal*, December 1970.

EQUAL PAY ACT 1970. An Act of Parliament designed to prevent, by 29 December 1975, discrimination on grounds of sex between the terms and conditions of employment of men and women; (see **equal pay**). The Act provides that equal treatment shall be given where women are employed on broadly similar work, or when a woman's job has been rated by **job evaluation** as equivalent to a man's, disputes as to equality of treatment being referred to **industrial tribunals**, and discrimination in collective agreements to the Industrial Court (now the **Central Arbitration Committee**). The UK government ratified the ILO **Equal Remuneration Convention** 1951 (No. 100) after the passing of the Act; see also **discrimination.**

EQUAL REMUNERATION CONVENTION 1951; see **Equal Pay Act 1970**, and **equal pay.**

EQUITY. British Actors' Equity Association; see **Actors' Equity Association, British.**

EQUITY SHOP CLAUSE; see **Actors' Equity Association, British.**

ERGONOMICS. Defined as the scientific study of the relationship between man and his working environment, K.F.H. Murrell (*Ergonomics: Man in His Working Environment*, Chapman and Hall, 1971) adds to this definition by describing 'working environment' to include tools, materials, and methods and organisation of work as well as ambient environment, and by describing 'man' to include both individuals and working groups and their characteristics, including capacities, abilities and limitations, and the more general environment of family life and relations with others. Defined in this way, ergonomics is seen as a focus for a number of technologies and fields of knowledge, from work study and design to anatomy, physiology and psychology.

ERLE COMMISSION. The **Royal Commission in Trade Unions, 1867-1869** under the chairmanship of Sir William Erle, former Lord Chief Justice of Common Pleas. The establishment of the Commission was a direct result of the **Sheffield Outrages** (q.v.). It produced eleven reports which led to the **Trade Union Act 1871** and the **Criminal Law Amendment Act 1871** which made changes in the law in favour of trade unions; see Sidney and Beatrice Webb, *History of Trade Unionism, 1666-1920*, 1919, p. 259 *et seq.* For other Royal Commissions on industrial relations generally; see **Cockburn Commission, Devonshire Commission, Dunedin Commission, Donovan Commission.**

ESA. Employment Service Agency (now **Department**) (q.v.).

ESCALATION CLAUSE. A clause in a contract for goods or services through which prices are automatically adjusted to take into account wage increases. The **National Board for Prices and Incomes** commented on the use of such clauses in the printing and other industries (*Wages, Costs and Prices in the Printing Industry*, Report No. 2, Cmnd. 2750, 17 August 1965, para 54), and proposed that such contracts should be reviewed for their effect upon the so-called wage-price spiral.

ESCALATOR CLAUSE. A provision found in many collective agreements in the United States designed to keep the real income of the worker constant during the period of a contract by providing for periodic wage adjustments to reflect changes in the BLS Consumer Price Index or other measure of living costs; sometimes accompanied by the device of the **annual improvement factor** (q.v.); see US Dept of Labor, *Escalator Clauses from Selected Collective Bargaining Agreements*, Washington DC, GPO (various dates). In Britain the nearest equivalent has been the **cost-of-living sliding scale** or, more recently, the notion of **threshold agreements** (q.v.); see also **indexation**.

ESCROW AGREEMENT. An arrangement in the United States whereby the parties agree to place a sum of money or valuables in the hands of a third party, especially during an industrial dispute, to be delivered in specified circumstances; e.g. to pay a wage increase if an arbitrator so awards, etc.

ESTABLISHED CIVIL SERVANT. A member of the Civil Service with a certificate from the Civil Service Department certifying that he satisfies the conditions laid down for permanent appointment; formerly a pensionable civil servant, but now no longer so, since the former division between established (pensionable) and unestablished (non-pensionable), has been abolished, all civil servants now being pensionable; see *The Civil Service*: Report of the Committee 1966-1968 (Chairman: Lord Fulton), Vol. 4 Section IV: Note by the Treasury. The Fulton Committee (Vol. I, Cmnd. 3638, June 1968, p. 48) recommended that the concept of establishment should be abolished on the grounds that it implied security of employment until retirement which went beyond what was genuinely needed; see **Fulton Report.**

ESTABLISHED SEAMAN; see **Established Service Scheme.**

ESTABLISHED SERVICE SCHEME. A scheme introduced in 1947 to provide security of employment and a single source of merchant seamen and designed to replace the Reserve Pool established by an Essential Work Order during the second world war. Under the scheme, the sup-

ply of seamen was jointly controlled by the British Shipping Federation, the Officers' Associations and the **National Union of Seamen**. An established seaman had priority of employment over an unestablished seaman and received a guarantee of employment in the form of a general service contract with the Merchant Navy Establishment Administration or a company service contract with a particular company. In 1973, however, all seamen were 'registered' and benefit became available for everyone. If no employment was available, an established seaman received **establishment benefit** (a supplement to unemployment benefit) related to his last earnings and enjoyed other privileges such as extra sickness benefits; in return he held himself ready for work and undertook to accept any suitable engagement offered; see D.H. Moreby, *Personnel Management in Merchant Ships*, Pergamon Press, 1968, pp. 199-200 and J. McConville, *The Shipping Industry in the United Kingdom*, International Institute for Labour Studies, 1977.

ESTABLISHMENT. (1) A unit of industry for certain statistical or industrial relations purposes, generally identifiable with a mine, plant, factory, etc. As used for the **Standard Industrial Classification** (SIC) (q.v.) and other official business statistics, the smallest unit which can provide the information normally required for an economic census, of, for example, employment, expenses, turnover, capital formation, at a particular address. Where distinct activities characteristic of different industries are carried out at one address, these are classified separately if separate data are available for them, and a single business carried on at a number of addresses may in certain circumstances be counted as a single establishment; see CSO, *Standard Industrial Classification 1968*, pp. iii-vi and *Statistical News*, November 1968. As used in federated engineering firms, under the 1922 Procedure Agreement, 'establishment' denoted a unit for industrial relations purposes and was described as 'the whole establishment, or sections thereof, according to whether the management is unified or sub-divided'. Handbook of National Agreements. *Procedure — Manual Workers*, II(3)(12). (2) The authorised numerical strength of a unit or department; hence 'below establishment', i.e. having fewer workers than authorised, etc., especially in the Civil Service or in the armed services; see also **established civil servant.**

ESTABLISHMENT BENEFIT; see **Established Service Scheme** (merchant navy).

ESTABLISHMENT OFFICER. An official responsible for all matters affecting the management and the employment of staff in a department, especially in the Civil Service.

ESTACODE. The name popularly given to regulations and instructions on pay and conditions of service in the Home Civil Service consolidated in the form of a manual and issued by the *Civil Service Department*. The regulations are subject to continuous review; see also **Crown Employment**.

EUROPEAN CONFEDERATION OF FREE TRADE UNIONS (ECFTU); see **International Labour Movement**.

EUROPEAN SOCIAL CHARTER. A document prepared by the Social Committee of the Council of Europe signed by member countries in 1961, ratified by the United Kingdom in July 1962 and coming into force following the fifth ratification in 1965. Part 1 contains a number of objectives which member states agree to accept, including the right of workers to safe and healthy working conditions; Part 2 provides for proper standards for those who work. Articles 5 and 6 deal with the right to organise and the right to bargain collectively; under Article 6 the contracting parties undertake to promote consultation and machinery for collective bargaining; it also recognises, with qualifications, the **right to strike** (q.v.). There is no machinery of enforcement of the Charter open to individuals, but the practice of states who are parties to the Charter is subject to examination by a committee of experts every two years. This committee found Britain in breach of a number of obligations in 1967, including Article 1, para. 2, employment discrimination on grounds of sex (since the subject of legislation under the **Equal Pay Act 1970** and the **Sex Discrimination Act 1975**), Article 10, para. 3, on grounds of inadequate facilities for the vocational training and retraining of adults, Article 18, paras 1, 2 and 3, on insufficiently liberal and over-complicated formalities for immigrant workers, Article 19, para. 8, on grounds that the UK had not done enough to promote co-operation between social services of different member states, and Article 29, para. 2, on difficulties put in the way of the reunion of migrant workers and their families; see D.J. Harris, 'The European Social Charter', 13 *International and Comparative Law Quarterly*, 1964.

EUROPEAN SOCIAL FUND. A fund established by the Treaty of Rome (arts 123-8) to improve employment opportunities for workers and thereby to raise standards of living; also to encourage spatial and occupational mobility within the European Community. On application by a Member State, the European Commission, which administers the Fund, meets 50 per cent of the expenditure incurred on such purposes as vocational re-training, resettlement, maintenance of income of workers while undertakings are being converted to other production etc. The UK has drawn on the Fund for various projects of this kind.

EUROPEAN TRADE UNION CONFEDERATION (ETUC). A confederation of 30 trade union federations from the 15 countries associated with the European Economic Community (EEC) and the European Free Trade Association (EFTA) established at Brussels on 9 February 1973. The ETUC replaced the European Confederation of Free Trade Unions formed in April 1969 and originally made up of seven free trade union federations in the six original members of the EEC. The countries involved are Austria, Belgium, the Federal Republic of Germany, Denmark, Finland, France, Great Britain, Iceland, Ireland, Italy, Luxembourg, Malta, the Netherlands, Norway, Switzerland, Sweden and Spain. The ETUC is said to represent almost 37 million organised workers. Its first President was Victor Feather, General Secretary of the **Trades Union Congress.** *Address:* 37 rue Montagne aux Herbes Potagères, 1000 Bruxelles, Belgium. *Tel:* 217.91.41 and 42.

EVENING SHIFT; see **part-time shift**.

EXCESS WORK ALLOWANCE (work study); see **allowances**. 'An addition to **standard time** for extra work occasioned by a temporary departure from standard conditions'. British Standards Institution, *Glossary of Terms Used in Work Study*, BS 3138, 1969, 36006.

EXCLUSION CLAUSE; see **disclaimer clause**.

EXCLUSIVE JURISDICTION AGREE-

MENT. An expression used in the Report of the Donovan **Royal Commission on Trade Unions and Employers' Associations 1965-1968,** Cmnd. 3623, June 1968, para. 691, p. 185. Defined by Victor Feather (Post Donovan Conference, *Private Sector,* Trades Union Congress March 1969, p. 22) as an agreement dealing with 'the right of a union to have the opportunity, without duplication of effort, to secure increased membership in a particular area in which they (sic) have been closely identified'; a variation on the idea of **spheres of influence** (q.v.).

EX-CRAFT UNION. A classification used by H.A. Clegg, A.J. Killick and Rex Adams (*Trade Union Officers,* Basil Blackwell, 1961, p. 17) to describe craft unions which have altered the basis of their membership, either by change of rule, or through amalgamation, or both, to embrace semi-skilled and unskilled workers, but which have maintained the constitutional provisions customary to craft unions (such as periodic re-election of officers) and whose councils, committees and full-time officer force are still dominated by apprenticed craftsmen, e.g. the **Amalgamated Engineering Union** (now the **Amalgamated Union of Engineering Workers,** Engineering Section), and the Electrical Trades Union (now the **Electrical, Electronic Telecommunication and Plumbing Union**).

EX GRATIA PAYMENT. A 'free-gift' payment made by management to a worker or workers; a device used in circumstances in which the employer wishes to make it known that the sum involved is discretionary and not subject to negotiation, e.g. a Christmas bonus, or a payment made in circumstances in which management wishes to provide recompense without conceding a principle. S.W. Lerner, J.R. Cable and S. Gupta (*Workshop Wage Determination,* Pergamon Press, 1969, pp. 48-9) doubt whether managements find it easy in practice to remove ex gratia payments from the negotiating area.

EX PARTE INJUNCTION. An **injunction** (q.v.) granted in the absence of the defendants under the 'interlocutory' jurisdiction of judges to give a remedy to a plaintiff for a short period, full argument of the case by both sides being heard at the end of that time; sometimes known as 'labour injunctions'. Ex parte injunctions were a feature of many of the leading cases in industrial relations in the 1960s - see, for example, **Ford v. Amalgamated Engineering and Foundry Workers' Union,** Torquay Hotels Ltd v. Cousins: K.W. Wedderburn *The Worker and the Law,* 2nd ed. Pelican, 1971. They may have the effect of resolving the dispute in the employer's favour before both sides can be heard in court on the legal merits of what workers have done, and have been outlawed in a number of countries, e.g. Canada and the USA. The **Trade Union and Labour Relations Act 1974,** s. 17 prohibits the use of ex parte injunctions in **trade disputes** unless all steps reasonable in the circumstances have been taken to notify the person or organisation concerned and give him or it an opportunity to make representations. A similar provision was made in the **Industrial Relations Act 1971.**

EXPECTANCY THEORY. An approach to **job-structuring** and job design adopted by J.R. Hackman and E.E. Lawler ('Employee relations to job characteristics', *Journal of Applied Psychology,* Vol. 5, No. 3, 1971, pp. 259-86) adopting the **hierarchy of needs** of Maslow, but not, like Herzberg (see **job enrichment**) and McGregor, assuming that all people have high order needs, want more responsibility, etc. While some people have such needs, and would therefore respond favourably to attempts to enrich their jobs, other people might respond better to improvements in pay, opportunities for forming social relationships on the job etc. Expectancy theory therefore makes the commonsense assumption that people will choose to behave in any situation in a way in which they believe that they will maximise the outcomes which they value most highly. It suggests that it may be wise to look at the needs of particular employees before coming to conclusions about increasing their responsibilities, etc. to increase **job satisfaction.**

EXPERIENCE CURVE; see **learning curve.**

EXPERIMENTAL RATE; see **temporary rate.**

EXPRESS TERMS; see **implied terms.**

EXTENDED HOURS. Hours worked by women and young persons in excess of the limits imposed by the Factories Acts in respect of daily hours or overtime. The **Factories Act 1961** limits the employment of women and young persons to 8 hours in any day or 48 hours in any week, lays down that working hours are to be between 7 a.m. and 8 p.m. (7 a.m. and 1 p.m. on Saturdays), that there is to be no Sunday work and that a maximum period of work without a break is 4½ hours; there is also a limit to weekly overtime of 6 hours, and an annual limit of 100 hours in any calendar year. (see Ian Fife and E.A. Machin, *Redgrave's Health and Safety in Factories,* Butterworths 1976, p. 279, *et seq.*). These hours can be varied by the Secretary of State for Employment by Exemption Order.

EXTENSION PROCEDURE; see Schedule 11 Claims.

EXTERNAL CONFERENCE. Under the **Engineering Procedure Agreement** — Manual Workers, 1 March 1976, Clause 15, a conference involving representatives of the local employers' association and local trade union officials as well as management representatives and shop stewards held on any appropriate issue when failure-to-agree has been recorded domestically. External Conferences differ from Local Conferences under the former 1922 Engineering Procedure Agreement principally in constituting the final stage in the procedure in all cases except those involving the interpretation or application of national agreements. After such a Conference, procedure is therefore exhausted, unless a special meeting of national representatives is called for (Clause 17).

EXTERNAL JOB REGULATION; see job regulation.

EXTERNAL MOBILITY; see labour mobility.

F

FAA. Film Artistes Association (q.v.).

FACILITIES FOR TRADE UNIONS. A topic which came into prominence in the late 1960s as a result of the growth of **workplace bargaining** and the Report of the Donovan **Royal Commission on Trade Unions and Employers' Associations 1965-1968** (Cmnd. 3623, June 1968) which recommended the review of such facilities by managements (para. 182). The **Commission on Industrial Relations,** in its report on *Facilities Afforded to Shop Stewards* (Cmnd. 4668, May 1971), while stressing that facilities arise from stewards' functions and need to be related to particular industrial environments, found that there was a general need to clarify the stewards' role and to formalise practices which were tacitly accepted, as well as to extend facilities in many instances. For an illustration of the general informality of facilities in engineering; see A.I. Marsh, E.O. Evans and P. Garcia, *Workplace Industrial Relations in Engineering*, Engineering Employers' Federation and Kogan Page, November 1971, p. 34 *et seq.* In June 1972 the United Kingdom government announced its intention to ratify International Labour Organisation Convention No. 135 (1971) and accept Recommendation No. 143 (1971) concerning the Protection and Facilities to be Afforded to Workers' Representatives in the Undertaking. The Convention supplements Convention No. 98 (Rights to Organise and Collective Bargaining, 1949), by providing that representatives shall enjoy effective protection against any act prejudicial to them, including dismissal, and such facilities as will enable them to carry out their functions promptly and efficiently, the Recommendation suggesting detailed measures to be adopted and listing the facilities concerned. This theme was taken up in the Employment Protection Act 1975, s. 53 which protects the activities of members of **independent trade unions** (q.v.) against their employers and (s. 58) provides for time off for members of such unions for these activities, guidance on this being given in a Code of Practice (see **Codes of Practice**). This Code entitled *Time-off For Trade Union Duties and Activities*, replaces paras 116-18 of the 1972 Industrial Relations Code of Practice, and came into effect on 1 April 1978.

FACTOR COMPARISON. An analytical method of **job evaluation** (q.v.), said to be little used in Britain. Jobs are examined in terms of selected factors, normally five factors in the case of manual workers — mental, physical and skill requirements, responsibility and working conditions. Key jobs are then identified and analysed, and on this basis, a scale of cash values prepared for each factor in the jobs, these values being subsequently applied to other jobs.

FACTORIES ACT 1961. An Act consolidating previous Factories Acts of 1937, 1948 and 1959 and the last of a long line of such Acts setting standards of cleanliness, overcrowding, temperature, ventilation and other factory conditions dating from the Health and Morals of Apprentices Act 1802; also concerned with safety, with the notification of accidents (see **accident book** and **notifiable accident**) and with the hours and holidays of women and young persons (see shift working). The **Health and Safety at Work Act 1974** (q.v.) contains powers to repeal or modify existing statutory provisions, including those of the Factories Act 1961. Under these powers the functions of factory inspectors have been transferred to inspectors appointed by the **Health and Safety Executive**. Penalties for offences previously committed under the 1961 Act have been transferred to the 1974 Act and also the making of subordinate legislation by Statutory Instruments. Since it is implicit in the 1974 Health and Safety at Work Act that existing statutory provisions will be progressively replaced by a system of regulations and approved Codes of Practice along the lines suggested by the Robens Committee (see **Robens Report**), the relevance of the 1961 Act is likely to diminish; see Ian Fife and E.A. Machin, *Redgrave's Health and Safety in Factories*, Butterworths, 1976. On the early history of factory legislation see B.L. Hutchins and A. Harrison, *A History of Factory Legislation*, King, 1926 and Frank Cass, 1966; also **Offices, Shops and Railway Premises Act 1963**.

FAIR COMPARISONS; see Priestley Formula.

FAIR DAY'S PAY; see fair day's work.

FAIR DAY'S WORK. A concept common to exponents of work study in the practice of the establishment of **standard times** acceptable to both workers and management; often associated with the concept of a **fair day's pay**, i.e. with the notion that, to be fair to both workers and management, an acceptable day's work ought to be accompanied by acceptable remuneration; 'A fair day's wage is for a fair day's work, the old time-honoured watchword', F. Engels, *Labour Standard*, 7 May 1881: hence the 'fair day's work' policy adopted by some companies (e.g. by subsidiaries of General Motors in Britain), that they seek to establish fair remuneration (usually as a **day rate**) for a fair level of performance; see also J.J. Gracie, *A*

Fair Day's Pay, Management Publications Trust, 1949, where the notion is extended to argue for a national **wages policy**, Hilde Behrend ('A Fair Day's Work', *Scottish Journal of Political Economy*, Volume VIII, June 1961, pp. 102-18), discussing the problems of defining a fair day's work, points out that the contract of employment lacks definition on the matter and that, although normative pressures in the workplace act as a guide, the notion of a fair day's work is abstract and vague, adding that 'factory production standards are considered fair, not because they are based on work measurement, but because they are judged and accepted as fair by all the parties concerned', and that it is 'mutual agreement which determines what production standards are accepted as right and are adopted'. A lengthy discussion of the concept of 'fairness' is to be found in R. Hyman and I. Brough, *Social Values and Industrial Relations*, Basil Blackwell 1975; see also **just wage, felt-fair pay.**

FAIR DEAL AT WORK. A policy statement on industrial relations issued by the Conservative Party in April 1968. The statement, which anteceded by two months the report of the Donovan **Royal Commission on Trade Unions and Employers' Associations 1965-1968** (q.v.), proposed a new legislative framework for British industrial relations in a comprehensive Industrial Relations Act. The **Industrial Relations Act 1971** subsequently enacted by the Heath government owed much to the thinking of *Fair Deal at Work*, though considerable changes of detail were made as a result of the Donovan Report and further consideration.

FAIR DISMISSAL; see unfair dismissal.

FAIR EMPLOYMENT AGENCY. A body established in Northern Ireland under the Fair Employment Act 1976 to promote equality of opportunity in employment between persons of different religious beliefs. The Agency is the primary enforcement body of the Act, which made illegal discrimination on political or religious grounds, though it can ultimately refer a case to the county court. It maintains a Register of Equal Opportunity Employers which have signed a Declaration of Principle and Intent to that effect.

FAIRFIELDS EXPERIMENT. Revolutionary changes in the use of modern management techniques, in inter-craft flexibility, and in relations between management and trade unions introduced into Fairfields shipyard from January 1966 when the assets and existing contracts of the bankrupt Fairfields Shipbuilding and Engineering Company were, with governmental support, purchased by a new company, Fairfields (Glasgow) Ltd. The changes were particularly associated with the initiatives of Sir Iain Stewart and James D. Houston who resigned shortly after the yard was merged into the **Upper Clyde Shipbuilders** group in February 1968; see Sydney Paulden and Bill Hawkins, *Whatever Happened at Fairfields?*, Gower Press, 1969, and Oliver Blandford and C.L. Jenkins, *The Fairfields Experiment,* Industrial Society, 1969, K.J.W. Alexander, *Fairfields: A Study in Industrial Change*, Allen Lane, The Penguin Press, 1970; see also **work-in.**

FAIR LIST. A form of **boycott** through which trade unions seek to discourage trading with unorganised firms. In Britain it is used in printing, but not apparently in other industries; see K.G.J.C. Knowles, *Strikes*, Blackwell, 1952, p. 16. In 1928 the TUC General Council reported to Congress on **fair lists** and **union labels** (q.v.) but took no further action on the matter.

FAIR WAGES CLAUSE; see **fair wages principle.**

FAIR WAGES PRINCIPLE. The principle that terms and conditions of employment of employees of government contractors should be not less favourable than those established for the particular trade or industry in the district concerned or, if there are no established standards, then the general level of terms and conditions observed by other employers whose general circumstances in the trade or industry are similar. The application of the fair wages principle has been secured by a succession of **Fair Wages Resolutions** of the House of Commons, the first dating from 1891 and the most recent passed in 1946. The current Resolution also provides that a government contractor must recognise the freedom of his workers to join trade unions and that he should be responsible for the observance of the Resolution by his sub-contractors. Questions arising out of the observance of the Resolution, which itself has no statutory force, are normally referred to the Central Arbitration Committee, if not otherwise settled e.g. by conciliation. The British Government has recommended that local authorities should incorporate **Fair Wages Clauses**

into their contracts; this has been generally, but not universally, implemented. The principle of the Resolution has been incorporated into a number of Acts, and nationalised industries normally insert a clause based on the Resolution in their contracts; see Ministry of Labour, *Industrial Relations Handbook*, HMSO, 1961 Ch. IX. In 1910 the government undertook to apply the Resolution to its own industrial employees, and this was confirmed in 1948, though the system was criticised by the National Board for Prices and Incomes (*Pay of Industrial Civil Servants*, Report No. 18, Cmnd. 3034, June 1966) as often failing to give industrial civil servants pay comparable with their counterparts in private industry; see also **Road Haulage Wages Act 1938, statutory fair wages,** and P.B. Beaumont, 'Experience under the Fair Wages Resolution of 1946', *Industrial Relations Journal*, Vol. 8, No. 3, Autumn 1977, pp. 34-42 and Brian Bercusson, *Fair Wages Resolutions*, Mansell, 1978.

FAIR WAGES RESOLUTION; see **fair wages principle.**

FALL-BACK PAYMENT; see **guarantee.**

FAMILIARISATION CURVE; see **learning curve.**

FAMILY WAGE; see **just wage.**

FARAMUS v. FILM ARTISTES ASSOCIATION (1964) AC 925. A case in which it was ruled by the House of Lords that the plaintiff, who had been treated as a member of the union for a number of years, had no grounds for claiming that he was in fact a member since he had been admitted contrary to rule. K.W. Wedderburn, *Cases and Materials on Labour Law*, CUP, 1967 p. 573 *et seq.*

FARMERS' UNION, NATIONAL (NFU). An employers' organisation formed in 1908 primarily to offset the political, economic and marketing disadvantages of the small scale and fragmented nature of agricultural production. Its present membership is in the region of 140,000 in some 1,200 local and 48 County Branches, and includes some 80 per cent of full-time commercial farmers, including horticulturalists, in England and Wales where it is regarded by governments as the official voice of agriculture (the National Farmers' Union of Scotland being also recognised north of the Border, the Ulster Farmers' Union in Northern Ireland and since 1978 the Farmers' Union of Wales in the Principality). The NFU combines the activities of a trade association and an **employers' association** for industrial relations purposes and has a statutory right to nominate the employer representatives on the **Agricultural Wages Board** (q.v.). *Address*: Agriculture House, Knightsbridge, London SW1X 7NJ. *Tel*: 01-235 5077.

FAST. Function Analysis System Technique; see **value analysis**.

FAT also **fat work; fat money.** Extra payment for handling difficult or 'advantageous' printing matter (leaded matter, standing headings, advertisements, table work and small type, for example), compared with the 'Jean' — solid matter, large type etc. A.E. Musson, *The Typographical Association*, OUP, 1954, p. 174). Hence jobs which for one reason or another earn better money than others; sometimes by extension, payment for work not done, e.g. in national newspapers a charge made by piece case and linotype **ships**, for material already set and delivered for insertion (Economist Intelligence Unit; *Survey of the National Newspaper Industry*, 1966 pp. 120-1). Also in payment by result schemes, **fat rates**, rates which are loose by contrast with rates which are 'lean' or 'tight'.

FAT MONEY; see **fat.**

FAT RATES; see **fat.**

FAT WORK; see **fat.**

FATHER OF THE CHAPEL (FOC); see **chapel.**

FATIGUE ALLOWANCE; see **relaxation allowance.**

FAWLEY PRODUCTIVITY AGREEMENTS; see **productivity bargaining.**

FBU; see **Fire Brigades Union,** also Federation of Broadcasting Unions (see **Broadcasting Staff, Association of**).

FEATHERBEDDING. Practices by trade unions or work groups resulting in payment for work not performed, overmanning of machines, or the existence of non-essential jobs, particularly in the USA; see also **restrictive labour practices, protective practices, underemployment,**

make-work practices, P. Jacobs, *Dead Horse and the Featherbird*, Santa Barbara Center for the Study of Democratic Institutions, 1962; Paul A. Weinstein (ed.), *Featherbedding and Technological Change*, D.C. Heath and Co, Boston, 1965.

FEDERATED CHAPEL or **federated house chapel;** see **chapel.**

FEDERATED FIRM. A firm or establishment which, in its dealings with trade unions, is in membership of an employers' organisation established for purposes of industrial relations or an **employers' association** (q.v.); hence **non-federated firm**, a firm which is not associated with such an organisation and negotiates with trade unions directly and without any direct relationship with other employers; (see A.I. Marsh, *Industrial Relations in Engineering*, Pergamon Press, 1965, p. 51 for reasons for firms being non-federated). The obligations of a federated firm to its employers' organisation may vary from one industry to another, and also the services received. The expression 'federated firm' is in two senses a misnomer: it is frequently the case that the **establishment** rather than the firm is a basis for membership, and membership itself is frequently to a federated association rather than directly to a federation.

FEDERATED UNION OF EMPLOYERS (FUE). An employers' association in the Republic of Ireland representing industry and business on all questions relating to industrial relations and to labour and social matters. Where necessary it participates on the management side in negotiations with trade unions in addition to giving advice to member companies and branches on industrial relations. The FUE is the most important, and in membership terms the most substantial of the 20 or so employers' unions holding negotiating licences in the Republic. *Address*: 8 Fitzwilliam Place, Dublin 2. *Tel*: Dublin 65126.

FEDERATION. A form of organisation, either of trade unions or of employers' associations, in which limited authority is given to a central body for negotiating or other purposes, each constituent organisation retaining substantial autonomy, e.g. in the former **Printing and Kindred Trades Federation, National Federation of Building Trades Employers, Engineering Employers' Federation** (q.v.). Described by the Trades Union Congress (*Trade Union Structure and Closer Unity*, TUC, 1947, p. 21) as 'a loose form of industrial unionism . . . where the industrial, craft or the general workers' unions who are concerned in any industry may get together to pursue jointly the problems affecting the industry with which they are all concerned'. Sidney and Beatrice Webb (*Industrial Democracy*, 1898, p. 837 *et seq.*) considered federation the best and most likely solution to problems of fragmentation of trade union organisation. In practice it has played a more uncertain role, and the future of federations is difficult to predict; (see John Hughes, *Trade Union Structure and Government*, Royal Commission on Trade Unions and Employers' Associations, Research Paper 5 (Part 1), 1967 p. 34 *et seq.*). **Confederation**, as in **Confederation of British Industry** (q.v.) is sometimes taken to imply a federation of federations; Fowler's *Modern English Usage*, 2nd ed., revised by Sir Ernest Gowers, OUP, 1965, comments: 'Whether there is, or ever has been, any precise difference in the ways in which confederation and federation are used may well be doubted'; see also **employers' association**.

FEDERATION OF BROADCASTING UNIONS; see **Broadcasting Staff, Association of.**

FEDERATION OF CIVIL ENGINEERING CONTRACTORS; see **Civil Engineering Contractors, Federation of.**

FEDERATION OF EMPLOYERS' ORGANISATIONS; see **federation.**

FEDERATION OF INDEPENDENT TRADE UNIONS; see **Independent Trade Unions, Federation of.**

FEDERATION OF INSURANCE STAFF ASSOCIATIONS; see **Insurance Staff Associations, Federation of.**

FEDERATION OVERTIME; see **overtime.**

FELT-FAIR PAY. A concept attributable to Elliott Jaques (*Equitable Payment*, Heinemann, 2nd ed., 1970) and resulting from studies in the **Glacier Project** (q.v.). Jaques suggests that individuals have subjective standards of fair payment which relate to the degree of responsibility of their work, and that this can be assessed by the time-span during which they exercise discretion without reference to their superior; see **time-span, fair day's pay, effort bargain.** Some critics regard the phenomenon of felt-fair pay as observable, but the suggested basis for it too narrow, e.g. G. Routh (*Occupation and Pay in Great Britain 1906-60*, CUP, 1965, p. 149): 'We can accept the existence of this intuitive knowledge (or something answering to that description) without accepting Dr Jaques' ascription of it to a single variable - the "time-span of discretion"'.

FELT HATTERS AND ALLIED WORKERS, AMALGAMATED SOCIETY OF JOURNEYMEN. A trade union formed by the amalgamation of the Hatters' Mutual Association and the Felt Hat Body Makers in 1879. Trade union organisation in the industry dates from the nineteenth century, first as the United Felt Makers of Great Britain and Northern Ireland and later as the Journeymen Hatters of Great Britain and Northern Ireland, a union which split as a result of mechanisation into the two organisations forming the 1879 amalgamation. The union is said to have been the first in the country to employ the **union label** (q.v.). It organises men only and shares a common general secretary with the **Amalgamated Felt Hat Trimmers and Wool Formers of Great Britain**, which organises only women. F. Worthington, 'The Hatters', *Federation News*, Vol. 1, No. 2, 1951. *Address*: 14 Walker Street, Denton, Manchester M34 3LH. *Tel*: 061-336 2450. *TUC Affiliated Membership 1977*: 689.

FELT HAT TRIMMERS AND WOOL FORMERS, AMALGAMATED ASSOCIATION OF. A trade union for women in the felt hat trade, formed in 1888 from a number of district organisations dating from 1884. The union shares a common general secretary with the **Amalgamated Society of Journeymen Felt Hatters and Allied Workers** (q.v.) which organises male workers in the industry. *Address*: 14 Walker Street, Denton, Manchester M34 3LH. *Tel*: 061-336 2450. *TUC Affiliated Membership 1977*: 642.

FERRYBRIDGE SIX. Six former industrial staff employees at Ferrybridge 'C' power station, members of the unrecognised Electrical Supply Union (ESU) who alleged that their dismissal by the Central Electricity Generating Board for non-membership of any of the four unions signatory to the National Joint Industrial Council for the Electricity Supply Industry Agreement was unfair (see **unfair dis-**

missal). An industrial tribunal meeting in Leeds in February 1976 found that Part 14 of the Agreement, under whose provisions the men were dismissed, was a valid **union membership agreement** within the terms of the Trade Union and Labour Relations Act 1974, but that the dismissal was unfair on the grounds that there did not exist under Part 14 a consistent practice for the CEGB to insist that employees should be members of the four signatory unions. The tribunal made an award of compensation, but not reinstatement. The ESU has subsequently ceased to operate.

FIET. International Federation of Commercial, Clerical and Technical Employees; see **International Trade Secretariats.**

FIFTH DIRECTIVE. A description commonly applied to a proposal for a Fifth Directive of the European Economic Community to co-ordinate the laws of member states as regards the structure of their limited liability companies and especially on the role of employees in relation to that structure, i.e. to **workers' participation** (q.v.). The proposal was submitted to the Council of Ministers in October 1972 (Supplement 10/72, Bull. EC.) and became part of the social action programme which it had adopted in January 1974 to involve workers or their representatives in the life of undertakings in the Community. It proposed, *inter alia*, that companies should be required to organise themselves into a two-tier structure, i.e. in the form of a supervisory (or policy) board consisting of non-executive directors to control the company and a management (or executive) board responsible for its day-to-day activities. Worker participation on the supervisory board should be compulsory in companies employing 500 or more workers, either on the basis of one-third of its members being appointed by the workers as representatives as in the Federal Republic of Germany (see **Betriebsräte**) or by the supervisory board appointing, as in the Netherlands, its own worker representatives, subject to the right of enterprise councils of employees to oppose the candidates put forward. These proposals were strongly resisted by employers in the United Kingdom. In September 1975 the Commission issued a 'green paper' (Bull. EC. Supplement 8/75) entitled *Employee Participation and Company Structure*, explaining the rationale of its position and the principles involved in the Fifth Directive and suggesting that, to meet differing national positions, an attempt should be made to construct a framework which should 'leave discretion to member states as to the precise models which they may adopt' (p. 46); see also **industrial democracy, Bullock Report.** The Callaghan government's White Paper *Industrial Democracy* (Cmnd. 7231, May 1978) represents a positive step in the direction of British reconciliation with the Fifth Directive.

50-50 SHARING PLAN see **Halsey Premium Bonus System.**

FILM ARTISTES' ASSOCIATION (FAA). A trade union catering almost entirely for crowd artistes which was founded in 1932; it is subject to widely fluctuating membership, but this rarely falls below 1,500. *Address:* 61 Marloes Road, London W8 6LF. *Tel:* 01-937 4567/8. *TUC Affiliated Membership 1977:* 1,858.

FINAL OFFER ARBITRATION; see **employer's final offer.**

FINE TUBES DISPUTE. A dispute beginning in 1970 between the Amalgamated Union of Engineering Workers and the Transport and General Workers Union and Fine Tubes Ltd a federated engineering firm and a wholly owned subsidiary of the Superior Tube Company of Norristown Pennsylvania, USA. Sanctions by the unions against the company began in June 1970 and were still continuing when a Committee of Inquiry under the chairmanship of Professor A.D. Campbell met in September 1971. The unions complained that the company had refused to honour the engineering national agreement of December 1968, had obstructed trade union recognition and locked out striking members. The Inquiry concluded that the issue of the 49 members involved had to be settled and that the unions should remove the duress of which the company complained and criticised negotiation and consultation arrangements at the company.

FINES; see **deductions.**

FIRE BRIGADES UNION (FBU). A trade union originating in the Firemen's Trade Union in 1918 and changing to its present title in 1930. The union spread from London to the provinces between the wars, but its growth was especially rapid after the creation of wartime National Fire Service in 1941, and it now claims to organise over 85 per cent of whole-time firemen in Britain, in addition to part-time (retained) firemen. It represents the workers' side of the National Joint Council for Local Authorities Fire Brigades and negotiates pay, conditions and hours for the ranks of firemen, leading firemen and sub officers. For matters affecting Station Officers and higher ranks, the FBU representatives on the NJC are joined by the National Association of Fire Officers. As a result'of the Board of Arbitration under the Chairmanship of Sir William Ross (the **Ross Award**), 23 January 1952 it lost its claim to a traditional parity between the pay and conditions of firemen and police constables which it asserted had existed until the application of Industrial Court Award 2249, 1950; the union had its first national strike at the end of 1977; see Frederick Radford, *Fetch the Engine*, FBU, 1950, and Fire Brigades Union, *Fifty Years of Service, 1918-1968*. *Address*: Bradley House, 59 Fulham High Street, London SW6 3JN. *Tel*: 01-736 2157. *TUC Affiliated Membership 1977*: 30,000.

FIRE OFFICERS, NATIONAL ASSOCIATION OF. An association formed in 1942 to represent officers of the National Fire Service in England, Wales and Scotland. When the NFS reverted to local authority control in 1948, a single National Joint Council was formed as the negotiating body on which all ranks except Chief Fire Officers and Firemasters were represented. The Association became the fire officers' representative organisation on this body, with a separate and autonomous Officers' Committee within the NJC. It has concerned itself mainly with the maintenance of differentials and claims a membership of more than two-thirds of serving officers. *Address*: 6 Westow Hill, Upper Norwood, London SE19 1RX. *Tel*: 01-670 5474.

FIRE PRECAUTIONS ACT 1971. An Act restricting the use of certain classes of premises unless there is in force for them a fire certificate under the Act. The original Act provided that no fire certificate could be required in respect of factory premises; an amendment effected by the Health and Safety at Work Act 1974 gave the Secretary of State the power to bring premises within the scope of the Act by designating 'use as a place of work' and this has been done with respect to factories, shops, offices and railway premises except where these involve fewer than 20 people. Fire safety is now supervised by fire authorities which control the issue of fire certificates (Fire Precautions (Factories, Offices, Shops and Railway Premises) Order 1976, SI 1976, No. 2009).

FIRST DIVISION ASSOCIATION. The Association of First Division Civil Servants; see **First Division Civil Servants, Association of.**

FIRST DIVISION CIVIL SERVANTS, ASSOCIATION OF (FIRST DIVISION ASSOCIATION). A trade union formed in 1918 to represent senior grades within the Administrative Class of the Civil Service and since that time extended to include museum keepers, statisticians, economists, lawyers, HM Inspectors of Schools and HM Inspectors of Taxes. It is a constituent member of the Civil Service National Whitley Council Staff Side and affiliated to the Trades Union Congress in July 1977. *Address*: Minster House, 272-4 Vauxhall Bridge Road, London SW1. *Tel*: 01-834 8843/4.

FIRST LINE SUPERVISOR; see **supervisor** and **foreman.**

FITU. Federation of Independent Trade Unions; see **Independent Trade Unions, Federation of.**

FIXED PAYMENT SYSTEM. Any **pay structure** or **payment system** in which earnings do not vary or fluctuate over the pay period, i.e. in which the worker is paid a straight **time rate**, an **upstanding wage**, a fixed **salary** etc., including most forms of **measured daywork.**

FIXED SHIFT. An arrangement whereby an individual, or a group of individuals, in a plant or establishment working more than one shift, works continuously on the same shift, e.g. on permanent days or permanent nights; the opposite of **rotating shift** and **alternating shift** (q.v.); see also **shift working.**

FIXED-TERM AGREEMENTS. Collective agreements remaining in force for an agreed period of time, say for one, two or three years, as distinct from agreements on which no termination date is put, it being. open to either party to request revision or replacement of an agreement on notice or when required (**open-ended agreements**). Fixed-term agreements were traditionally rare in British industrial relations. Long term agreements came briefly into favour in the 1960s; see R.F. Banks, 'Long Term Agreements and Package Deals', *Industrial Welfare*, Vol. XLVII, October 1965. The onset of inflation after that period, and the development of **incomes policy** encouraged annual agreements; see **twelve month rule**. Sometimes abbreviated to **term agreements** or described as **fixed-period agreements**, e.g. in J.F.B. Goodman and T.G. Whittingham, *Shop Stewards in British Industry*, McGraw-Hill, 1969, p. 147.

FIXED WAGES; see incentive payment system.

FIXED WORKING HOURS. An arrangement whereby **working hours** are fixed between a set starting and set finishing time each day, as contrasted with some forms of **shift work, staggered hours, rational working hours, variable working hours** and **flexible working hours**; see J. Harvey Bolton, *Flexible Working Hours*, Anbar Publications Ltd, 1971.

FLAT RATINGS; see rating.

FLEXIBLE WORKING HOURS (FWH, FLEXTIME OR FLEXITIME). A practice according to which workers are allowed to arrange their starting and stopping times to suit their personal requirements, provided that they work for a 'core time' each day (say 10 a.m. to 4 p.m.), and make up within a given period the total number of hours for which they have contracted to work; mostly found among white collar workers, but not limited to them. The system, which is intended partly to stagger working hours and partly as a form of **job enrichment**, has been adopted by a number of German, Austrian, Swiss and French companies; in Britain some 500 organisations employing about 100,000 employees are said to have adopted FWH by the beginning of 1974; see P.J. Sloane, *Changing Patterns of Working Hours*, Department of Employment Manpower Paper No. 13, 1975; see also J. Harvey Bolton, *Flexible Working Hours*, Anbar Publications Ltd, 1971 and Institute of Personnel Management, *Flexible Working Hours*, IPM Information Report 12, September 1972; also **fixed working hours, staggered working hours, rational working hours, variable working hours.**

FLEXIBILITY. The relaxing of **demarcation** between crafts, trades or jobs by workers being willing to perform tasks which are ancillary to these crafts, trades or jobs as defined or customary in their particular establishments, e.g. for a fitter to perform simple electrical work, for a painter not to wait for an electrician to remove an electrical fitting. Flexibility provisions have been a feature of some **productivity agreements**, e.g. the Vosper Thornycroft Woolston Works, Labour and Wages Structure Agreement, 30 August 1967, which places trades into groups, and provides that 'all workers within a group of trades shall be versatile in their employment and may, within the limits of their own capabilities, perform any work normally carried out by their group. They will also carry out any work to further their job, using such necessary tools within their capabilities'. Flexibility is, of course, advocated in order to make more efficient use of manpower; see **restrictive practices**. It may be associated with, or overlap into, provisions for **interchangeability** (q.v.).

FLEXTIME (FLEXITIME); see flexible working hours.

FLINT GLASS WORKERS, NATIONAL UNION OF. A union formed in 1948 by amalgamation of two old established organisations, the National Union of Glass Cutters and Decorators and the National Flint Glassmakers' Friendly Society. It is mainly based in the Stourbridge area, where the manufacture of crystal glass is centred, but also has members in other parts of the country. *Address*: 4 Prospect Hill, Stourbridge, Worcs. *Tel*: Stourbridge 3467.

FLIXBOROUGH DISASTER. An explosion at the Flixborough chemical plant of Nypro (UK) Ltd on 1 June 1974, which killed 28 people, injured many more and caused damage valued at more than £30m; claimed as Britain's worst industrial accident above ground. A Court of Inquiry under s. 84 of the Factories Act 1961, with Mr Roger Parker, QC as Chairman, concluded that the explosion was caused by the ignition of a massive vapour cloud of cyclohexene escaping under pressure from a temporarily installed and faulty by-pass assembly. A failure of this kind was not covered by the factory legislation then in force and no prosecutions therefore resulted. It was subsequently claimed by the Health and Safety Commission that legislation under the **Health and Safety at Work Act 1974** would ensure better control over major hazard plants of the Flixborough kind.

FLOATER. A casual worker on the docks who prefers this status and 'floats' from gang to gang picking up the jobs which he thinks will bring in the most money; T.S. Simey (ed.), *The Dockworker,* Liverpool University Press, 1954, pp. 70-9, and Final Report of the *Committee of Inquiry under the Rt Hon. Lord Devlin into certain matters concerning the Port Transport Industry,* Cmnd. 2734, 1965, p. 6.

FLOOR-TO-FLOOR TIME; see **allowed time**.

FLYING PICKETS. Squads moved from site to site, often in coaches, to act as strike pickets (see **picketing**). The use of such mobile pickets in Britain first became evident during the national miners' and building workers' strikes of 1972. While nothing in the law of picketing requires that pickets should consist exclusively of workers employed at each factory or site to be picketed, flying pickets became associated at that time with violent behaviour and **mass picketing** (see **Saltley Incident, Shrewsbury Pickets** and **Grunwick Dispute**), by 'turning picketing into an offensive action': Robert Taylor, 'Pickets and the Law', *New Society,* 21 November 1974.

FOC; see *chapel*.

FOC LISTS. Lists of preferred trade union members awaiting employment kept by **fathers of the chapel** in the national newspaper industry; sometimes known as **buddy lists**.

FOLDED-ARMS STRIKE; see **ca'canny**.

FOOTINGS. Entrance or gratitude money, payable when a man took up a new job (Works Rules, 1840) see Kenneth Hudson, *Working To Rule; Railway Workshop Rules, A Study of Industrial Discipline,* Adams and Dart, 1970, p. 19. OED dates this term from 1710.

FOOTPLATEMEN; see **Locomotive Engineers and Firemen, Associated Society of.**

FOOTWEAR, LEATHER AND ALLIED TRADES, NATIONAL UNION OF (NUFLAT). A union formed in January 1971 as a result of a merger between the National Union of Boot and Shoe Operatives (NUBSO), the Society of Leatherworkers and the Union of Leather-

workers and Allied Trades. NUBSO, the major partner in the merger, was formed in 1874, having originally been called the National Union of Boot and Shoe Riveters and Finishers. It was principally organised in order to cope with the problems arising from the trend from a hand-sewn craft industry into a machine-made trade, especially the need for satisfactory systems of payment. Until the 1890s, development was mainly through local joint **Boards of Conciliation and Arbitration**. A major conflict between the union and the Manufacturers' Federation in 1895 led to Terms of Settlement which included the establishment of a **Guarantee Fund** to which each side contributed £1,000. On default by either side a claim can be made by the Federation or by the Union if a notified strike at a factory lasts for more than three days, and fines have varied in the fifteen cases to date from £5 to £300. The National Agreement negotiated in February 1919 established the pattern of wages structure for the industry which has remained ever since. Agreements also cover ancillary industries concerned with cut sole, built heel, last, toe puff and stiffener and heel design and manufacture; see *Fifty Years, The History of the National Union of Boot and Shoe Operatives 1875-1924,* NUBSO, 1924; Alan Fox, *History of the National Union of Boot and Shoe Operatives,* Basil Blackwell, 1958. *Address:* The Grange, Earls Barton, Northampton NN6 0JH *Tel:* 0604 810326. *TUC Affiliated Membership, 1977:* 66,553.

FOOTWEAR MANUFACTURERS' ASSOCIATION; see **British Footwear Manufacturers' Association.**

FORD v. AMALGAMATED ENGINEERING AND FOUNDRY WORKERS' UNION AND OTHERS (1969) IWLR 339. A case involving injunctions sought by the Ford Motor Company in February 1969 to restrain the Amalgamated Engineering and Foundry Workers Union and the Transport and General Workers' Union from furthering an official strike against the company and to make mandatory the countermanding of the strike declaration. Legal action was subsequently dropped by the company after judgement by Lane J. that collective agreements of the kind involved were unenforceable because of the lack of intention of the negotiators to create legal relations. For discussion of the case; see Roy Lewis, 'The Legal Enforceability of Collective Agreements, *British Journal of Industrial*

Relations, Vol. VIII, No. 3, November 1970; see also **injunction**.

FOREIGNERS. (1) Objects worked or repaired in works time without consent, or made and taken out of factories without permission: (2) **illegal men** (q.v.) '. . . such a one as hath not served seven years at the art of printing, under a lawful master printer, as an apprentice'; *The Case and Proposal of the Free Journeymen Printers in and about London,* 1666.

FOREMAN. A **supervisor** (q.v.); an employee charged to oversee the work of others, not usually expected to operate machines or work with tools, and hence superior to a **chargehand,** or working chargehand, but not normally considered managerial in status; usually classed as **staff** and monthly rather than hourly paid, but not invariably so. The precise status of the foreman varies from one company and factory or workplace to another, and may span more than one grade; see **first-line supervisor** and **second-line supervisor.** The origin of the term is said to be hybrid, one meaning being associated with the 'foreman' or lead man who had the forward position in gangs of ditch diggers and tow rope pullers, another with the ganger who obtained labour and hired this to entrepreneurs (see **contract system** and **labour-only contracting**) and a third with the still current notion of the foreman of a jury. The decline in status of the foreman has been variously associated with the growth of mass production, with trade union development and the **shop steward,** with the proliferation of staff specialists arising out of expanding technology and **scientific management,** and with the hierarchical structures of modern management. A. Hamlin, K. Thurley and D. Voon (*Essential Facts on the British Foreman,* Institute of Industrial Supervisors, 1965) in a survey of 'shop floor supervisors', found one-in-five recruited from outside his company, and two-thirds without paper qualifications, almost 60 per cent being selected by informal methods only. For a study of the changing role of the foreman, see D. Dunkerley, *The Foreman,* Routledge and Kegan Paul, 1975.

FOREMEN AND STAFF MUTUAL BENEFIT SOCIETY LTD. (FSMBS). A company limited by guarantee registered on 30 January 1970 under the Company Acts 1948 to 1967 to provide benefits and transact insurance business for its members. The FSMBS was formerly registered as a Friendly Society. It was originally instituted in 1899 to provide foremen with benefits comparable to those provided by trade unions, and eligibility for membership was later extended to all employees in the engineering, shipbuilding and allied trades holding positions of trust or employed in management, technical or commercial capacities. The Society was criticised by trade unions as anti-union in providing benefits, under Rule 7, for non-union members only, and such a rule was considered by the **Royal Commission on Trade Unions and Employers' Associations, 1965-1968** (Cmnd. 3623, 1968 pp. 62-4) to be incompatible with Friendly Society status. Rule 7 was subsequently (May 1969) removed by the Society following a private Bill promoted in Parliament by the **Association of Supervisory, Technical and Managerial Staffs,** the society later changing its legal form to one of a limited company. *Address:* 190 West George Street, Glasgow C2.

FORMALISATION. In the Donovan **Royal Commission on Trade Unions and Employers' Associations 1965-1968** (Cmnd. 3623, June 1968) regarded principally as the process of moving from the use of informal **custom and practice** on industrial relations in a company or establishment to that of written and formal agreements either on substantive matters, or procedural, or both. Such formalisation inevitably also suggests more detailed agreements; see *Examination of Grievances and Communications within the Undertaking,* International Labour Office, Geneva, 1965, which in this context describes 'formality' as 'the nature and extent of procedural details such as written submissions and the number of possible steps' in procedure. Some writters suggest that formality may not be confined to the criterion that agreements or arrangements are committed to paper; for example, H.A. Clegg (*The System of Industrial Relations in Great Britain,* Basil Blackwell, 3rd ed. 1976) considers that 'formality implies that an arrangement is explicit, not that it must be written down or signed'. In his view commitment to writing and the addition of signatures assist formality, but are not essential to it.

FORM OF INQUIRY. A written sheet of particulars formerly used by **employers' associations** and particularly by the **Engineering Employers' Federation,** for use by a firm proposing to hire a particular worker; the form was sent for comment to his previous employer, including a note on whether he was willing to release him from employment or on his previous conduct if he had already left or been sacked. The Form, now generally abandoned, was designed in part to prevent **enticement of labour;** it could also be used to operate a black list of workers whom employers considered undesirable; see **enticement of labour**.

FORTY-HOUR WEEK CONVENTION (No. 47) 1935; see **hours of work**.

FOUNDRY WORKERS, AMALGAMATED UNION OF (AUFW). A trade union which became, by amalgamation, the Foundry Section of the **Amalgamated Union of Engineering and Foundry Workers** (AEF), in 1968, and of the **Amalgamated Union of Engineering Workers** in April 1970. The union traces its origins to the formation of the Friendly Iron Moulders' Society in 1809, the earliest of craft organisations in the trade. It was established by amalgamation of the Ironfounding Workers' Association and the United Metal Founders' Society in 1946 and, before merging in the AEF, could claim to be the only large union (almost 63,000 members) *exclusively* organising foundry workers, the remaining unions having no more than 8,000 members; see H.J. Fyrth and Henry Collins, *The Foundry Workers: A Trade Union History,* AUFW, 1959.

FOUR-DAY WEEK. The rearrangement of total weekly working hours on a four-rather than, as currently, on a five- (or sometimes five-and-one-half) day basis. It is claimed by some observers that the 4-day, 40-hour workweek is a growing development in the United States; see Riva Poor (ed.), *4 Days, 40 Hours,* Pan Books, 1972. In Britain, few firms have adopted the practice, except some of those with continuous shift working. It has, however, been referred to by the Trade Union Congress (*Review of Collective Bargaining Developments,* No. 1, May 1972), linked to the priority to be given to the objective of a 35-hour week.

FRACTIONAL BARGAINING. (1) Defined by Neil W. Chamberlain (*The Union Challenge to Management Control,* Harper and Row, 1948 and Archon Books, p. 277, 1967) as synonymous with **specialised bargaining** as used by Paul H. Norgren (*The Swedish Collective Bargaining System,* 1941, p. 216), i.e. as a process

'in which union representatives at several administrative levels and locations negotiate for rates applicable to categories of workers who represent only fractions of the total bargaining unit'. (2) Now more usually in the United States context, used in the sense employed by James Kuhn (*Bargaining in Grievance Settlement* Columbia University Press, 1961, pp. 79-83) as **grievance bargaining,** i.e. a situation in which the settlement of grievances arising out of labour contracts becomes the subject of bargaining rather than of a judicial type approach based upon the facts and upon interpretation of the terms of the agreement. Kuhn prefers the term fractional bargaining to grievance bargaining 'because a single bargain involves workers only as members of work groups, not as trade union members, and union representatives operate more as leaders of work groups than union leaders', i.e, it tends to be unofficial **work group bargaining** rather than official trade union bargaining. Compare both definitions of fractional bargaining with **fragmented bargaining** and **sectionalism** and (2) with **autonomous bargaining.**

FRAGMENTED BARGAINING. A term used to describe a number of situations in which work groups, grades of workers, different trade unions, or individual employees, are free to bargain for themselves within a single bargaining unit; an expression generally broader than, but sometimes similar to, the meanings attributed to **fractional bargaining** (q.v.). Its use has been popularised by Allan Flanders' description, in evidence to the Donovan **Royal Commission on Trade Unions and Employers' Associations 1965-1968,** Cmnd. 3623, June 1968, p. 18, of workplace bargaining in Britain as 'largely informal, largely fragmented and largely autonomous', fragmentation arising because 'it is conducted in such a way that different groups in the works get different concessions at different times'. Acceptance of this analysis was related to the Commission's recommendation that greater formality should be introduced into collective bargaining structures; see also National Board for Prices and Incomes, *Third General Report,* August 1961 to July 1968. Cmnd. 3715, July 1968 para. 42, **sectionalism** and **comprehensive agreement.**

FREE AREA; see **travelling time**.

FREE-CALL; see **blue-eyed boys**.

FREEDOM OF ASSOCIATION. In a general sense, the right of citizens of a state to assemble in public or private for the purpose of joining together in a common cause, and to associate one with another to achieve their objectives; in the more specific context of industrial relations, the **right to organise** in trade unions and employers' associations and to bargain collectively. The constitution of the **International Labour Organisation** contains a statement of the principle of freedom of association (currently deriving from the **Declaration of Philadelphia** 1944), and this has been supported by a number of conventions; the Right of Association (Agriculture) Convention, 1921 (No. 11), the Right of Association (Non-Metropolitan) Convention 1947 (No. 84), the Freedom of Association and Protection of the Right to Organise Convention 1948 (No. 87), and the Right to Organise and Collective Bargaining Convention 1949 (No. 98). Complaints about alleged infractions of the conventions submitted to the ILO are referred to a special Committee on Freedom of Association. Such complaints were made by the Aeronautical Engineers' Association against the government of the United Kingdom in 1954 (Case No. 96, International Labour Office, *Official Bulletin,* Vol. XXXVII, No. 4, 30 November 1954) and by the **National Union of Bank Employees** against four British banks in 1962 alleging that the union was being prevented from exercising its normal trade union function because of the existence of internal **staff associations,** contrary to ILO Convention 98, Article 2 Clause 2. (*Report of the Inquiry by the Hon. Lord Cameron into the Complaint made by the National Union of Bank Employees on 12 March 1962 to the Committee on Freedom of Association of the International Labour Organisation,* Cmnd. 2202, HMSO, November 1963; see also C. Wilfred Jenks, *The International Protection of Trade Union Freedom,* Stevens, 1957, *Human Rights and International Labour Standards,* 1960, *Social Justice in the Law of Nations,* OUP, 1970, and International Labour Office, *Freedom of Association, A Workers' Education Manual,* ILO, Geneva, 1972. It was not until the passing of the **Industrial Relations Act 1971** that a legal right to belong to a trade union was introduced in Great Britain. That legislation, however, also gave a legal right *not* to belong which led to a number of clashes between trade unions and the **National Industrial Relations Court.** Following the repeal of that Act, this second right has now lapsed, and, under the **Trade Union and Labour Relations Acts 1974 and 1976** and the **Employment Protection Act 1975** employees have the following individual rights: (a) the dismissal of an employee for membership or trade union activities at an appropriate time is unfair (see **unfair dismissal**); (b) officials and members have the right to time off to participate in trade union activities (see **Codes of Practice**), and (c) every employee has the right not to be penalised for, deterred or prevented from joining a trade union or taking part in its activities at an appropriate time. All these rights exist in relation to **independent trade unions** only.

FREE LABOURERS; see **strike-breaking.**

FREE-RIDER. A non-unionist; a worker who receives the benefits of the union's activities in collective bargaining without paying the contributions which union membership implies, hence getting something for nothing; see also **closed shop, agency shop.**

FRICTIONAL UNEMPLOYMENT or **search unemployment.** A type of **unemployment** in which individuals are temporarily without work, or are between jobs; short-term unemployment arising because a worker, on leaving a job, has insufficient information to secure suitable alternative employment, or is seeking improved wages or working conditions, etc. Economists are concerned to point out that frictional unemployment is inevitable if there is to be **mobility of labour,** and that it is not irreconcilable with **full-employment;** they may differ on some of the situations which they would regard as 'frictional'; temporary **lay-offs** due to shortage of work·or industrial action, and lay-offs due to seasonal causes (see **seasonal unemployment**) may, for example, be regarded as 'frictional' by some and not by others. **Employment services** are in large measure concerned to minimise frictional unemployment. **Technological unemployment** is sometimes regarded as at least partly frictional, i.e. as arising from a failure to offer the right skill at the right time and place; see also **structural unemployment, underemployment, concealed unemployment** (or **disguised unemployment**).

FRIENDLY BENEFITS or **provident benefits. Benefits,** especially those paid by a friendly society or a **trade union** to its members in return for contributions, and in the latter case distinguished from **trade benefits.** The friendly benefits more frequently recognised are **sickness and accident benefit, death benefit** or **funeral benefit** and **superannuation benefit,** but tool benefit, marriage dowry, **unemployment benefit,** provision of convalescent homes and legal aid may also be recognised in some cases. In 1970, friendly benefits formed 16.1 per cent of the total expenditure per member of registered unions; in 1976 the proportion was 13.0 per cent. The percentage fall over a long period of time reflects the diminishing role of benefits in union affairs and rising levels of working expenses; see Arthur Marsh and Peter Cope, 'The Anatomy of Trade Union Benefits in the 1960s', *Industrial Relations Journal,* Summer 1970.

FRINGE BENEFITS. Benefits received by workers from their employer, either in cash, in kind, or in services, over and above straight payment for work done. The expression is said not to have come into use until the 1950s (see J.C. Hill, 'Stabilisation of Fringe Benefits', *Industrial and Labor Relations Review,* 7, 2; p. 221). The term **'employee benefits'** is preferred by some on the grounds that 'fringe benefits' have become associated with the perquisites of top management (see H. Murlis, *Employee Benefits Today.* Management Survey Report No. 19, BIM, 1974). It seems doubtful whether this view is widely held. What are thought to constitute fringe benefits varies from one situation to another and raises difficulties of calculating both cost to the employer and value to the employee (see A. Rubner, 'A Working Definition of Fringe Wages', *Journal of Industrial Relations,* Sidney, Australia, November 1965, G.L. Reid, 'The Concept of Fringe Benefits', *Scottish Journal of Political Economy,* Vol. IX, 1962 pp. 208-18 and D. Robinson, *Wage Drift, Fringe Benefits and Manpower Distribution,* OECD, 1968, pp. 41-64). Main benefits usually included are **sick pay schemes, retirement pensions,** medical care and treatment, **holidays with pay,** private unemployment benefit; but 'welfare' benefits may also be included, e.g. housing, social and recreation facilities, and **perks** (q.v.). In a sample of 350 firms G.L. Reid and J.A. Bates (G.L. Reid and D.J. Robertson (eds) *Fringe Benefits, Labour Costs and Social Security,* George Allen and Unwin, 1965, Ch. 3) found that in 350 companies in seventeen industrial groups total fringe benefit expenditure varied from 5 per cent to over 40 per cent of total

payroll, with two-thirds of the firms between 7½ and 15 per cent. A Department of Employment Labour Cost Survey in 1975 (see **Labour Costs**) showed that in manufacturing industries 87.5 (91.3) per cent of average labour costs expenditure per employee went on wages and salaries (including payment for holidays, sickness, injury and when attending classes) 6.4 (4.4) per cent on statutory national insurance contributions, 4.2 (3.2) per cent on private social welfare payments and the remaining 1.9 (1.0) per cent on payments in kind, subsidised services, recruitment and training and other labour costs. (Figures from the 1968 Survey (*Employment and Productivity Gazette,* August 1970) given in parentheses.) Non-wage benefits given by the employer in the nineteenth century were mainly associated with paternalism or various forms of exploitation; some like **tied cottages** are still so regarded by trade unions which in Britain, unlike the USA, have traditionally been reluctant to incorporate fringe benefits into collective bargaining, a phenomenon which may also be related to state provision in such areas. The position in relation to **occupational pensions** (q.v.) may now be changing. Fringe benefits appear to have grown principally because of government encouragement in two world wars, because of the desire of managements to be good employers, and because of their willingness to compete for labour by means other than money wages. On fringe benefits for executives, see BIM, *Information Summary 120,* December 1965; also Jane Moonman, *The Effectiveness of Fringe Benefits in Industry,* Gower Press, 1973.

FSMBS; see **Foremen and Staff Mutual Benefit Society Ltd.**

FTATU. Furniture, Timber and Allied Trades Union (q.v.).

FUE. Federated Union of Employers (q.v.).

FULLY PAID-UP MEMBER; see **paid-up member.**

FULTON REPORT. The *Report of the Committee on the Civil Service,* 1966-1968 (Cmnd. 3638, June 1968) under the chairmanship of Lord Fulton. The committee recommended a more managerial attitude towards the running of the Civil Service, the establishment of a separate **Civil Service Department** (q.v.) to deal with manpower and staff matters, and was critical of some aspects of **Whitleyism** (q.v.). In proposing a common grading structure, manning work by **job evaluation** rather than by reference to membership of a class, career management to open up promotion prospects, and other changes, it foreshadowed considerable alterations in industrial relations in the non-industrial Civil Service.

FUNCTION ANALYSIS SYSTEM TECHNIQUE (FAST); see value analysis.

FUNERAL BENEFIT; see death benefit.

FUNERAL SERVICE OPERATIVES, NATIONAL UNION OF (NUFSO). A trade union formed in 1917 and originally known as the British Funeral Workers' Association. For some time it was confined to the South East, with the bulk of its membership in the Co-operative Movement; more recently it has become national in scope. The majority of its members are drivers, but it recruits all grades, including supervisors, and has in the past few years also accepted car hire workers, florists and allied trades. *Address:* 16 Woolwich New Road, London, SE18 6HD. *Tel:* 01-854 5870. *TUC Affiliated Membership 1977* 1,375.

FURNITURE, TIMBER AND ALLIED TRADES UNION. A trade union formed in 1971 from the merger of the **National Union of Furniture Trades Operatives** and the **Amalgamated Society of Woodcutting Machinists.** *Address:* Fairfields, Roe Green, Kingsbury, London NW9 0PT. *Tel:* 01-204 0273. *TUC Affiliated Membership 1977:* 87,398.

FURNITURE TRADES OPERATIVES, NATIONAL UNION OF (NUFTO). A trade union formed in 1947 by the amalgamation of the National Amalgamated Furnishing Traders' Association and the Amalgamated Union of Upholsterers. NAFTA was established in 1902 as an amalgamation of the Alliance Cabinet Makers (which had two recorded branches in 1868) and the United Operative Cabinet and Chairmakers' Society of Scotland (1875), and the AUU as a federation of local trade unions in 1891. The United French Polishers (1911) transferred their engagements to NUFTO in March 1969, and the Midlands Glass Bevellers' and Kindred Trades Society (1901), in January 1970. In September 1971, NUFTO (TUC affiliated 1970 membership 60,754), together with the **Amalgamated Society of Woodcutting Machinists,** transferred their engagements to the **Furniture, Timber and Allied Trades' Union,** forming a new union with a membership of almost 84,000.

FWH. Flexible Working Hours (q.v.).

G

GAIN SHARING; see gain sharing plans.

GAIN SHARING PLANS also **gain sharing** and **sharing plans.** An expression originally used to describe incentive payment systems such as the **Halsey Premium Bonus System,** the **Rowan System** and the **Barth Premium Plans** (q.v.) in which, on completing a job in less than **standard time,** the worker receives payment for the actual time taken plus a proportion of the time saved (R. Marriott, *Incentive Payment Systems,* Staples Press, 3rd (revised) ed., 1968, pp. 56-7). The term has been attributed to H.R. Towne, president of the Yale and Towne Manufacturing Company of Connecticut. It is said, in the United States, currently to be applied to any method in which workers participate with management in gains due to increased productivity and to be associated with **profit sharing;** see H.S. Roberts, *Roberts' Dictionary of Industrial Relations,* Bureau of National Affairs, 1966.

GALVANISING CONCILIATION BOARD. A joint board of operatives and employers constituted in 1921 to arbitrate on the wages and conditions of workers in galvanising steel sheet and strip production. Together with the **Sheet Trade Board,** the Galvanising Conciliation Board made up the **Sheet Makers' Conference.** As a result of the nationalisation of the steel industry the board became part of the British Steel Corporation in 1968, but continues to function as an independent entity making agreements covering some 3,400 operatives represented by the **Transport and General Workers' Union.** *Addresses:* Joint Secretaries (Employers' Secretary); British Steel Corporation, 33 Grosvenor Place, London SW1. (Operatives' Secretary): Transport and General Workers' Union, Transport House, Smith Square, London SW1.

GANG PIECEWORK; see **group piece-work.**

GANG MASTER; see **labour-only sub-contracting.**

GANG SYSTEM; see **labour-only sub-contracting.**

GANTT TASK AND BONUS PLAN; see **differential piece-rate plan.**

GARTON MEMORANDUM. The memorandum of the Garton Foundations on the *Industrial Situation after the War,* October 1916. The Memorandum is particularly of interest in anticipating some of the principles of **Whitleyism** (q.v.) and some features of collective bargaining structure proposed in the Whitley Report. There is some circumstantial evidence of a connection between the work of the Foundation and the setting up of the Whitley Committee; see D. Carnegie, *The Promotion of Industrial Harmony,* 1919, p. 14, B.G.De Montgomery, *British and Continental Labour Policy,* 1912, p. 406 and Lord Esher, *Journals and Letters,* ed. M.V. Brett, 1934-38, Vol. 4, p. 393.

GAW. Guaranteed Annual Wage (q.v.).

GCA. Group Capacity Assessment (q.v.).

GEARED INCENTIVE SCHEME. An **incentive payment system** in which the rate of payment is not directly proportionate to the rate of working. EPA, *Glossary of Work Study Terms.*

GEDDES REPORT. The report of the **Shipbuilding Inquiry Committee, 1965-1966** (Cmnd. 2937, March 1966), under the chairmanship of Sir Reay Geddes. The main task of the committee was to recommend what action should be taken by employers, trade unions and government to make the shipbuilding industry competitive in world markets. Its proposals included regrouping, a Shipbuilding Industry Board with grants for reorganisation and, *inter alia,* a number of suggestions on **joint consultation, productivity bargaining** and trade union representation. The Commission on Industrial Relations (*Shipbuilding and Shiprepairing,* Report No. 22, Cmnd. 4756, August 1971) reported that progress had been made

under Geddes, but that major areas of reform remained, espcially at company and yard level, arising from independent action and **sectionalism.** It proposed company joint councils and procedures, strengthened consultative and demarcation arrangements, review of company industrial relations strategies and improved joint action within and among unions.

GENERAL COUNCIL OF BRITISH SHIPPING. A national representative organisation of United Kingdom merchant shipowners (excluding the fishing fleet) on all matters of a corporate nature including recruitment, training, and pay and conditions of seamen. It was formed as the **Shipping Federation Ltd** in 1890, principally to contain the militant trade union activities of J. Havelock Wilson and his associates (see **Seamen, National Union of**). In 1967 it became the **British Shipping Federation** and adopted its present title in 1975 when it merged with the United Kingdom Chamber of Shipping. The General Council nominates representatives to all but two of the seats on the employers' side of the **National Maritime Board** which regulates conditions of employment throughout the Merchant Navy and is responsible for administering the **Established Service Scheme** and meeting the costs involved. It is also responsible for the recruitment, selection and shore training of most of the rating personnel in merchant ships and nominates a shipowners' representative to the Merchant Navy Training Board; see L.H. Powell, *The Shipping Federation; A History of the First Sixty Years, 1890-1950* and D.H. Moreby, *Personnel Management in Merchant Ships,* Pergamon Press, 1968. *Address*: 30/32 St Mary Axe, London, EC3A 8ET. *Tel*: 01-283 2922.

GENERAL FEDERATION OF TRADE UNIONS (GFTU). A federation of trade unions originally formed in 1899 as a result of a resolution of the **Trades Union Congress** of 1897. The principal object of the GFTU on its inception was to act as a centralised holder of strike funds for its affiliates, a function which the TUC itself was unwilling to assume. In this role the GFTU was ineffective, and its main function in recent times has been to provide services for small trade unions. A Management Committee decision to approach small TUC affiliates dates from 1956. Since that time it has recruited a number of organisations and in December 1976 had 43 affiliated unions with a total membership of 469,282. For the early history of the Federation, see E.H. Phelps Brown, *The Growth of British Industrial Relations*, Macmillan, 1965 and for recent developments, A.I. Marsh and M. Speirs, 'The General Federation of Trade Unions, 1945-1970', *Industrial Relations Journal*, Vol. 2, No. 3. Autumn, 1971 and M. Speirs, 'The GFTU and the Future', *Federation News* Vol. 22, No. 1, January, 1972. A history of the organisation is in preparation. *Address*: Central House, Upper Woburn Place, London WC1H 0HY. *Tel*: 01-387 2578 & 01-388 0852.

GENERAL INDEX OF RETAIL PRICES; see **retail prices index.**

GENERAL AND MUNICIPAL WORKERS' UNION (GMWU). A trade union descended from Will Thorne's Gasworkers' Union of 1889 which took its present form on the amalgamation of three unions, the National Union of General Workers, the National Amalgamated Union of Labour and the Municipal Employees' Association, in 1924. Membership was originally drawn from unskilled and semi-skilled workers, notably from gas and local government. Non-craft manual workers still predominate, drawn from a wide range of industries, with the largest concentrations in engineering, public administration and defence and in public utilities, but with considerable numbers in chemicals, glass, bricks, construction, food, drink and tobacco. The union has skilled membership in edge tool, cutlery, wool, glass and other industries, and in 1976, 314,272 female members. It has been notable for the predominantly regional basis of its policy making and administration and for the absence in its constitution of organisation to deal separately with different trades. These characteristics were partially modified at the 1969 Congress which set up a system of Regional and National Industrial Conferences to act as forums for discussions and advisory bodies on industrial policy, to deal with the specialised demands of plant bargaining, to improve vertical communication, and to stimulate flagging recruitment. The same Congress established a Productivity Services Centre to provide technical assistance for negotiators and shop stewards in productivity techniques. In 1972, it announced the formation of a new section of the union for non-manual workers, the **Managerial, Administrative, Technical and Supervisory Association.** The most recent unions to amalgamate with the GMWU are the National Union of Water Works Employees (4,000 members, 1972), the Rubber, Plastic and Allied Workers (1975) and the Scottish Professional Footballers' Association (1976). The union is the third largest in Britain; see H.A. Clegg, *General Union*, Basil Blackwell, 1954 and *General Union in a Changing Society*, Basil Blackwell, 1964; G and MWU, *Evidence to the Royal Commission on Trade Unions and Employers' Associations*, 1966. *Address:* Thorne House, Ruxley Ridge, Claygate, Esher, Surrey KT10 0TL. *Tel:* 0372 62081/5. TUC Affiliated Membership, 1977: 916,438.

GENERAL-PURPOSE MANNING. A system of manning merchant ships in which all ratings form one work team and in which, while it is not common for 'traditional sailors' and firemen to be used on catering duties, stewards may be employed on deck during berthing and unberthing operations; see also **dual-purpose manning;** both have formed part of **productivity agreements** (q.v.) D.H. Moreby, *Personnel Management in Merchant Ships*, Pergamon Press, 1968, p. 181.

GENERAL STRIKE. A strike of a political, and usually revolutionary, nature, involving an overall strategy of mass action against both employers and government; alternatively, as expounded by the International Workers of the World (see **Wobblies**) 'the general lockout of the master class' (see J. Connolly, *Labour Nationality and Religion*, Dublin 1910, Chapter 6, para. 2). In particular the name popularly given to the strike in support of the miners called by the General Council of the Trades Union Congress and lasting from 3 May 1926 to 12 May 1926, known to the TUC as the **National Strike** (see Lord Citrine, *Men and Work*, Greenwood Press, 1976) and described by K.G.J.C. Knowles (*Strikes*, Basil Blackwell, 1952, p. 8) as 'not so much a revolutionary strike as a peaceful demonstration of civil disobedience'; see W.H. Crook, *The General Strike*, University of North Carolina Press, 1931; J.G. Murray, *The General Strike of 1926*, Lawrence and Wishart, 1951 and J. Symons, *The General Strike*, Cresset Press, 1957, Christopher Farman, *The General Strike, May 1926*, Panther, 1974 and Margaret Morris, *The General Strike*, Penguin, 1976. The thesis that the General Strike of 1926 formed a watershed in British industrial relations, and especially in the attitudes of unions towards strikes and **syndicalism** and of employers to organised labour (see **Mond Turner Conferences**), has been discussed by H.A. Clegg ('Some Consequences of the General Strike', *Manchester Statistical Society,* January 1954), who considers it to be one factor among others influencing the course of events, while conceding that it may have marked the end of the theory of the revolutionary general strike in Britain, and reduced the prestige of postwar advocates of **workers' control** (q.v.); see also Anthony Mason, *The General Strike in the North East,* University of Hull Occasional Paper in Economic and Social History, 1970.

GENERAL UNION. A trade union whose basis of membership recruitment is unlimited by occupation or industry; in practice a trade union which recruits over a wide range of occupations and industries, e.g. the **Transport and General Workers' Union,** the **General and Municipal Workers' Union,** and, less evidently, the **Union of Shop, Distributive and Allied Workers** (see H.A. Clegg, A.J. Killick and Rex Adams, *Trade Union Officers,* Basil Blackwell, 1961, pp. 14-15). Such unions have historically originated with unskilled workers and can be seen as a method of spreading risks as well as a form of **open union** well suited for growth.

GENERAL UNION OF ASSOCIATIONS OF LOOM OVERLOOKERS; see **Loom Overlookers, General Union of Associations of.**

GENERAL UNION OF OPERATIVE CARPENTERS AND JOINERS v. O'DONNELL (1877) 1 ILTJ 282; see **benefits**.

GEOGRAPHICAL MOBILITY or **spatial mobility.** Movement of labour from one geographical area to another. Relatively low geographical mobility, especially from one town to another, appears to be a characteristic of the British labour market, greater mobility being related to higher educational standards reached: A.I. Harris and R. Clausen, *Labour Mobility in Britain, 1953-1963,* SS 333, HMSO, March 1966; see also **labour mobility**.

GFTU. General Federation of Trade Unions (q.v.).

GHOST MACHINES; see **ghost workers.**

GHOST PAYMENTS; see **ghost workers.**

GHOST WORKERS also **ghost payments, ghost machines.** Descriptions arising in situations in which payments are made to crews of existing machines on behalf of workers or machines which are notionally, but not actually, employed in producing an edition of a newspaper of more than a normal number of pages; a pretext for extra payment commented on by the Shawcross *Royal Commission on the Press,* 1961-62, Cmnd. 1811, September 1962, pp. 38-9.

GIFT HOURS (iron and steel industry): premiums paid by crediting workers with more hours than are actually worked, e.g. by paying 9 hours for an afternoon shift and 10 hours for a night shift when the normal working hours expected are 8 hours (i.e. 1 gift hour and 2 gift hours respectively), for **shift premiums,** for weekend work **(weekend extras),** holiday **(holiday extras),** overtime **(overtime extras),** rest days **(rest day extras);** also **cumulative extras** (i.e. any two or more time extras which are payable together at the same time).

GILDS; see **craft gilds.**

W. GIMBER AND SONS LTD v. SPURRETT (1967) ITR 308 (DC); see **seniority**.

GLACIER PROJECT. An on-going project of action research into industrial organisation carried out by the Glacier Metal Co. Ltd, with Wilfred (now Lord) Brown as its Chairman, in collaboration first with the **Tavistock Institute of Human Relations,** and later with the leader of its research team, Dr Elliott Jaques. The project was begun on a long term basis in 1948, and was initially concerned with the nature of executive authority. This led to the creation of a new structure of management-worker-union relations in the company, based on the notion that management operates within three distinct roles - executive, representative and legislative - each with its own distinctive system; to a change from **piecework** to **timework,** and to the abandonment of **clocking** and later to the development of theories on **time-span** and product analysis pricing. The project has developed an extensive literature of which the principal studies are: Wilfred Brown, *Exploration in Management,* Heinemann, 1960, and *Piecework Abandoned,* Heinemann, 1962; Wilfred Brown and Elliott

Jaques, *Product Analysis Pricing*, Heinemann, 1964, and *Glacier Papers*, Heinemann, 1965 (which includes an exhaustive bibliography); Elliott, Jaques, *The Changing Culture of a Factory*, Tavistock, 1951, *Measurement of Responsibility*, Heinemann Education, 1972, and *Equitable Payment*, Heinemann, 2nd ed., 1970, see also A.D. Newman and R.W. Rowbottom, *Organisation Analysis*, Heinemann, 1968; J. Kelly, *Is Scientific Management Possible?*, Faber and Faber, 1968, and Wilfred Brown, *Organisation*, Heinemann, 1971 and J.L. Gray, *The Glacier Project, Concepts and Critiques*, Heinemann, 1976.

GLCSA. Greater London Council Staff Association (q.v.).

GMWU. General and Municipal Workers' Union (q.v.).

GOING RATE. The rate of wages, or of payment, assumed to be general, or modal, in a particular town or district, especially for labour of a particular skill or grade. The concept of the going rate is closely involved in the reasons given by employers for 'staying in line' over wages or earnings, and hence with concepts of local **labour markets**. The validity of the reasoning and practice concerned in the concept has been challenged by some labour economists; see Derek Robinson (ed.), *Local Labour Markets and Wage Structures*, Gower Press, 1970.

GOLDBRICKING. A form of **ca'canny** in which working groups, by agreement or tacit understanding between workers, put minimum effort into jobs on which piecework prices are thought to be too low to produce quota earnings (**stinkers**), while they produce up to quota earnings on those which have looser or more generous prices (**gravy jobs**). Among dayworkers, or timeworkers, goldbricking takes the form of working to levels of production which would ensure a good price if the jobs concerned were put on **piecework;** see also **working daywork,** and **quota restriction;** see Donald Roy, 'Quota Restriction and Goldbricking in a Machine Shop', *American Journal of Sociology*, Vol. 67, No. 2, 1952 (reprinted in Tom Lupton (ed.), *Payment Systems,* Penguin Modern Management Readings, 1972) and W. Baldamus, *Efficiency and Effort,* Tavistock, 1967, p. 106; see also **restrictive practices.**

GOLD, SILVER AND ALLIED

TRADES, NATIONAL UNION OF (NUGSAT). A trade union dating as a national and composite body from 1910 when a number of local trades unions were consolidated and led by the Silversmiths and Britannia Metal Smiths. The union was originally known as the Amalgamated Society of Gold, Silver and Kindred Trades (1912), which brought together the Silversmiths, Britannia Metal Smiths, Silver and EP Finishers, Spoon and Fork Filers and Stampers, Holloware Buffers, Holloware Stampers, Platers and Gilders. It adopted its present title in 1914 after amalgamation with the Birmingham Silversmiths and Electroplate Operatives. In 1969 the union absorbed the Society of Goldsmiths, Jewellers and Kindred Trades. *Address:* Kean Chambers, 11 Mappin Street, Sheffield S1 4DT. *Tel:* 0742 21668. *TUC Affiliated Membership 1977:* 2,447.

GOOD-FAITH BARGAINING. Collective bargaining in which the parties make serious and sincere attempts to arrive at a mutually agreeable settlement. The concept of good-faith bargaining has become especially important in the United States, where the parties have a legal obligation 'to meet at reasonable times and confer in good faith with respect to wages, hours, and other terms of employment', an obligation which does not, however, require either side to agree to a proposal or make a concession. The National Labour Relations Board has developed under the Wagner and Taft-Hartley Acts a number of criteria, including dilatory behaviour, refusal to meet at convenient and reasonable times, actions designed to weaken unions, refusal to incorporate terms into a written contract, to determine whether good-faith bargaining is taking place; the concept, however, remains a difficult one; see 'Good Faith Bargaining in Labor Relations', 61 *Harvard Law Review*, 1224, 1948; 'The Good Faith Bargaining Requirements', *Virginia Law Review*, January 1957; US President's Advisory Committee on Labor Management Policy, *Collective Bargaining*, Washington DC: CPO 1962. The concept of 'good faith bargaining' was reflected in s. 55 of the **Industrial Relations Act 1971** in connection with trade union recognition but, since the repeal of that Act, has no counterpart in current legislation.

GOON. A thug hired by a trade union or by a management to create or resist violence during a labour dispute by terrorist methods: **goon squad**, a group of thugs hired for this purpose (USA).

GOON SQUAD; see **goon**.

GO-SLOW; see **ca'canny**.

GOVERNMENT SEIZURE; see **presidential seizure**.

GOVERNMENT SUPERVISORS AND RADIO OFFICERS, ASSOCIATION OF (AGSRO). A trade union formed in 1956 by amalgamation of the Government Foremen and Technical Supervisors and the Civil Service Radio Officers' Association. It caters primarily for Civil Servants and staff in closely related organisations under the control of Ministers of the Crown. *Address:* 90 Borough High Street, London SE1 1LL. *Tel:* 01-407 4866/7. *TUC Affiliated Membership 1977:* 11,964.

GOVERNMENT TRAINING CENTRES; now renamed **Skillcentres** (q.v.).

GRACE PERIOD; see **lateness**.

GRADE CREEP. An expression, said to have originated in the United States, and used to describe a situation in which, within a standard pay system, pressures for regrading result in increased take-home pay; hence a form of **wage drift** (q.v.), linked in Britain particularly with that taking place for salaried jobs in the public sector (**salary drift**); see T.L. Johnston, 'Public Sector and White Collar Bargaining', in D.J. Robertson and L.C. Hunter (eds), *Labour Market Issues in the 1970s,* Oliver and Boyd, 1970, and National Board for Prices and Incomes, *Pay of Staff Workers in the Gas Industry,* Report No. 86, Cmnd. 3795, 1968.

GRADE REPRESENTATIVES. Workers representing trade union members on Local Joint Committees of British Road Services and acting, since 1969, as **shop stewards** (q.v.). The relevant agreement makes provision for annual election, minimum age and length of service, and for grievance handling, disciplinary representation, and local negotiation by grade representatives.

GRADING. A form of **job evaluation** (q.v.) in which grades are determined in the light of predetermined definitions of functions, skill and responsibility, and jobs subsequently described and allocated to appropriate grades. An inexpensive and popular system of job evaluation, especially among salaried workers employed in government departments. Other examples are the clerical workers' grading scheme introduced by the Institute of Office Management in 1942, and the day-wagemen's scheme in coal mining (1955); see W.H. Sales and J.L. Davies, 'Introducing a New Wage Structure into Coalmining', *Bulletin of the Oxford University Institute of Statistics,* August, 1957 pp. 201-24.

GRADUATE APPRENTICE; see **apprenticeship**.

GRADUATED MEASURED DAYWORK; see **Premium Pay Plan**.

GRADUATED PENSION SCHEME; see **retirement pensions**.

GRAPEVINE. A popular description of the informal communication of information downwards in an enterprise or establishment by word of mouth, by-passing official channels of communication. Some commentators attest to the usefulness as well as the disadvantages of the grapevine which, although it may develop rumours, may also correct some of the shortcomings of formal communications; see L.R. Sayles and G. Strauss, *Human Behaviour in Organisations,* Prentice Hall, 1966, p. 369; see also **briefing groups**.

GRAPHICAL AND ALLIED TRADES, SOCIETY OF (SOGAT). A trade union originally formed in 1966 by amalgamation of the **National Society of Operative Printers and Assistants** (NATSOPA) and the **National Union of Printing, Bookbinding and Paper Workers,** (NUPB and PW) the former making up Division I and the latter Division A of the amalgamation. Constitutional differences between the two divisions led to an announcement in October 1970 that the amalgamation was at an end. The terms of the separation were arrived at in November 1971 during the course of one of the three High Court actions then being pursued between them, the title Society of Graphical and Allied Trades being retained by Division A, and Division I being again known as NATSOPA. The NUPB and PW was the shortened title adopted in 1928 for the National Union of Printing, Bookbinding, Machine Ruling and Paper Workers, an amalgamation in 1921 of the National Union of Bookbinders and Machine Rulers (1911) and the National

Union of Printing and Paper Workers (1914), to which was added in 1937 the (Reunited) Amalgamated Society of Paper Makers (1894), in 1943 the Society of Women Employed in the Bookbinding and Printing Trades (1896), in 1948 the (Reunited) Original Society of Papermakers (1837) and in 1962 the Monotype Casters and Typefounders' Society; (see C.J. Bundock, *The National Union of Printing, Bookbinding and Paper Workers*, OUP, 1959). The Scottish Typographical Association amalgamated with SOGAT in 1975. The union's membership has been traditionally found among paper workers in paper mills, bookbinders, machine rules and among some provincial printing machine assistants. *Address*: 274-288 London Road, Hadleigh, Benfleet, Essex SS7 2DE. *Tel*: 0702-553131. *TUC Affiliated Membership 1977*: 194,312.

GRAPHICAL ASSOCIATION, NATIONAL (NGA). A trade union formed in 1964 by the amalgamation of the Typographical Association (originally established as the Provincial Typographical Association in 1849) and the London Typographical Society, itself an amalgamation of the London Society of Compositors (originally established in 1845 and re-established in 1848) and the Printing Machine Managers' Trade Society in 1955. Since 1964 a number of unions have transferred their engagements to the NGA - the National Union of Press Telegraphists and the Association of Correctors of the Press in June 1965, the National Society of Electrotypers and Stereotypers in October 1967 and the Amalgamated Society of Lithographic Printers in December 1968. The formation of the NGA represents part of a move from multi-unionism in the printing industry encouraged by the Trades Union Congress and occasioned, *inter alia*, by the breakdown of horizontal craft demarcations due to technological change in the industry. Broadly speaking, it now organises craft workers in printing, publishing and packaging. It has an Executives, Technicians and Overseers' Section. *History and Progress of the Amalgamated Society of Lithographic Printers, 1880-1930*, ASLP, 1930; Ellic Howe (ed.), *The London Compositor, 1875-1900*, OUP 1947; Ellic Howe and Harold Waite, *The London Society of Compositors*, Cassell, 1948; A.E. Musson, *The Typographical Association*, OUP, 1954. *Address*: Graphic House, 63-67 Bromham Road, Bedford MK40 2AG. *Tel*: 0234 51521. *TUC Affiliated Membership 1977*: 107,723.

GRASS; see **grass-hands.**

GRASS-HANDS. Assistants or substitutes for regularly employed compositors, temporarily employed; hence **grassing,** the use of grass-hands; see Ellic Howe and Harold E. Waite, *The London Society of Compositors,* Cassell and Co., 1948, p. 221. A term used generally in the newspaper industry to describe casual workers in any department, sometimes simply as **grass.**

GRASSING; see **grass-hands.**

GRAVEYARD SHIFT or **lobster shift, midnight shift** or third shift; the third shift on a **continuous shift system,** the **night shift,** beginning around midnight and ending early in the morning; see **shift system.**

GRAVY JOBS. Workshop slang for piecework jobs on which prices or times are relatively slack or loose, thereby making it easy for workers to make money; the opposite of **stinkers;** see also **goldbricking.** Donald Roy, 'Quota Restriction and Goldbricking in a Machine Shop' *American Journal of Sociology,* Vol. 67, No. 2, 1952 (reprinted in Tom Lupton (ed.), *Payment Systems,* Penguin Modern Management Readings, 1972).

GREATER LONDON COUNCIL STAFF ASSOCIATION (GLCSA). A trade union formed in May 1909 and organising the staff of the London County Council. The present title was adopted when the LCC became the Greater London Council. *Address:* 164/168 Westminster Bridge Road, London SE1 7RW. *Tel:* 01-633 5927. *TUC Affiliated Membership, 1977:* 18,504.

GREEN BOOK AGREEMENT. A name used to describe a number of agreements made in 1969 between trade unions in the steel industry and the British Steel Corporation which resulted from proposals set out by the Corporation in a green coloured booklet. The agreements made provision for a rationalised wages structure, for conditions of employment providing greater security and stability of earnings, for the acceptance of work study and for the acceptance of the best manning arrangements.

GREEN BOOK PROCEDURE. An **emergency disputes procedure** formerly used in the building industry and dating from 1927. This provided that either party at the site might notify its officials that a strike existed or was likely to exist, and thereby set in train emergency steps for its resolution or prevention by both sides. The Green Book Procedure was unusual in that it did not include a **no-strike clause**, and hence involved no distinction between a **constitutional** and **unconstitutional** strike (q.v.); see A.I. Marsh and W.E.J. McCarthy, *Disputes Procedures in Britain*, Royal Commission on Trade Unions and Employers' Associations, Research Papers 2 (Part 2), 1968 p. 53 *et seq.* It was replaced in 1970 by a more orthodox site procedure *(National Working Rules, 2 March 1970, Rule 7 (10))*.

GREENER. A sweated worker: Alan Fox, *History of the National Union of Boot and Shoe Operatives, 1874-1957*, Blackwell, 1958, p. 106; see **sweating**.

GRIEVANCE. A complaint, usually by a worker or workers, about wages, conditions of employment or actions of management: hence **grievance procedure**, a procedure for handling grievances (see **disputes procedure**), **grievance machinery**, and **grieving** (USA: the presentation of grievances). Within this general description, the word grievance may have a more or less specific meaning, depending on the industrial relations system in which it is employed. In the United States, it is usually considered to refer only to formal complaints about violations or difficulties in applying contracts or collective agreements or, in some cases, laws and regulations. It may sometimes, therefore, be identified as an **arbitrable grievance**, i.e. a grievance required by contract to be taken to arbitration, and be thought of as involving a **conflict of right** (q.v.). But it may also be used in a wider sense in the USA. Harold S. Roberts (*Dictionary of Industrial Relations*, BNA, 1966) defines a grievance as 'any complaint by an employee or by a union (sometimes by the employer or employer association) concerning any aspect of the employment relationship'. In other countries the word may be confined to complaints *outside* any formal regulation or agreement; see International Labour Office, *Examination of Grievances and Communications within the Undertaking*, ILO, 1965, Ch. I: 'The Concept of Grievance'. In Britain usage is as wide as that given by Roberts, no distinction being generally made between issues which involve the application or interpretation of collective agreements and those which do not. A few company or plant

agreements distinguish between a general grievance procedure, and a **claims procedure**, i.e. a procedure dealing with complaints arising out of formal collective agreements; some writers equate a grievance procedure with an **appeals procedure**, and distinguish this from a **negotiating procedure**, i.e. a procedure for negotiating new agreements (see D.T.B. North and G.L. Buckingham, *Productivity Agreements and Wage Systems*, Gower Press, 1969). This latter distinction is common enough in practice, though rarely made explicit in principle.

GRIEVANCE ARBITRATION. Arbitration designed to administer the terms of existing contracts or collective agreements, and hence concerned with **conflicts of rights** arising out of interpretations and applications of these contracts; sometimes used in the United States of America in contrast to **contract arbitration** (q.v.); also known as **judiciable arbitration**.

GRIEVANCE BARGAINING; see **fractional bargaining**.

GRIEVANCE MACHINERY; see **grievance**.

GRIEVANCE PROCEDURE; see **grievance** and **procedural terms**.

GRIEVING; see **grievance**.

GRIMSBY STEAM AND DIESEL FISHING VESSELS ENGINEERS' AND FIREMEN'S UNION; see **Engineers' and Firemen's Union, Grimsby Steam and Diesel Fishing Vessels.**

GROSS RATE. Base rate of payment adjusted according to the prevailing sliding scale, i.e. **selling price sliding scale** or **cost of living sliding scale** (q.v.) (steel industry).

GROUP CAPACITY ASSESSMENT (GCA). A technique for improving the utilisation of labour in offices and other white collar and indirect areas devised by Arthur Young and Company in the United States in the early 1950s. It is said to make possible in such areas a continuing week by week comparison of the amount of work accomplished by a group and the time available; see J.E. Bayhylle, *Productivity Improvements in the Office*, Engineering Employers' Federation, Research Paper 2, December 1968, pp. 23-9; also **Variable Factor Programming**

(VFP), **Clerical Work Improvement Programme** (CWIP) and **Clerical Work Evaluation** (CWE).

GROUP DYNAMICS; see T group.

GROUP INCENTIVE SCHEMES or **group bonus schemes.** Payment schemes based upon considerations of output or performance, but related and applied to groups of workers, or to all workers in a plant, rather than to individuals. Schemes include **group piece-work, contract piece-work, production bonuses,** and may sometimes be taken to include **measured day-work** and schemes of the **Scanlon** and **Rucker Plan** type; see **share of production plans.** It has been said for some years that there exists in Britain a trend from individual to group incentive schemes (see, for example, N.C. Hunt, *Methods of Wage Payment in British Industry,* Pitman, 1951, p. 99; *The Director,* 1950, p. 37) partly on the grounds that individual incentive schemes are unsatisfactory, e.g. D. Pym, 'Is there a Future for Wage Incentive Systems?', *British Journal of Industrial Relations,* Vol. II, 1964, pp. 379-97. It is doubtful, however, whether such a movement has taken place (see Sylvia Shimmin, Chapter 10 in R. Marriott, *Incentive Payment Systems,* Staples Press, 3rd ed. 1968).

GROUP LEADER. A term used in some companies to describe a **leading hand** or **working chargehand** (see **chargehand**).

GROUP PIECEWORK or **gang piecework.** An incentive system of payment in which the total piecework earnings of a squad or gang are computed, and shared between members of the gang. For an example from the shipbuilding industry; see N.C. Hunt, *Methods of Wage Payment in British Industry,* Pitman, 1951, p. 101, and in the motor industry, S. Melman, *Decision-making and Productivity,* Blackwell, 1958; see also **contract piecework.**

GROUP RELATIONS TRAINING; see **T Group.**

GROUP TECHNOLOGY (GT). Defined by the Mechanical Engineering Economic Development Committee (*Why Group Technology?* National Economic Development Office, August 1975) as 'The organisation of production facilities in self-contained and self-regulating groups or cells [hence **'cellular manufacture'**], each

of which undertakes the complete manufacture of a family of components with similar manufacturing characteristics. The cell staff are often each capable of using several machines or processes, so that there are usually fewer men than machines'. GT appears to have developed in two principal stages. Early uses of the expression were concerned to improve machine tool utilisation by reducing setting time by classifying and grouping 'technologically similar parts' to be manufactured together (e.g. in S.P. Mitrofanov, *The Scientific Principles of Group Technology* published in the USSR in 1959) or, by classification of components, to reduce duplication at the point of design. Later it became increasingly synonymous with cellular manufacture, i.e. of a reorganisation of batch production to allow workers to be organised, together with machines, into self-contained, specialist groups making the most of the manufacturing technology available to each group. In connection with this approach Audley Engineering of Newport, Shropshire (later Serck Audio Valves Ltd) is said to have invented the term **cellular group production.** It is claimed that the principle of giving each group of men in a 'cell' the responsibility for making components from start to finish increases their versatility and interest as well as reducing manufacturing time and increasing output; see also **job enlargement, job enrichment, job rotation.** By 1975, some 150 UK companies were said to be making use of GT, among those fully committed being Herbert Machine Tools, Edgwick Works, a development associated with the name of Frank W. Craven.

GROVES v. WIMBORNE (LORD) (1898) 2 QB 402; see **employers' liability.**

GRUNWICK DISPUTE. A dispute at the Grunwick Processing Laboratories beginning in August 1976 and involving issues of mass picketing, blacking of mail by members of the Union of Post Office Workers contrary to ss. 58 and 68 of the Post Office Act 1953 and recognition of the Association of Professional, Executive, Clerical and Computer Staff under s. 11 of the Employment Protection Act 1975. The union, having been rebuffed by the employer, referred the recognition issue to the Advisory, Conciliation and Arbitration Service, which recommended that this should be conceded at both Willesden establishments of the company without, however, having obtained the opinions of the employees still working at the factories (as distinct from those on strike) because of its inability to persuade the company's management to provide their names and addresses. In subsequent proceedings, the House of Lords found for the company in its continued refusal to recognise the union after this ACAS recommendation on the grounds of its interpretation of the requirement of the Employment Protection Act, s. 14(1) that ACAS 'shall ascertain the opinions of workers to whom the issue relates' (**Grunwick Processing Laboratories Ltd v. ACAS**, *The Times,* 15 December 1977). In addition to its refusal to recognise the union, the company also rejected the findings of a Court of Inquiry chaired by Lord Justice Scarman (see **Scarman Report**) which recommended in August 1977 that all the strikers who wished to return should be taken back by the company, and which approved the principle of recognition, claiming that the court was acting as an instrument of the 'corporate state'. The dispute was notable for the detailed involvement of the National Association for Freedom as well as for the questions it posed on picketing and on the status of ACAS in s. 11 recognition questions where employer co-operation cannot be obtained; see Joe Rogaly, *Grunwick,* Penguin Special, 1977 and an account of the situation by Grunwick's managing direction, George Ward, *Fort Grunwick,* Maurice Temple Smith, December 1977.

GRUNWICK PROCESSING LABORATORIES LTD v. ACAS see **Grunwick Dispute.**

GT. Group Technology (q.v.)

GTCs; Government Training Centres; see **Skillcentres.**

GUARANTEE PAYMENT. A payment required to be made to individual employees in the **guaranteed week** provisions of the Employment Protection Act 1975. The payment is calculated by multiplying the number of normal working hours on any workless day by the 'guaranteed hourly rate', i.e. by a rate calculated by dividing the amount of one week's pay by the normal weekly working hours of the employee concerned, or, if the number of working hours varies from week to week, by the average number worked over the previous 12 weeks. The maximum guarantee payment required to be paid for any one day is £6.60 and, in any

quarter, an employee cannot receive under the Act guaranteed payments for more than five days. These limitations are subject to annual review. Any payments due under voluntary guaranteed week arrangements can be offset against guarantee payments, and *vice versa.* In April 1978 the Department of Employment issued a consultative document proposing a permanent statutory scheme to compensate workers on short time similar to those operating in other European countries. Under the scheme employers would be required to pay employees 75 per cent of normal gross pay for each working day lost provided that there was not more than one week's continuous lay off, employers being able to claim back one-half of the amount paid from a Short-Time Working Fund.

GUARANTEED ANNUAL WAGE (GAW). In its most rigorous form, an agreement for guaranteed all-the-year-round employment at specific rates, assuring a minimum annual income; more loosely as 'annual wage' a variety of approaches towards stabilisation of workers' incomes by collective agreement. In the United States new prominence was given to GAW by a demand for a guarantee of employment on an annual basis made to the National War Labour Board by the United Steel Workers of America in 1944, though there were instances of GAW plans before that time. In its most rigorous form GAW remains rare in the USA, but has been for some years an important bargaining issue. In Britain the pattern of collective bargaining and of wages and employment and income guarantees have lent themselves less to the GAW approach, though it has been mentioned in the motor industry; see A.D.H. Kaplan, *The Guarantee of Annual Wages,* The Brookings Institution, Washington DC, 1947; Don A. Seastone, 'The History of Guaranteed Wages and Employment', *Journal of Economic History,* Vol. 15, No. 2, 1955 and Richard M. Bourne, 'Wage Guarantees - a Re-examination', *Labor Law Journal,* February 1960.

GUARANTEED WAGE. A wartime arrangement introduced as a result of the Essential Work Order (S.R. and O. 1941, No. 302), as a result of which workers capable of and available for work and willing to perform any reasonable services outside their normal occupation were paid a weekly wage if no work could be found for them; see H.M.D. Parker, *Manpower,* HMSO, 1957, Chs. 6 and 7. Trade unions sought to maintain the guaranteed wage principle in post-war agreements, ultimately in the form of a **guaranteed week** (q.v.) though the expression guaranteed wage is still used in some cases, e.g. in cotton manufacturing.

GUARANTEED WEEK. A device, origi- nating in the wartime **guaranteed wage,** whereby a worker is, subject to certain con- ditions, guaranteed by collective agree- ment, either a certain number of days or shifts of employment during a week, or payment in lieu at an agreed rate. Many such agreements were made in British industries after the second world war, the concept of a guaranteed wage being replaced generally in the middle 1950s by that of a guaranteed week (though some- times without change of title) after con- flicts with the National Insurance Commissioners over unemployment bene- fit, and sometimes becoming known as a **guarantee of employment.** Guarantees of this kind (not to be confused with other types of **guarantee** (q.v.)) are now usually for a full working week or for payment for equivalent hours. The rate at which pay- ment is guaranteed varies from one indus- try to another. Guarantees are often, under the terms of national agreements, suspended or reduced when approved short-time is being worked as an alterna- tive to redundancy, or where there is a strike within the establishment concerned or at another associated establishment, e.g. another federated establishment in engineering. The courts are usually reluct- ant to imply the power to suspend and tend to require express terms in an agree- ment, e.g. in **Powell Duffryn Ltd v. House;** see Trade Union Research Unit, 'The Guaranteed Week', *Federation News,* October 1972, and **short-time working.** Under the **Employment Protection Act 1975** ss. 22-8, the right to a **guarantee pay- ment** is given to all employees who have been continuously employed more than four weeks, provided that he is available for work, that no suitable alternative work can be found for him and that the reason for lack of work does not involve a **trade dispute** involving any employee of his employer or an associated employer. In April 1978 the Department of Employ- ment published a consultative document proposing a statutory scheme to compen- sate workers put on short time. All employ- ers would be required to pay employees 75 per cent of normal gross pay for each work- ing day lost provided there was not more than one week's continuous lay off. Employers would be able to claim back half of this amount from a short-time working fund to be financed by employers and the government equally. During times of high unemployment, an employer would be reimbursed completely where workers were put on short time rather than made redundant. In these cases half the money would come from the fund and half from the government directly.

GUIDELINES; see criteria.

GUIDE-CHART PROFILE METHOD. A method of **job evaluation** associated with the name of Dr E.N. Hay and prac- tised by Hay-MSL Limited. Three factors, know-how, problem-solving and accoun- tability are each divided into eight degrees or levels, and qualified by an assessment of the breadth and type of decision-making involved, the whole being built up on a Guide-Chart and compared with a copy- righted distribution of salaries related to firms of different sizes; see E.N. Hay and D. Purves, 'A New Method of Job Evalua- tion - the Guide Chart Profile Method', *Personnel,* Vol. 28, 1951, pp. 162-70, Vol. 31, 1954, pp. 72-80 and Vol. 35, 1958, pp. 63-72; discussed in T.T. Paterson, *Job Evaluation* - Vol. 1, *A New Method,* Busi- ness Books, 1972.

GUILD OF INSURANCE OFFICIALS; see **Union of Insurance Staffs.**

GUILDS; see craft gilds.

GUILD SOCIALISM. A workers' con- **trol** movement which followed from about 1913 the decline of **syndicalism** (q.v.) and was particularly associated with G.D.H. Cole, its principal publicist (*inter alia, Self- Government in Industry,* 1917, Hutchin- son, ed. J. Corina, 1972, and *Guild Social- ism Re-stated,* Leonard Parsons Ltd, 1920). Guild Socialists rejected the apocal- yptic general strike as the means to work- ers' control, preferring peaceful 'encroaching' control through the **collec- tive contract** (q.v.) and through the exten- sion of guilds which should include all classes of worker, whether by hand or by brain, and which should take over one industry after another, controlling these within the terms of contracts between them and the state, the latter being the instrument of protection for the public and of consumers. The main effects of Guild Socialism were felt in coal mining, building and in the post office, but little practical result of these experiments was left by 1922, partly because of government opposition, partly because of post-war depression and partly because, in G.D.H. Cole's own words, 'the Guild Socialists never faced the fundamental problem of power and of large scale organisation and planning'; see Branko Pribićević, *The Shop Stewards' Movement and Workers' Control*, Basil Blackwell, 1959, H.A. Clegg, *A New Approach to Industrial Democracy*, Basil Blackwell, 1960, and Ken Coates and Anthony Topham (eds), *Industrial Democracy in Great Britain*, Bertrand Russell House, 1974.

GUILLEBAUD FORMULA. A comparability formula for the pay of railwaymen with wages and salaries in outside industry reached by the Guillebaud Committee in March 1960 (*Report of the Railway Pay Committee of Inquiry;* see **Guillebaud Report**). The National Board for Prices and Incomes (*Pay and Conditions of British Railways Staff,* Cmnd. 2873, January 1966) found that, in the interests of the **prices and incomes policy,** the use of the formula should be discontinued.

GUILLEBAUD REPORT. A name given to the findings of a number of committees and **Courts of Inquiry** under the chairmanship of Mr C.W. Guillebaud, the best known of which is probably the *Railway Pay Committee of Inquiry, 1958-1960.* The object of this inquiry was to investigate the question of relativity of railway pay to that in other industries and to review wages and salary structure. It established new standards in **comparability** or **fair comparisons** which later became a matter for concern in **incomes policy.** On developments in British Rail; see Charles McLeod, *All Change: Railway Industrial Relations in the Sixties,* Gower Press, 1970.

H

HAGMAN SYSTEM. An alternative expression for the **contract system** used in the nineteenth century foundry trade; a system by which foremen (or **hagmasters**) 'worked on sub-contract to foundry masters, hired and paid their own moulders' and which 'still persisted in the 1880s'

(H.J. Fyrth and H. Collins, *The Foundry Workers,* Amalgamated Union of Foundry Workers, 1959, p. 23).

HAGMASTER; see **hagman system.**

HALF-TIME BRITAIN; see **underemployment.**

HALF-TIME SYSTEM. The practice of employing children half-time in mills which resulted from the partial restriction of working hours of young persons under the provisions of the 1844 Factory Act. The **Education Act 1918** abolished half-time working of children under 14 as from January 1921. E. Hopwood, *History of the Lancashire Cotton Industry and the Amalgamated Weavers' Association,* AWA, 1969.

HALSEY PREMIUM BONUS SYSTEM. An **incentive payment system** based, like the **Bedeaux System,** upon providing the worker with a bonus for time saved. It was introduced by Mr F.A. Halsey, superintendent of the Rand Drill Company of Canada in 1890 and to Britain by Messrs G. and J. Weir of Cathcart, being sometimes therefore known as the **Weir System** or the **Halsey-Weir System.** Halsey suggested percentage bonus of $33\frac{1}{3}$ per cent; following Weir many employers have preferred 50 per cent, hence the method is sometimes known as the **50-50 Sharing Plan,** the general formula being (time taken *plus* half of time saved) x rate per hour. Under this system the price per unit diminishes, as under Bedeaux, for each successive unit of output; see N.C. Hunt, *Methods of Wage Payments in British Industry,* Pitman, 1951, R. Marriott, *Incentive Payment Systems,* Staples Press, 3rd (revised) ed. 1968, and W.J. Reader, *The Weir Group: A Centenary History,* Weidenfeld and Nicolson, 1971.

HALSEY-WEIR SYSTEM; see **Halsey Premium Bonus System.**

HAND-OVER PAY. A payment to a shift worker for remaining on the job after the end of his shift either to keep machines in operation, or to give information and advice to the on-coming shift in order to ensure continuity of production. Hand-over pay may apply to either, or both of these situations; under **coupling-up** in engineering (q.v.), it is confined to the latter.

HANLEY v. PEASE AND PARTNERS

LTD (1915) 1 KB 696; see **suspension**. K.W. Wedderburn, *Cases and Materials on Labour Law*, CUP, 1967, p. 143.

HARDMAN REPORT. The report of the Committee of Inquiry set up jointly by the Post Office and the **Union of Post Office Workers** with Sir Henry Hardman, KCB, in the chair, which was published on 5 May 1971. The Inquiry followed the prolonged dispute between the Post Office and the UPW earlier in 1971 and recommended, Mr John Hughes dissenting, a pay increase of 9 per cent, with differential rates in areas of labour shortage outside the London area and (all three members of the committee in agreement), scale shortening over two years, accelerated mechanisation and productivity measures, reduction of excessive overtime and a system of linking pay locally with productivity.

HASTINGS AGREEMENT. An agreement adopted at the 1933 Labour Party Conference laying down the terms under which affiliated trade unions might sponsor Labour candidates. Such arrangements were required to be made by written agreement, terminable on three months' notice on either side. The Constituency Labour Party concerned was required to pay not less than 20 per cent and the affiliated union not more than 80 per cent of a candidate's maximum expenses allowed by law. Maximum sums were also laid down which unions might pay as contributions to a Constituency Labour Party for organisation and registration expenses and for a full-time agent. A separate agreement governs the position of Labour and Co-operative candidates; see Martin Harrison, *Trade Unions and the Labour Party since 1945*, Allen and Unwin, 1960; also **Political Fund**.

HAWTHORNE EFFECT; see **Hawthorne Experiment**.

HAWTHORNE EXPERIMENT. A series of experimental studies carried out between 1927 and 1932 by the Research Division of the Harvard Business School at the Hawthorne Works of the Western Electric Company which formed the basis for a school of thought on **human relations** associated with the name of Elton Mayo. The studies were originally described in his Lowell Lectures published as *Human Problems of an Industrial Civilisation* (Macmillan, 1933) and written up at length in F.J. Roethlisberger and W.J.

Dickson, *Management and the Worker*, Harvard University Press, 1939; see also Henry Landsberger, *Hawthorne Revisited*, New York State School of Industrial Relations, 1958. They were little known in Britain until after the second world war. The essence of the Hawthorne findings was that physical and monetary factors alone were insufficient to explain changes in out-put and employee morale. Their effect was to lay emphasis on the informal social organisation of work groups and upon the resolution of conflict, which was regarded as undesirable, by management attention to the social needs of workers. The Hawthorne Experiment had considerable impact on academic and management thinking in the 1940s and 1950s, but its influence has declined since that time; see **human relations. Hawthorne Effect:** the effect which management attention to problems may have in improving production and morale before, or after, better methods or working techniques are introduced, or, more generally, the tendency of people to behave in an artificial way when they know that they are the subject of an experiment.

HEAD SHOPMAN; see **shop steward**.

HEAD TEACHERS, NATIONAL ASSOCIATION OF. Formed in 1897 and now includes 370 local associations of head teachers of schools recognised by the Department of Education and Science, whether local authority or independent. It is represented on the appropriate **Burnham Committee** for pay and conditions, on the Schools' Council for curricula and on every major national body concerned with education. *Address:* Maxwelton House, 41-43 Boltro Road, Haywards Heath, Sussex RH16 1BJ. *Tel:* Haywards Heath (0444) 5391-2. *Membership:* more than 19,000.

HEALDERS AND TWISTERS TRADE AND FRIENDLY SOCIETY, HUDDERSFIELD. A textile trade union founded in 1896 as the Huddersfield and District Healders and Twisters Trade Union and changing to its present title in 1911. The union had its highest membership of 530 members in 1928; since that time numbers have steadily declined. *Address:* 20 Uppergate, Hepworth, Huddersfield HD7 1TG. *Tel:* 048-489 4509. *TUC Affiliated Membership, 1977:* 221.

HEALTH AND SAFETY COMMIS-

SION; see **Health and Safety at Work Act 1974.**

HEALTH AND SAFETY EXECUTIVE; see **Health and Safety at Work Act 1974.**

HEALTH AND SAFETY AT WORK ACT 1974. An Act of Parliament resulting from the report of the Robens Committee of Inquiry into Health and Safety at Work 1922 (see **Robens Report**) and following that Committee's approach to health and safety issues in contrast to the more fragmented approach broken down by industry and hazard which was favoured in previous legislation, e.g. the Factories Act 1961, Shops, Offices and Railway Premises Acts etc. Such legislation was to be replaced by regulations and Codes of Practice under the new Act. The Act applies to all places of work and to all employers and all workers with the exception of domestic workers in private houses and lays a positive statutory requirement on employers, so far as practicable, to ensure the health, safety and welfare of his employees. Employees have an unqualified duty to take reasonable care while at work. From 1 October 1974 a **Health and Safety Commission** was required to provide an effective general information and advisory service and to submit to the Secretary of State for approval and necessary regulations and Codes of Practice. From 1 January 1975 a **Health and Safety Executive** was charged with enforcing the legislation and appointing inspectors with suitable qualifications with power, if they think it necessary, to issue **improvement notices** and, in more extreme cases, **prohibition notices**, the latter prohibiting activities which would, in the inspector's opinion, give rise to serious personal injury until they were rectified. The Act also provides for the appointment of **Safety Representatives** in the workplace (q.v.) and for the taking over of the **Employment Medical Advisory Service**; see Ian Fife and E.A. Machin, *Redgrave's Health and Safety in Factories* Butterworth's 1976 and R. Howells and B. Barrett, *The Health and Safety at Work Act: A Guide for Managers*, IPM, 1975.

HEALTH SERVICE EMPLOYEES, CONFEDERATION OF (COHSE). A trade union formed in 1946 as a result of the merger of the Mental Hospital and Institutional Workers' Union (1930, founded as the National Asylum Workers' Union in 1910) and the National Union of County Officers (1930, originally the Poor Law Workers' Trade Union, founded 1918, which changed its name to the Poor Law Officers' Union in 1922). The union is represented on National Joint and Whitley Councils for Local Authorities and the National Health Service. *Address:* Glen House, High Street, Banstead, Surrey SM7 2LH. *Tel:* 25-53322. *TUC Affiliated Membership 1977:* 200,455.

HEALTH VISITORS' ASSOCIATION. An organisation founded in London in 1896 as the Women Sanitary Inspectors' Association. Increasing membership among health visitors resulted in a change of name to the Women Sanitary Inspectors' and Health Visitors' Association in 1914 and four years later the organisation registered as a trade union, though still maintaining to the present many characteristics of a **professional association**. In 1929 the organisation became known as the Women Public Health Visitors' Association as a result of recruitment among school nurses, domiciliary midwives and matrons of day nurseries. Its present title was adopted in 1962. Health visitors now make up the vast majority of membership and many ancillary grades have become ineligible. M.F. Weller, 'Seventy Years On: Inaugural Lecture at the Annual Conference of 1966', *International Journal of Nursing Studies,* Vol. 4, 1967, pp. 233-43. *Address:* 36 Eccleston Square, London SW1V 1PF. *Tel:* 01-834 9523. *TUC Affiliated Membership 1977:* 9,719.

HEATON TRANSPORT (ST HELENS) LTD v. TGWU (1972), 2 All ER 1217-1267 and ICR 285. A judgement by the House of Lords arising out of the action of dockers in blacking disputed work at Liverpool and Hull, the activities of shop stewards in organising such blacking and the question of Transport and General Workers Union responsibility for these actions of its stewards. Earlier a Court of Appeal judgement had found that the union was not so responsible, leading to the imprisonment of five London dockers ('The Pentonville Five') for contempt of court. This was reversed by the House of Lords, on appeal, finding the union responsible. On the legal issues involved, see Bob Hepple, 'Union Responsibility for Shop Stewards', *Industrial Law Journal,* December 1972 and case note by P.L. Davies, 36 *Modern Law Review,* 78, 1973.

HEIGHT MONEY. Allowances paid for working at heights, e.g. in the National Working Rules for the Building Industry (Rule 3), which allows for extra payments for working at various heights over 40 feet on 'detached work' (i.e. on detached tower-like structures), and over 125 feet on 'exposed work' (i.e. on buildings with no outside cladding or protection from weather conditions); see also **differentials**.

HEWLETT v. ALLEN; see check-off.

HIGGLING OF THE MARKET. A phrase used by Sidney and Beatrice Webb (*Industrial Democracy*, 1902 ed., Part III, Chap. II) to describe the process in which workers are involved in **individual bargaining**, to their disadvantage, as both they and Alfred Marshall note (*Principles of Economics*, 3rd ed., 1895, Book VI, Ch. IV, p. 649), the urgency of workers coming to terms with their employers necessarily leading to their getting the worst of the bargain. The Webbs saw the chain of bargaining between the levels of the worker and the private customer as demanding resort to the methods of **mutual insurance** and **collective bargaining** if the standard of life of workers was to be maintained and raised. For a critique of the limitations of an economic argument of this kind; see Allan Flanders, 'Collective Bargaining - A Theoretical Analysis', *British Journal of Industrial Relations*, March 1968.

HIGH-FLIER or **cowboy**, or **ratebuster** (q.v.); a worker whose main object is maximum earnings rather than security of employment; Innis Macbeath, *The Times Guide to the Industrial Relations Act*, 1971, p. 15.

HIGH TASK RATING METHOD. A work study procedure whereby the time study man compares the actual rate of working of an operator with his concept of the rate necessary to earn the normal incentive earnings, as contrasted with a **low task rating method** (q.v.) EPA, *Glossary of Work Study Terms*.

HILL v. C.A. PARSONS AND CO. LTD (1971) 3 WLR 995, (1971) 3 All ER 1345 (CA). A legal case in which an injunction was granted by the Court of Appeal to restrain the employer from terminating the contract of an employee of 35 years standing, under pressure from the Draughtsmen and Allied Technicians' Association. In a reserved judgement, it was maintained that the notice to terminate was invalid on the grounds that it constituted an exception (per **Francis v. Kuala Lumpur Councillors** (1962) 1 WLR 1411, 1417-1418, and **Lumley v. Wagner** (1852) De

G.M. and G 604) to the principle of the court that **specific performance** could not be claimed in cases involving a contract for personal employment (**Stocker v. Brocklehurt** (1851) 3 Mac and G 250) unless the case fell within some recognised exception (**Whitwood Chemical Co. v. Hardman** 1891, 2 Ch. 416). Lord Denning, Lord Justice Sachs concurring, maintained that the length of notice was insufficient and that, had it been in force at the time, the **Industrial Relations Act 1971** would have made the 100 per cent agreement of DATA with the company, which precluded Mr Hill from joining the **United Kingdom Association of Professional Engineers** unlawful, and ss. 5 and 22 would have protected him against dismissal by his employers on grounds of his refusal to join DATA.

HILTON v. ECKERSLEY (1855) 6 E and B 47; see **conspiracy**.

HIVING-OFF. The separation from the Civil Service of particular areas of work which were formally its province and their transfer to independent boards or agencies. The Fulton Committee (*The Civil Service, Vol. 1, Report of the Committee, 1966-1968*, HMSO, Cmnd. 3638, pp. 61-2) discussed the issue of hiving-off, noted that many activities were 'hived-off' (e.g. the Post Office, the Atomic Energy Authority, etc.) and recommended that the whole question should be reviewed.

HOLIDAY CREDITS; see holidays with pay.

HOLIDAY EXTRAS. Gift hours paid over and above **clocked hours** for work performed on certain agreed holidays (steel industry).

HOLIDAYS WITH PAY (HWP). **Annual holidays** (excluding **Bank Holidays** or other **paid holidays**) for which workers receive payment while absent from work; also used of the movement of opinion which led to these conditions of work. The development of holidays with pay is described by G.C. Cameron in G.L. Reid and D.J. Robertson, *Fringe Benefits, Labour Costs and Social Security*, George Allen and Unwin, 1965, Ch. 10. The **Amulree Committee** in 1938 (q.v.) estimated 7¾ million out of a total of 18½ million employed workpeople to be in receipt of holidays with pay, and made recommendations for its extension (see also **Holidays with Pay Act 1938**), which has mainly resulted from collective agreements, and which is now thought to be virtually complete. In April 1977 1 per cent of all manual workers were estimated to be entitled to 2 to 3 weeks' basic annual holiday, 18 per cent to 3 weeks, 47 per cent to 3 to 4 weeks, 34 per cent to more than 4 weeks (Department of Employment, *Time Rates of Wages and Hours of Work*, 1977). In the engineering industry, annual holiday pay has traditionally been by a system of **holiday credits**, every manual worker being credited for each full week's work performed, with one-twenty-fifth of the sum of the appropriate time rate plus one-third, or one-twenty-fifth of any domestic rate used for calculating holiday credits, whichever is the greater, each federated firm being required to keep accumulated credits in a trust fund for disbursement; this arrangement was ended by a new national holiday agreement of April 1978 which bases holiday pay on individual normal average earnings, full pay being given to employees in the service of a company on 1 January in any year, with proportionate pay for new starters and for **accrued holiday pay**. In the building and civil engineering industry holiday credits are managed by the **Building and Civil Engineering Holidays Scheme Management Limited**, through a system of stamps representing each week of credit accumulated. **International Labour Convention No. 132** revises earlier conventions on annual holidays by raising the standards to three weeks and giving detailed guidance for determining the duration of the holiday and for calculating holiday pay; it has not been ratified by the UK government on the grounds that it is not consistent with the way in which conditions of work are determined in the UK.

HOLIDAYS WITH PAY ACT 1938. An Act empowering all statutory wage authorities (Trade Boards, Agricultural Wages Committees and the Road Haulage Wages Board), to make provisions for holidays with pay in addition to any other holidays or half-holidays to which such workers might be entitled under other enactments, e.g. the Shops Act. The statutes at present empowering the statutory fixing of holidays with pay are the **Wages Councils Act 1959**, the **Agricultural Wages Act 1948** and the **Agricultural Wages (Scotland) Act 1949; see holidays with pay** and **Amulree Committee** for the origins of the statute.

HOLLAND-MARTIN REPORT. The report of a *Committee of Inquiry into Trawler Safety*, Final Report Cmnd. 4114, July 1969, under the Chairmanship of Admiral Sir Doric Holland-Martin.

HOMEWORKING. A type of **outworking** (q.v.) in which workers receive work and perform tasks in their own homes for manufacturing or other producers or service trades; work done by **homeworkers**. The Commission onn industrial Relations has confined the definition to those so employed directly by manufacturing establishments, but it may logically be extended to other work than manufacturing (e.g. to typing, addressing envelopes etc.) and to those who do work at home and are paid by middlemen or contractors; see Trades Unions Congress, *Homeworking; A TUC Statement*, 1978. The Employment Protection Act 1975 (Schedule 7, Part IV 9 (6)(b)) brings within the scope of the Wages Council Acts all persons who work at home in industries covered by **Wages Councils.**

HOMEWORKER; see homeworking.

HONOUR CARDS; see clocking.

HORIZONTAL DEMARCATION; see demarcation.

HORIZONTAL UNIONISM. Trade union structure based upon the organisation of workers with similar interests, without regard to the industry in which they are employed; the opposite of **vertical** or **industrial unionism.** Craft unions have commonly been thought of as an expression of horizontal unionism (see **craft union**); another form may appear as a variant of occupational unionism (see **occupational union**). It is in this sense that the Civil Service Clerical Association, in its evidence to the Donovan Royal Commission on Trade Unions and Employers' Associations, favoured five unions in the civil service: *viz*, for messengers, manipulative and allied grades; clerical and allied grades; executive and allied grades; administrative and allied grades; and professional and allied grades (see CSCA, *Memorandum*, December 1965, p. 4).

HORNBY v. CLOSE (1867) 2 QB 153. In which it was ruled that the United Order of Boilermakers could not recover £24.18s. 5½d. from a member of the union on the grounds that the rules of the union were illegal in the sense that they could not be legally enforced. K.W. Wedderburn,

Cases and Materials on Labour Law, CUP, 1967, p. 538.

HORSMAN STRIKE. A stoppage of work at the Morris Cars Branch of the British Motor Corporation following the dismissal of Mr Frank Horsman, Senior Shop Steward of the Transport and General Workers' Union at the factory on 15 July 1959. The issue of the dismissal was never completely resolved, and formed part of the background to the establishment of the **Motor Industry Joint Labour Council** in November 1965.

HOSIERY AND KNITWEAR WORKERS, NATIONAL UNION OF. An amalgamation of five district unions in the Midlands and one branch in Scotland, in 1945, first known as the National Union of Hosiery Workers and later given its present title in order to assist the organisation of knitwear workers. Since 1945 the union has, by transfer of engagements, taken into membership a number of trade unions on the finishing side of the industry, in 1970 the Nottingham and District Hosiery Finishers' Association and the Leicester and Leicestershire Hosiery Trimmers and Auxiliary Association and in 1971 the **Amalgamated Society of Operative Lacemakers and Textile Workers** (q.v.). The majority of members of the union are covered by the wages and conditions of the National Joint Industrial Council for the Hosiery Trade, but because of the importance of the Courtauld Group of companies, separate agreements are made with this group also. *Address:* 55 New Walk, Leicester LE1 7EB. *Tel:* 0533 56791. *TUC Affiliated Membership, 1977:* 71,626; see also **Robinson Inquiry.**

HOSIERY AND TEXTILE DYERS' AND AUXILIARY ASSOCIATION. A union previously known as the Hinckley and District Dyers' and Auxiliary Workers' Union, and founded in 1912. Its membership represents dyers, finishers and auxiliary workers in hosiery, knitwear and fabric dyeing and finishing in the Leicester and Nottinghamshire areas. It organises all grades of staff, including drivers, in those textile firms in which it is represented. It had 450 members in December 1977. It is affiliated to the **General Federation of Trade Unions** and the National Federation of Hosiery Dyers and Finishers. *Address:* 67 Station Road, Hinckley, Leics.

HOSPITAL CONSULTANTS AND SPECIALISTS, ASSOCIATION OF. Formed as the Regional Hospital Consultants and Specialists Association on the inception of the National Health Service and taking its present title in 1972 when Senior Hospital Doctors from Teaching Hospitals became eligible to join. *Address:* The Old Court House, London Road, Ascot, Berks. *Tel:* Ascot 25025. *Membership 1977:* about 5,000.

HOURS OF EMPLOYMENT (CONVENTIONS) ACT 1936; see **night work.**

HOURS OF WORK. Working hours, in relation to length (especially in the day or the **working day**), and also in relation to patterns of hours worked, e.g. **fixed working hours, variable working hours, shift work, staggered hours, flexible working hours, rational working hours,** etc., or both, e.g. in relation to the **working week.** In general, no limits are set by legislation to the length or pattern of hours worked by men in Britain, though there are exceptions where seamen are concerned, and in baking, coal mining, road haulage, automatic sheet glass manufacture, and in shops; the hours of women and young persons in factories have, however, been subject to limitations since 1833, currently in the **Factories Act 1961,** the **Employment of Women, Young Persons and Children Act 1920** and the **Hours of Employment (Conventions) Act 1936.** These enactments provide, in summary, that women and young persons in factories may not work more than 9 hours in any day or 48 hours in any week, that working hours are to be between 7 a.m. and 8 p.m. (7 a.m. and 1 p.m. on Saturdays, that there is to be no Sunday work, and that the maximum period of work without a break is to be 4½ hours; there is also a weekly overtime limit of 6 hours and an annual limit of 100 hours **statutory overtime** in any calendar year, not to be worked in more than 25 weeks (see also **federation overtime** and **night work**); see Department of Employment and Productivity, *Hours of Employment of Women and Young Persons Employed in Factories, A Report,* HMSO, 1969. Hours of work are determined for the majority of workers by industry-wide collective bargaining and in **Wages Council** industries by Wage Regulation Orders. Currently, the great majority of workers have a normal or standard working week of 40 hours or less: in April 1976, over 79 per cent of full-time male manual workers had a normal working week of 40 hours, almost 15 per cent having a working week shorter than this and 6 per cent a working week longer than this. At the same time, some 22 per cent of non-manual workers had a normal working week of 37½ hours, that of somewhat less than 54 per cent being shorter than this and about 25 per cent longer (Department of Employment, *New Earnings Survey*, HMSO, 1977). A working week of 47 or 48 hours was extensively adopted in Britain during the period 1919 and 1920, sometimes with an eighthour day; the period immediately after the second world war saw the reduction of normal working hours for manual workers generally to 44, and then to 42 in the later 1950s and early 1960s, to 40, together with a 5-day week, while non-manual hours moved towards the 37½ hour position, or less. Actual hours worked have, since the war, commonly been considerably in excess of normal working hours (see **overtime**). The International Labour Organisation has adopted a number of Conventions and Recommendations relating to hours of work: the **Hours of Work (Industry) Convention 1919 (International Labour Convention No. 1),** not ratified by the UK; the **Forty-Hour Week Convention 1935 (No. 47),** which came into force in 1951 and has been ratified by a few countries only, not including the UK, and the **International Labour Recommendation No. 116, 1962,** which was designed to speed up the advance of the 40-hour week; the European Social Charter (Art. 2(1)) obliges member states to 'provide for reasonable daily and weekly working hours, the working week to be progressively reduced to the extent that the increase of productivity and other relevant factors permit', see Clyde E. Dankert, Floyd C. Mann, Herbert R. Northrup (eds), *Hours of Work,* Harper and Row, Industrial Relations Research Association Publication No. 32, 1965, and National Board for Prices and Incomes, *Hours of Work, Overtime and Shiftworking,* Report No. 161, Cmnd. 4554, December 1970, and P.J. Sloane, *Changing Patterns of Working Hours,* DE Manpower Paper No. 13, 1975; see also **Eight Hours Day Movement, shiftworking, guaranteed week, moonlighting.**

HOURS OF WORK (INDUSTRY) CONVENTION 1919; see **hours of work.**

HOUSE UNION; see **company union.**

HUDDERSFIELD HEALDERS AND TWISTERS TRADE AND FRIENDLY SOCIETY; see **Healders and Twisters Trade and Friendly Society, Huddersfield.**

HULL MAIN PRINCIPLES; see **Bridlington Agreement.**

HUMAN RESOURCE ACCOUNTING. A system of accounting for 'people' as organisational resources or of measuring the cost and value of people to organisations. The notion underlying Human Resource Accounting is that boards of directors and chief executives should be encouraged to regard human resources less as an expense than as assets which have returns as well as costs and which, if properly deployed and developed, can increase in value to the organisation. If, therefore, suitable measurements can be found to enable the costs and value of, for example training, to be correctly evaluated, and for the effectiveness of management's use of manpower to be monitored, the role and status of personnel specialists might be enhanced and productivity and profitability increased. Theory in the field appears to be developing from two directions, the one based upon a study of the variables which determine the effectiveness of human organisation, e.g. in Rensis Likert and David G. Bowers, 'Organisation Theory and Human Resource Accounting', *American Psychologist,* September 1968, pp. 585-92, and the other on the assessment of the individual's value to an organisation, e.g. in the work of Eric Flamholtz; see Eric Flamholtz, 'Human Resource Accounting: A Review of Theory and Research', *Journal of Management Studies,* Vol. 11 No. 1, February 1974, pp. 44-61. Variations on the American approaches are suggested by W.J. Giles and D. Robinson, *Human Asset Accounting,* IPM, 1972.

HUMAN RELATIONS. (1) Relationships between workers and workers, between groups of workers and between workers and managements and groups of workers and managements in industry of an informal and unstructured kind, i.e. in contrast with, and sometimes in opposition to, **labour relations** and/or **industrial relations,** where these are regarded as involving formal regulation by collective agreement or by formal managerial or trade union institutions; (2) a school of thought, associated originally with Elton Mayo (see **Hawthorne Experiment**) but subsequently further developed by others, and concerned with the notion that, by contrast with the tenets of **scientific management,** workers have many needs other than the purely economic, and that managements may, by paying attention to their non-economic, social and cultural needs, increase worker satisfaction and productivity (see A. Etzioni, *Modern Organisations,* Prentice Hall, 1964, p. 20 *et seq.*); sometimes also extended to refer to means of human relations training, e.g. role-playing, **T Groups,** etc., to embrace an ethical orientation to work ('the positive good which may result from the right kind of inter-relationship between people'; 'a spirit of understanding between individuals and groups'; 'the attitude of one human being to another'), or to claim the disciplinary approach of a science concerned with an holistic rather than partial approach to inter- and intra-personal behaviour (see Robert Tannenbaum, 'Some Current Issues in Human Relations', *California Management Review,* Vol. II, No. 1, Fall 1959). Early human relations thought was criticised for ignoring external economic variables, ignoring class and other conflict, disregarding the existence of trade unions, being manipulative, etc. (see Henry Landsberger, *Hawthorne Revisited,* New York State School of Industrial and Labor Relations, 1958). Much of this criticism can still be heard, but in the 1960s the tendency was to take more structured approaches (e.g. Rensis Likert, *The Human Organisation,* McGraw-Hill, 1967), to emphasise more directed training, to accept that **conflict** is normal, and even healthy, to propose new organisational patterns and to admit the role of technology (C. Argyris, *Integrating the Individual and the Organisation,* Wiley, 1964, R. Blauner, *Alienation and Freedom,* University of Chicago Press, 1964, J. Woodward, *Industrial Organisation,* OUP, 1965, W. Bennis, *Changing Organisations,* McGraw-Hill, 1966, T. Burns and G.M. Stalker, *The Management of Innovation,* Tavistock, 1966). In the 1970s this trend has continued, though with more discussion of **industrial democracy, workers' participation,** and **job enrichment.**

HUMAN RELATIONS. The journal of the **Tavistock Institute of Human Relations** (q.v.) containing articles of industrial relations interest.

HUMBUGGING; see **driving.**

HUNGER MARCHES; see **National Unemployed Workers' Movement.**

HUNT COMMITTEE; see **assisted areas.**

HWP; holidays with pay (q.v.).

HYGIENE FACTORS. Factors in work motivation distinguished by Frederick Herzberg from **motivators** (see **job enrichment**). Herzberg's theory (see F. Herzberg, B. Mausner and B. Snyderman, *The Motivation to Work,* John Wiley and Sons, 1969, and F. Herzberg, *Work and the Nature of Man,* Crosby Lockwood Staples, 1974) supposes that one set of factors, hygiene factors, are concerned with job context, e.g. wages, working conditions, status, security, etc., while another set are motivators and relate to job content. Hygiene factors, Herzberg argues, can reduce job *dis*satisfaction; motivators, on the other hand, can create job satisfaction, and are related to achievement, work content, recognition, responsibility, advancement and personal growth. Each set of factors operates in its own dimension, and may have its value, but for positive effects, motivators are needed; see W.J. Paul and K.B. Robertson, *Job Enrichment and Employee Motivation,* Gower Press, 1970.

I

IAB. Industrial Arbitration Board (q.v.).

IAM. INSTITUTE OF ADMINISTRATIVE MANAGEMENT; see **Administrative Management, Institute of.**

ICF. International Federation of Chemical and General Workers' Unions; see **International Trade Secretariats.**

ICFTU. International Confederation of Free Trade Unions (q.v.).

ICTU. Irish Congress of Trade Unions (q.v.).

IDLE TIME. An expression used generally (as in British Standards Institution, *Glossary of Terms Used in Work Study,* BS 3138, 1969, No. 33018) to mean 'that part of attendance time when the worker has work available but does not do it', or more specifically to mean **machine idle time,** i.e. the time when a machine is available but is not used, e.g. because of shortage of material. In both senses it is the opposite of **machine running time,** but not usually considered to be identical with **down time** (q.v.).

IDT. Industrial Disputes Tribunal (q.v.).

IFBWW. International Federation of Building and Woodworkers; see **International Trade Secretariats.**

IFFTU. International Federation of Free Teachers' Unions; see **International Trade Secretariats.**

IFPAAW. International Federation of Plantation, Agricultural and Allied Workers; see **International Trade Secretariats.**

IFPCW. International Federation of Petroleum and Chemical Workers; see **International Trade Secretariats.**

IFTU. International Federation of Trade Unions (q.v.).

IGF. International Graphical Federation; see **International Trade Secretariats.**

ILFORD AGREEMENT. An agreement negotiated in 1965 between Ilford Ltd and the General and Municipal Workers' Union providing, *inter alia,* that the company would accept the principle of **100 per cent membership** in return for union undertakings in relation to **job evaluation** and other items, and that a failure of a union member to abide by union rules and by its agreements with the company would free the latter from its 100 per cent obligation. The Ilford Agreement was an early example of a type of productivity package deal (see **productivity bargaining**) containing some unusual features; see K.W. Wedderburn, *Cases and Materials on Labour Law,* CUP, 1967, p. 665.

ILLEGAL MEN. Men who have not by apprenticeship gained the right to follow a trade; Sidney and Beatrice Webb, *History of Trade Unionism, 1666-1920,* 1920 ed., p. 59; **foreigners;** A.E. Musson, *The Typographical Association,* CUP, 1954.

ILJ. Industrial Law Journal (q.v.).

ILO. International Labour Organisation (q.v.).

IMF. International Metalworkers' Federation; see **International Trade Secretariats.**

IMI. Irish Management Institute (q.v.).

IMPERIAL CHAPEL; see **chapel.**

IMPINGEMENT MONEY. Payment made in circumstances in which a shift impinges on the Christmas holiday (national newspaper industry).

IMPLIED TERMS. Terms of a contract, e.g. a **contract of employment,** which are not **express terms,** i.e. which have not been formulated by the parties, orally or in writing (including terms in correspondence, **works rules,** collective agreements etc.); hence terms of a contract which are inferred by a court. Authorities appear to agree that terms may be implied by reference to the presumed intention of the parties, from duties imposed by the law (including general legal duties in a contract of employment, such as co-operation, care and fidelity), and from custom; see, for example, B.A. Hepple and Paul O'Higgins, *Employment Law,* Sweet and Maxwell, 1976, Ch. 7. In certain cases legislation exists which enables the **Central Arbitration Committee** to make awards which have effect as implied terms of contract of the workers concerned; see also **Schedule 11 Claims.**

IMPROVEMENT CURVE; see **learning curve.**

IMPROVEMENT FACTOR; see **annual improvement factor.**

IMPROVEMENT NOTICE; see **Health and Safety at Work Act 1974.**

IMPROVER. Either (1) a young journeyman who has served the full time of his apprenticeship, but is required by agreement or custom to spend some time as an improver before attaining a full journeyman's (or craftsman's) rate. Improver status of this kind was usual in the engineering industry in the 1920s: 'the young man usually served as an improver for a period which might be anything from 6 months to 2 years on conditions and at wage rates agreed by the local unions, which usually meant that the rate was 10/- less than that earned by the qualified men' (Gertrude Williams, *Recruitment to Skilled Trades,* Routledge and Kegan Paul, 1957, p. 68); see also **loosing rate.** Such a status is not now normal, though some such workers may be given a differential rate if they complete their training before the accepted age, e.g. 21 or 20 in some cases; or (2) an adult or mature trainee over apprentice age who attains the necessary skill to be accepted to perform particular jobs (e.g. in the manufacture of stationery) or, as in the gas industry, who is recruited (e.g. as an improver mainlayer where there is no apprenticeship for young people) and undergoes training for a specified period of time.

IMS MONITOR. A quarterly review of the British labour market, commenting on current and recent trends and written for practical decision-makers who have to deal directly with employees in business or government service (1972-). It is published by Chapman and Hall for the Institute of Manpower Studies, University of Sussex, Mantell Buildings, Falmer, Brighton, BN1 9RF.

IN PLACE OF STRIFE; see **Donovan Commission.**

INCENTIVE PAYMENT SYSTEM, incentive scheme or **incentive plan.** Any system of payment which provides the individual worker with an incentive to increased effort or increased production; hence any system of **payment by results** in which such increases are associated with increased earnings, in whatever form, i.e. any system other than one involving plain time rates or fixed remuneration by the hour, week, month or other period. R. Marriott (*Incentive Payment Systems,* 3rd (revised) ed., Staples Press, 1968) classifies systems into individual or group weekly wage incentive schemes (**straight piecework, money piece-work, standard hour, bonus, premium bonus** and other systems in which earnings vary, depending on the scheme used, in different proportions in relation to output); long-term collective schemes (**share of production plans, cost reduction plans,** e.g. **Scanlon, Rucker, profit sharing** and **co-partnership**); and systems not directly based on production (**merit rating, attendance bonuses** etc.). Incentive payment systems rest upon an individualistic theory of work and motivation the operation of which has been questioned from a number of different points of view: confusion of issues (e.g. W.M. Leiserson, 'Wage Decisions and Wage Structure in the United States' in E.M. Hugh-Jones, *Wage Structure in Theory and Practice,* North-Holland Publishing Co., 1966); narrowness of assumptions (W.F. Whyte, *Money and Motivation,* Harper, 1955, H. Behrend, 'Financial

Incentives as a System of Beliefs', *British Journal of Sociology,* June 1959, T. Lupton, *Money for Effort,* HMSO, 1961, S. Shimmin, *Payment by Results,* Staples Press, 1959, W. Baldamus, *Efficiency and Effort,* Tavistock, 1967); technical inadequacies (D. Pym, 'Is there a Future for Wage Incentive Systems?', *British Journal of Industrial Relations,* November 1964, G.L. Mangum, 'Are Wage Incentives Becoming Obsolete?' *Industrial Relations,* October 1962; see also **effort bargain**). The general situation is discussed in R. Marriott (op. cit. *supra*), National Board for Prices and Incomes, *Payment by Results (Supplement),* Cmnd. 3627-1, December 1968, Paper 1), H. Behrend, 'An Assessment of the Current Status of Incentive Schemes', *Journal of Industrial Relations,* October 1963 and SAF, *The Condemned Piecework,* Svenska Arbetsgivareföreningen, 1970, in which a study of 73 plants in Swedish industry revealed falls in efficiency where changes had been made from piecework systems to **fixed wages** and increases in efficiency where changes had been made from one incentive payment system to another and where fixed wages had been changed to incentive systems suggesting, *inter alia,* that much still remained to be learned about alterations in wage payment forms; see also D. McGregor, *The Human Side of Enterprise,* McGraw Hill, 1960, and the work of F. Herzberg, *Work and the Nature of Man,* Crosby Lockwood Staples, 1974; see **job enrichment** for alternative views of worker motivation; also **wage drift, measured daywork.**

INCENTIVE PLAN; see **incentive payment scheme.**

INCENTIVE RATE. A rate of payment arising, over and above **basic rate** or **standard rate** or **standard performance,** from an **incentive payment system** or **bonus scheme.**

INCENTIVE SCHEME; see **incentive payment system.**

INCE PLAN. A proposal in 1954 by Sir Godfrey Ince, Permanent Secretary to the Ministry of Labour, that in order to restrain wage demands, all industries should make use of **arbitration** as a final step in the settlement of disputes. The proposal followed a period in which wage arbitration awards had been small in amount (see Allan Flanders, 'Wage Movements and Wage Policy in Post-war Britain', *Annals* *of the American Academy,* March 1957). It was rejected, though for different reasons, both by the Trades Union Congress and the British Employers' Confederation; see **terminal arbitration.**

INCE REPORT; see **Youth Employment Service.**

INCIDENTAL OVERTIME ALLOWANCE. An additional annual payment made to all staff except foremen, apprentices and juniors, carrying with it an obligation to work short periods of overtime of not more than 30 minutes a day, or more than one hour a week: *Electricity Supply Agreement, 1964/65.*

INCOMES POLICY. An attempt by government to provide criteria for influencing, in the national interest, the outcome of income determination, whether such income is derived from wages, salaries or **non-wage incomes,** principally in order to restrain inflation by keeping increases within limits or **norms,** or within the bounds of productivity increases, but also in some instances with other objectives in mind, e.g. dealing with problems of **low pay,** the adjustment of **differentials** in the interests of equity etc.; sometimes regarded as synonymous with **wage restraint** or with **wage policy,** but more usually distinguished from the latter in that the expression 'wage policy' suggests the exclusion of non-wage incomes. The term 'incomes policy' became generally preferred to 'wage policy' in the 1960s, particularly after 1963 when at the Labour Party Conference, trade union support was forthcoming, not for a wage policy but for 'an incomes policy to include salaries, wages, dividends and profits and social security benefits' (Frank Cousins, General Secretary, Transport and General Workers' Union). Since 1965 it has been generally synonymous with the term **prices and incomes policy** as practised by the Wilson administration until 1970 and abandoned by the Heath government in that year; see Lloyd Ulman and Robert J. Flanagan, *Wage Restraint; A Study of Incomes Policy in Western Europe,* University of California Press, 1971, H.A. Clegg, *How to run an incomes policy and why we made such a mess of the last one,* Heinemann, 1971, John Corina, *The Development of Incomes Policy,* Institute of Personnel Management, 1966 and Campbell Balfour, *Incomes Policy and The Public Sector,* Routledge and Kegan Paul, 1972. The idea of an incomes policy, voluntarily

agreed between the government, the Trades Union Congress and the Confederation of British Industry was revived by the Heath government in the second half of 1972 in tripartite talks at Chequers and in Downing Street (see **Chequers and Downing Street Talks**); these broke down in November 1972 and led to the imposition of a statutory incomes standstill (see **Counter-Inflation (Temporary Provisions) Act 1972**), followed by a second stage in a programme for controlling inflation (Cmnd. 5205, January 1973) under the **Counter-Inflation Act 1973** and the establishment under it of a **Pay Board** to oversee the application of the remuneration aspects of a Prices and Pay Code. This phase of incomes policy, a third phase having foundered in the miners' national strike in January 1974, ended with the fall of the Heath government and the advent of a Labour government in February of that year which until 1977 developed a policy on voluntary lines under the **Social Contract** (q.v.), relating to pay only, prices remaining subject to the Counter-Inflation Act 1973.

INCOMES POLICY COMMITTEE. A committee established by the **Trades Union Congress** in October 1965 to examine claims by affiliated unions upon employers for improvements in wages, hours and holidays in implementation of the TUC's policy of pursuing voluntarily its own **criteria** in incomes policy. Until it was wound up in February 1970 and replaced by a **Collective Bargaining Committee** (q.v.) the Incomes Policy Committee examined 1,800 claims covering nearly seven million workers each year.

IN COMPLIANCE. To be in good standing as a trade union member, as distinct from being out-of-compliance (see **out-of-compliance men**); not to be in arrears of contribution, or to be in arrears within the limits allowed by trade union rule (usually 13 weeks), and hence able to claim such benefits as the **paid-up member** is entitled to.

INCONSISTENT RATING; see **rating.**

INCONVENIENCE ALLOWANCE. An allowance paid to a worker for specified circumstances causing him inconvenience, e.g. in occasional alteration of working hours, starting and stopping times, etc.

INCONVENIENCE PAYMENT. A term preferred by F.P. Cook (*Shift Work,* Institute of Personnel Management, 1954) to shift differential, on the grounds that differential (q.v.) has come to mean a reward for particular skill or responsibility.

INCREMENTAL PAYMENT SYSTEM.
A generic expression sometimes used to describe various types of incremental scale or wage-for-age scale arrangements and variants on them. The Office of Manpower Economics (Incremental Payment Systems, HMSO, 1973) divides such systems into fixed scales with automatic progression, fixed scales with limited flexibility (e.g. double or treble increments, parallel scales, etc.), and more variable arrangements, with or without guidelines.

INCREMENTAL SCALE.
A payment structure, particularly in the public sector, in which individuals in each grade are placed upon a scale of pay in which each moves from a given minimum, or appropriate age-pay point, on entry, to a given maximum through a number of predetermined incremental stages. In most cases such increments are expressed in terms of fixed monetary amounts and are annual; not to be confused with wage-for-age scales (q.v.) which, while applying increments, do so on age criteria only, while incremental scales are usually designed to be more flexible in use, e.g. to allow for other criteria in fixing an individual's starting point on the scale in addition to age, and often include provision for the withholding of increments for inefficiency and for an efficiency bar, blocking progress beyond a given point on the scale unless a given standard of efficiency or accomplishment can be demonstrated; see Hilda Kahn, Salaries in the Public Services in England and Wales, Allen and Unwin, 1962, p. 275 et seq.

INDEMNITY FUND.
A fund maintained by an employers' association or federation to indemnify its members against pecuniary losses through strikes, especially those incurred by acting in conformity with an association's policies or decisions; see K.C.J.C. Knowles, Strikes, Basil Blackwell, 1952, pp. 121-3, and A.I. Marsh, Industrial Relations in Engineering, Pergamon Press, 1965, p. 53 for historical and current examples. Sometimes employers' associations have provided for financial assistance to workers employed by a member firm who have suffered loss or injury in the firm's interest in connection with a strike (J.H. Richardson, Industrial Relations in Great Britain, 1938, p.

86). For the United States, see mutual strike aid.

INDENTURED APPRENTICE.
An apprentice subject to a written agreement of apprenticeship, the parties usually being the employer, the parent or guardian, and the apprentice, under which he agrees to serve the employer as an apprentice to a particular trade, the employer to accept and instruct him, the guardian giving his consent to this arrangement; such an agreement as contrasted with a verbal agreement of apprenticeship only. The word 'indenture' is now archaic, and 'it is quite immaterial whether a formal written agreement constituting the relationship of master and apprentice is referred to as an apprenticeship indenture, an instrument of apprenticeship, an apprenticeship agreement, or a contract of apprenticeship' (Andrew Beveridge, Apprenticeship Now, Chapman and Hall, 1963, p. 61). It derives from the former practice of engrossing such agreements on to parchment, which was then torn in two, each party retaining half as proof of the contract; the term was later applied to every deed, whatever its nature.

INDEPENDENT MEMBERS.
Persons, apart from those representing employers and workers, appointed to Wages Councils and Agricultural Wages Boards (see Agricultural Wages Act 1948 and Agricultural Wages (Scotland) Act 1949) by the Secretary of State for Employment in the one case and the Minister of Agriculture, Fisheries and Food in the other. The appointment of such members was begun under the Trade Board Acts. The role of the independent members is to ensure that the Councils or Boards arrive at decisions, since employers' and workers' representatives vote by sides. The number of independent members is an odd one, normally on Wages Councils a Chairman, Deputy-Chairman and a third independent member. Hence, in case of a deadlock between employers' and workers' sides, the votes of the three independents are decisive; they first attempt, however, to assist the parties to arrive at their own settlement and their position has been described as that of 'conciliators with casting votes' (F.J. Bayliss, British Wages Councils, Basil Blackwell, 1962, Ch. 7); see also C.W. Guillebaud, The Wages Council System of Great Britain, Nisbet, 1962; also members, other than those representative of employers and workers, of arbitration boards and tribunals, Courts of Inquiry, Committees

of Investigation, Joint Industrial Councils etc.; see also **wingmen**.

INDEPENDENT NATIONAL UNION; see **independent union**.

INDEPENDENT REVIEW COMMIT-TEE. A body set up by the Trades Union Congress to consider appeals from individual trade union members who have been dismissed or who face dismissal from their jobs as a result of being expelled from, or having been refused admission to a trade union in a situation in which union membership is a condition of employment, i.e. in which there is a **closed shop** (q.v.). The Committee's decisions have no legal force but the majority of affiliated unions have agreed to abide by its decisions on admission, expulsion and readmission. It consists of three members, Lord Wedderburn, Lord McCarthy and Mr George Doughty, formerly General Secretary of the Draughtsmen's and Allied Technicians' Association. The IRC made its first decision in August 1976; see Brian Weekes, 'Law and Practice of the Closed Shop', *Industrial Law Journal*, Vol. 5, No. 4, December 1976, pp. 211-22.

INDEPENDENT STAFF ORGANISA-TIONS, CONFEDERATION OF (CISO). A confederation of associations outside the **Trades Union Congress** the formation of which was discussed at a conference of some 40 organisations in December 1972. The establishment of CISO appears to have drawn its impetus from staff associations in banking and insurance, from the growth of the TUC unions in commercial employment and from the desire to express a form of trade unionism unencumbered by the conventions and traditions associated with the TUC; see **Federation of Insurance Staff Associations, Federation of Independent Trade Unions** and **Conference of Professional and Public Service Organisations**. CISO was reconstituted in June 1973 as the **Confederation of Employee Organisations** (CEO) q.v.

INDEPENDENT TRADE UNION. Defined by the **Trade Union and Labour Relations Act 1974,** s. 30(1) as a trade union which is not under the domination or control of an employer or group of employers or one or more employers' associations and is not liable to interference by an employer by financial or other means. The interpretation of this definition in practice, and especially of the words 'domi-nation', 'control' and 'interference', rests substantially with the **Certification Officer** whose role it is to issue (and withdraw) certificates of independence to (or from) **listed trade unions** (and only listed trade unions) who make application for them according to a procedure laid down in the Employment Protection Act, though a trade union which is refused may appeal to the **Employment Appeal Tribunal** on a matter of fact or of law. 'Independence' bears no necessary relationship to the concept of a **bona fide trade union** as understood within the trade union movement and those with certificates, while for the most part consisting of TUC affiliated and other similar organisations, include some **staff associations.** For a note on the procedure for obtaining a certificate and of the position of the Certification Officer, see *First Annual Report of the Certification Officer, 1976,* HMSO, 1977. The primary advantages of independent status are that only unions with such status can use the **Section 11** (recognition) procedure, the **Schedule 11 Claims** procedure, demand **disclosure of information** consultation on **redundancy,** etc. under the Employment Protection Act 1975 ss. 11, 98, 17, 99; also on individual rights, ss. 53, 57 and 58 (trade union membership and activities); see also **independent union.**

INDEPENDENT TRADE UNIONS, FEDERATION OF (FITU). An organisation, formed in 1946, and catering for trade unions unrecognised in formal negotiating machinery, outside the **Trades Union Congress** and **breakaway unions.** At the peak of its existence, FITU claimed to include 45 unions with a combined membership of 400,000, including the Aeronautical Engineers' Association, the Union of Railway Signalmen, the Gas Industrial Union and a number of unrecognised staff associations in the civil service. It obtained no support from the principal unions at that time outside the TUC, and is said to have gone out of existence some time in the 1950s.

INDEPENDENT UNION. (1) In the United States of America, an organisation of workers, usually in a single plant or company, which is not affiliated to any national or international organisation, and which may frequently, though not always correctly, be thought of as company-dominated; Leo Troy, 'Local Independent Unions and the American Labor Movement', *Industrial and Labor Relations Review,* April 1961 and H.P.

Cohany and J. Neary, 'Unaffiliated Local and Single-employer Unions in the United States', *Monthly Labor Review,* September 1962. Also in the USA, **independent national union,** a labour organisation not affiliated to the **AFL-CIO** and not a company dominated union. (2) In Great Britain defined in the **Industrial Relations Act 1971,** s. 167 (now repealed) as a union 'not under the domination or control of an employer or a group of employers or of one or more organisations of employers'. Section 67 of the same Act debarred the **Registrar of Trade Unions and Employers' Associations** from registering any organisation of workers which is not independent and has no 'power, without the concurrence of any parent organisation, to alter its own rules and to control the application of its own property and funds'; see now **independent trade union;** also **company union, house union, bona fide trade union, Spencer Union, staff association.**

INDEX OF RETAIL PRICES; see **retail prices index.**

INDEXATION; see **cost of living sliding scale.**

INDIRECT LABOUR. Any labour cost which is not specifically charged to any operation or department, but is a charge to general works' operation; alternatively an **indirect worker,** the opposite of a **production worker** (q.v.).

INDIRECTS. Indirect workers; workers who are not directly concerned with production, the grades of labour falling in this category as distinct from **production workers** (q.v.) varying from one industry and establishment to another.

INDIRECT WORK MEASUREMENT. The measurement of work of **indirect labour,** and particularly of clerical and other similar workers; see **Clerical Work Evaluation (CWE), Clerical Work Improvement Programme (CWIP), Group Capacity Assessment (GCA),** and **Variable Factor Programming (VFP).**

INDIRECT WORKER; see **indirect labour.**

INDIVIDUAL ASSESSMENT BONUS SCHEME; see **merit rating.**

INDIVIDUAL BARGAINING. The situation which pertains when the individual worker endeavours to sell his labour as dearly as possible, and the employer to purchase that labour as cheaply as possible (Sidney and Beatrice Webb, *Industrial Democracy,* 1898, p. 173). The Webbs contrasted individual bargaining with **collective bargaining** (q.v.) in which 'a group of workmen concert together and send representatives to conduct bargaining on behalf of the whole body' and 'the foreman is prevented from taking advantage of competition ... to beat down the earnings of workmen'; see also Allan Flanders, 'Collective Bargaining: A Theoretical Analysis', *British Journal of Industrial Relations,* March 1968 and *Management and Unions: The Theory and Reform of Industrial Relations,* Faber and Faber, 1975 and **higgling of the market.**

INDIVIDUAL CONCILIATION. Conciliation (q.v.) arising from employment issues provided for by statute, particularly not to be unfairly dismissed under the Trade Union and Labour Relations Act 1975 (see **unfair dismissal**) and complaints under the Equal Pay Act 1970, and The Sex Discrimination Act 1975; contrasted with **collective conciliation** (q.v.).

INDIVIDUAL RATE. A wage rate paid to an individual outside the rate or wage structure applying to similar workers in the establishment, or where no such structure formally exists; may sometimes be a **red circle rate** (q.v.).

INDUCTION. The introduction of a new employee to his place of work, to his conditions of employment, and to his job. Induction is increasingly thought of as a continuing process and as involving not only the giving of basic information, but also social reorientation and job training; see W.R. Marks, *Induction - Acclimatizing People to Work,* Institute of Personnel Management, Practical Handbook No. 3, April 1970. It is also thought of as a means of reducing **labour turnover;** see P.J. Samuel, *Labour Turnover? Towards a Solution,* Institute of Personnel Management, 1969; also **induction crisis.**

INDUCTION CRISIS. A source of labour wastage or **labour turnover** (q.v.) arising from new recruits to an organisation leaving within the first few months of their employment and hence from the initial, or early, reactions of recruits to the employing company. The point at which the induction crisis may be said to have ended raises questions of definition; for examples, see A.K. Rice, J.M.N. Hill and E.L. Trist, 'The representation of labour turnover as a social process', *Human Relations*, Vol. 3, No. 4, 1959 and Angela M. Bowey, *A Guide to Manpower Planning*, Macmillan, 1974, p. 20. For other discussion on the process, see: H. Silcock, 'The recording and measurement of labour turnover', *Journal of the Institute of Personnel Management*, Vol. 37, No. 3, 1955; Elliott Jaques, *The Changing Culture of a Factory*, Routledge and Kegan Paul, 1951 and P.F. Brissenden and E. Frankel, *Labour Turnover in Industry*, Macmillan, New York, 1922.

INDULGENCY PATTERN. An expression used by A.W. Gouldner (*Patterns of Industrial Bureaucracy*, The Free Press: Collier-Macmillan, 1964 and *Wildcat Strike*, Antioch Press and Harper and Row, 1965), to describe a situation in which management is 'lenient', not supervising work too closely or exercising discipline for its own sake, giving second chances, and not standing on its dignity or rights. Gouldner regards the indulgency pattern as disposing workers to regard the plant favourably. Anne Crichton (*Personnel Management in Context*, Batsford, 1968, p. 17) thinks of it as 'an area of silent bargaining', and A.I. Marsh, E.O. Evans and P. Garcia (*Workshop Industrial Relations in Engineering*, Engineering Employers' Federation and Kogan Page, 1971) as related to informal workshop relations practices.

INDUSTRIAL ARBITRATION. Arbitration of matters arising out of terms and conditions of employment, i.e. labour arbitration, as distinct from arbitration on other subjects and in other areas, e.g. commercial arbitration, civil arbitration, international arbitration; see **arbitration**.

INDUSTRIAL   ARBITRATION BOARD (IAB). The title, between 1971 and 31 January 1976 of the **Central Arbitration Committee**, successor to the Industrial Court established under the **Industrial Courts Act 1919** (q.v.). The IAAb had, in addition to the functions of the Industrial Court, special jurisdictions under the Industrial Relations Act 1971 which disappeared when that Act was repealed in 1974.

INDUSTRIAL CIVIL SERVANT. A civil servant engaged on manual work. Manual workers employed by government departments are mostly classed as industrial civil servants, as opposed to **non-industrial civil servants** who are predominantly management, supervisory and office workers. Most industrial civil servants are employed by the Ministry of Defence, in industrial defence establishments, or by the Department of the Environment on the maintenance of office and industrial accommodation. The pay and conditions of government industrial employees are determined separately from those for non-industrial civil servants and they belong, as a general rule, to trade unions whose membership is not confined to government employees (e.g. to the **Transport and General Workers' Union,** the **Amalgamated Union of Engineering Workers,** Engineering Section etc.) whereas non-industrials belong to trade unions whose membership is derived from the appropriate grades of the civil or other closely related public services.

INDUSTRIAL CONFLICT. Defined by Arthur Kornhauser as '... the total range of behaviour and attitudes that express opposition and divergent orientations between industrial owners and managers on the one hand and working people and their organisations on the other' (Arthur Kornhauser, Robert Dubin and Arthur M. Ross (eds) *Industrial Conflict*, McGraw-Hill, 1954, p. 13). Clark Kerr also defines industrial conflict in terms of the conflicting interests of management and labour, but adds that the term has been loosely used to mean at least three things: (a) the sources of discontent, e.g. grievances, managerial prerogatives, wage payment; (b) all forms of opposed action, whether violent or non-violent (e.g. strikes and collective bargaining) and hence 'the battle which finds its source in incompatible views'; and (c) conflict as opposed to peace. 'Thus a strike is said to constitute industrial conflict, while bargaining is peaceful' (*American Journal of Sociology*, November 1954). Alan Fox *A Sociology of Work in Industry*, Collier-Macmillan, 1971, Ch. V) traces in various writers changing interpretations of the significance and meaning of conflict and analyses the dynamics of conflict regulation, tracing the former from Marx (conflict as the dynamic of constructive social change) and G. Sorel and G. Simmel, *Reflections on Violence*, Collier Macmillan, 1961, and *Conflict*, Glencoe, Illinois Free Press, 1955 (conflict forging group identities, maintaining boundaries and leading to institutions of regulation and stability), through Talcott Parsons (conflict as the study of 'tensions', 'strains' and psychological malfunctioning) and Elton Mayo, *The Human Problems of an Industrial Civilisation*, Macmillan, 1933, *The Social Problems of an Industrial Civilisation*, Routledge and Kegan Paul, 1975 (the breakdown of traditional society by competition, individualism and urban-industrialisation and the desirability of collaborative systems in the workplace, with social harmony and co-operation), to more recent tendencies of industrial sociologists to take up more neutral positions, conflict being seen as making a constructive contribution to a healthy social order (Robert Dubin, 'Constructive Aspects of Industrial Conflict', in Kornhauser, Dubin and Ross, op. cit., 1954, Clark Kerr, *Labour and Management in Industrial Society*, Doubleday, New York, 1964, and F.H. Harbison, 'Collective Bargaining and American Capitalism', in Kornhauser, Dubin and Ross, op. cit. 1954). Alan Fox sees **collective bargaining** as the most important change in regulating conflict in the West, and exmines its problems as a dynamic institution; see also **strikes, human relations, constructive conflict**.

INDUSTRIAL CO-PARTNERSHIP ASSOCIATION; see **Industrial Participation Association**.

INDUSTRIAL COUNCIL. A national body consisting of equal numbers of representatives of employers and of workers, established by the Board of Trade in 1911 'for the purpose of considering and of inquiring into matters referred to them affecting trades disputes and especially of taking suitable action in regard to any dispute referred to them affecting the principal trades of the country . . .' The Council issued a single report in July 1913 and was then allowed to lapse; see Lord Amulree, *Industrial Arbitration*, OUP, 1929 p. 114 *et seq.* and R. Charles *The Development of Industrial Relations in Britain 1911-1939.* Hutchinson, 1973.

INDUSTRIAL COURT; see **National Industrial Relations Court;** also the former title of the **Central Arbitration Committee** (q.v.).

INDUSTRIAL COURTS ACT 1919. An Act passed as a result of the Fourth Report of the **Whitley Committee** (1916-18) (see **Whitleyism**) and extending the provisions for **voluntary arbitration** in Britain beyond those provided in the **Conciliation Act 1896.** Part I of the Act established a standing Industrial Court (known from 1971 to 1974 as the Industrial Arbitration Board and now under the Employment Protection Act 1975 renamed the **Central Arbitration Committee** (q.v.)) to which the Minister of Labour (now the Secretary of State for Employment) might refer for settlement a **trade dispute** reported to him by the parties, provided that the relevant **disputes procedure** had been exhausted; s. 2(2)(b) and (c) of the Act also empowered the Minister to establish a panel of arbitrators and to use them as an alternative to the Court, either as **single arbitrators** or as **boards of arbitration** in like circumstances, and in Part II to set up **Courts of Inquiry** (ss. 4 and 5). The Court at first endeavoured to give grounds for its decisions (Lord Amulree, *Industrial Arbitration*, OUP, 1929, p. 183) as the 'first tentative step towards the formation of a body of industrial case law'. These intentions were later abandoned; see M.T. Rankin, *Arbitration Principles and the Industrial Court*, P.S. King and Son, 1931; also H.A. Turner, *Arbitration*, Fabian Research Series No. 153, 1952 and K.W. Wedderburn and P.L. Davies, *Employment Grievances and Disputes Procedures in Britain*, University of California Press, 1969. The Employment Protection Act repealed Part I of the Act placing the Central Arbitration Committee and power to appoint arbitrators under the control of the **Advisory, Conciliation and Arbitration Service** (q.v.), but left ss. 4 and 5 of the Act intact.

INDUSTRIAL DEMOCRACY. An expression with a number of meanings and usages all concerned with the role and status of workers in industrial society and all implying, to a greater or lesser extent, the participation of those who work in industry in determining the conditions of their working lives. Hence industrial democracy may imply **workers' control**, in the form of **industrial unionism, syndicalism, guild socialism**, or any of their variants; or it may imply **workers' participation** as understood in **Whitleyism, joint-consultation, cownership, co-partnership** or **co-determination** (q.v.). 'Any theory or scheme as long as it is based on a genuine concern for the rights of workers in industry, particularly their right to share in the control of industrial decisions'; H.A. Clegg, *A New Approach to Industrial Democracy*, Basil Blackwell, 1960, p. 3. Even more broadly, '. . . industrial democracy means a nation in which men are equal in dignity and opportunity, but in which rewards go to effort, enterprise, brains skill and qualifications'; Quintin Hogg, quoted in Ken Coates (ed.), *Can the Workers Run Industry?* Bertrand Russell House, 1976. Aims in advancing industrial democracy centre mainly on the desire to break up concentration of industrial power as a safeguard against self-interest and arbitrary action, and on the need to increase social as well as material satisfaction in industrial society. The first of these aims may be seen as requiring the break-up of capitalist society, the increase of accountability, either by governmental action or by encouragement of opposition to the authoritarian tendencies of management, or the wider involvement of workers in decision-making, or simply as the development of techniques to bring the two sides of industry closer together; the second lays emphasis on the importance of the workplace as a unit of social organisation, on the need to encourage personal development and job satisfaction, and of achieving a proper balance between industry and community; see also Sidney and Beatrice Webb, *Industrial Democracy,* 1898, W.H. Scott, *Industrial Democracy; a Revaluation,* Liverpool University Press, 1955, The Labour Party, *Industrial Democracy, A Working Party Report,* June 1967, for a reader in literature on the field, Ken Coates and Anthony Topham (eds), *Industrial Democracy in Great Britain,* Bertrand Russell House, 1974, and R.O. Clarke, D.J. Fatchett and B.C. Roberts, *Workers' Participation in Management in Britain,* Heinemann, 1972; see also **dual unionism, rival unionism.** For a bibliography; see R.O. Clarke, D.J. Fatchett and S.G. Rothwell, *Workers' Participation and Industrial Democracy, A Bibliography,* 1969. The Labour government, returned to office in 1974, accepted a commitment to industrial democracy as a third stage of reform of Labour Law in Britain (see **Trade Union and Labour Relations Acts 1974 and 1976** and **Employment Protection Act 1975**). In May 1978 a White Paper from the Callaghan government modified the approach of the **Bullock Report** (q.v.), (*Industrial Democracy,* Cmnd. 7231).

INDUSTRIAL DISPUTE. In general, a dispute between an employer or employers and employees and their trade union, about their terms and conditions of work. Precise definitions differ from one country to another; see H.A. Turner, *Is Britain Really Strike Prone?* CUP, 1969 and W.E.J. McCarthy, 'The Nature of Bri-

tain's Strike Problem', *British Journal of Industrial Relations,* Vol. VIII, No. 2, June 1970. With this qualification **International Labour Office** data are given in the table opposite. The **Industrial Relations Act 1971,** now repealed, employed the term 'industrial dispute' in place of the more familiar '**trade dispute**' previously used in British Labour legislation and now restored in the **Trade Union and Labour Relations Acts 1974 and 1976.**

INDUSTRIAL DISPUTES ORDER 1376 (1951); see **Industrial Disputes Tribunal** and **Compulsory Arbitration.**

INDUSTRIAL DISPUTES TRIBUNAL (IDT). An arbitration tribunal established under Statutory Rules and Orders, 1951. No. 1376 (**Order 1376**) to replace the **National Arbitration Tribunal** (q.v.). Order 1376 contained no prohibition of strikes but retained an element of **compulsory arbitration** in that one party could refer a difference to the IDT without the agreement of the other. Awards on disputes and on **issues** relating to the observance of **recognised terms and conditions** became an **implied term** of contract, and hence legally enforceable. The IDT eventually became unpopular with employers, who believed that it unduly favoured trade unions; trade unions were less opposed to it and some, particularly the **National and Local Government Officers' Association,** considered it a 'charter for trade unionism' (see Alec Spoor, *White Collar Union,* Heinemann, 1967). It was disbanded in 1959, when Order 1376 was revoked, and the issues procedure incorporated into s. 8 of the **Terms and Conditions of Employment Act** of the same year; see W.E.J. McCarthy, *Compulsory Arbitration in Britain; The Work of the Industrial Disputes Tribunal,* Royal Commission on Trade Unions and Employers' Associations, Research Papers 8, 1968, pp. 31-44, H.A. Clegg, 'The End of the IDT', *Personnel Management,* March 1959.

INDUSTRIAL ENGINEERING; see **work study.**

INDUSTRIAL INJURIES ACTS. The National Insurance (Industrial Injuries) Act 1946, now replaced by the **National Insurance (Industrial Injuries) Act 1965,** as amended in 1966 and 1967. Acts replacing the system of **workmen's compensation** by a statutory scheme in which insured persons are entitled to benefit if

INTERNATIONAL COMPARISON OF DAYS LOST
THROUGH INDUSTRIAL DISPUTES

Days lost per 1,000 people employed

| | 1976† | . Average for | | |
		5 years 1967-1971	5 years 1972-1976	10 years 1967-1976
Australia*	1,490	796	1,502	1,131
Belgium	(a)	394	348 (c)	373 (c)
Canada	2,270	1,682	2,130	1,906
Denmark‡	390	64	1,078	571
Fed. Rep. of Germany	40	80	32	56
Finland	1,310	886	1,028	957
France	420	313 (b)	338	327 (b)
India	(a)	1,346	1,635 (c)	1,419 (c)
Irish Republic	840	952	782	867
Italy	2,200	1,692	1,956	1,824
Japan	150	194	294	244
Netherlands	10	42	82	62
New Zealand	940	350	504	427
Norway	60	20	114	67
Sweden**	10	62	16	39
Switzerland	20	—	—	—
United Kingdom	300	608	968	788
United States	1,190	1,644	1,054	1,349

*   Including electricity and gas, excluding communication.
†   Preliminary figures
‡   Manufacturing only.
** All industries included until 1971.
(a) Figures not available.
(b) 1968 figure unavailable and not included in averages.
(c) 1976 figure unavailable and not included in agerages.

Note: Where no figure is given the number of days lost per 1,000 employed is less than five.

they can show that they have suffered (a) a personal injury caused after 4 July 1948 by accident arising out of and in the course of employment, or (b) a prescribed disease or a prescribed personal injury, not caused by accident arising out of and in the course of employment, but being a disease or injury due to the nature of that employment, and developed after 4 July 1948; see also **injury benefit, disablement benefit, death benefit.** For a summary see: C.D. Drake, *Labour Law,* Sweet and Maxwell, 2nd ed. 1973; see also **employers' liability.**

INDUSTRIAL JURISPRUDENCE. A term employed by Sumner H. Slichter (*Union Policies and Industrial Management,* Brookings Institution, 1941, p. 1) to describe the system whereby trade unions and managements in a workplace formulate rules on union recognition, wages and conditions, shop institutions and procedures for handling grievances: 'When labor and management deal with labor relations analytically and systematically after such a fashion, it is proper to refer to the system as "industrial jurisprudence".'

INDUSTRIAL AND LABOR RELATIONS REVIEW. A quarterly journal published by the New York State School of Industrial Relations, Cornell University, Ithaca, New York (1947 -). The **Cornell Review** is recognised as the major journal in the industrial relations field in the United States and contains learned articles, communications from readers, book reviews and information on most aspects of the subject. For notes on industrial relations journals in general, see George Sayers Bain and Gillian B. Woolven, 'The Literature of Labour Economics and

Industrial Relations, A Guide to its Sources', *Industrial Relations Journal,* Summer 1970 and in J. Fletcher (ed.), *The Uses of Economics Literature,* Butterworths, 1971.

INDUSTRIAL LAW; see **labour law.**

INDUSTRIAL LAW JOURNAL (ILJ). A journal first issued in March 1972 and published for the Industrial Law Society by Sweet and Maxwell Ltd, 11 New Fetter Lane, London EC4. It replaced the former Bulletin of the Society, and has as its object to provide a forum in which the theory and practice of **labour law** are brought together, for analysis, criticism and in functional studies of the way in which the law actually operates in labour relations. *Editor:* Paul Davies, Balliol College, Oxford.

INDUSTRIAL MISCONDUCT. In general at common law, misbehaviour of a serious character which would entitle an employer to dismiss an employee on the spot without notice or wages in lieu (i.e. would justify **summary dismissal** or **instant dismissal**); more broadly in industrial relations, a kind of behaviour which would, on this or some subsequent occasion, involve a worker in disciplinary action of some kind, possibly including dismissal (see **disciplinary procedure**). The National Insurance Commissioners, in the case of disqualification from unemployment benefit, have interpreted misconduct more comprehensively than the common law to include 'such misconduct as would lead a reasonable employer to terminate a claimant's employment', including an act by a bus driver on holiday, leading to conviction for a drinking offence when driving his own car, drunkenness outside working hours, theft unconnected with the job, etc. (for examples of disqualification for misconduct for unemployment benefit, sickness benefit, etc., see B.A. Hepple and Paul O'Higgins, *Employment Law,* Sweet and Maxwell, 1976, and Olga Aikin and Judith Reid, *Employment, Welfare and Safety at Work, Labour Law 1,* Penguin, 1971).

INDUSTRIAL PARTICIPATION ASSOCIATION. An organisation founded in 1884 to disseminate knowledge and information and to initiate, encourage and maintain investigation and research into **co-partnership** and until 1972 known as the **Industrial Co-partnership Association.** It is an incorporated voluntary society registered as a charity and membership is open to any corporate body or individual who wishes to support its work. *Address:* 25/28 Buckingham Gate, London SW1. *Tel:* 01-828 8754.

INDUSTRIAL PSYCHOLOGY, NATIONAL INSTITUTE OF (NIIP). A non-profitmaking scientific association founded in 1921 with the object of developing **occupational psychology** in the United Kingdom. The Institute undertook research, teaching and advisory work, particularly in **vocational guidance,** personnel selection, accidents and ergonomics, into wages of recording performance and in the making of surveys and diagnostic studies of general use in industry and had a journal, **Occupational Psychology.** It went out of existence for lack of funds in 1973.

INDUSTRIAL REHABILITATION UNITS. Units, mostly non-residential, designed to provide facilities for preparing those disabled by accidents or other handicapped persons for full-time work in industry. The first unit was opened at Egham in 1943; there are now 26 with accommodation for 2,542. About 14,000 people pass through the units each year; also **disabled persons, Remploy Ltd.**

INDUSTRIAL RELATIONS. The practice, or the study, of relationships within and between workers, working groups and their organisations and managers, employers and their organisations. Thus defined, industrial relations is an all-inclusive term covering all aspects of the employment relationship and its associated institutions and social and economic environment, whatever its nature. Some writers tend to approve this type of definition, though not necessarily with equal enthusiasm or emphasis (e.g. Hilde Behrend, 'The Field of Industrial Relations', *British Journal of Industrial Relations,* Vol. 1, No. 3, October 1963, A.N.J. Blain and John Gennard, 'Industrial Relations Theory; A Critical Analysis', *British Journal of Industrial Relations,* Vol. VIII, No. 3, November 1970, L. Reed Tripp, 'The Industrial Relations Discipline in American Universities', *Industrial and Labor Relations Review,* Vol. 17, No. 4, July 1964); others, for a number of reasons prefer different definitions. **Labour relations** are sometimes abstracted from 'industrial relations' as describing organised or institutionalised relationships within the whole, though sometimes the two terms are used as if they were interchangeable (e.g. in H.A. Turner, Garfield Clack and Geoffrey Roberts, *Labour Relations in the Motor Industry,* Allen and Unwin, 1967, Ch. 10 'Industrial Relations in Foreign Car Firms'). A distinction is often made between industrial relations and **human relations,** the former being understood to refer to collective relations between the parties and the latter to interpersonal relations, both being subsumed under **labour-management relations** or labour relations (see an ILO definition quoted by Hilde Behrend, op. cit.). The distinction being made here seems to suggest a qualitative difference based on both a collective/non-collective criterion and upon degrees of formality. But it and other distinctions may also imply a difference of academic discipline, e.g. be regarding industrial relations as primarily a branch of sociology (J.H. Smith, *The University Teaching of Social Sciences: Industrial Sociology,* UNESCO, 1961) or of the psychology of inter-personal relations (P.H. Cook, *Australian Quarterly,* December 1955), or as a factor in economic analysis (e.g. in L.C. Hunter, G.L. Reid and D. Boddy, *Labour Problems of Technological Change,* Allen and Unwin, 1970). The difficulties of containing a definition of industrial relations within the scope of existing disciplines has led some writers to suggest that it is principally concerned with problem areas, for example, the securing of 'civilised disagreement about the things to be disagreed about, and civilised recognition of common interest' (Tom Lupton, *Industrial Behaviour and Personnel Management,* Institute of Personnel Management, 1964, p. 45), or, somewhat similarly, that 'conflict is the basic concept, and should form the basis of a study of industrial relations' (C.J. Margerison, 'What do we mean by Industrial Relations?', *British Journal of Industrial Relations,* Vol. VII, No. 2, July 1969). Margerison, like many other writers, evidently feels that the problem approach is one way out of the difficulty that industrial relations is inevitably interdisciplinary in character; others consider that its many-sidedness conceals a particular logic (Hilde Behrend, op. cit., p. 394) and a need for unification, which is 'slowly evolving into an inter-disciplinary subject in its own right' centred (Kingsley Laffer, 'Industrial Relations, Its Teaching and Scope; an Australian Experience'. *International Institute for Labour Studies Bulletin,* November 1968) around the notion of industrial relations as one of a number of interrelated social systems concerned

with the development and administration of rules concerned with people in their working environments as developed by J.T. Dunlop (*Industrial Relations Systems,* Holt-Dryden, 1958). A modified version of this has been developed by Allan Flanders, with a broad view of what constitutes industrial relations: 'Market, collective, formal and informal work relations together comprise the subject matter of industrial relations'; (*Industrial Relations, the Nature of the Subject,* Ruskin College, January 1960), but with the word 'system' principally used to describe formal rather than informal relationships (*Industrial Relations — What is Wrong with the System?,* Faber and Faber, 1965, p. 10); see also R. Hyman and I. Brough, *Social Values and Industrial Relations,* Blackwell, 1975 and V.L. Allen, *The Sociology of Industrial Relations,* Longmans, 1971 and, for a Marxist view, R. Hyman., *Industrial Relations: A Marxist Interpretation,* Macmillan, 1975.

INDUSTRIAL RELATIONS. A journal published three times a year by the Institute of Industrial Relations, University of California, Berkeley, USA (1961-). It publishes articles on all aspects of the employment relationship, gives special attention to developments in labour economics, sociology, psychology, political science and law. For notes on industrial relations journals in general; see George Sayers Bain and Gillian B. Woolven, 'The Literature of Labour Economics and Industrial Relations: A Guide to its Sources', *Industrial Relations Journal,* Summer 1970 and in J. Fletcher (ed.), *The Uses of Economics Literature,* Butterworths, 1971.

INDUSTRIAL RELATIONS ACT 1971. An Act of Parliament resulting from the policy on industrial relations of the Conservative Heath government of 1971-74, based substantially on that Party's document **'Fair Deal at Work'** (q.v.), and subsequently repealed with effect from 16 September 1974 by the succeeding Labour government by the **Trade Union and Labour Relations Act** of that year as an item in the **Social Contract** between the Labour Party and the General Council of the Trades Union Congress. The Act followed the success of the Conservatives at the polls in June 1970 after the fall of the Wilson government which was itself in large measure due to a rift in relations between the Labour Party and the trade union movement caused by the incomes policy of 1966-70 (see **National Board for Prices and Incomes**) and by trade union opposition to its policy statement on industrial relations **'In Place of Strife'** (q.v.). In attempting to shift the emphasis in British industrial relations from its traditional **voluntarism**, or freedom from legal intervention, to that of a more positive 'framework' of law, the Act followed very largely institutions and practices developed in the United States since the **Wagner Act** (q.v.), e.g. in its emphasis on **unfair industrial practices (unfair labor practices** in the USA), its **National Industrial Relations Court (NIRC or Industrial Court)** (an equivalent in some of its functions of the National Labor Relations Board). Other provisions were more clearly derived from the Donovan Royal Commission on Trade Unions and Employers' Associations 1965-1968 (see **Donovan Commission**), e.g. in legislating on **unfair dismissal** (q.v.). It followed closely on Conservative Party thinking of the time in laying emphasis on the freedom of the individual to join or not to join trade unions, and hence made illegal **closed shops**, except under stringent conditions as **'approved closed shops'**, attempting to bridge the gap between principle and reality by making possible the legal development of **'agency shops'** on the United States model. In repealing the **Trades Disputes Act 1906**, the IRA attempted to limit the 'immunities' generally enjoyed by trade unions under that Act in **industrial disputes** to **registered trade unions** and their accredited officials (see **shop steward**) and it provided an elaborate system for reforming collective bargaining through the intervention of the **Commission on Industrial Relations** (already established by Royal Warrant by the previous Labour government, but now given additional functions and powers) and the Industrial Court. The **Trades Union Congress,** followed by almost all its affiliated organisations, committed itself to a policy of non-registration and (except in self defence) of non-co-operation with the institutions set up under the Act. Partly as a result, some of its provisions failed to work effectively. Others, however, proved inadequate in conception or enforcement. In practice it had little effect on existing closed shop practices and attempts to apply legal sanctions in notable cases proved ineffective (see, for example, **Langston v. AUEW**); the widened legal liability for strikes proved difficult to enforce (see **Pentonville Five**) and little seems to have been achieved in reforming collective bargaining, though

the **Industrial Relations Code of Practice** which was drawn up as a result of the Act, and which still remains in effect, may have assisted developments among more progressive companies; **national emergency procedures,** bearing considerable resemblance to those in the United States, were used on one occasion only and then, it seems, abandoned for practical purposes. It is possible to see the failure of the Act in terms of overweening trade union power which it was inadequate to control, in terms of the inherent conservatism of the British industrial relations system in which neither managements nor unions were willing, in practice, to admit the validity of the interventions for which the Act so clearly stood, or simply as the result of an inadequate view of 'the law', and more particularly of the 'rule of law' and of its normative and restraining role in industrial society. As a positive educational experience, the Act had some results. Unfair dismissal procedures became well established between 1971 and 1974 and the theme of protection of individuals at work has been taken up in the **Employment Protection Act 1975,** the **Health and Safety at Work Act 1974** and other subsequent legislation. Numerous legal guides to the Act appeared after it became law; see H.A. Clegg, *The System of Industrial Relations in Great Britain,* Basil Blackwell, 1972, Ch. 12 for a brief description of the Act and its background in layman's terms; also a short account of the case for and against it in W.E.J. McCarthy and N.D. Ellis, *Management By Agreement,* Hutchinson, 1973. The most complete analysis of its total experience and effect is by B. Weekes, M. Mellish, L. Dickens and J. Lloyd, *Industrial Relations and the Limits of the Law,* Basil Blackwell, 1975; also A.W.J. Thomson and S.R. Engleman, *The Industrial Relations Act,* Martin Robertson, 1975. The basic philosophy of the Act can be examined in *Fair Deal at Work* (see above) and in the earlier Inns of Court Conservative and Unionist Society's study, *A Giant's Strength,* Christopher Johnson Publisters Ltd, 1958. See also M. Moran, *The Origin, Life and Death of the 1971 Industrial Relations Act,* Macmillan Press, 1977.

INDUSTRIAL RELATIONS CODE OF PRACTICE; see Codes of Practice.

INDUSTRIAL RELATIONS JOURNAL. An industrial relations journal intended to provide a forum for the reflections of those involved in the day-to-day practice of industrial relations and for opinions, findings and conclusions from the general field of industrial relations research (1970-). Published by Business Publications Ltd, Mercury House, Waterloo Road, London SE1, and edited from the Department of Adult Education, University of Nottingham. For notes on industrial relations journals in general; see George Sayers Bain and Gillian B. Woolven, 'The Literature of Labour Economics and Industrial Relations', *Industrial Relations Journal,* Summer 1970 and in J. Fletcher (ed.), *The Uses of Economics Literature,* Butterworths, 1971.

INDUSTRIAL RELATIONS, NORTHERN IRELAND ORDERS; see Labour Relations Agency.

INDUSTRIAL RELATIONS RESEARCH BULLETIN. The journal of the Research Department of the **Engineering Employers' Federation,** bringing together fact and opinion, findings and conclusions, information and advice from the general field of industrial relations research (1969-). Published by the Engineering Employers' Federation, Broadway House, Tothill Street, London SW1. For notes on industrial relations journals in general; see George Sayers Bain and Gillian B. Woolven, 'The Literature of Labour Economics and Industrial Relations', *Industrial Relations Journal,* Summer 1970 and in J. Fletcher (ed.) *The Uses of Economics Literature,* Butterworths, 1971.

INDUSTRIAL RELATIONS TRAINING RESOURCE CENTRE. A Centre established to encourage industrial relations training at company level by advice, guidance and the building of links between industry and academic institutions. It originated in a recommendation of 1975 from the National Economic Development Council. *Address:* Ashridge Management College, Berkhamsted, Herts HP4 1NS. *Tel:* Little Gaddesden (044 284) 2511/5.

INDUSTRIAL SOCIETY. The journal of **The Industrial Society,** formerly 'Industrial Welfare' (1918-).

INDUSTRIAL SOCIETY, THE. An independent and non-profitmaking body founded in 1918 as the Industrial Welfare Society, with the object of improving relations in all places of employment so that workers may give their best to their work. The Society believes in the encouragement of effective leadership, positive management-union relationships. effective terms of employment and conditions of work, adequate communication, and the development of young employees. It provides an advisory and information service, runs courses and conferences on subjecs relevant to personnel and industrial relations, some of them in-plant, and issues publications in these fields; see Elizabeth Sidney, *The Industrial Society, 1918-1968,* The Industrial Society, 1968. *Address:* 48 Bryanston Square, London W1. *Tel:* 01-262 2401.

INDUSTRIAL TRAINING ACT 1964. An Act empowering the Secretary of State for Employment to establish **Industrial Training Boards** with the objects of ensuring an adequate supply of properly trained men and women at all levels of industry, of improving the quality and efficiency of industrial training, and of sharing the cost of training, by means of grants and levies, more evenly between firms. Under the Act, the ITBs, which in January 1978 numbered 24 (excluding the Agricultural Training Board), were originally free to determine their own levies and grants, and their own training arrangements, subject to ministerial approval on levy proposals and general policy, the Secretary of State carrying out his functions with the advice of a **Central Training Council** which gave the lead on training in occupations common to all industries, on research into training problems and on matters of general policy. The Industrial Training Act marked a change in training policy from that accepted by the **Carr Report** (q.v.) of 1958 which recommended that training functions should remain within industry and that government should concentrate on proving and expanding facilities for technical education. In 1972 the Heath government, in a consultative document 'Training for the Future', expressed the view that the levy-grant system had secured a permanent change in the attitude of British industry towards training and might be substantially brought to an end. It suggested that Training Boards should continue primarily as advisory bodies working under a National Training Agency and operating on selective financial incentive schemes approved by the Agency. This scheme was later (August 1972) modified to allow exemption from levy-grant of smaller firms and of any firm carrying out such training as judged reasonable for its own needs, other firms being required to pay a levy not exceeding

1 per cent of payroll. The **Employment and Training Act 1973** brought these proposals into being under the **Manpower Services Commission** (delegated to the **Training Services Agency**). From 1 April 1978 the Training Services Agency ceased to be a separate executive agency and became an operating division of the Manpower Services Commission.

INDUSTRIAL TRAINING BOARD (ITB); see Industrial Training Act 1964.

INDUSTRIAL TRIBUNALS. Tribunals originally established to hear appeals by employers against assessments of training levies under the terms of the **Industrial Training Act 1964** (s. 2), and later extended to a number of other jurisdictions as follows, the most recent being created by the **Industrial Relations Act 1971**: (a) **Contracts of Employment Act 1963** (s. 4; questions regarding written particulars of employment); (b) **Redundancy Payments Act 1965** (right to payment, amount of payment and employer's right to rebate); also s. 41 and 42 and Schedule 7 (equivalent payments to civil servants and employees of nationalised industries); (c) **Docks and Harbours Act 1966** (disputes about meaning of 'dock work'); (d) **Sex Discrimination Act 1975** (complaints of unlawful discrimination); (e) **Equal Pay Act 1970** (dispute between employer and employee as to equal treatment of men and women, s. 2); (f) **Trade Union and Labour Relations Act 1974** (Schedule Part III, Complaint of **unfair dismissal**); (g) **Employment Protection Act 1975** (s. 27, **guarantee payments**, s. 32, medical suspension payments, s. 38 **maternity pay**, s. 54 trade union rights, ss. 57 and 58 time off for trade union officials and members etc., s. 66 employee's rights on insolvency, s. 70 refusal to provide a written statement of reasons for dismissal, s. 84, failure to provide an itemised pay statement etc. The tribunals have been described as a type of **labour court,** and in their pre-Industrial Relations Act form as a 'useful device for dealing with certain problems affecting individual employees quickly and informally' (K.W. Wedderburn, *The Worker and the Law,* Pelican, 2nd ed., 1971, p. 151), though the first of these characteristics may not be immediately evident (see C. E. McCormick, 'The Redundancy Payments Act in the Practice of the Industrial Tribunals', *British Journal of Industrial Relations,* Vol, VIII, No. 3, November 1970). The tribunals have traditionally taken the tripartite form of a legally quali-

fied chairman flanked by **wingmen** drawn from panels of employers and employed persons. In March 1971, before the **Industrial Relations Act 1971** became law, the **Trades Union Congress** adopted the policy of advising affiliated unions that trade union members should withdraw from the employed persons' panel, advice which was followed after the relevant portions of the Act came into force on 28 February 1972, but withdrawn following the repeal of the 1971 Act; see also R.W. Rideout, 'The Industrial Tribunals', *Current Legal Problems,* 1968, S. Weisbard, 'Industrial Tribunals', *New Law Journal,* 1969 and K.W. Webberburn and P.L. Davies, *Employment Grievances and Disputes Procedures in Britain,* University of California Press, 1969, Part IV, K. Whitesides and G. Hawker, *Industrial Tribunals,* Sweet and Maxwell, 1975.

INDUSTRIAL UNION. A trade union whose membership is organised on the basis of representing all grades of workers in a particular industry, and hence includes unskilled, semi-skilled, skilled, and sometimes non-manual employees; a **vertical union,** as distinct from a **horizontal** union or a **general union;** see also **industrial unionism.** The point has often been made that Britain, has, in any strict sense, no industrial unions, even if these are described as embracing all **manual workers** in an industry, though the **National Union of Mineworkers** and the **National Union of Footwear, Leather and Allied Trades** come near to the mark, and others, notably the **National Union of Railwaymen,** the **Iron and Steel Trades Confederation,** the **Union of Post Office Workers,** have long-standing aspirations in this direction; see H.A. Clegg, A.J. Killick and Rex Adams; *Trade Union Officers,* Basil Blackwell, 1961. The advantages claimed for industrial unions as an ideal form of trade union organisation are ones of solidarity, avoidance of craft exclusiveness, and capacity to participate in the running of industry; see, for example, Noah Barou, *British Trade Unions,* Gollancz, 1947. Some writers have been sceptical of such claims, e.g. J.D.M. Bell, *Industrial Unionism, a Critical Analysis,* Department of Economic and Social Research, University of Glasgow, n.d. [1948?]. Major 'industrial unions' have been subject to membership decline in recent years, e.g. in the coalmining and railway industries. John Hughes (*Trade Union Structure and Government,* Royal Commission on Trade Unions and Employers' Associations, Research Papers 5, Pt 1, 1967) notes that the industrial union arrangement is likely to appeal to workers where there are production skills peculiar to an industry (e.g. in coalmining and iron and steel), and where promotion is most easily available by experience and seniority; also that **dual membership agreements** may (as in coal mining) be necessary to secure completeness of membership.

INDUSTRIAL UNIONISM. (1) A theory of social revolution evolved by Daniel De Leon, Eugene Debs and other leaders of the American Socialist Labour Party, associated with the Industrial Workers of the World or **Wobblies,** and advocated in Britain by the Socialist Labour Party. A new society was to be developed along industrial lines, industries being organised by industrial unions. The SLP made little progress in the British labour movement, and after about 1910 such advocates as Tom Mann moved in the direction of **syndicalism,** others moving into **Guild Socialism;** see Branko Pribićević, *The Shop Stewards' Movement and Workers' Control,* Basil Blackwell, 1959, p. 12 *et seq.* (2) A theory of trade union organisation involving **industrial unions** (q.v.).

INDUSTRIAL WORKERS OF THE WORLD (IWW); see Wobblies.

INDUSTRY-WIDE AGREEMENT; see industry-wide bargaining.

INDUSTRY-WIDE BARGAINING. An expression, originally used in the United States, to describe collective bargaining which takes place on an industry-wide basis and regulates terms and conditions of work for a substantial proportion of employees in that industry by **industry-wide agreements;** commonly known in Great Britain as **national bargaining** (q.v.) but increasingly in recent years by its American nomenclature. An early use in the British context is to be found in Milton Derber, *Labor-Management Relations at the Plant Level under Industry-wide Bargaining, A Study of the Engineering Industry in Birmingham, England,* University of Illinois, 1955; it was freely employed by the Donovan Royal Commission on Trade Unions and Employers' Associations 1965-1968 (see **Donovan Commission**). It has the advantage of distinguishing, where that is appropriate, national bargaining from **company bargaining** where company agreements (as in

the Ford Motor Company) have been described as 'national'.

INFORMATION AGREEMENT; see **information, disclosure of.**

INFORMATION, DISCLOSURE OF. In its most general form, the practice by companies of keeping employees informed about financial and other aspects of their business affairs by **joint consultation, employee reports,** or by other means; more specifically, the practice of making such information available to recognised trade unions for the purposes of collective bargaining. In the latter sense, provision was made in the **Industrial Relations Act 1971** whereby companies were required to disclose such information where trade union representatives would, in its absence, be materially impeded in collective bargaining and where it would be in line with good industrial relations practice, to disclose. Following the repeal of this Act, the same general requirement was included in the **Employment Protection Act 1975,** ss. 17-21, and with the same reservations, i.e. that companies are not required to disclose information communicated in confidence, where it relates specifically to an individual, where it would cause substantial injury to the employer's own undertaking or where national security is concerned. Nor are employers required to produce or copy original documents or to assemble unreasonable amounts of information. A **Code of Practice** (q.v.) on *Disclosure of Information to Trade Unions for Collective Bargaining Purposes* (Code of Practice 2), drawn up by the Advisory, Conciliation and Arbitration Service, was approved by Parliament in August 1977. On the history, development and general problems of disclosure, see A.I. Marsh and R. Rosewell, 'A Question of Disclosure', *Industrial Relations Journal,* Vol. 7, No. 2, Summer 1976, pp. 4-16. The Commission on Industrial Relations reported on the subject in September 1972 (*Disclosure of Information,* Report No. 31, 1972). Arising out of the 1977 Code of Practice (Clause 22) is the suggestion of **disclosure agreements,** i.e. joint understandings on how disclosure provisions can be implemented most effectively. Some unions have preferred to lodge **information claims** before the beginning of substantive bargaining, i.e. claims to the information which they require in the circumstances relevant to that particular claim. The Industry Act 1975 also contains provisions (ss. 28-34) requiring specific information to be provided to a minister of the Crown, and, at his direction, to authorised representatives of relevant trade unions, under similar, but not identical, safeguards to those in the Employment Protection Act. In July 1977 the government issued a Green Paper, *The Future of Company Reports,* Cmnd. 6888 including references to the development of **employee reports.**

INJUNCTION. An order of the court by which a person or group of persons who are committing, or threatening to commit, an act against the legal or equitable rights of another person or group are restrained from continuing or commencing such a wrongful act or are commanded to restore matters to the position at which they stood before the wrongful act was committed. In the United States of America, prior to the Norris-La Guardia Act of 1932, the injunction was the normal employer response to picketing and boycotts by unions. The Act forbade the federal courts to issue injunctions in labour disputes unless certain prior conditions had been fulfilled. The **Taft-Hartley Act 1947** (as amended by the Landrum-Griffin Act 1959) established a detailed code of law regulating strikes, picketing and boycotts, and allows for injunctions primarily in relation to **unfair labour practices** and national emergency disputes (see **cooling-off periods**). In Britain it was generally thought until 1963 that the **Trades Disputes Act 1906,** s. 4, gave general immunity to trade unions from actions in tort, and that this covered the process of injunction. In **Boulting v. Association of Cinematograph, Television and Allied Technicians** (1963) 2 QB 606 (q.v.) it was held that the words of the Act did not forbid an action for an injunction on a tort *about to be committed,* and a number of labour injunctions followed including **Torquay Hotels Ltd v. Cousins,** (1968), 3 WLR, 506 CA (q.v.) and those issued by the Ford Motor Company restraining the TGWU and AEF from picketing and persuading other unions to strike which were later withdrawn (see **Ford v. Amalgamated Engineering and Foundry Workers' Union and others).** On such injunctions; see K.W. Wedderburn and P.L. Davies, *Employment Grievances and Disputes Procedures in Britain,* University of California Press, 1969. For injunctions during this period restraining trade union officials from acting contrary to trade union rules; see Cyril Grunfeld, *Modern Trade Union Law,* Sweet and Max-

well, 1970. The effect of the **Trade Union and Labour Relations Act 1974,** s. 16, is to remove from the courts the possibility of injunctions arising out of proceedings in contract where this involves compelling an employee to do any work or to attend any place for the purpose of doing any work, or restraining him from committing a breach or threatened breach of contract, in relation, for example, to an **industrial dispute.** The Act does not prohibit the use of injunctions against employers, or against trade unions or employees in other circumstances; but see **ex parte injunction;** also P.L. Davies and S.D. Anderman, 'Injunction Proceedings in Labour Disputes', *Industrial Law Journal,* Vol. 2, No. 1, December 1973, pp. 213-28.

INJURY BENEFIT. One of the three main types of benefit provided by the **Industrial Injuries Acts** for insured persons injured by accidents at work and suffering from prescribed industrial diseases, the others being **disablement benefit** and **death benefit.** Payment is not normally made for the first three days of incapacity, and only if two or more days of incapacity or unemployment occur within a period of six consecutive days; it may be made for 26 weeks from the date of accident, but finishes earlier if the incapacity for work ends within the 26 weeks and disablement benefit is claimed; see Department of Health and Social Security, Leaflet N15.

INLAND REVENUE STAFF FEDERATION (IRSF). A recognised civil service departmental staff association originating as the Association of Tax Clerks in 1892. In 1936 the Association of Officers of Taxes, as the union was then called, and the National Association of Taxes Assessing and Collecting Services formed a Federation which was joined by the Valuation Officer Clerical Association in the following year; in 1938 these unions amalgamated though without changing the 1936 title. The IRSF claims to organise over 92 per cent of potential among Inland Revenue Staff. *Address:* 7 St George's Square, London SW1V 2HY. *Tel:* 01-834 8254. *TUC Affiliated Membership, 1977:* 63,984.

INQUIRY, COMMITTEE OF; see Committee of Inquiry.

INQUIRY, COURT OF; see Court of Inquiry.

INSTANT DISMISSAL; see **summary dismissal.**

INSTITUTE OF OFFICE MANAGE-MENT (IOM) now Institute of Administrative Management; see **Administrative Management, Institute of.**

INSTITUTE OF PERSONNEL MANAGEMENT; see **Personnel Management, Institute of.**

INSTITUTE OF SUPERVISORY MANAGEMENT; see **Supervisory Management, Institute of.**

INSTITUTION OF PROFESSIONAL CIVIL SERVANTS; see **Professional Civil Servants, Institution of.**

INSURANCE OFFICIALS, GUILD OF; see **Insurance Staffs, Union of.**

INSURANCE STAFF ASSOCIATIONS, FEDERATION OF. A body formed in the late 1950s to provide for exchange of information between staff associations in the insurance industry and as a channel for communication to outside bodies. Its constitution provided that it could be invited by affiliates to negotiate with employers on their behalf. In practice it seems never to have done so. In 1971 it comprised 10 staff associations with a total membership of about 34,000. After the merger of some insurance staff associations into the **Association of Scientific, Technical and Managerial Staff** (q.v.), the Federation declined and was replaced in 1972 by the **Confederation of Independent Staff Organisations** (CISO) (q.v.).

INSURANCE STAFFS, UNION OF (UIS) A trade union founded in 1919 as the Guild of Insurance Officials and taking the title Union of Insurance Staffs in 1969. In the following year it merged with the **Association of Scientific, Technical and Managerial Staffs** as its ISS Section. The UIS reached its peak membership of 21,000 in 1963. It was affiliated to the **Trades Union Congress** and had 13,840 members on amalgamation.

INSURANCE TRADE UNIONS, CONFEDERATION OF (CITU). A body established in 1946-47 to provide machinery for liaison between unions affiliated to the **Trades Union Congress** with interests in the insurance industry. It now meets periodically to discuss matters of general interest and consists of the **Association of**

Scientific, Technical and Managerial Staffs (ISS Section), the **National Union of Insurance Workers,** the **Union of Shop, Distributive and Allied Workers,** and the insurance section of the **Transport and General Workers' Union.** *Address:* Transport House, Smith Square, London SW1P 3JB. *Tel:* 01-828 7788.

INSURANCE WORKERS, NATIONAL UNION OF. A trade union formed on 1 October 1964 by amalgamation between the National Federation of Insurance Workers and National Amalgamated Union of Life Insurance Workers. The total membership of the union is employed in Industrial Life Offices which provide home service insurance, and is basically a federation now comprising 14 sections, one for each Office. All members work away from their Societies' head office, in which employees are organised by the **Association of Scientific, Technical and Managerial Staffs** (q.v.); they do not include agents and officials of the Co-operative Insurance Society which are respectively organised in the **Union of Shop, Distributive and Allied Workers** and in the **Transport and General Workers' Union** in the form of the **National Union of Co-operative Insurance Society Employees** (q.v.). *Address:* 185 Woodhouse Road, N. Finchley, London N12 9BA. *Tel:* 01-368 1098. *TUC Affiliated Membership 1977:* 25,061.

INTEGRATIVE BARGAINING. One of four models of collective bargaining behaviour advanced by Richard E. Walton and Robert B. McKersie. (*A Behavioral Theory of Labor Negotiations,* McGraw-Hill, 1965) in an attempt to provide predictive hypotheses on how people will tend to behave in varying situations and bargaining conditions, the others being **distributive bargaining, intraorganisational bargaining** and **attitudinal structuring.** Integrative bargaining consists of problem-solving behaviours and other activities which identify, enlarge and act upon the common interests of the parties.

INTERCHANGEABILITY. The relaxation of **demarcation** between crafts, trades or jobs by workers being willing to do jobs alternative to those which they normally do by agreement or custom, so as to ensure continuity of employment or make more economical use of labour, e.g. a striker with no immediate work to do might do rough painting on a ship's side, or a caulker be temporarily employed as a burner. Interchangeability has something in common with **flexibility** (q.v.) and provisions about them have sometimes appeared in the same **productivity agreements;** see also **restrictive practices.**

INTEREST DISPUTES also **disputes of interest, conflicts of interest.** Disputes or conflicts in **collective bargaining** arising out of the making of new agreements on terms and conditions of work, or the renewal of those which have expired, as distinct from **rights disputes** (q.v.), i.e. disputes about alleged violations of rights already established in employment contracts. Some writers prefer the term **nonjudiciable disputes** on the grounds that 'interest' exists in disputes involving existing as well as new agreements, e.g. T.L. Johnston, *Collective Bargaining in Sweden,* Allen and Unwin, 1962, p. 139; others distinguish them as **economic disputes.** The distinction between conflicts of rights and conflicts of interest has been drawn in the United States of America and in other counties with legal systems recognising the enforceability of collective agreements; it has not commonly been made in Britain. The **Industrial Relations Code of Practice 1972,** para. 126 provides, however, a definition 'disputes . . . which relate to claims by employees or proposals by management about terms and conditions of employment'.

INTERFERENCE   ALLOWANCE (work study); see **allowances.** 'An allowance of time for production unavoidably lost through the simultaneous requirements for service of two or more operations, machines or processes'. British Standards Institution, *Glossary of Terms Used in Work Study,* BS 3138, 1969, No. 36009.

INTERMEDIATE AREA; see **assisted areas.**

INTERNAL JOB REGULATION; see **job regulation.**

INTERNAL MOBILITY; see **labour mobility.**

INTERNATIONAL   CONFEDERATION OF FREE TRADE UNIONS (ICFTU). An international trade union organisation comprising 114 affiliated organisations in 89 countries and territories outside the Soviet bloc, with a total individual membership of more than 48 millions. The ICFTU was formed in 1949

after non-communist affiliates withdrew from the **World Federation of Trade Unions** (q.v.). It has a number of regional organisations, and associated with it are 16 autonomous **International Trade Secretariats.** The **AFL-CIO** withdrew from the ICFTU in 1969 following a dispute over the application for affiliation of the International Union, United Automobile, Aerospace and Agricultural Implement Workers of America (UAW) (ICFTU, *Report of the Ninth World Congress,* July 1969, pp. 15-16). The ICFTU is notable for its support of trade union independence from government and for its opposition to communist and fascist regimes and to racialism. It is also concerned with union building and economic growth in developing countries. *Address:* 37-41 rue Montagne aux Herbes Potagères, Bruxelles 1, Belgium. *Tel:* 17.80.85.

INTERNATIONAL FEDERATION OF BUILDING AND WOODWORKERS (IFBWW); see **International Trade Secretariats.**

INTERNATIONAL FEDERATION OF CHEMICAL AND GENERAL WORKERS' UNIONS (ICF); see **International Trade Secretariats.**

INTERNATIONAL FEDERATION OF COMMERCIAL, CLERICAL AND TECHNICAL EMPLOYEES (FIET); see **International Trade Secretariats.**

INTERNATIONAL FEDERATION OF FREE TEACHERS' UNIONS (IFFTU); see **International Trade Secretariats.**

INTERNATIONAL FEDERATION OF PETROLEUM AND CHEMICAL WORKERS (IFPCW); see **International Trade Secretariats.**

INTERNATIONAL FEDERATION OF PLANTATION,   AGRICULTURAL AND ALLIED WORKERS (IFPAAW); see **International Trade Secretariats.**

INTERNATIONAL FEDERATION OF TRADE UNIONS (IFTU). An international trade union organisation formally constituted in 1913 and reconstituted in 1919 as a federation of national centres in 14 countries with a membership of 17,668,000, and associated with a number of **International Trade Secretariats.** The IFTU came to an end on the establishment of the **World Federation of Trade Unions** (q.v.) in 1945. Walter Schevenels, *Forty-*

five Years, 1901-1945; International Feder-ation of Trade Unions, Brussels, Board of Trustees, 1956.

INTERNATIONAL GRAPHICAL FEDERATION (IGF); see **International Trade Secretariats.**

INTERNATIONAL INSTITUTE FOR LABOUR STUDIES; see **Labour Studies, International Institute for.**

INTERNATIONAL LABOUR CONVENTION NO. 1. A convention on **hours of work** in industry (1919) requiring the limitation of working hours to a maximum of eight in a day and 48 in a week, with provisions for certain exceptions. The United Kingdom has not ratified this convention.

INTERNATIONAL LABOUR CONVENTIONS NOS 11, 84, 87 and 98; see **freedom of association** and **right to strike.**

INTERNATIONAL LABOUR CONVENTION NO. 14. A convention on **weekly rest** in industry (1921), providing for a rest period of at least 24 hours in every period of seven days. The United Kingdom has not ratified this convention.

INTERNATIONAL LABOUR CONVENTION NO. 47; see **hours of work.**

INTERNATIONAL LABOUR CONVENTION NOS 89 and 90; see **night work.**

INTERNATIONAL LABOUR CONVENTION NO. 100 on equal remuneration, 1951. The Convention requires ratifying governments to promote and, so far as is consistent with national methods of wage determination, to ensure the application to all workers of the principle of equal pay for men and women for work of equal value; see **equal pay** and **Equal Pay Act 1970.**

INTERNATIONAL LABOUR CONVENTION NO. 132; see **holidays with pay.**

INTERNATIONAL LABOUR MOVEMENT. A complex of some sixty organisations, differing in structure, purpose, ideology, political independence and cohesiveness, but all representing in one way or another the interests of organised labour on an international scale. The Workingmen's International Association (the First

International) remained in existence from 1864 to 1876 and a second (socialist) International was created in Paris in 1889; but no international trade union organisation, except for sectional **International Trade Secretariats** (q.v.) existed until the beginning of the present century. Development was interrupted by the first world war (the International Trade Union Secretariat (1903) and its successor, the **International Federation of Trade Unions** (1913) being located in Berlin), and affected between the wars by the growth of Soviet trade unionism. The IFTU (reconstituted with European and United States membership in 1919) was paralleled by the Red Trade Union International (1921) devoted to opposition to reformist trade unionism and to the overthrow of capitalism, and by the International Federation of Christian Trade Unions which condemned any liberal, socialist or communist regime and favoured systematic collaboration of all classes. Today these three divisions of thought are continued in the **International Confederation of Free Trade Unions** (1949) q.v., the **World Federation of Trade Unions** (1945), and the **World Confederation of Labour** (WCL), usually known as the Christian International. 'Regional' internationals also exist which limit their membership to trade union centres in particular regions, e.g. the International Confederation of Arab Trade Unions, the All-African Trade Union Federation, and the African Trade Union Confederation, which are predominantly political in character. Industrial internationals exist in the WFTU (11 Trade Union Internationals, formerly trade departments), in the WCL and in the ICFTU, though in the first they are centrally administered, and in the second thought to be weak. A fourth category of international trade union organisation is represented by trade union groups which are linked to the existence of various supranational organisations, e.g. to the **Organisation for Economic Co-operation and Development** (q.v.), the Organisation of American States, the Eastern bloc's Council for Mutual Economic Aid (COMECON), and the **European Confederation of Free Trade Unions** (1969), now the **European Trade Union Confederation** (1973), made up of ICFTU-affiliated centres in countries of the European Economic Community. In recent years parts of the international labour movement have become increasingly concerned with the emergence of the **multinational corporation** (q.v.).

INTERNATIONAL LABOUR ORGANISATION (ILO). An international organisation founded at the Paris Peace Conference in 1919 and therefore the oldest of the agencies associated with the League of Nations and the United Nations Organisation. The suggestion that nations should act together to improve and to legislate labour conditions was formerly thought to have originated with Robert Owen but is now with greater certainty attributed to Charles Hindley in England (Member of Parliament for Ashton-under-Lyne, 1835-57) in 1833, and some ten years later to Daniel Legrand in France. It was later developed by the First and Second Internationals (formed in 1864 and 1889 respectively) and by the **International Federation of Trade Unions** which had its origins in a conference in 1901 and was formally constituted in 1913. In 1969, 118 countries were in membership of the ILO which functions by collecting and distributing information on labour and industrial conditions and by establishing international labour standards through the International Labour Conference in the form of Conventions and Recommendations which member states are under an obligation to submit to their competent national authorities, Conventions becoming binding when ratified by them; see *inter alia:* B. Beddington Behrens, *The International Labour Office,* Leonard Parsons, 1924; G.N. Barnes, *History of the International Labour Office,* Williams and Norgate, 1926; C.W. Jenks, *The International Protection of Trade Union Freedom,* Stevens, 1957, and *Human Rights and International Labour Standards,* Stevens, 1960; David A. Morse, *The Origin and Evolution of the ILO and its Role in the World Community,* New York State School of Industrial and Labor Relations, Cornell University, Ithaca, New York, 1969. The USA withdrew from the organisation in November 1977 alleging that it had departed from its original principles as a result of the erosion of tripartite representation, a growing lack of objectivity and increasing politicisation.

INTERNATIONAL LABOUR RECOMMENDATION NO. 91. An ILO Recommendation on collective bargaining providing for the establishment of machinery for the negotiation of collective agreements and procedures for the settlement of disputes arising out of them; see **collective bargaining.**

INTERNATIONAL LABOUR RECOMMENDATION NO. 92. An ILO Recommendation providing for the establishment of voluntary conciliation and arbitration machinery to assist in the prevention and settlement of labour disputes.

INTERNATIONAL LABOUR RECOMMENDATION NO. 116; see **hours of work.**

INTERNATIONAL LABOUR RECOMMENDATION NO. 119; see **termination of employment.**

INTERNATIONAL LABOUR RECOMMENDATION NO. 143; see **facilities for trade unions.**

INTERNATIONAL METALWORKERS' FEDERATION (IMF); see **International Trade Secretariats.**

INTERNATIONAL ORGANISATION OF EMPLOYERS (IOE); see **Employers, International Organisation of.**

INTERNATIONAL SECRETARIAT OF ENTERTAINMENT TRADE UNIONS (ISETU); see **International Trade Secretariats.**

INTERNATIONAL STANDARD CLASSIFICATION OF LABOUR COST; see **labour costs.**

INTERNATIONAL STANDARD CLASSIFICATION OF OCCUPATIONS (ISCO); see **Occupations, International Standard Classification of.**

INTERNATIONAL TEXTILE, GARMENT AND LEATHER WORKERS' FEDERATION (ITGLWF); see **International Trade Secretariats.**

INTERNATIONAL TRADE SECRETARIATS (ITS). International trade union organisations based upon a federal structure of national trade unions in particular trades or industries. Attempts to form such secretariats date from the end of the 1860s, and the idea of a common secretariat took form at a Labour Congress held in Copenhagen in 1901. The arrangements which developed had close relations with the **International Federation of Trade Unions** up to the second world war. At the end of that war attempts to integrate the secretariats with the newly formed **World Federation of Trade Unions** raised questions of the autonomy of individual secretariats as well as of communist domination. The formation of the **International Confederation of Free Trade Unions** in 1949 enabled secretariats to retain their independence by recognising their autonomy within the organisation on a definition agreed at its second World Congress in Milan in 1951. The following secretariats are currently associated with the ICFTU:

International Federation of Building and Woodworkers (IFBWW) founded 1934; 27-29 rue de la Coulouvrenière, CH 1204 Geneva, Switzerland. *Tel:* 21.16.11. *Membership:* 3,000,000.

International Federation of Commercial, Clerical and Technical Employees (FIET) founded in its present form in 1921; 15 avenue de Balexert, CH-1210 Geneva-Châtelaine, Switzerland. *Tel:* 96.27.34. *Membership:* 5.9 millions.

Universal Alliance of Diamond Workers (UADW) founded 1905; Plantin-en-Moretuslei 66-68 Antwerpen, Belgium. *Tel:* 32.91.51. *Membership:* (31.12.1968) 10,400.

International Secretariat of Entertainment Trade Unions (ISETU) founded 1965; 2nd Floor, King's Court, 2 Goodge St, London W1P 2AE. *Membership:* 471,516.

International Union of Food and Allied Workers' Associations (IUF) founded 1920; Rampe du Pont-Rouge 8, CH-1213 Petit-Lancy, Switzerland. *Tel:* 93.22.23. *Membership:* 2,198,378.

International Graphical Federation (IGF) founded 1949; Monbijoustrasse 73, CH-3007 Berne, Switzerland. *Tel:* 45.99.20. *Membership:* 838,000.

International Federation of Chemical and General Workers' Unions (ICF) founded 1947; 58 rue de Moillebeau, CH-1211 Geneva, Switzerland. *Tel:* 33.77.60. *Membership:* 3,000,000.

International Metalworkers' Federation (IMF) founded 1904; route des Acacias 54 bis, CH-1227 Geneva, Switzerland. *Tel:* 43.61.50. *Membership:* 13 millions.

Miners' International Federation (MIF) founded 1890; 75-76 Blackfriars Road, London SE1 8TE. *Tel:* 01-928 2262-3. *Membership:* 1,280,000.

International Federation of Petroleum and Chemical Workers (IFPCW) founded 1954; Madison Plaza, Suite 215, Denver, Colorado, United States of America. *Tel:* 388-9237. *Membership:* Affiliated and Cooperating Unions, 2,000,000. Regional Office 54 rue Moillebeau, Ch 1121, Geneva, Switzerland.

International Federation of Plantation, **Agricultural and Allied Workers** (IFPAAW) founded 1959; 17 rue Necker CH-1201, Geneva. *Tel:* 31.31.05. *Membership:* 3,500,000.

Postal, Telegraph and Telephone International (PTTI) founded 1920; 36 avenue du Lignon, CH 1209, Geneva, Switzerland. *Tel:* (022) 96.83.11. *Membership:* 3,292,394.

Public Services International (PSI) founded as International Federation of Unions in Public and Civil Services, 1935, renamed, 1958; 26/30 Holborn Viaduct, London EC1. *Tel:* 01-583 1841/2. *Membership:* 3,700,000.

International Federation of Free Teachers' Unions (IFFTU) re-established 1951; Ave. G. Bergmann 111, 1050 Bruxelles, Belgium. *Tel:* 648.68.73. *Membership:* 2,200,000.

International Textile, Garment and Leather Workers' Federation (ITGLWF) founded as merger of secretariats in 1960 including leather workers in 1970; 8 rue Joseph Stevens, 1000 Bruxelles, Belgium. *Membership:* 5 millions.

International Transport Workers' Federation (ITF) founded 1896; Maritime House, Old Town, Clapham, London SW4 0JR. *Tel:* 01-622 5501. *Membership:* 6.5 millions.

Some five ITSs (the IMF, ICF and to a lesser extent IFPCW, IUF and FIET) have developed in the past few years policies for dealing with the **multinational corporation** (q.v.); see also **international trade union movement.**

INTERNATIONAL TRANSPORT WORKERS' FEDERATION (ITF); see **International Trade Secretariats.**

INTERNATIONAL UNION. A term used in the United States to describe most unions which have affiliated **locals** in the United States and in some other countries, mostly in Canada; also referred to as 'national unions'; see Jack Barbash, *Labor Unions in Action,* Harper, New York, 1948.

INTERNATIONAL UNION OF FOOD AND ALLIED WORKERS' ASSOCIATIONS (IUF); see **International Trade Secretariats.**

INTER-UNION DISPUTES. Disputes between trade unions, usually about membership but also about claims to exclusive rights to perform particular jobs or types of work; **jurisdictional** and **demarcation disputes** (q.v.); see S. Lerner, *Breakaway*

Unions and the Small Trade Union, George Allen and Unwin, 1961, p. 66. Sometimes also used of situations in which trade unions fall out of line in the custom of negotiating jointly or of following a common agreement, e.g. in the case of maintenance workers in the newspaper industry in 1955 who refused to follow the agreement negotiated by the printing unions, thereby bringing the industry to a standstill; see H.A. Turner, *Trade Union Growth, Structure and Policy,* George Allen and Unwin, 1962, p. 304. **Rule 12** of the **Trades Union Congress** gives the General Council power to use its influence to settle disputes between affiliated organisations, to investigate cases in dispute if invited by an affiliated organisation and to invite contending organisations to appear before the General Council's Disputes Committee; in extreme cases power exists under **Rule 13** to suspend an offending union; see also **Bridlington Agreement.** An average of 25 cases of disputes between unions were reported to the TUC each year in the 1960s (see TUC, *Trade Unionism,* Evidence to the Royal Commission on Trade Unions and Employers' Associations, 1966, p. 21) but this has now greatly increased. There were 111 such cases in 1976-77. Other trade union machinery concerned with aspects of inter-union disputes is to be found, for example, in **Minute 741** (q.v.) of the **Confederation of Shipbuilding and Engineering Unions,** and in Rule 8 of the **General Federation of Trade Unions.** The **Royal Commission on Trade Unions and Employers' Associations, 1965-68** examined the problems of multi-unionism and recommended mergers, agreements on rights of representation, and more intense efforts by the TUC to obtain closer working between unions. In *In Place of Strife,* Cmnd. 3888, January 1969, the Labour government rejected the suggestion that inter-union disputes involving recognition should be tackled by amending the legal definition of 'trade dispute' to exclude disputes between 'workmen and workmen' (and thus open strikers to legal action), and preferred action·by the TUC and the **Commission on Industrial Relations** (q.v.). Such a change was made in the definition of **industrial dispute** in the **Industrial Relations Act 1971.** This was removed when the Act was repealed in 1974 and the words 'worker' and 'worker' reintroduced into the definition of a **trade dispute** along the lines of the **Trade Disputes Act 1966** (Trade Union and Labour Relations Act 1974, s. 29). Even under the Industrial Relations Act the **Industrial**

Relations Code of Practice (para. 11 (iv)) emphasises, nevertheless, the responsibility of unions in '[maintaining] effective procedures for resolving particular issues with other unions, and [making] full use of the procedures established by the Trades Union Congress for settling inter-union disputes'. This has remained the policy of Labour governments since 1974, though complications have sometimes arisen from legislation on **transfer of engagements** (see **Rothwell v. APEX and TUC (1976)** and from the recognition procedure of the Employment Protection Act 1975 (see **Section 11 Procedure**).

INTIMIDATION. An expression variously used at different times in the context of industrial relations. Where **picketing** (q.v.) is concerned, a narrow definition confined to threat of personal violence was contained in the Criminal Law Amendment Act 1871. That Act was repealed by the **Conspiracy and Protection of Property Act 1875** which covered not only the use of violence or intimidation to persons, their wives and children, but also injury to property. An even wider definition in the **Trade Disputes and Trade Unions Act 1927** lapsed on repeal of that Act in 1946, leaving the situation substantially based on the 1875 Act. Where threats of action in collective bargaining are concerned, it was held by the House of Lords in the case of **Rookes v. Barnard** that threats to break a contract constituted *civil* intimidation. This resulted in the **Trades Disputes Act 1965** which provided that in contemplation or furtherance of a **trade dispute** neither a threat that a contract of employment would be broken nor a threat to induce another to breach a contract of employment would in themselves be actionable in tort, thus restoring the law to what it was generally believed to be before Rookes v. Barnard. The **Industrial Relations Act 1971,** repealed the 1965 Act, extended the protection from action in the ordinary courts to any contract and to prevention of its performance (s. 132(1)(b)), but in s. 96 made it an **unfair industrial practice** for any person, other than a **registered trade union** or someone acting within the scope of his authority on behalf of such a union, in contemplation or furtherance of an **industrial dispute,** to induce or threaten to induce another person to break a contract to which he was a party, such a contract including so much of a contract of employment as was implied or incorporated from a collective agreement, with remedy available from the **National Industrial Relations Court.** In repealing the Industrial Relations Act 1971, the **Trade Union and Labour Relations Act 1974** restored the position to that of the 1965 Act.

INTRAORGANISATIONAL BARGAINING. One of the four models of collective bargaining behaviour advanced by Richard E. Walton and Robert B. McKersie (*A Behavioral Theory of Labor Negotiations,* McGraw-Hill, 1965) in an attempt to provide predictive hypotheses on how people will tend to behave in varying circumstances and bargaining conditions, the others being **distributive bargaining, integrative bargaining,** and **attitudinal structuring.** Intraorganisational bargaining is described as comprising the behaviour of a negotiator intended to achieve consensus within his own organisation.

INVESTIGATION, COMMITTEE OF; see **Committee of Investigation.**

IOE. International Organisation of Employers; see **Employers, International Organisation of.**

IOM. Institute of Office Management; see **Office Management, Institute of.**

IPCS. Institution of Professional Civil Servants; see **Professional Civil Servants, Institution of.**

IPM. Institute of Personnel Management; see **Personnel Management, Institute of.**

IRISH CONGRESS OF TRADE UNIONS (ICTU). The central body representative of the trade union movement in Ireland. The ICTU was founded as the Irish Trade Union Congress in 1894. A split in 1945 which resulted in the formation of two Congresses, the Irish Trade Union Congress (representative of unions which had their head office in Britain and a number of Irish-based unions) and the Congress of Irish Unions (composed of the main Irish-based unions), was healed in 1959 when the present Irish Congress of Trade Unions was established. The main function of the ICTU is to co-ordinate the work of trade unions operating in Ireland; it has no power over the internal affairs of its affiliates and the Congress resolutions do not bind them unless ratified by individual organisations. Congress does not engage in collective bargaining although it may, when requested by affiliated unions,

negotiate at national level with employers' organisations on policy and principles relating to wages and conditions of employment. It also helps in resolving **inter-union disputes,** and proposes names to the government for nomination as delegates to the International Labour Conference and as workers' members of the **Labour Court.** In 1976 there were 89 trade unions, operating in the Republic of Ireland, these unions having a total membership of 465,400. Of these 71 were affiliated to the ICTU, making Congress representative of 371,500 members, 93 per cent of all trade unionists. The main affiliated unions were the **Irish Transport and General Workers' Union,** the **Amalgamated Transport and General Workers' Union,** the **Workers' Union of Ireland,** the Irish Union of Distributive Workers and Clerks, and the Irish National Teachers' Organisation, these five unions making up more than one-half of that total, the main non-affiliated organisations being the Irish Bank Officials' Association, the National Busmen's Union and the Marine, Port and General Workers' Union. Of the 89 trade unions operating in the Republic in 1976 73, with a membership of 388,100, were Irish-based and 16, with a membership of 77,300 had their head office in Britain. The principal British unions with Irish Membership were the **Transport and General Workers' Union** (33,600 members), the **Union of Construction, Allied Trades and Technicians** (10,300), the **Association of Scientific, Technical and Managerial Staffs** (9,500), the **Electrical, Electronic, Telecommunication and Plumbing Union** (3,000), the **General and Municipal Workers' Union,** the **Union of Shop, Distributive and Allied Workers** and the **Amalgamated Union of Engineering Workers** (Engineering Section (3,400). The constitution of the ICTU requires affiliated unions with head offices in Britain to devolve certain functions upon their Irish membership. *Address:* 19 Raglan Road, Ballsbridge, Dublin 4. *Tel:* Dublin 680641.

IRISH MANAGEMENT INSTITUTE (IMI). An independent body of businessmen and firms controlled by an annually elected Council and founded in 1952 with the objective of raising the standard of management in Ireland. The IMI conducts a programme of courses on all aspects of industrial and commercial management, including industrial relations, and also provides an information service, and library as well as a monthly business Journal. *Address:* 186 Orwell Road, Dublin 14. *Tel:* Dublin 904681.

IRISH TRANSPORT AND GENERAL WORKERS' UNION (ITGWU). A trade union formed in Dublin by James Larkin in January 1909, as a breakaway of dockers and carters from the National Union of Dock Labourers, and at first called the Irish Transport Workers' Union. The union was reorganised in 1918 after its involvement in the nationalist risings during the first world war and developed into a mass organisation for general workers. It now claims a financial membership of over 100,000 and a book membership of up to 150,000, organised in six industrial groups covering workers in substantially all industries in Ireland. ITGWU, *Fifty Years of Liberty Hall 1909-1959,* 1959. *Address:* Liberty Hall, Dublin 1. *Tel:* Dublin 749731. *ICTU Affiliated Membership: 1977:* 150,000.

IRON LAW OF OLIGARCHY. A theory attributed to Robert Michels (*Political Parties,* New York, International Library, 1915, reprinted Collier Macmillan, 1966) and restated by a number of writers to explain the supposed tendency within trade unions for power to move from the membership to executive committees and paid officials; see Will Herberg, 'Bureaucracy and Democracy in Labor Unions', *Antoich Review* III, Fall 1943, pp. 405-17; Bernard Karsh and Jack London, 'The Coal Miners; a Study in Union Control', *Quarterly Journal of Economics,* LXVIII, August 1954, pp. 415-36. Martin A. Trow and James S. Coleman (*Union Democracy: The Internal Politics of the International Typographical Association,* Glencoe, The Free Press, 1956) and G. Wootton ('Parties Union Government, the AESD', *Political Studies,* Vol. IX, No. 2, June 1961) contrast the tendency towards oligarchy with the notion of a two party system in union government; see also Malcolm Warner, 'The Big Trade Unions: Militancy or Maturity?', *New Society,* 11 December 1969.

IRON LAW OF WAGES; see subsistence theory of wages.

IRON AND STEEL TRADES CONFEDERATION (ISTC). A trade union operative from January 1917, created to take responsibility for trade questions affecting wages and conditions of work in the iron and steel industry. The Confederation arose out of the need of the government during the first world war to consult the many unions then existing in the industry. This resulted in a scheme of confederation whereby existing members of confederating unions were transferred to the **British Iron, Steel and Kindred Trades Association** (BISAKTA), the same union being the only affiliate of the ISTC, and all new members being recruited into it, the ISTC taking over all the officials of the amalgamating unions. The ingenuity of this scheme was notably successful in reducing difficulties caused by the multiplicity of unions in steel; it also made possible a long period of close co-operation between union and managements in the industry. It did not, however, succeed in producing an industrial union in the complete sense, the **National Union of Blastfurnacemen, Ore Miners, Coke Workers and Kindred Trades** (NUB) remaining outside the Confederation, and other manual workers being members of the **Transport and General Workers' Union,** the **General and Municipal Workers' Union,** the **Amalgamated Union of Building Trade Workers** and a number of other craft unions. At the end of 1976, ISTC manual worker membership in the British Steel Corporation was reckoned at 80,000, out of a total TUC affiliated membership of 104,000. Particularly since the establishment of the Corporation by the **Iron and Steel Act 1967,** this situation, and the problem of union jurisdiction over various grades of staff workers, claimed both by the ISTC, and by other unions two of which (the **Association of Scientific, Technical and Managerial Staffs** and the **Association of Professional, Executive, Clerical and Computer Staffs**) are not nationally recognised by the Corporation, have tended to upset the previous smoothness of relations and to reintroduce the problem of inter-union conflict; see *Report of the Court of Inquiry under Lord Pearson into the dispute between the British Steel Corporation and certain of their employees,* Cmnd. 3754, August 1968. Sir Arthur Pugh, *Men of Steel,* ISTC, 1951. *Address:* Swinton House, 324 Gray's Inn Road, London WC1X 8DD. *Tel:* 01-837 6691. *TUC Affiliated Membership, 1977:* 104,073.

IRON, STEEL AND WOOD BARGE BUILDERS' AND HELPERS' ASSOCIATION. A trade union founded in 1872 as the River Thames Barge Builders. In 1916 it became the Barge Builders' Trade Union but reverted to its original title in 1918 and retained this until 1941 when the above name was adopted. The union amalgamated with the **Transport and General Workers' Union** in 1972.

IRREGULAR INDUSTRIAL ACTION SHORT OF A STRIKE; see strike.

IRRITATION STRIKE. Sometimes known as a **pearl strike.** 'A mild form of industrial sabotage . . . which the Syndicalists [see **Syndicalism**] defined as remaining at work and doing everything wrong'; (K.G.J.C. Knowles, *Strikes,* Blackwell, 1952, p. 14), for example, cinema projectionists deliberately missing reels and showing films upside down. Or a form of **ca'canny** (q.v.), as in *The Miners' Next Step,* 1912, 'remaining at work, reducing their output, and so contrive by their general conduct to make the colliery unremunerative'; see also **working without enthusiasm.**

IRSF. Inland Revenue Staff Federation (q.v.).

IS. The Industrial Society (q.v.).

ISCO. International Standard Classification of Occupations; see **Occupations, International Standard Classification of.**

ISETU. International secretariat of Entertainment Trade Unions; see **International Trade Secretariats.**

ISM. Institute of Supervisory Management; see **Supervisory Management, Institute of.**

ISSUE. In broad terms, any **difference** or **dispute** between the employer, union or worker, i.e. any question at issue. More specifically, an **issue** as provided for in Order 1376; see **Industrial Disputes Tribunal.**

ISSUES OF RIGHTS; see rights disputes.

ISTC. Iron and Steel Trades Confederation (q.v.).

IT. industrial tribunal (q.v.).

ITB. Industrial Training Board; see **Industrial Training Act 1964.**

ITF. International Transport Workers' Federation; see **International Trade Secretariats.**

ITGLWF. International Textile, Garment and Leather Workers' Federation; see **International Trade Secretariats.**

ITGWU. Irish Transport and General Workers' Union (q.v.).

ITS. International Trade Secretariat(s) (q.v.).

IUF. International Union of Food and Allied Workers' Associations; see **International Trade Secretariats.**

IWW. Industrial Workers of the World: see **Wobblies.**

J

JACK REPORT. Name given to the reports of a number of Courts of Inquiry under the chairmanship of Professor D.T. Jack, especially those concerned with the national engineering stoppage of 1957, (Cmnd. 159 for *Engineering,* and Cmnd. 160 for *Shipbuilding;* see also H.A. Clegg and Rex Adams, *The Employers' Challenge,* Basil Blackwell, 1957), and with the *Ford Motor Company* (Cmnd. 1999, April 1963) arising out of the dismissal of Kevin Halpin and a number of other trade union members; also the Committee of Inquiry into the *Dispute at Spitalfields, Borough, Stratford, Brentford and King's Cross Markets* in July 1964, and inquiries into two air transport disputes, *British Overseas Airways Corporation and the Merchant Navy and Airline Officers' Association* (Cmnd. 105, 1957) and at *London Airport* (Cmnd. 608, November 1958), and a steel industry dispute about the lining of furnaces (*Steel Company of Wales and the Amalgamated Union of Building Trades Workers,* 1966, January 1967).

JE. Job evaluation (q.v.).

JENKINSON v. NEILD; see blacklisting.

JEWEL CASE AND JEWELLERY DISPLAY MAKERS' UNION, LONDON. A trade union founded in 1894 and in 1977 having 18 members, making it probably the smallest union in existence in Britain. It recruits only craftsmen in a few firms in the London area, and reached a peak of membership in 1949 (72 members). It is affiliated to the **General Federation of**

Trade Unions. *Address*: 3 Montague House, Whitmore Road, London N1 5QE. *Tel*: 01-739 8164.

JIC. Joint Industrial Council; see **Whitleyism.**

JOB. A piece of work, particularly one designed to be performed by a particular individual; British Standards Institution, *Glossary of Terms Used in Work Study*, BS 3138: 1969, defines as 'all the work carried out by a worker or group of workers in the completion of their prescribed duties and grouped together under one title or definition' and in **work study** techniques, 'a part of these duties' (No. A3002).

JOB ANALYSIS. The analysis of a job to provide a **job description** in order to facilitate the choice of a job by individuals, personnel selection, the development of training schemes, the definition of work methods etc. Methods of job analysis may vary according to the purpose of the job description, e.g. for training purposes aspects of the job will be selected which are trainable and which determine success or satisfaction, and involve fact-finding observation, recording of essential factors, and assessment of emergent needs; see G.A. Randell, 'Job Analysis' in *Industrial Training Handbook*, ed. John W. Barber, Iliffe Books, 1968; G. McBeath and D.M. Rands, *Salary Administration*, Business Books Ltd, 3rd ed., 1976.

JOB-AND-FINISH. The practice of allowing workers to go home when they have completed a fixed amount of work in less than the number of hours contracted for. Early finish may apply on a daily or on a week by week basis. In either event, workers on time rates are paid as if a full day or week has been worked, and payment by result workers receive full piecework earnings; see also **stint wage system**. W.W. Daniel (*Beyond the Wage-Work Bargain*, PEP Broadsheet 519, July 1970, pp. 25-6) comments on the dramatic increases which job-and-finish may achieve in the short run, and the long run problems which it may create.

JOB CREATION PROGRAMME. A scheme introduced in October 1975 and administered by the **Manpower Services Commission** to provide temporary jobs of social value, at the appropriate local rate of pay, for people who would otherwise be unemployed and who would benefit from such work, paying particular attention to young unemployed between 16 and 24 years old and the over 50s. Sponsors, which include local authorities, voluntary organisations, private employers, community groups and individuals can submit projects and, if approved, are given a grant to cover approved wage costs and the equivalent of up to 10 per cent of that figure for running costs where these cannot be provided from other sources. Projects must provide new employment opportunities. By the end of February 1977 over 6,500 projects had been started, 60 per cent of them by local authorities and 29 per cent by voluntary organisations. In January 1978 it was claimed that 122,200 jobs had been safeguarded by the Programme (*Department of Employment Gazette*, February 1978).

JOB DESCRIPTION. A statement of the purpose, scope, duties, responsibilities etc., of a particular job, the product of **job analysis** (q.v.).

JOB DESIGN. The use by management of such discretion as is available in planning the content of jobs to obtain a number of possible results, e.g. maximum job specialisation, maximum interchangeability or mobility, linkages between job and job, or maximum **job satisfaction;** see also **work structuring**, L. Davis, 'The Design of Jobs', *Industrial Relations*, Vol. 6, 1966.

JOB ENGINEERING. An expression used to describe the process of fitting the **job** to the man, by changing the required duties and responsibilities, methods, procedures, equipment etc., rather than finding the man to suit the job as originally designed and available; may be thought of as an alternative to recruitment, or training, or as a supplement to them; M.M. Mandell, *The Selection Process*, American Management Association, 1964.

JOB ENLARGEMENT. A form of **work-structuring**, sometimes referred to as 'horizontal job enlargement', in which a job is expanded by the addition of operations similar to those already being undertaken, thus increasing the total cycle time of the operator. Job enlargement involves a reversal of the conventional process of increasing efficiency by breaking down jobs into smaller and smaller operations performed by different workers and thus questions the validity of greater and greater specialisation on the grounds that it tends to increase tensions and frustrations. Job enlargement has been practised in Britain by Philips, by Hoover (who, in 1964 changed from a traditional assembly line to a carousel conveyor method of assembling a popular model of vacuum cleaner) and in Imperial Chemical Industries along with the technique of **job enrichment** (q.v.); see also S. Cotgrove, J. Dunham and C. Vamplew, *The Nylon Spinners*, George Allen and Unwin, 1971 (ICI).

JOB ENRICHMENT. A practice advocated by Frederick Herzberg (*Work and the Nature of Man*, Crosby Lockwood Staples, 1974) as preferable to **job enlargement** (q.v.). It is alleged that job enrichment, by 'vertical loading' or providing positive motivational factors such as responsibility, achievement, and recognition (or motivations as distinct from **hygiene factors**, q.v.), provides an opportunity for an employee's psychological growth. Herzberg does not claim that all jobs can, or need, to be enriched, and summarises his advice to management as follows: 'If you have someone on a job, use him. If you can't use him on the job, get rid of him, either *via* automation or by selecting someone of lesser ability. If you can't use him and you can't get rid of him, you will have a motivational problem'. ('One More Time: How do you Motivate Employees?', *Harvard Business Review*, January-February 1968, p. 62); see also W.J. Paul and K.W. Robertson, *Job Enrichment and Employee Motivation*, Gower Press, 1970, based upon experience in Imperial Chemical Industries, and John R. Maher (ed.) *New Perspectives in Job Enrichment*, Van Nostrand Reinhold, 1971.

JOB EVALUATION (JE). A technique used, normally within companies, and sometimes at industry level, to determine the relationships between jobs and to establish for them a systematic structure or hierarchy of wage and/or salary rates. In some countries, including the Netherlands, the Soviet Union and Eastern Europe, national job evaluation schemes have been developed. JE schemes can be divided broadly into those which are non-analytical, such as **ranking** and **grading** or classification, and those which are analytical, such as **factor comparison** and **points rating**, but there are those which are composite in character or involve **time-span** (q.v.). Interest in job evaluation in Britain has increased as managements have sought to achieve acceptable pay struc-

tures sufficiently logical to reduce discontent over pay **differentials** and to prevent leapfrogging claims. The National Board for Prices and Incomes, (*Job Evaluation*, Report No. 83, Cmnd. 3772, September 1968) found 25 per cent of workers in a sample of firms employing 6.5 millions covered by job evaluation, 47 per cent of schemes using points rating, 28 per cent grading, 20 per cent ranking, and only 5 per cent factor comparison. Industry schemes included those in coal mining, jute, woven wire, cotton weaving (see **CMC Wage Scheme**) and electrical cable making. The Board did not consider a national scheme to be relevant to Britain's needs; see also British Institute of Management, *Job Evaluation, A Practical Guide*, 1970; Trades Union Congress, *An Outline of Job Evaluation and Merit Rating*, 1964, International Labour Office, *Job Evaluation*, 1969 and B. Livy, *Job Evaluation; A Critical Review*, Allen and Unwin, 1975; see also **Guide-Chart Profile Method** (Hay-MSL), **Castillion Method** and **Paterson Method**.

JOB GRADING; see **grading**.

JOB INSTRUCTION. A term used in **Training Within Industry** (q.v.).

JOB METHODS. A term used in **Training Within Industry** (q.v.).

JOB PRICE CONTRACT. A system of payment in which a worker or a group of workers is paid a fixed price for completing an agreed job, their incentive to finish the work being their desire to claim their price and to start on a new job. The practice can be associated with **labour-only sub-contracting** (q.v.), but is also employed in the construction industry with gangs of regularly employed workers; see also **contract piecework**.

JOB REGULATION. The process whereby the rules are made which regulate the content of **jobs**; Allan Flanders, *Industrial Relations; What is Wrong with the System?*, Institute of Personnel Management, and Faber and Faber, 1965, p. 15 *et seq.*, explains the process in terms of the institutions of **internal job regulation**, e.g. those producing rules which are domestic to the enterprise, **work rules**, factory **wage structures**, **grievance procedures** etc. and of **external job regulation**, e.g. provisions of the **Factories Acts**, trade union rules, employers' association rules, **collective agreements** made outside the factory etc.

JOB RELATIONS. A term used in **Training Within Industry** (q.v.).

JOB RELEASE SCHEME. A special measure to reduce unemployment introduced on 3 January 1977. The scheme enables full-time employed workers who are within one year of the statutory pensionable age, i.e. at age 64 for men and 59 for women, to leave their jobs and to receive a tax-free allowance (currently £26.50 a week from April 1978 - and from 1 July 1978 £35.00 for married applicants). In agreeing to release a worker under JRS the employer also agrees to recruit as a consequence someone who is registered as unemployed for full-time work as soon as possible - usually within a month - though not necessarily for the job the former worker had vacated. The scheme is due to close for applications on 31 March 1979.

JOB REQUIREMENTS. The characteristics required by a worker if he is to perform the **job** satisfactorily, e.g. vision, skill etc. E.J. McCormick and J. Tiffin, *Industrial Psychology*, Allen and Unwin, 6th ed., 1975.

JOB ROTATION. A form of **work-structuring** in which the activities of a worker are widened by enabling him to work in turn at several different operations performed in a production area. The technique has been used in Britain by Philips with small work groups; see also **job enlargement** and **job enrichment**.

JOB SATISFACTION. Described by Alan Fox as 'that vaguest of much-used concepts' (*A Sociology of Work in Industry*, Collier-Macmillan, 1971, p. 75). V.H. Vroom (*Work Motivation*, John Wiley and Sons, 1964) regards job satisfaction as the positive orientation of an individual towards the work role which he is at present occupying. Absolute levels of job satisfaction are difficult to measure (see R. Blauner, 'Work Satisfaction and Industrial Trends in Modern Society', in R. Bendix and S.M. Lipset (eds), *Class Status and Power*, Routledge and Kegan Paul, 1967), but it is generally agreed that it falls at successively lower levels in the occupational scale, *inter alia*; see A. Etzioni (ed.), *A Sociological Reader on Complex Organisations*, 2nd ed. Holt, 1969, pp. 223-49. Improvement of job satisfaction has been approached from a number of angles; **incentive payment systems**, in the **motivators** and **hygiene factors** of Herzberg's theory (q.v.), in terms of leadership style (see

for example, F. Fiedler, *A Theory of Leadership Effectiveness*, McGraw-Hill, 1967, etc.), Enid Mumford considers the hypothesis that job satisfaction is related to the degree of 'fit' between organisational demands and individual needs; 'Job Satisfaction — A New Approach Derived from an Old Theory', *Sociological Review*, Vol. 18, No. 1, March 1970, pp. 71-101; or a general reader in the area, see Mary Weir (ed.), *Job Satisfaction*, Fontana, 1976; also **work-structuring**, **Work Research Unit**.

JOB SPECIFICATION. A **job description** (see **job analysis**) used to define the functional limits and terms of reference of a job and also the requirements of the person who would perform it most effectively. Job specifications for manual workers might include such factors as the nature of the operations to be performed, the types of material to be used, the machinery to be operated, the time standards required, the environmental features of the work and its possible effects on individuals; also such items as the vision, dexterity, physical characteristics, hearing, education and training, previous experience, hours and wages required or offered for the job; i.e. all the vital characteristics and requirements of the job to which a worker is to be matched; see **manpower planning**.

JOB STRESS; see **occupational stress**.

JOBBING MASTER. A trade union branch official, particularly in the baking industry, whose task it is to keep a list of members out of employment and to send members to available jobs.

JOBCENTRE. Modernised employment offices administered by the Employment Service Division of the **Manpower Services Commission**, see **employment service**. The first Jobcentre was opened in Reading in May 1973. Jobcentres were preceded by experiments with self-service employment offices from 1968 to 1969, the first being at St Helens, Lancs and at Ashford, Kent. Their objective has been to follow up the principle of self-selection of jobs by providing attractive offices in busy shopping areas in the centre of towns, backed up by information, interviewing and guidance, in order to increase the use made of the employment service. The aim is to replace 80 per cent of local employment offices with Jobcentres by 1980. By the end of 1977 389 had been opened. It is claimed that they are handling 20 per cent more vacancies than older style offices (May 1978).

JOHN LEWIS PARTNERSHIP. An enterprise based on common ownership and founded by Spedan Lewis in 1914, all his interests in the company being finally transferred to the John Lewis Partnership Trust Ltd to which all members of the Partnership indirectly elect a majority of the board. The Partnership own all the equity shares but (unlike the practice in the **Scott Bader Commonwealth** q.v.) debenture and preference stocks are owned by outsiders. Rates of pay determine the share of individual partners in distributed profits, and the principle is observed that managers are completely accountable to the partners, though not appointed by them; see Spedan Lewis, *Partnership for All,* Kerr-Cross Publishing, 1948 and *Fairer Shares,* Staples Press, 1954. A critical outside analysis of the Partnership is to be found in Allan Flanders, Ruth Pomeranz and Joan Woodward, *Experiment in Industrial Democracy, A Study of the John Lewis Partnership,* Faber and Faber, 1968.

JOHNSON v. LINDSAY AND CO. (1891) AC 371; see **employers' liability**.

JOINT BOARDS OF CONCILIATION AND ARBITRATION; see **Boards of Conciliation and Arbitration**.

JOINT BOARD FOR THE NATIONAL NEWSPAPER INDUSTRY; see **Newspaper Industry, National Joint Board for.**

JOINT CBI/TUC CONCILIATION AND ARBITRATION SERVICE. A non-governmental conciliation and arbitration service set up jointly by the **Confederation of British Industry** and the **Trades Union Congress** to deal with disputes at national and other levels. A joint CBI/TUC committee of sixteen members to administer the scheme was announced in April 1972 and formally began work in the following September. It formed part of a dialogue between the two bodies which from July 1972 developed into tripartite talks between them and the Heath administration on economic management (see **Chequers and Downing Street Talks**) which broke down on 2 November and led to a 90-day standstill on prices and incomes (*A Programme for Controlling Inflation,* Cmnd. 5125, November 1972 and the **Counter-Inflation (Temporary Provisions) Act 1972**). The service seems to have

been employed on only one occasion, though a bipartite approach has been retained in the **Advisory Conciliation and Arbitration Service** (q.v.); see also **conciliation, arbitration, prices and incomes policy.**

JOINT CONCILIATION. A procedural situation in which trade unions and employers take matters arising to joint panels of employers and trade union representatives, with or without an independent chairman, e.g. in the chemical industry or the building industry; the opposite of **employer conciliation** (q.v.); see A.I. Marsh and W.E.J. McCarthy, *Disputes Procedures in Britain,* Royal Commission on Trade Unions and Employers' Associations, Research Papers 2 (Part 2), HMSO, 1968.

JOINT CONSULTATION. A form of **workers' participation,** formally popularised during the 1939-45 war as a result of the 1942 agreements on **Joint Production Consultative and Advisory Committees** (JPCs) made between trade unions and the Director-General of Ordnance Factories on the one hand and trade unions and the Engineering and Allied Employers' National Federation on the other (see Wal Hannington, *The Rights of Engineers,* Gollancz, 1944); also implicitly a theory of worker-management relations. In both senses **joint consultation** had antecedents dating from the 1914-18 war; see **Whitleyism,** though this was by no means confined to consultative notions only. (H.A. Clegg and T.E. Chester, Joint Consultation, in A.D. Flanders and H.A. Clegg, *The System of Industrial Relations in Great Britain,* Basil Blackwell, 1954 and W.H. Scott, *Industrial Democracy, a Revaluation,* Liverpool University Press, 1955). World War II developments produced, however, a special type of machinery for formal consultation, the essence of which was embodied in the 1942 engineering agreement (*Handbook of National Agreements,* 2.81 and A.I. Marsh, *Industrial Relations in Engineering,* Pergamon Press, 1965, p. 109 *et seq.*). This distinguished strictly between consultation and negotiation, excepting from the former 'trade questions such as wages, and like subjects, which are covered by agreements with trade unions or normally dealt with by the approved machinery of negotiations', making consultation advisory on matters concerned with production and increasing efficiency only, and providing for representation independent of **shop ste-**

wards, concepts also built into the Acts setting up nationalised industries since the war. In engineering the concept was so far modified in 1955 as to approve the development of informal consultation in procedure (A.I. Marsh, op. cit, p. 94) and, with some industries and companies excepted, formal consultative machinery is often claimed now to have been abandoned, or, where shop steward organisation has intervened, become increasingly difficult to separate from negotiation (H.A. Clegg, *A New Approach to Industrial Democracy,* Basil Blackwell, 1960, p. 33 *et seq,* and W.E.J. McCarthy, *The Role of Shop Stewards in British Industrial Relations,* Royal Commission on Trade Unions and Employers' Associations, Research Papers No. 1, 1966, p. 32 *et seq.*), This in turn has led to claims that separation of negotiation and consultation is either impractical or undesirable (Labour Party, *Industrial Democracy, a Working Party Report,* 1967), or that the success of formal consultation depends on the importance ascribed to it by managements (Ministry of Labour, *Evidence to the Royal Commission on Trade Unions and Employers' Associations,* 1965 HMSO, p. 24). Theoretically the distinction between consultation and negotiation depends on the proposition that consultation is non-competitive and integrative in nature, whereas negotiation is competitive and concerned with temporary and unsatisfying compromise, consultation therefore being equipped to resolve conflict and negotiation merely to contain it (National Institute of Industrial Psychology; *Joint Consultation in British Industry,* Staples Press, 1952, p. 28, and Mary Parker Follett, *Dynamic Administration,* Metcalf and Urwick (eds), Pitman, 1973); see H.A. Clegg (op. cit.) for a contrary view. A Confederation of British Industry working party has taken the view that consultation cannot be separated from communication and negotiation, but that it is necessary to plan for each. It also rejected a merging of consultation and negotiation on the grounds that it might lead to too early negotiation, that it might make all management plans and decisions negotiable, and that negotiations may not be fully representative of all groups (*Communication and Consultation,* 1966, p. 11).

JOINT CO-ORDINATING COMMITTEE FOR GOVERNMENT INDUSTRIAL ESTABLISHMENTS: see **Whitleyism.**

JOINT INDUSTRIAL COUNCIL; see **Whitleyism.**

JOINT INDUSTRY BOARD FOR THE ELECTRICAL CONTRACTING INDUSTRY; see **Electrical Contractors' Association.**

JOINT PRODUCTION CONSULTATIVE AND ADVISORY COMMITTEE (Joint Production Committees, or JPCs); see **Joint Consultation.**

JOINT SHOP STEWARDS' COMBINE COMMITTEES; see **Combine Committees.**

JOINT SHOP STEWARDS' COMMITTEES; see **Joint Shop Stewards' Works Committees.**

JOINT SHOP STEWARDS' WORKS COMMITTEES. Commonly known as **Joint Shop Stewards' Committees;** committees of **shop stewards** belonging to different unions within an establishment in the engineering industry first allowed for by the **Confederation of Shipbuilding and Engineering Unions** in an Executive Council minute of 19 February 1947 (see A.I. Marsh, *Industrial Relations in Engineering,* Pergamon Press, 1965, Appx A4 for the text of this minute). An inquiry covering 432 federated engineering establishments in 1969 showed 68 per cent of these establishments to have Joint Shop Stewards' Committees, 82 per cent of these meeting in the works and 73 per cent meeting their managements regularly. (A.I. Marsh, E.O. Evans and P. Garcia, *Workplace Industrial Relations in Engineering,* EEF and Kogan Page, 1971). Similar committees of shop stewards exist in other industries, usually by tacit agreement between unions, and sometimes with managements also; in federated engineering Joint Shop Stewards' Works Committees are not nationally recognised by the **Engineering Employers' Federation.**

JOINT STATEMENT OF INTENT ON PRODUCTIVITY, PRICES AND INCOMES; see **Declaration of Intent.**

JOURNALISTS, NATIONAL UNION OF (NUJ). A trade union founded in 1907 and catering for journalists, whether freelance, or employed by newspapers, by radio or television, or in public relations, and affiliated to the **Trades Union Congress** (q.v.). It takes no part in politics and has no political fund. In the 1950s the union departed from its former practice of negotiating minimum rates only, in favour of all-round increases, and in the late 1960s it developed a new policy of negotiating career structures to provide at national or house level guaranteed increments for journalists based on service, experience and responsibility, as well as agreements on redundancy compensation and transferable or preservable pensions. Together with other journalists' and proprietors' organisations it set up the National Council for the Training of Journalists in 1952, and in 1966 agreed on dual membership with the Institute of Journalists, the latter taking prime responsibility for technical matters. Rivalry has nevertheless continued. In the middle 1970s, closed shop demands from some branches led to the provision of a **Press Council** in the Trade Union and Labour Relations Act 1976; see F.J. Mansfield, *Gentlemen — The Press!* W.H. Allen, 1944, and C.J. Bundock, *The National Union of Journalists 1907-1957*, OUP, 1957. *Address*: Acorn House, 314/320 Gray's Inn Road, London WC1X 8DP. *Tel*: 01-278 7916. *TUC Affiliated Membership, 1977*: 28,520.

JOURNEYMAN. A skilled worker who has completed his apprenticeship and is qualified to work for day wages; for example, in the printing industry 'a compositor or pressman who has completed his apprenticeship; derived from the French — "Journée", a day, day's work, or day's pay' (*Dictionary of Printing Terms*, Print Buyer Magazine Ltd, revised 1976). In modern usage, more loosely applied to qualified workers generally who work as employees.

JPC (JPC and AC). Joint Production Committee, or **Joint Production Consultative and Advisory Committee;** see **joint consultation.**

JUDICIABLE ARBITRATION; see **grievance arbitration.**

JUDICIABLE DISPUTES; see **rights disputes.**

JUNIORITY; see **seniority.**

JURISDICTIONAL DISPUTE. In the United States an **inter-union dispute** over the assignment of, or the right to perform, certain types of work; also a dispute over the right to represent employees in a particular company or industry. Broadly speaking, the term would seem to cover, in the British context, both **demarcation disputes** and **membership disputes.** S.W. Lerner, however (*Breakaway Unions and the Small Trade Union*, Allen and Unwin, 1961, p. 66) reserves jurisdictional disputes for 'conflicts which arise when rival unions claim the right to organise the same group of workers', and demarcational disputes for 'situation in which 'rival unions claim the same jobs for their members', placing the former within the competence of the Disputes Committee of the Trades Union Congress (see **Bridlington Agreement**), though they can also arise between different occupations within the same union.

JURORS' ALLOWANCES. Rates of travelling allowances, day and night subsistence and compensation for loss of earnings made to jurors under the Juries Act 1974. Present allowances (from 12 December 1977) are as follows:

Travelling:
Public conveyance - fare actually paid.
Train - 2nd class fare unless otherwise directed by the court.
Steamer (Scotland only) - when cabin is occupied cabin fare.
Hired Vehicle - in case of urgency and when no public service is available - fare and reasonable gratuity.
Private Conveyance - Motor-car up to
  1000cc............................ 10.6p per mile
  1000-1750cc.................. 12.3p per mile
  over 1750cc.................... 13.4p per mile
when substantial saving of time results: otherwise 2.6p per mile.
(Also lesser rates for private motor cycles.)

Subsistence:
Daily absence from home or place of employment of   per day
- up to 4 hours........................... £0.75
- over 4 and up to 8 hours......... £1.65
- over 8 and up to 12 hours....... £2.90
- over 12 and up to 16 hours...... £4.10
- over 16 hours.......................... £4.90
- overnight................................ £10.40

Loss of Earnings:
- the amount of the loss or additional expense but with a maximum of £10.78 per day (or £5.38 per day where the period is 4 hours or less). For service over 10 days, the maximum may be raised to £21.50 per day in respect of any one day after the tenth day.

JUST WAGE. An ethical teaching based upon the notion that the economic system ought to enable each family to provide for itself sufficient income to meet its own needs and those of its dependants, whether children, widows, aged etc.; hence usually synonymous with the **family wage.** Pre-industrial society, it is supposed, allowed wives and children to contribute to family income. In an industrial wage economy greater reliance is placed on the father of the family and his employer and injustice arises if wage earners are unemployed cannot earn sufficient for ordinary family needs. Hence, the employer owes a worker the value of his potential contribution to the product and, where this contribution falls short, it is the duty of all concerned (employers, workers and the state) to maximise it and to raise it where necessary. Justice therefore requires (a) freely functioning labour markets from which monopolistic and monopsonistic power is eliminated or in which they are at least controlled; (b) levels of employment high enough to eliminate chronic unemployment but not so high as to cause inflation; (c) fiscal policies which neither overburden efficient employers nor favour the inefficient; and (d) adequate training facilities to enable workers to meet changing labour markets. Employers are ethically required to pay according to the skills they are buying, irrespective of considerations of sex etc.; see also **Catholic Industrial Relations Teaching.** Origins of the doctrine of the just wage are to be found in the writings of St. Thomas Aquinas (1227-74), Henry of Langenstein (1340-97), and Antonio of Florence (1389-1459). A modern discussion is to be found in M.P. Fogarty, *The Just Wage,* Greenwood Press, 1976, and a briefer reference in J.-Y. Calvez and J. Perrin, *The Church and Social Justice,* Burns Oates, 1961.

JUTE, FLAX AND KINDRED TEXTILE OPERATIVES, UNION OF (UJFKTO). A trade union formed in 1906 and more commonly known as the Dundee Union of Jute and Flax Operatives, its membership being confined to Angus in Scotland and to the jute and flax industry in that area. *Address:* 93 Nethergate, Dundee DD1 4DH. *Tel:* 0382 22273. *TUC Affiliated Membership 1977:* 1,740.

K

KARMEL COMMITTEE. The Committee on the **Truck Acts** (q.v.) under the chairmanship of David Karmel, QC, which reported in 1961 and recommended the repeal of these Acts and their replacement by more modern legislation. Change was opposed by the **Trades Union Congress** and none has been made.

KAVANAGH v. HISCOCK (Divisional Court) (1974) ICR 282; (1974) 2 All ER 177. A case in which it was emphasised that the picket (see **picketing**) involved in a **trade dispute** (q.v.) has no special rights over and above any other person and that statute confers on him only the liberty to communicate and freedom from certain technical liabilities he might otherwise incur by standing upon the highway for this purpose.

KELLY v. NATSOPA (1915) 31, TL 632; see **Bonsor v. Musicians' Union.**

KEY WORKERS SCHEME. One of the three transfer schemes operated by the **Employment Service Division** of the **Manpower Services Commission** (the others being the **Employment Transfer Scheme** and the **Nucleus Labour Force Scheme,** q.v.), each operating a system of grants. The Key Workers Scheme assists workers who transfer, temporarily or permanently, to key supervisory or training posts beyond daily travelling distance in Development or Intermediate Areas, by means of financial assistance in the form of allowances.

KINDERSLEY COMMITTEE. The Review Body on Doctors' and Dentists' Remuneration appointed in March 1962 to advise the Prime Minister on the pay of doctors and dentists in the National Health Service, with Lord Kindersley as Chairman. A standing committee of this kind was advised by the **Pilkington Commission** (q.v.) in 1960 as the only means of 'the settlement of remuneration without public dispute, the provision of some assurance for the professions that their remuneration is not determined by considerations of political convenience and the provision of some safeguard for the community as a whole against medical and dental earnings rising higher than they should'. The Committee produced twelve reports between 1962 and 1970, when resignations followed the rejection of the May 1970 report by the Wilson administration. In November 1970 a new review body was proposed by the Heath government and later established as the **Doctors' and Dentists' Review Body** (q.v.).

KIRKBY CO-OPERATIVE; see **workers' co-operatives.**

KNIGHTS OF LABOR. A trade union organisation having its origin in Philadelphia, USA, in 1869 which grew to a membership of some 700,000 by 1886 and declined rapidly thereafter. The prime object of the Knights of Labor was to develop **one big union** of all workers regardless of nationality, creed, race, sex or skill. On their impact in Britain; see Henry Pelling, 'The Knights of Labor in Britain, 1880-1901', *Economic History Review*, 2nd series, Vol. 9, No. 2, December 1956, pp. 313-31.

L

LABOR-MANAGEMENT   RELATIONS ACT 1947; see **Taft-Hartley Act 1947.**

LABOUR COSTS. The costs, both voluntary and statutory, incurred by employers because they employ labour. The first comprehensive survey of employers' labour costs in Great Britain was made in 1964 (*Labour Costs in Great Britain in 1964*, HMSO, 1968); a second survey in 1968 included separate information for Northern Ireland (*Employment and Productivity Gazette*, August 1970, October 1970 and January 1971) and, so far as practicable, followed the **International Standard Classification of Labour Cost** ('Resolution concerning Statistics of Labour Cost; Studies and Notes', *International Labour Office Bulletin of Labour Statistics,* 1967). The first British survey to be conducted on the European pattern (and the third in the British series) was held in 1973 (*Department of Employment Gazette*, September 1975, pp. 873-85 and October 1975, pp. 1013-29) and covered manufacturing, mining and quarrying,

construction, gas, electricity and water and a second in 1974 for distribution, banking and insurance. The results of the 1975 survey, comparable to that of 1973 and made under Regulation 328/1975 of the Council of Ministers of the EEC were, in broad outline, published in the *Gazette* for September 1977, pp. 927-40, and included the following: wages and salaries (87.5 per cent of costs), statutory national insurance contributions (6.4 per cent), provisions for redundancy (0.5 per cent), employers' liability insurance (0.4 per cent), private social welfare payments (4.2 per cent), payments in kind (0.3 per cent), subsidised services to employees (1.1 per cent), and vocational training costs (0.3 per cent); see also **fringe benefits**.

LABOUR COURT. A court established in the Irish Republic by the Industrial Relations Act 1946 which performs a number of functions of which the provision of a conciliation service and the investigation of trade disputes are the most important. Having investigated a dispute, the Court may make a recommendation which is not legally enforceable; with the agreement of the parties to a dispute it may also arbitrate, in which case its award is binding, though no court has yet tested whether this is legally so (see R.J.P. Mortished, 'The Industrial Relations Act, 1946', *Public Administration in Ireland, Vol. II,* p. 85, and D. O'Mahony, *Industrial Relations in Ireland; The Background,* The Economic Research Institute Paper No. 19, May 1964). In 1970 the Labour Court dealt with 569 disputes, 451 (or 79 per cent) of which were settled by conciliation, and 509 (or 89 per cent) were settled by conciliation or investigation; see also **registered agreement.**

LABOUR COURTS. Judicial institutions established by the state for the settlement of labour disputes, especially those relating to disputes on existing rights, i.e. rights arising from the interpretation, application or enforcement of collective agreements, from individual contracts of employment, from torts alleged to have been committed in connection with industrial relations or employment with statutory employment rights, etc., but excluding, in most definitions, courts or other bodies concerned primarily with the resolution of **conflicts of interest** by **conciliation, mediation** or **arbitration.** The history of labour courts is said to have begun in 1806 with the **conseils de prud'hommes** in France; other examples are to be found in the three level system of the German **Arbeitsgerichte** (regular labour courts), **Landesarbeitsgerichte** (appellate labour courts) and **Bundesarbeitsgerichte (Federal Labour Court),** dating from 1926, and in the single Swedish **Arbetsdomstolen,** or Labour Court. **Industrial tribunals** in Britain were formerly thought by some to be too limited in jurisdiction to be called labour courts; since the **Industrial Relations Act 1971,** extension of this jurisdiction and the establishment of an **Employment Appeals Tribunal** may have modified this judgement to some extent. Labour Courts in different countries have, within the general area defined above, widely differing coverage and methods of handling disputes; see Benjamin Aaron (ed.), *Labor Courts and Grievance Settlement in Western Europe*, University of California Press, 1971.

LABOUR FORCE; see working population.

LABOUR LAW. That part of the law which treats of persons in their capacity as workers or as employers; defined by K.W. Wedderburn (*The Worker and the Law,* 2nd ed. Pelican Books, 1971, p. 17), as including the employment relationship between worker and employer arising from the contract of employment and the problems of job security connected with its termination, collective bargaining and the legal effect of collective agreements, statutory provisions relating to particular conditions of employment, the law concerning strikes, lock-outs and industrial conflict and the law about the status and membership of trade unions. Currently a distinction is usually made between labour law and **industrial law**, the former confining itself to the employment relationship and the latter including also such topics as company law and industrial property and taxation; nevertheless the two headings are sometimes treated as if they were substantially synonymous (e.g. in D.J. Keenan and L. Crabtree, *Essentials of Industrial Law*, Pitman, 1972). The expression **trade union law** is normally confined to the law relating to trade unions and to trade disputes (e.g. as in M.A. Hickling, *Citrine's Trade Union Law*, 3rd ed., Stevens, 1967 and in Cyril Grunfeld, *Modern Trade Union Law*, Sweet and Maxwell, 1970).

LABOUR-MANAGEMENT RELATIONS; see industrial relations.

LABOUR MARKET. An economic concept used to describe the mechanisms and conditions under which labour is demanded and supplied both within the firm (internal labour market) and in an economy or locality (external labour market). Labour markets have conventionally been regarded as principally external, subject to the theory that changes in distribution will occur when the balance of net advantages to workers can be improved by movement, a view derived ultimately from Adam Smith (*Wealth of Nations*, 1776-78, Everyman edition, 1910) and subsequently regarded as a special case of the general economic theory of value (see J.R. Hicks, *The Theory of Wages*, Macmillan, 1963, p. 1). Such a theory has long been regarded as inadequate both as an explanation of wage determination (see Hicks, op. cit. p. 10) and of the behaviour of labour markets, the latter being subject to **collective bargaining** (A.M. Ross, *Trade Union Wage Policy*, Berkeley, University of California Press, 1948) and to a complex of institutional and social forces affecting behaviour - **labour turnover**, recruitment, mobility (see **labour mobility**), company **manpower planning**, personal and social incentives, etc; see Derek Robinson (ed.), *Local Labour Markets and Wage Structures*, Gower Press, 1970, Dan Gowler, 'Determinants of the Supply of Labour to the Firm', *Journal of Management Studies*, Vol. 6, No. 1, February 1969, pp. 73-95, A.J. Brown, 'Further Analysis of the Supply of Labour to the Firm', *Journal of Management Studies,* Vol. 8, No. 3, October 1971, and a most comprehensive survey and inquiry in D.I. Mackay, D. Boddy, J. Brack, J.A. Diack and N. Jones, *Labour Markets under Different Employment Conditions*, George Allen and Unwin, 1971; also D. Robinson, 'Myths of the Local Labour Market', *Personnel,* Vol. 1, No. 1, 1967, and J. Corina, *Labour Market Economics,* Heinemann, 1972. The American literature in this area is extensive, but mostly relates to the postwar period or before; e.g. D. de Schweinitz, *How Workers find Jobs*, University of Pennsylvania Press, 1932, Clark Kerr, *Migration to the Seattle Labor Market Area 1940-42*, University of Washington, 1942, H. Hineman Jr., H. Fox and D. Goder, *Patterns of Labor Mobility*, Minneapolis, 1948, L. Reynolds, *The Structure of Labor Markets*, Harper, 1951, G. Myers and G.P. Shultz, *The Dynamics of a Labor Market*, Prentice Hall, 1951; (for a summary of US research, see H.S. Parnes, *Research on Labor Mobility, An*

Appraisal of Research Findings in the United States, American SSRC, 1954.

LABOUR, MINISTRY OF. Now the Department of Employment; see **Employment, Department of.**

LABOUR MOBILITY. Movement of labour involving a change of occupation (**occupational mobility**), or of location (**spatial mobility** or **geographical mobility**), hence in status or place of work, either within an establishment or undertaking (sometimes known as **internal mobility**) or between establishments or undertakings (**external mobility**) and associated with **labour turnover.** M. Jefferys, *Mobility in the Labour Market, Employment Changes in Battersea and Dagenham,* Routledge and Kegan Paul, 1954, G. Thomas, *Labour Mobility in Britain, 1945-1949,* Social Survey Report 134, A.I. Harris and R. Clausen, *Labour Mobility in Britain, 1953-63,* HMSO, SS. 333, March 1966, and D.I. Mackay, D. Boddy, J. Brack, J.A. Diack and N. Jones, *Labour Markets under Different Employment Conditions,* George Allen and Unwin, 1971. For a summary of US research in the field see H.S. Parnes, *Research on Labour Mobility, An Appraisal of Research Findings in the United States,* American SSRC, 1954.

LABOUR-ONLY SUB-CONTRACTING. A system in which a main contractor does not employ workers directly as his own employees, but either through a sub-contractor who supplies labour only (i.e. works with equipment and material provided by the main contractor), or on the basis that each worker is self-employed (hence the expression 'self-employed labour-only sub-contracting', workers involved being collectively known as **the lump,** or as working 'on the lump'). Such systems are not new; the **contract system** was formerly common in iron and steel, textiles and shipbuilding; it also exists in agriculture as the **gang system,** in which **gangmasters** provide labour, e.g. for the clamping of potatoes; the **butty** system (q.v.) in the coal mining industry and sub-contracting for labour-only has for a considerable time been traditional among some building crafts, e.g. tiling. In most industries (such as those quoted above) such practices have died out; in construction labour-only sub-contracting, particularly of the self-employed type, has increased since the war, the latter, it has been estimated by 60 per cent between

1961 and 1966 until the number of workers under labour-only sub-contract may be 165,000-200,000 (*Report of the Committee of Inquiry under Professor E.H. Phelps Brown into certain matters concerning Labour in Building and Civil Engineering,* Cmnd. 3714, July 1968). Labour-only sub-contracting has usually been opposed by trade unions, is alleged to give rise to abuse, including tax evasion, lack of insurance cover and job security and in the construction industry has become a threat to organised industrial relations (see Phelps Brown Report and A.I. Marsh and W.E.J. McCarthy, *Disputes Procedures in Britain,* Royal Commission on Trade Unions and Employers' Associations, 1965-68, Research Papers 2 (Part 2) 1968, p. 61); see also **Emerald Construction Co. Ltd v. Lowthian,** and **co-operative contracting.** In 1973 the National Federation of Building Trades Employers opened a voluntary register of employers who were prepared to inform the unions about labour-only sub-contractors and to allow **check-off** of union dues, and an attempt was made in 1971 to prevent income tax and national insurance evasion by obliging a contractor making a payment to a sub-contractor to deduct tax at source of 35 per cent unless the sub-contractor held a certificate as a self-employed building worker. From April 1977 under the Finance (No. 2) Act 1975 this arrangement was tightened up by making a certificate dependent on a clean tax record for three years and requiring the certificate to carry a photograph of the holder. Companies which were exempt from the 1971 scheme are now included.

LABOUR RELATIONS; see industrial relations.

LABOUR RELATIONS AGENCY (LRA). A body in Northern Ireland broadly equivalent to the **Advisory, Conciliation and Arbitration Service,** in Great Britain, established under the Industrial Relations (No. 1) Northern Ireland Order 1976 with effect from 1 October of that year. Its full-time chairman is Mr Brendan Harkin. Like ACAS it has a governing council of employer and employee representatives and independent members. *Address*: Windsor House, Bedford Street, Belfast BT2 7NU. *Tel*: Belfast 21442.

LABOUR STUDIES, INTERNATIONAL INSTITUTE FOR. An institute established by the **International Labour Organisation** in 1960 as a centre for advanced studies in the social and labour field, and with two broad aims; education for leadership in labour and industrial relations and research for developing useful social and labour policies. It also organises conferences and has published a *Bulletin* (1966-). *Address*: route des Morillons, CH-1200 Geneva 22, Switzerland. *Tel*: (022) 98.52.11.

LABOUR TURNOVER. The rate at which workers move in and out of employment at a plant, or sometimes in an industry; of particular interest as an element in **labour costs** and as a possible indication of low morale or poor industrial relations. Many formulae for measuring percentage labour turnover exist, most of them variants on the **separation rate** (T = S/W x 100, where (S) = quits [resignations or voluntary terminations of employment by workers] plus **discharges** [termination by the employer for the worker's fault] plus **lay-offs** or **redundancies**, plus other wastage over a period [deaths, retirements etc.] (W) = number of workers over a period), or the **accession rate** (T = A/W x 100, where (A) = new hirings [plus rehirings in some cases] over a period); see also '**BIM Index**'. The Department of Employment collects and publishes data on labour turnover consisting of variants on these two measures in the *Department of Employment Gazette* to which it has now added estimates based on the **New Earnings Survey** ('Labour Turnover: Estimates based on Employment Surveys and New Earnings Surveys', *Department of Employment Gazette,* April 1972). In recent years it has been claimed that for some purposes percentage leaving rates of cohorts of entrants may give more information about withdrawal from work; see A.K. Rice, J.M.M. Hill and E.L. Trist, 'The Representation of Labour Turnover as a Social Process', *Human Relations,* 1953, pp. 349-72 and Food Manufacturing Economic Development Committee, *A Study of Labour Turnover,* National Economic Development Office, 1968. On the relation between labour turnover and local labour markets; see H. Silcock, 'The Phenomenon of Labour Turnover', *Journal of the Royal Statistical Soceity,* A, 117, 1954, pp. 429-40, H. Behrend, 'Absence and Labour Turnover in a Changing Economic Climate', *Occupational Psychology,* 1953, and R. Hyman, 'Economic Motivation and Labour Stability', *British Journal of Industrial Relations,* Vol. VIII, No. 2, July 1970, pp. 159-78, D.I. Mackay, D. Boddy, J. Brack, J.A. Diack and N. Jones,

Labour Markets under Different Employment Conditions, George Allen and Unwin, 1971, Part III, and P.J. Samuel, *Labour Turnover? Towards a Solution,* Institute of Personnel Management, 1969, James L. Price, 'The Meaning of Turnover', *Industrial Relations Journal,* Vol. 6, No. 2, Winter 1975/6, pp. 33-46, B.O. Pettman (ed.), *Labour Turnover and Retention,* Gower Press, 1975, also **induction crisis.**

LAC. Local Advisory Committee (q.v.).

LACE MAKERS AND TEXTILE WORKERS, AMALGAMATED SOCIETY OF OPERATIVE (LACE MAKERS' SOCIETY). A trade union tracing its origins to the Lacemakers' Union of 1831, and continuously from the Amalgamated Society of Operative Lace Makers founded in 1874. The Society changed its name to Amalgamated Society of Lace Makers and Auxiliary Workers on merger with the Auxiliary Society of Male Lace Workers and the Female Lace Workers' Society in 1933, and to the above title in 1963. It was notable for its continuous tradition of conciliation, negotiation and arbitration pioneered by the earlier lace unions even before the influence of A.J. Mundella in the 1860s. It merged with the **National Union of Hosiery and Knitwear Workers** in June 1971; see Norman H. Cuthbert, *The Lace Makers' Society,* Amalgamated Society of Operative Lace Makers and Auxiliary Workers, 1960. At the time of the merger it had about 1,300 members.

LACE MAKERS' SOCIETY; see **Lace Makers and Textile Workers, Amalgamated Society of Operative.**

LAMINATED AND COIL SPRING WORKERS' UNION. A trade union founded in 1911 and organising workers involved in the manufacture and repair of heavy laminated and coil springs for railway and road vehicles. On 1 January 1977 the union transferred its engagements to the **Amalgamated Union of Boilermakers, Shipwrights, Blacksmiths and Structural Workers.**

LANCASTER v. LONDON PASSENGER TRANSPORT BOARD (1948) 2 All ER 796; see **employers' liability.**

LANDESARBEITSGERICHTE: see **labour courts.**

LA SOLENNITÀ DELLA PENTE-COSTE; see **Catholic industrial relations teaching.**

LAST-IN-FIRST-OUT; see **seniority.**

LATENESS. Being late for work. What is reckoned as lateness varies from one situation to another. Arrival after starting time may constitute lateness in one case; in others there may be a **grace period** or period of **allowable lateness.** Lateness of any considerable length may constitute voluntary or avoidable **absence** (q.v.); the British Institute of Management (*Absence from Work*, BIM, 1955) has suggested that an hour's lost time through lateness is sufficient to constitute absence. British industry appears to produce no systematic data on lateness. Glacier Metal (see **Glacier Project**), found that 40 per cent of all lateness was caused by between 3 and 5 per cent of workers employed; Wilfred Brown, *Piecework Abandoned*, Heinemann, 1962, p. 88; see also **clocking, quartering.**

LAW REFORM (CONTRIBUTORY NEGLIGENCE) ACT 1945. An act modifying the doctrine of contributory negligence in relation to accidents which may have been caused both by the defendant and by the plaintiff's failure to take reasonable care for his own safety. Before the Act, contributory negligence was a complete defence, and, if proved, freed the defendant from all liability; under the Act damages are divided in proportion to the respective degrees of responsibility, and the plaintiff is entitled to recover damages according to the extent of his own negligence; see J. Munkman, *Employers' Liability at Common Law*, Butterworth, 8th ed., 1975, and **employers' liability.**

LAW REFORM (PERSONAL INJURIES) ACT 1948); see **employers' liability.**

LAY-OFF. Temporary, indefinite or permanent exclusion from a particular employment because of shortage of work, or of materials, or due to other factors over which the worker has no control; usually distinguished from **suspension, dismissal** or **discharge** in so far as these are associated with disciplinary action or normal unsuitability for jobs. Both **redundancy** (q.v.) and more temporary lay-off and **short-time working** are catered for in the **Redundancy Payments Act 1965**, a temporarily laid-off employee being one who earns no pay in any week through lack of work (s. 5). A tradition for temporary lay-off without pay (or **lost periods**) appears to exist in most British industries, though not, for example, in the national newspaper industry. Pressure from trade unions in industries where lay-offs without pay have been common in the past (e.g. in motor manufacturing) has led to demands for **lay-off pay** both on a company and a national scale. On legal aspects of lay-off and remuneration; see B.A. Hepple and Paul O'Higgins, *Employment Law*, Sweet and Maxwell, 1976, p. 132 *et seq.*; see also **temporarily stopped** and **guaranteed week.**

LAY-OFF PAY; see **lay-off.**

LAY OFFICIAL. Sometimes used to describe officials of a trade union who are elected by their members but who are not full-time or entirely paid by their union; most frequently applied to branch secretaries and **shop stewards** (q.v.). In the latter case may be extended to apply to full-time shop stewards (or **conveners** and **senior stewards**) provided that these are paid, wholly or in part, by the individual employer in whose establishment the steward is employed.

LAZY STRIKE; see **ca'canny.**

LDCs; see **Local Department Committees.**

LEADING HAND; see **chargehand** and **supervisor.**

LEAD-IN PAYMENT. A type of payment as recommended for the electricity supply industry by the Wilberforce Inquiry (*Report of a Court of Inquiry into a dispute between the parties represented on the National Joint Electricity Council for the Electricity Supply Industry*, Cmnd. 4594, February 1971), in order to accelerate the application of incentive schemes. Under the arrangement suggested, workers formally accepting conditions laid down for incentive schemes would receive a lead-in payment to be stopped as soon as particular schemes were introduced and replaced by bonus payment arising from them; see **Wilberforce Report.**

LEADING TOOLSETTER; see **chargehand.**

LEAD RATE. A payment made in addition to the basic rate for a particular class of worker for such factors as skill and responsibility.

LEAN. Difficult work on which a man on piece rates cannot expect to get high earnings (printing industry); the opposite of **fat** (q.v.).

LEAPFROGGING; see **whipsawing.**

LEARNER ALLOWANCE (work study); see **allowances.** 'A temporary benefit given to workers while they develop their ability', British Standards Institution, *Glossary of Terms Used in Work Study*, BS 3138, 1969, A 1018.

LEARNING CURVE. An expression used both for the graphical representation of the output of individuals and working groups over time and as a basis for quantification in theories about the learning process. Commonly in the former sense employed to measure the performance of workers under training against that of experienced operators (Ministry of Labour, *Glossary of Training Terms,* HMSO, 1967); where the latter is concerned, it was formerly thought that learning curves showed that the learning process lasted for a comparatively short time and was followed by a 'plateau' of skill and productivity, but studies begun by L. McDill and continued by T.P. Wright at the Curtiss-Wright Corporation (*Journal of Aeronautical Sciences*, February 1936), by J.R. de Jong (*Time and Motion Study*, September 1964), by P.J.D. Cooke of Urwick Orr and Partners, and others, have suggested that, on the contrary, the process is a continuous one and conforms closely to the law that the cumulative average of unit direct labour cost, or time taken, decreases by a fixed percentage (for wholly manual work, according to de Jong, by 20 per cent, i.e. by following an 80 per cent learning curve), each time the cumulative output is doubled. This has possible implications for several aspects of industrial relations. On long product runs falling unit costs and built-in earnings increases for payment by result workers becomes inevitable without any necessary increase in effort (hence National Board for Prices and Incomes, *Payment by Results,* Report No. 65, May 1968, p. 14, has pointed to the learning curve as a factor in the 'autonomous' rise of piecework earnings), while the notion that there is an absolute or **standard time** for a job seems no longer to be logically tenable (P.J.D.

Cooke, 'Learning Curves', *Management Today,* November 1967). Some observers challenge the term learning curve on the grounds that it deals with improvement beyond or after 'threshold' learning. It is sometimes referred to in other terms e.g. **cost curve, experience curve, familiarisation curve, repetition curve, efficiency curve, performance curve,** which suggest different angles from which the phenomenon can be viewed.

LEAVE; see **leave of absence.**

LEAVE OF ABSENCE ... or simply **leave:** permission to be away from work or duty (see also the opposite; **unauthorised absence** or **absenteeism**). It seems reasonable to distinguish between leave which is given collectively (e.g. **bank** and **public holidays,** annual holidays, etc.), and that which is asked for by individuals in particular circumstances (to meet civic obligations or functions, for domestic or personal reasons, or for sport or recreation). Practice in 37 British companies, including arrangement for payment, is examined in British Institute of Management, *Information Summary 118,* October 1965; see also **sabbatical leave.**

LEE v. SHOWMEN'S GUILD OF GREAT BRITAIN (1952) 2 QB 329. A leading case in which the plaintiff, who had been expelled from the union for 'unfair competition' was upheld by the court on the grounds that it was for the court to tell the union what the rule meant, and that in its opinion 'unfair competition' had not been involved. K.W. Wedderburn, *Cases and Materials on Labour Law,* CUP, 1967, p. 640; also **membership of a trade union.**

LEGAL ENACTMENT. A trade union method described by Sidney and Beatrice Webb (*Industrial Democracy,* 1897, Ch. IV) and involving the use of parliament to enforce common rules about hours, working conditions etc. The Webbs regarded legal enactment as involving prolonged and uncertain struggle (1902 ed., p. 253), to be a more peaceful method than **collective bargaining,** but to lack its flexibility in securing the 'Rent of Ability', or 'Rent of Opportunity', pp. 797-806); see also **mutual insurance.**

LEGAL MINIMUM WAGE; see **national minimum wage.**

LEGALISED UNIFORM LIST; see **Uniform List.**

LETCH REPORT. Report of the Committee on the Earnings of Pilots under the Chairmanship of Sir Robert Letch, 1 May 1957. The Committee recommended figures of net earnings for 1st class pilots in 32 pilotage districts in the United Kingdom with review of pilotage rates when actual earnings were 10 per cent higher or 10 per cent lower than these figures. Net recommended earnings were, the Committee further recommended, to be altered only when there was an increase in **National Maritime Board** scales of pay for navigating officers, substantial change in the character of trade in a port or in the way in which pilots derived their earnings.

LEVER AMENDMENTS. Two Opposition amendments to the Trade Union and Labour Relations Bill during its passage through the House of Commons in 1974 (see **Trade Union and Labour Relations Act 1974**) resulting from defeats by the Wilson government and associated with voting confusion in the division lobbies. The amendments, one allowing an individual in a closed shop situation to become a member of a minority union or 'other independent trade union' and the other allowing workers the right 'on reasonable grounds' not to belong to a trade union, were carried following the discovery that a tied vote on each had resulted from 'nodding through' the lobbies Mr Harold Lever, a senior government Minister, who was not in fact in the Palace of Westminster at the time. The amendments were later removed in the Trade Union and Labour Relations (Amendment) Act 1976; see A.W.J. Thomson and S.R. Engleman, *The Industrial Relations Act*, Martin Robertson, 1975, p. 16.

LIAISON COMMITTEE FOR THE DEFENCE OF TRADE UNIONISM. A 'broad left' committee in which the Communist Party plays an important part and which originated in 1966 as a parliamentary lobby against the incomes policy of the Labour government at that time. In 1969 the Committee was also involved in organising stoppages of work against the Labour government's policy white paper **In Place of Strife** (q.v.) and in 1972 against the Conservative government's **Industrial Relations Act 1971**. It disclaims any intention of regarding itself as an alternative to the official trade union movement but continues to exist as left-wing political watchdog on events affecting trade unionists.

LIAISON REPRESENTATIVES; see **shipboard liaison representatives.**

LICENSED HOUSE MANAGERS, NATIONAL ASSOCIATION OF (NALHM). A trade union of public house managers formed in 1970, and by 1972 claiming a national membership of over 10,000. Membership of the union was encouraged by the larger brewing groups and it has been recognised by the Brewers' Society; in some areas it has been in competition with the **Transport and General Workers' Union**. It affiliated to the TUC in 1976; see Kevin Hawkins, 'Brewer-Licensee Relations: A Case Study in the Growth of Collective Bargaining and White Collar Militancy', *Industrial Relations*, Spring 1972. *Address*: 9 Coombe Lane, London, SW20 8NE. Tel: 01-947 3080/5941. *TUC Affiliated Membership, 1977*: 13,329.

LIEU BONUS; see **lieu rate.**

LIEU DAYS. Days holiday taken either in lieu of unpaid overtime, or where the practice of working longer hours than those nationally or generally agreed has been maintained because of the requirements of the methods of production, e.g. in the steel industry, where some continuous working plants agreed to continue to work 42 hours on average after the 40 hour shorter working week agreement, the two hours per week, together with ½ of weekly gross earnings, being accumulated and taken as lieu days.

LIEU PAYMENT; see **lieu rate.**

LIEU RATE, also **lieu bonus** and **lieu payment;** an additional hourly payment (or **timeworkers' bonus**) made to a timeworker who cannot be employed on **payment by results**, hence a form of recompense for not being able to supplement earnings by payment by results. Lieu rates may be fixed or variable; see National Board for Prices and Incomes, *Payment by Results,* Report No. 65, pp. 5-6 and S.W. Lerner, J.R. Cable and S. Gupta, *Workshop Wage Determination*, Pergamon Press, 1969, p. 50; see also M.L. Yates, *Wages and Labour Conditions in British Engineering*, Macdonald and Evans, 1937, p. 91, a 'term also applied to special allowances above time rates paid to certain workers, normally engaged on piecework, on occasions for which no piece prices have been fixed'.

LINE-STAFF DOCTRINE. A form of management organisation (hence **line and staff organisation**) based upon the principle that line departments are directly concerned with accomplishing the objectives of the company, while staff departments are auxiliary, thus suggesting that normative rules can be applied to line and staff behaviour, e.g. that line management gives orders while staff are advisory. The terms line and staff were originally military. Joan Woodward (*Industrial Organisation: Theory and Practice,* OUP, 1965, p. 99) suggests that the doctrine emerged from the failure of the joint-accountability-of-specialists notion of management of F.W. Taylor (see **scientific management**) to gain general acceptance. E. Rhenman, L. Strömberg and G. Westerlund (*Conflict and Co-operation in Business Organisations,* Wiley-Interscience, 1970) argue that it arose as a compromise between the beliefs of early management theorists in unitary command (one man, one boss) and the growth of supervision and administration. Both works criticise the doctrine in practice.

LINE AND STAFF ORGANISATION; see **line-staff doctrine.**

LINWOOD PLAN. A version of the **Scanlon Plan** (q.v.) introduced into the Linwood, Paisley, assembly plant of the Pressed Steel Company in September 1963, and subsequently abandoned in February 1966; see R.B. Gray, 'The Scanlon Plan, A Case Study', *British Journal of Industrial Relations,* Vol. IX, No. 3, November 1971, pp. 291-313.

LIST SYSTEM. A form of **check-off** (q.v.) operated for **National Union of Seamen** members operating under the **National Maritime Board** on foreign-going ships as a result of SR and O 635, 1943; see Temperley's *Merchant Shipping Acts,* Stevens, 3rd ed., 1976.

LISTED EMPLOYERS' ASSOCIATION; see **listed trade union.**

LISTED TRADE UNION. A trade union accepted on to a list maintained by the Certification Office under the provision of s. 8 of the Trade Union and Labour Relations Act 1974. The essential requirement for listing is that the body concerned must be an organisation of workers which has regulation of relations between workers and employers as one of its principal objects. There is no test of size or effectiveness. Listing carries entitlement to tax relief on provident benefits. It does not imply status as an **independent trade union** (q.v.), but without it no application for such status can be made. There were 485 listed unions at 31 December 1977. Current lists may be inspected free of charge at the Certification Office, Vincent House Annexe, Hide Place, London SW1P 4NG and for unions having their headquarters in Scotland at the Office of the Assistant Certification Officer for Scotland, 19 Heriot Row, Edinburgh, EH3 6HT, **Employers' associations** (q.v.) may be listed under the same statutory provision though with no corresponding advantages; 196 were so listed at 31 December 1977.

LITHOGRAPHIC ARTISTS, DESIGNERS, ENGRAVERS AND PROCESS WORKERS, SOCIETY OF (SLADE and PW). A craft union in the printing industry representing those employed in the production of artists' work, photoengraving, gravure and litho printing plates or cylinders, and engraved plates for security printing, etc. The society was originally founded in Manchester in 1885 as the National Society of Lithographic Artists, Designers and Writers, Copperplate and Wood Engravers, its principal London-based rival, of the same name going out of existence in 1898. Its title was changed to include the growing class of process workers in 1903. A Wallpaper and Textile Section was formed in 1972 following the transfer of engagements by the United Society of Engravers; see also **SLADE Art Union.** *Address*: 55 Clapham Common, South Side, London SW4 9DF. *Tel*: 01-720 7551. *TUC Affiliated Membership 1977*: 18,239.

LIVING-IN, also **living-in system.** The practice, originating in the tradition of the apprentice living with his master's family, of requiring workers, particularly in warehousing and retail trade, to live in the premises of tradesmen as part of their contract of employment. Living-in was not covered by the **Truck Acts** (q.v.), though similar abuses attached to it. It was the subject of much adverse propaganda and many strikes during the first decade of the twentieth century, and was largely eliminated by conditions during the first world war, though some instances remained in the 1920s; see H.G. Wells; *Kipps,* 1905 and P.C. Hoffman, *They Also Serve*: *The*

Story of the Shop Workers, Porcupine Press, 1949, pp. 18-66.

LIVING-IN SYSTEM; see **living-in.**

LLOYD v. BRASSEY (1969) ITR 100 CA; see **Redundancy Payments Act 1965.**

LOAD FACTOR; see **work load.**

LOBSTER SHIFT; see **graveyard shift.**

LOCAL or **local union.** The basic unit of labour organisation in the United States, generally made up of a single plant unit (especially in industrial unions) or a small geographical unit (especially in craft unions). Locals are the basic unit for all national and **international unions**, chartered by the international union and affiliated to it; see Joel Seidman, Jack London and Bernard Karsh, 'Leadership in the Local Union', *American Journal of Sociology*, November 1950, Leonard Sayles and George Strauss, *The Local Union: Its Place in the Industrial Plant*, Harper, New York, 1953.

LOCAL ADVISORY COMMITTEE (LAC). The lowest level of joint consultative committee in the electricity supply industry established under the Electricity Act 1947 (see **joint consultation**). The reinforcement of LACs by more informal meetings between management and primary working groups at power stations is described by H. Sallis, 'Joint Consultation and Meetings of Primary Working Groups in Power Stations', *British Journal of Industrial Relations*, Vol. III, pp. 326-44.

LOCAL AGREEMENT. An expression used in two primary senses: (1) Any collective agreement or the result of any collective bargaining between a trade union or trade unions and an employer or employers in a particular locality; in this sense a local agreement may be identical to a **district agreement**, or it may be a **plant agreement** within a company bargaining structure, or an area agreement covering several plants, factories, depots, etc., whether or not this falls within the general jurisdiction of a **national agreement** or a **company agreement;** (2) In a looser sense, the result of any collective bargaining which takes place below national or industry-wide level; in this sense, local agreements can be regarded as covering both (1) and also **works** or **plant agreements,** **domestic agreements,** etc.; i.e. any agreement which is *not* arrived at at the highest level recognised for collective bargaining in a given situation. Usage varies from one industry to another and from one company to another.

LOCAL DEPARTMENTAL COMMITTEES (LDCs). Local negotiating and consultative committees operating in British Rail. The Committees consist of elected representatives of workers (in this context the equivalent of **shop stewards** (q.v.)) and of British Railways Board officials, and are empowered to negotiate issues within the framework of national agreements. F.V. Pickstock, *British Railways - The Human Problem*, Fabian Research Series 142, 1950 and Charles McLeod, *All Change: Railway Industrial Relations in the Sixties*, Gower Press, 1970, p. 15.

LOCAL PANEL COMMITTEES. Joint committees established under an agreement on the national Joint Council for Civil Air Transport dated 20 September 1948 to consider and decide matters of local concern within the framework of agreements made by **National Sectional Panels** in the industry, and primarily of a consultative nature; see *Civil Air Transport Industry, Handbook of National Agreements*, II/1.

LOCAL UNION; see **local.**

LOCK AND METAL WORKERS, NATIONAL UNION OF (NULMW). A trade union founded in 1889 and amalgamated with the Birmingham Locksmiths' Society and the Wolverhampton Locksmiths' Society in 1912 to form the national union. It organises all grades of worker in the lock, latch and key industry, including, in recent years, non-manual workers, for whom a full-time officer was appointed in 1971. At the end of the 1950s its membership had declined to about 2,000, since when it has continued to increase. *Address*: Bellamy House, Wilkes Street, Willenhall, Staffs. WV13 2BS. *Tel*: 0902 66651/2. *TUC Affiliated Membership, 1977*: 7,041.

LOCK-OUT. The denial of the possibility of working by an employer to his employees in connection with a **trade dispute.** There is no current legal definition of the term. The **Trade Union and Labour Relations Act 1974** however (Schedule I, para. 7) provides that industrial tribunals have no power to judge whether a dismissal is fair or unfair if a strike or lock-out is in progress, provided that the dismissal concerned is not selective; i.e. provided that the employer dismisses *all* the employees concerned in industrial action. Students of industrial relations have usually noted that lock-outs are one side of a total conflict situation and difficult to distinguish from **strikes**, the question of which party makes a declaration to act being in practice immaterial (see, for example, K.G.J.C. Knowles, *Strikes*, Basil Blackwell, 1952, p. 299 *et seq*), and each party tending to place the responsibility on the other. Hence more general definitions of lock-out, e.g. '... the employer's side of the economic pressure when the parties are unable to resolve their problems in negotiations or agree on the terms and conditions of employment' (H.S. Roberts, *Dictionary of Industrial Relations*, Bureau of National Affiars, 1966). The infrequency of lock-outs is sometimes attributed to the fact that 'employers can gain the same end by other means - for instance by imposing conditions which would provoke a strike' (Williamson and Harris, *Trends in Collective Bargaining*, New York, 1945, p. 58), but the reluctance of employers to use lock-outs as a counterweapon also appears to have declined Knowles (op. cit., p. 3) notes that the *Oxford English Dictionary* has no record of lock-out being used as a term before 1860, **turn off** being used much earlier.

LOCK-OUT PAY; see **victimisation benefit.**

LOCOMOTIVE ENGINEERS AND FIREMEN, ASSOCIATED SOCIETY OF (ASLEF). A trade union of locomotive drivers and of staff in the line of promotion to that grade (secondmen, traction trainees), founded in 1880, and party to negotiation with the British Railways Board through the **Railway Staff Joint Council** and the **Railway Staff National Council** (q.v.) and also in London Transport; often referred to as the **footplatemen's** union. ASLEF has consistently sought to preserve its craft traditions, and pursues the policy that the technical and organisational changes which have taken place on the railways since the second world war have not affected the craft nature and status of the work performed by footplatemen. The union claims to organise 90 per cent of eligible staff on British Railways; see *Report of a Court of Inquiry under Mr. A.J. Scamp*, HMSO, Cmnd. 2779, 1965; Norman McKillop, *The*

Lighted Flame: A History of the Associated Society of Locomotive Engineers and Firemen, Thomas Nelson and Sons, 1950. *Address*: 9 Arkwright Road, Hampstead, London NW3 6AB. *Tel*: 01-435 6300 and 2160. *TUC Affiliated Membership, 1977*: 28,189.

LOGGING. The entry into the official log book by the master of a ship of an offence or indiscipline by a merchant seaman. Entries may be accompanied by a fine in the form of forfeiture of pay. The Pearson Report (*Final Report of the Court of Inquiry Concerning the Shipping Industry*, Cmnd. 3211) of 1967 recommended that seamen should have the right to be accompanied by a friend during logging procedure, though gave no special recommendation that **Shipboard Liaison Representatives** (q.v.) should carry out this function. Opinions in the industry differ on the advisability of this; see D.H. Moreby, *Personnel Management in Merchant Ships*, Pergamon Press, 1968, pp. 72-3 and 113-14. *The Report of the Working Group on Discipline in the Merchant Navy*, Department of Trade, November 1975 recommended that firms should be abolished; see J. McConville, *The Shipping Industry in the United Kingdom*, International Institute for Labour Studies, 1977.

LONDON JEWEL CASE AND JEWELLERY DISPLAY MAKERS' UNION; see **Jewel Case and Jewellery Display Makers' Union, London.**

LONDON SOCIETY OF TIE CUTTERS; see **Tie Cutters, London Society of.**

LONDON WEIGHTING. The practice of paying differentially high rates to those employed in the London area (usually divided into Inner London and Outer London), on grounds of higher living costs or other considerations involved in living there; a practice common among non-manual workers employed in London. National Board for Prices and Incomes, Report on *London Weighting in the Non-Industrial Civil Service* (No. 44, Cmnd. 3436, November 1967) recommended that the practice (originally introduced in 1920) should be continued and the levels of London Weighting be reviewed every three years on a cost-of-living basis.

LOOM OVERLOOKERS, GENERAL UNION OF ASSOCIATIONS OF. A

union of local associations of loom over-lookers originally formed in 1885 and now comprising 14 such associations princi-pally in Lancashire. *Address*: 6 St Mary's Place, Bury BL9 0DZ. *Tel*: 061-764 4244. *TUC Affiliated Membership, 1977*: 2,960. See also **British Federation of Textile Technicians.**

LOOSE RATING; see **rating.**

LOOSE TIMES; see **rating.**

LOOSING RATE. A special rate paid to young journeymen between the time when their apprenticeships end and the time when they attain the full adult rate. Loos-ing rates in the engineering industry were suspended in 1940. A.I Marsh, *Industrial Relations in Engineering*, Pergamon Press, 1965, p. 150; see also **improver.** In the case of draughtsmen and tracers in the engineering industry, the loosing rate represented the minimum salary on the completion of apprenticeship at the time when no national minimum **wage-for-age scale** existed.

LOST PERIOD; see **lay-off** and **short-time working.**

LOW PAY. An imprecise term used to describe the situation of those who, for one reason or another, are at the lower end of pay scales or distributions of earnings; low pay may, therefore, be thought of as absolute (i.e. too low to support a given, or a reasonable, standard of living) or rela-tive (i.e. lower than is reasonable in rela-tion to the pay of other workers engaged in the same occupation, or trade or industry, or locality). In these senses, low pay is in part related to concepts of poverty and in part to notions of proper **differentials.** As an issue it was highlighted by **incomes pol-icy** and by the activities of the **National Board for Prices and Incomes** which in its final reference (*General Problems of Low Pay*, Report No. 169, Cmnd. 4648, April 1971) concluded that low pay was the result of a variety of factors and that improvement required the establishment of causes of the situation industry by indus-try. In earlier references the Board had fre-quently advocated narrowing of differentials or **tapering** (q.v.) (e.g. in *Pay and Conditions in Clothing Manufactur-ing Industries*, Report No. 110, Cmnd. 4002, April 1969) and such devices as the **minimum earnings levels** adopted in the engineering industry (see, for example, Report No. 63, *Pay of Municipal Busmen*,

Cmnd. 3605, April 1968); see also J. Edmonds and G. Radice, *Low Pay*, Fab-ian Research Series 270, July 1972; E.A.G. Armstrong; 'Birmingham and some of its low-paid workers', *Manchester School*, December 1968, pp. 365-82, and H. Lydall, *The Structure of Earnings*, OUP, 1968. Also **national minimum wages** and **Wages Councils.** In April 1977, 1.4 per cent of full-time manual workers unaf-fected by absence earned less than £30 a week and 9.0 per cent less than £40 per week, average earnings being £75.8 for men and £49.8 for women (New Earnings Survey, 1977, *Department of Employ-ment Gazette*, October 1977); see also N. Bosanquet and R.J. Stephens, 'Another Look at Low Pay', *Journal of Social Pol-icy*, January-July 1972, and **Low Pay Unit.**

LOW PAY UNIT (LPU). An independent body established from the beginning of 1975 with funds from the Seebohm Rown-tree Studentship Fund to draw attention to the extent of low pay, especially in the sectors covered by **Wages Councils** (q.v.). The Unit issues a Low Pay Bulletin and has produced a number of pamphlets, including Alan Fisher and Bernard Dix, *Low Pay and How to End It*, Pitman, 1974. *Address*: 9 Poland Street, London W1V 3DG. *Tel*: 01-437 1780.

LOW TASK RATING METHOD. A work study procedure whereby the time study man compares the actual rate of working of the operator with his concept of the rate necessary to earn the basic wage, as contrasted with a **high task rating method** (q.v.) EPA, *Glossary of Work Study Terms.*

LPU. Low Pay Unit (q.v.).

LRA. Labour Relations Agency (q.v.).

LUDDISM; see **Luddites.**

LUDDITES. Groups of workers, said to be directed by one Ned Ludd, whose iden-tity or existence is unknown, involved in a campaign of smashing machines, princi-pally in Nottinghamshire, Yorkshire, Lan-cashire and Cheshire, in 1811 and 1812; also applied to handloom weavers involved in machine breaking and protests against the factory system, especially between 1815 and 1826 (G.D.H. Cole and R. Postgate, *The Common People, 1746-1946*, Methuen, 1949, 4th ed.). Currently used in a loose and pejorative sense to describe workers who resist the introduction of new machinery or methods, or employ **restrictive labour practices** (q.v.).

LUMLEY v. WAGNER (1852) De G M and G 604; see **Hill v. C.A. Parsons and Co. Ltd** and **specific performance**.

THE LUMP. Workers in the construction industry operating on a self-employed **labour-only sub-contracting** basis (q.v.).

LYING-IN MONEY (iron and steel industry): money kept in hand where workers are paid a week in arrears.

M

MACHINE ANCILLARY TIME. The time when a machine is temporarily out of productive use owing to change overs, setting, cleaning etc,; usually distinguished from **machine down time**, and **machine idle time** (work study).

MACHINE CALICO PRINTERS, TRADE SOCIETY OF. A trade union of calico printers, founded in 1840, which absorbed in 1937 the Federated Board of English and Scottish Machine Calico Printers. The union has members in Great Britain, Ireland and overseas. Its membership has declined steadily in recent years. It was suspended from the **Trades Union Congress** in 1972 and later withdrew. *Address*: 317 Corn Exchange Buildings, Manchester M4 3BT. *Tel*: 061-832 4979.

MACHINE DOWN TIME; see **down time.**

MACHINE IDLE TIME; see **idle time.**

MACHINE QUESTION. A phrase popularly used to describe the historical issues of **demarcation, dilution** (q.v.), and sometimes payment, arising out of the introduction of new machines in the engineering industry, the craft unions (especially the Amalgamated Society of Engineers and its successor the Amalgamated Engineering Union) claiming 'the right to the tools of the trade' (one aspect of the **right to work**, q.v.), and the employers the right to introduce whatever new machines they wished, and to use whatever labour, whether skilled or semi-skilled, was appropriate;

see J.B. Jefferys, *The Story of the Engineers,* EP Publishing, 1971; also **craft control, restrictive practices, practice, relaxation agreements.**

MACHINE RUNNING TIME. The time during which a machine is actually operating, i.e. the total time during which the machine is available, less any **machine down time, machine idle time**, or **machine ancillary time** (work study).

McHUGH DISPUTE. A dispute at Austin, Longbridge in 1952-53 over the dismissal of Mr John McHugh (Secretary of the Austin Motor Joint Shop Stewards' Committee) as part of a redundancy in connection with the ending of production of the A90 Atlantic Model. The issue led to a strike in February 1953, and to a Court of Inquiry (Cmd. 8839, May 1953) see also H.A. Turner, Garfield Clack and Geoffrey Roberts, *Labour Relations in the Motor Industry,* Allen and Unwin, 1967, p. 271 *et seq.*

MACKENZIE REPORT. The report of the Court of Inquiry under the Chairmanship of Sir William Mackenzie into the dispute between the Engineering and National Employers' Federation and the Amalgamated Engineering Union, Cmd. 1653, May 1922, sometimes known as the 'Overtime and Managerial Functions' dispute, which gave rise to the 1922 Procedure Agreement, Manual Workers (see **Engineering Procedure Agreement**). The Inquiry came to the conclusion that managements alone were in a position to judge whether overtime was necessary, though overtime beyond the 30 hours in four weeks limit might be thought unreasonable, and that good sense and good will were necessary in operating the overtime agreement. The text of the report is reprinted in *Thirty Years of Industrial Conciliation,* Engineering and Allied Employers' National Federation, December 1927.

MACLELLAND v. NATIONAL UNION OF JOURNALISTS: MILLS v. NATIONAL UNION OF JOURNALISTS (1975) ICR 116; *The Times,* 21 November 1974. A case in which it was ruled that members of a trade union cannot lawfully be disciplined for failure to attend a mandatory meeting unless such a meeting has been properly convened under the union rules; see **membership of a trade union.**

MAGENTA BOOK. A booklet of agreements and understandings involving a productivity bargain between the Amalgamated Engineering Union, the Electrical Trades Union and the management of the Corby Iron and Steel Works, July 1965 to December 1967; see **Blue Book.**

MAINTENANCE OF MEMBERSHIP. A form of union security (see **union security clauses**) devised by the public members of the National War Labor Board in the United States to resolve conflict between the labour and industry members of the Board over the **closed shop**. The compromise was that individuals who were members of the union or who subsequently joined would continue their membership until the end of the contract, a clause being inserted in the agreement to the effect that employees would have a 15-day period in which to decide whether they wanted to leave or to remain in the union, or some variation on this formula.

MAJOR TRADES; see **differential.**

MAKE-UP PAY. Generally applied to a payment made to a payment by results worker who has failed to earn sufficient to reach his **guarantee** (q.v.) of fall-back level of payment; see also **pieceworkers' guarantee.** Make-up pay is usually to be distinguished from a **make-up payment** (q.v.).

MAKE-UP PAYMENT; see **compensatory payment.**

MAKE-WORK PRACTICES. Activities of trade unions or individuals in limiting production or creating unnecessary work or jobs in order to create or maintain employment, to spread available work, or to maintain earnings; **restrictive labour practices;** see **restrictive practices,** also **fat, featherbedding, dead horse rule, welting, spelling, blow.**

MANAGEMENT BY CONSENT. Management by positive agreement and co-operation of workers (by analogy with 'government by consent'); may include various forms of **workers' participation** (q.v.) and the narrowing of areas in which management considers itself free to take unilateral action - see **managerial prerogatives.** (*Management by Consent - A report by a research group appointed jointly by ASSET and the Fabian Society,* Fabian Research Series No. 125, 1948; The Labour Party, *Industrial Democracy - A Working Party Report,* 1967, p. 20 *et seq.*).

MANAGEMENT BY EXCEPTION (MBE). A technique of management which involves only exceptional happenings being referred to managers, all other situations being dealt with in accordance with precise instructions previously laid down, or where there are deviations from budgets or plans already established. The broad object of the system is to reduce the quantity of detail requiring to be handled by management; see L.R. Bittel, *Management by Exception: Systematizing and Simplifying the Managerial Job,* McGraw-Hill, 1965.

MANAGEMENT BY OBJECTIVES (MBO). A generic title used to express both the methods of philosophy of management which embrace the continuous review of management objectives and achievement, management training, and the reinforcement of management motivation by systematic approaches to selection, salary and succession. MBO in Britain is particularly associated with the name of John Humble, a director of Urwick, Orr and Partners Ltd, who defines it as 'a dynamic system which seeks to integrate the company's need to clarify and achieve its profit and growth goals with the manager's need to contribute and develop himself. It is a demanding and rewarding style of a business' John W. Humble (ed.), *Management by Objectives in Action,* McGraw-Hill, 1970.

MANAGEMENT STUDIES, JOURNAL OF. An academic journal on management subjects designed also to be of use and value to practising managers and businessmen, and containing articles and reviews, some of which are on industrial relations (1964-). Published by Basil Blackwell, Broad Street, Oxford. For notes on industrial relations journals in general; see George Sayers Bain and Gillian B. Woolven, 'The Literature of Labour Economics and Industrial Relations', *Industrial Relations Journal,* Summer 1971 and in J. Fletcher (ed.), *The Uses of Economics Literature,* Butterworths, 1971.

MANAGERIAL, ADMINISTRATIVE, TECHNICAL AND SUPERVISORY ASSOCIATION (MATSA). The non-manual worker section of the **General and Municipal Workers' Union.** MATSA was inaugurated by the union in April 1972 with the intention of recruiting all levels of managerial, administrative and supervisory employees, both in traditional GMWU areas in engineering and the public sector, and also in such areas as Civil Air Transport, finance, distribution and nursing. It claimed to have 72,000 members in 1977.

MANAGERIAL FUNCTIONS; see **managerial prerogatives.**

MANAGERIAL FUNCTIONS AGREEMENT; see **Engineering Procedure Agreement.**

MANAGERIAL FUNCTIONS CLAUSE; see **managerial prerogatives.**

MANAGERIAL GRID. A training device invented by Robert Blake and Jane Moulton (*The Managerial Grid: Key orientations for achieving production through people,* Gulf Publishing Company, Houston, Texas, 1977), also known as the **Blake Grid.** The Grid identifies five types of organisational structures based on two key variables, concern for performance and concern for people, and aims to improve management performance by allowing the executive to plot his own behavioural style and to improve it in relation to that of his colleagues. The Grid method is sometimes thought of as 'convergent' in that it tends to direct individuals and groups towards common objectives, and is sometimes contrasted with **T Groups** (q.v.), which are said to be 'divergent', in that they encourage spontaneity and creativity in the individual.

MANAGERIAL PREROGATIVES. Also referred to as **managerial rights** and **managerial functions.** Rights or functions which managements assert to be exclusively theirs and hence not subject to **collective bargaining** with trade unions, nor to **joint regulation** with unions or employees (see also **trade union functions**). Such rights have been taken to include hiring and firing, promotions, discipline, manning of machines, production control, decisions on overtime etc. Overt conflict over the issue of managerial prerogatives has been more notable in the United States than in Britain, where it has mainly attracted attention in the engineering industry, especially in the lock-out of 1897-98 (see R.O. Clarke, 'The Dispute in the British Engineering Industry 1897-1898,' *Economica*, May 1957, pp. 128-37) and in that of 1922, when it was related to the workers' control movement (see Carter L. Goodrich, *The Frontier of Control,* and Dent/Pluto Press 1975, Harcourt, Brace and Howe, 1920, A. Shadwell, *The Engineering Industry and the Crisis of 1922,* John Murray, 1922 and B. Pribicevic, *The Shop Stewards' Movement and Workers' Control, 1910-1922,* Basil Blackwell, 1959); see also **managerial functions clause** i.e. the clause (II) (1) (d), of the 1922 **Engineering Procedure Agreement** which required workers raising issues in procedure to work on the management's terms, except in specified circumstances, until procedure had been exhausted; A.I. Marsh, *Industrial Relations in Engineering, A collection of Teaching Documents and Case Studies,* Pergamon Press, 1966, Document 8. The notion of managerial prerogatives carries with it the implication that there are actions or areas for action so essential to management that these must remain unilaterally the property of management if management itself is to continue to exist. Academic writers have usually tended to question either whether such a 'frontier' can be said absolutely to exist, or whether such a view is conducive to the most constructive attitude to the task of management or management-union relations. N.W. Chamberlain (*The Union Challenge to Management Control,* 1948, Archon Books, 1967) has argued that there is no logical limit to union penetration into the function of management and that the question is one of functional integration - a recommendation broadly in line with developments in Britain. Margaret Chandler (*Management Rights and Union Interests,* McGraw-Hill, 1964) suggests that it would be relevant to discard the idea of management as a keeper of property rights and to concentrate on its more dynamic function as a 'promoter of process'.

MANAGERIAL, PROFESSIONAL AND STAFF LIAISON GROUP. A loose federation of non-TUC unions and staff associations formed in January 1978 with the object of establishing the right of employees to belong to the trade union of their choice, or to no trade union, their right to maintain their own ethical standards and their right not to be discriminated against on grounds of non-affiliation to any specific federation of trade unions. The **British Medical Association** and the **Confederation of Employee Organisations** were prominent among the founding organisations. *Address*: c/o British Medical Association, BMA House,

Tavistock Square, London WC1H 9JP. *Membership, 1977*: 240,000 approx.

MANAGERIAL RIGHTS; see **managerial prerogatives.**

MANAGERS' AND OVERLOOKERS' SOCIETY. A textile trade union founded in 1912 as the Yorkshire Managers' and Overlookers' Society which changed to its present title in 1921. Membership in the early 1920s was as high as 50,000 but has now declined. *Address*: Textile Hall, Westgate, Bradford, Yorks. BD1 2RG. *Tel*: 0274 27967. *TUC Affiliated Membership, 1977*: 1,185.

MANCHESTER AND DISTRICT CARETAKERS' ASSOCIATION; see **Caretakers' Association, Manchester and District.**

MANCHESTER PIECEWORK REGULATIONS. An agreement on the application of piecework in Manchester and District between engineering unions and the Manchester Engineering Employers' Association in January 1918 and still in force. The agreement is unusual in that it commits the Amalgamated Engineering Union (now the **Amalgamated Union of Engineering Workers Engineering Section**) to **demonstrations** by the employer during the timing of a job and to some other provisions not accepted by the union nationally; see A.I. Marsh, *Industrial Relations in Engineering,* Pergamon, 1965, pp. 292-3.

MANCHESTER SCHOOL OF ECONOMIC AND SOCIAL STUDIES. The journal of the Faculty of Economic and Social Studies of the University of Manchester, published three times a year since 1930 and principally concerned with applied economics with some interest in the labour field. For notes on labour economics and industrial relations journals generally; see George Sayers Bain and Gillian B. Woolven, 'The Literature of Labour Economics and Industrial Relations', *Industrial Relations Journal,* Summer 1971, and J. Fletcher (ed.), *The Uses of Economic Literature,* Butterworths, 1971.

MANPOWER FORECASTING; see **manpower planning.**

MANPOWER PLANNING. Defined by the Department of Employment (*Company Manpower Planning,* Manpower Papers No. 1, 1968) 'as strategy for the acquisition, utilisation, improvement and preservation of an enterprise's human resources' and as involving three main stages: an evaluation or appreciation of exiting resources, an assessment or forecast of labour requirements if the organisation's overall objectives are to be achieved (**manpower forecasting**), and measures to ensure that all the necessary resources are available as and when required, the whole exercise making necessary attention to recruitment, redundancy and dismissal policy, training, management development, etc. For an assessment of the current position of company manpower planning see D.I. Mackay, D. Boddy, J. Brack, J.A. Diack, and N. Jones, *Labour Markets under Different Employment Conditions,* George Allen and Unwin 1971, Part V, Gareth Stainer, *Manpower Planning,* Heinemann, 1971 and J. Bramham, *Practical Manpower Planning,* IPM, 1975. D.J. Bartholomew and A.F. Forbes, *Statistical Techniques of Manpower Planning,* Wiley, 1978, is written as a manual of basic techniques; for a bibliography, see *Department of Employment Gazette,* 1977, pp. 1095—96. On manpower forecasting; see J. Stuart Wabe (ed.), *Problems in Manpower Forecasting,* Saxon House, 1974.

MANPOWER AND PRODUCTIVITY SERVICE (MPS). A service provided confidentially and free of charge by the Department of Employment to promote higher productivity and greater efficiency in industry and commerce through the provision of a central consultancy service and regional field force to give advice to managements on management techniques and controls essential for increasing productivity. Facilities for conciliation and arbitration were included. The service became fully operational on 1 January 1969, and incorporated its predecessor, the Industrial Relations Service of the Ministry of Labour. It was also designed to undertake responsibilities arising out of the registration of procedural agreements and arrangements recommended by the Donovan Commission (**Royal Commission on Trade Unions and Employers' Associations, 1965-1968**, Cmnd. 3623, June 1968). Para. 182, and to follow up the findings of the **Commission on Industrial Relations** (q.v.). In May 1971, the consultancy and advisory functions of the MPS were revised to concentrate on such matters as efficient use of manpower, labour turnover and absenteeism, payment systems, work study, job evaluation and personnel practices. The name of the Service was changed to the **Conciliation and Advisory Service** (q.v.) on 1 March 1972. Its functions are now performed by the **Advisory, Conciliation and Arbitration Service.**

MANPOWER SERVICES COMMISSION. A Commission established by the **Employment and Training Act 1973** (q.v.) and representative of both sides of industry, local authority and educational interests, with the function of taking responsibility for the **Employment Service** and **Training Services Agencies** in planning, developing and operating the public employment services, for the area of training covered by the Agency and for advising the Minister on manpower questions. From 1 April 1978 the Training Services Agency and the Employment Service Agency ceased to be separate executive agencies and became operating divisions of the Commission.

MANPOWER UTILISATION AND PAYMENT STRUCTURE AGREEMENT (MUPS). A type of **productivity agreement** made at company level between Imperial Chemical Industries Ltd and its manual worker unions in the later 1960s which envisaged at each site greater flexibility in the use of manpower both within crafts and between craft and non-craft workers. The agreement proved difficult to implement, in part because of existing traditions of ICI personnel policy, in part because, as a company level agreement, MUPS had no basis of plant acceptance, and in part because of resistance to some of the changes it required. MUPS was followed in 1969 by a more successful **Weekly Staff Agreement** (q.v.); see J. Roeber, *Steps to a New Social Contract,* Duckworth, 1974.

MANSFIELD MILLS DISPUTE. A dispute arising at Mansfield Hosiery Mills, Ltd, Loughborough, in which it was claimed by Asian workers that they were being discriminated against in being refused progression from bar-loading to better-paid knitting jobs. Mr Kenneth Robinson, sitting as a **Committee of Inquiry** into the dispute between the employees of Mansfield Hosiery Mills Ltd, Loughborough, and the employer, reported in December 1972 and recommended that the company and the union, the **National Union of Hosiery and Knitwear Workers,** should negotiate immediately a new training agreement guaranteeing that trainee knitters should

be selected on merit regardless of race, colour, creed or ethnic or national origin.

MANUAL WORKER. In general usage, a worker who works with his hands, or earns his living by physical labour, as distinct from one who employs his intellectual abilities; a **blue-collar worker,** as distinct from a **white-collar worker;** a worker who is not **staff.** Such distinctions may be ones of degree ('The term essentially indicates that more physical dexterity and ability than mental manipulation are required'; H.S. Roberts, *Dictionary of Industrial Relations,* BNA Incorporated, 1966), or ones of statistical convenience; see, for example, Office of Population Censuses and Surveys, *Classification of Occupations* 1966, HMSO, p. 130 *et seq.* Department of Employment Earnings Surveys (see **earnings**) use the term as broadly synonymous with 'wage earner' (Office of Population Censuses and Surveys, *Sample Census 1966 (Great Britain),* Economic Activity Tables, Part III, p, xlii), including **operatives** and some manual workers, like shop assistants, who, for occupational purposes, are treated as non-manual; see also **staff status, staff conditions, mensualisation.**

MANUAL WORKERS ON STAFF CONDITIONS. An aspect of **mensualisation** (q.v.).

MARGINAL PRODUCTIVITY THEORY OF WAGES. The theory that wage rates tend, in the long run, to equal the value of the marginal product of labour, i.e. that they are determined by competitive forces acting in conformity with the general theory of value applied to the four factors of production, land, labour, capital and business enterprise; hence, according to the theory, wages tend to be fixed at the point which represents what an employer needs to pay for the marginal unit of labour and to be determined by the loss of production which would occur if one worker were withdrawn from a specific combination of the other factors of production; see J.R. Hicks, *The Theory of Wages,* Macmillan, 1963. The theory is an abstraction rather than a model drawn from observation and experiment, and has been much criticised on this account as ignoring the imperfections of **labour markets** and the effects of **collective bargaining;** see J.W.F. Rowe, *Wages in Theory and Practice,* Routledge, 1928, A.M. Ross, *Trade Union Wage Policy,* University of California Press, 1948, Barbara

Wootton, *The Social Foundations of Wage Policy,* Allen and Unwin, 1962. Also **wage theories, bargaining theory of wages.**

MARLOW ASSOCIATION; see **Marlow Declaration.**

MARLOW DECLARATION. A statement of aims and principles on social and industrial relations originally signed by eighteen men representative of the churches, of industry, of trade unions and of education as a result of a conference held at Marlow, Bucks, in January 1963. It laid emphasis upon the responsibilities of the individual and concern for the moral welfare of people in industry, and outlined the conditions of a happy and smooth working industrial partnership. The **Marlow Association** subsequently issued a number of papers entitled 'Redundancy or Redeployment', 'The Church, Industry and Technology', 'Industry and the Individual', 'Conflict or Co-operation in Industry', 'Human Engineering', and 'Sense of Belonging'.

MARRIAGE GRANT or **dowry grant** (q.v.).

MARSHALL v. ENGLISH ELECTRIC CO. LTD (1945) 61 TLR 379; (1945), 1 All ER 653; see **suspension.** K.W. Wedderburn, *Cases and Materials in Labour Law,* CUP, 1967, p. 144.

MARTIN v. SCOTTISH TRANSPORT AND GENERAL WORKERS' UNION (1952) 1 All ER 691. A leading case in which it was ruled that the plaintiff could not possibly be a member of the union since the union had no power under its rules to admit him to temporary membership and was thus acting *ultra vires* in doing so. K.W. Wedderburn, *Cases and Materials on Labour Law,* CUP, 1967, p. 564 *et seq.*; also **membership of a trade union.**

MASS DISMISSAL DIRECTIVE; see **Collective Redundancy Directive.**

MASS PICKETING. The attendance for purposes of **picketing** of a factory or site of large numbers of persons, such as occurred at the Saltley Depot in 1972 (see **Saltley Depot Incident**) and at Grunwick Ltd in 1977 (see **Grunwick Dispute**), usually to prevent the entry of vehicles, but also, in respect of other incidents during the miners' strike of 1972, to prevent members of other unions from entering premises. It has normally been the practice of both trade unions and of the police to attempt to limit numbers of pickets in order to minimise the possibility of civil disturbance and this has usually been effective, though nowhere is the number of pickets legally restricted. Arguments that such a change might be made, or that a statutory right to detain vehicles (e.g. in Chris Ralph, *The Picket and the Law,* Fabian Research Series 331, April 1977) would remove most of the problems of mass picketing, have received little support.

MASTER PRINTERS, BRITISH FEDERATION OF (BFMP); now the **British Printing Industries Federation** (q.v.).

MASTER PRINTERS OF SCOTLAND; see **British Printing Industries Federation.**

MASTER STANDARD DATA (MSD). A simplified **Predetermined Motion Time System;** see R.M. Crossan and H.W. Nance, *Master Standard Data,* McGraw-Hill, 1972 revised.

MATER ET MAGISTRA; see **Catholic Industrial Relations Teaching.**

MATERNITY AGREEMENT; see **maternity leave.**

MATERNITY LEAVE. Leave from work of an employee during and after pregnancy. Employees in Britain had no statutory right to such leave, to the protection of their jobs or to maternity pay until 6 April 1977 when ss. 34-52 of the Employment Protection Act 1975 came into effect. Under the Act an employee with two years' service on the eleventh week before confinement who informs her employer at least three weeks before her pregnancy absence begins, is entitled to return to work up to 29 weeks after her confinement, to the job she was originally employed to do, or to a suitable alternative job. Dismissal on grounds of pregnancy is statutorily unfair (see **unfair dismissal**), the provision of alternative employment where return to the original is impracticable is mandatory and the burden of proof on the offer rests on the employer before an **industrial tribunal**. A temporary replacement may be fairly dismissed if the employer acts reasonably in so doing. The employee is also entitled to maternity pay at 90 per cent of her weekly pay for six weeks, less the state maternity allowance, whether or not she returns to work, the payment being made by the employer who can claim back the full amount from a Maternity Pay Fund maintained by the Secretary of State for Employment. An International Labour Convention on the protection of women in employment during pregnancy and after confinement has existed since 1919 and was revised in 1952. It has not yet been accepted by the United Kingdom. The maternity leave arrangements under the Employment Protection Act appear to fall short of the standards laid down in the Convention in several respects. They also seem to fall short of those applying in many other member states of the European Economic Community. The proportion of women in Britain affected by the current legislation cannot be large. Some 80 per cent of women giving birth between 1966 and 1971 were not gainfully employed. Some of these would have been disqualified by the two-year service requirements; others would not have wished to return to work after pregnancy. The provisions of the Act have stimulated some interest in the making of voluntary **maternity agreements** providing for reductions in service qualifications in some cases, and to longer periods of paid leave; a few provide for **paternity leave**; see *Industrial Relations Review and Report*, No. 162, October 1977, pp. 2-8.

MATERNITY PAY; see **maternity leave.**

MATSA. Managerial, Administrative, Technical and Supervisory Association (q.v.).

MATURITY CURVES or **salary growth curves.** Curves showing median salaries of professional staff, especially those for whom ordinary grades and salary ranges may be thought not to provide satisfactory salary progression, at various age levels; curves showing career salary paths. Such curves, compiled from local or national salary data, can be compared with curves for comparable staff within companies or organisations, thus providing a guide to the salary progressions which may be appropriate; see G. McBeath and D.N. Rands, *Salary Administration,* Business Books Ltd, 3rd ed., 1976.

MBE. Management by Exception (q.v.).

MBO. Management by Objectives (q.v.).

MDW. Measured Daywork (q.v.).

MEASURED DAYWORK (MDW). A system of payment in which the worker is given a flat agreed hourly rate of payment for an explicit and agreed performance set by time study. Some writers (e.g. T. Lupton, 'Methods of Wage Payment, Organisational Change and Motivation', *Work Study and Management,* December 1964, pp. 543-9) distinguish between measured daywork and **controlled daywork,** defining the former as a system in which the worker receives less if his performance falls short of the agreed level, and the latter as one in which no such sanction is applied, the arrangement being regarded as contractual, failures of performance requiring proof as to cause, and being followed by disciplinary measures only if a worker's responsibility can be shown. Others include the possibility of combining MDW with a measure of incentive payments, e.g. D. Blyth (*Remuneration and Incentives,* Editype, 1969) who, while describing a flat payment as one type of MDW system, includes another in which, after the work has been measured, 'the operator's earnings are based on his performance during a previous work period, say a four-weekly period, and where his earnings are stable during each particular period'; see also **stepped measured daywork** and **Premium Pay Plan.** A report from Sweden (SAF, *The Condemned Piecework,* Svenska Arbetsgivareföreningen, 1970), casts doubt upon the virtues of moving to daywork systems in some instances. Reports of the growth of measured daywork are difficult to confirm; also its effectiveness in practice (see S.H. Slichter, J.J. Healy and E.R. Livernash, *The Impact of Collective Bargaining on Management,* The Brookings Institution, Washington, 1960, Anne Shaw, 'Measured Daywork - A Step Towards a Salaried Workforce', *The Manager,* 32, 1964, pp. 39-41, Sylvia Shimmin, 'Case Studies in Measured Daywork,' *Personnel Magazine,* October 1966, pp. 32-3, 42, and A. Flanders, 'Measured Daywork and Collective Bargaining', *British Journal of Industrial Relations,* Vol. XI, No. 3, November 1973, pp. 368-92). There is no doubt, however, that technical change, problems of **wage drift** (q.v.) and of controlling conventional payment by results systems have brought an increase of interest in measured daywork.

MEDIATION. Defined in **Royal Commission on Labour, 1891-1894** as 'the exercise of good offices by some outside agency with a view to avert an impending rupture between the parties, or, if the rupture has taken place, to bring them together as soon as possible, without itself acting as arbitrator or making an award' or more currently by the **Advisory, Conciliation and Arbitration Service (ACAS)** as 'a method of settling disputes whereby an independent person makes recommendations as to a possible solution, leaving the parties to negotiate a settlement'. Hence **mediator:** '. . . a kind of technical consultant to both sides, helping them to find a solution, rather than a judge deciding who is right' (Ross Stagner and Hjalmar Rosen, *The Psychology of Union-Management Relations,* Tavistock, 1965, p. 113). 'Mediator' and 'mediation' have not until recently been terms in common use in Britain, their place having been occupied by **conciliator** and **conciliation** (q.v.). Recently ACAS has tended to revive the distinction and reported in 1977 four Boards of Mediation and 27 cases referred to single mediators. In the USA, conciliation and mediation are usually employed interchangeably. Sometimes, however, it is suggested that conciliation is merely an attempt to bring the two sides together, whereas mediation involves the further step of making proposals for settlement; see Edgar L. Warren, 'The Role of Public Opinion in Relation to the Mediator', *Proceedings of the Fifth Annual Meeting, Industrial Relations Research Association* and on Denmark, Walter Galenson, *Comparative Labour Movements,* Prentice-Hall Inc., 1952.

MEDIATOR; see mediation.

MEDICAL ASSOCIATION, BRITISH (BMA). An association of doctors with a membership of some 64,000 in all branches of medical practice throughout the United Kingdom and an overseas membership of 14,000. The BMA was originally founded at Worcester in 1832 as the Provincial Medical and Surgical Association. It moved to London and adopted its present title in 1856 and is now constituted as a limited liability company with a licence from the Department of Trade and Industry to dispense with the word 'Limited' in its title. It is also a listed trade union. Its aims are to promote the medical and allied sciences and to maintain the honour and interests of the medical profession, and it negotiates on behalf of doctors in all branches of medicine on questions of pay and conditions of service. *Address*: BMA House, Tavistock Square, WC1H 9JP. *Tel*: 01-387 4499.

MEDICAL PRACTITIONERS' UNION (MPU). A union of medical practitioners now merged with the **Association of Scientific, Managerial and Technical Staffs** as its Medical Practitioners' Section. *Address*: 10-26A Jamestown Road, London NW1 7DT. *Tel*: 01-267 4422. *TUC Affiliated Membership, 1977*: 5,502.

MEL. Minimum earnings level (q.v.).

MELTERS' BROWN BOOK AGREEMENT. A national agreement between the Iron and Steel Trades Employers' Association and the **Iron and Steel Trades Confederation** as a result of negotiations in 1928 and 1929 and coming into force on 2 February 1930. The agreement established a standard tonnage and a standard equivalent melting rate for each process (see **tonnage payments**) and was subsequently superseded by locally negotiated agreements in most steel works in the country.

MELTERS' SLIDING SCALE. A selling price sliding scale in the steel industry originating in an agreement between 13 companies in membership of the Steel Ingot Makers' Association and the British Steel Smelters' Mill, Iron, Tinplate and Kindred Trades Association in March 1905. The agreement related to the selling price of steel plates ¼" thick and upwards and was later extended to cover practically every class of labour in the steel industry directly related to production; see Sir Arthur Pugh, *Men of Steel,* Iron and Steel Trades Confederation, 1951, p. 137 and Appx 1; also **Brown Booklet Agreement** and **change of practice principle**. The Melters' Sliding Scale was stabilised as from 3 March 1940, when a cost of living payment was introduced.

MEMBERSHIP DISPUTE; see representation dispute.

MEMBERSHIP OF A TRADE UNION. A matter subject to a number of legal cases, both in relation to **admission to a trade union, discipline of trade union members** and other issues. For admission cases, see **Nagle v. Fielden, Spring v. National Amalgamated Stevedores and Dockers, Martin v. Scottish Transport and General Workers' Union, Faramus v. Film Artistes Federation, Lee v. Showmen's Guild, Bonsor v. Musicians' Union;** see R.W. Rideout, 'Admission to Non-Statutory Associations Controlling Employment', 30 *Modern Law Review*, 1967, 'The Content of Trade Union Disciplinary Rules,' *British Journal of Industrial Relations,* Vol. 3, July 1965, 'The Content of Trade Union Rules Regulating Admission', *British Journal of Industrial Relations,* Vol. 4, March 1966. S. 7 of the **Trade Union and Labour Relations Act 1974** provides for the right of a trade union member to resign from his union with reasonable notice and complying with any reasonable conditions; see also **Barger v. TGWU** and **Ashford v. ASTMS.** Complaints against expulsions or discrimination, formerly subject to s. 5 of the Industrial Relations Act 1971 (now repealed) are now left to the unions themselves and, failing satisfaction, to the **Independent Review Committee** (q.v.) or to the courts at common law. The courts commonly take the view that in relation to members, the rules of the union ought to be abided by (see **MacLelland v. National Union of Journalists, Weakley v. Amalgamated Union of Engineering Workers, Brown v. Amalgamated Union of Engineering Workers**) and fairly applied, including a right of a member to state his case (e.g. in **Radford v. NATSOPA**); see Roger W. Rideout, *Principles of Labour Law*, 2nd ed., 1976, Ch. 11.

MENSUALISATION. A term originating in France to describe the practice of putting an 'horaire', or hourly paid worker, on a 'mensuel', or monthly paid, basis; hence also to the process of extending **staff status** (q.v.), to manual workers, or of putting manual workers, wholly or partly, on **staff conditions**, either by agreement or as an act of management policy. The narrowing of the gap between manual and staff conditions is said to have accelerated in the past 25 years, partly as a result of general social policy, partly (as in France, Switzerland and Austria) as a consequence of more direct governmental initiative, and partly by collective agreement, usually on management initiative. In Britain mensualisation is usually partial, and is not widespread; in engineering a national agreement on **Manual Workers on Staff Conditions** dates from 1941 (*Handbook of National Agreemenets*, Ref. 1.16) and provides a definition designed to distinguish staff workers proper from manual workers on staff conditions, only the latter being representable by manual worker unions. It has been estimated that in 1961, 2 per cent of manual workers in federated engineering establishments were on staff conditions of some kind, usually for sick pay and pensions; in 1966 the proportion was 2.3 per cent and

in 1969 3.4 per cent; all were on conditions lying between those of hourly rated manual and weekly staff; see also Michael Hand, *Staff Status for Manual Workers, Productivity Progress,* Pergamon Press, 1968, H.J. Schotranger, *Staff Status for Manual Workers,* Industrial Society, 1967.

MERCHANT NAVY AND AIRLINE OFFICERS' ASSOCIATION (MNAOA). A trade union originating as the Navigators' and Engineers Officers' Union in 1936 and taking its present title on amalgamation with the Marine Engineers' Association in April 1956. It caters for navigating, engineer, purser and medical officers and engineer cadets in the merchant navy and for navigators and flight engineers employed by civil airlines. Apart from the more usual trade union functions, the Association provides indemnity payments for members in respect of cancellation or suspension of certificates or licences; see D.H. Moreby, *Personnel Management in Merchant Ships,* Pergamon Press, 1968, pp. 212-7. *Address*: Oceanair House, 750-760 High Road, London E11 3BB. *Tel:* 01-989 6677. *TUC Affiliated Membership, 1977:* 36,050.

MERCHANT SHIPPING ACT 1894. An Act of which Part II, Part V, Part VI, Part XIII and Part XIV contain provisions relating to masters and seamen, especially on contracts of employment, and on discipline. The latter makes a wide variety of acts a criminal offence and under Regulations approved by the Department of Trade and Industry, authorises monetary fines for certain disciplinary offences, s. 225 of the Act limits the seaman's right to strike by making wilful disobedience of lawful commands, and combination to do this or to neglect duty, a criminal offence. The **Pearson Report** (q.v.) in 1967 recommended a newly drafted Act, jettisoning obsolete provisions and leaving many matters to be dealt with by contractual arrangements and industrial negotiation, disobedience of a limited class of orders only being regarded as a criminal offence (Part II); see also *Merchant Shipping Acts,* Stevens, 3rd ed., 1976.

MERGERS; see multi-establishment company.

MERIDEN   CO-OPERATIVE;   see **workers' co-operatives.**

MERIT PAY; see merit rate.

MERIT RATE. Most properly used to describe an addition to the rate of a worker for personal merit which is periodically reassessed according to a **merit rating scheme** (see **merit rating**); **merit pay**. Sometimes used to describe a wage supplement given for rough job grading or differential purposes (see *Workshop Wage Determination*, S.W. Lerner, J.R. Cable and S. Gupta (eds), Pergamon Press, 1969, pp. 49-50), and in the sense of **merit rate commonly applied** i.e. as a euphemism for a wage element in a shop or factory, added to the basic rate, which may have arisen either from pressure to generalise individual merit rates or made to disguise a general wage increase. In principle merit rates, in their individual form, are non-negotiable and can formally both be given and taken away, though these characteristics are not always maintained in practice.

MERIT RATE COMMONLY APPLIED; see **merit rate.**

MERIT RATING. Also known as **efficiency rating, personal employee** or **individual assessment bonus schemes, merit rating schemes**; a system of providing an incentive or reward to individual workers by the systematic assessment of employees in terms of the performance, aptitudes and other qualities necessary for the successful carrying out of his job (British Institute of Management, *Merit Rating: A Practical Guide*, Personnel Management Series, 1954, p. 5). R. Marriott, *Incentive Payment Systems*, Staples Press, 3rd (revised) ed., 1968, pp. 78-91) records that such systems were rare in Britain before 1939, except as a basis for promotion in the Civil Service, and examines their current use and performance, advantages and disadvantages. Research underlines the importance of management's initial approach to the worker, and the need for continued co-operation (Norah M. Davies, 'A Study of a Merit Rating Scheme', *Occupational Psychology*, 27, 1953, pp. 57-68; R. Marriott, 'An Exploratory Study of Merit Rating Systems in Three Factories', *Occupational Psychology* 36, 1962, pp. 180-214). Outside the Civil Service merit rating is seldom popular with trade unions since it appears to be basically subjective in operation, and schemes have frequently failed; see also E.B. Knauft, 'A Classification and Evaluation of Personnel Rating Methods': *Journal of Applied Psychology*, 31, 1947, pp. 617-25. Recently there has been a tendency to regard merit rating as concerned less with the measurement of

merit than with **performance appraisal** (q.v.).

MERIT RATING SCHEME; see **merit rating.**

MERRICK DIFFERENTIAL PIECE PLAN or **Merrick Multiple Piece-rate Plan**; see **differential piece-rate plan.**

METAL WORKERS' UNION, ASSOCIATED (AMU). A trade union founded in 1868 as the Iron, Steel and Metal Dressers' Society. Shortly after changing its name to the Metal Dressers' and Kindred Trades' Society, it was enlarged by the transfer to it of the engagements of the Associated Metal Workers and Allied Trades (then 380 strong, and historically known as the Amalgamated Society of Brassworkers), the resultant organisation adopting the title Associated Metalworkers' Society in 1964. This was changed in 1974 to its present title; see also **Cartledge v. Jopling**. *Address*: 92 Deansgate, Manchester 3. *Tel*: 061-834 6891. *TUC Affiliated Membership, 1977*: 5,057.

METAL MECHANICS, NATIONAL SOCIETY OF (NSMM). A trade union founded in Birmingham in April 1872 as the Amalgamated Society of Brass Workers and now having membership in the metal and engineering trades generally, especially in the Midlands and Greater London area. In 1874 the name of the union was changed to the National Society of Amalgamated Brass Workers, and in 1906, as membership grew outside the brass industry proper, to the National Society of Amalgamated Brass Workers and Metal Mechanics, and again in 1919 to the National Society of Brass and Metal Mechanics. The present title was adopted about 1945. See Malcolm Totten, *Founded in Brass. The First Hundred Years of the National Society of Metal Mechanics*, NSMM, 1972. *Address*: 70 Lionel Street, Birmingham B3 1JG. *Tel*: 021-236 0726. *TUC Affiliated Membership, 1977*: 47,882.

METHOD STUDY. Defined by the British Standards Institution, *British Standard Glossary of Terms Used in Work Study*, BS 3138, 1969 No. 10002 as 'the systematic recording and critical examination of existing and proposed ways of doing work as a means of developing and applying easier and more effective methods of reducing costs'. The term has been attributed to Frank and Lillian Gilbreth, who coined it to distinguish the technique from the 'time study' of F.W. Taylor. Method Study is currently regarded as a necessary part of work study which precedes work measurement, the object being to ensure that the job is being performed in the best and most economical way before work measurement is applied; see International Labour Office, *Introduction to Work Study*, Geneva, 1969, Part Two.

METHODS TIME MEASUREMENT (MTM). A **Predetermined Motion Time System** devised by the Methods Engineering Council in the United States which analyses manual operations and methods into the basic motions required to perform them. A predetermined time standard is given to each basic motion and the conditions under which it is made. Basic MTM motions are nine in number: reach, grasp, move, turn and/or apply pressure, position, disengage, eye control, leg and body movement; see also **Universal Standard Data**.

MIDLAND IRON AND STEEL WAGES BOARD. A Joint Conciliation Board covering some 3,146 operatives in some 18 companies in hot rolling and cold rolling in the private sector of the steel industry in the Midland, Derbyshire and Yorkshire areas. The Board is thought to be one of the oldest Joint Conciliation Boards in the country, dating from the establishment of a joint board in South Staffordshire in 1872. It has existed under its present title at least from 1917, when the **Iron and Steel Trades Confederation** was formed. The President of the Board is appointed from outside the steel industry, the Chairman by the employers (subject to ISTC approval), and both employers and union appoint Secretaries, the Board's expenditure being met by both sides equally on the basis of a levy of 4p per operative per week. A **neutral committee** procedure is operated similar to that in other parts of the steel industry; see Eric Taylor, *The Better Temper, a commemorative history of the Midland Iron and Steel Wages Board 1876-1976*, ISTC, 1976. *Address*: London Works Steel Co. Ltd., Tividale, Warley, West Midlands. B69 3HU. *Tel*: 021-557 2871.

MIDNIGHT SHIFT; see **graveyard shift**.

MIF. Miners' International Federation; see **International Trade Secretariats**.

MIJLC. Motor Industry Joint Labour Council (q.v.).

MILITANCY. Combative or warlike attitudes by trade unions or their members, taking the form of strikes, overtime bans, go-slows, withdrawal of co-operation or demonstrations in order to bring pressure to bear on employers. V.L. Allen (*Militant Trade Unionism,* Merlin Press, 1966, pp. 18-20) considers that belief in the effectiveness of militancy is inherent in trade unionists in their efforts to improve income and conditions. R.M. Blackburn, *Union Character and Social Class*, Batsford, 1967, discusses the reasons for variations in trade union militancy.

MILITARY AND ORCHESTRAL MUSICAL INSTRUMENT MAKERS' TRADE SOCIETY. A trade union founded in 1894 and formerly known before 1926 as the Military Musical Instrument Makers' Trade Society. *Address*: 56 Avondale Crescent, Enfield, Middx. *TUC Affiliated Membership, 1977*: 185.

MILLER v. AMALGAMATED ENGINEERING UNION (1938) Ch. 669; see **benefits**.

MILTON PLAN. A plan for the successful running down and closure of the British Aluminium rolling mill at Milton near Stoke-on-Trent and development and transfer of labour to the company's more modern plant at Rheola in the Vale of Neath put into operation between September 1962 and January 1964. Alan Fox *The Milton Plan: An Exercise in Manpower Planning and Transfer of Production*, Institute of Personnel Management, 1965.

MINERS' COAL; see **concessionary coal**.

MINERS' INTERNATIONAL FEDERATION (MIF); see **International Trade Secretariats**.

MINEWORKERS, NATIONAL UNION OF (NUM). A trade union founded in 1945 from the member unions of the Miners' Federation of Great Britain (MFGB formed in 1888) after prolonged efforts towards greater centralisation (see George B. Baldwin, 'Structural Reform in the British Miners' Union', *Quarterly Journal of Economics*, November 1953, pp. 576-96). The NUM is an industrial union negotiating directly with the National Coal Board, and including coalmining staffs, clerical workers and cokemen in its organisation. Both as the NUM and as the MFGB, the union has played a notable role in the British labour movement; see R. Page Arnot, *The Miners: A History of the Miners' Federation of Great Britain, 1889-1910,* Allen and Unwin, 1949; *The Miners: The Years of Struggle,* Allen and Unwin, 1953; *The Miners in Crisis and War,* Allen and Unwin, 1961; *A History of the Scottish Miners from the Earliest Times,* Allen and Unwin, 1955; J.E. Williams, *The Derbyshire Miners,* Allen and Unwin, 1962. W.R. Garside, *Durham Miners, 1919-1960,* Allen and Unwin, 1972; Sidney J. Webb, *The Story of the Durham Miners, 1662-1921,* Fabian Society, 1921; E. Welbourne, *The Miners' Unions of Northumberland and Durham,* CUP, 1923; J.A. Wilson, *A History of the Durham Miners' Association, 1870-1904,* Veitch and Sons, Durham, 1907; R. Challinor, *The Lancashire and Cheshire Miners,* Frank Graham, 1972; J. Davison, *Northumberland Miners 1919-39,* NUM, 1973; A.R. Griffin, *The Miners of Nottinghamshire; a History of the Nottinghamshire Miners' Association, Vol.* 1, 1881-1914, Nottinghamshire Printers Ltd 1957, Vol. 2, 1914-1944, Allen and Unwin, 1962; R. Page Arnot, *South Wales Miners, 1893-1914,* Allen and Unwin, 1967; Ness Edwards, *History of the South Wales Miners' Federation,* Vol. 1, Lawrence and Wishart, 1938; Eric Wyn Evans, *Miners of South Wales,* University of Wales Press, 1961; Frank Machin, *The Yorkshire Miners: A History,* Vol. 1, NUM, 1958. Membership of the NUM has fallen sharply in recent years with the contraction of the coal mining industry. The Colliery Officials and Staffs Area of the union was established at the beginning of 1947 and had in 1978 some 18,200 members. *Address:* 222 Euston Road, London NW1 2BX. *Tel:* 01-387 7631. *TUC Affiliated Membership, 1977:* 259,966.

MINIMUM EARNINGS LEVEL (MEL). A device, introduced into the engineering industry by the national agreement of 22 December 1964 for raising the effective minimum earnings level for different classes of worker over a period of three years in order to benefit the lower paid. New and higher MELs were introduced at six-monthly intervals, workers' remuneration, however made up, being increased to these levels. In January 1968, the MEL arrived at became the **minimum time rate** for each of the classes concerned. The National Board for Prices and Incomes (*Pay and Conditions of Service for Engineering Workers,* Report No. 49, Cmnd. 3495, December 1967) approved the method of raising the pay of the lower paid worker, but considered that the 1964 settlement had failed in its purpose because its objectives were set too low (p. 33); see also **tapering, pro-tanto settlement.** The MEL principle was continued in the engineering national agreement of December 1968 and August 1972; it has also been introduced into other industries, e.g. rubber.

MINIMUM ENTITLEMENT. A term used by the Department of Employment to refer to the minimum income assured to a worker for a normal working week. Arrangements relating to this minimum income may vary from one situation to another; e.g. they may relate to **basic rates,** to **standard rates,** to **minimum time rates,** to **minimum earnings levels,** to the **guaranteed week,** etc.

MINIMUM LIST HEADING (MLH); see **Standard Industrial Classification.**

MINIMUM PIECEWORK STANDARD (MPS). An agreed yardstick of earnings for the payment by results worker of average ability in the engineering industry to be borne in mind when fixing piecework prices or times. An MPS of 25 per cent over basic time rates (excluding **War Bonus**) was increased to 27½ per cent by National Arbitration Tribunal Award No. 326 of 20 March 1943, to 45 per cent by the national wage agreement of 28 November 1950, and from 1 January 1968 altered to 15 per cent over new and higher times rates established as a result of the **Engineering Package Deal** Agreement of 1964. A national MPS ceased to exist as a consequence of the second engineering package deal agreement of December 1968, and has not been subsequently restored, piecework incentive being 'a matter for determination domestically' (*Memorandum of Agreement,* IV, para. 7). The MPS was neither a part of the wages structure of the engineering industry, nor a guarantee. It should be distinguished from the **pieceworkers' guarantee** (q.v.) in engineering: A.I. Marsh, *Industrial Relations in Engineering,* Pergamon Press, 1965, pp. 148, 199 and 208-9.

MINIMUM RATE; see **minimum time rate.**

MINIMUM TIME RATE (MTR) or minimum rate or simply **time rate.** The lowest rate of pay, by national, local, or work-place agreement, and sometimes by **custom and practice** or by law, which a particular worker or class of workers may be paid; also the rate on which **premium payments** for overtime, shiftwork, etc., are usually paid. In the engineering industry, the name given to the rate resulting from the conversion of **minimum earnings levels** into minimum time rates from 1 January 1968, as a result of the Package Deal Agreement (see **Engineering Package Deal**) of 1964 subsequently increased as a result of further agreements in 1968 and 1972. In some industries payment by results systems may be based on the (minimum) time rate; in engineering they have been traditionally related to the **base** (or **basic** or **bonus**) **rate** (q.v.) but this may now in many cases be identical to the relevant MTR.

MINIMUM WAGE. An expression used in a number of circumstances in which a worker's remuneration is not allowed to fall below a given amount. The most common are those which arise out of minimum wage legislation (see **national minimum wage**) and from agreements guaranteeing payment by result workers a minimum payment in the event of their being unable to achieve a higher level of piecework earnings, e.g. in engineering and cotton (see **guarantee** and **pieceworkers' guarantee**). May sometimes be used loosely to describe **guaranteed wage**, or **guaranteed week** payments (q.v.).

MINISTRY OF LABOUR (MOL) now the Department of Employment; see **Employment, Department of.**

MINOR TRADES; see **differential.**

MINUTE 741. A Minute of the Executive Council of the **Confederation of Shipbuilding and Engineering Unions** approved by the General Council in February 1947 enabling the machinery of the Confederation to be used in cases of stoppages affecting more than one union. The Minute was primarily intended to prevent disputes between unions arising out of the payment of strike pay, and was specifically not arranged to cover **demarcation disputes** (q.v.); A.I. Marsh, *Industrial Relations in Engineering*, Pergamon Press, 1965, p. 35, and *A Collection of Teaching Documents and Case Studies, Industrial Relations in Engineering*, 1966, pp. 31-3; see also **inter-union disputes.**

MISCELLANEOUS TRADES JOINT COUNCIL (MTJC); see **Whitleyism.**

MITBESTIMMUNG; see **co-determination.**

MIXED ESTABLISHMENT; see **mixed offices.**

MIXED HOUSE; see **mixed office.**

MIXED OFFICE also **mixed house; mixed establishment.** Either (1) a combined news and jobbing office in the printing industry, or (2) a printing office in which both trade unionists and non-unionists are employed, e.g. an **open house** or **open shop** (q.v.); see A.E. Musson, *The Typographical Association*, OUP, 1954, p. 174. Also an office paying both by time and by piece (John Child, *Industrial Relations in the British Printing Industry*, George Allen and Unwin, 1967).

MNAOA. Merchant Navy and Airline Officers' Association (q.v.).

MNC. Multi-national Corporation (q.v.).

MOBILITY OF LABOUR; see **labour mobility.**

MODULE TRAINING; see **apprenticeship.**

MOL. Ministry of Labour; now the Department of Employment; see **Employment, Department of.**

MONDISM. The doctrine emphasising the common interests between workers and management put forward by Sir Alfred Mond; see **Mond Turner Conferences.**

MOND TURNER CONFERENCES. So called after Sir Alfred Mond (later Lord Melchett), of Imperial Chemical Industries, and Ben Turner, Chairman of the Trades Union Congress, the respective leaders of the two sides of the **Conference on Industrial Reorganisation and Industrial Relations** 1928-29. The Conference was a response by Sir Alfred Mond and a group of other individualists to a passage in a TUC Presidential Address by George Hicks in 1927, drawing attention to the advantages of direct exchanges between labour and capital 'in a common endeavour to improve the efficiency of industry and raise the workers' standard of life'. Its broad object was to improve the climate of industrial relations after the **General Strike** and the **Trade Disputes and Trade Union Act 1927**. On the TUC side, its prime instigator was the General Secretary, Walter (later Lord) Citrine (Lord Citrine, *Men and Work,* Greenwood Press, 1976.) After three sets of meetings, the Conference petered out into joint discussions between the TUC, the Federation of British Industries, and the National Confederation of Employers' Organisations (later the British Employers' Confederation) which continued for some years, and, it is claimed by Citrine, provided the basis for 'a friendly intimacy and a confident relationship without any sacrifice of principle'; see also H.A. Clegg and T.E. Chester, Joint Consultation, in A.D. Flanders and H.A. Clegg, *The System of Industrial Relations in Great Britain*, Basil Blackwell, 1964, pp. 335 *et seq.*

MONEY PIECEWORK; see piecework.

MONEY STEWARD. A trade union branch official whose task it is to receive members' contributions, sign their cards, and sometimes also to enter contributions into a contribution book.

MONTHLY STAFF; see staff.

MOONLIGHTING or **double-jobbing;** the practice of holding a second job. A good deal is known about moonlighting in the United States, where it is said to be increasing, particularly where working hours are short, e.g. in J.C. Deiter, 'Moonlighting and the Short Work Week', *South Western Social Science Quarterly*, December 1966. In May 1963, The Bureau of Labour Statistics counted 3.9 million moonlighters (see F.A. Bragan and H.R. Hamel, 'Multiple Job Holders in May 1963', *Monthly Labor Review*, March 1964, pp. 247-57); most likely on the **afternoon and night shifts** (P.E. Mott, F.C. Mann, Q. McLoughlin and D.P. Warwick, *Shift Work*, Ann Arbor, University of Michigan Press, 1965, p. 62); see also H.A. Wilensky, 'The Moonlighter; A Product of Relative Deprivation', *Industrial Relations,* Vol. 3, No. 1, October 1963, pp. 105-24. Little is known about moonlighting in Britain, though it is thought that one reason for it may be payment in cash for evening or week-end work, so avoiding Pay-As-You-Earn. About 1½ million second employment jobs are known to Inland Revenue (excluding self-employed); the *Family Expenditure Survey* of 1973 showed that 6.9 per cent of the working population had second jobs; the *General Household Survey* of the same year showed only 3.1 per cent and 3.5 per cent in 1973 compared with 5.1 per cent in the USA for both these years; see J. Alden, 'The Extent and Nature of Double Jobholding in Great Britain', *Industrial Relations Journal*, Vol. 8, No. 3, Autumn 1977, pp. 14-33.

MORGAN v. FRY AND OTHERS (1968) 3 All ER 452. A leading case in which it was held that a strike notice, if of a length equal to that required to terminate the contract, would have the effect of suspending the contract, thereby not involving the strikers in liability for breach.

MORRIS REPORT. Name given to reports of one of two Courts of Inquiry under the chairmanship of the Rt Hon. Lord Justice Morris, CBE, into a national engineering and shipbuilding dispute in 1953 (Cmd. 9084, February 1954, and Cmd. 9085, February 1954.)

MOTION TIME ANALYSIS (MTA). A **predetermined motion time system** (q.v.).

MOTION AND TIME STUDY; see work study.

MOTIVATORS. The alternative, in the motivational theory of Frederick Herzberg, to **hygiene factors** (q.v.).

MOTOR INDUSTRY JOINT LABOUR COUNCIL (MIJLC or SCAMP COUNCIL). A joint council of the principal motor vehicle manufacturers and national trade union representatives in the motor industry set up in November 1965 under the independent chairmanship of Jack (later Sir Jack) Scamp, to promote good relations in the motor-car industry, including in its functions that of inquiring into particular disputes leading to serious unofficial strikes, reviewing the state of industrial relations in particular firms, and keeping the general state of relations under review. The Council had its origin in a Joint Statement on Industrial Relations issued in April 1961 after a meeting of the parties convened by the Minister of Labour, which was followed by a Joint Study Group of managing directors and trade union national officials. The MIJLC undertook 15 investigations. Three of these took the form of **Courts of Inquiry** carried out by Sir Jack Scamp (Cmnd. 2905, 1966, Longbridge Delivery Agents;

Cmnd. 2935, 1966, Motor Vehicle Collections Ltd. and Avon Car Transporters Ltd; Cmnd. 3749, Ford Sewing Machinists), and of the remaining 12 investigations by the Council proper, three dealt with particular plants, and 9 with specific disputes; see **Motor Industry Joint Labour Council**, First Report December 1966, Second March 1968. The industry's own Council which replaced the MIJLC and which is known as the **Motor Vehicle Industry Joint Council** came into being in December 1969. This ceased to operate after a short time.

MOTOR VEHICLE INDUSTRY JOINT COUNCIL. The successor to the **Motor Industry Joint Labour Council** (q.v.).

MPS. Minimum piecework standard; Manpower and Productivity Service (q.v.).

MPU. Medical Practitioners' Union (q.v.).

M RATES. Time rates for unskilled labourers in industrial employment in government industrial esablishments (derived from 'miscellaneous'), calculated by taking a simple arithmetic average of the agreed minimum time rates in a selected number of industries outside the Civil Service. The M Rate represented an application by government of the **fair wages principle** (q.v.). It was criticised by the National Board for Prices and Incomes (*Pay of Industrial Civil Servants*, Report No. 18, Cmnd. 3034, June 1966) for relating pay to wage rates rather than earnings and subsequently abolished. The NBPI recommended new pay structures for the industrial civil service.

MSC. Manpower Services Commission (q.v.).

MSD. Master Standard Data (q.v.).

MTA. Motion Time Analysis (q.v.).

MTM. Methods Time Measurement (q.v.).

MTR. Minimum time rate (q.v.).

MU. Musicians' Union (q.v.).

MUDD v. GENERAL UNION OF OPERATIVE CARPENTERS AND JOINERS (1910) 26 TLR 518; see **benefits.**

MULTI-EMPLOYER BARGAINING or **association bargaining**. An expression used, particularly in the United States, to describe collective bargaining which takes place between a union and a group or groups of employers, sometimes combined in an **employers' association**. Very often it is synonymous with **industry-wide bargaining.**

MULTI-ESTABLISHMENT COMPANY. A company having more than one **establishment** for industrial relations purposes, a **multi-plant company** where the plant is the basic unit for such purposes. The growth of multi-establishment companies has produced new problems of company industrial relations policy in Britain which have only been partially investigated; see A.I. Marsh, 'The Staffing of Industrial Relations Management in the Engineering Industry', *Industrial Relations Journal*, Vol. 2, No. 2, Summer 1971, A.I. Marsh, E.O. Evans and P. Garcia, *Workplace Industrial Relations in Engineering*, EEF and Kogan Page, 1971, and J.C. Ramsey, 'Negotiating in a Multi-Plant Company', *Industrial Relations Journal*, Vol. 2, No. 2, Summer 1971; Commission on Industrial Relations, *Industrial Relations in Multi-Plant Undertakings*, Report No. 85, 1974. In so far as multi-establishment status involves mergers and takeovers, a separate literature began to emerge in the 1960s and 1970s; see D. Brooks and R. Smith, *Mergers: The Impact on the Shop Floor*, Action Society Trust, 1966, and P.F. Barrett, *The Human Implications of Mergers and Takeovers*, IPM, 1973. It has been suggested by N. Milward and J. McQueeney ('The Industrial Effects of Mergers and Takeovers,' *Department of Employment Gazette*, September 1977, pp. 944-6) that the impact of mergers on employees is given little consideration when acquisitions are made and that there might be fewer failures if this were done; see also G. Meeks, *Disappointing Marriage: A Study of the Gains from Merger*, CUP, 1977.

MULTINATIONAL CORPORATION (MNC) or multinational company, or multinational firm. An imprecise expression used to describe a corporation, company or firm (but not a cartel), which has branches, divisions or subsidiaries in a number of countries, subject to a greater or lesser degree to the control or influence of the management of its country of origin. The increasing size and number of such corporations has occasioned concern in the 1960s and in the early 1970s, particularly from trade unions, on the grounds that democratic control may pass out of the hands of host countries, that employment opportunities and collective bargaining may be manipulated by transferring production facilities from one country to another, and that fair labour standards may not be observed; see Malcolm Warner, 'Towards Transcontinental Unions', *New Society*, 15 October 1970, Hans Günter (ed.), *Transcontinental Industrial Relations*, Macmillan, 1971, and Trades Union Congress, *International Companies*, TUC, 1970; John H. Dunning (ed.); *The Multi-National Enterprise*, George Allen and Unwin, 1971; Charles Levinson, *Capital Inflation and the Multi-Nationals*, George Allen and Unwin, 1971 and *International Trade Unionism*, Allen and Unwin, 1972, J. Gennard, *Multi-nationals: Industrial Relations and the Trade Union Response*. Occasional Papers in Industrial Relations, 1, Institute of Personnel Management, 1976, B.C. Roberts, 'Multi-national Collective Bargaining: A European Prospect' and (with J. May) 'The Response of Multi-national Enterprises to International Trade Union Pressure', *British Journal of Industrial Relations*, March 1973 and November 1974; also **International Trade Union Movement**. The Governing Body of the **International Labour Organisation** adopted a Tripartite Declaration of Principles concerning *Multinational Enterprises and Social Policy* in November 1977, in effect internationalising the industrial relations section of the OECD's *Guidelines on International Investment for Multinational Enterprises*, commended in the UK government's White Paper Cmnd. 6525, June 1976.

MULTI-PLANT COMPANY; see multi-establishment company.

MULTIPLE PIECE RATES; see differential piece-rate plan.

MULTIPLE TIME PLAN; see differential piece-rate plan.

MUNC. Sometimes used as an abbreviation for **multi-national corporation** (q.v.) more usually MNC.

MUPS. Manpower Utilisation and Payment Structure Agreement (q.v.).

MUSICIANS' UNION (MU). A trade union formed in 1921 as a result of the amalgamation of the National Orchestral Union of Professional Musicians and the Amalgamated Musicians' Union, both founded in 1893. The union's membership grew to about 22,000 in the 1920s, but declined after the advent of the talkies and was only 7,000 in 1940, since when it has grown to its present figure. Early problems of the union were the immigration of foreign musicians and the use of military bands and orchestras; currently it is concerned especially with the effects of recorded, broadcast and 'wired' music. It was recognised at a very early stage by the BBC, and negotiates, *inter alia*, with the Independent Television Contractors' Association, the Society of West End Theatre Managers, Mecca Ltd (and other ballroom proprietors), the British Resorts' Association, the Film Production Association, the British Phonographic Industry, the Orchestral Employers' Association, the Royal Opera House, Sadler's Wells Theatre, the Shipping Federation, circus proprietors, etc. On the early history of the union, see E.S. Theale, 'The Story of the Amalgamated Musicians' Union'. *Musicians' Journal*, April 1929. *Address*: 29 Catherine Place, Buckingham Gate, London SW1. *Tel*: 01-834 1348. *TUC Affiliated Membership, 1977*: 37,019.

MUTUALITY. The principle, accepted by federated engineering employers since 1898, that piecework prices or times must be agreed by mutual arrangement between the management and the worker who is to perform the work. The principle is currently embodied in a number of agreements with individual engineering unions and, by implication in the case of new prices and times, in an agreement between the **Engineering Employers' Federation** and the **Confederation of Shipbuilding and Engineering Unions** (*Handbook of National Agreements*, 2.5 to 2.581). The original intention of engineering employers was both to assure the worker that prices and times would not be imposed upon him, and to discourage union control over them. The arrangement is now thought in some quarters to stimulate fragmented workshop bargaining and be partly responsible for **earnings drift**, as well as hampering the development of payment systems such as **measured daywork** (q.v.) in which individual mutuality is inappropriate or restricted; see A.I. Marsh, *Industrial Relations in Engineering*, Pergamon Press, 1965, and Coventry and District Engineering Employers' Association, *Wage Drift, Measurement and Systems of Payment*, 1967, pp. 21-2.

MUTUAL INSURANCE. A method of trade union action described by Sidney and Beatrice Webb (*Industrial Democracy*, 1898, Ch. 1), other methods being **collective bargaining** and **legal enactment**. Mutual insurance involved the use of trade union benefits, both as positive and negative sanctions to enforce membership discipline, and as a means whereby union terms and working rules could be imposed on employers (see Allan Flanders, 'Collective Bargaining: A Theoretical Analysis', *British Journal of Industrial Relations*, March 1968, and *Management and Unions: The Theory and Reform of Industrial Relations*, Faber and Faber, 1975, and A.I. Marsh and P.J. Cope, 'The Anatomy of Trade Union Benefits in the 1960s', *Industrial Relations Journal*, Summer 1970). The Webbs appear not to have envisaged that mutual insurance might evolve into collective bargaining, but they conceded that it might be associated with other trade union methods and be 'in its economic aspect ... hardly distinguishable from collective bargaining' (p. 797).

MUTUAL STRIKE AID or **employer strike insurance** (United States). A private agreement by which competing employers contract that, if one of them is the subject of a strike, the others will indemnify him by some predetermined sum of money to help him to withstand its effects. Mutual strike aid arrangements have been growing in the United States, particularly in public services; see Frank M. Tuerkheimer, 'Strike Insurance and the Legality of Inter-Employer Economic Aid under the Present Federal Legislation', *New York University Law Review*, Vol. 38, No. 126, January 1963 and John S. Hirsch Jr, 'Strike Insurance and Collective Bargaining', *Industrial and Labor Relations Review*, Vol. 22, No. 3, April 1969. For similar arrangements in Britain, see **indemnity fund**.

N

NACE; Nomenclature Générale des Activités Économiques des Communautés Européennes (q.v.).

NACODS. National Association of Colliery Overmen, Deputies and Shotfirers; see **Colliery Overmen, Deputies, and Shotfirers, National Association of.**

NAGLE v. FIELDING (1966) 1 All ER 689, W 579. A leading case involving the Jockey Club in which it was held that if the rules of an association exercising monopoly control over admission to an occupation do not expressly preclude a particular group from admission (in this case a woman), then the exercise of the discretion to membership, if used to exclude such a group, would be arbitrary and capricious and, as such, invalid; see K.W. Wedderburn, *Cases and Materials on Labour Law*, CUP, 1967, p. 579; see also **membership of a trade union.**

NALGO; see **National and Local Government Officers' Association.**

NALHM. National Association of Licensed House Managers; see **Licensed House Managers, National Association of.**

NAS. National Association of Schoolmasters; see **Schoolmasters, and Union of Women Teachers, National Association of.**

NASD. National Amalgamated Stevedores and Dockers; see **blue union.**

NAS/UWT. National Association of Schoolmasters and Union of Women Teachers; see **Schoolmasters and Union of Women Teachers, National Association of.**

NAT. National Arbitration Tribunal (q.v.).

NATIONAL AGREEMENT; see **national bargaining.**

NATIONAL AMALGAMATED STEVEDORES AND DOCKERS (NASD); see **blue union.**

NATIONAL ARBITRATION TRIBUNAL (NAT). An arbitration tribunal established under the **Conditions of Employment and National Arbitration Order 1305 (1940)** to operate a system of **compulsory arbitration** which it continued to do until 1951. Part II of the Order prohibited strikes and lock-outs unless the difference had been reported to the Minister and not referred by him for settlement within twenty-one days. The NAT was empowered to make awards which became an **implied term** of contract between the employer and the workers concerned in a reference, and enforceable at law. Employers were required to observe **recognised terms and conditions** (q.v.) such references to be raised as 'questions'. Under the Order one party could report a difference to the Minister for reference to the NAT without the agreement of the other; see Ministry of Labour, *Industrial Relations Handbook*, 1944, 1953 and 1961 editions.

NATIONAL ASSOCIATION OF COLLIERY OVERMEN, DEPUTIES AND SHOTFIRERS (NACODS); see Colliery Overmen, Deputies and Shotfirers, National Association of.

NATIONAL ASSOCIATION OF CO-OPERATIVE OFFICIALS; see Co-operative Officials, National Association of.

NATIONAL ASSOCIATION OF FIRE OFFICERS; see Fire Officers, National Association of.

NATIONAL ASSOCIATION OF HEAD TEACHERS; see Head Teachers, National Association of.

NATIONAL ASSOCIATION OF LICENSED HOUSE MANAGERS (NALHM); see Licensed House Managers, National Association of.

NATIONAL ASSOCIATION OF SCHOOLMASTERS AND UNION OF WOMEN TEACHERS; see Schoolmasters and Union of Women Teachers, National Association of.

NATIONAL ASSOCIATION OF THEATRICAL, TELEVISION AND KINE EMPLOYEES (NATTKE); see Theatrical, Television and Kine Employees, National Association of.

NATIONAL BARGAINING. Collective bargaining involving the regulation of terms and conditions of work for substantial groups of workers at national level in particular industries, or **industry-wide bargaining**, e.g. in engineering, chemicals, etc., as distinct from **district bargaining**, **plant bargaining**, **domestic bargaining**, etc. Also traditionally used to describe bargaining at head office level in some companies, e.g. in Fords and in Imperial Chemical Industries, where a more precise description might be **company bargaining** or company-wide bargaining. National bargaining in the former sense rarely covers all the companies in an industry, some preferring company bargaining, independent **plant bargaining** or other forms of bargaining. National bargaining machinery began to develop in Britain in the latter part of the nineteenth century (see H.A. Clegg, Alan Fox and A.F. Thompson, *A History of British Trade Unions Since 1889*, Vol. 1, 1889-1910, OUP, 1964), and reached its peak between the wars, partly as a result of developments from the first world war and from **Whitleyism** (q.v.), remaining embodied in the official institutions represented by trade unions and employers' associations. The Donovan Royal Commission on Trade Unions and Employers' Associations, 1965-1968 (see **Donovan Commission**), Cmnd. 3623, June 1968, Ch. III, was concerned to contrast the decline of the formal system represented by national bargaining of this kind with the growth of 'the informal system created by the actual behaviour of trade unions and employers' associations, of managers, shop stewards and workers'. It is to be doubted whether, in some industries, the formal national bargaining system ever exercised the control attributed to it, while in others such control remained comparatively intact for a considerable period of time.

NATIONAL BOARD FOR PRICES AND INCOMES (NBPI or PIB). A body, constitutionally independent of government, first established by Royal Warrant in April 1965 and later by Act of Parliament (see **Prices and Incomes Act 1966**), to keep incomes, prices and charges under constant review. The Board was the principal instrument of the **prices and incomes policy** inaugurated by the Wilson administration in the Joint Statement of Intent on Productivity, Prices and Incomes of December 1964 (see **Declaration of Intent**), and was proposed in the White Paper on *Machinery of Prices and Incomes Policy*, Cmnd. 2577, February 1965. It was dissolved by the Heath administration and ceased to operate in March 1971. During its life it published 170 reports, 79 on pay, 67 on prices, 10 related to both pay and prices, and 9 general studies of such subjects as **job evaluation, payment by results, productivity agreements**, etc. The general effect of the Board was to inject considerations of productivity into pay, by linking it with higher individual and managerial performance, by discouraging **comparability** as a sole basis for wage determination, and by emphasising the inflationary results of higher wages unaccompanied by higher productivity, and to deter price increases to some extent. In the process of securing this effect it probably accelerated an improvement in management and industrial relations practice, particularly at company and plant level, and as an investigatory body it made a considerable contribution to the development of this aspect of public administration. This, and the possibilities of developing NBPI techniques are discussed in Allan Fels, *The British Prices and Incomes Board,* Department of Applied Economics, Occasional Paper 29, CUP, 1972. The winding-up of the Board resulted from the Heath government's abandonment of the prices and incomes policy; see also Aubrey Jones, 'The Price of Prosperity', *The Observer,* 1 November 1970, and Hugh Clegg, *How to Run an Incomes Policy and Why We Made Such a Mess of the Last One,* Heinemann, 1971, and R.J. Liddle and W.E.J. McCarthy, 'The Impact of the Prices and Incomes Board on the Reform of Collective Bargaining', *British Journal of Industrial Relations.* Vol. X, No. 3, November 1972, pp. 412-39.

NATIONAL BONUS; see piecework supplement.

NATIONAL CONFEDERATION OF EMPLOYERS' ORGANISATIONS (NCEO). A national employers' organisation which came into being in 1919 as a direct result of the **National Industrial Conference** (q.v.) called in that year. The objects of the Confederation were principally to provide for consultation between employers' organisations, and to keep watch over government policies, particularly in labour matters. During the 1920s, the NCEO increasingly assumed the role of national spokesman for employers on labour relations, leaving the Federation of British Industries as the main national trade association. It became the **British Employers' Confederation** (q.v.) in 1939, and in that form was later merged into the **Confederation of British Industry.**

NATIONAL COUNCIL OF LABOUR COLLEGES (NCLC). A body formed in 1921 to provide independent working-class education, originally on a Marxist basis and as 'a partisan effort to improve the position of labour in the present and to assist ultimately in the abolition of wage slavery'. The NCLC was established as a consequence of a series of events beginning with the forced resignation of the Principal of Ruskin College in 1909 and the subsequent coalition between the Central Labour College and the Plebs League, and in opposition to the Workers' Educational Association (and its trade union linked organisation, the **Workers' Education Trade Union Committee,** q.v.), which worked in co-operation with universities and the Board of Education. In 1969 both NCLC and WETUC interests were taken over by the TUC Education Committee; see J.F.C. Harrison, *Learning and Living, 1790-1960,* Routledge and Kegan Paul, 1961.

NATIONAL DOCK LABOUR BOARD; see **Dock Labour Scheme.**

NATIONAL DOCK LABOUR SCHEME; see Dock Labour Scheme.

NATIONAL EMERGENCY PROCEDURES. Procedures authorised by the **Industrial Relations Act 1971** (ss. 138-45) in circumstances in which a strike, threatened strike, lock-out or irregular industrial action short of a strike was likely to cause grave injury to the national economy, create a serious risk of public disorder, or endanger the lives of a substantial number of persons. In such circumstances the Secretary of State for Employment could apply to the **Industrial Court** for an order directing those persons responsible not to call, organise, procure or finance such an action, or to discontinue or defer it, for a period not longer than 60 days (see **cooling-off period).** The Secretary of State might also (s. 141) in circumstances similarly defined, apply to the Industrial Court for a ballot to be taken among the workers concerned, to be conducted under the supervision of the **Commission on Industrial Relations.** The procedures were discontinued from 31 July 1974 on the repeal of the Industrial Relations Act by the **Trade Union and Labour Relations Act 1974;** see also **employers' final offer.**

NATIONAL EXAMINATION BOARD IN SUPERVISORY STUDIES (NEBSS); see **Supervisory Studies, National Examination Board in.**

NATIONAL FARMERS' UNION (NFU); see **Farmers' Union, National.**

NATIONAL FEDERATION OF BUILDING TRADES EMPLOYERS

(NFBTE); see **Building Trades Employers, National Federation of.**

NATIONAL FEDERATION OF BUILDING TRADES OPERATIVES (NFBTO); see **Construction Unions, National Federation of.**

NATIONAL FEDERATION OF CONSTRUCTION UNIONS (NFCU); see **Construction Unions, National Federation of.**

NATIONAL FEDERATION OF PROFESSIONAL WORKERS (NFPW); see **Professional Workers, National Federation of.**

NATIONAL GRAPHICAL ASSOCIATION (NGA); see **Graphical Association, National.**

NATIONAL INCOMES COMMISSION (NIC). A body of five independent members set up in November 1962 to examine pay claims submitted to it by the two sides in the industry concerned, to examine the pay of groups of public servants when requested to do so by the government, and to comment on wage settlements already made. The Commission was formally abolished on the establishment of the **National Board for Prices and Incomes** in 1965. During its 2½ years of life the NIC, which formed one aspect of the Macmillan government's **wages policy** (q.v.) and a companion organisation to the **National Economic Development Council** (NEDC) (q.v.), reported on three settlements and acted in an arbitral capacity on the pay of university teachers. It was boycotted by trade unions on the advice of the Trades Union Congress as an agency of government and therefore lacking in real independence in its judgements on the outcome of collective bargaining, and was also criticised for its legalistic approach and slowness of operation; see Allan Fels, *The British Prices and Incomes Board*, CUP, 1972, Ch. 2.

NATIONAL INDUSTRIAL CONFERENCE. A conference of industries threatened by strikes called by the Lloyd George government in February 1919. The occasion for the Conference was a resurgence of industrial unrest after the end of the first world war, especially in engineering and mining. It appointed a provisional joint committee charged principally to consider hours, wages and conditions, unemployment and the best methods of promoting co-operation between capital and labour. This recommended, *inter alia*, a maximum legal working week, a national minimum wage, and an advisory National Industrial Council. The provisional joint committee lingered on until July 1921, but its recommendations were never adopted by government; see Rodger Charles, *The Development of Industrial Relations in Great Britain, 1911-1939*, Hutchinson, 1973.

NATIONAL INDUSTRIAL RELATIONS COURT (NIRC) or **Industrial Court.** A court with the status of the High Court established by the **Industrial Relations Act 1971**, s. 99 and Schedule 3, and abolished in 1974 when that Act was repealed. It was empowered to function as a court of original jurisdiction in cases involving collective disputes, **unfair industrial practices**, and in proceedings brought by one party to a collective agreement against another. Its appellate jurisdiction (s. 114) covered appeals on questions of law from an **industrial tribunal** in respect of all statutory and other claims over which such a tribunal has jurisdiction (except the Docks and Harbours Act, 1966, and the **Industrial Training Act 1964**), and certain appeals from the decisions of the then **Chief Registrar of Trade Unions and Employers' Associations** (s. 115). Where its appellate jurisdictions were concerned the NIRC was in 1976 replaced by the **Employment Appeal Tribunal** (q.v.); see R.W. Rideout *The Practice and Procedure of the National Industrial Relations Court,* Sweet and Maxwell, 1973.

NATIONAL INSTITUTE OF INDUSTRIAL PSYCHOLOGY (NIIP); see **Industrial Psychology, National Institute of.**

NATIONAL INSURANCE ACT 1911; see **unemployment benefit.**

NATIONAL INSURANCE ACT 1965; see **unemployment benefit** and **sickness benefit.**

NATIONAL INSURANCE (INDUSTRIAL INJURIES) ACT 1965; see **Industrial Injuries Acts.**

NATIONAL JOINT ADVISORY COUNCIL (NJAC). A formal and permanent body consisting of representatives of the **Confederation of British Industry** and of the **Trades Union Congress** sitting under the chairmanship of the Secretary of State for Employment 'to advise the Government on matters in which employers and workers have a common interest'. The Council was originally formed in October 1939, and has several times been reconstituted. In the 1950s and 1960s Committees of the NJAC published reports on *Practices Impeding the Full and Efficient Use of Manpower*, November 1958, *Sick Pay Schemes*, 1964, *Dismissal Procedures*, 1967, *Introduction of Shift Working*, 1968, *Pension Rights*, 1966, and *Hours of Employment of Women and Young Persons Employed in Factories*, 1969. In 1971, a small sub-committee was engaged in considering methods of payment of wages. The Council itself appears not to have met for upwards of ten years though it seems not to have been formally disbanded.

NATIONAL JOINT COUNCIL FOR THE BUILDING INDUSTRY (NJCBI); see **Building Industry, National Joint Council for the.**

NATIONAL LABOR RELATIONS ACT 1935; see **Wagner Act.**

NATIONAL LEAGUE OF THE BLIND AND DISABLED; see **Blind and Disabled, National League of the.**

NATIONAL AND LOCAL GOVERNMENT OFFICERS' ASSOCIATION (NALGO). A trade union founded in 1905 as the National Association of Local Government Officers and still retaining the initials NALGO as its short title, although changing its name to National and Local Government Officers' Association in 1952. As first conceived, the union catered solely for local government officers and the change of name was a recognition of the fact that the union had followed its members into the National Health Service, and into electricity, gas, water and other industries formerly associated with local government, but after the war made into national social services or public corporations. It claims to be the largest white collar union in the world and the fourth largest union in Britain. Affiliation to the Trades Union Congress was first raised in the union in 1921 and finally agreed to by the membership in 1964 (see D. Volker, 'NALGO's Affiliation to the TUC', *British Journal of Industrial Relations*, Vol. IV, No. 1, March 1966, pp. 59-76). The union has been notable for its moderation and for the extensiveness of its legal, voca-

tional, educational, educational and other services to members; in recent years, however, it has adopted more militant attitudes and in 1970 sanctioned its first official strike. Alec Spoor, *White Collar Unions: Sixty Years of NALGO*, Heinemann, 1967. *Address*: 1 Mapledon Place, London WC1H 9AJ. *Tel*: 01-388 2366. TUC Affiliated Membership, 1977: 683,011.

NATIONAL MARITIME BOARD (NMB). Originating in 1916 as the Mercantile Marine Conditions Committee and established with its present title on a permanent basis in 1920 as a joint negotiating body for wages and conditions of service in the Merchant Navy, to prevent and adjust differences between shipowners, masters, seamen and apprentices, and to establish a single source of supply of seamen controlled by shipowners and unions. The Board's agreements (to be found in the *National Maritime Board Year Book*) do not, except by special arrangement, apply to vessels under 200 tons gross or to certain other ships, including tugs and salvage vessels. It is composed of equal numbers of owners' representatives elected by the **General Council of British Shipping** (with one additional representative for the British Railways Board and one Naval Director of Stores), and of employees' representatives from the trade unions concerned. Its detailed operation is carried on in six panels for shipmasters (employees represented by the Mercantile Marine Service Association and the **Merchant Navy and Airline Officers' Association**; navigating officers (MNAOA); engineer officers (MNAOA and MMSA and AUEW); radio officers (**Radio and Electronic Officers' Union**); sailors and firemen (**National Union of Seamen**, plus one seat for the Shipconstructors' and Shipwrights' Association - **Amalgamated Union of Boilermakers, Shipwrights, Blacksmiths and Structural Workers**); and for catering (NUS); see D.H. Moreby, *Personnel Management in Merchant Ships*, Pergamon Press, 1968, pp. 197-9 and J. McConville, *The Shipping Industry in the United Kingdom*, International Institute for Labour Studies, 1977, pp. 3-10, *Address*: 17-18 Bury Street, London EC3. *Tel*: 01-283 9610.

NATIONAL MINIMUM WAGE. A governmental provision whereby wages are not allowed to fall below a national minimum level, thereby relieving poverty among low paid employed workers.

National minimum wage systems operate, for example, in France, the Netherlands, Canada and the United States of America. In Britain the principle of the national minimum wage has not so far been accepted, though the **Royal Commission on Trade Unions and Employers' Associations, 1965-1968** (p. 71, para. 280) recommended that it should be considered, and Rule 2 of the **Trades Union Congress** contains as an object 'a legal minimum wage for each industry or occupation' dating from the early 1920s when the question was under active discussion (see R.L. Bowlby, 'Union Policy Toward Minimum Wage Legislation in Post-war Britain', *Industrial and Labor Relations Review*, Vol. 11, No. 1, October 1957, pp. 72-84, and the reply by F.J. Bayliss and rejoinder, *Review* Vol. 12, No. 1, October 1958, pp. 113-23), other methods being preferred to deal with problems of low paid workers (see **Wages Councils, Agricultural Wages Acts, fair wages principle, Schedule 11**). The preference given to the lowest paid workers by prices and incomes policy after 1965, increased the extent of evidence about them (see, for example, Derek Robinson, 'Low Paid Workers and Incomes Policy', *Oxford University Institute of Statistics Bulletin*, Vol. 29, No. 1, February 1967, pp. 1-30), and growing criticism of the effectiveness of Wages Councils have revived interest in the national minimum wage concept, which was reported on by an Inter-Departmental Working Party in 1969 (DEP, *National Minimum Wage*, HMSO, 1969). No **International Labour Conventions** or **Recommendations** bear directly on a national minimum wage, though some deal with minimum wage fixing machinery, both generally and in particular industries; see (**International Labour Convention No. 131** and **Recommendation 135**, 1970, not accepted by the UK Government); see also **low pay**, and in the United States, C. and R. Campbell, 'State Minimum Wage Laws as a Cause of Unemployment', *Southern Economic Journal*, 1969 and D.E. Kaun, *Economics of the Minimum Wage: the Effects of the Fair Labour Standards Act, 1945-1960*, PhD Thesis, Stanford University, 1963.

NATIONAL MINORITY MOVEMENT. A militant left wing movement of trade unionists begun by the miners in 1923, launched in 1924 and associated with the names of Tom Mann as president and Harry Pollitt as general secretary, with the object of uniting the workers through factory committees, strengthening **trades councils,** and achieving **workers' control of** industry, Allen Hutt, *Postwar History of the British Working Class,* EP Publishing, 1974; Alan Fox, *History of the National Union of Boot and Shoe Operatives*, Blackwell, 1958, p. 466 *et seq.*; Wal Hannington, *Never On Our Knees*, Lawrence and Wishart, 1967, p. 182 *et seq.*, and Roderick Martin, *Communism and the British Trade Unions, 1924-1933,* Clarendon Press, Oxford, 1969.

NATIONAL MODERNISATION COMMITTEE. A body established by the National Joint Council for the Port Transport Industry to carry through a two-stage programme of reform of industrial relations in the docks as recommended by the **Devlin Report** (*Report of the Committee of Inquiry into certain matters concerning the Port Transport Industry*, Cmnd. 2734, August 1965). Stage I envisaged modifications and tightening up of the **Dock Labour Scheme** (q.v.), transferability of dock labour, work-sharing and abolition of casual practices; Stage II, beginning in December, 1968, proposed abolition of all other restrictions on the effective use of labour on the docks, and a review of the wages structure of the industry; see also, Report of a *Court of Inquiry into a dispute between the parties represented on the National Joint Council for the Port Transport Industry*, Cmnd. 4429, July 1970, and D.F. Wilson, *Dockers; The Impact of Industrial Change,* Fontana/Collins, 1972, M. Mellish, *The Docks After Devlin*, Heinemann, 1972, and **Aldington-Jones Report**.

NATIONAL NEWSPAPER INDUSTRY, JOINT BOARD FOR THE. A joint committee of managements and trade union officials in the national newspaper industry established in 1964 under the independent chairmanship of Lord Devlin, with the object 'to examine all the circumstances of publication and production of national newspapers with the intention of making recommendations to the Newspaper Proprietors' Association and to the printing trade unions which will lead to increased efficiency'. The Board was a follow-up to the criticisms aroused by the **Shawcross Report** of 1962 (q.v.). It was responsible for the Economist Intelligence Unit's survey *The National Newspaper Industry*, 1966, but was relatively ineffective in promoting change in the industry. It went into abeyance in 1967.

NATIONAL NEWSPAPER STEER-

ING GROUP. A joint committee of printing trade unions, the **Newspaper Publishers' Association** and individual managements of national newspapers, established after the settlement of the stoppage of work by members of the **Society of Graphical and Allied Trades** in June 1970, with the object of achieving greater stability in the industry by developing an improved wages structure, securing more effective utilisation of labour and technical resources, providing adequate training and introducing workable written procedures. The Group ceased to operate after early meetings had been held.

NATIONAL POWERLOADING AGREEMENT; see Powerloading Agreements.

NATIONAL PRODUCTION ADVISORY COUNCIL ON INDUSTRY (NPACI). A body first formed in 1941 on which the Chancellor of the Exchequer formerly met representatives of employers and workers and which acted as a forum for consultation on government policy and procedure affecting industrial production. At one time the NPACI met quarterly, but no meetings have taken place for some years. It now seems that it is defunct.

NATIONAL SECTIONAL PANELS; see Sectional Panels.

NATIONAL SOCIETY OF BRUSHMAKERS AND GENERAL WORKERS (NSBGW); see Brushmakers and General Workers, National Society of.

NATIONAL SOCIETY OF METAL MECHANICS (NSMM); see Metal Mechanics, National Society of.

NATIONAL SOCIETY OF METAL MECHANICS against NEWTOWN POLISHING CO. LTD Industrial Court Awards 3026 and 3069; see **claims procedure.**

NATIONAL SOCIETY OF OPERATIVE PRINTERS AND ASSISTANTS (NATSOPA); see Operative Printers, Graphical and Media Personnel, National Society of.

NATIONAL STRIKE; see general strike.

NATIONAL UNEMPLOYED WORKERS' MOVEMENT. A militant movement, originating in 1920, associated particularly with the name of Wal Han-

nington and demanding 'Work or Full Maintenance'. The methods of the movement were rejected by the Labour Party and by the **Trades Union Congress.** Its original title, National Unemployed Workers' Committee Movement, was adopted at a conference of local unemployed organisations in Manchester in November 1921, and the word 'Committee' dropped some years later. It was responsible for the National **Hunger Marches** of 1922, of 1927 (with the South Wales Miners), 1930, 1932, 1934 and 1936 and conducted its last campaign in 1939. Its activities were partly responsible for the '**Black Circular**' (q.v.). A first hand account of the NAWM by its chief organiser is given in Wal Hannington, *Never On Our Knees*, Lawrence and Wishart, 1967.

NATIONAL UNION OF AGRICULTURAL AND ALLIED WORKERS; see Agricultural and Allied Workers, National Union of.

NATIONAL UNION OF BANK EMPLOYEES (NUBE); see Bank Employees, National Union of.

NATIONAL UNION OF BASKET, CANE AND FIBRE FURNITURE MAKERS OF GREAT BRITAIN AND IRELAND (NUB); see Basket, Cane and Fibre Furniture Makers of Great Britain and Ireland, National Union of.

NATIONAL UNION OF BOOT AND SHOE OPERATIVES (NUBSO); see Footwear, Leather and Allied Trades, National Union of.

NATIONAL UNION OF DOMESTIC APPLIANCE AND GENERAL METAL WORKERS (NUDAGMW); see Domestic Appliance and General Metal Workers, National Union of.

NATIONAL UNION OF DYERS, BLEACHERS AND TEXTILE WORKERS (NUDB and TW); see Dyers, Bleachers and Textile Workers, National Union of.

NATIONAL UNION OF FLINT GLASS WORKERS; see Flint Glass Workers, National Union of.

NATIONAL UNION OF FOOTWEAR, LEATHER AND ALLIED TRADES; see Footwear, Leather and Allied Trades, National Union of.

NATIONAL UNION OF FUNERAL SERVICE OPERATIVES (NUFSO); see Funeral Service Operatives, National Union of.

NATIONAL UNION OF FURNITURE TRADES OPERATIVES (NUFTO); see Furniture Trades Operatives, National Union of.

NATIONAL UNION OF GENERAL AND MUNICIPAL WORKERS; see General and Municipal Workers' Union.

NATIONAL UNION OF GOLD, SILVER AND ALLIED TRADES; see Gold Silver and Allied Trades, National Union of.

NATIONAL UNION OF HOSIERY AND KNITWEAR WORKERS; see Hosiery and Knitwear Workers, National Union of.

NATIONAL UNION OF INSURANCE WORKERS (NUIW); see Insurance Workers, National Union of.

NATIONAL UNION OF JOURNALISTS (NUJ); see Journalists, National Union of.

NATIONAL UNION OF LOCK AND METAL WORKERS (NULMW); see Lock and Metal Workers, National Union of.

NATIONAL UNION OF MINEWORKERS (NUM); see Mineworkers, National Union of.

NATIONAL UNION OF PRINTING, BOOKBINDING AND PAPER WORKERS (NUPB and PW); see Graphical and Allied Trades, Society of.

NATIONAL UNION OF PUBLIC EMPLOYEES (NUPE); see Public Employees, National Union of.

NATIONAL UNION OF RAILWAYMEN (NUR); see Railwaymen, National Union of.

NATIONAL UNION OF RAILWAYMEN v. SULLIVAN AND OTHERS; see Negotiating Licence.

NATIONAL UNION OF SCALEMAKERS (NUS); see Scalemakers, National Union of.

NATIONAL UNION OF SEAMEN (NUS); see Seamen, National Union of.

NATIONAL UNION OF SHEET METAL WORKERS, COPPERSMITHS, HEATING AND DOMESTIC ENGINEERS (NUSMWC H AND DE); see Sheet Metal Workers, Coppersmiths, Heating and Domestic Engineers, National Union of.

NATIONAL UNION OF TAILORS AND GARMENT WORKERS (NUTGW); see Tailors and Garment Workers, National Union of.

NATIONAL UNION OF TEACHERS (NUT); see Teachers, National Union of.

NATIONAL UNION OF TEXTILE AND ALLIED WORKERS (NUTAW); see Textile and Allied Workers, National Union of.

NATIONAL UNION OF VEHICLE BUILDERS (NUVB); see Vehicle Builders, National Union of.

NATIONAL UNION OF WALLCOVERINGS, DECORATIVE AND ALLIED TRADES; see Wallcoverings, Decorative and Allied Trades, National Union of.

NATIONAL WAGES POLICY; see wage policy.

NATIONAL WHITLEY COUNCIL; see Whitleyism.

NATIONAL WOOL SORTERS' SOCIETY; see Wool Sorters' Society, National.

NATSOPA. National Society of Operative Printers and Assistants; see Printers Graphical and Media Personnel, National Society of Operatives.

NATTKE. National Association of Theatrical Television and Kine Employees; see Theatrical, Television and Kine Employees, National Association of.

NATURAL WASTAGE; see wastage.

NAVVY. Abbreviation of 'navigator'. A labourer employed in the work of excavating and constructing a 'navigation' or canal; later extended to cover excavation and construction of other kinds, for railways, drains, roads, etc; see Terry Coleman, *The Railway Navvies*, Hutchinson, 1965; Donall Macamhaigh, *An Irish Navvy*, Routledge and Kegan Paul, 1976; A.J.M. Sykes, 'Navvies: their work attitudes', *Sociology*, Vol. 3, pp. 21-35, and 'Navvies: their social relations', *Sociology*, Vol. 3, pp. 157-72.

NBPI. National Board for Prices and Incomes (q.v.).

NCEO. National Confederation of Employers' Organisations (q.v.).

NCLC. National Council of Labour Colleges (q.v.).

NEBSS. National Examination Board in Supervisory Studies; see **Supervisory Studies, National Examination Board in.**

NEGATIVE STRIKE. A strike to prevent the worsening of wages and conditions by an employer - a **defense** or **defensive strike.** The opposite of a **positive strike,** i.e. a strike with the object of improving wages and conditions. Principally USA.

NEGOTIATING LICENCE. A licence to negotiate provided for in the Republic of Ireland under the Trade Union Act 1941. The Act makes it unlawful for any body of persons to carry on negotiations on the fixing of wages or other conditions of employment without such a licence, under penalty of an immediate fine and a continuing penalty for every day on which the offence is committed. It also provides for a special tribunal to resolve jurisdictional disputes; s. 3 of the Act, incorporating this provision, was declared unconstitutional by the Supreme Court in the case of **National Union of Railwaymen v. Sullivan and others,** SC, IR, p. 77 (in which that union was contesting a claim of the **Irish Transport and General Workers Union to** have the sole right to represent workers in the statutory transport undertaking, CIE) on the grounds that no law could take away the citizen's **freedom of association.** This decision has inhibited the use of negotiating licences to limit numbers of trade unions. G.F. Daly, *Industrial Relations, Comparative Aspects*, The Mercier Press, 1968.

NEGOTIATING   PROCEDURE. Strictly defined, a procedure for negotiating new collective agreements (see D.T.B. North and G.L. Buckingham, *Productivity Agreements and Wage Systems,* Gower Press, 1969); most frequently not, however, explicitly distinguished from other procedures; see **grievance.**

NEGOTIATION. A method of joint decision making involving bargaining between representatives of workers and representatives of management or of employers, with the object of establishing mutually acceptable terms and conditions of employment, including wages, hours, working conditions, etc.; the process involved in **collective bargaining** and resulting in **collective agreements.** A distinction is often made between negotiation and **consultation** (q.v.), the former being regarded as implying competitive rivalry for domination between conflicting interests, or an **adversary situation,** bargaining resulting in compromise seldom entirely satisfactory to either side, and the latter as being noncompetitive and concerned with common interests and wholly integrated conclusions; see National Institute of Industrial Psychology, *Joint Consultation in British Industry*, Staples Press, 1952, p. 28. Such a distinction has not necessarily been borne out in practice or accepted in theory; see **joint consultation**; R.E. Walton and R.B. McKersie, *A Behavioral Theory of Labor Negotiations,* McGraw-Hill, 1965 and J.Z. Rubin and B.R. Brown, *The Social Psychology of Bargaining and Negotiation*, Academic Press, 1975.

NETWORK ANALYSIS. A generic term used to describe a number of management techniques used to plan and control complex processes and projects consisting of a set of inter-related activities. The object is to reduce to diagrammatical form on paper the paths followed by the component parts of the different activities on a time scale which will indicate how and where they can be brought together at the appropriate points, the whole taking the form of a complex of lines and circles from which a critical path can be chosen; hence **Critical Path Method** (CPM). **Programme Evaluation Review Technique** (PERT) acknowledges, while following a similar system, that the time allowed to complete a particular activity cannot be predicted exactly, and makes appropriate allowance for this. Network Analysis techniques can be used in a wide variety of circumstances, such as the launching of new products, production scheduling, construction projects, etc; see K.G. Lockyer, *An Introduction to Critical Path Analysis*, Pitman, 3rd ed., 1969.

NEUTRAL COMMITTEES. A device

built in to the disputes procedure in many sections of the iron and steel industry, formerly accepted between the Iron and Steel Employers' Association and the **Iron and Steel Trades Confederation** and agreed in 1946 between the ISTEA and the **National Union of Blastfurnacemen**, and now continued by the British Steel Corporation. The procedure establishes that, after failure-to-agree upon a difference at the works and by a joint district committee, the parties may appoint a neutral committee consisting of two employers' and two union representatives, none of the representatives being officials of either side or appointed from the works concerned, the committee having plenary powers to issue a memorandum of settlement signed by all parties. Failing such a settlement, the difference can be referred back to the employer and the union concerned and, if necessary, passed on to their head offices and ultimately to arbitration for settlement. Ministry of Labour, *Industrial Relations Handbook*, HMSO, 1961, p. 43 *et seq*.

NEW EARNINGS SURVEY; see earnings.

NEW MODEL UNIONS; see New Unionism.

NEW UNIONISM. An expression used to describe a number of experimental or formative periods in trade union structure and activity, especially 1830-34 (attempts to set up federations, national unions, and **one big union**, the Grand National Consolidated Trade Union, ending in a succession of strikes and a shift of attention to political rather than trade union methods); 1845-52 (the building of new unions with practical industrial aims, often relatively centralised, with high dues, benefits, craft consciousness and permanent officials, of which the Amalgamated Society of Engineers of 1851 has come to be considered the most pattern-setting for the mid-Victorian period - sometimes called **new model unions**); and 1889-90 (the wave of enthusiasm for organising unskilled workers which followed the Dock Strike of 1889 into more militant unions with strike rather than friendly benefits and relatively low dues and socialist aims, out of which emerged the general unions of today and the direct trade union sponsorship of candidates for parliament); see Sidney and Beatrice Webb, *History of Trade Unionism, 1666-1920*, 1919; G.D.H. Cole, *A Short History of the British Working Class*

Movement, 1789-1947, George Allen and Unwin, revised ed., 1948 and W. Milne Bailey, *Trade Union Documents*, G. Bell and Sons, 1929; also on new model unions, J.B. Jefferys, *Story of the Engineers*, Lawrence and Wishart, 1945 and EP Publishing 1971, and on general unionism after 1889, E.J. Hobsbawn, 'General Labour Unions in Britain, 1889-1914', *Economic History Review* (2), 1, 2, and 3, 1948-49.

NEWSPAPER PUBLISHERS' ASSOCIATION (NPA). Known until 1968 as the Newspaper Proprietors' Association. An employers' association formed in 1906 as a result of the decision by a number of national newspaper proprietors to secede from the London Master Printers' Association. Membership of the NPA is confined to national daily and Sunday newspapers (some, however, with offices in Manchester), and to evening papers published in London (provincial morning, evening and London suburban weekly newspapers being in membership of the **Newspaper Society** (q.v.) and Scottish newspapers of the **Scottish Daily Newspaper Society** or the Scottish Newspaper Proprietors' Association). The NPA holds collective agreements with printing, maintenance and journalists' unions (see NPA, *Handbook of Agreements*) and is responsible for settlement of all labour disputes in national newspaper offices in London and Manchester. Since 1959 negotiations and day-to-day action on industrial relations have been handled by a Labour Executive Committee composed of representatives of each major newspaper group at management level, meeting weekly and advised by a London Labour Committee and a Manchester Managers' Committee of labour specialists. In the 1960s the NPA became closely involved in the development of plant (or house) bargaining in the industry, both in an advisory and problem resolving role, especially in relation to **comprehensive agreements** (q.v.). On the situation in Fleet Street during and since that time, see K. Sisson, *Industrial Relations in Fleet Street*, Blackwell, 1975. The NPA also negotiates collectively with wholesalers and with rail and freight organisations on arrangements for the distribution of national newspapers and provides for the joint recognition of advertising agencies. It maintains a Marketing Department with the object of increasing advertising and sales and provides a training service to all national newspaper offices. *Address*: 8 Bouverie Street, London EC4Y 8AY. *Tel*: 01-583 8132.

NEWSPAPER SOCIETY. An organisation of provincial newspaper proprietors (outside Scotland) originating as the Provincial Newspaper Society in 1836 and taking its present title in 1889. Until 1917 the Newspaper Society did not concern itself with labour matters so that national newspaper proprietors saw nothing inconsistent in being members both of the Society and of their own Newspaper Proprietors' Association (see **Newspaper Publishers' Association**) for labour purposes. After two reconstructions in 1916 and 1917, the Society made the decision to negotiate on behalf of its members and made its first national agreement in 1919 in conjunction with the British Federation of Master Printers (now the **British Printing Industries Federation** q.v.). It still negotiates jointly with the BFMP on many matters through a Joint Labour Committee. In 1921 it amalgamated with the Linotype Users' Association (1894), the Northern Federation of Newspaper Owners (1904) and the Newspaper Federation (earlier the Federation of Southern Newspaper Owners, 1909), all of which had earlier broken away to negotiate independently with trade unions. The scope of the Society's work expanded considerably during and after the 1939-45 war, and it now maintains specialised departments dealing with technical questions, work study, training, industrial relations, advertising and editorial matters; see the following Newspaper Society publications: *The Provincial Newspaper Society*, 1886; *The Newspaper Society, 1836-1936*; *Yesterday, Today, Tomorrow*, 1948; *Newspaper Society's 125 Years of Progress*, 1961, and a quarterly technical journal, *Newspaper Society Production Journal. Address:* Whitefriars House, 6 Carmelite Street, London EC4Y 0BL. *Tel:* 01-353 4722.

NEWTOWN POLISHING CO. LTD AND NATIONAL SOCIETY OF METAL MECHANICS. Industrial Court Awards 3026 and 3069; see **claims procedure.**

NFBTE. National Federation of Building Trades Employers; see **Building Trades Employers, National Federation of.**

NFBTO; see **Construction Unions, National Federation of.**

NFCU. National Federation of Construction Unions; see **Construction Unions, National Federation of.**

NFPW. National Federation of Professional Workers; see **Professional Workers, National Federation of.**

NFU. National Farmers' Union; see **Farmers' Union, National.**

NGA. National Graphical Association; see **Graphical Association, National.**

NIGHT SHIFT. Either the alternative to **dayshift,** i.e. a second shift, or the third of three shifts, i.e. in **double day shifts,** or in **three shift systems.**

NIGHT WORK. Defined by **International Labour Convention No. 89,** for women, as work with a period of at least 11 consecutive hours including an interval of 7 consecutive hours beween 10 p.m. and 7 a.m. and for young persons (**International Labour Convention No. 90**) as a period of at least 12 consecutive hours including an interval of at least 7 consecutive hours between 10 a.m. and 7 p.m. These Conventions have not been ratified by the United Kingdom, but the **Hours of Employment (Conventions) Act 1936** prohibits night work for women as a general rule and the **Employment of Women, Young Persons and Children Act 1920** performs a similar function for young persons, though the **Factories Act 1961** permits male young persons to be employed at night in certain industries (s. 117). The **Trades Union Congress** would prefer a more limited definition of 'night', namely the period 6 p.m. to 8 a.m. A Report of a Working Party of the National Joint Advisory Council, *Hours of Work of Women and Young Persons employed in Factories,* HMSO, 1969, recommended the adoption of the definition of 'night' in Convention No. 89, but differed on other restrictions for young persons.

NIIP. National Institute of Industrial Psychology; see **Industrial Psychology, National Institute of.**

NINE HOURS MOVEMENT. A movement for a 54-hour working week or nine hour working day among the engineering workers of Tyneside which led in 1871 to a strike lasting some five months and to the claim being conceded. The Amalgamated Society of Engineers appears to have stood aloof from the claim of the Nine Hours' League in 1871 though this resulted in a general reduction of engineering hours which the union later defended;

see E. Allen, J.F. Clarke, N. McCord and D.J. Rowe, *The North-East Engineers' Strike of 1871*, Frank Graham, 1971.

1922 PROCEDURE AGREEMENT - MANUAL WORKERS; see **Engineering Procedure Agreement.**

NIRC. National Industrial Relations Court (q.v.).

NJAC. National Joint Advisory Council (q.v.).

NJCBI. National Joint Council for the Building Industry; see **Building Industry, National Joint Council for the.**

NOB. Abbreviation for 'not on bonus'.

NOMENCLATURE GÉNÉRALE DES ACTIVITÉS ÉCONOMIQUES DES COMMUNAUTÉS EUROPÉENNES (NACE). A classification of production units by industry developed for common use in the European Economic Community; the EEC equivalent of the **Standard Industrial Classification** (q.v.) currently in use in the United Kingdom. NACE was developed in a number of stages beginning in 1961 and completed in 1970 for the six original EEC members; see Statistical Office of the European Communities, *NACE: General Industrial Classification of Economic Activities within the European Communities*, Luxembourg, January 1970. It is likely to be adopted for UK use in 1983 in place of the current 1968 SIC.

NOMINATION PROCEDURE. A procedure enabling members of trade unions to nominate people to receive money due from the union on the member's death other than under a will or on intestacy. The sum covered by the procedure is at present limited to £1,500 (**Administration of Estates (Small Payments) Act 1965**). The Industrial Relations (Nomination) Regulations 1977, SI No. 789, makes provision for the revocation of a nomination, the making of nominations to one or several people, and protection for a union which makes a payment in ignorance of a marriage; see also **benefits.**

NON-COMPLIANCE MEN; see **out-of-compliance men.**

NON-CONTINUOUS THREE SHIFT SYSTEM; see **three shift system.**

NON-DISCRIMINATION NOTICE; see **Sex Discrimination Act 1975** and **Race Relations Acts.**

NON-FEDERATED FIRM. A firm not in membership of an **employer's association** or federation for industrial relations purposes, and hence one which negotiates directly with a trade union or trade unions without such intermediary assistance or advice; see also **federated firm.** Non-federated firms may also, of course, be unorganised. Reasons for remaining nonfederated frequently include the consideration that federation would inhibit the kind of relationships bargaining preferred by the firm concerned; see A.I. Marsh, *Industrial Relations in Engineering*, Pergamon Press, 1965, p. 51.

NON-INDUSTRIAL CIVIL SERVANT; see **industrial civil servant.**

NON-JUDICIABLE ARBITRATION; see **contract arbitration.**

NON-JUDICIABLE DISPUTES; see **interest disputes.**

NON-MANUAL WORKER; see **white collar worker.**

NONS. Workers who are not members of trade unions; non-unionists; see also **out-of-compliance men.**

NON-SERVICE WORKERS; see **service workers.**

NON-WAGE INCOMES. Incomes derived from rents, interest, fees, dividends, profits, capital or speculative gains and similar sources independent of wage and salary determination in collective bargaining, and therefore forming an important part of the theory and application of **incomes policy;** see D. Robinson, *Non-Wage Incomes and Prices Policy, Report of a Trade Union Seminar*, Organisation for Economic Co-operation and Development, 1966.

NON-WORKING CHARGEHAND; see **chargehand.**

NO-POACHING AGREEMENT. An agreement or understanding between trade unions not to attempt to recruit each other's members; sometimes known as a **no-raiding agreement.** In Britain, such an arrangement is principally represented by the **Bridlington Agreement** (q.v.) though non-poaching agreements exist in writing between particular unions and also informally, particularly at workplace level; see also **spheres of influence agreement** and **inter-union disputes**. Similar agreements between employers concerned with 'enticement of labour' are sometimes known as **anti-pirating agreements** (q.v.); see also **form of inquiry**.

NO-RAIDING AGREEMENT; see **no-poaching agreement**.

NORM. A rule, a standard, or a pattern for action (*International Encyclopaedia of the Social Sciences*, Macmillan and Free Press, 1968, p. 204); hence a **normative system**: a set of integrated norms consistently related according to certain principles (Alan Fox and Allan Flanders 'Collective Bargaining: From Donovan to Durkheim', *British Journal of Industrial Relations*, July 1969). 'Norm' as used in **incomes policy** (q.v.): an overall average in conformity with which incomes might be allowed to rise within a specified period.

NORMATIVE SYSTEM; see **norm**.

NORTHERN CARPET TRADE UNION; see **Carpet Trade Union, Northern**.

NOS NOD. Abbreviation for 'no shillings and no pence'. A system of pay-day or **payroll simplification** (q.v.) doing away with all coins in the wage packet and paying (before decimalisation) to the nearest 10s. note; H.P. Cemach, 'Nos Nod Needed Now', *Office Management*, March 1957. The usual practice was to round off to the nearest 10s. *above*; to round off downwards might be considered a breach of the **Truck Acts** (q.v.).

NO-STRIKE CLAUSE or **PEACE CLAUSE.** A clause in a **collective agreement**, and usually in a **procedure agreement**, to the effect that the parties to the agreement undertake not to take industrial action against each other, either by way of **strike, lock-out** or other means, or, more usually, that they undertake not to take such action until the procedure laid down has been exhausted, i.e. that the specified procedural stages have been followed, a failure-to-agree recorded at the final stage, and, in some cases, recourse to **conciliation** and/or **arbitration** having been tried without success. The existence of a no-strike clause of the former kind suggests that all industrial action is unconstitutional, while the latter implies that such action after procedure has been exhausted is constitutional but that before or during the time procedure is being operated, unconstitutional; see **constitutional strike, unconstitutional strike**. Under s. 18(4) of the **Trade Union and Labour Relations Act 1974**, no-strike clauses in collective agreements are legally unenforceable unless the relevant collective agreement is in writing, expressly permits the incorporation of the clause into the individual contract, is accessible and available to the employee and unless the individual contract expressedly or impliedly incorporates the clause.

NOTIFIABLE ACCIDENT. An accident causing loss of life or disabling a worker for more than three days from earning full wages from the work at which he was employed which the **Factories Act 1961**, s. 80, requires shall be reported to an inspector appointed by the Health and Safety Executive (see **Health and Safety at Work Act 1974**).

NOTTINGHAM AND DISTRICT DYERS' AND BLEACHERS' ASSOCIATION; see **Dyers' and Bleachers' Association, Nottingham and District**.

NPA. Newspaper Publishers' Association (q.v.).

NPACI. National Production Advisory Council on Industry (q.v.).

NSBGW. National Society of Brushmakers and General Workers; see **Brushmakers and General Workers, National Society of**.

NSMM. National Society of Metal Mechanics; see **Metal Mechanics, National Society of**.

NUAAW. National Union of Agricultural and Allied Workers; see **Agricultural and Allied Workers, National Union of**.

NUB. National Union of Blastfurnacemen, Ore Miners, Coke Workers and Kindred Trades; see **Blastfurnacemen, Ore Miners, Coke Workers and Kindred Trades, National Union of**, and National Union of Basket, Cane and Fibre Furniture Makers of Great Britain and Ireland; see **Basket, Cane and Fibre Furniture Makers of Great Britain and Ireland, National Union of**.

NUBE. National Union of Bank Employees; see **Bank Employees, National Union of.**

NUBSO. National Union of Boot and Shoe Operatives; see **Footwear and Allied Trades, National Union of.**

NUCISE. National Union of Co-operative Insurance Society Employees; see **Co-operative Insurance Society Employees, National Union of.**

NUCLEUS LABOUR FORCE SCHEME. One of three transfer schemes administered by the Employment Service Division of the **Manpower Services Commission** (the others being the **Employment Transfer Scheme** and the **Key Workers Scheme** (q.v.). The Nucleus Labour Force Scheme assisted unemployed workers recruited in areas of high unemployment who moved temporarily for training to the parent factories of firms setting up new establishments in the workers' home areas. It has now been discontinued.

NUDAGMW. National Union of Domestic Appliance and General Metal Workers; see **Domestic Appliance and General Metal Workers, National Union of.**

NUDB and TW. National Union of Dyers, Bleachers and Textile Workers; see **Dyers, Bleachers and Textile Workers, National Union of.**

NUFLAT. National Union of Footwear, Leather and Allied Trades; see **Footwear, Leather and Allied Trades, National Union of.**

NUFSO. National Union of Funeral Service Operatives; see **Funeral Service Operatives, National Union of.**

NUFTO. National Union of Furniture Trades, Operatives; see **Furniture Trades Operatives, National Union of.**

NUGSAT; National Union of Gold, Silver and Allied Trades; see **Gold, Silver and Allied Trades, National Union of.**

NUGMW. National Union of General and Municipal Workers; see **General and Municipal Workers' Union.**

NUHKW. National Union of Hosiery and Knitwear Workers; see **Hosiery and Knitwear Workers, National Union of.**

NUIW. National Union of Insurance Workers; see **Insurance Workers, National Union of.**

NUJ. National Union of Journalists; see **Journalists, National Union of.**

NUJJER. A member of the **National Union of Journalists** (q.v.).

NULMW. National Union of Lock and Metal Workers; see **Lock and Metal Workers, National Union of.**

NUM. National Union of Mineworkers; see **Mineworkers, National Union of.**

NUMBER 10 AGREEMENT. National Agreement No. 10 on Wages and Working Conditions between the Employers' Federation of Papermakers and Boardmakers (now the **British Paper and Board Industry Federation**) and the Society of Graphical and Allied Trades, Transport and General Workers' Union and General and Municipal Workers' Union. The Agreement had its origin in a Memorandum of Agreement of September 1943 on Wages and Working Conditions in Board Mills.

NUPB and PW. National Union of Printing, Bookbinding and Paper Workers; see **Graphical and Allied Trades, Society of.**

NUPE. National Union of Public Employees; see **Public Employees, National Union of.**

NUR. National Union of Railwaymen; see **Railwaymen, National Union of.**

NURSERIES AND CHILD MINDERS' REGULATION ACT 1948; see **Day Nurseries.**

NUS. National Union of Seamen; see **Seamen, National Union of;** also National Union of Students, and National Union of Scalemakers; see **Scalemakers, National Union of.**

NUSMWC H AND DE. National Union of Sheet Metal Workers, Coppersmiths, Heating and Domestic Engineers; see **Sheet Metal Workers, Coppersmiths, Heating and Domestic Engineers, National Union of.**

NUT; see **Teachers, National Union of.**

NUTAW. National Union of Textile and

Allied Workers; see **Textile and Allied Workers, National Union of.**

NUTGW. National Union of Tailors and Garment Workers, see **Tailors and Garment Workers, National Union of.**

NUVB. National Union of Vehicle Builders; see **Vehicle Builders, National Union of.**

O

O AND M. Organisation and Methods (q.v.).

OB. Organisational Behaviour (q.v.).

OBSERVATION RATIO STUDY; see **activity sampling.**

OCCUPATION. A term usually applied to a person's trade, vocation, or principal way of making a living, e.g. a carpenter, teacher or bookmaker. For purposes of statistical or **occupational analysis,** a collection of 'jobs' or 'positions' having sufficiently similar task content or status to be grouped under a common title, for example in the **International Standard Classification of Occupations** (q.v.) or **Classification of Occupations and Directory of Occupational Titles** (CODOT) Arthur Salz, in S. Nosow, and W.H. Form (eds), *Man, Work and Society, A Reader in the Sociology of Occupations,* Basic Books Inc., 1962, Ch. III, 1, points out that the word 'occupation' can be fixed for limited periods only and must cover three different sets of facts, 'technological - the specific manual or mental operations involved in the execution of occupational work; economic - the income yield of the occupation which serves to provide a livelihood; and social - the prestige attaching to a person or group by virtue of occupation'; see also J.H. Goldthorpe and K. Hope, *The Social Grading of Occupations. A New Approach and Scale,* OUP, 1974, and D. Dunkerley, *Occupations and Society.* Routledge and Kegan Paul, 1975.

OCCUPATIONAL ANALYSIS. Defined by the **Department of Employment** as 'the process of examining in detail all available evidence, including job descriptions and specifications concerning jobs in order to identify those that are sufficiently similar with regard to their main tasks to be grouped together under a common occupation-title. When the analysis is completed an occupational description can be produced', *Glossary of Training Terms,* HMSO, 1967.

OCCUPATIONAL COMMUNITY. A concept centring around the notion that there are groups of workers who are affected by their work in such a way that their non-work lives are dominated by their work relationships, or to such an extent that they would reject the idea that any distinction between 'non-work' and 'work' properly exists. Definitions differ in emphasis; e.g. J. Gerstl ('Determination of Occupational Community in High Status Occupations', *Sociological Quarterly,* 1961, pp. 37-48);) 'an occupational community means that people who are members of the same occupation or who work together have some sort of common life together and are to some extent separate from the rest of society - [involves] the convergence of informal friendship patterns and colleague relations'; or C.W. Mills (*White Collar: The American Middle Classes,* Galaxy, 1956, pp. 222-3) 'the craftsman pattern [in which] there is no split between work and play'. Graeme Salaman (*Community and Occupation,* CUP, 1974, Ch. 2) develops the idea of degree of occupational community and attempts to describe its components and determinants.

OCCUPATIONAL EARNINGS SURVEYS; see **earnings.**

OCCUPATIONAL GUIDANCE also Occupational Guidance Service, and Occupational Guidance Units; see **vocational guidance.**

OCCUPATIONAL INTEREST ASSOCIATIONS. A term used by the Organisational Behaviour Research Group of the London Graduate School of Business Studies to describe both **trade unions** and **professional associations;** see Malcolm Warner and Lex Donaldson, 'Dimensions of Organisation in Occupational Interest Associations', *Third Joint Conference on Industrial Relations and Manpower Organisation,* London 21 December 1971 and Malcolm Warner, 'An Organisation Profile of the Small Trade Union', *Industrial Relations Journal,* Winter 1972.

OCCUPATIONAL MOBILITY. Mobility of labour between occupations or jobs. Occupational mobility appears to be inversely related to skill where manual workers are concerned: G.Bancroft and S. Garfinkle, 'Job Mobility in 1961', *Monthly Labor Review*, Vol. 86, 1963; see also **labour mobility**.

OCCUPATIONAL PENSION SCHEMES. Retirement benefits provided for employees in private industry, in the public services or in nationalised industries in addition to, or in substitution for, state retirement pensions; a type of **fringe benefit**. A civil service scheme was initiated as long ago as 1834; 1.6 million employees in private employment were members of occupational pension schemes in 1936, 5 millions in 1958 (a total of 8.75 millions, including the public sector), a total of 12.2 millions in 1967, and 12.8 millions in 1970 (*Occupational Pension Schemes;* Surveys by the Government Actuary, 1958, 1968 and 1971), though the figures may have been overestimated (the **New Earnings Survey, 1970** estimated a total of 9.8 millions in Great Britain, excluding members of the Armed Forces, employees in Northern Ireland, and those working overseas: *Department of Employment Gazette,* 'Occupational Pension and Sick Pay Schemes', August 1971). The characteristics of pension schemes have always differed, and have been affected by the development of state retirement pensions and the tax treatment of savings for retirement (see 'The History of Retirement Pensions', *Midland Bank Review*, J. Wiseman, Occupational Pension Schemes, in G.L. Reid and D.J. Robertson (eds), *Fringe Benefits, Labour Costs and Social Security,* George Allen and Unwin, 1965). The nature of occupational pension schemes has been criticised, *inter alia,* for its possible effects on **labour mobility**. In the public sector this is being overcome by provisions for transfer of acquired pension rights on moving from one employer to another and the situation generally is now affected by the **Social Security Pensions Act 1975**. Under this Act, retirement pensions are made up of a basic flat-rate state pension and an additional element related to earnings. Occupational pension schemes may continue either by contracting-in with a 'ride on top' scheme in addition, or by contracting-out with a scheme structured to provide benefits better than the minimum level necessary to contract out, in either event after consultation, with 'recognised independent trade unions'. The approval of the Occupational Pen-

sions Board is necessary before a scheme can be contracted out. The principle of trade union participation is a new one (see Department of Health and Social Security, *Occupational Pension Schemes: the role of members in running schemes,* Cmnd. 6514, June 1976). British unions appear to have paid very little attention to pensions until a 'State Reserve Scheme' proposed by the Heath government in the early 1970s brought trade union opposition and until the negotiation of pensions was arranged to fall outside the pay limits of Stage 2 of the *Programme for Controlling Inflation*; see Harry Lucas, *Pensions and Industrial Relations,* Pergamon, 1977.

OCCUPATIONAL PENSIONS BOARD; see **occupational pensions**.

OCCUPATIONAL PSYCHOLOGY. The journal (formerly *The Human Factor* and before that the *Journal of the National Institute of Industrial Psychology,* 1922-37), formerly published by the **National Institute of Industrial Psychology**. It contained articles of industrial relations interest and has been incorporated in the **Journal of Occupational Psychology**.

OCCUPATIONAL PSYCHOLOGY, JOURNAL OF. A journal of the British Psychological Association reconstituted from **Occupational Psychology**, formerly published by the **National Institute of Industrial Psychology**, now disbanded; published quarterly and containing articles on all aspects of industrial, organisational and applied psychology.

OCCUPATIONAL SICK PAY SCHEMES; see **sick pay schemes**.

OCCUPATIONAL STRESS or **job stress.** An expression used to describe the psychological and physiological effects of overload, insecurity, conflict and danger at work upon individuals and associated with various states of anxiety and ill health, e.g. ulcers and heart disease. The term 'stress' is apparently being used in its engineering sense in applying to human beings the inherent capacity of a metal or material to stand up to a defined amount of strain, which, if exceeded, results in a rupture or break. In the context of work it appears to have no precise meaning as a concept, but rather to indicate a collection of related problems involving a number of systems and disciplines; see R.S. Lazarus, 'Environmental Planning in Stress and

Adaptation' in Lennart Levi (ed.), *Society, Stress and Disease*, OUP, 1971, and Alan McLean (ed.), *Occupational Stress*, Charles C. Thomas, Illinois, 1974.

OCCUPATIONAL UNION. A type of trade union in which the workers organised belong to a particular occupational classification, or to a related group of occupations, almost invariably non-manual. The description may include unions to be found in a particular service, e.g. national or local government, whether these seek to organise only one grade or group (e.g. the **Confederation of Health Service Employees**) or many grades or groups (e.g. the **National and Local Government Officers' Association**). In the latter case it may approach the concept of an **industrial union** (q.v.) for non-manual workers. But it may also be taken to include unions which have a membership cutting across service or industry boundaries, e.g. the **Association of Professional, Executive, Clerical and Computer Staff** and thus give an appearance of **horizontal unionism.** The concept of occupational unionism is therefore somewhat indefinite and of limited descriptive and analytical use; see John Hughes, *Trade Union Structure and Government*, Royal Commission on Trade Unions and Employers' Associations, Research Papers No. 5 (Part 1), HMSO, 1967. The term is also sometimes applied to manual worker unions of the 'craft' type.

OCCUPATIONS, INTERNATIONAL STANDARD CLASSIFICATION OF (ISCO). An international system for classifying occupations designed to facilitate comparisons of occupational data between countries. The current Classification, issued by the **International Labour Office,** was published in 1968, and replaces that published in 1958 and reprinted in 1962. It divides occupations into eight major groups, Professional and Technical, Administrative and Managerial, Clerical, Sales, Service, Agricultural etc., Production, Transport, and labourers and workers not classifiable by occupation. An additional section is provided for the Armed Services. The work of compiling the Classification dates from the Seventh International Conference of Labour Statisticians, convened by the ILO in 1949.

OD. Organisation Development (q.v.).

ODD. Organising District Delegate (q.v.).

OECD. Organisation for Economic Co-operation and Development (q.v.).

OEEC. Organisation for European Economic Co-operation; now **Organisation for Economic Co-operation and Development** (q.v.).

OFFICE MANAGEMENT, INSTITUTE OF (IOM) now the Institute of Administrative Management; see **Administrative Management, Institute of.**

OFFICER CADET; see **cadet.**

OFFICES, SHOPS AND RAILWAY PREMISES ACT 1963. An Act regulating working conditions in offices and shops, the first comprehensive legislation of its kind in Britain. Before 1963 employers were required by the Shops Acts 1912-36, consolidated in the Shops Act 1950, to maintain proper ventilation, reasonable temperature, proper lighting and suitable and sufficient washing facilities and sanitary conveniences. Under the 1963 Act detailed provisions are made about conditions necessary for health, welfare and safety and protection against fire; see H. Samuels and N. Stewart Pearson, *The Offices, Shops and Railway Premises Act, 1963* (2nd ed.), Charles Knight and Co., 1971. Under the **Health and Safety at Work Act 1974** regulations under the Act will gradually be replaced by new regulations and approved Codes of Practice.

OFFICIAL STRIKE. A strike with approval by the union in accordance with the union's rules and usually accompanied by the payment of **strike pay** or **dispute benefit** (q.v.): the opposite of an **unofficial strike** (see also **wildcat strike**). An official strike is not necessarily synonymous with a **constitutional strike** (q.v.).

OLD AGE PENSIONS; see **retirement pensions.**

OLD v. ROBSON (1890) 59 LJMC 41; see **benefits.**

ON CALL. To be standing by, immediately available for work, outside normal working hours; hence **on-call allowance,** or **standby allowance.**

ON-CALL ALLOWANCE; see **on call.**

ONE BIG UNION; see **class unionism.**

100 PER CENT SHOP; see **closed shop.**

ONE-MAN ARBITRATION; see **single arbitration.**

ONE-SHOT AGREEMENT. A collective agreement in which a single, once-for-all payment is made to workers in return for a change in working practice, i.e. one in which payment for such a change is not continuous. R.B. McKersie, 'Productivity Bargaining: Deliverance or Delusion?', *Personnel Management,* Supplement, 1966, evidences a productivity bargain between the West Coast shipping companies in the United States and the International Longshoremen's and Warehousemen's Union as such an agreement; see also **productivity bargaining.**

ONE-STEP AGREEMENT. A collective agreement, particularly at plant or works level, at which widespread comprehensive changes (see **comprehensive agreement**) in procedure or in terms or conditions of employment are made in a single negotiating period; by contrast with a situation in which, in order to achieve similar change, several **sequential agreements** are needed over a period of time, each modifying terms and conditions by partial changes; see P.A.L. Parker, W.R. Hawes and A.L. Lumb, *The Reform of Collective Bargaining at Plant and Company Level,* Department of Employment, Manpower Papers No. 5, HMSO, 1971.

OPEN DOOR POLICY. The principle that it should be possible for any employee to communicate with any executive of the company for which he works, including the chairman or managing director, on any matter of concern to him, including the handling of a personal grievance, or query about the attitude or policy of the company itself; more loosely an arrangement whereby shop stewards may see the chief executive of an establishment or company on matters of urgency. The first of these forms is characteristic of some non-federated firms, usually those who do not recognise trade unions, and is often associated with American ownership; see also **grievance, 24 hour rule.**

OPEN-ENDED AGREEMENT. A collective agreement on which no termination date is put, it being open for the parties to request a new agreement either as they think necessary, or after appropriate notice is given; by contrast with a **fixed-term agreement** (q.v.).

OPEN HOUSE; see **open shop.**

OPEN SHOP. A workshop, office or establishment in which the employer gives employment to any worker whether a trade unionist or not (J.H. Richardson, *Introduction to the Study of Industrial Relations,* Allen and Unwin, 1954, p. 228); in this usage identical with a **mixed shop, open house** or **mixed office,** e.g. in printing; see A.E. Musson, *The Typographical Association,* OUP, 1954, p. 174. Also used to mean a non-union shop: e.g. 'a workplace or factory where the employer will not formally recognise the union in any way'; International Confederation of Free Trade Unions, *Trade Union Handbook.*

OPEN UNION. A trade union with few or no restrictions on, or qualifications for, membership, and hence the opposite of a **closed union,** i.e. one in which recruitment is limited to a particular grade or grades of worker, or to workers in a particular industry or region. The distinction has been commonly made in the USA to distinguish between unions with freedom of entry and those which might seek to be exclusive or discriminatory in their membership, or to operate **closed shops,** and which might therefore come into conflict with **right to work laws** (q.v.). In Britain, it has been developed by H.A. Turner (*Trade Union Growth, Structure and Policy,* Allen and Unwin, 1962, p. 249 *et seq.*) to explain aspects of trade union structure and behaviour, open unions being thought of as more preoccupied with wages, closed unions with issues affecting the control of labour supply and employment, open unions with **100 per cent membership** and closed unions with the **closed shop,** etc. The concepts have been further developed by John Hughes (*Trade Union Structure and Government,* Royal Commission on Trade Unions and Employers' Associations, Research Paper 5, Pt I, HMSO, 1967) as a partial explanation of the dynamics of trade union growth and decline; see **typology of unions.**

OPERATIONAL RESEARCH (OR). Defined by the Operational Research Society (founded in 1947) as 'the attack of modern science on complex problems arising from the direction and management of large systems of men, machines, materials and money in industry, government and defence. The distinctive approach is to develop a scientific model of the system, incorporating measurement of factors, such as chance and risk, with which to predict and compare the outcomes of alternative decisions, strategies or controls. The purpose is to help management determine its policy and actions scientifically'; see E. Duckworth, *A Guide to Operational Research,* Methuen, 3rd ed. 1976; P. Rivett and R.L. Ackoff, *A Manager's Guide to Operational Research,* Wiley, 1963; M.J. Sargeaunt, *Operational Research for Management,* Heinemann, 1965 and Stafford Beer, *The Theory of Operational Research,* SIGMA Paper, 1964. The term was first invented to describe the activities of a small section of the Air Ministry at Bawdsey in 1937-1939 concerned to make the best use of the newly invented radar according to M.G. Bennett, 'Operational Research in Industry', in *Society: Problems and Methods of Study,* A.T. Welford (ed.), Routledge and Kegan Paul, 1967.

OPERATIVE. A term used broadly to describe employees in manufacturing industries other than those of an administrative, technical and clerical category; **manual workers** generally. In some industries (as operative or **operator**) used to refer to manual workers with varying degrees of skill and knowledge, but of lesser skill and adaptability than craftsmen.

OPERATIVE PRINTERS AND ASSISTANTS, NATIONAL SOCIETY OF (NATSOPA); see Operative Printers, Graphical and Media Personnel, National Society of.

OPERATIVE PRINTERS, GRAPHICAL AND MEDIA PERSONNEL, NATIONAL SOCIETY OF OPERATIVE (NATSOPA); see Printers, Graphical and Media Personnel, National Society of Operative.

OPERATOR; see **operative.**

OR. Operational Research (q.v.).

ORANGE BOOK; see **blue book.**

ORDER 1305 (1940); see **National Arbitration Tribunal** and **compulsory arbitration.**

ORDER 1376 (1951); see **Industrial Disputes Tribunal** and **compulsory arbitration.**

ORGANISATION DEVELOPMENT (OD). The effort to improve organisational effectiveness through the long-term, planned and systematic application of behavioural science knowledge and techniques with the collaboration of skilled consultants. Broadly speaking, OD attempts to assist managers in any particular enterprise to identify and evaluate their own managerial styles, e.g. through the use of the **Managerial Grid** (q.v.), and, over a period of time to train them in appropriate problem solving, communication and group process skills, thereby moving towards an improvement of interpersonal and inter-group skills, to an improvement plan for the enterprise, to the implementation of this plan and finally to a review of the total result obtained as a basis for further action. The approaches involved are eclectic, drawing on whatever aspects of **organisational behaviour** (q.v.) or other thinking as required, participative, and rely heavily on feedback of information and progressive training. The consultancy role involved is one of general collaboration, research, mutual diagnosis and discussion rather than the more usual single problem, single technique, set-solution approach of more traditional consultants, i.e. it involves '**process consultancy**'. Key components of the OD movement, e.g. **action research** and **sensitivity training** (q.v.) can be traced back to the 1940s, but the term was probably used with a distinct meaning in the United States in the late 1950s and began to grow rapidly in that country in the 1960s, reaching Britain in the latter part of that period; see Richard Beckhard, *Organisation Development; Strategies and Models,* Addison-Wesley, 1969, G. Warren Bennis, *Changing Organisations,* Addison-Wesley, 1969, Paul R. Lawrence and Jay W. Lorsch, *Organisation and Environment,* Addison-Wesley, 1969, E.H. Schein, *Process Consultation: Its Role in Organisation Development,* Addison-Wesley, 1969, Richard D. Walton, *Interpersonal Peacemaking: Confrontation and Third Party Consultation,* Addison-Wesley, 1969 and, more recently, Wendell L. French and Cecil H. Bell, *Organisation Development,* Prentice-Hall, 1973 and Manab Thakur, *OD: The Search for Identity,* Information Report 16, Institute of Personnel Management, 1974.

ORGANISATION AND METHODS (O and M). Described by the O and M Group of the Institute of Work Study Practitioners as 'a generic term for those techniques, including Method Study and Work Measurement, which are used in the examination of clerical, administrative and management procedures and organisation in order to effect improvement'; 'office work study' (Harry Cemach, *Work Study 'n the Office,* Anbar Publications, 4th ed. 1969). The expression O and M is said to have been coined in 1941, and to have originated from N. Baliol Scott, a member of the Treasury Investigation Section originally established in 1919 to promote the better use of office methods and equipment (see T.P. Sherman, *O and M in Local Government,* Pergamon Press, 1969, p. 4). O and M had spread to most government departments by 1943, departments without their own staff being assisted by the Treasury O and M Division; in the 1950s it was taken up by nationalised industries; the Local Government Manpower Committee (*First Report,* Cmd. 7870, January 1950, *Second Report* Cmd. 8421, HMSO, December 1951) recommended its extension to local authority work; see also G.E. Milward (ed.), *Organisation and Methods: A Service to Management,* Macmillan, 1967. Some recent approaches to O and M lay emphasis upon the social effects of the changes achieved, e.g. M.E. Addison, *Essentials of Organisation and Methods,* Heinemann, 1971.

ORGANISATION FOR ECONOMIC CO-OPERATION AND DEVELOPMENT (OECD).

An organisation established in 1961 as successor to the Organisation for European Economic Co-operation (OEEC) originally set up in 1948 to administer the Marshall Aid plan and the co-operative effort for European recovery after the second world war. It now consists of 24 countries, Australia, Austria, Belgium, Canada, Denmark, Finland, France, Germany, Greece, Iceland, Ireland, Italy, Japan, Luxembourg, Netherlands, New Zealand, Norway, Portugal, Spain, Sweden, Switzerland, Turkey, United Kingdom, and United States of America. Yugoslavia is a participating member. The aim of OECD is to harmonise national policies and contribute towards economic growth, employment and living standards by providing information and opportunities for discussion on which rational policies can be built, especially where the environment, aid to developing countries, trade, financial affairs, etc., are concerned. Its interest in industrial relations is the responsibility of a Manpower and Social Affairs Committee and recent publications in the field include a series on industrial relations aspects of manpower policy (including W.H. Scott, *Office Auto-*

mation, July 1965; A.D. Smith, *Redundancy Practices in Four Countries,* October 1966; Dorothy Wedderburn, *Enterprise Planning for Change,* April 1968); on job opportunities, and a number of studies on labour markets (including Derek Robinson, *Non-Wage Incomes and Prices Policy,* 1966; G. Bowen Thomas, *Manpower Problems in the Service Sector,* 1967; John Corina, *Forms of Wage Payment for High Productivity,* 1970, and Derek Robinson, *Wage Drift, Fringe Benefits and Manpower Distribution,* 1968). *Address:* 2 rue Andre-Pascal, 75, Paris 16e, France.

ORGANISATION FOR EUROPEAN ECONOMIC CO-OPERATION (OEEC); see **Organisation for Economic Co-operation and Development** (OECD).

ORGANISATION OF EMPLOYERS.

Under the terms of the **Industrial Relations Act 1971,** an unregistered **employers' association.** The term is no longer in use.

ORGANISATION OF WORKERS.

Under the terms of the **Industrial Relations Act 1971,** an organisation of employees not legally a 'trade union' i.e. not registered as a trade union under the Act, and hence classified as enjoying, *inter alia,* a less protected legal status, e.g. in relation to strike action. The term is no longer in use.

ORGANISATIONAL BEHAVIOUR (OB).

An imprecise term which began to emerge among students of management in the early 1960s to express both a reaction against traditional theories of **scientific management** (q.v.) and **human relations** (q.v.) and an attempt to combine the approaches of the former ('organisation') with those of the latter ('people'), taking the best from each and adopting a flexible approach to problem solving rather than one involving a search for the 'one best way'. Writers in the field vary in the emphasis which they place upon these two aspects and in the extent to which they apply theoretical or 'action' frameworks to their scholarship. 'People' oriented writers include human resource theorists such as Chris Argyris (*Personality and Organisation,* Harper, 1957), Douglas McGregor (*The Human Side of Enterprise,* McGraw-Hill, 1960 and Rensis Likert (*New Patterns of Management,* McGraw-Hill 1961) who stress the human need for recognition and fulfilment through meaningful work and those who have argued that variations in this thesis have to be accepted to meet different groups and conditions, e.g. Warren G. Bennis and Philip E. Stater (*The Temporary Society,* Harper and Row, 1968), Robert Blauner (*Alienation and Freedom,* University of Chicago Press, 1964), William F. Whyte (*Money and Motivation,* Harper 1955), and others. Among those who have emphasised 'organisation' rather than 'people' are Leonard Sayles and Margaret K. Chandler (*Managing Large Systems,* Harper and Row, 1971) and Joan Woodward (*Industrial Organisation,* OUP, 1965). While these latter may be thought of as organisational sociologists, other 'people' oriented writers, e.g. Harold Leavitt (*Managerial Psychology,* University of Chicago Press, 1958 and subsequent editions), would consider themselves to be psychologists. Similarly there is no accepted understanding as to whether OB should be concerned primarily with theory or action, whether it should or should not be value free, or whether it falls within the ambit of industrial relations. The American Industrial Relations Research Association published a synopsis of some parts of the field in 1974 (*Organisational Behaviour,* IRRA, 1974), including chapters on **job satisfaction, supervision,** formal participation, conflict and its resolution and **Organisation Development** (q.v.).

ORGANISING DISTRICT DELEGATE or **ODD.** A term formerly used by trade unions, and still in use by a few, to describe a local trade union official or organiser. The term until recently survived in the engineering *1922 Procedure Agreement-Manual Workers* (II(3)(c)(7)(c)), this part of the text deriving from 1917-19.

OSBORNE v. AMALGAMATED SOCIETY OF RAILWAY SERVANTS (1910) AC 87: known as the **Osborne Judgment.** A leading case in which it was declared *ultra vires* and void under the Trade Union Acts for a registered trade union to have a rule purporting to confer the power to collect and administer funds for the'purpose of parliamentary representation. The decision was extended to local government representation in the following year (**Wilson v. Amalgamated Society of Engineers** (1911) 2 Ch. 324) and was also applied to unregistered unions (**Wilson v. Scottish Typographical Association** (1912) ISLT 203, (1912) SC 534: **Parr v. Lancashire and Cheshire Miners' Federation** (1913) 1 Ch. 366); see W.M. Geldart, *The Osborne Judgment and After,* Manchester Guardian Ltd (1911?). The Osborne Judgment flooded the courts with injunctions against trade unions and resulted in pressure which terminated in the **Trade Union Act 1913** (q.v.).

OSBORNE JUDGMENT; see **Osborne v. Amalgamated Society of Railway Servants.**

OUT-OF-COMPLIANCE MEN. Trade union members who are in arrears with contributions and have exceeded the period of time allowed by rule in which to make these good (usually 13 weeks); hence by extension, **nons** or non-unionists; also known as **non-compliance men:** steel industry and elsewhere.

OUT-OF-HOURS WORK. Overtime work; a term used, for example, in the electricity supply industry; e.g. the electrical power engineers' ban on out-of-hours work, 1 November to 28 December 1973.

OUT-OF-HOURS PAYMENTS. A name given to a form of overtime payment, especially among doctors in the National Health Service, e.g. for evening or night visits to patients; see *Report of the Review Body on Doctors' and Dentists' Pay* (**Kindersley Committee**), Twelfth Report, paras 140-3.

OUT-OF-OFFICE PAYMENT. Any payment made to a payment by result worker in the engineering industry which is unaffected by effort, e.g. **merit pay** or good **timekeeping bonus,** and especially the **piecework supplement** (q.v.).

OUT-OF-WORK BENEFIT; see **unemployment, tramping.**

OUT-OF-WORK DONATION; see **donation.**

OUTWORKER; see **outworking.**

OUTWORKING. (1) Outwork or work done by an **outworker,** i.e. by a worker working at home, or away from the factory, shop or premises where the items made are handled or assembled for sale; a **homeworker** (see also **sweating**); (2) work done by men employed in an establishment or factory, who are sent out to do jobs, e.g. on lift maintenance or repair, on servicing machinery etc., and often paid **outworking allowances,** i.e. allowances, usually at a daily rate, for working over and above certain distances from home, establishment or place of work, payment also in most cases taking account of the length of the job, if this exceeds an agreed period; see also **travelling time, travelling allowance, travelling expenses.**

OUTWORKING ALLOWANCES; see **outworking.**

OVERMAN. A foreman or overseer, especially in a colliery, as in the title of the union **NACODS** (q.v.); also, sometimes as 'oversman', an arbitrator or umpire, especially in Scotland (see s. 12, Industrial Courts Act 1919: 'In the application of this Act to Scotland, a reference to an oversman shall be substituted for any reference to an umpire').

OVERMANNING; see **underemployment.**

OVERTIME. Hours worked in excess of normal standard or basic hours (and usually calculated on a daily basis), such normal, standard, or basic hours being determined by collective agreement (e.g. a standard working week of 40 hours consisting of 5 days of 8 hours), or by statute or regulation (e.g. the case of **women and young persons** or in **Wages Council** industries); hence the distinction in engineering between **federation overtime** (i.e. overtime hours calculated over and above the normal working day) and **statutory overtime** (i.e. overtime hours over and above the normal daily working hours stated on the factory notice: see A.I. Marsh, *Industrial Relations in Engineering,* Pergamon Press, 1965, p. 155); also **systematic overtime,** i.e. regularly worked overtime, or overtime used 'as a method of production'; **overtime premium,** an enhanced payment made for overtime hours worked (e.g. time-and-one-third for the first two hours and time-and-one-half thereafter, or other proportions as laid down in collective agreements); **overtime guarantee,** i.e. a guaranteed payment of an agreed number of hours (e.g. in engineering, three hours' pay at overtime rate), when a worker is required, without prior notice, to return to work after he has finished his shift and gone home. In Britain reductions in the standard working week (see **hours of work**) since the war were until 1970 accompanied by rising levels of overtime - from an average of one hour per worker in manufacturing in 1947 to 6½ hours in 1969 since when overtime hours have fallen to 4.2 in 1977. Recent surveys (e.g. National Board for Prices and Incomes, *Hours of Work, Overtime and Shiftworking,* Report No. 161, Cmnd. 4554, December 1970), have attributed high levels of overtime to labour shortage, to policies of supplementing **low pay** to attract and retain labour, to the attempt to increase machine utilisation without **shiftworking,** and to the willingness of workers to increase take-home pay by working longer than standard hours. It has increasingly been thought of as a source of inefficiency and as a problem to be tackled by management (see NPBI, op. cit., and E.G. Whybrew, *Overtime Working in Britain,* Royal Commission on Trade Unions and Employers' Associations, Research Papers 9, 1968, who also discusses the possibility of legislation to set an upper limit of overtime worked). Overtime has historically involved the issue of managerial functions in some industries; see **Clause (j).** On the legal obligation to work overtime, see **Pearson and another v. William Jones** (1967) 2 All ER 1962.

OVERTIME EXTRAS. Overtime premiums in the steel industry, i.e. **gift hours** payable over and above clocked hours for any time worked prior to or after normal shift or day, currently shift rate plus 50 per cent.

OVERTIME GUARANTEE; see **overtime.**

OVERTIME PREMIUM. An additional payment, or allowance, made to workers who work overtime; see **premium payment;** usually made by expressing overtime as fractions of flat rate from the first to the sixth (or later) hours of overtime inclusive. The National Board for Prices and Incomes (*Hours of Work, Overtime and Shiftworking,* Report No. 161, Cmnd. 4554, December 1970) examined premium rates for overtime in 1970 in 88 major agreements for manual dayworkers (p. 98). Overtime premiums on weekdays commonly start at time-and-a-quarter, but up to one-quarter (including engineering) specify time-and-a-third and another quarter time-and-a-half, with proportionately higher rates for increased hours of overtime worked; see Department of Employment, *Time Rates of Wages and Hours of Work,* HMSO (annual); see also **overtime, overtime extras.**

OXFORD ECONOMIC PAPERS. A journal, 1937, new series 1949 - published three times a year covering economic theory and applied economics; published by

Oxford University Press. For notes on labour economics and industrial relations journals generally; see George Sayers Bain and Gillian B. Woolven, 'The Literature of Labour Economics and Industrial Relations', *Industrial Relations Journal,* Summer 1971 and J. Fletcher (ed.), *The Uses of Economic Literature,* Butterworths, 1971.

OXFORD UNIVERSITY INSTITUTE OF ECONOMICS AND STATISTICS BULLETIN. A journal begun in 1939, becoming quarterly in 1955/56 and including from time to time articles of interest to labour economists, especially of a statistical nature; published by Basil Blackwell Ltd, Broad Street, Oxford. For notes on labour economics and industrial relations journals generally; see George Sayers Bain and Gillian B. Woolven, 'The Literature of Labour Economics and Industrial Relations', *Industrial Relations Journal,* Summer 1971 and J. Fletcher (ed.), *The Uses of Economic Literature,* Butterworths, 1971.

P

PACERS. Exceptionally fast workers who may be introduced by employers to set norms or production standards in incentive or piece work systems, and usually catered for in arrangements for these systems by provisions that 'normal' workers or 'workers of average ability' should be used in setting job times. The word appears to be more common in the United States than in Britain and in Canada the expressions **speeders** and **bellhorses** are sometimes used.

PACKAGE DEAL. A collective agreement in which workers receive a combination of benefits rather than an improvement in one aspect only of wages and conditions of work, e.g. the **Engineering Package Deal Agreement** of 1964, which allowed for movement towards new **minimum time rates,** a shortening of the working week, additional holidays, etc., and on the employers' side, a change in the Guarantee of Employment Agreement (see **guaranteed week**) and assurances on the economic utilisation and transfer of labour; see also **productivity bargaining.**

PAID HOLIDAYS. In some industries used to describe **holidays with pay** (q.v.).

In engineering, where annual holidays have traditionally been financed out of **holiday credits,** usually confined to those holidays on which workers continue to be paid by the employer, e.g. 'Bank or other paid holidays' or 'recognised holidays', though this usage is not entirely consistently applied (e.g. in the *National Agreement* of 18 August 1972, Section III, para. 1, where it was applied to the total of 22 days of paid holidays provided for in 1972 and 23 days in 1973).

PAID-UP MEMBER. A member of a trade union who is up to date with his contributions (a **fully paid-up member**), or is **in compliance** (q.v.); hence **paid-up membership,** the membership of a trade union which is paid-up, as distinct from a higher figure of membership which comprises those who are on the books of the union, but including some who are not in good standing financially, conditions for which vary from one union to another.

PAID-UP MEMBERSHIP; see **paid-up member.**

PANEL OF INVESTIGATION. A form of investigation into industrial disputes adopted by the **Advisory, Conciliation and Arbitration Service** containing some of the features of former **Committees of Inquiry** or **Committees of Investigation** and of **Courts of Inquiry,** but with characteristics of its own, e.g. those carried out in 1976 into mechanical rectifiers at British Leyland, Cowley (*ACAS Report No. 1*) and into difficulties affecting London Docks (*ACAS Report No. 2*). ACAS sees the Panels as a form of mediation, on a basis of voluntary agreement by the parties, in which an active secretariat with inquiry functions goes beyond the evidence produced at hearings to produce a settlement. Ideas and draft reports produced by the secretariat are discussed with the parties before publication.

PAPERMAKERS AND BOARDMAKERS, EMPLOYERS' FEDERATION OF; now the **British Paper and Board Industries Federation** (q.v.).

PARALLEL UNIONISM. An expression used to describe a situation in which official trade union organisation is paralleled, within the same union or unions, by unofficial organisation at the workplace 'and by a network of unofficial joint committees ... regarded as a threat to the existing institutions of trade unionism and to the control which they are expected to exercise over their membership'; Peter Anthony and Anne Crichton, *Industrial Relations and the Personnel Specialists,* Batsford, 1969, p. 49.

PARR v. LANCASHIRE AND CHESHIRE MINERS' FEDERATION; see Osborne v. Amalgamated Society of Railway Servants.

PARTICIPANT OBSERVER STUDY; see participant observation.

PARTICIPANT OBSERVATION or participant observer study. A method of social research in which the researcher takes up temporary residence as a member of the community which he is concerned to study. The technique derives from social anthropology and from the necessity, or desire, to investigate social behaviour, for language and for other reasons, from within, rather than without, the social group. Participant observer studies in industrial relations include those by Tom Lupton (*On the Shop Floor,* Pergamon, 1963) and Garfield Clack (*Industrial Relations in a British Car Factory,* CUP, 1967); see J. Friedrichs and H. Lüdtke, *Participant Observation; Theory and Practice,* Saxon House, 1975.

PARTICIPATION AGREEMENT. A type of collective agreement suggested by the **Confederation of British Industry** in its evidence to the Bullock Committee of Inquiry into Industrial Democracy which reported in January 1977 (see **Bullock Report**). The CBI favoured the company by company · establishment of bodies representative of all employees in of a size over 2,000 where they would be practicable, the form of these bodies to be determined by voluntary participation agreement; see CBI, *Evidence to the Bullock Committee of Inquiry,* March 1976, paras 19-22.

PARTICIPATION RATE; see activity rate.

PARTSMAN. An employee who receives, identifies and sells parts and accessories in the parts department of a motor vehicle retailer, or in the stores of a motor factor or in those of a haulage or road passenger transport companies.

PART-TIME SHIFT. A shift, usually of shorter duration than normal, especially an **evening shift** performed by women between 5 p.m. and 10 p.m. to increase utilisation of machinery, particularly where there is too little female labour to permit a **double-day shift** system or where it is necessary to offer acceptable hours to suitably trained women. For part-time workers in the engineering industry; see *Handbook of National Agreements,* 2.6 and 2.61.

PART-TIME WORKER. A worker who is employed for some part only of each, or of some, working days in a working week or one who is employed on particular working days only; see also **casual worker** and **peripheral worker**.

PASSING PICKETS; see picketing.

PASSOVER. The promotion of a person lower in the **seniority list** (q.v.) before the next senior candidate, especially of airline pilots where passover rules usually regulate such a practice.

PATENTS ACT 1977. An Act seeking to clarify the question of ownership of inventions as between the employee and the employer. Before the passing of the Act, the question of ownership was conclusively determined by an express provision in the employee's contract of employment, or in the absence of such a clear contractual provision, by reference to the employee's duties. Most contracts which included references to inventions assigned those made by employees to the employer. Where no such provision existed the Courts tended to hold that where *senior* employees were concerned and where invention could be construed as falling within the duty of the employee, the invention also belonged to the employer (**Worthington Pumping Engine Co. v. Moore (1930) 20 RPC 41. Sterling Engineering Co. v. Patchett [1955] AC 534**). S. 39 of the Act now provides a new statutory test of ownership which applies irrespective of any terms on the contract of employment, namely that in all cases except those in which an invention results from an employee's duties or those in which the nature of his responsibilities is such that he has a special obligation to further the interests of the employer's undertaking, the invention belongs to the employee; see *Industrial Relations Review and Report,* No. 161, October 1977, p. 2 *et seq.*

PATERNALISM. Defined by the National Institute of Industrial Psychology (*Joint Consultation in British Indus-*

try, Staples Press, 1952) as 'a situation in which management maintains authoritarian leadership but at the same time provides generous welfare amenities and frequently maintains close social contact with workers ... there is sometimes the implication that [this] is a means of maintaining or increasing the dependence of workers on employers and, occasionally, of weakening the activities of trade unions'. A word now normally used in a pejorative sense, either for the reasons above, because it is considered to be demeaning to workers (see Clinton S. Golden and Harold J. Ruttenberg, *The Dynamics of Industrial Democracy,* New York, Harper and Bros, 1942), or because it may corrupt the paternalist; see Norman J. Ware, *Labor in Modern Industrial Society,* Boston (D.C. Heath and Co., 1935), who maintains that an initial sense of superior wisdom and of benevolence may move through a sense of indignation to despotism.

PATERNITY LEAVE; see **maternity leave.**

PATERSON METHOD. A method of **job evaluation** developed by Professor T.T. Paterson of the University of Strathclyde. The method is based upon the notion that the common denominator for all jobs is decision-making, and that six bands of decision-making are clearly discernible in all organisations - E: *Policy Making;* D: *Programming;* C: *Interpretative;* B: *Routine;* A: *Automatic* and O: *Defined,* the proper relationship between the average basic pay of each band, plotted on a logarithmic scale being a straight line. The method and its application are discussed in T.T. Paterson, *Job Evaluation:* Vol. 1, *A New Method,* and Vol. 2, *A Manual for the Paterson Method,* Business Books, 1972.

PATTERN BARGAINING. An expression used, particularly in the United States, to describe a situation in which a trade union or trade unions use an agreement particularly favourable to them as a model for imitation elsewhere and turn their collective bargaining strategy and tactics to this end. The terms for pattern-setting in the USA may be derived from the agreement made with one particular company (e.g. in the motor industry or in steel), or by a request for a model contract for a particular group of employees in an industry, local unions and employers being expected to conform to the pattern

set. The latter practice is considered by some to be invalid under the judgement of the Supreme Court in the case of United Mine Workers v. Pennington (1965) as a violation of the anti-trust laws; see W.H. Carpenter Jr. and E. Handler, *Small Business and Pattern Bargaining,* Babson Institute Press, 1961, Harold Levinson, 'Pattern Bargaining: A Case Study of the Automobile Workers', *Quarterly Journal of Economics, 1960.* Pattern bargaining in Britain is more familiar under the headings **trade movement, whipsawing, comparability, wage rounds** and **leapfrogging** (q.v.).

PATTERN WEAVERS' SOCIETY. A textile trade union founded in 1930 and organising only male union members from hand and power loom pattern weaving departments, having broken away from the National Union of Textile Workers. The union had over 350 members in 1931. *Address:* New Field End, Hill Top, Cumberworth, Nr. Huddersfield, HD8 8YE. *Tel:* Holmfirth 048-489 2547. *TUC Affiliated Membership, 1977:* 150.

PATTERNMAKERS AND ALLIED CRAFTSMEN, ASSOCIATION OF (APAC). A craft union for patternmakers originating in the United Kingdom Pattern Makers' Association established in 1872 as a result of a strike on the Wear and Tyne for a nine-hour day in the previous year and of dissatisfaction of patternmakers about their representation by other unions. Until adopting its present title in 1968, effective from 1 January 1969, the union was known as the United Patternmakers' Association. It has remained a union entirely confined to craftsmen concerned with patternmaking skills; see W. Mosses, *The History of the United Patternmakers' Association,* UPA, 1922: UPA, *Seventy-Five Years Progress, 1872-1947,* 1947. *Address:* 15 Cleve Road, West Hampstead, London NW6 1YA. *Tel:* 01-624 7085. *TUC Affiliated Membership, 1977:* 9,757.

PAY BOARD. An Agency established under the **Counter-Inflation Act 1973,** with the two main functions of checking that the remuneration provisions of a Price and Pay Code designed to restrain inflation under the Act were implemented, and of advising the Secretary of State for Employment about pay problems, including the treatment of anomalies and relativities both within and between groups of workers in Stage Three of the Heath government's counter-inflation policy (see **incomes policy** and relativities). The Board began operation on 2 April 1973, with Sir Frank Figgures as chairman. It operated until 26 July 1974, when it was abolished along with all statutory pay controls after the return of a Labour government to office.

'PAY CLUB'. A name sometimes given to a group of employers who voluntarily agree to exchange information on the pay of particular groups of employees, the information so collected being used separately by each employer in the process of pay determination in his own business or establishment. The role of 'pay clubs' and of pay surveys in general is discussed in Pay Board, *Relativities,* Pay Board Advisory Report No. 2, Cmnd. 5535, January 1974.

PAY-DAY SIMPLIFICATION. A movement towards more economical and secure ways of paying employees, especially manual workers, than by the customary weekly wage packet. Until the **Payment of Wages Act 1960** (q.v.), the **Truck Acts** (q.v.) etc. ruled out alternatives to payment in 'current coin of the realm' for manual workers falling within their scope. Payment by cheque, legal for such workers since 1 March 1963 (see **Payment of Wages Act 1960**), appeared at that time to be a less promising possibility than bank transfer. Progress towards simplification was initially slow among manual workers. Some firms developed a **nos nod** system (q.v.), or variations on it. J.M. Stamford, *Pay-Day Simplified,* Productivity Progress,' Pergamon Press, March 1968.

PAY INDEXATION; see **indexation, threshold agreement, cost of living sliding scale.**

PAY STRUCTURE. Generally synonymous with **wage structure** (q.v.), but sometimes used to indicate that the notion of structure is to be extended to **salaries** as well as to **wages** more narrowly defined, e.g. in the White Paper *Productivity, Prices and Incomes after 1969* (Cmnd. 4237, Dec. 1969), para. 54 *et seq.,* which drew attention to 'pay structures which have grown up over years, even decades, and which bear little relation to the realities of present day working methods' ... making necessary '... a thorough-going rationalisation of the whole grading and pay structure'; see also **productivity bargaining, job evaluation.**

PAYMENT BY RESULTS (PBR or P by R). An expression used with both broad and restricted meanings. At its broadest 'any system of wages and salaries under which payment is related to factors in a worker's performance other than time spent at his employer's disposal' (National Board for Prices and Incomes, *Payment by Results,* Report No. 65. Cmnd. 3627, May 1968, p. 3), i.e. any payment system other than straight time rates, or any **incentive payment system** (q.v.). More narrowly defined, may be restricted to payment systems which attempt to establish a formal and direct relationship between pay and output or effort, i.e. to exclude systems which are not directly dependent on production such as those based on profits, valued added, or personal assessment (merit rating, attendance bonuses, length of service bonuses and the like), or quality and waste bonuses, for example. The **Engineering Employers' Federation** confines PBR solely to those schemes in which earnings vary directly with the effort of the individual or gang in which there is **mutuality** (q.v.) in the fixing of prices, times and other measurements; see **payment by results workers.** In April 1961, 33 per cent of all wage earners in Britain were paid under PBR systems broadly defined (*Ministry of Labour Gazette,* September 1961, pp. 369-73). The NBPI (op. cit.) confirmed that PBR contributed to **wage drift** (q.v.) and was sometimes under inadequate control, but was able neither to commend or condemn it generally. It suggested guidelines to test whether particular PBR schemes were working successfully or otherwise. No clear evidence exists that the use of PBR is declining; see R. Marriott, *Incentive Payment Systems,* Staples, 3rd (revised) ed. 1968, pp. 260-3.

PAYMENT BY RESULTS WORKERS. Defined by the Department of Employment for statistical purposes (*Department of Employment and Productivity Gazette,* October 1969, p. 912) as 'workers paid under piece-work arrangements, output bonus schemes or any payment schemes which vary according to the output of individuals, groups or departments: contract and lieu workers (those workers receiving compensatory payment in lieu of payment by results), in shipbuilding and ship repairing and lieu workers in iron and steel manufacture are also included'. The **Engineering Employers' Federation**

adopts a narrower definition: 'workers whose earnings vary directly by their own effort, either as individuals or as a group and in which there is a feature of **mutuality** (q.v.) in the negotiation and agreement of prices, times, targets or other measurements of production'.

PAYMENT IN KIND. Defined by the Department of Employment and Productivity (*Labour Costs in Britain,* HMSO, 1968) as 'goods provided by employers, free or below cost, to employees, their dependants and former employees, for example, articles of food or fuel'. The DE's 1975 *Labour Costs Survey* showed that 0.1 per cent of labour costs per employee in manufacturing industries were incurred as a result of payment in kind and 0.3 per cent in all industries covered. The former proportion was identical in a previous survey conducted in 1968 (*Employment and Productivity Gazette,* August 1970, p. 665); see also **Truck Acts, concessionary coal, labour costs.**

PAYMENT OF WAGES ACT 1960. An Act to allow an employed person, at his request in writing and with the agreement of his employer, to be paid by bank transfer, postal order, money order, or, by cheque. Redgrave's *Health and Safety in Factories,* 1976, p. 1775 *et seq.* Manual workers covered by the **Truck Acts** (q.v.), the Hosiery Manufacture (Wages) Act 1874, and miners to whom the Stannaries Act 1887 applied could previously be paid lawfully only in 'current coin of the realm'. The Act was part of a movement to simplify pay-day arrangements; see **pay-day simplification.**

PAYMENT OF WAGES IN PUBLIC HOUSES PROHIBITION ACT 1883. An Act making it an offence to pay the wages of any workman at or within any public house or place for the sale of intoxicating liquor unless the wages are paid by the resident owner or occupier to a workman *bona fide* employed by him; see also **butty.**

PAYMENT ON ACCOUNT. Payment of some part of a wage or salary increase in advance of the conclusion of final negotiations; may be agreed in order to preempt some part of **retrospective payment,** or to assist the course of negotiations by providing financial relief during protracted discussions and in the latter sense be difficult to distinguish from **talking money.**

Employers were cautioned on the problems of payment on account during the period of the **prices and incomes policy.**

PAYMENT SYSTEM. Any method of payment determination, whether involving **timework, piecework,** or **payment by results, measured daywork,** or whether **work study** is employed or not. While payment systems result in payment structures as defined by some observers (see **wage structure**), these may be of an unplanned rather than a planned variety, and susceptible to **wage drift** or **earnings drift,** and the encouragement of conflict over **differentials;** see National Board for Prices and Incomes, *Payment By Results,* Report No. 65, Cmnd. 3627, May 1968.

PAY PAUSE. A temporary pause in pay increases in the public sector announced by Mr Selwyn Lloyd in July 1961, which came to an end eight months later in March 1962. The pay pause was intended to be followed in the private sector, and to allow time for the Macmillan administration to work out a longer-term wages policy. The pay pause, while it lasted, was effective, but caused much resentment among public employees; see Bernard Donoughue, 'Wages Policies in the Public Sector', *Planning,* PEP, Vol. XXVIII, No. 467, 19 November 1962.

PAYROLL DEDUCTION SCHEMES; see **check-off.**

PAYROLL SIMPLIFICATION; see **pay-day simplification.**

PBR; payment by results (q.v.).

PEACE CLAUSE; see **no-strike clause.**

PEACER. Petroleum Employers' Advisory Council on Employee Relations (q.v.).

PEARL STRIKE; see **irritation strike.**

PEARSON AND ANOTHER v. WILLIAM JONES (1967) 2 All ER 1062. A leading case in which it was held, on appeal to Queen's Bench Division, that **overtime** was not obligatory upon the workers concerned in circumstances in which their normal working hours were stated in **works rules** along with the provision that the relevant engineering industry national agreement would apply, Waller J finding that in order that overtime should be compulsory there should either be an

express term that an employee shall work overtime, or possibly an **implied term**, but that there was no such provision in the contract concerned.

PEARSON REPORT. Name given to a number of reports of **Courts of Inquiry** under the chairmanship of the Rt Hon. Lord Pearson, CBE, on the *Electricity Supply Industry* (Cmnd. 2361, May 1964), on a *Dispute between the British Overseas Airways Corporation and the British Airline Pilots' Association* (Cmnd. 3551, 1968), and especially on the *Shipping Industry* (First Report Cmnd. 3025, 1966; Final Report, Cmnd. 3211, 1967). The last report recommended that companies should plan, develop and implement effective personnel policies and man their ships more effectively, that the scheme of **shipboard liaison representatives** (q.v.) should be extended and that the **Merchant Shipping Acts** should be extensively redrafted; see also **complaints procedure**; also a report into a *Dispute between the parties represented on the National Joint Council for the Port Transport Industry* (Cmnd. 4429, July 1970).

PENALTY CLAUSES. Provision or clauses in collective agreements which provide for monetary or other penalties to either workers or management in the event of particular action or behaviour; hence **penalty rates,** overtime rates (see **overtime**) which being at premium rates, make overtime more costly to the employer than normal time. In engineering, the term 'penalty clauses' is used to describe Clauses (f) and (g) of the Overtime and Nightshift Agreement (*Handbook.* Ref. 2.2) which provide for payment up to 6 a.m. for dayshift workers released after midnight or after 2 a.m. In the Ford strike of 1969, the proposals of the company that payments during period of lay-off and short-time and the annual holiday bonus should be dependent on workers refraining from strike action were also popularly known as penalty clauses; see Roy Lewis, 'The Legal Enforceability of Collective Agreements', *British Journal of Industrial Relations,* Vol. VIII, No. 3, November 1970, p. 322; also the provisions proposed in *In Place of Strife*, Cmnd. 3888, January 1969, para. 94, for financial penalties against those failing to observe a **conciliation pause** (q.v.).

PENALTY PAY; see **premium payment.**

PENALTY RATE; see **premium payment.**

PENSION SCHEMES; see **occupational pension schemes.**

PENSIONER INDICES; see **retail prices index.**

'PENTONVILLE FIVE'; see **Heaton Transport (St Helens) Ltd v. TGWU.**

PENZANCE AGREEMENT. An agreement arrived at between the British Railways Board and the **National Union of Railwaymen** at Penzance on 5 July 1968. The Agreement, in which the British Railways Board took the unusual step of flying to meet the NUR Executive Committee at the union's Annual General Meeting, marked the turning point in pay and efficiency negotiations in the industry and set a new pattern both in pay and grading structure and in collective bargaining methods. Charles McLeod, *All Change: Railway Industrial Relations in the Sixties,* Gower Press, 1970, pp. 140-65.

PER. Professional and Executive Recruitment; see **Professional and Executive Register.**

PERFORMANCE APPRAISAL, performance rating or **efficiency rating.** An assessment of the performance of employees (and particularly staff employees, hence **staff appraisal** and **staff assessment**) with a view to the making of decisions on their pay or salary adjustment, promotion, transfer, training, etc.; see also **merit rating.** Appraisal may be more or less systematic, and more or less regular (see **employee appraisal**). It may involve appraisal by superiors only, or by the individual employee himself in addition. Where either method is used, but particularly where joint appraisals are done, this may also result in the setting of targets for work to be done and of performance for the achievement of these targets, following a style of approach often associated with **management by objectives** (q.v.), in which such targets may commonly be agreed between the individual concerned and his superior; see E. Anstey, *Staff Reporting and Staff Development,* Allen and Unwin, 1969, M.R. Williams, *Performance Appraisal in Management,* Heinemann, 1972, and G.A. Randell, P.M.A. Packard, R.L. Shaw and A.J. Slater, *Staff Appraisal,* Institute of Personnel Management. Revised ed., 1974.

PERFORMANCE CURVE; see **learning curve.**

PERFORMANCE RATING; see **performance appraisal.**

PERFORMING RIGHTS SOCIETY LTD v. MITCHELL AND BOOKER LTD (1924) 1 KB 762; see **contract of service.**

PERIPHERAL WORKERS. Defined by Dean Morse (*The Peripheral Worker,* Columbia University Press, 1969) as 'for the most part, those individuals who have had work experience of any kind other than full-time work for a full year' (p. 5). The classification as used by Professor Morse includes **casual workers** of all kinds (q.v.), many married women and students, the handicapped and the old, a total of 38 millions in the United States in 1965 (Special Labor Force Report No. 76, *Work Experience of the Population in 1965),* compared with 48 millions in full-time jobs.

PERKS or **perquisites.** A type of **fringe benefit** (q.v.) which may be enjoyed by employees arising either out of formal or informal use of the employer's facilities or equipment (use of, or repairs to, vehicles, use of telephone, etc.) or out of rewards by third parties flowing from their employment (e.g. tips, gifts from suppliers or customers, 'change left behind by absent minded or hastening passengers. Knighthoods for senior civil servants . . . to compensate them for low money salaries'. A. Rubner, *Fringe Benefits: The Golden Chains,* Putnam, 1962).

PERMS. Workers on the docks in permanent employment and usually employed by the week; weekly workers on the docks as distinct from those hired as casual labour for the 'turn' or half-day from 8 a.m. to noon, or 1 p.m. to 5 p.m.

PERQUISITES; see **perks.**

PERSONAL EMPLOYEE ASSESSMENT; see **merit rating.**

PERSONAL LIABILITY, doctrine of; see **employers' liability.**

PERSONAL NEEDS ALLOWANCE; see **relaxation allowance.**

PERSONAL RATE. A rate of payment retained by an individual worker, although out of line with an agreed structure of rates or payments, and sometimes known as a **red circle rate.** Personal rates are frequently used to protect workers whose levels of earnings prove to be too high to be accommodated in their appropriate positions or groups when job evaluation or grading is being instituted. They are usually temporary or conditional on the worker concerned staying in the same job, and are often kept constant when other collectively agreed rates are increased. Such a device was used in implementing a new daywage structure in the coal mining industry in 1955; see W.H. Sales and J.L. Davies, 'Introducing a New Wage Structure into Coal Mining', *Bulletin of the Oxford University Institute of Statistics,* August 1957, pp. 201-24; Jules Backman, 'Red Circle Rates', *Labor Law Journal,* June 1961.

PERSONNEL   MANAGEMENT. Defined by the **Institute of Personnel Management** (*Personnel Magazine,* March 1963) as 'that part of management which is concerned with people at work and with their relationships within an enterprise. Its aim is to bring together and develop into an effective organisation the men and women who make up an enterprise and, having regard for the well-being of the individual and of working groups, to enable them to make their best contribution to its success'. The IPM considers personnel management as concerned with recruitment, selection, placement and termination, training, education and promotion, terms of employment, working conditions, communication, negotiation and grievance settlement; see Anne Crichton, *Personnel Management in Context,* Batsford, 1968, Ch. 1. On the extent of personnel management as a specialism, see Anne Crichton and R.G. Collins, 'Personnel Specialists - A Count by Employers', *British Journal of Industrial Relations,* Vol. IV, No. 2, July 1966, A.I. Marsh, 'The Staffing of Industrial Relations Management in the Engineering Industry', *Industrial Relations Journal,* Vol. 2, No. 2, Summer 1971, and J. Eaton, C.R. Gill and R.S. Morris, 'The Staffing of Industrial Relations Management in the Chemical Industry', *Chemistry and Industry,* 17 September 1977, pp. 751-4; for a sociological study of the values, attitudes and influence of personnel managers as a profession see Tony J. Watson, *The Personnel Managers,* Routledge & Kegan Paul, 1977; and, for a recent British text-book, G. Thomason, *A Textbook of Personnel Management,* IPM, 1975.

PERSONNEL MANAGEMENT. The journal of the **Institute of Personnel Management** (1920-) published by Business Publications Ltd, Mercury House, Waterloo Road, London SE1. *Personnel Management* absorbed in 1969 *Personnel and Training Management* (formerly *Personnel Magazine* and earlier *Personnel Management and Methods*, 1945-). For notes on industrial relations journals in general; see George Sayers Bain and Gillian B. Woolven, 'The Literature of Labour Economics and Industrial Relations', *Industrial Relations Journal,* Summer 1971 and in J. Fletcher (ed.), *The Uses of Economic Literature,* Butterworths, 1971.

PERSONNEL MANAGEMENT, INSTITUTE OF (IPM). A professional management association including practising personnel specialists, training officers, graduate members who have completed courses of training approved by the Institute, and student members who are taking such courses. The Institute was founded in June 1913 and provides a number of publications, an information service and courses and conferences on all aspects of training, management and industrial relations relevant to personnel work. In June 1978, the IPM had a membership of 19,152, including 1,579 Fellows and Hon. Fellows, 6,875 members, 3,776 associate members, and 1,406 Affiliate members, the balance being made up principally of student members of various kinds; see G.R. Moxon, *The Growth of Personnel Management in Great Britain during the War,* IPM, 1946; Anne Crichton, 'Changes in the Status of the Personnel Officer since 1939', *Personnel Management,* December 1952, and 'The IPM in 1950 and 1960'. *Personnel Management,* December 1961, and M.M. Niven, *Personnel Management 1913-1963,* IPM, 1967. *Headquarters:* Central House, Upper Woburn Place, London WC1H 0HX. *Tel:* 01-387 2844.

PERSONNEL REVIEW. A professional journal reporting new developments in research, theory and practice of personnel management (1971-). The Review is published quarterly by Gower Press for the **Institute of Personnel Management** and is edited from the Manchester Business School, Booth Street West, Manchester M15 6PB. For notes on industrial relations journals in general; see George Sayers Bain and Gillian B. Woolven, 'The Literature of Labour Economics and

Industrial Relations', *Industrial Relations Journal,* Summer 1971 and in J. Fletcher (ed.), *The Uses of Economic Literature,* Butterworths, 1971.

PERT. Programme Evaluation and Review Technique (q.v.).

PETROLEUM EMPLOYERS' ADVISORY COUNCIL ON EMPLOYEE RELATIONS (PEACER). A body formed in December 1967 by oil companies operating in the United Kingdom for the exchange of views and information on labour relations, and for the purpose of representation of the industry on the Labour and Social Affairs Committee of the **Confederation of British Industry** (q.v.). *Address:* Suite 321-323 Grand Buildings, Trafalgar Square, London WC2. *Tel:* 01-930 0594.

PFA. Professional Footballers Association (q.v.).

PHELPS BROWN REPORT. Name given to the reports of one of two Committees of Inquiry under the chairmanship of Professor E.H. Phelps Brown; *Pay and Conditions of London Busmen* (12 December 1963 and 28 February 1964), and *Building and Civil Engineering* (Cmnd. 3714, and Research Supplement, July 1968) - see **labour-only sub-contracting.**

PHILADELPHIA, DECLARATION OF. A declaration adopted at the 26th Session of the International Labour Conference in Philadelphia in 1944 redefining the aims and purposes of the **International Labour Organisation** and reaffirming that labour is not a commodity, freedoms of expression and association (see **freedom of association**), the danger of poverty to prosperity everywhere, and the need for war on want. For the text of the Declaration, see *The ILO in the Service of Social Progress,* ILO, 1969, Appx 1.

PHILLIPS CURVE. An econometric model developed by A.W. Phillips and R.G. Lipsey based upon studies showing a fairly stable empirical relationship between the rate of change of money wages and the rate of unemployment in the United Kingdom since 1861 (A.W. Phillips, 'The Relation between Unemployment and the Rate of Change of Money Wage Rates in the United Kingdom, 1861-1957', *Economica,* Vol. 25, November 1958; R.G. Lipsey, 'The Relation between Unemployment and the Rate of Change of Money Wage Rates in the United Kingdom 1861-1957: A Further Analysis', *Economica,* Vol. 27, February 1960). These studies suggested that **full-employment** rather than cost-push factors or collective bargaining institutions were responsible for post-war inflation. There is evidence that the Phillips and other econometric wage models all under-predicted wage increases between 1962 and 1967 (see J.H. Pencavel, 'A Note on the Comparative Predictive Performance of Wage Inflation Models in the British Economy', *Economic Journal,* March 1971); this and the **wage explosion** with rising unemployment after late 1969 called into question the validity of the assumptions underlying the Phillips Curve relationships.

'PHOSSY JAW'. Necrosis of the jaw acquired by working with 'The Phos' or yellow phosphorus, especially in the lucifer match trade in the later nineteenth and early twentieth century. Exposure to the chemical led to decay of the teeth and jaw and ultimately in some cases to abscesses on the brain.

PIB. Prices and Incomes Board; see **National Board for Prices and Incomes.**

PICKERING v. THE BISHOP OF ELY; see **specific performance.**

PICKETING. Attendance by pickets during a dispute at a place where persons are working or carrying on business in order to dissuade them or others from doing so; hence **picket line,** a group of pickets, and **passing pickets** by workers not so persuaded or deterred. The legality of peaceful picketing now rests upon s. 15 of the **Trade Union and Labour Relations Act 1974.** Picketing must be done in contemplation of furtherance of a **trade dispute** as defined in the Act, and only for the purposes of peacefully obtaining or communicating information, or for peaceful persuasion, and not done at the home of the persons concerned. See, for example **Broome v. DDP** (1974) and **Kavanagh v. Hiscock** (1974). The **Conspiracy and Protection of Property Act 1875,** s. 7, makes it a criminal offence, while picketing, to use violence or intimidation, see **R. v. Jones** (1974), persistently to follow a person from place to place, to hide tools, clothes or other property owned by another person, to 'watch or beset' another person's house, or to follow such other person in a disorderly manner in any street or road, and pickets have been convicted (though

not often) of other offences under the general law, such as obstructing the police in the execution of their duty (**Piddington v. Bates** (1960) 3 All ER 660 and **Tynan v. Balmer** (1965) 3 All ER and (1966) 3 All ER 133). **Consumer picketing** is aimed at dissuading would-be customers from resorting to picketed premises. It is protected if confined to the peaceful communication of information. The practice of picketing appears greatly to have increased in the 1970s in Britain and many demands have been made that a law specifying both the rights of pickets and the penalties to be incurred for unlawful picketing. In practice the law was proved difficult to amend in ways which might not occasion greater problems than at present and the situation remains very much as laid down in 1906. On picketing since 1972 see: Charles D. Drake, 'The Right to Picket Peacefully', *Industrial Law Journal,* Vol. 1, No. 4, December 1972, pp. 212-18; R. Barber, *Picketing: The Law of Violence.* Bow Group, 1972; R. Taylor, 'Pickets and the Law', *New Society,* 21 November 1974, P. Wallington, 'Criminal Conspiracies and Industrial Conflict', *Industrial Law Journal,* June 1977 and Chris Ralph, *The Picket and the Law,* Fabian Research Series, 331, April 1977; also, **Saltley Depot Incident, Shrewsbury Pickets, mass picketing, flying pickets, Grunwich Dispute.**

PICKET LINE; see **picketing.**

PICKET MONEY. Money paid by trade unions to members engaged in **picketing** duties, especially to 'flying squads' of pickets, e.g. in the miners' strike of January/ February 1972.

PIDDINGTON v. BATES; see **picketing.**

PIECEWORK. Most properly used to refer to incentive payment or payment by result systems which stipulate a price for each unit or each piece of work (**money piecework**), but also by extension to systems in which a worker is given a fixed time in which to do a job but is paid the same amount if he finishes it earlier (**time piecework** or **standard hour system**) (q.v.) and often used loosely to describe incentive payment or payment by results schemes generally (see, for example, P.S. Florence, *Labour,* Hutchinson University Library, 1950, p. 109), perhaps, it is suggested by R. Marriott (*Incentive Payment Systems,* Staples, 3rd (revised) ed., 1968, p. 34) in the first instance to disguise unpopular types of bonus systems. Both money piecework and time piecework are often referred to as **straight piecework** (e.g. in Ministry of Labour, *Industrial Relations Handbook*, 1953, HMSO, p. 182).

PIECEWORK STROKE. The speed or effect expected while working on piecework, compared with the lower speed or effort to be expected on timework or daywork (**timework stroke** or **daywork stroke**); *Committee of Inquiry into Certain Matters concerning the Port Transport Industry* (Devlin Report), Final Report, Cmnd. 2734, August 1965, p. 17.

PIECEWORK SUPPLEMENT. An **out-of-office payment** to payment by results workers in engineering, paid for all hours worked. It ceased to be nationally determined as a result of the agreement between the **Engineering Employers' Federation** and the **Confederation of Shipbuilding and Engineering Unions** of 18 August 1972 (Section II, 7), which left such supplements to be determined domestically. It originated in an award of 5s. per week made by the Committee on Production in 1917, which was called **War Bonus** and added to the basic rate of timeworkers and to the earnings of payment by results workers without being taken into account for overtime premium. After a number of fluctuations, the War Bonus became known as **National Bonus**, and in 1950, the National Bonus of timeworkers was consolidated into the time rate as the **consolidated time rate**, while the 33s. National Bonus of payment by result workers was retained as a national piecework supplement. National increases were thereafter added to the piecework supplement so as to increase the pay of payment by result workers by the same amount as timeworkers. From 1954 until 1972, three national piecework supplements existed for adult males according to grade of skill; see A.I. Marsh, *Industrial Relations in Engineering*, Pergamon Press, 1965.

PIECEWORK WAGE DRIFT. The rise of earnings of production workers under systems of payment by results when the rate at which earnings increase is higher than the rate at which production increases; the extent to which increases in earnings are not matched by a corresponding increase in the rate of production; Coventry and District Engineering Employers' Association, *Wage Drift, Work Measurement and Systems of Payment, 1967*.

PIECEWORKERS' GUARANTEE. A guarantee of minimum fall-back payment to a payment by results worker in the engineering industry; see also **guarantee**. Under the principle established by National Arbitration Tribunal Award No. 470, 1943, a pieceworker is now guaranteed a minimum payment of the **minimum time rate** for his class, or the appropriate domestic rate where higher, whatever his level of production. It is customary to apply the guarantee in accordance with the practice of each establishment on settlement of earnings, e.g. if settlement is on a weekly basis, the guarantee will be applied weekly; but it may be applied, say, monthly or job by job. Where the period of settlement is longer than a week **subbing** is usual.

PILKINGTON COMMISSION. The *Royal Commission on Doctors' and Dentists' Remuneration*, which reported in February 1960 (Cmnd. 939), the Chairman of which was Sir Harry (now Lord) Pilkington. The Commission advised, *inter alia*, the establishment of a standing Review Body to advise the Prime Minister on the pay of doctors and dentists, a recommendation which resulted in the **Kindersley Committee** (1962-70) (q.v.).

PILKINGTON STRIKE. A classic case of a **wildcat strike** (q.v.) involving challenge to union leadership and alienation from the union, occurring at Pilkington Brothers Ltd, St Helens and other establishments of the same company in the spring of 1970. The strike originally arose over an error in wage calculations but rapidly turned into a wage claim on which the actions of the General and Municipal Workers' Union failed to satisfy its members. It ultimately spread to seven Pilkington factories employing 11,000 workers and was remarkable for threats of community violence in St Helens as well as a dramatic breakdown of relationships between the union and its members and between the company and its employees; see *Report of a Court of Inquiry under Professor John C. Wood into a Dispute between Pilkington Brothers Ltd. and certain of their employees*, HMSO, May 1970, and Tony Lane and Kenneth Roberts, *Strike at Pilkingtons*, Collins/Fontana, 1971.

PILOTS; see Letch Report.

PITCHER. A worker who takes meat from the tailboard or a vehicle and who works with other pitchers in taking it to the stalls of market tenants, either by hand or by mechanical means; see National Board for Prices and Incomes, *Smithfield Market*, Report No. 126, Cmnd. 4171, October 1969; see also **pitching**.

PITCHING; see **retaining wage**.

P and KTF. Printing and Kindred Trades Federation (q.v.).

PLAIN SHIFT EARNINGS. The earnings for a shift which are subject to the increase in **gift hours** or premiums for a particular shift worked (steel industry).

PLAIN TIME RATE. Minimum time rate (q.v.).

PLANNED MAINTENANCE. The ordering of the maintenance of buildings and equipment in a satisfactory condition by monitoring the man-hours spent on maintenance tasks and organising these with clear objectives and priorities, thus avoiding maintenance on a 'breakdown' or 'fire fighting' basis; advocated, *inter alia,* to make better use of working time and to reduce **overtime;** see National Board for Prices and Incomes, *Hours of Work, Overtime and Shiftworking*, Report No. 161, Cmnd. 4554-1, December 1970.

PLANT AGREEMENT; see **plant bargaining.**

PLANT BARGAINING. In its most formal sense, bargaining about wages and conditions of work for all or for significant groups of employees at plant or works level, resulting in written **plant** or **works agreements.** Sometimes more loosely used to mean, in addition or in whole, a more-or-less informal state of affairs involving **domestic bargaining.** On the development of such bargaining in Britain; see B.C. Roberts and John Gennard, 'Trends in Plant and Company Bargaining', *Scottish Journal of Political Economy,* Vol. XVII, No. 2, June 1970; Department of Employment, *The Reform of Collective Bargaining at Plant and Company Level,* Manpower Papers No. 5, 1971 and A.I. Marsh, E.O. Evans and P. Garcia, *Workplace Industrial Relations in Engineering,* EEF and Kogan Page, 1971.

PLAY. Not being at work; unemployment, e.g. in the pottery industry.

PLURAL SOCIETY. A term derived from political theory and currently tending to refer to any community with a plurality of centres of power (see B.A. Shils, *Torment of Secrecy,* Heinemann, 1957) and hence to any complex organisation, including the industrial. On the view that all industrial undertakings should be treated as plural societies and that the role of management is to reconcile individual and group objectives; see N. Ross, in *Human Relations and Modern Management,* E.M. Hugh Jones (ed.), North Holland Publishing Co., 1958 and Alan Fox, *Industrial Sociology and Industrial Relations,* Royal Commission on Trade Unions and Employers' Associations, Research Papers 3, HMSO, 1966. Fox discussed the enterprise both as a **unitary** and as a **pluralistic system** and concluded that industrial relations must be based on the latter view of the firm, the former being founded on unreal assumptions about social behaviour and the nature of authority. In a later consideration of the subject Fox has criticised the view he took in the Donovan paper, principally on the grounds that pluralism is not 'value free' as a concept and that by adopting pluralistic attitudes and frameworks, the parties might simply be refining and legitimising the *status quo,* thus ignoring the possibility that 'a radical analysis beyond pluralism is not only of greater intellectual validity but is also a necessary stimulus and guide to the pursuit of more fundamental change' (p. 229); see also the development of his thinking on **trust relations,** and the response of H.A. Clegg, 'Pluralism in Industrial Relations', *British Journal of Industrial Relations,* Vol. XIII, No. 3, November 1975, pp. 309-11.

PLURALISTIC SYSTEM; see **plural society.**

PMTS. Predetermined motion time systems (q.v.).

POA. Prison Officers' Association (q.v.).

POACHING. The act of a trade union in recruiting members by influencing them to leave another union, and particularly a transfer contrary to the morally binding code of the **Bridlington Agreement** (q.v.); S.W. Lerner, *Breakaway Unions and the Small Trade Union,* Allen and Unwin, 1961, pp. 68-9; also used of employers inducing workers to work for them by leaving other employers; see **enticement of labour.**

POEU. Post Office Engineering Union (q.v.).

POINT PREMIUM SYSTEM. A type of incentive payment system similar to premium bonus systems but employing points value to units of work rather than units of time; it is particularly associated with the name of Charles Bedeaux (see **Bedeaux System**). For a description of point premium systems, see N.C. Hunt, *Methods of Wage Payment in British Industry*, Pitman, 1951, Ch. X.

POINTS RATING. A method of **job evaluation** (q.v.) more commonly practised in Britain. It requires the selection and definition of the factors considered relevant in determining the relative degrees of difficulty, responsibility or contribution in different jobs, and the allocation of points to these factors and to appropriate sub-factors with appropriate weightings and against appropriate benchmarks. A total point score can therefore be worked out for each job, and these ranked in order, money values being placed upon the jobs afterwards.

POLICE ACT 1964. An Act amending and adding to the Police Act 1919, and the Police (Scotland) Act 1956. Following an outbreak of discontent and the formation of a Police Union in 1918, the 1919 Act made it unlawful for a member of a police force in Great Britain to be a member of a trade union, or of any assocation having as one of its objects to control or influence pay and conditions in the police service; it also virtually prohibited strike action (s. 3). In recompense for these losses of freedom each country was permitted to establish a **Police Federation** representative of policemen, to consult and advise on all matters concerning welfare and efficiency (but not on discipline and promotion). Each Federation was to be independent of the authorities, but not a trade union within the statutory definition. In 1953 a non-statutory **Police Council for Great Britain** was set up as a negotiating body on pay and conditions. The 1964 Act placed this on a statutory basis, with Police Advisory Boards for England and Wales and Scotland, and reaffirmed the status of the Police Federations, as well as the prohibition against policemen joining trade unions (s. 47) and against striking (s. 53). The Police Federation of England and Wales and the Northern Ireland Police Federation withdrew from the Police Council in 1976 on the grounds that the employing sides of the Council were failing to face up to their responsibilities to ensure fair conditions for the police and in October 1977 an inquiry, chaired by Lord Edmund-Davies, was announced which would look into police pay, negotiating machinery and the rights and duties of the Police Federations; see also **Police Act 1972.**

POLICE ACT 1972. An Act Schedule I of which modifies s. 44(a) of the **Police Act 1964** forbidding association of the **Police Federations** with any body or person outside the police service. The Home Secretary may now authorise such association to bodies specified by himself.

POLICE COUNCIL FOR GREAT BRITAIN; see **Police Act 1964.**

POLICE FEDERATIONS; see **Police Acts 1964** and **1972.**

POLICY ALLOWANCE (work study); see **allowance**; 'an increment, other than a bonus increment (q.v.), applied to **standard time** (or some constituent part of it, e.g. work content) to provide a satisfactory level of earnings for a specified level of performance under exceptional circumstances'. British Standards Institution, *Glossary of Terms Used in Work Study*, BS 3138, 1969, A 1015.

POLICY OVERTIME. Overtime which is systematically worked as a matter of managerial policy, in order to retain labour, maintain earnings, etc.

POLITICAL FUND. A trade union fund for use on political objects authorised under the **Trade Union Act 1913** (q.v.), and supervised by the Chief Registrar of Friendly Societies (now by the **Certification Officer** (q.v.). The Act reversed the House of Lords judgement in the case of **Osborne v. Amalgamated Society of Railway Servants**, by making political objects lawful but confining expenditure on them to the political fund. The Certification Officer reported that for 1976 all listed unions had a political fund income of £2,942,000 and an expenditure of £2,278,000. Under the Act trade union members not wishing to make contributions to political funds authorised by approved rules (i.e. to the **political levy**) must be permitted to contract out of payment (see **contracting-out**). On the use of political funds, see Martin Harrison, *Trade Unions and the Labour Party,*

George Allen and Unwin, 1960, and on the law relating to the political levy, Cyril Grunfeld, *Modern Trade Union Law*, Sweet and Maxwell, 1970.

POLITICAL LEVY; see **political fund.**

POLITICAL STRIKE. A stoppage of work for political ends. K.G.J.C. Knowles (*Strikes*, Basil Blackwell, 1952, pp. 291-2) distinguishes between consciously political and unconsciously political strikes, including among the former revolutionary general strikes, strikes with political objects designed to force a government's hand and strikes with economic objects but called for political reasons, and among the latter, strikes connected with workers' living standards but where government action is necessary to effect improvement and strikes with economic objectives but likely to provoke government action because of their effects at home and abroad. Strikes for purely political objects are not **trade disputes** under the **Trade Union and Labour Relations Act 1974;** neither union officials nor strike leaders nor rank and file members are legally protected. The problem continues to be one of distinguishing the objective of a strike; a strike to prevent a company from contributing to the funds of a political party, or to compel a trade union member so to contribute would not be protected; one primarily concerned with terms and conditions of work, but with political overtones, might be protected. The Emergency Powers Acts 1920 and 1964 could, however, be used in any emergency situation, whether an industrial dispute or not.

POLYTECHNIC TEACHERS, ASSOCIATION OF (APT). An association formed in 1973 to represent teachers in the 30 Polytechnics of England and Wales and the Polytechnic of Northern Ireland. Its main objectives have been national control of Polytechnics and parity of provision between Polytechnics and universities. *Address*: Throgmorton House, 27 Elphinstone Road, Southsea, Hants, PO5 3HP. *Tel*: 0705 818625. *Membership, 1977*: 3,500.

POPULORUM PROGRESSIO; see **Catholic industrial relations teaching.**

PORTERAGE; see **retaining wage.**

PORTS INDUSTRY, JOINT SPECIAL COMMITTEE ON THE; see **Aldington-Jones Committee.**

POSITIVE STRIKE. A strike to improve wages and conditions; the opposite of a **negative strike,** i.e. a strike to prevent the worsening of wages and conditions; principally in USA.

POST-DONOVAN CONFERENCES. Conferences of affiliated unions called by the **Trades Union Congress** in 1969 to discuss the conclusions and recommendations of the (Donovan) **Royal Commission on Trade Unions and Employers' Association 1965-1968** on the reform and extension of collective bargaining. The conferences were held in six sectors: *Engineering and Shipbuilding*, the *Construction Industries*, the *Public Sector*, the *Wages Council Sector*, the *Private Non-Manual Sector*, and *'Other Private Sector' industries*. In 1970, a **Collective Bargaining Committee** (q.v.) of the TUC was established, *inter alia*, to follow up the Post-Donovan Conferences.

POST-ENTRY CLOSED SHOP; see **closed shop.**

POST OFFICE ENGINEERING UNION (POEU). A trade union originating in 1887 as the Postal Telegraph Linemen's Movement which, after a number of subsequent changes, took its present title in 1919. It organises all engineering grades concerned with telecommunications in the Post Office Corporation below supervisory level and co-operates with other unions in the Post Office in the **Council of Post Office Unions** (COPOU) (q.v.). It claims 95 per cent organisation among staff eligible for membership. The union has been notable in recent years for its campaign for increased capital expenditure on telecommunications, for its advocacy of technical change and for its comprehensive educational service. A view of its historical problems with breakaways, especially the Engineering Officers' (Telecommunication) Association (EO(T)A) has been given by S.W. Lerner, 'Fission and Fusion in the Post Office Engineering Union', in *Breakaway Unions and the Small Trade Union*, George Allen and Unwin, 1961, Ch. 4. The union had its first one-day official stoppage in 1969; see POEU, *75 Years: A Short History of the Post Office Engineering Union, 1962*, and F. Bealey, *The Post Office Engineering Union*, Bachman and Turner, 1976. *Address*: 150 Brunswick Road, Ealing, London W5 1AW. *Tel*: 01-998 2981. *TUC Affiliated Membership, 1977*: 124,535.

POST OFFICE EXECUTIVES, SOCIETY OF (SPOE). A Post Office trade union with negotiating rights for first line supervising officers in the Engineering Department and the Motor Transport Division, for all grades in the Traffic Class, for all supervising grades in the Supplies Division and, since September 1971, grades above draughtsmen in the Drawing Office Class. The Association was originally known as the Society of Post Office Engineering Inspectors and was first recognised by the Postmaster General in March 1911. Until 1939 it was affiliated to the Institution of Professional Civil Servants along with a sister organisation, the Society of Post Office Engineering Chief Inspectors, with which it amalgamated in 1943 to form the Society of Post Office Engineering Inspectorate, later renamed the Society of Telecommunication Engineers. Its present title was adopted in 1969 on amalgamation with the Telecommunications Traffic Association. *Address:* 116 Richmond Road, Kingston-on-Thames, KT2 5HL. *Tel:* 01-549 3323. *TUC Affiliated Membership, 1977:* 22,583.

POST OFFICE UNIONS, COUNCIL OF (COPOU). From March 1969 the title of the former Post Office Joint Trade Union Council, charged with co-ordinating the views of Post Office Unions on matters of common concern, including conditions of service, operational issues, planning and financial programme of the Post Office. COPOU now consists of the **Union of Post Office Workers,** the **Post Office Engineering Union,** the Post Office Management Staffs Association, the Society of Post Office Executives, the National Federation of Sub-Postmasters and the Postal and Telecommunications Group of the **Civil and Public Services Association** which joined the Council towards the end of 1971. In addition, there are now two associate member unions, the Telephone Contract Officers' Association, and the Society of Civil and Public Servants (Post Office Executive Group). The council represents almost all employees of the Post Office Corporation. *Address:* 113 Tottenham Court Road, London W1P 9HG. *Tel:* 01-387 2533/4.

POST OFFICE WORKERS, UNION OF (UPW). A trade union representing postmen, postmen higher grade, postal and telegraph officers, telephonists, telegraphists, cleaners, and other small grades employed by the Post Office Corporation.

The union, which traces its origins in the first of the permanent associations to be formed in the Post Office in 1881, was formed by amalgamation and came into being on 1 January 1920. It was notable at this time for the emphasis which it placed on **workers' control,** an aspiration which still remains among the objects of the union. (See Branko Pribićević, *The Shop Stewards' Movement and Workers' Control,* Basil Blackwell, 1959.) It is now organised in some 1,200 branches throughout Great Britain and Northern Ireland, which conduct negotiations with local managers on purely local matters. Its Annual Conference is organised into a Main Conference, and three Sectional Conferences, one for postmen and postmen higher grade, one for postal and telegraph officers, overseas telegraph operators and radio operators, and one for telephonists and telegraphists. It is a constituent union of the **Council of Post Office Unions** (COPOU); see UPW, *Official Recognition - How it was Gained,* UPW n.d.; UPW, *How we Began: Postal Trade Unionism, 1870-1920,* UPW, 1920, and Michael Moran, *The Union of Post Office Workers,* Macmillan, 1974. *Address:* UPW House, Crescent Lane, Clapham, London SW4 9RN. *Tel:* 01-622 2291. *TUC Affiliated Membership, 1977:* 201,099.

POSTAL, TELEGRAPH AND TELEPHONE INTERNATIONAL (PTTI); see **International Trade Secretariats.**

PROFESSIONAL AND PUBLIC SERVICE ORGANISATIONS, CONFERENCE OF (COPPSO). A conference of public service workers' and allied unions representing 750,000 members convened by the **National Union of Teachers** in August 1961 to seek joint action against attempts of the Treasury to impose a **pay pause.** Two only of the 18 organisations originally attending were affiliated to the **Trades Union Congress.** COPPSO was ineffective in its attempts to obtain membership of the National Economic Development Council and to achieve a permanent liaison machinery with government over pay in the public sector. After some member organisations previously unaffiliated joined the TUC, the Conference became progressively less workable and, as an experiment in pursuing joint policies outside the TUC framework, ceased to hold meetings in July 1964.

POST OFFICE WORKERS' UNION

(POWU). A trade union in Ireland formed in 1923 by amalgamation of the Irish Postal Union (originally in 1900, the Dual Workers' Association, which became the Association of Irish Post Office Clerks in 1904, and the Irish Postal Union in 1920), and the Irish Postal Workers' Union, an all Irish organisation resulting from a conference of March 1922, in which the Union of Post Office Workers in Ireland, after the setting up of the Provisional Government of the Irish Free State on 1 March of that year, resolved upon establishing a union unrelated to a British organisation. *Address:* 52 Parnall Square, Dublin 1. *Tel:* Dublin 747841. *ICTU Affiliated Membership, 1977:* 10,000.

POWELL DUFFRYN LTD v. HOUSE (1974) ICR 123; see **guaranteed week.**

POWERLOADING AGREEMENTS. Collective agreements between the National Coal Board and the National Union of Mineworkers, first at district level, and in 1966 at national level (hence **National Powerloading Agreement**) relating to mechanised faces. The 1966 agreement progressively replaced pit level piecework in coal mining by offering inclusive shift rates to members of powerloading teams; A.I. Marsh and W.E.J. McCarthy, *Disputes Procedures in Britain,* Royal Commission on Trade Unions and Employers' Associations, Research Papers 2(2), 1968, pp. 76-7.

POWER LOOM CARPET WEAVERS' AND TEXTILE WORKERS' ASSOCIATION. A trade union founded in 1866 and until 1917 known as the Power Loom Carpet Weavers' Mutual Defence and Provident Association. The union is strongly organised in the carpet trade. It reached the peak of its membership in 1966. *Address:* Carpet Weavers' Hall, Callows Lane, Kidderminster, Worcs. *Tel:* 0562 3192. *TUC Affiliated Membership, 1977:* 6,475.

POWER LOOM OVERLOOKERS, SCOTTISH UNION OF. A trade union originating in 1911. In 1943 the constituents of the Scottish Federation of Power Loom Tenters (Dundee and District, Dunfermline and District, Forfar, Kirriemuir and District, Perth and District, Katrine and District, and Glasgow and West of Scotland) amalgamated to form the Scottish Union of Powerloom Tenters which adopted its present title in 1968. *Address:* 857 Turnberry Avenue, Dundee, Angus. *Tel:* 0382 86489. *TUC Affiliated Member-*

ship, 1977: 300; see also **British Federation of Textile Technicians.**

POWER LOOM OVERLOOKERS, YORKSHIRE ASSOCIATION OF. An association of loom overlookers with branches in Huddersfield and Dewsbury (which combined in 1918), Halifax, Keighley, Leeds and Bradford. It was originally formed in 1911. *Address:* Textile Hall, Westgate, Bradford BD1 2RG. *Tel:* 0274-27966. *TUC Affiliated Membership, 1977:* 1,376.

POWU. Post Office Workers' Union (q.v.).

PREDETERMINED MOTION TIME SYSTEMS (PMTS). Any work measurement technique in which **synthetic times** established for basic human motions, and arrived at by statistical methods, are used to build up the **standard time** for a job at a defined level of performance. The notion of universal elementary motions is said to have been conceived by Frank B. Gilbreth, whose 'therbligs' were developed by A.B. Segur (*Manufacturing Industry,* 1927) into a system which he called **Motion Time Analysis** (MTA), other practical systems emerging being later known as **Work Factor System, Methods-Time Measurement** (MTM), (or MTM2), **Dimensional Motion Times** (DMT), **Basic Motion Time Study** (BMT), **Master Standard Data** (MSD), etc. In essence, synthetic times are provided for application to component motions as discovered by minute method study analysis. PMTS has advantages of universality and precision, though identical time standards do not exist from one country to another in practice (it has been suggested that American times may have to be increased by approximately 11 per cent to satisfy European conditions); it also has the disadvantage of restriction to repetition jobs on grounds of uneconomy of application to non-repetitive jobs and small batch jobs, and it has been questioned whether it is valid to add together times for individual small motions in a way which PMTS requires; see International Labour Office, *Introduction to Work Study,* Geneva, 1969; see also British Standards Institution, *Glossary of Terms Used in Work Study,* BSI No. 31003, 1969; H.B. Maynard, G.J. Stegemerten and J.L. Schwab, *Methods-Time Measurement,* McGraw-Hill, 1948, R.M. Currie, *Simplified PMTS,* British Institute of Management, 1963, and Department of Employment, *An Introduction to*

Predetermined Motion-Time Systems, HMSO, 1976.

PRE-ENTRY CLOSED SHOP; see **closed shop.**

PREFERENTIAL HIRING. A form of union security practised in the United States under which the employer agrees to give first preference to workers who are members of the union, or made available by the union, so long as the union is able to supply employees of the required number and quality, non-unionists being taken on only after all qualified union members have been found work; hence **preferential shop;** a company or shop in which **preferential hiring** is used. Harold S. Roberts, *Dictionary of Industrial Relations,* BNA, 1966, p. 332.

PREFERENTIAL SHOP; see **preferential hiring.**

PREMIUM BONUS PLAN (SYSTEM). An **incentive payment** or **payment by results** system (q.v.). Authorities differ on whether a difference exists between a **bonus system** (q.v.) and a **premium bonus system,** and on whether the expression should be confined to **time-saved systems** or **task-bonus systems.** Marriott (*Incentive Payment Systems,* Staples, 1968, 3rd (revised) ed., pp. 35-6) observes that the words 'bonus' and 'premium' are synonymous in common usage and concludes that in classifying incentive payment systems they should both be regarded as 'bonus systems', the word 'premium' being added when this was included by the originator of any particular scheme. N.C. Hunt (*Methods of Wage Payment in British Industry,* Pitman, 1951, p. 78) notes that 'the essence of premium bonus systems is that piece-rate per unit of output declines as output goes up', that they were opposed by trade unions at the end of the nineteenth century (though accepted in 1902 by the Amalgamated Society of Engineers) and officially condemned by the Trades Union Congress in 1909. Hunt considers premium bonus plans to be of declining importance in the majority of industries.

PREMIUM PAY; see **premium payment.**

PREMIUM PAY PLAN. A 'stepped' or 'graduated' **measured daywork** system of payment associated with Philips Industries Limited, designed to overcome the main shortcomings of conventional **payment by results** systems, but allowing individual workers some measure of choice in effort and pay, and demanding a high standard of supervision. The system works on a basis of job evaluated grades and work measurement by a **predetermined motion-time system** resulting in a number of standard performance levels. Workers are then paid on the following type of matrix (illustrated from one factory in December 1967) (see table below).

After training, each worker contracts with his foreman to maintain a given performance level, and his performance is measured daily. His pay does not vary with output until performance has been maintained for two weeks. The system is said to put pressure on management to organise production efficiently, and, despite the need to correct loss of performance by workers, to be applied equitably; see National Board for Prices and Incomes, *Payment by Results,* Report No. 65, Cmnd. 3627, May 1968, p. 42 *et seq.*

PREMIUM PAYMENT or, in some industries, **premium pay.** In the engineering industry, payment, in addition to payment for work done, made in circumstances provided for in national agreements, e.g. for **overtime, nightshift** working, etc., and **coupling-up;** more generally, an **allowance** made to the worker as extra payment to compensate for working outside normal hours on shifts, on holidays, or under dangerous or unpleasant conditions; see **overtime premium, shift differential.** Premium payment is some-

Class	Rate on Engagement	Level of Performance:								
		60	65	70	75	78	81	84	87	90
A	198/6	198/6	198/6	206/6	216/6	222/6	228/6	234/6	240/6	246/6
B	—		198/6	201/1	212/4	222/9	229/0	235/3	241/6	247/9	254/0
C	—		198/6	207/4	218/2	229/0	235/6	242/0	248/6	255/0	261/6
D	—		201/6	212/9	224/0	235/3	242/0	248/9	255/6	262/3	269/0

times referred to as **penalty pay,** and the rates paid as **penalty rates;** it is also applied occasionally to plus rates paid to employees for exceptional skill or ability.

PREMIUM WAGE SYSTEM. Any incentive payment system which provides a bonus or premium for work in excess of the norm and for extra effort; see also **premium bonus system.**

PRE-PRODUCTION RATE; see temporary rate.

PRESIDENTIAL   SEIZURE or **government seizure.** A procedure by which the government of the United States of America, or the President, may seize certain properties in the national interest. Such procedure in peacetime requires specific statutory authority (Youngstown Sheet and Tube Co. v. Sawyer, 343 US 579, 30LRRM2172). A considerable literature on seizure of this kind exists in the US (see Harold Roberts, *Dictionary of Industrial Relations,* 1966, pp. 127 and 334, and J.L. Blackman, *Presidential Seizure in Labour Disputes,* Harvard UP, 1967). It has rarely been referred to in Britain, but see H.A. Turner, *Is Britain Really Strike Prone?,* CUP, 1969, p. 47.

PRESS CHARTER. A provision for a Charter of Freedom of the Press introduced into the Trade Union and Labour Relations (Amendment) Act 1976 s. 2 (now s. 1A of the **Trade Union and Labour Relations Acts 1974 and 1976**). The Charter resulted from fears for the independence of the Press arising from actions of the National Union of Journalists in relation to the trade union membership of editors which brought pressures in Parliament for the amendment of provisions in the 1974 Act on union membership agreements and linked provisions on unfair dismissal. The Charter, to be drawn up by the parties, or failing this by the Secretary of State for Employment after consultation with them and with the Press Council, is required to contain practical guidance for trade unions, employers and editors on matters relating to press freedom and to contain provision for a body to which complaints of breach of the Charter can be made. It has no direct legal force, but may be quoted in evidence in any legal proceedings.

PRESSED   GLASSMAKERS, SOCIETY OF. A trade union founded as a craft society in1872 for makers of hand-made glassware and currently affiliated to the **General Federation of Trade Unions.** Automation has caused a decline in its membership. *Address:* 11 Oakfield Road, Lobley Hill, Gateshead NE11 0AA. *Tel:* Dunston 605099. *Membership, 1977:* 504.

PRICE PLATEAU. A form of **wage policy,** associated with the name of Mr Harold Macmillan which followed the White Paper *The Economic Implications of Full Employment,* Cmd. 9725, 1956, and taking the form of an appeal that nationalised industries and private employers should forego price increases for at least a year, while unions should adopt a policy of wage restraint. The **Trades Union Congress** rejected restraint and a strike in engineering and shipbuilding following stands by employers which they felt that the government had encouraged, were followed by Courts of Inquiry and the establishment of the **Cohen Council** Council on Prices, Productivity and Incomes (see H.A. Clegg and Rex Adams, *The Employers' Challenge,* Basil Blackwell, 1957).

PRICES AND INCOMES ACTS. Three Acts of Parliament of 1966, 1967 and 1968 concerned with the statutory implementation of the Wilson administration's **prices and incomes policy** 1965-70. The Act of 1966 established the **National Board for Prices and Incomes** on a statutory basis, and gave the government power to delay pay or price increases for one year; the 1967 Act enabled it to impose a 30-day standstill on such rises while they were examined, further delay of up to three months if they were referred to the NBPI and a further delay if the Board so recommended; the 1968 Act increased the power to delay after an NBPI recommendation to eight months and gave further powers to order price reductions on an NBPI recommendation. A motion calling for the repeal of the 1966 and 1967 Acts was carried at the **Trades Union Congress** in 1967, and the policies implied in them were phased out before the Labour Government was defeated in the General Election of June 1970.

PRICES AND INCOMES BOARD (PIB); see National Board for Prices and Incomes.

PRICES AND INCOMES POLICY. A policy outlining the considerations which, in the national interest, should guide all those concerned with prices and incomes, announced by the Wilson administration in a White Paper, *Prices and Incomes Policy*, Cmnd. 2639, April 1965, following the **Declaration of Intent** (q.v.) of December 1964. The policy lasted until 1970, and was characterised by a number of further white papers setting down the **criteria** for the policy (*Prices and Incomes Policy - An Early Warning System*, Cmnd. 2808, November 1965, *Prices and Incomes Standstill: Period of Severe Restraint*, Cmnd. 3150, November 1966, *Prices and Incomes Policy after 30th July 1967*, Cmnd. 3235, March 1967, *Productivity, Prices and Incomes Policy in 1968 and 1969*, Cmnd. 3590, April 1968, and *Productivity Prices and Incomes after 1969*, Cmnd. 4237, December 1969), by three Prices and Incomes Acts in 1966, 1967 and 1968), establishing the policy on a statutory basis, by the setting up of **norms**, by the activities of the **National Board for Prices and Incomes**, and by the growing opposition of trade unions which eventually resulted in the decline of the policy and its subsequent abandonment by the Heath administration during the early part of its period in office. The policy attempted to avoid negative wage restraint, and a 'stop-go' attitude to economic growth and to operate with the consent of the **Confederation of British Industry** and the **Trades Union Congress**. It developed through five stages - a voluntary stage between April 1965 and June 1966, when the Prices and Incomes Act of that year gave the government power to delay price and pay increases for one year, and suspended exceptional criteria for such increases as a short-term standstill measure following a sterling crisis; a third stage of moderate restraint followed between July 1967 and March 1968, with a zero norm but more moderate criteria for exceptional increases and statutory delaying powers; a fourth phase (March 1968 to end 1969) followed a further sterling crisis after devaluation, and a fifth at the beginning of 1970, when voluntary restraint was substantially restored to meet growing opposition to the policy. Opinions differ on the effectiveness of the policy while in operation. Trade unions were of the view that it acted principally to increase productivity and unemployment and to hamper the role of bargaining in improving the real income of their members. Some observers have reckoned it moderately successful in restraining rises in incomes and rather more successful in restraining price rises (J. Corina, *The Times*, 5 March 1970); others, using unemployment series to explain wage movements (see **Phillips Curve**) have reckoned it counter-produc-

tive (R.G. Lipsey and J.M. Parkin, 'Incomes Policy: A Reappraisal', *Economica*, May 1970); see also Department of Employment, *Prices and Earnings in 1951-1969; An Econometric Assessment*, HMSO, 1971; Hilde Behrend, Harriet Lynch, Howard Thomas and Jean Davies, *Incomes Policy and the Individual*, Oliver and Boyd, 1967; John Corina, *Incomes Policy - Problems and Prospects*, Parts I and II, Institute of Personnel Management, 1966, and Hugh Clegg, *How to Run an Incomes Policy and Why we made such a Mess of the Last One*, Heinemann, 1971. The Heath government revived approaches to a voluntary prices and incomes policy in 1972; see **Chequers and Downing Street Talks, Pay Board, wage restraint**. For the prices and incomes policy of the Labour government after 1974 see **Social Contract**.

PRIESTLEY FORMULA. A formula for the remuneration of civil servants introduced by the Priestley *Royal Commission on the Civil Service, 1953-1955*, Cmd. 9613, November 1955 based upon 'fair comparisons' with the current pay of outside staffs on broadly comparable work, taking into account differences in other conditions of service. The Priestley Formula replaced the **Tomlin Formula** laid down by the Tomlin Commission in 1931 (q.v.). In order to provide facts relating to job comparability and pay and conditions, the Commission proposed the establishment of an independent **Civil Service Pay Research Unit** (q.v.), information from the unit being used in subsequent negotiation on rates of pay. This method of determining Civil Service pay has been used since 1956; see B.V. Humphreys, *Clerical Unions in the Civil Service*, Blackwell and Mott, 1958, pp. 212-22.

PRIESTLEY v. FOWLER (1837) 3 M and W 1; see **employers' liability**.

PRIESTMAN PLAN. A classical example of a group **production bonus** introduced by Messrs Priestman Bros of Hull in 1917 in which, in consultation with the Works Committee, a bonus was paid on all output higher than a fixed standard, both the standard and the bonus being reviewed every four weeks; see N.C. Hunt, *Methods of Wage Payment in British Industry*, Pitman, 1951, p. 107.

PRIMARY BOYCOTT; see boycott.

PRIMARY WORK GROUPS; see **work groups.**

PRINTERS, GRAPHICAL AND MEDIA PERSONNEL, NATIONAL SOCIETY OF OPERATIVE (NATSOPA). A trade union tracing its origin from the Printers' Labourers' Union of 1889 which ten years later became the Operative Printers' Assistants' Society, and in 1904 the National Society of Operative Printers' Assistants, an ampersand being inserted in 1912 between 'Printers' and 'Assistants' as a token of the society's unwillingness to accept that its jurisdiction was confined to assistants only and not to operative printers or machine managers; see R.B. Suthers, *The Story of NATSOPA,* NATSOPA, 1929 and James Moran, *NATSOPA, 75 Years,* OUP, 1964. In 1966 NATSOPA became Division 1 of the **Society of Graphical and Allied Trades** (q.v.), but reverted to its old title when the amalgamation with the National Union of Printing, Bookbinding and Paper Workers broke up in 1970 and took its present title in 1972. It organises principally machine assistants, clerks, messengers and photo-printers in national newspapers, workers in ink and roller manufacture and in general printing, machine assistants and clerks in some areas. *Address:* Caxton House, 13-16 Borough Road, St George's Circus, London SE1 0AL. *Tel:* 01-928 1481. *TUC Affiliated Membership, 1977:* 53,396.

PRINTING, BOOKBINDING AND PAPER WORKERS, NATIONAL UNION OF (NUPB AND PW); see **Graphical and Allied Trades, Society of.**

PRINTING AND KINDRED TRADES FEDERATION (P and KTF). A federation of trade unions established in 1901, after attempts lasting some 15 years, to provide co-ordination between a number of printing unions, especially in relation to national agreements. The Federation after 1919, when the first national agreement on hours and holidays was signed, followed a policy of representing constituent unions on matters of common interest, while allowing them to pursue their own individual policies on such matters as pay negotiations. As a result of the amalgamation of a number of trade unions in the industry the Federation became The Printing Trade Unions Co-ordinating Bureau in February 1974 and was subsequently dissolved. See P and KTF, *Sixty Years of Service, 1901-1961,* P and KTF, 1961.

PRISON OFFICERS' ASSOCIATION (POA). An association catering for members of the prison officer class, nursing sisters and non-industrial civilian employees in the prison service in Great Britain and Northern Ireland, and the staffs of special hospitals. An early Police and Prison Officers' Union foundered in 1919 after a police strike (see **Police Act 1964**), and there was no effective representation of prison officers until 1938, the right to set up a Prison Officers' Association being accepted by the Home Secretary in 1939. The Association secured a full seat on the Staff Side of the Civil Service National Whitley Council in 1969, and affiliated to the **Trades Union Congress** in 1967. *Address:* Cronin House, 245 Church Street, Edmonton, London N9 9HW. *Tel:* 01-807 3383 and 3101. *TUC Affiliated Membership, 1977:* 20,686.

PRO TANTO SETTLEMENT. A collective agreement in which wage increases are related inversely to the individual's earnings; see also **tapering.** Pro tanto settlements were a feature of National Arbitration Award No. 326 of 1943 and of the 1950 national agreement in the engineering industry: T.P. Hill and K.G.J.C. Knowles, 'The Variability of Engineering Earnings', *Bulletin of the Oxford University Institute of Statistics,* Vol. 18, No. 2, May 1956. A modified form of the principle of the graduated increase was also applied in the Engineering National Agreement of 22 December 1964; see **minimum earnings level.**

PROCEDURAL RECOGNITION; see **trade union recognition.**

PROCEDURAL TERMS or procedural rules which, taken together, constitute **procedure** (or procedural) **agreements.** Terms of a collective agreement which refer to the adjustment of differences between the parties, whether arising from the making of new agreements (see **conflicts of interest**), from the application or interpretation of existing agreements (see **conflicts of rights**), of the processing of individual grievances (see **grievance procedures;** usually contrasted with **substantive terms** (q.v.), i.e. those relating to rates of pay, etc. Allan Flanders (*Collective Bargaining: Prescription for Change,* Faber and Faber, 1968, p. 63) summarises the position of procedural terms as regulating conflict between the parties to collective bargaining, and distinguishes three more detailed functions; definition of the bargaining unit, determination of the status of and facilities for representatives, and the regulation of behaviour in the settlement of disputes; see also J.T. Dunlop, *Industrial Relations Systems,* Dryden, Holt, 1958, and **substantive terms** for elements of overlapping with procedural terms.

PROCEDURE AGREEMENT; see **procedural terms.**

PROCESS CONSULTANCY; see **Organisation Development.**

PROCESS WORKER. A worker, usually of a non-craft kind, who works on a process, e.g. in the chemical industry. In the printing industry a craftsman engaged on the preparation of the printing surfaces of gravure cylinders or litho and letterpress plates.

PRODUCTION BONUS. A bonus, or additional payment, made for additional production, e.g. for tonnage (see **tonnage payments**) or for production over and above standard output as fixed or agreed, e.g. in the **Priestman Plan,** a type of **group incentive scheme. Stabilised production bonus,** or **consolidated production bonus,** a production bonus which has been fixed at a given level and is paid as a part of, or regularly in addition to, the **base rate** or **time rate.**

PRODUCTION WORKERS often also referred to as **direct labour,** or **directs** (as opposed to **indirect workers** or **indirects**). A group of workers whose work is in 'direct' production, e.g. processing, assembling, fabricating, receiving, handling, etc., as contrasted with the groups whose work is in 'indirect' labour, e.g. in clerical work or offices, in supervision or professional occupations, and, sometimes, in maintenance and security. Classification as 'directs' and 'indirects' may vary from one industry to another and one establishment to another. Where payment by results for production workers is the practice, application to indirects may be difficult, leading to **lieu rates** and sometimes to schemes of overall factory bonuses; see National Board for Prices and Incomes, *Payment by Results,* Report No. 65, Cmnd. 3627, May 1968.

PRODUCTIVITY AGREEMENT; see **productivity bargaining.**

PRODUCTIVITY BARGAINING. A type of collective bargaining resulting in a **productivity deal, productivity package deal, productivity agreement, comprehensive agreement, efficiency agreement,** etc. The term originated in the **Blue Book** deal concluded between the Esso Petroleum Company and the unions at its Fawley Refinery in 1960 (see Allan Flanders, *The Fawley Productivity Agreements,* Faber and Faber, 1964), in which increased pay was given in return for specified changes in working practices, e.g. for elimination of mates and of overtime, greater **interchangeability** and **flexibility** of workers and unions in performing jobs, direct reductions in manning scales, etc., the whole being regarded as a single package at plant level. It was originally conceived as a form of **wage-work bargaining** of a type contrasting with **effort bargaining** (q.v.) though the latter might be considered 'productivity bargaining of an elementary type' (Allan Flanders, 'How Dangerous is Productivity Bargaining?', *British Industry,* 18 March 1966). Fawley type productivity bargaining was confined to particular situations and the use of the term gradually extended, particularly as a result of the Wilson administration's **prices and incomes policy,** to include in practice the application of work standards in incentive schemes, wage and salary restructuring, etc., with a consequent increase in the acceptability of the concept among employers' associations (see A.I. Marsh, 'The Contribution of Employers' Associations', in B. Towers, T.G. Whittingham and A.W. Gottschalk, *Bargaining for Change,* Allen and Unwin, 1972). Productivity bargaining was the most dynamic concept in British industrial relations in the 1960s, and was especially favoured in government policy because of its emphasis on management initiative and because of its possibilities in developing **plant bargaining** with links between higher earnings and higher productivity. Guidelines on productivity deals were issued by the National Board for Prices and Incomes in its three reports on productivity bargaining (No. 23, *Productivity and Pay During the Period of Severe Restraint,* Cmnd. 3167, 15 December 1966; No. 36, Cmnd. 3311, 13 June 1967 and No. 123, Cmnd. 4136, 5 August 1969) emphasising the need to relate agreements to specific changes in working practice and to relevant indices of performance, to provide effective controls and to guard against repercussions elsewhere, as well as protecting the consumer (see *Report* 123, pp. 39-40). 3,788 such agreements were reported to the Department of Employment and Productivity between 1 January 1967 and 24 October 1969 covering 7 million workers (see B.C. Roberts and John Gennard, 'Trends in Plant and Company Bargaining', *Scottish Journal of Political Economy*, Vol, XVII, No. 2, June 1970 and D.J. Robertson and L.C. Hunter (eds), *Labour Market Issues of the 1970s*, Oliver and Boyd, 1970). *Report* 123 also made allowance for **efficiency agreements** (q.v.). Productivity bargaining has been regarded by some as a form of **integrative bargaining,** a view adopted early by F.E. Oldfield in connection with the Mobil, Coryton, Agreement (*New Look Industrial Relations*, Mason Reed Ltd, 1966) and by R.B. McKersie (op. cit.); also W.W. Daniel, *Beyond the Wage-Work Bargain*, PEP Broadsheet 519, July 1970, and Stephen Cotgrove, Jack Dunham and Clive Vamplew, *The Nylon Spinners*, George Allen and Unwin, 1971, for the possible relationship between productivity bargaining and attitudes to work. Yves Delamotte, *The Social Partners Face the Problems of Productivity and Employment*, OECD, Paris, 1971, discusses the contrasting attitudes of Britain and the continent to productivity bargaining; see also Tony Cliff, *The Employers' Offensive: Productivity Deals and How to Fight Them*, Pluto Press, 1970. In the later 1960s and early 1970s the attitude of employers to the productivity bargaining approach became increasingly critical, and the enthusiasm of most unions for the practice declined. Nevertheless goverments in pursuing **incomes policies** continue to lay emphasis on the need to link pay and productivity; see for example, **self financing productivity deals**.

PRODUCTIVITY DEAL; see productivity bargaining.

PRODUCTIVITY PACKAGE DEAL; see **productivity bargaining.**

PROFESSION. A term historically used to describe the learned professions of divinity, law and medicine and sometimes also the military profession; now commonly applied to other non-manual occupations of high status involving advanced training and education and related to defined areas of concern and application to the community. Opinions differ on the precise attributes of a profession. Those most commonly suggested are a basis of theoretical knowledge, assured standards of competence achieved by examination, the existence of a **professional association** (q.v.) or organisation, integrity resulting from the application of an agreed code of conduct, professional authority and a professional culture (see, for example, G. Millerson, *The Qualifying Associations*, Routledge and Kegan Paul, 1964, Barrington Kaye, *The Development of the Architectural Profession in Britain*, Allen and Unwin, 1960, p. 17 and E. Greenwood, 'Attributes of a Profession', *Social Work*, Vol. 2, July 1957, pp. 45-55). How these attributes should be stressed or combined, and whether particular occupations should be judged professional or otherwise remain matters in dispute. Some writers maintain that the difference between a professional and non-professional occupation is simply a matter of the **degree** to which it possesses professional attributes (E. Greenwood, op. cit.); others suggest that one attribute, e.g. a moral code, is of overwhelming importance (R. Lewis and A. Maude, *Professional People*, Phoenix House Ltd 1952), or that a complex of characteristics is responsible (A.M. Carr-Saunders, D. Caradog Jones and C.A. Moser, *Social Conditions in England and Wales*, OUP, 1958, p. 108); see also A.M. Carr-Saunders and P.A. Wilson, *The Professions*, OUP, 1933 and K. Prandy, *Professional Employees*, Faber and Faber, 1965.

PROFESSIONAL ASSOCIATION. Defined by G. Millerson (*The Qualifying Associations*, Routledge and Kegan Paul, 1964, p. 33) as 'any organisation which directly aims at the improvement of any aspects of professional practice: for example by providing a qualification, by controlling conduct, by co-ordinating technical information, by pressing for better conditions of employment'. As thus broadly defined, professional associations would therefore include such organisations as the Royal Society, study associations, **qualifying associations** (i.e. those seeking to control entry to a profession by setting standards of competence for entry), associations to co-ordinate professional activity and those which are 'protective' and attempt to exercise pressure to protect and improve the working conditions and remuneration of their members, e.g. the **British Medical Association.** For discussion of the **protective associations** and their likeness to **trade unions,** see K. Prandy, *Professional Employees*, Faber and Faber, 1965 and R.M. Blackburn, *Union Character and Social Class*, Batsford, 1967. The tendency for such associations to acquire more resemblance to trade unions has grown in recent years.

PROFESSIONAL CIVIL SERVANTS, INSTITUTION OF (IPCS). A Civil Service union formed in 1919 from some of the departmental associations of professional civil servants to form a single organisation representing specialists on the Staff Side of the National Whitley Council set up as a result of the reports of the Whitley Committee (see **Whitleyism**). Membership is now drawn both from the Civil Service and from other bodies financed wholly or partly by the government whose staff pay and grading structures and conditions of service are related to those of the Civil Service, e.g. the United Kingdom Atomic Energy Authority, the Agricultural Research Council, the Civil Aviation Authority. It amalgamated with a TUC affiliated union, the Society of Technical Civil Servants, in 1970, the whole organisation becoming affiliated in May 1976. *Address:* 3-7 Northumberland Street, London WC2N 5BS. *Tel:* 01-930 9755. *TUC Affiliated Membership 1977:* 100,233.

PROFESSIONAL ENGINEERS, UNITED KINGDOM ASSOCIATION OF (UKAPE). A union of professional engineers, managers and associates of acceptable status developed from the Engineers' Guild founded in 1938 to give personal advice to professional engineers on salaries and conditions of employment. UKAPE was first registered under the **Trade Union Act 1871** in May 1969, and later under the **Industrial Relations Act 1971.** It worked closely with the **Association of Supervisory and Executive Engineers** (now merged into the **Engineers' and Managers' Association** (q.v.)), with which it had a **spheres of influence** agreement, and had been in conflict since its inception with other white collar unions, particularly the Draughtsmen's and Allied Technicians' Association (now Amalgamated Union of Engineering Workers, Technical and Supervisory Section) e.g. at C.A. Parsons and Co. Ltd (see **Hill v C.A. Parsons and Co. Ltd**). Linda Dickens, 'UKAPE: A Study of a Professional Union', *Industrial Relations Journal,* Vol. 3, No. 3, Autumn 1972, pp. 2-16 and B.C. Roberts, Ray Loveridge and John Gennard, *Reluctant Militants,* Heinemann, 1972. *Address:* 32 High Street, Bookham, Leatherhead, Surrey KT23 4AG. *Membership, 1977:* 5,500; see also **professional association.**

PROFESSIONAL AND EXECUTIVE RECRUITMENT (PER). A nationwide service for the recruitment of professional, administrative, managerial, executive and technical staff introduced from 1 March 1973 as a specialist and separately managed branch of the **Employment Service Agency** (now a Division of the **Manpower Services Commission**) in succession to the placing service previously provided directly by the Department of Employment and known as the **Professional and Executive Register.** The Professional and Executive Register was replaced on grounds of its limited coverage (49,040 on the Register in September 1971), its limited success (one-in-six only of those registered being found a job), and on grounds of expense (£100 per placing compared with £12 for the general employment service). PER as at present organised lays emphasis on the marketing of the service to employers and potential candidates for jobs and fees are charged for employers making engagements through the service on a percentage scale depending on salary. No charge is made to candidates using the service, which is open to applicants aged 18 years and over who are qualified either academically or by experience, ex-regular offices of HM Forces having a prescriptive right of enrolment. The PER Executive Secretaries Agency specialises in the recruitment of top secretaries and 'Reward' (annual subscription £35); clients and participatory firms £30) provides market information on managerial, professional and executive pay and benefits. PER *Head Office Address:* 4-5 Grosvenor Place, London SW1X 7SB. *Tel:* 01-235 7030.

PROFESSIONAL AND EXECUTIVE REGISTER; see Professional and Executive Recruitment.

PROFESSIONAL, EXECUTIVE, CLERICAL AND COMPUTER STAFF, ASSOCIATION OF (APEX). A trade union founded in 1890 as the National Union of Clerks and claiming to be the oldest-established white collar workers' union in Great Britain. The National Union of Clerks added to its title the words 'and Administrative Workers' in 1920, merged with the Women Clerks' and Secretaries' Association to become the Clerical and Administrative Workers' Union in 1941, and assumed its present title in 1972. The NUC was the first staff workers' union to be nationally recognised in the engineering industry (1920), and the union has about 70 per cent of its membership in manufacturing (particularly in engineering, metal manufacture and in food and drink), the remainder being principally confined to coal mining, Co-operative employment, trade union staffs and insurance. Rather less than one-half of its members are women; see Fred Hughes, *By Hand and Brain, The Story of the Clerical and Administrative Workers' Union,* Lawrence and Wishart, 1953 and G.S. Bain, *The Growth of White Collar Unionism,* OUP, 1970. Since the 1972 change of name emphasis has been placed on the recruitment of lower and middle management. A new history is in preparation. *Address:* 22 Worple Road, London SW19 4DF. *Tel:* 01-947 3131-6. *TUC Affiliated Membership, 1977:* 141,766.

PROFESSIONAL FOOTBALLERS ASSOCIATION (PFA). A trade union originally founded in 1898, and re-established in 1907, gaining influence particularly since 1945 (see *Association Football, Report of a Committee of Investigation into a Difference regarding the Terms and Conditions of Association Football Players* (Forster Report), 1952: *Report of the Committee on Football* (Chester Report), Department of Education and Science, 1968). It organises professional footballers in England and Wales only. *Address:* 124 Corn Exchange Buildings, Hanging Ditch, Manchester 4 3BN. *Tel:* 061-834 7554. *Current Membership, 1977:* 2,500. The union was suspended from membership of the TUC by decision of the 1972 Congress for failing to comply with Congress policy of non-registration under the **Industrial Relations Act 1971** and has not reaffiliated.

PROFESSIONAL SCIENTISTS AND TECHNOLOGISTS, ASSOCIATION OF (APST). An organisation set up in 1972 by the Council of Science and Technology Institutes to act in a trade union capacity for professional scientists and technologists, i.e. for those with a degree or equivalent qualification in science and technology working at professional or managerial levels. Managers holding appointments at these levels may also become members even though otherwise unqualified. APST was at July 1976 recognised by Imperial Chemical Industries and by 24 other companies, almost all in chemicals and pharmaceuticals, with sole bargaining rights in nine of them; see C. Gill, R.S. Morris and J. Eaton, 'APST; the rise of a professional union', *Industrial Rela-*

tions Journal, Vol. 8, No. 1, Spring 1977, pp. 50-61. It has a certificate of independence under the Trade Union and Labour Relations Act 1974. *Address:* Hinchley House, 14 Harley Street, London W1N 2BE. *Tel:* 01-636 7021. *Membership, 1977:* approximately 10,000.

PROFESSIONAL WORKERS, NATIONAL FEDERATION OF (NFPW). A federation representing some 1.5 million affiliated members in 41 trade unions employed in professional, clerical, and administrative grades in industry and service employment, and recognised by the **Trades Union Congress** as a body representative of white collar workers. The NFPW was founded in 1920 on the initiative of G.D.H. Cole, and is mainly concerned in communicating the views of its affiliated membership, expressed in its annual conference, to the TUC, to government departments and to employing bodies, e.g. on the preservation or transfer of pension rights, on office legislation, arbitration, education and training, etc. Membership has more than doubled in the past decade. *Address:* 30a Station Road, Harpenden, Herts AL5 4SE. *Tel:* Harpenden 3692.

PROFIT SHARING. A method which attempts to reconcile employer-employee interests in privately owned industry by schemes which, in addition to wages and salaries, arrange that payments to workers shall also be made out of profits. Opinions differ on detailed definition. In 1889 an International Congress on Profit Sharing defined profit sharing as 'payment made in accordance with freely agreed schemes . . . fixed in advance and not variable by decision of the employer . . . to a substantial proportion of, ordinary employees', thus excluding unilateral schemes, goodwill bonuses from profits, casual arrangements and those making payment only to managerial staff. In Britain it has, since 1945, become customary to extend the definition to include schemes which may apply to certain groups of employees only, and those which distribute profits regularly but not on a strictly predetermined basis, on the grounds that both these arrangements conform to the general aims and principles of profit sharing. Schemes are sometimes associated with share distribution, with or without voting rights, and with the notion of **co-partnership** (q.v.). In 1955, an official investigation was made into the subject (COI, *Profit Sharing and Co-Partnership Schemes in the U.K.,*

1956); see also C.G. Hanson, 'Profit Sharing Schemes in Great Britain', *Journal of Management Studies,* October 1965, pp. 331-50. The number of British firms which have adopted profit sharing is small and there is no indication that profit sharing is on the increase. The effect of shareholding schemes on attitudes appears also to be small (see Acton Society Trust and Guy Naylor, *Sharing the Profits,* Garnstone Press, 1968). Profit sharing has generally been disliked by trade unions on grounds that it might be used to resist trade unionism or to undercut collective bargaining. In the USA profit sharing is also associated with **share of production plans**; e.g. **Scanlon** and **Rucker** (q.v.) see also J.N. Scanlon, 'Profit Sharing under Collective Bargaining: Three Case Studies,' *Industrial and Labor Relations Review,* Oct. 1948, pp. 58-75; see also **capital sharing**. The 1978 Finance Bill included tax incentives to encourage profit sharing.

PROGRAMME EVALUATION AND REVIEW TECHNIQUE (PERT); see **network analysis.**

PROGRESS PAYMENT SCHEME. A kind of **profit sharing** (q.v.) introduced into some national newspapers in January 1955; see Economist Intelligence Unit, *Survey of the National Newspaper Industry,* 1966, Pt. III, p. 95.

PROHIBITION NOTICE; see **Health and Safety at Work Act 1974.**

PROMOTION LADDER, seniority rule or **seniority ladder.** A system of promotion of manual workers to better paid and more responsible jobs by seniority customary in the iron and steel industry, and regulated by union rule. The system is said to have been introduced with the ending of the **contract system** (q.v.). It is convenient in that it accords both with the need for on-the-job training and with the necessity for each man, in a continuous shift situation, to be able to cover the job of the next above him in experience and skill in case of sickness, accident, or absence. It has the disadvantage that a worker displaced for any reason from the promotion ladder, has no choice but to begin again at the bottom. This not only inhibits mobility of labour; it also hampers redeployment when mill productive capacity is being reduced or reorganised; see L.C. Hunter, G.L. Reid and D. Boddy, *Labour Problems of Technological Change,* George Allen and Unwin, 1970, pp. 171 and 179; see also **sticker.**

PROPENSITY TO STRIKE. A concept attributed to Clark Kerr and Abraham Siegel ('The Inter-Industry Propensity to Strike', Ch. 14 in Arthur Kornhauser, Robert Dubin and Arthur M. Ross (eds), *Industrial Conflict,* McGraw-Hill, 1954), and measured in terms of man-days due to strikes and lock-outs. Kerr and Siegel find (with exceptions) similar propensities to strike in the same industries in different countries and, while acknowledging that strikes are complex phenomena, that the most general explanation of this is that high propensities are associated with workers who live in 'isolated masses' and low propensities with integration in the general community. They conclude that the 'effort should be to increase vertical and horizontal mobility, to encourage a wide variety of mixed associations, to break down barriers between individuals, to create the mixed community instead of the 'Gold Coast' or the 'back of the yards' which alike inspire ideological thinking' (p. 205); see **strikes.**

PROTECTION SOCIETIES. A name given to a number of district associations of workers in Lancashire established as rivals to existing cotton unions and sometimes breakaways from them. The last such society was the Blackburn Protection Society, which became affiliated to the Weavers' Amalgamation in 1920 and merged with the original Blackburn Weavers' Association in 1949. E. Hopwood, *A History of the Lancashire Cotton Industry and the Amalgamated Weavers' Association,* AWA, 1969, pp. 78-9.

PROTECTIVE ASSOCIATION; see **professional association.**

PROTECTIVE PRACTICE. A trade union or work group practice designed to protect the jobs or the status of workers, or of particular groups of workers. Use of the expression emphasises the desire of workers, especially through organisation, for self protection rather than the desire to 'restrict' for its own sake, or contrary to the public interest; hence it is sometimes used in the trade union movement to counter allegations of **restrictive practices** in the use of labour (q.v.). The problem is evidently one of determining where 'protection' ends and market exploitation begins; e.g. 'At times the use of overmanning goes beyond this to serve as a device for raising earnings. In printing, for instance, where manning complements are excessive it can happen that a smaller number of men actually perform the job and they share between themselves the pay of the full complement'. (Donovan **Royal Commission on Trade Unions and Employers' Associations 1965-1968,** Cmnd. 3623, June 1968, para. 309).

PROVIDENT BENEFIT or **friendly benefit** (q.v.).

PROVISIONS FOR AVOIDING DISPUTES. An expression used in some industries, and particularly in engineering, to describe a procedure for handling grievances or a grievance procedure (see **grievance**). The first such provisions in engineering date from the Terms of Settlement of 1898; they were expanded in the Carlisle Agreement of 1907, reconstituted in the **York Memorandum** of 1914, and elaborated in the Shop Stewards and Works Committee Agreements of 1917 and 1919, the latter two agreements being incorporated into the 1922 Procedure Agreement Manual Workers, now terminated (see **Engineering Procedure Agreement**); see A.I. Marsh, *Industrial Relations in Engineering,* Pergamon Press, 1965.

PRU; see **Civil Service Pay Research Unit.**

PSI. Public Services International; see **International Trade Secretariats.**

PTTI. Postal, Telegraph and Telephone International; see **International Trade Secretariats.**

PUBLIC EMPLOYEES, NATIONAL UNION OF. A trade union catering for local government workers and hospital ancillary and clerical grades first formed by the secession in 1907 of a number of branches of the Municipal Employees Association (in 1924 to merge as part of the **General and Municipal Workers' Union,** q.v.), to form the National Union of Corporation Workers, later changing its title to NUPE. From 1934 to his retirement in 1962, the history of the union was dominated by its General Secretary, Bryn Roberts (d. 26 August 1964), whose negotiating and expansionist membership policies brought him into conflict both with the G and MWU and with the **Transport and General Workers' Union** which regarded the union as a breakaway and sought to exclude it from joint machinery in local government, also excluding it for

some time from membership of the **Trades Union Congress.** Bryn Roberts' controversial views on this are to be found in *At the TUC,* NUPE, 1947 and *The Price of TUC Leadership,* Allen and Unwin, 1961; see also, W.W. Craik, *Bryn Roberts and the National Union of Public Employees,* Allen and Unwin, 1955. *Address:* Civic House, 8 Aberdeen Terrace, Blackheath, London SE3 0QY. *Tel:* 01-852 2842. *TUC Affiliated Membership, 1977:* 650,530.

PUBLIC HOLIDAYS. In England, Wales, and Northern Ireland, Good Friday and Christmas Day; see **bank holidays.**

PUBLIC SERVICES INTERNATIONAL (PSI); see **International Trade Secretariats.**

PUFFLER; see **butty.** But also said to be applied only to a miner in charge of hand-stripping a face, or to a miners' representative to negotiate contracts; usually said to be confined to Warwickshire usage (also 'fuffler').

PULLER-BACK. A worker employed to work inside vehicles and pull the meat back to the tailboard of the delivering vehicle, where it is handed to the **pitcher** (q.v.); see National Board for Prices and Incomes, *Smithfield Market,* Cmnd. 4171, October 1969.

PURE DRIFT; see **wage drift.**

Q

QUADRAGESIMO ANNO; see **Catholic industrial relations teaching.**

QUALIFIED MANPOWER. A term defined in the 1966 sample Census of Population as all persons holding recognised degrees, diplomas, associateships or other professional and vocational qualifications usually obtained after the age of 18; a **Unit for Manpower Studies** within the Departments of Employment is concerned to investigate employment prospects for highly qualified people: see the report of the Unit *Employment of the Highly Qualified, 1971-1986,* May 1978. Financed by the Department of Employment, the Institute of Manpower Studies has carried out a series of studies to explore the present and potential employment of qualified manpower; see 'The role of graduates in Industry,' *Department of Employment Gazette*, January 1975, and 'Qualified Manpower in Employment', *Department of Employment Gazette*, March 1976; also E.G. Whybrew, 'Qualified Manpower: Statistical Sources', *Statistical News*, HMSO, May 1972.

QUALIFYING ASSOCIATION; see **professional association.**

QUALIFYING DAYS. The provision to be found in a number of agreements about payment for **Bank Holidays** or other **paid holidays,** and sometimes for **annual holidays** also, which requires attendance on the working days immediately preceding and following the holiday, in default of which, with certain exceptions, holiday payment is withheld. The object of the provision is to discourage early leaving and late return from holiday; see, for example, in engineering, 'Workpeople shall not qualify for payment for the six Bank or other paid holidays who fail to work the full normal working day immediately preceding and the full working day immediately following the holiday, unless they can produce evidence to the satisfaction of the employer that their absence was due to causes beyond their control' (*Holiday Agreements*, before 1978).

QUANTIFIABLE EMOLUMENTS. A Civil Service Pay Research Unit term meaning any emolument, other than the service rate of pay, which can be expressed in monetary terms, e.g. pension, bonus, merit pay, luncheon vouchers, etc., and excluding unquantifiables to which no precise monetary value can be assigned, e.g. sick leave, discounts on firm's products, etc. Geoffrey Walker, *Pay Research in the Civil Service,* National Association of Local and Government Officers, TUE 6, 1968, p. 16; see also **true money rate.**

QUARTERING. A form of fining for bad timekeeping in which an employee loses a quarter of an hour's pay if he is late by a laid down number of minutes, in some cases 3, and in others 5 or 6; see **clocking** and **lateness.**

QUESTION. In broad terms, any **difference, dispute** or **issue** arising between the employer, union or worker, i.e. any question at issue. More specifically a question

as provided for in Order 1305; see **National Arbitration Tribunal and recognised terms and conditions.**

QUESTIONS PROCEDURE. A procedure under the **Sex Discrimination Act 1975** (s. 74) and the Race Relations Act 1976 (s. 65) whereby in order to help a person who considers he may have been discriminated against whether to institute proceedings or not, he may question the 'respondent' on a form prescribed by the Secretary of State. A similar form may be provided on which the respondent may reply if he so wishes (Sex Discrimination (Questions and Replies) Order 1975, SI 1975, No. 2048; Race Relations (Questions and Replies) Order 1977, SI 1977, No. 842).

QUINN v. LEATHAM (1901) AC 495. A case in which union officials, in attempting to get rid of non-union men, were found guilty of civil conspiracy by inflicting economic damage upon the plaintiff for purposes other than that of advancing their own legitimate trade interests, and by combining to induce a worker to break his contract of employment and a customer to break his commercial contract; K.W. Wedderburn, *Case and Materials on Labour Law*, CUP, 1967, p. 443 *et seq.*

QUIT RATE. The rate of resignation or voluntary termination of employment by workers; an element in **labour turnover** (q.v.).

QUOTA RESTRICTION. A form of ca'canny in which working groups restrict output by limiting this to a 'quota' or 'bogey' agreed or understood between members of the group, the object being to maintain a control of production in order to avoid **speed-up** on piecework, to share work (see **work sharing**), to retain a basis for argument for higher piecework prices, or simply to avoid working themselves out of a job; see Donald Roy, 'Quota Restriction and Goldbricking in a Machine Shop', *American Journal of Sociology*, Vol. 67, No. 2, 1952 (also reprinted in Tom Lupton (ed.), *Payment Systems*, Penguin Modern Management Readings, 1972), and W. Baldamus, *Efficiency and Effort*, Tavistock, 1967, p. 106; see also **goldbricking, restrictive practices.**

R

R. v. BUNN (1872) 12 Cox 316. A case in which employees of a gas company threatened to withdraw their labour and were, despite the **Criminal Law Amendment Act 1871**, indicted for conspiracy to coerce and convicted. The decision was reversed by the **Conspiracy and Protection of Property Act 1875** which removed the application of the doctrine of criminal conspiracy from acts done 'in contemplation or furtherance of a trade dispute'; see also K.W. Wedderburn, *Cases and Materials on Labour Law*, CUP, 1967, p. 380.

R. v. JONES AND OTHERS (1974) ICR 310, CA. A case involving the **Shrewsbury Pickets** (q.v.). The Court of Appeal quashed the convictions of three of the pickets for affray, but dismissed other appeals for unlawful assembly and intimidation, the latter under s. 7 of the **Conspiracy and Protection of Property Act 1875**. The judgement had the effect of confirming the prison sentences on John Jones, Eric Tomlinson (two years) and Dennis Warren (three years) and resulted in an amendment to the 1875 Act in the **Criminal Law Act 1977** (q.v.) restricting sentences under that Section within a statutory limit. Previously, the drafting of the Act allowed for unlimited sentences where trial by jury rather than by magistrates' court was adopted, as in this case.

RACE RELATIONS ACTS. Acts of 1965, 1968 and 1976. The first Act applies mainly to discrimination in places of public resort and incitement to racial hatred: the second contains specific provisions relating to employment. Under the latter Act it became unlawful to discriminate against any person on the grounds of colour, race or ethnic or national origin in refusing employment for which he is available and qualified, to deny him equal opportunities of training, or to dismiss him in circumstances in which other persons doing similar work would not be dismissed (s. 3). Trade unions, employers' associations and trade associations can also act unlawfully in denying by discrimination, any person from equal access to membership, or to benefits (s. 4) and discrimination in advertisements and notices are also unlawful (s. 6). The 1976 Act extended the meaning and scope of discrimination to include indirect discrimination (s. 1(1)(b)) and discrimination by way of victimisation (s. 2). It also abolished

both the Race Relations Board and the Community Relations Commission in favour of a **Commission for Racial Equality** with power to conduct formal investigations, to issue **non-discrimination notices** where discrimination is found to exist and, in cases of persistent discrimination lasting five years, to apply to designated county courts for an injunction. Individual complaints about discrimination are no longer channelled through a central body or a conciliation procedure, but taken to **industrial tribunals**. See Sheila Patterson, *Immigrants in Industry*, OUP, 1968; P.L. Wright, *The Coloured Worker in British Industry*, OUP, 1968; S. Allen *The Trade Union Movement and Discrimination, Collected Essays*, Runnymede Trust, 1971, and **Mansfield Mills Dispute** and **discrimination**.

RADCLIFFE v. RIBBLE MOTOR SERVICES LTD (1939) AC 215; (1939) 1 All ER 637; see **employers' liability**.

RADFORD v. NATIONAL SOCIETY OF OPERATIVE PRINTERS, GRAPHICAL AND MEDIA PERSONNEL (1972) 116 SJ 695, ChD. A case in which the plaintiff had acted contrary to an arrangement made between his union and his employer relating to the closure of his works and contrary to a union direction that he should accept transfer rather than take a redundancy payment and was excluded from membership. It was held by the court that if a rule provided for an automatic forfeiture of membership without the necessity for a charge and a hearing, it would be *ultra vires*; see **membership of a union**.

RADIO AND ELECTRONIC OFFICERS' UNION (REOU). A trade union of radio officers at sea having a continuous existence since 1912 and adopting its present title in 1967. From 1921 to 1937 it was known as the Association of Wireless and Cable Telegraphists and from 1937 to 1967 as the Radio Officers' Union. The union claims to have in membership some 75 per cent of such officers, and nominates the employees' representatives on the Radio Officers' Panel of the **National Maritime Board** (q.v.). *Address*: 4-6 Branfill Road, Upminster, Essex RM14 2XX. *Tel*: 86-22321-2. *TUC Affiliated Membership, 1977*: 3,620.

RADIUS AGREEMENT. An agreement forming part of a contract of service in which an employer seeks to bind an employee not to accept similar employment, or to set up in a similar business for himself, for a prescribed period within a given radius from his present work. Attempts to bind employees by such agreements in the retail trade and to a lesser extent in commercial houses before the first world war led to strong opposition from the trade unions concerned. The unions supported their members in fighting through the courts limitations which they considered unreasonable, especially where multiple firms were concerned. Use of the practice seems now to have reached reasonable proportions.

RAILWAYMEN, NATIONAL UNION OF (NUR). A trade union originally founded in 1871 as the Amalgamated Society of Railway Servants, and taking its present title in 1913 as a result of a merger with the General Railway Workers' Union (1889) and the United Pointsmen's and Signalmen's Society (1880). The NUR was at its foundation regarded by many as a new model for British trade union structure (see Sidney and Beatrice Webb, *The History of Trade Unionism*, 1920 ed., p. 531) as a form of **industrial unionism**, or **employmental unionism**. It has fallen short of its original aim to 'secure the complete organisation of all workers employed on or in connection with any railway in the United Kingdom', though it represents all **conciliation grades** with the exception of those footplatemen and locomotive engine staff in membership of the **Associated Society of Locomotive Engineers and Firemen** and some employees of National Carriers Limited and Freightliners Limited, salaried staff in the **Transport Salaried Staffs Association** and some engineering workshop staff (see **Railway Shopmen's National Council**). Its predecessor the ASRS was notable for its involvement in the **Taff Vale Case** and the Osborne Judgement (see **Osborne v. ASRS**). Membership of the union reached a peak in 1947 (462,205) and declined thereafter with the contraction of the railway system; see, G.D.H. Cole and R. Page Arnot, *Trade Unionism on the Railways*, Labour Research Department, 1917; G.W. Alcock, *Fifty Years of Railway Trade Unionism*, Co-operative Printing Society Ltd., 1922; Philip S. Bagwell, *The Railwaymen, A History of the National Union of Railwaymen*, Allen and Unwin, 1963. *Address*: Unity House, Euston Road, London WC1 2BL. *Tel*: 01-387 4771. *TUC Affiliated Membership, 1977*: 180,000.

RAILWAY SHOPMEN'S NATIONAL COUNCIL. A joint negotiating body between British Rail, the **Confederation of Shipbuilding and Engineering Unions**, and the **National Union of Railwaymen** responsible for determining wages and conditions of work for wages staff in railway workshops, and for dealing with questions arising from shop, works, and departmental line committees at lower levels. The machinery dates from 1927; on railway nationalisation it was agreed that existing machinery should continue, pending the completion of a new agreement. With some modification, it is still in operation, Charles McLeod, *All Change; Railway Industrial Relations in the Sixties*, Gower Press, 1970; A.I. Marsh, *Industrial Relations in Engineering*, Pergamon Press, 1965, p. 26.

RAILWAY STAFF CONFERENCE. A body appointed by the British Railways Board to act on its behalf on all schemes of Machinery of Negotiation for staff. It consists of the Staff Officers of British Railways Board Headquarters and the Staff Officers of the five Regions, British Rail Engineering Ltd, and British Railways Shipping and International Services Division. *Address*: 222 Marylebone Road, London NW1. *Tel*: 01-262 3232.

RAILWAY STAFF JOINT COUNCIL. The first stage in national negotiations in British Rail. The council meets in four sections at which officials of appropriate unions are present (**Nationa Union of Railwaymen, Associated Society of Locomotive Engineers and Firemen and Transport Salaried Staffs Association**). In the event of disagreement, the **Railway Staff National Council** (at which representatives of all three unions are present), attempts to resolve the issue, and is specially convened to deal with claims for general pay increases. A third, **arbitration**, stage is catered for by the **Railway Staff National Tribunal**. Until 1969, awards of the Tribunal were not formally binding; since that time they have been accepted as such in cases in which reference is made by both parties on agreed terms of reference. These negotiating arrangements date in their present form from an agreement on Machinery for Negotiation for Railway Staff, arrived at in 1956 between the (then) British Transport Commission and the three railway unions. Charles McLeod, *All Change; Railway Industrial Relations in the Sixties*, Gower Press, 1970.

RAILWAY STAFF NATIONAL COUN-CIL; see **Railway Staff Joint Council.**

RAILWAY STAFF NATIONAL TRIB-UNAL; see **Railway Staff Joint Council.**

RANDOM OBSERVATION METHOD; see **activity sampling.**

RANKING. A simple form of **job evaluation** described by the National Board for Prices and Incomes (*Job Evaluation*, Report No. 83, Cmnd. 3772, September 1968) as follows: 'A job description is usually prepared to distinguish each job and to define its duties, responsibilities and the qualities needed for its successful performance. 'Key jobs' are then identified . . . the remainder of the jobs are then grouped around the key jobs, with ranking carried out within each sub-group . . . the ranked jobs are then divided into grades and allocated pay levels or ranges.'

RAT. A worker who turns strike-breaker, who works under the rate, or who behaves in a way regarded as traitorous or anti-social by his workmates; see preamble to the Rule Book of the London Operative Tin-Plate Workers, 1839; 'The following is a Description of Persons in the Trade Known by the Name of "Rats". A rat is to his Trade, what a Traitor is to his Country, and although both may be useful to one party in troublesome times, when peace returns they are detested alike by all; so when help is wanted, a Rat is the last to contribute assistance and the first to grasp a benefit he never laboured to procure. He cares only for himself, but sees not beyond the extent of a day, and for a momentary and worthless approbation would betray friends, family and Country; in short he is a traitor on a small scale; he first sells the journeymen and is himself afterwards sold in turn by the master, until at last he is despised by both, and deserted by all. He is an enemy to himself - to the present age - and to posterity'. A.T. Kidd, *History of the Tin-Plate Workers and Sheet Metal Workers and Braziers Societies,* National Union of Sheet Metal Workers and Braziers, 1949, p. 27.

RATEBUSTER. A worker who exceeds the limit on earnings accepted by the workshop or by his fellow workers, hence running the risk of suggesting to management the rates are too high and might be reduced (see **rate cutting**). The term derives from the shop floor usage in the United States. The suggestion may be that the **ratebuster** is a **pacer** or **whip** encouraged by the management to speed up the rate of work, but seems usually to be confined to workers who, by choice or otherwise, expend more effort than their fellows without such encouragement. The classical study of the ratebuster is that of Melville Dalton, 'The Industrial "Ratebuster"; a Characterisation', *Applied Anthropology,* Winter 1948, pp. 5-18 (reprinted in Tom Lupton (ed.), *Payment Systems,* Penguin Modern Management Readings, 1972).

RATE CUTTING. The arbitrary reduction by an employer of a **piecework** price or time where there has been no change in the means, method or material employed on the job. Early resistance to **payment by results** in the engineering industry and elsewhere owed much to the fear of workers and their unions that employers would cut rates (see G.D.H. Cole, *Workshop Organisation,* A.I. Marsh (ed.), Hutchinson, 1973); engineering employers sought to counter such fears by guaranteeing that **mutuality** would be observed in the setting of time and/or prices, and that these times and/or prices would not be changed unless a mistake in calculation on either side could be shown, or the material, means, or method of production, or quantities, had been changed (*Handbook of National Agreements,* 2.51, 2.54(3) and (4), 2.55(3), (4) and (5), 2.57(3) and (4), 2.58(3), (4) and (5)), further protection against rate cutting for general workers being also assured, 2.54(5) guaranteeing that no change would result in a reduction in a worker's earnings. Workers may sometimes refer to rate cutting in circumstances in which managements desire to reduce rates or times in circumstances in which material, means, methods or quantities have been changed; see also **speed up.**

RATED ACTIVITY SAMPLING; see **activity sampling.**

RATED TIME STUDY. A work study measurement technique attributed to Charles Bedeaux for establishing values for common units of work ('B Units') by adjusting the elements arrived at by time study by rating assessment as well as by making a rest allowance for fatigue (see also **Bedeaux System**); R.M. Currie, *Work Study,* Pitman, 4th ed., 1977.

RATE-FIXER; see rate-fixing.

RATE-FIXING. The setting of a rate or a

time for a job by a rate-fixer or **supervisor** without the use of the stop watch or of time and motion study or **work study** methods, e.g. from estimates based on experience, past records, etc. Rate-fixing by such 'guesstimating' has evidently survived the development of more systematic work study methods, especially in heavy engineering (see R. Marriott, *Incentive Payment Systems*, Staples, 3rd ed., 1968, p. 96 *et seq.*), and may be particularly susceptible to **effort bargaining**, especially in engineering, where *Handbook of National Agreements* 2.51 involves agreement of the piecework price or time allowed with the individual worker concerned (see **mutuality**).

RATE FOR THE JOB. Usually the **basic rate** or standard **time rate** agreed or established for a particular job or occupation and of general application; hence a rate which is a fair rate, involving no element of **sweating** or undercutting, or working under the rate; may sometimes be applied to a wage or **salary scale**, and hence to a point of any established scale, or even in some cases to particular earnings or to a level of earnings generally accepted as attainable by a particular grade or class of worker.

RATING. Defined in the *British Standard Glossary of Terms Used in Work Study*, BS 3138, 1969 as 'the assessment of the worker's rate of working relative to the concept of the rate corresponding to **standard rating**', The International Labour Office (*Introduction to Work Study*, Geneva, 1969, p. 258) prefers to substitute **standard pace** for standard rating in this definition (see **standard performance**). Rating is also the word used to describe the numerical value of the symbol used to denote the rate of working, e.g. 'a 100 rating', 'an 80 rating'. Note also **loose rating**, leading to **loose times**, i.e. inaccurate rating which is too high and therefore results in over-generous times for the completion of jobs; **tight rating**, leading to **tight times**, i.e. inaccurate rating which is too low, and therefore results in times inadequate for the performance of a job; **inconsistent rating**, i.e. a mixture of loose, tight and accurate ratings; **flat ratings** i.e. a set of ratings in which the observer has underestimated the variations in the worker's rate of working; **steep ratings**, i.e. a set of ratings in which the observer has overestimated the worker's rate of working.

RATING SCALE. (1) A method of presenting an employee's qualifications by means of a graphic chart or other form, the scale measuring the individual's ability, personality, performance and potential compared with a standard previously set. (2) A series of numerical indices given to various rates of working in the practice of **work study**; see **rating**. Many such scales are in use, the 100-133 scale, the 60-80 scale, the 75-100 scale, and the British Standard Scale, 0-100, a restatement of the 75-100 scale. In the 100-133, 60-80 and 75-100 scales, the lower figure in each case represents the rate of working of an operator on time rates of pay (e.g. steady, unhurried performance, under proper supervision, but not intentionally slow), and the higher figure represents the standard rate of working, i.e. that of an average qualified worker on incentive who is suitably motivated to apply himself to work. The underlying assumption on each scale is that workers on incentive perform, on average, about one-third more effectively on incentive than on plain time work, and that all scales are linear. In the British Standard Scale, 0 represents zero activity and 100 **standard rate**; this is claimed to have advantages over previous scales; see International Labour Office, *Introduction to Work Study*, Geneva, 1969, Ch. 16.

RATIO-DELAY STUDY; see **activity sampling.**

RATIONAL WORKING HOURS. An arrangement or system of working hours which conforms to fluctuations in work load; an approach said to have been pioneered by Dr Robert Rosencranz, a German **O and M** consultant. The notion is that it is possible to predict changes in activity levels, so that contracts of employment should provide, subject to an agreed maximum, for more hours to be worked in some periods than others, or on some days rather than others. German banks are said to have conducted experiments along these lines; see J. Harvey Bolton, *Flexible Working Hours*, Anbar Publications Ltd, 1971.

RATTENING. Defined by Sidney and Beatrice Webb (*History of Trade Unionism, 1666-1920*, 1919, p. 260) as 'the temporary abstraction of the wheelbands or tools of a workman whose subscription to his club was in arrear ... the recognised method of enforcing, not merely the payment of contributions, but also compliance with the trade regulations of the club', especially in Sheffield. This practice might extend to more violent intimidation, and was considered a factor in the **Sheffield Outrages** of 1866.

READY MIXED CONCRETE v. MINISTER OF PENSIONS (1968) 2 WLR 775; (1968) 1 All ER 433; see **contract of service.**

REBUTTAL CLAUSE; see **disclaimer clause.**

RECOGNISED ASSOCIATION. A **staff association** formally recognised either nationally by the Civil Service Department, or on a departmental basis, to take part in discussion, negotiation, agreements and arbitration for the grade or grades of civil servants it represents; contrasted with an **unrecognised association**, i.e. a staff association which is free to make representations to the government, but which has no prescriptive right to a reply and no negotiating rights. In the non-industrial Civil Service, recognition has depended generally on numerical strength, though no precise membership proportions have ever been laid down. HM Treasury, *Staff Relations in the Civil Service*, HMSO, 1965.

RECOGNISED TERMS AND CONDITIONS; see **Schedule 11 Claims**. For examples of cases arising under the extension of recognised terms and conditions; see K.W. Wedderburn, *Cases and Materials on Labour Law*, OUP, 1967, p. 345 *et seq*. A somewhat similar use of the **Central Arbitration Committee** on recognised terms to that provided for in Schedule 11 of the Employment Protection Act 1975 is to be found in Part II of the **Road Haulage Wages Act 1938** and the **Civil Aviation Act 1949.**

RECOGNITION; see **trade union recognition.**

RECOGNITION OF CARDS. An arrangement between unions whereby they mutually agree to recognise the cards of trade unionists transferred from one employment to another, whether these are cards of the same or different unions from those in the employment to which they are transferred. Recognition of cards was advocated by the **Trades Union Congress** in 1924 in the Hull Main Principles, as one means of avoiding inter-union competition, and was repeated in the **Bridlington Agreement** (q.v.). General recognition of cards was appealed for in a memorandum

by the TUC to affiliated unions in 1940, and some measure of co-operation was obtained; some unions, however, declined to adopt the scheme; see Trade Union Congress, *Trade Union Structure and Closer Unity*, TUC, 1947, p. 8.

RECRUITMENT RATE or **accession rate**; see **labour turnover.**

RECRUITMENT SUBSIDY FOR SCHOOL LEAVERS (RSSL). A scheme introduced in October 1975 to alleviate unemployment among school leavers by encouraging employers to provide more employment opportunities for young people by paying to them £5 per week for 26 weeks for each recruit; see also **Youth Employment Subsidy.**

RED BOOK; see **blue book.**

RED CIRCLE RATE; see **personal rate.**

RED FRIDAY. The name given by trade unionists to 31 July 1925, when a threat of the **Trades Union Congress** to support the miners' resistance to a wage cut led to a reversal of the Baldwin government's policy and a decision to subsidise the colliery owners in order to allow existing wages and conditions to be maintained; the same date was dubbed on the political right **Blackmail Friday**; see K.G.J.C. Knowles, *Strikes*, Basil Blackwell, 1952, p. 110 *et seq*.

REDEPLOYMENT. The redistribution of labour, particularly with the object of finding jobs for workers as an alternative to **redundancy** (see R. Thomas, *An Exercise in Redeployment*, Pergamon Press, 1969), or of producing a more efficient labour distribution or use of labour resources. In the latter usage, may be interpreted as a euphemism for **unemployment** or redundancy, since these may be associated with or result from, redeployment policies; see also **shake-out.**

REDEPLOYMENT PAYMENT. A payment offered to trade unions in the steel industry by the British Steel Corporation in its 'Productivity Programme' (*Proposals for Increasing Productivity, Modernising the Wages Structure and Improving Conditions of Employment*) May 1968. The object of the payment was to compensate a worker required to move from his normal occupation to another occupation not in the same promotion line (see **promotion ladder**), and involved making up loss of earnings on a diminishing scale over four thirteen-week periods. Similar payments are made under the terms of redundancy agreements in other industries, e.g. printing.

REDUNDANCY. Reduction in the labour force of an enterprise, company, factory or office owing to closure, technical change, reorganisation or a diminution in economic activity: a situation in which for any of these reasons (as distinct from dismissal for disciplinary or suitability causes), there is a surplus of labour to be made redundant, either because their continued employment or because the particular skills which they possess are no longer required; **collective redundancy. Redundancy agreement:** a collective agreement between an employer or employers and a trade union or trade unions, to regulate jointly the circumstances in which redundancy will take place; the procedures to be followed in implementing redundancy (hence **redundancy procedure**), or the terms on which labour is to be discharged; (see also, **last-in-first-out, severance pay, redundancy pay**); **redundancy policy**: a unilateral policy by management covering similar contingencies and procedures. Attention to problems of redundancy in Britain increased in the 1950s and 1960s as a result of prolonged **full-employment**, which both raised workers' expectations of employment security (see also **right to work**), emphasised the relationships between redundancy and **mobility of labour** (q.v.) in economic growth, and as a result of **automation**, which induced fears of **technological unemployment**. The slow growth of redundancy agreements and policies (see 'Redundancy in Britain', *Ministry of Labour Gazette*, February 1963, pp. 50-5), added to these considerations, led to the **Redundancy Payments Act 1965**; see British Institute of Management, *Company Redundancy Policies*, Information Summary, 137, March 1969; Acton Society Trust, *Redundancy, A Survey of Problems and Practices*, 1958, and *Three Studies on Redundant Workers*, 1959; Hilda Kahn, *Repercussions of Redundancy*, Allen and Unwin, 1965; D. Wedderburn, *Redundancy and the Railwaymen*, CUP, 1965; F. Herron, *Labour Market in Crisis; Redundancy at Upper Clyde Shipbuilders*, Macmillan, 1975; see also **redeployment**.

REDUNDANCY AGREEMENT; see **redundancy.**

REDUNDANCY PAY; see **Redundancy Payments Act 1965** and **severance pay.**

REDUNDANCY PAYMENTS ACT 1965. An Act establishing for the first time in Britain a general statutory right of workers dismissed for reasons of **redundancy**, to payment, such payment being made by the employer concerned with a rebate of (as at January 1978) 41 per cent from a Redundancy Fund, a lump sum related to weekly pay, age and length of service on termination of employment. The Act also provides that in the event of an employee's entitlement being resisted by his employer, the employee is entitled to claim his payment before one of the **industrial tribunals**. Substantially all employees are covered by its provisions, except those over retiring age, employees with less than 104 weeks' continuous employment with their employers, and certain excluded classes (principally Crown servants, employees of the National Health Service and registered dock workers. The intention of the Act has been variously interpreted as compensation for loss of accrued rights in a job (Lord Denning MR in **Lloyd v. Brassey** (1969) ITR 100 (CA)), as compensation for loss of security and as an encouragement to workers to accept redundancy (see **Wynes v. Southrepps Hall Boiler Farm Ltd** (1968) ITR 407), and remains puzzling to some (see K.W. Wedderburn, *The Worker and The Law*, Pelican, 2nd ed. 1971, pp. 125-6; 'The rationale of the curious Act of 1965 is still shrouded in mystery ...') An official survey carried out in 1969 (S.R. Parker, C.G. Thomas, N.D. Ellis and W.E.J. McCarthy, *Effects of the Redundancy Payments Act*, HMSO, 1971) regards the Act as having broadly achieved its objects in both economic and social spheres in that it has had some impact on the attitudes of the parties involved in redundancy and has led to increased flexibility and mobility of labour, though it had been subject to criticism about anomalies in payments, selectivity, and alleged abuse of the scheme. For a criticism of the Act see R.H. Fryer, 'The Myths of the Redundancy Payments Act', *Industrial Law Journal*, Vol. 2, No. 1, March 1973 and for a general view of its legal development, Cyril Grunfeld, *The Law of Redundancy*, Sweet and Maxwell, 1971? The **Employment Protection Act 1975**, ss. 99-107, provides a procedure for handling redundancies in order to comply with the EEC's **Collective Redundancy Directive** of 1975 (q.v.). This allows for prior consultation of at least 90 days in redundancies involving more than 100 employees and of 60 days in those involving 10 to 100; the employer is also required to disclose in writing to representatives of recognised trade unions his reasons, the numbers and descriptions of employees concerned, the method of selecting them and the proposed method of bringing the redundancy about.

REDUNDANCY POLICY; see **redundancy.**

REDUNDANCY REBATES ACT 1977. An Act enabling the Secretary of State for Employment to vary the amount of rebate payable to employers under the **Redundancy Payments Act 1965** (q.v.) by selecting one of different rates in the range 35 per cent to 80 per cent. Rates of rebate payable to employers have been steadily reduced from 70 per cent in 1965 to 50 per cent in 1969 and now (January 1978) stands at 41 per cent.

REDUNDANCY SIT-IN; see **sit-in.**

REFERABLE DISPUTE. In general a difference between two parties in collective bargaining which may be referred for settlement through an agreed procedure, i.e. excluding those which are not thought to be, or are not constitutionally designed to be, referred through such a procedure. In the building industry, formerly a dispute which was handled through National Joint Council machinery rather than through the emergency, or **Green Book Procedure** (q.v.); see A.I. Marsh and W.E.J. McCarthy, *Disputes Procedure in Britain*, Royal Commission on Trade Unions and Employers' Associations, Research Papers 2 (Part 2), 1968, Ch. 5.

REFEREE. An **arbitrator**; rarely used today except as the title of a **single arbitrator** at the final stage in the District Conciliation Scheme in the Coal Mining Industry.

REGIONAL EMPLOYMENT PREMIUM (REP). A subsidy on labour costs introduced in 1967 for manufacturing employers in **development areas**. Payment of the premium ceased with effect from 2 January 1977.

REGISTERED AGREEMENT. A collective agreement registered in the Irish Republic under the terms of the Industrial Relations Act 1946. Under Part III of the Act the **Labour Court** is empowered to register an agreement if the parties consent, if the agreement applies to all workers of a particular class, if it contains a no-strike clause, and on a number of other conditions. Once registered the agreement applies to every worker and employer of the class concerned, whether party to the agreement or not, as an **implied term** of contract; see David O'Mahony, *Industrial Relations in Ireland: the Background*, The Economic Research Institute, Paper No. 19, May 1964.

REGISTERED TRADE UNION. A **trade union** (q.v.) as defined in the **Industrial Relations Act 1971 ss. 61** and **67** (as distinct from an unregistered organisation of workers), registered with the **Chief Registrar of Trade Unions and Employers' Associations** under the terms of that Act (now repealed), and meeting the requirements as to rules in its Schedules 4 and 5 in order to remain registered, or a federation of trade unions in which all constituent or affiliated organisations were trade unions within the meaning of the Act. Registration gave the advantages of corporate status, and *inter alia* the capacity to enter into **agency shop** and **approved closed shop** agreements, exemptions from actions for inducing breaches of contract (s. 96), protection for officials and a limit on awards made against the organisation in actions before the **National Industrial Relations Court**, and exemptions from income tax, corporation tax and capital gains tax in respect of certain provident funds under the Income and Corporation Taxes Act, 1970, s. 338; see C.G. Heath, *A Guide to the Industrial Relations Act, 1971*, Sweet and Maxwell, 1971, p. 48 *et seq.* No corresponding status now exists under the current **Trade Union and Labour Relations Act**; but see **independent trade union.**

REGISTERED UNEMPLOYED. Defined by the Department of Employment as persons who are seeking employment with an employer, are capable and available for work, are registered for employment at an employment exchange or youth employment service careers office on the day of the monthly count and are not in employment on that day. The count includes both claimants for unemployment benefit and persons who are not claiming benefit, but excludes non-claimants who are registered only for part-time work; it also excludes those persons who are severely disabled and unlikely to obtain work other than in special conditions. It distinguishes between the **wholly unemployed** and the **temporarily stopped.** Registered unemployment figures are calculated monthly; they include **casual workers,** but these are excluded from analyses of unemployment by occupation, age and duration of unemployment. For a recent survey of the prospects of registered unemployed persons obtaining work, see 'Characteristics of the unemployed: sample survey June 1976', *Department of Employment Gazette,* June 1977. Fifty-five per cent of men and 70 per cent of women seeking full-time longdterm work were reckoned to have good, fair or reasonable prospects of obtaining it; 21 per cent of men and 16 per cent of women who were, like the previous group, keen to get work were reckoned to have poor prospects of obtaining it, and 24 per cent of men and 13 per cent of women were assessed as having poor prospects and being somewhat unenthusiastic for work.

REGISTRAR OF FRIENDLY SOCIETIES; see **Chief Registrar of Friendly Societies.**

REGISTRAR OF TRADE UNIONS AND EMPLOYERS' ASSOCIATIONS; see **Chief Registrar of Trade Unions and Employers' Associations.**

REGULARS. Casual workers who are regularly employed; see **blue-eyed boys.**

REHABILITATION OF OFFENDERS ACT 1974. An Act making it unlawful for an employer to discriminate against a person for a conviction which is 'spent', i.e. a conviction in respect of which a 'rehabilitation period' of up to 10 years has elapsed after the end of the sentence, during which there has been no further conviction. It is also potentially actionable under the Act to make any unauthorised disclosure to a third party, thus involving the question of giving references. All convictions for periods longer than two years are excepted from the provisions of the Act; also excepted are convictions for certain offences under the Children and Young Persons Act and the Prevention of Fraud (Investments) Act. Certain occupations or professions are also excepted, e.g. accountants, solicitors, doctors, barristers.

RELAXATION AGREEMENTS. Also known as **dilution** agreements (q.v.). Agreements with trade unions on the relaxation of existing customs on the employment of skilled workers, including the use of alternative classes of labour (or **dilutees**) on jobs previously regarded as skilled, the use of unskilled or semi-skilled labour to assist skilled workers, and sometimes the easing of restrictions on the manning of machines, on overtime and on the employment of women on work previously done by men. Relaxation Agreements were made during both the 1914-18 and 1939-45 wars, especially in the engineering and printing industries in order to augment the supply of labour (P. Inman, *Labour in the Munitions Industries,* HMSO and Longmans, Green and Co., 1957, Part I; *Engineering Handbook of National Agreements,* Section 7; A.I. Marsh, *Industrial Relations in Engineering,* Pergamon Press, 1965; John Child, *Industrial Relations in the British Printing Industry,* George Allen and Unwin Ltd, 1967). During the first world war the **Treasury Agreement,** March 1915, subsequently embodied in the Munitions of War Act, gave the government compulsory powers to introduce a general dilution scheme; this was not particularly successful and in the second world war voluntary methods only were used.

RELAXATION ALLOWANCE (work study); see **allowances.** 'An addition to basic time intended to provide the worker with opportunity to recover from the physiological and psychological effects of carrying out specified work under specified conditions and to allow attention to personal needs' British Standards Institution, *Glossary of Terms Used in Work Study,* BS 3138, 1969, No. 35004); hence its alternative nomenclature **compensating rest.** Relaxation allowance is usually considered to have two components, **personal needs allowance** (a constant factor allowing, for example, for washing, going to the lavatory and getting a drink), and a **fatigue allowance** (a variable addition made according to the circumstances of the job).

RELIEF SHIFT. An extra shift made necessary at periodic intervals to facilitate shift rotation (see **three shift system**), in which case it may overlap regular shifts in the establishment; sometimes applied to various other arrangements whereby workers are given relief in their shift patterns, e.g. by rotating day and night shifts, or by giving relief in a continuous shift system by giving workers different days off pin the week.

REMPLOY LTD. The **Disabled Persons' Employment Corporation** (known as

Remploy Ltd), a public corporation established under the Ministry of Labour, now the **Department of Employment**, to provide sheltered employment for the severely disabled, but also empowered to employ a small percentage of able-bodied and less severely disabled people to fill key posts or to provide essential staff. The **Disabled Persons (Employment) Act 1944** provided that Remploy was to be a commercial undertaking, making goods for sale on the pen market, and meeting its costs out of such sales, losses being made good from public funds. Eighty-seven Remploy factories provided in 1978 sheltered employment for 10,400 employees including over 8,000 severely disabled men and women and have met the numerous dilemmas involved in their operation with a good deal of skill and success; (see Department of Employment Leaflet DPL 12); see also **Industrial Rehabilitation Units** and **disabled persons.**

REMUNERATION. Payment for services rendered; often used generically to describe different types of **take home pay, wages, salaries, earnings,** etc.

REMUNERATION OF TEACHERS ACT 1965; see **Burnham Committees.**

RENT (AGRICULTURE) ACT 1976; see **tied cottage.**

RE-OPENER CLAUSE. A clause in a collective agreement providing that, if there is over a specified time a given rise in the cost of living (or in an index of prices) a new wage claim may be submitted by the union side, e.g. in the **Engineering Package Deal Agreement** of 1964; see also **threshold agreement** and **indexation.**

REOU. Radio and Electronic Officers' Union (q.v.).

REP. Regional Employment Premium (q.v.).

REPETITION CURVE; see **learning curve.**

REPRESENTATION DISPUTE. A dispute between unions over the representation of a particular group of workers; a **membership dispute**, whether this is **jurisdictional** or **demarcational** (q.v.). In practice the former have frequently been dealt with by trade unions themselves under the terms of the **Bridlington Agreement** while the latter have frequently been referred for conciliation by the **Department of Employment** and now by the **Advisory Conciliation and Arbitration Service** (q.v.).

RERUM NOVARUM; see **Catholic industrial relations teaching.**

RESETTLEMENT ALLOWANCE or Resettlement Payment. A payment made to a worker as part of a scheme of compensation for being made redundant (see **redundancy**) i.e. in combination with the giving of a payment in lieu of notice, and a **severance payment**, the resettlement allowance being related to the time lag expected in finding a new job, e.g. in Imperial Chemical Industries and the steel industry.

RESETTLEMENT TRANSFER SCHEME now **Employment Transfer Scheme** (q.v.).

REST DAY EXTRAS. Gift hours payable over and above **clocked hours** for all time worked during the period of eight hours after the end of the worker's last shift in his rota turn to the beginning of his first shift of the next rota turn (stel industry).

RESTITUTIONAL OVERTIME PAYMENT. Payment to compensate for a withdrawn or lost opportunity to work overtime; national newspaper industry.

RESTRICTIONS. A word which can be applied to all sanctions by workers against managements short of actual withdrawal of labour; hence the distinction made in National Coal Board statistics between **stoppages of work** and **restrictions.** Depending on the situation restrictions in British industry may range from withdrawal of co-operation, insistence on formal rights and customs, to limitations of output and on hours of work; see **restrictive practices.**

RESTRICTIVE LABOUR PRACTICES; see **restrictive practices.**

RESTRICTIVE PRACTICES. Defined by the **Confederation of British Industry** in its evidence to the Donovan **Royal Commission on Trade Unions and Employers' Associations, 1965-1968** as any work practice, collectively operated, which hinders or acts as a disincentive to the more effective use of labour, technical skill, machinery, or other resources, i.e. such practices as trade union reluctance to accept manpower economies when new methods or machines are introduced, **demarcation**

rules, systematic time wasting, resistance to work study, etc. leading to overmanning or under-utilisation of manpower resources. Such a definition appears to suggest that restrictive practices are confined to action or inaction by trade unions or by workers, i.e. to **restrictive labour practices**, strictly interpreted, and could be removed by unions or workers if they so wished. Other commentators have pointed out that any type of organisation is in itself a set of restrictive practices in that it allocates defined responsibilities to certain individuals and groups and not to others, and that such practices should be judged on their immediate appropriateness, total effect, and on the attitudes engendered by them, rather than in absolute terms (see for example W.W. Daniel, *Beyond the Wage-Work Bargain*, Political and Economic Planning, Broadsheet 519, July 1970, p. 6), others that they involve at least acquiescence by management (and therefore might better be thought of as 'arrangements') and are sometimes justifiable on social grounds. Hence the definition: 'an arrangement under which labour is not used efficiently and which is not justifiable on social grounds' (Royal Commission on Trade Unions and Employers' Associations, *Restrictive Labour Practices*, Research Papers 4, HMSO, 1967, p. 47). The Royal Commission itself preferred the definition 'rules and customs which unduly hinder the efficient use of labour' (Cmnd. 3623, HMSO June 1968, para. 296), using the word 'unduly' to except justifiably restrictive rules, stressing the specific relation of restrictions to particular circumstances and their removal as one element in the task of management in securing the efficient use of resources, especially by **productivity bargaining**. For a general view of trade union attitudes; see J.E. Mortimer, *Trade Unions and Technological Change*, OUP, 1971 and A. Aldridge, *Power, Authority and Restrictive Practices*, Basil Blackwell, 1978; see also **machine question, dilution, craft control, relaxation agreements, ca'canny, work sharing, welting, spelling, under-employment, overmanning, soldiering, continuity rule, protective practice, fat, featherbedding, dead horse rule, make-work practices.**

RETAIL BOOK, STATIONERY AND ALLIED TRADES EMPLOYEES' ASSOCIATION. A trade union for bookstall and bookshop employees founded in 1919, which has grown from a membership of less than 1,000 in the 1920s to 7,000

approximately in 1977. *Address*: 7 Grapes Street, Shaftesbury Avenue, London WC2H 8DW. *Tel*: 01-836 4897. The union was suspended from membership of the TUC by decision of the 1972 Congress, for failing to comply with Congress policy of non-registration under the **Industrial Relations Act 1971**, and has not since become re-affiliated. All its members are currently employed by W.H. Smith with whom it has a post-entry closed shop.

RETAIL PRICES INDEX. An index measuring the movement of retail prices. Three indices of retail prices are currently in use in the United Kingdom, a **General Index of Retail Prices**, published monthly in the *Department of Employment Gazette*, and two indices for one-person and two-person pensioner households. For a description of the latter, see the *Department of Employment and Productivity Gazette*, June 1969. The General Index of Retail Prices measures the change from month to month in the average level of retail prices of the commodities and services purchased by all types of households in the UK, except certain higher income households and those of retired persons mainly dependent on social security payments. Its base date is now January 1974 and the weights used are revised each January on the basis of the Family Expenditure Surveys for the three years ended in the previous June, revalued at the prices obtaining at the date of revision (see Department of Employment, *Method of Construction and Calculation of the Index of Retail Prices*, Studies in Official Statistics, No. 6, HMSO, 1967). The Department is insistent that the Index measures price changes only and that it is not a **cost of living index** though it is often popularly regarded as such. The earliest index of the kind officially compiled in the UK bore that title and was designed to measure the percentage increase month by month in the cost of maintaining unchanged the standard of living prevailing among working-class households in July 1914 (see Ministry of Labour, *Industrial Relations Handbook*, HMSO, 1944 edition, p. 187 *et seq.*). An Interim Index, 17 June 1947 = 100, was submitted as a temporary measure on the advice of the *Report of the Cost of Living Advisory Committee* in March 1947 (Cmd. 7077), pending the holding of a large scale postwar household expenditure inquiry, the advisory Committee prefering in subsequent reports the term 'Index of Retail Prices' to 'Cost of Living

Index' on the grounds that the latter gave rise to suggestions that it should be based on basic necessities only. A new Index of Retail Prices was started from January 1956 with the average level of prices at that date = 100, and based on a household expenditure inquiry in 1953. The Index was subsequently re-based in January 1962 and now has a reference base of January 1974; see *Reports of the Cost of Living Advisory Committee*, Cmd. 7077, March 1947, Cmd. 8328, June 1951, Cmd. 8481, September 1952, Cmnd. 9710, February 1956, Cmnd. 1657, March 1962 and Cmnd. 3677, 1968; also **cost of living sliding scales, threshold agreements** and **indexation**.

RETAIN AND TRANSFER. A system of regulating the labour market for professional association footballers in which the transfer of players from one club to another only takes place if a player's present club approves the transfer and receives a satisfactory fee from the club to which he is being transferred. The system is a controversial one. It was broadly approved by the Forster Committee of 1952 (*Report of a Committee of Investigation into a difference regarding the Terms and Conditions of Association Footballers*, HMSO) but modified as a result of a High Court decision in **Eastham v. Newcastle United Football Club** ((1964) Ch. 413; (1963) 3 WLR 574; 107 SJ 574; (1963) All ER 139) to allow for an option period after an initial period of contract and adjudication by the Management Committee of the Football League in the event of a club wishing to retain a player but no agreement being arrived at between the parties; see Peter J. Sloane, 'The Labour Market in Professional Football', *British Journal of Industrial Relations*, Vol. VII, No. 2, July 1969, pp. 181-99. The Commission on Industrial Relations (*Professional Football* Report No. 87, 1974) criticised the system as did the Chester *Report of the Committee on Football*, 1968. A revised system replaced retain and transfer arrangements from July 1967.

RETAINER. A sum paid to secure special services if required, either in advance of a particular engagement (e.g. of a barrister) or to obtain advice, treatment, maintenance or other attention on need or on demand. Seems mainly to be used in relation to professional or technical services but a similar concept can be applied to manual workers where these have historically worked as independent contractors e.g. market porters; see **retaining wage.**

RETAINING WAGE. London Area Wholesale Markets: the minimum weekly rate of pay of a porter, net of **porterage** (i.e. piecework payment based upon weights and kinds of commodities carried on the *inside* of the market) and **pitching** (i.e. a similar payment made on the *outside* of the market).

RETENTION BONUS. A compensatory payment sometimes made to workers who, as a result of a factory run-down, are required or encouraged to continue in employment until closure while other workers are free to accept redundancy terms, it being supposed that this is to the employer's advantage in retaining key employees over this period and will, perhaps, compromise the chances of such employees in finding alternative work; see **redundancy.** Such bonuses are usually paid on the length of the retained services involved.

RETIREMENT BENEFITS. Sums paid by trade unions to members, usually as a single payment on their retirement from work; amounts paid out per head are usually small, and payment is sometimes based on years of service, e.g. in the case of the **National Union of Railwaymen**; see Arthur Marsh and Peter Cope, 'The Anatomy of Trade Union Benefits in the 1960s', *Industrial Relations Journal*, Summer 1970.

RETIREMENT PENSIONS. Payments made to men over 65 and women over 60 under the **National Insurance Act 1965** (after 6 April 1978 under the **Social Security Pensions Act 1975**) or under **occupational pensions schemes**; see also **superannuation. Old age pensions** provided by the State began in 1908 with a non-contributory scheme for persons over 70 and contributions made compulsory for those in the National Health Insurance Scheme in 1925; retirement pensions proper were introduced in 1948 and a **Graduated Pensions Scheme** in April 1961. Under this scheme a 'graduated pension' was added to basic or flat-rate pension for employees with earnings initially in excess of £9 per week, the amount of pension payable varying according to the total amount paid in graduated contributions, which in turn depended on the worker's level of earnings and the length of his contributory membership. This scheme, much criticised by contributors, was brought to an end in April 1975 and all accrued benefits frozen at that date. Under the Social Security Pension Act 1975 the existing flat rate pension is to be replaced from 6 April 1978 by a 'basic pension' which all contributors meeting contribution conditions will receive and an 'additional pension' which is earnings related. (Department of Health and Social Security *Leaflets* NP15, 22, 23, 24, 29 and 30).

RETROACTIVE PAY; see **retrospective payment.**

RETROSPECTION. The pre-dating of all or part of the application of a collective agreement or some aspect of it. Retrospection may involve **retrospective payment** (q.v.), but it may also be more indirect in its operation, e.g. it may be an expression of the principle that a new wage, salary or bonus rate shall be so fixed from the date on which an agreement is made as to take into account co-operation or increases in productivity which have taken place in the past.

RETROSPECTIVE PAYMENT. A payment made under a wage or salary agreement which allows for an increase in remuneration to be applied from a date earlier than that on which the agreement was made; known in the United States as **retroactive pay;** see also **retrospection.** Retrospective payment is to be distinguished from **back pay** (q.v.).

REVIEW BODIES. The name given to a number of standing committees or boards whose role it has been to review the remuneration and pay structures of particular groups of workers, especially those for whom it is thought that collective bargaining is not appropriate. From 1962 to 1970 the **Kindersley Committee** (q.v.) acted as Review Body on Doctors' and Dentists' Remuneration and the **National Board for Prices and Incomes** performed a similar function for university teachers between November 1967 and May 1970, and for the armed forces. The three current Review Bodies the **Top Salaries Review Body** (q.v.), the **Armed Forces Review Body** and the **Doctors and Dentists Review Body,** were set up by the Heath government and made their first reports in 1972.

RICHARDSON v. KOEFOD (1969) 3 All ER 1264. A case finally overruling the mediaeval judgement that if no duration was fixed for a contract of employment it should be presumed to be for a fixed period of one year only, Lord Denning, Master of the Rolls: 'The time has now

come to state explicitly that there is no presumption of a yearly hiring. In the absence of express stipulation, the rule is that every contract of service is determinable by reasonable notice. The length of notice depends on the circumstances of the case'; see **termination of employment.**

RIDGE v. BALDWIN; see **specific performance.**

RIGHTS COMMISSIONERS. Persons appointed by the Minister of Labour of the Republic of Ireland to investigate disputes and to make recommendations. The investigations of a Rights Commissioner almost always take place in private and his recommendations may be appealed to the **Labour Court,** but in such event the parties are bound by the Court's decision.

RIGHTS DISPUTES also **disputes of rights, conflicts of rights, issues of rights, rights issues.** Disputes or conflicts arising in an industrial relations system out of alleged violations of rights established in contracts of employment, by law or by collective agreement, as distinguished from **interest disputes,** i.e. disputes involved in making new terms and conditions of employment or renewing those which have expired, and which are thus subject to a process of negotiation rather than of adjudication. Such a distinction is said to be fundamental in most national industrial relations systems. In Britain it has had little significance where collective agreements are concerned, in part because they are not considered to be legally enforceable, in part because procedures make no such distinction in most cases, and in part because the predominance of informal custom and practice makes it impracticable (**Royal Commission on Trade Unions and Employers Associations, 1965-68,** Cmnd. 3623, June 1968, p. 121). They are now referred to in the **Industrial Relations Code of Practice,** 1972 (para. 126) as relating 'to the application on interpretation of existing agreements or contracts of employment'. K.W. Wedderburn, 'Conflicts of Rights and Conflicts of Interest in Labor Disputes', in *Dispute Settlement Procedures in Five Western European Countries,* ed. Benjamin Aaron, Institute of Industrial Relations, University of California, Los Angeles, 1969, argues that the distinction may be of more limited value than has been generally supposed. Some writers prefer the term **'judiciable disputes',** see T.L. Johnston, *Collective Bar-*

gaining in Sweden, Allen and Unwin, 1962, p. 139.

RIGHTS ISSUES; see **rights disputes.**

RIGHT TO MANAGE; see **managerial prerogatives.**

RIGHT TO ORGANISE; see **freedom of association.**

RIGHT TO STRIKE. The right of a worker to withdraw his labour in the protection of his interests, widely regarded as a fundamental freedom connected with **freedom of association.** The approach to the question differs from one country to another, though all countries impose some limitations (see Otto Kahn-Freund (ed.), *Labour Relations and the Law: A Comparative Study,* Stevens, 1965). In Britain there is no law laying down the right to strike but rather as 'a right to withdraw labour in combination without being subject to legal consequences' (*Donovan Royal Commission on Trade Unions and Employers Association Report,* Cmnd. 3623, 1968, para. 935) or as 'an essential element in the principle of collective bargaining.' (Lord Wright, Crofter Harris Tweed Co. v. Veitch (1942) A.C. 435 at p. 463.) (see **strikes**). International Labour Conventions dealing with **freedom of association** (q.v.) make no reference to the right to strike, but the ILO's Committee of Experts on the Application of Conventions and Recommendations has stated that 'the law of the land shall not be such as to impair, nor shall it be applied as to impair, the guarantees provided for' in **International Labour Convention No. 87,** 'and especially the freedom of action of trade union organisations in defence of their occupational interests; it is therefore necessary that in every case in which workers are prohibited from striking, adequate guarantees should be accorded to such workers in order fully to safeguard their interests' (*Report III, Part IV, to the 43rd Session of the International Labour Conference,* 1959, para. 68). The right to strike is recognised in the **European Social Charter,** limited to **conflicts of interest** between employers and workers, and subject to obligations arising out of collective agreements previously entered into, such as the use of agreed negotiating procedures to settle disputes; see **no-strike clauses, constitutional strikes, unconstitutional strikes.**

RIGHT TO WORK. An expression used in two principal senses: (1) The right of a worker *not* to be excluded from employment by the refusal of a particular trade union to admit him to membership by the operation of a **closed shop** (q.v.) or by other discrimination, e.g. **preferential hiring** arrangements, excessive initiation fees, etc. Hence **right to work laws** such as those contained in ss. 7 and 8 of the **Taft-Hartley Act 1947** the United States, or in State legislation authorised under the Act; see F. Meyers, '*Right to Work' in Practice,* New York: The Fund for the Republic, 1959; R.W. Rideout, *The Right to Membership of a Trade Union,* University of London, the Athlone Press, 1963; Ronald L. Miller, 'Right-to-work' laws and compulsory union membership in the United States', *British Journal of Industrial Relations,* Vol. XIV, No. 2, July 1976, pp. 186-93. (2) The right of workers to employment, to make a living, or to a living wage; hence also to job protection, income maintenance, compensation in the event of loss of job, or even more generally, to satisfying work or industrial relationships (*droit au travail*); see F. Meyers, *Ownership of Jobs,* Institute of Industrial Relations, University of California, Los Angeles, 1964, for a comment on the modern tendency to extend property-like rights to jobs; also K.W. Wedderburn, *The Worker and the Law,* Pelican, 2nd ed. 1971, p. 137 *et seq.,* and A. Sykes, 'The Ideological Basis of Industrial Relations in Great Britain', *Management International,* 1965, Vol. 5, No. 6.

RIGHT TO WORK LAWS; see **right to work.**

RIVAL UNIONISM. Described by Walter Galenson (*Rival Unionism in the US,* New York; American Council on Public Affairs, 1940) as 'the co-existence of two or more unrelated labor organisations actively competing for the control of the workers employed or the work habitually performed within a particular trade or occupation', distinguishing this from **dual unionism** (q.v.), which he regards as non-competitive. Some writers in the USA confine the term rival unionism to situations which give rise to inter-union disputes about membership and not to disputes about claims to particular jobs or types of work (commonly known in the USA as **jurisdictional dipsutes**); see Florence Peterson, *American Labor Unions,* New York, Harper 1963. The term is not commonly used in Britain.

ROAD HAULAGE WAGES ACT 1938.

An Act applying to workers employed on vehicles of which Part II remains in force and provides that any such worker employed in connection with a vehicle operated 'on own account' (i.e. a vehicle used for the carriage of goods in connection with any trade or business carried on by an employer) or a trade union of which he is a member, may make a complaint to the Secretary of State for Employment if he considers that the remuneration paid to him is unfair. Failing settlement of the complaint by any other method, the Secretary of State is then required to refer the matter to the Industrial Court (now the **Central Arbitration Committee**) which has the power to fix statutory minimum remuneration for a period of three years. Remuneration shall not be considered to be unfair if it is equivalent to what would have been paid by **Wages Councils** to workers employed on similar work; see also **fair wages principle**. The employer's licence to run a road haulage business may be revoked if he fails to comply with a CAC award and he may be convicted of the crime of failing to comply.

ROBENS REPORT. The **Report of the Committee on Safety and Health at Work 1970-1972** (Cmnd. 5034, July 1972). The Committee drew attention to the inadequacies of existing safety and health arrangements at work and recommended more self-regulation at work and involvement of management and workers, under a system of unified legislation, with existing health and safety inspectorates for factories, mines, agriculture, explosives, nuclear installations and alkali works operating within a single independent national Safety and Health at Work Authority which should also promote a more co-ordinated research effort in occupational safety and health. A feature of the Report was the emphasis which it placed on the development of non-statutory codes of practice. It fell short of the demands from some quarters that legislation should provide for safety committees representing employees at each place of work (see, for example, Society of Labour Lawyers, *Occupational Accidents and the Law*, Fabian Research Series 280, January 1970). A number of research papers were commissioned by the Committee, those published to September 1972 being, P.J. Shipp and A.S. Sutton, *A Study of the Statistics relating to Safety and Health at Work*, HMSO, 1972 and A.R. Hale and M. Hale, *A Review of the Industrial Accident Research Literature*, HMSO, 1972; see also

R.W.L. Howells, 'The Robens Report', *Industrial Law Journal*, Vol. 1, No. 4, December 1972. The **Health and Safety at Work Act 1974** (q.v.) follows the recommendations of the Report both in its general approach and in establishing a **Health and Safety Commission**.

ROBERTS ARUNDEL DISPUTE. A dispute at the Roberts Arundel textile machinery factory at Stockport in 1966-67. The dispute arose over the management's attempts to introduce female labour and American management. This led to a strike, the dismissal of 149 employees and the withdrawal of recognition from the Amalgamated Engineering Union. Negotiation failed to solve the problem and in October 1967 it was announced that production at the factory would cease from January 1968.

ROBERTSON REPORT. Name given to the reports of several **Courts of Inquiry** under the chairmanship of Professor D.J. Robertson, including two inquiries in the motor industry (*Rootes Motors, Linwood*, Cmnd. 3692, 1968, and *Girling Ltd., Bromborough*, Cmnd. 3855, 1968), *Railway guards and shunters* (Cmnd. 3426, 1967), and *Heathrow, London Airport firemen* (Cmnd. 4405, July 1970); also a Committee of Investigation in a dispute between the *Steel Company of Wales and the Amalgamated Union of Building Trades Workers*, 1966.

ROCHDALE REPORT. The report of the committee under the chairmanship of Lord Rochdale, to review the organisation and structure of the United Kingdom shipping industry (Cmnd. 4337, May 1970). The committee made recommendations about manpower and training of seafarers and shore staff, approved the development of inter-union co-operation through the **British Seafarers' Joint Council**, recommended a merger between the Merchant Marine Service Association (representing shipmasters), the **Merchant Navy and Airline Officers' Association** (q.v.) and the **Radio and Electronics Officers' Union**, and considered that there was 'much to be said for all ratings to be members of the **National Union of Seamen**'.

ROLL TURNERS' TRADE SOCIETY, BRITISH (BRTTS). A trade union founded in 1898, and recognised in a number of works in the steel industry, principally in Lancashire, the Midlands and in South Wales. *Address*: 44 Collingwood

Avenue, Corby, Northants. *Tel*: 05366 2617. *TUC Affiliated Membership, 1977*: 776.

ROOKES v. BARNARD AND OTHERS (1964) 1 All ER 367. A leading case in which it was held that the defendants had used unlawful means to induce the British Overseas Airways Corporation to dismiss an employee, Mr Douglas Rookes, the House of Lords, on appeal, holding that they were guilty of unlawful intimidation because they had threatened to induce a breach of contract resulting in interference with the employment of Mr Rookes, that they were not protected by s. 3 of the **Trades Disputes Act 1906**, and that there was nothing to differentiate a threat of a breach of contract from a threat of physical violence or any other legal threat. The case resulted in the **Trades Disputes Act 1965**, the object of which was to restore the law to the position it was previously thought to occupy under the 1906 Act. Both the 1906 and the 1965 Acts were repealed by the **Industrial Relations Act 1971**. Following the repeal of the Industrial Relations Act itself, the 1965 position was again restored in the **Trade Union and Labour Relations Act 1974** (s. 13) which now applies. See also **intimidation**. The case of Rookes v. Barnard, and the changes in common law attitudes which it revealed, was one reason for the appointment of the Donovan **Royal Commission on Trade Unions and Employers' Associations 1965-68**, which included a particular attention to law in its terms of reference.

ROSS AWARD; see **Fire Brigades Union**.

ROSSENDALE UNION OF BOOT, SHOE AND SLIPPER OPERATIVES; see **Boot, Shoe and Slipper Operatives, Rossendale Union of**.

ROTATING SHIFT. Any arrangement of working periods in which the worker changes his shift hours on a regular basis; may be an **alternating shift** arrangement, e.g. alternating weeks of days and nights, or a more complex arrangement such as that involved in a so-called 'continental shift' system; see **three-shift system**.

ROTHWELL v. APEX AND TRADES UNION CONGRESS (1976) ICR 211 (QBD). A case in which it was argued by the plaintiff, the President of the Staff Association-General Accident (SAGA), that the action of the TUC Disputes Committee in awarding that a breach of the Bridlington Principles had been committed and that the Association of Professional, Executive, Clerical and Computer Staff ought to have discontinued the process of transferring the engagements of SAGA membership to itself under the terms of the Trade Union (Amalgamations etc.) Act 1964 and, this transfer having been completed, to expel the members so obtained, was *ultra vires* and void. Judgement was made in favour of the plaintiff. See Bridlington Agreement and Peter J. Kalis, 'The Bridlington Agreement and Awards of the TUC Disputes Committee', *Industrial Law Journal*, Vol. 5, No. 4, December 1976, pp. 246-9; see **Bridlington Agreement**.

ROUND-THE-CLOCK OPERATION. A production system which keeps the plant in operation for all twenty-four hours of the day, usually involving the use of a **three-shift system** (q.v.).

ROUSTABOUT. A worker in the petroleum industry who works on wells both as a drilling and production labourer.

ROWAN SYSTEM. A premium bonus or incentive payment system based, like the **Halsey Premium Bonus System** and the **Bedeaux System**, one providing the worker with a bonus on time saved. It was devised by Mr James Rowan of the firm of David Rowan and Co., Glasgow, and introduced into their marine engine plant in 1898. Rowan differs from Halsey in that the proportion of time saved is not fixed, the formula being time taken *plus*

$$\frac{\text{time taken x time saved}}{\text{time allowed}} \text{ x rate per hour.}$$

It gives a more generous payment than the **Halsey-Weir System** (50 per cent bonus), until the time saved is 50 per cent of time allowed, after which Rowan becomes less generous to the worker than Halsey, giving a more certain safeguard against loose time fixing; N.C. Hunt, *Methods of Wage Payment in British Industry*, Pitman, 1951, and R. Marriott, *Incentive Payment Systems*, Staples Press, 3rd ed. (revised) 1968.

ROYAL COMMISSION ON LABOUR, 1891-94; see **Devonshire Commission**.

ROYAL COMMISSION ON LABOUR LAWS, 1874-75; see **Cockburn Commission**.

ROYAL COMMISSION ON THE POLICE, 1960-62; see **Willink Commission.**

ROYAL COMMISSION ON TRADE DISPUTES AND TRADE COMBINATIONS, 1903-06; see **Dunedin Commission.**

ROYAL COMMISSION ON TRADE UNIONS, 1867-69; see **Erle Commission.**

ROYAL COMMISSION ON TRADE UNIONS AND EMPLOYERS' ASSOCIATIONS, 1965-68; see **Donovan Commission.**

RPAW. Rubber, Plastic and Allied Workers (q.v.).

RSSL. Recruitment Subsidy for School Leavers (q.v.).

RUBBER, PLASTIC AND ALLIED WORKERS (RPAW). A trade union founded in 1890 as the India Rubber, Cable and Asbestos Workers' Union, and later known as the United Rubber Workers of Great Britain. The organistion was almost destroyed in the industrial troubles in the early 1920s and the depression of the 1930s, having only 312 members in 1936. It recovered after the second world war, and was represented on the National Joint Council for the Rubber Manufacturing Industry having more than 4,000 members. It amalgamated with the **General and Municipal Workers' Union** in 1974.

RUCKER PLAN. A plant-wide bonus system involving productivity sharing which originated with Allan Rucker of Cambridge, Massachusetts, which has been widely publicised in Britain by F.R. Bentley Company Ltd. (see F.R. Bentley, *People, Productivity and Progress*, Business Publications Ltd, 1964), and is now said to be operating in 40 British companies. It is broadly similar in intention to the **Scanlon Plan** (q.v.); but the formula used is more engineered and precise, and takes account only of **value added** (q.v.) by manufacture, leaving out the cost of raw materials and supplies. It places less emphasis on formal union-management co-operation than the Scanlon Plan, but usually includes a Share of Production Committee for ideas on method improvement. The basic premise of the scheme is that there is a direct and proportional relationship between annual production value per worker and annual pay per worker in every company, the for-

mer being taken to be value added by the manufacturer, i.e. sales, *less* cost of materials and supplies. A ratio of wages to production value can therefore be set, and employees guaranteed a fixed percentage of any improvement on that ratio - say 40 per cent. This can be distributed in part on a monthly basis, and in part used as a reserve fund against deficits; see British Institute of Management, *Information Note 26*, 1964.

RULE 11. A rule of the **Trades Union Congress** on industrial disputes. Affiliated organisations are, under the Rule, obliged to keep the General Council informed on matters arising between them and employers, or between unions themselves, including unauthorised or unconstitutional stoppages. The General Council until 1969 had no power to intervene until other bodies of workpeople than those immediately concerned were involved. As a result of the undertaking given to the Labour government in Downing Street on 18 July 1969, the Rule was amended to allow the Council to take action to obtain the facts where a dispute was likely to lead to an unconstitutional stoppage of work which involved directly or indirectly large bodies of workers or which, if protracted, might have serious consequences and to tender its considered opinion and advice with a view to promoting a settlement. Affiliated organisations refusing the advice or assistance of the Council may be dealt with under **Rule 13** (q.v.).

RULE 12. A rule of the **Trades Union Congress** on disputes between affiliated organisations. The rule obliges affiliated unions to notify the General Council of such disputes, to authorise no stoppage of work until consideration of the matter by the Council, or to obtain a return to work if a stoppage has already taken place. It also authorises the General Council to refer cases to its Disputes Committee, dealing with a trade union under **Rule 13** (q.v.) in the event of non-compliance with the Committee's decision; see **inter-union disputes, Bridlington Agreement.**

RULE 13. A rule of the **Trades Union Congress** empowering the General Council to investigate the conduct of any affiliated organisation on the grounds that its activities are detrimental to the interests of the trade union movement or the principles and policy of Congress, and, after due process, if necessary suspend or exclude it from membership. The ultimate sanction in Rule 13 has rarely been applied. Recent cases are the National Amalgamated Stevedores and Dockers in 1959 (see **blue union**) and the Electrical Trades Union (see **Electrical, Electronic, Telecommunication and Plumbing Union**) and in 1973 20 affiliated unions with a total membership of 370,000 were expelled for failure to comply with the TUC's policy of non-registration under the **Industrial Relations Act 1971**. Almost all of them were subsequently readmitted; see also **inter-union disputes**.

RUN AGREEMENT. A National Maritime Board (q.v.) agreement covering **runners**, i.e. crew employed to take ships from one port to another only. 'Run' = single trip; 'Voyage' = round trip.

RUSSELL v. AMALGAMATED SOCIETY OF CARPENTERS AND JOINERS (1912) AC 421; see **benefits**.

S

SABBATICAL LEAVE or **sabbaticals.** Periodic time off for research, travel and study for professional people, and especially for university teachers; originally **sabbatical year,** by analogy with the seventh year prescribed by Mosaic law to be observed as a 'Sabbath'. In the United States the term has been applied to extended vacations negotiated by the Steelworkers' Union (see Robert A. Bedolis, 'The Steel Labor Agreement, 1963', *Business Management Record,* December 1963); recently discussed in Britain in relation to senior staff in industry; see British Institute of Management, *Information Summary 118,* October 1965; 'Next Step in Sabbaticals', *Business Week,* 3 August 1963; 'Pros and Cons of Executive Sabbaticals', *Management Review,* October 1963; 'Should Management take a Sabbatical?', *Personnel Practice Bulletin,* September 1964, E. Goldston, 'Executive Sabbaticals: about to take off?', *Harvard Business Review,* Sept./Oct. 1973 pp. 57-8. The practice seems to be rare in private industry in Britain: see J.M. Hill, *Special Leave Allowances,* Institute of Personnel Management, Information Report 15, 1974; see also C. Goyder, *Sabbaticals for All,* Fabian Society, 1977.

SABBATICAL YEAR; see **sabbatical leave.**

SABBATICALS; see **sabbatical leave.**

SACRIFICE; see **victimisation benefit.**

SAFETY AND HEALTH AT WORK, COMMITTEE ON; see **Robens Report.**

SAFETY REPRESENTATIVES. Representatives appointed by recognised trade unions (i.e. **independent trade unions** recognised by an employer for negotiating purposes) to represent employees on matters relating to health and safety under Regulations made under s.2(4) of the **Health and Safety at Work Act 1974** in 1976. The Act (s. 2(6)) requires employers to consult with such representatives with a view to making and maintaining arrangements which will promote co-operation over health and safety matters. The Regulations on Safety Representatives came into force in October 1978. There was previously in Britain no statutory obligation on employers to receive or consult employee representatives on health and safety, though many did so by voluntary arrangement. The appointment of representatives solely from trade unionists, unless the unions involved in any establishment agree to extend representation to non-unionists also, has been subject to considerable controversy. An original clause of the Act (s. 2(5)) making statutory provision for this alternative kind of representation also was later repealed. While they have a duty to report hazards to their employer, Safety Representatives take no legal responsibilities for any course of action subsequently taken by him.

SAGGERS v. BRITISH RAILWAYS BOARD (1977), EAT: TLR 17 May 1977. A case in which it was ruled that, in the application of a **union membership agreement** (q.v.), it was necessary, in determining whether a dismissal for refusal to join the appropriate union was unfair, to interpret the term 'religious belief' (Trade Union and Labour Relations Act 1974, Schedule I, para. 6(5)), to take into account both the beliefs of the religious sect to which the individual belonged and his own personal belief, the former being a strong pointer to the latter; see also **closed shop.**

SALARIED EMPLOYEE; see **white collar worker.**

SALARY. A form of **remuneration**, usually contrasted with **wages** in which a fixed payment is made, normally, but not invariably, by applying an annual rate of pay on a monthly basis, for non-manual, managerial, professional, or white collar work; hence 'salariat', those who are paid a salary, as distinct from wage earners, and to be 'salaried': also **salary administration, salary drift, salary growth curves** and **salary scales**, i.e. rates of remuneration, usually annual in character, and having intervals between them, employees being able to ascend the scale as a result of age, length of service, merit, grade promotion, etc. A distinction is sometimes drawn between the salary itself, which is fixed, and additional variable components of remuneration, such as **commission**, which form part of total earnings in some salaried occupations. Office of Population Censuses and Surveys, *Sample Census 1966 (Great Britain),* Economic Activity Tables, Part III, p. xlii, gives a list of occupations which are classified as salaried for the purposes of employment statistics.

SALARY   ADMINISTRATION. Defined by G. McBeath and D.M. Rands (*Salary Administration,* Business Books Ltd, 3rd ed., 1976) as 'the application of a systematic approach to the problem of ensuring that staff are paid in a logical, equitable manner for the work they do'. The techniques employed in this systematic approach may include **job analysis, job evaluation,** salary surveys and planning, **employee appraisal,** etc.

SALARY DRIFT; see **grade creep.**

SALARY GROWTH CURVES; see **maturity curves.**

SALARY SCALE; see salary.

SALTLEY DEPOT INCIDENT. A major instance of **'mass picketing'** occurring at the Nechells Lane Coke Depot of the West Midlands Gas Board beginning on 3 February 1972 and lasting for 8 days before, as a result of the presence of an estimated 15,000 strikers and sympathisers, the gates of the depot were closed. The incident occurred during the miners' strike (see **Wilberforce Report**) and raised a question of possible amendment of the law relating to peaceful picketing; see **picketing.** 76 persons were arrested including 61 miners; 16 policemen were injured.

SAU. SLADE Art Union (q.v.).

SAWMAKERS'   PROTECTION SOCIETY, SHEFFIELD. A trade union founded in 1911 with 280 members. It had some 500 members in 1951, but has since declined in numbers. *Address:* 27 Main Avenue, Totley, Sheffield. *Tel:* 0742 361044. *TUC Affiliated Membership, 1977:* 244.

SAYER   v.   AMALGAMATED SOCIETY OF CARPENTERS AND JOINERS (1902) 19 TLR 122; see **benefits.**

SCAB. An American term most commonly applied to workers who remain at work while their fellows are on strike, but also used to describe those who accept work during a strike, or even those who, in the absence of a strike accept less than union rates and conditions. Scabs are not necessarily thought of a strikebreakers; see **strikebreaking.** The more usual British expression is **blackleg.**

SCALEMAKERS, NATIONAL UNION OF (NUS). A trade union founded in 1909 and taking its present title in 1930. *Address:* 195 Walworth Road, London SE17 1RP. *Tel:* 01-703 8008. *TUC Affiliated Membership, 1977:* 1,842.

SCAMP COUNCIL. The **Motor Industry Joint Labour Council** (q.v.).

SCAMP REPORT. Name given to reports of a number of inquiries under the chairmanship of Sir Jack Scamp, some of which related to the work of the **Motor Industry Joint Labour Council** (q.v.) - *Longbridge Group of Delivery Agents* (Cmnd. 2905, 1966), *Motor Vehicle Collections Ltd and Avon Car Transporters* (Cmnd. 2935, 1966), *Ford Motor Company* (Cmnd. 3749, 1968). *Birmingham Aluminium Castings* (Cmnd. 3201, 1967), *Pressed Steel Fisher* (Cmnd. 3688, 1968). Other principal reports have been: *Vickers Ltd., Barrow in Furness* (Cmnd. 3984, 1969). *British Rail* (Cmnd. 2779, 1965). *British Airline Pilots* (Cmnd. 3428, 1967) *Liverpool Dock Workers* (1967) and in the 'Dustmen's Strike' (National Joint Council for Local Authorities Services), November 1970 awarding an increase of earnings of between 14.5 per cent and 15 per cent.

SCANLON PLAN. A system of bonus payment involving productivity sharing (see also **share of production plans, cost-reduction plans**) devised by Joseph N. Scanlon, at one time research director of the United Steelworkers of America, and latterly on the staff of the Massachusetts Institute of Technology, which has proved to be of limited use in the United States and has been employed only occasionally in Britain (see **Linwood Plan**). The Plan does not involve a unique formula which is applied in each company; in each instance a relationship is agreed by management and unions between labour costs and overall productivity, measuring the latter in terms of output by quality, or value, or operating profit (in which case it has something in common with **profit sharing** (q.v.). Bonus is then paid to *all* workers, whether directly or indirectly involved in production, on a basis of labour cost savings. In its original application in the Lapointe Machine Tool Company, bonus was paid on any reduction of percentage labour costs below an agreed figure. Supporters of the Plan regard it less as a payment system than as a philosophy of management and draw attention to the emphasis which it places on teamwork and participation on the shop floor and to the benefit of including both direct and indirect workers. Problems usually occur when continuous bonus reductions make the scheme unattractive to workers; see Frederick G. Lesieur (ed.), *The Scanlon Plan; A Frontier in Labor-Management Co-operation*, The Massachusetts Institute of Technology Press, 1969; British Institute of Management, *Information Note 26*, 1964; R.B. Gray, 'The Scanlon Plan. A Case Study', *British Journal of Industrial Relations*, Vol. IX, No. 3, Nov. 1971, pp. 291-313, and C.F. Frost, J.H. Wakeley and R.A. Ruh, *The Scanlon Plan for Organisation Development*, Michigan State UP, 1974.

SCARMAN REPORT. The Report of the Court of Inquiry under the chairmanship of the Rt Hon. Lord Justice Scarman into a *Dispute between Grunwick Processing Laboratories Ltd and members of the Association of Professional, Executive, Clerical and Computer Staff*, Cmnd. 6922, August 1977; see **Grunwick Dispute.**

SCHEDULE 11 CLAIMS. Claims made under Schedule 11 of the **Employment Protection Act 1975** by employers' associations or trade unions that an employer is observing 'terms and conditions of employment less favourable than the recognised terms and conditions or, where ... there are no recognised terms and conditions, the general level of terms and conditions' (para. 1). Such claims are reported to the

Advisory, Conciliation and Arbitration Service and, failing settlement, to the **Central Arbitration Committee** (q.v.) which, if it finds the claim well founded, may make an award that the appropriate terms and conditions shall be observed (hence the expression **extension procedure**). Such an award has effect as an implied term of contract (see **implied term**) from such date as the Committee may determine. Claims can be reported under the Schedule and referred to ACAS without the agreement or consent of the employer against whom the claim is made; hence the procedure represents a form of **compulsory arbitration** (q.v.). They refer to substantive, but not to recognition and procedural terms; see **Newtown Polishing Co. Ltd and National Society of Metal Mechanics,** Award 3026, 29 July 1964, as interpreted in Award 3069 (K.W. Wedderburn, *Cases and Materials on Labour Law*, CUP, 1967, p. 359 *et seq.*); also, on the **guaranteed week** in engineering, **Dawes Cycle Co. Ltd and National Society of Metal Mechanics,** Award 3110, 3 August 1966 and **Brook Motors Ltd and Transport and General Workers' Union,** Award 3168, 7 May 1968. The Claims Procedure originated in **questions** and **issues** to which similar procedures were applied under **Order 1305** (1940) and **Order 1376** (1951) respectively (see **National Arbitration Tribunal** and **Industrial Disputes Tribunal;** Ministry of Labour, *Industrial Relations Handbook*, HMSO, 1961, p. 143 *et seq.*). Following the ending of Order 1376 a **Claims Procedure** was operated in similar terms under the Terms and Conditions of Employment Act 1959, Section 8. The principal difference between Section 8 and Schedule 11 is that the latter is evidently intended to be of wider application in referring to 'the general level' of terms and conditions in any trade, industry or section of a trade and industry in any district in addition to other terms and conditions of a formally negotiated nature. Agriculture and **Wages Council** trade and industries (q.v.) are now included within the ambit of the Schedule. ACAS received 1,124 Schedule 11 cases in 1977, 727 of which were referred to the Central Arbitration Committee.

SCHOOLMASTERS AND UNION OF WOMEN TEACHERS, NATIONAL ASSOCIATION OF (NAS/UWT). A trade union formed in January 1976 by the merger of the National Association of Schoolmasters and the Union of Women Teachers to which the Scottish Schoolmasters joined in direct association. The NAS originated in 1919 as the National Union of Men Teachers in male opposition to the acceptance by the **National Union of Teachers** of equal pay for women in teaching. After a long struggle it was admitted to the **Burnham Committee** in 1961. It became affiliated to the Trades Union Congress in 1969. Bernard Morton (ed.), *Action, 1919-1969,* Educare, 1969. The new union's declared aim is to make teaching an attractive career for well-qualified men and women with salaries and prospects at least comparable to those in other professions. *Address:* PO Box 65, Swan Court, Hemel Hempstead, Herts HP1 1DT. *Tel:* 0442 2971/4. *TUC Affiliated Membership, 1977:* 86,098.

SCIENTIFIC MANAGEMENT. A term derived from an extention of the philosophy of management, motivation and incentives of F.W. Taylor (1856-1915), and sometimes referred to as **Taylorism.** B.M. Gross (*The Managing of Organisations,* Collier-Macmillan, 1964) attributes the coinage of the expression to Lovis Brandeis, a lawyer who supported his client's case before the Interstate Commerce Commission of the United States in 1910 by using Taylor's ideas and sought to make them more popular than Taylor's own description of his ideas as the 'task system'. Taylor accepted the change as broader and more appealing. Scientific management quickly became an international movement, spreading to most European countries where, as in the USA it encountered labour opposition; Lenin and Trotsky led a drive for scientific management in the Soviet Union. R.M. Currie (*Work Study,* Pitman, 4th ed. 1977) regards the following principles 'extended and applied, as forming the basis of scientific management'; the development of a science of each element of a man's work, thereby replacing rule-of-thumb methods; selecting the best worker for a task and then training, developing and teaching him, replacing the practice of workers selecting their own task and training themselves; the development of a spirit of co-operation between management and men; and the division of work between management and workers, each taking the work for which it is most fitted, rather than, as formerly, almost all work and responsibility being put on the men. The same principles have been presented elsewhere as attributable to the assumptions of orthodox economic theory that man is a rational animal who maximises his economic gains, that each individual responds individually to economic incentives, and that men can be treated in a standardised fashion (see for example, W.F. Whyte, *Money and Motivation,* Harper, 1955); others have doubted whether Taylor's thinking was so narrow; see R.M. Barnes, *Motion and Time Study,* John Wiley and Sons, 1949, pp. 8-9. The term 'scientific management' tends now to be employed very broadly to include any philosophy, principle or technique used in the systematic improvement of efficiency, reduction of operating costs, the maximum utilisation of human and material resources, etc.; see F.W. Taylor, *The Principles of Scientific Management,* Harper, 1911, R.F. Hoxie, *Scientific Management and Labor,* Merlin Kelley, 1970 and C.P. Snow, *The Two Cultures and the Scientific Revolution,* CUP, 1959; contrast with **human relations** (q.v.).

SCIENTIFIC, TECHNICAL AND MANAGERIAL STAFFS, ASSOCIATION OF (ASTMS). A trade union formed in January 1968 by merger between the Association of Scientific Workers (AScW) and the Association of Supervisory Staffs, Executives and Technicians (ASSET), AScW having been formed originally in 1918 as the National Union of Scientific Workers, and ASSET having its origins in 1917 as the National Foremen's Association. ASTMS, through the AScW part of the merger, represents scientific and technical employees in a number of industries and especially in the universities, the health services, chemicals and engineering; through ASSET it organises managers, supervisors and technicians, its main strength being in engineering and civil air transport. It has also, since 1968, absorbed a number of staff associations and smaller trade unions, especially the **Medical Practitioners' Union,** the Prudential Staff Association and the Union of Insurance Staffs, giving it new areas of recruitment. It has been notable for its rapid membership growth and vigorous policies associated with its General Secretary, Mr Clive Jenkins; see Clive Jenkins, 'Tiger in a White Collar?', *Penguin Survey of Business and Industry,* 1965; George Sayers Bain, *The Growth of White Collar Unionism,* OUP, 1970. *Address:* 10-26 Jamestown Road, London NW1 7DT. *Tel:* 01-267 4422. *TUC Affiliated Membership, 1977:* 396,000.

SCMU. Scottish Commercial Motormen's Union; see **Commercial Motormen's Union, Scottish.**

SCOTT BADER COMMONWEALTH LTD. A company formed in 1951 by the Bader family on the basis of worker-ownership, 90 per cent of the shares in the concern being given over to the company in that year, and the remaining 10 per cent in 1963, ultimate voting rights on constitution and finance now resting with seven trustees of the Commonwealth. The company raises no capital from outside sources except bank loans and income distribution is determined by a General Meeting of the Commonwealth at which every member is entitled to speak and vote, workers also being encouraged to accept managerial responsibilities as well as shared profits; see Fred H. Blum, *Work and Community; The Scott Bader Commonwealth and the Quest for a New Social Order,* Routledge and Kegan Paul, 1969.

SCOTTISH COMMERCIAL MOTORMEN'S UNION (SCMU); see Commercial Motormen's Union, Scottish.

SCOTTISH JOURNAL OF POLITICAL ECONOMY. The journal of the Scottish Economic Society (which was revived in 1953), published three times a year since 1954, and containing some articles on labour economics. For notes on labour economics and industrial relations journals generally, see George Sayers Bain and Gillian B. Woolven, 'The Literature of Labour Economics and Industrial Relations,' *Industrial Relations Journal,* Summer 1971 and J. Fletcher (ed.), *The Uses of Economic Literature,* Butterworths, 1971.

SCOTTISH TEACHERS' SALARIES COMMITTEE; see Burnham Committees.

SCOTTISH DAILY NEWSPAPER SOCIETY (SDNS). An **employers' association** open to all firms and companies printing morning or evening daily newspapers in Scotland, including the Scottish branches of firms or companies publishing newspapers elsewhere. The Society was formed in February 1915, but its effective participation in industrial relations dates from 1944 when specific changes were made to the constitution and an independent secretary appointed. In addition to industrial relations it deals with a variety of editorial, advertising and distribution matters of common interest to Scottish daily newspapers. In 1978 it had constitu-

ent members publishing the *Glasgow Herald* and *Glasgow Evening Times,* the *Scottish Daily Record* and the *Sunday Mail,* the *Scottish Daily Express* and *Scottish Sunday Express, The Scotsman,* the *Evening News,* the *Press and Journal,* the *Evening Express,* the *Dundee Courier,* the *Evening Telegraph,* the *Sunday Post,* the *Weekly News,* the *People's Journal* and the *Sporting Post. Address:* 90 Mitchell Street, Glasgow G1 3NQ. *Tel:* 041-221 9741.

SCOTTISH TRADES UNION CONGRESS (STUC). The national co-ordinating body for the trade union movement in Scotland, comprising in 1977 of 79 organisations affiliating on behalf of 1,011,438 members and in addition 43 trades councils throughout Scotland. The STUC was formed in 1897 as a result of a meeting of Scottish trades councils following the decision of the **Trades Union Congress** in 1895 to exclude **trades councils** (q.v.) from direct TUC representation. Since the 1920s it has been generally agreed between the TUC and the STUC that the latter should look after Scottish issues and make appropriate representations to the British government on such matters. Trade unions with membership both in Scotland and in the rest of the United Kingdom commonly affiliate to both STUC and TUC; a few unions wholly confined to operating in Scotland are affiliated to the STUC only. All trades councils in Scotland are directly affiliated to the Scottish Congress and are entitled to submit motions and vote both for these and for the General Council in the same way as affiliated unions. The activities of the General Council are similar to those of the General Council of the TUC, though its rules in relation to inter-union disputes and those affecting affiliated unions differ in some respects; see Scottish Trade Union Congress, *Submission to the Royal Commission on Trade Unions and Employers' Associations,* May 1966 and J.M. Craigen, *The Scottish TUC, 1897-1973,* MLitt Thesis, Heriot Watt, 1974. *Address:* 16 Woodlands Terrace, Glasgow G3 6DF. *Tel:* 041-332 4946/7/8.

SCOTTISH TYPOGRAPHICAL ASSOCIATION (STA). A printing trade union founded in 1853 and confining its membership to Scotland. The union was a founder member of the **Printing and Kindred Trades Federation** established in 1901. Its principal membership lay in the craft area of printing, but an Auxiliary Section set up in 1924 led, after conflict with the Paper Workers' Union and a brief period of expulsion from the P and KTF, to an agreement in 1928 whereby the Association limited membership of the Section in Aberdeen, Dundee, Edinburgh and Glasgow to assistants to its craft members in case and machine rooms, but organised all eligible workers elsewhere. The STA traditionally resisted any idea of merger with other printing unions south of the border, but eventually amalgamated with the Society of Graphical and Allied Trades in 1975. Sarah A. Gillespie, *A Hundred Years of Progress; The Record of the Scottish Typographical Association*, Robert Maclehose and Co. Glasgow, 1953.

SCOTTISH UNION OF BAKERS AND ALLIED WORKERS; now amalgamated with the Union of Shop, Distributive and Allied Workers; see **Shop, Distributive and Allied Workers, Union of.**

SCOTTISH UNION OF POWER LOOM OVERLOOKERS; see **Power Loom Overlookers, Scottish Union of.**

SCPS. Society of Civil and Public Servants; see **Civil and Public Servants, Society of.**

SCREW, NUT, BOLT AND RIVET TRADE UNION. A trade union founded in 1914 and currently having all its membership in Guest, Keen and Nettlefolds in Birmingham, where it recruits all grades of workers. *Address:* 368 Dudley Road, Birmingham B18 4HH. *Tel:* 021-429 2431. *TUC Affiliated Membership, 1977:* 2,524.

SDNS. Scottish Daily Newspaper Society (q.v.).

SDTU. Sign and Display Trades Union (q.v.).

SEAMEN, NATIONAL UNION OF (NUS). A union first established as the National Amalgamated Sailors' and Firemen's Union of Great Britain and Northern Ireland by Joseph Havelock Wilson in 1887. Havelock Wilson's union had a stormy passage, giving rise to the opposition of the **Shipping Federation** and many years of strikes and strike breaking as well as the union's expulsion from the **Trades Union Congress,** to which it returned after his death in 1929. Joint national machinery in the form of the **National Maritime Board** (q.v.) was finally established in 1920. Since the 1939-45 war the union has

been mainly concerned with improved wages and conditions for its members, and the decasualisation of the industry (see **Established Service Scheme**). Unofficial strikes in 1947, 1955 and 1960 have resulted in the introduction of the concept of 'ship steward at sea' in the form of **shipboard liaison representatives** (q.v.); see J. Havelock Wilson, *My Stormy Passage Through Life,* Vol. 1 (Vol. 2 not published), Co-operative Press, 1925; National Union of Seamen, *The Story of the Seamen,* NUS, 1964; Basil Mogeridge, 'Militancy and Inter-Union Rivalries in British Shipping, 1911-1929' *International Review of Social Science,* Vol. 6, No. 3, 1961. pp. 375-412. *Address:* Maritime House, Old Town, Clapham, London SW4 0JP. *Tel:* 01-622 5581. *TUC Affiliated Membership, 1977:* 41,919.

SEALIFE PROGRAMME. A programme of investigation, experiment and development launched in March 1975 as a joint initiative by employers and trade unions in the shipping industry and by the Department of Trade to examine ways in which life at sea can be made more attractive to the UK seafarer and from which the effective use of manpower on ships can be developed. The programme has led to suggestions for changes both in the central institutions of the industry and within shipping companies themselves to ensure greater crew stability. *Address:* 17-18 Bury Street, London EC3A 5AH. *Tel:* 01-283 9512.

SEARCH UNEMPLOYMENT; see **frictional unemployment.**

SEASONAL TRADES; see **seasonal unemployment.**

SEASONAL UNEMPLOYMENT. **Unemployment** which arises in particular trades and industries (hence **seasonal trades**), through seasonal variations in activity, e.g. in the construction industry, agriculture, hotels, catering, etc. The classical study of seasonal unemployment is that by C.T. Saunders, *Seasonal Variations in Employment,* Longmans, Green and Co., 1936.

SECOND LINE SUPERVISOR; see **supervisor** and **foreman.**

SECONDARY BOYCOTT; see **blacking.**

SECONDARY STRIKE; see **sympathetic strike.**

SECRETARY OF STATE FOR EMPLOYMENT v. ASLEF (NO. 2) (1972) 2 WLR 1370, 1403 (CA); see **work-to-rule.**

SECTION 8; Terms and Conditions of Employment Act 1959; see **Schedule 11 Claims.**

SECTION 11 PROCEDURE; A procedure for handling issues of **trade union** recognition under ss. 11-16 of the **Employment Protection Act 1975.** This procedure is a successor to that laid down in the Industrial Relations Act 1971 (now repealed) which made provision for such cases to be referred to the Commission on Industrial Relations for investigation and ultimately to enforceable orders granted by the National Industrial Relations Court. References are currently restricted to independent trade unions only (i.e. they cannot be made by employers or by unions not in possession of certificates of independence), to the **Advisory Conciliation and Arbitration Service** which is required to examine the issue, consult the parties concerned, to make such inquiries as it thinks fit, and to report, settling the matter by negotiation if possible. Enforcement is, in the last resort, by an award by the **Central Arbitration Committee** which becomes an implied term of contract of the workers concerned as in the **Schedule 11 Procedure** (q.v.). ACAS has considered its obligation to encourage the extension of collective bargaining (Employment Protection Act 1975, s. 1(1)) as implying a commitment to recognition as a matter of principle. Both this and the methods of inquiry used have been criticised by employers' organisations and at present the future of the procedure appears to be in doubt, partly as a result of the case of **Grunwick Processing Laboratories Ltd v. ACAS,** *The Times,* 15 December 1977. In 1977 ACAS received 589 applications for recognition. Of the 1,038 such applications received from 1 February 1976 to 31 December 1977 408 (39 per cent) were withdrawn, rather more than one-half of these having resulted in full or partial recognition. Final reports had been issued in respect of 100 cases.

SECTIONAL BEHAVIOUR; see **sectionalism.**

SECTIONAL PANELS or **National Sectional Panels;** Joint Bodies set up under the National Joint Council for Civil Air Transport with plenary powers to negotiate and settle terms and conditions of employment for particular groups of workers in the industry. Twelve panels have been set up; for Engineering and Maintenance, Supervisory, Engineering and Technical, Clerical and Clerical Administrative, Catering, Draughtsmen, Planners and Tracers, General Service Workers, Surface Transport and Goods Handling, Pilot Officers, Navigating and Engineering Officers, Radio Officers, M1 and M4 Grades, and M5 to M6 Grades.

SECTIONALISM or **sectional behaviour.** Action taken by individual unions or individual work groups working in isolation from, and sometimes in conflict with, other unions and work groups; similar attitudes and behaviour within management between supervisors and managers relating to different crafts and at different managerial levels. For an analysis of sectionalism in shipbuilding; see Commission on Industrial Relations, *Shipbuilding and Shiprepairing,* Report No. 22, Cmnd. 4756, August 1971, Ch. 21; also **fractional bargaining, fragmented bargaining.**

SECTOR-GENERAL UNION; see **sectoral union.**

SECTORAL UNION or **sector-general union.** An expression suggested by John Hughes (*Trade Union Structure and Government,* Royal Commission on Trade Union and Employers' Associations, Research Papers, 5 (Part 1), 1967, p. 6) to describe unions which have historically concentrated on a particular sector of the economy, but are prone to take an open approach to their sectoral definition and extend into 'allied' fields, for instance the **National Union of Public Employees,** and the **Union of Shop, Distributive and Allied Workers.**

SELECTIVE EMPLOYMENT PAYMENT ACT 1966; see **selective employment tax.**

SELECTIVE EMPLOYMENT TAX (SET). A payroll tax introduced in 1966 and designed, by refunds in respect of certain types of employment and refunds with a premium in respect of others, to redistribute labour in the interests of the economy, particularly from service to manufacturing employment. Under s. 1 of the Selective Employment Payments Act 1966, establishments engaged in eligible activities (those falling within Orders III to XVI of the 1958 **Standard Industrial Classification** or Orders III to XIX of the

1968 SIC) and certain other stated manufacturing activities, could attract refunds of SET (and until 1968 an additional payment), if more than half of their employees were engaged in connection with such activities or in related scientific research or training, and less than half in office work, sales and transport (see also **Regional Employment Premium**). Disputes relating to refund entitlement were referred to **industrial tribunals** (q.v.). The Heath government abolished SET from 1 April 1973 as part of the development of a new Value Added Tax. It is claimed to have reduced employment substantially in various sectors, e.g. in the distributive trades by 9.4 per cent and in miscellaneous services by 17.7 per cent between June 1966 and June 1970 (J. Pellegrini, *The Effects of SET on British Manufacturing Industry,* unpublished PhD Thesis, University of London, 1972) and W.B. Reddaway and Associates, *Effects of the Selective Employment Tax, Final Report,* CUP, 1973.

'SELF-FINANCING PRODUCTIVITY DEALS'. Defined in *Department of Employment News,* No. 45, 1977 as 'schemes whereby the savings achieved in unit costs outweigh the costs of the schemes such as extra payments to those directly or indirectly involved, and any extra capital or running costs'. Deals of this kind were referred to in the Callaghan Labour government's White Paper *The Attack on Inflation after 31 July 1977* as permissible outside the 10 per cent pay guideline provided for; see also **productivity bargaining**.

'SELF-FUNDING'. A principle enunciated by the Department of Employment in the application of some **incremental scales** (q.v.) outside the civil service and local government under the provisions of the Callaghan Labour government's **incomes policy** (q.v.), viz. that such payments might only be made if they made no addition to the salary cost of the employer over a given period, the suggestion being that he was only permitted to distribute in increments such sums as he had saved in the previous period out of savings resulting from staff leaving and being replaced by new staff engaged at lower salary levels.

SELF-GOVERNMENT IN INDUSTRY. A form of **workers' participation** advocated by the Whitley Committee on the Relations Between Employers and Employed, 1917-18; see **Whitleyism**.

SELLING-PRICE SLIDING SCALE. An arrangement whereby it is agreed in advance that wage rates shall vary in a specific relationship to changes in the market price of the product. Such arrangements were not uncommon in the earlier part of the nineteenth century, but came into more general use in the coal industry and in the iron and steel trade in the 1860s and 1870s (see also **Melters' Sliding Scale**). They are said to have been best suited to single product trades which were subject to market fluctuations and had a high ratio of labour to total costs; they had the advantage of automatic application and were favoured for a time as contributing to industrial peace, diminishing in popularity as trade union strength grew and as notions of minimum rates and living standards became accepted; see E.H. Phelps Brown, *The Growth of British Industrial Relations,* Macmillan, 1965: Sir A. Pugh, *Men of Steel,* Iron and Steel Trades Confederation, 1951 and W.J. Ashley, *The Adjustment of Wages,* Longmans, 1903. Selling-price sliding scales in the steel industry were stabilised in 1940 and replaced by a **cost of living sliding scale** (q.v.); in heavy steel the stabilised payment (67½ per cent, later increased to 75 per cent) was merged with rates for blast-furnacemen in 1955 and for steel workers in 1966.

SEMI-SUPERVISOR; see **supervisor**.

SENIOR SHOP STEWARD; see **convener**.

SENIOR STEWARD or **senior shop steward**; see **convener**.

SENIORITY. An employee's standing in a company, plant or department, acquired through length of service or continuous employment, and resulting, by agreement or by custom and practice, in particular rights or privileges, especially in relation to pay, promotion (see **seniority rule, seniority list**), transfer (where the practice may also be known as **juniority,** i.e. the movement of the most junior worker before the more senior) and **redundancy,** or **lay-off.** In Britain, seniority in the case of **redundancy** is usually considered in terms of **last-in-first-out,** and this very rarely by collective agreement. In the United States seniority in such circumstances is more often found to be regulated by such an agreement under provisions for **bumping,** i.e. by providing that an employee has the right to displace a shorter service employee at time of lay-off, or that an employee whose job is discontinued may take over the job of another employee with less seniority than his own; in turn the displaced worker can bump a more junior employee, and so on. Where job transfer is involved, bumping implies lateral movement or demotion in most cases, and this is referred to in some studies of workplace redeployment in Britain; see L.C. Hunter, G.L. Reid and D. Boddy, *Labour Problems of Technological Change,* George Allen and Unwin, 1970, p. 309; see also **promotion ladder.** The High Court regards an employee who is dismissed as a result of bumping to be redundant within the terms of the **Redundancy Payments Act 1965** (per **W. Gimber and Sons v. Spurrett** (1967) ITR 308 (D.C.); see Cyril Grunfeld, *The Law on Redundancy,* Sweet and Maxwell, 1971).

SENIORITY ALLOWANCE. A monetary allowance paid to doctors in the National Health Service after periods of service. Its principal object is to induce older doctors to remain in the service; see **Kindersley Committee,** *Twelfth Report* (Review Body on Doctors' and Dentists' Remuneration, Cmnd. 4352, May 1970), para. 144.

SENIORITY LADDER; see **promotion ladder.**

SENIORITY LIST. A list of employees, usually according to length of service and used to regulate promotions, transfers and benefits of various kinds, e.g. car parking facilities; see also **seniority promotion ladder** and **passover.**

SENIORITY PREMIUMS. An expression used in Economist Intelligence Unit, *Survey of the National Newspaper Industry,* 1966 Pt III, p. 24, to describe weekly increments of 10s. given on all newspapers to adult members of SOGAT clerical chapels during each of the first five years of service and set increases given to juniors, learners and apprentices as age and service grows. The former might properly be thought of as **service increments** (q.v.) and the latter as **wage-for-age scales** (q.v.).

SENIORITY RULE; see **promotion ladder.**

SENSITIVITY TRAINING; see **T Group.**

SEPARATION ALLOWANCE. An allowance paid to married servicemen who are separated from their wives and families for Service reasons, and intended as a compensation for the personal and emotional disadvantages of separation. National Board for Prices and Incomes, Report No. 116 (*Standing Reference on the Pay of the Armed Forces,* Second Report, Cmnd. 4079, June 1969) advocated more generous allowances. NBPI *Fifth Report* (Cmnd. 4529, November 1970) recommended the introduction of proposals made by the Ministry of Defence to this effect.

SEPARATION; see **wastage** and **labour turnover.**

SEPARATION RATE; see **labour turnover.**

SEQUENTIAL AGREEMENTS; see **one-step agreement.**

SERVANT; see **contract of service.**

SERVICE INCREMENTS. Additional payments made, usually to manual workers, after given periods of service with a company or enterprise. May be modest in scope, e.g. after 3 months' and 6 months' service only (see S.W. Lerner, J.R. Cable and S. Gupta, *Workshop Wage Determination,* Pergamon Press, 1969, p. 40, for such an example), or spread over a long period, as with municipal busmen, for whom a service bonus scheme has given an additional 4 per cent on basic pay after 6 months increasing to 12 per cent after 20 years' service (see National Board for Prices and Incomes Report No. 16, Cmnd. 3012, May 1966, p. 27); also known as **service pay.** Not to be confused with **incremental scales** or **wage-for-age scales** (q.v.); see also **seniority premiums,** and for local authority manual workers, **service supplement.** The usual aim of service increments is to reduce labour turnover and reward experience.

SERVICE PAY; see **service increments.**

SERVICE SUPPLEMENT. Service increments (q.v.) applied by the National Joint Council for Local Authority Services (Manual Workers); in 1970, 35p per week for all full-time workers with 5 years' service.

SERVICE WORKERS. Workers in licensed residential establishments and licensed restaurants subject to **Wages**

Council orders such as cloakroom attendants, waiters and porters, as distinct from **non-service workers,** e.g. barmen and kitchen staff. Minimum remuneration for the former is fixed at a lower level than that for the latter, principally on the grounds that, coming into direct contact with the public, they are likely to be in receipt of gratuities.

SESSION MONEY; see **compensatory payment.**

SET. Selective Employment Tax (q.v.).

SETTLING-IN GRANT; see **Employment Transfer Scheme.**

SEVEN POINT PLAN. A system advocated by Alec Rodger (*The Seven Point Plan,* National Institute of Industrial Psychology, Paper No. 1, 3rd ed. 1970) as providing a rough sketch of a scientifically defensible method of assessing the occupational potentialities of candidates for jobs. The Plan, which involves an assessment of the interviewee's circumstances and attributes under seven heads (physical make-up, attainments, general intelligence, special aptitudes, interests, disposition and domestic and family circumstances), is not claimed to be the only reasonable assessment system available, nor to be an exceptionally good one: used with caution, however, it is asserted to be useful and practical.

SEVERANCE PAY. Redundancy pay or **dismissal pay.** Payment made to a worker who is made redundant (see **redundancy**), or sometimes part of such a payment, e.g. where the total sum paid to a redundant worker is composite, part of it being made up of a sum payable (say) according to the terms of the **Contracts of Employment Act 1963,** part of a **resettlement allowance** related to time taken to get a new job, and part (**severance pay**) as an additional allowance for long service.

SEX DISCRIMINATION ACT 1975. An Act making unlawful discrimination on grounds of sex, marital status or by way of victimisation is a wide range of employment and activities and establishing an **Equal Opportunities Commission** (EOC). It supplements the **Equal Pay Act 1970** by prohibiting discrimination in the offering of, and in acts preparatory to the making of, contracts of employment, e.g. in the advertising of jobs, while the Equal Pay Act provides for equal treatment when the contract has been entered into. It applies equally to men and women and substantially all employees and contract workers except midwives and where sex can be regarded as a genuine occupational qualification. The EOC is primarily an educational and investigatory body. If it finds discrimination taking place as a result of an investigation, it can issue a **non-discrimination notice** specifying what has to be done to eliminate it and requiring the recipient to comply within five years, at the end of which time the Commission may seek an injunction restraining the employer from continuing the discriminatory practices concerned. Complaints of discrimination by individuals are subject to reference to conciliation and reference, if necessary, to **industrial tribunals.** *Address:* Overseas House, Quay Street, Manchester M3 3HN. *Tel:* 061-833 9244; see M. Nash, *The Sex Discrimination Act 1975: A Guide for Managers,* IPM, 1975; also **discrimination.** For a review of the experience of and literature on women in employment, see *Women at Work: A Review,* DE Manpower Paper No. 11, 1975 and *Women at Work; Overseas Practice,* DE Manpower Paper No. 12, 1975.

SHAKE-OUT. Redeployment; the object of the Labour government's policy on redeployment of labour in 1966 being to 'shake-out' labour from areas of over-manning into high-productivity firms and industries, especially in the export sector; *Hansard,* July 20, 1966, p. 628. See also D.I. Mackay, 'Redundancy and Re-engagement: A Study of Car Workers', *Manchester School,* Vol. 40, September 1972, pp. 295-312.

SHANKS v. UNITED OPERATIVE MASONS' ASSOCIATION (1874) 1 R. 823; see **benefits.**

SHARE OF PRODUCTION PLAN. A collective bonus scheme in operation in a small number of British companies and virtually indistinguishable from the **Rucker Plan** (q.v.); see Trades Union Congress, *The Share of Production Plan,* 1959.

SHARE OF WAGES. A controversy centred around the question whether trade union action is capable of increasing the share of national income going to workers, and therefore of reducing the share available for other income recipients, i.e. of affecting **distributive shares.** The consensus of academic opinion is that the effect of direct, i.e. **collective bargaining,**

activity by trade unions on distributive shares tends to be slight. Some commentators believe that it has substantially no effect (e.g. A.M. Cartter, *Theory of Wages and Employment,* Irwin, Inc., 1959, p. 178, and L.G. Reynolds and G.H. Taft, *The Evolution of Wage Structure,* Yale University Press, 1956, p. 190); others that effects have been confined to low income brackets only (J.T. Dunlop, *Wage Determination under Trade Unions,* A.M. Kelly Inc., 1970; D.J. Robertson, *The Economics of Wages and the Distribution of Income,* Macmillan, 1961); others that it can affect shares only under certain conditions, e.g. when unions are aggressive and markets are sufficiently 'hard' for employers not to be able to escape easily through higher prices (E.H. Phelps Brown and P.E. Hart, 'The Share of Wages in National Income', *Economic Journal,* June 1952). P.J. Loftus ('Labour's Share in Manufacturing,' *Lloyds Bank Review,* No. 92, April 1969) derives from a study of the ratio of total wages and salaries paid in manufacturing industry to total value added in manufacturing industry that the former has a clear tendency to remain much the same (about 50 per cent) in situations and economies which vary in other respects, and concludes *inter alia* that government action against labour as a monopoly appears to be unnecessary; see Clark Kerr, 'Trade Unionism and Distributive Shares', *American Economic Review, May 1954,* also **wages fund.**

SHARING PLANS; see **gain sharing plans.**

SHAVING; see **continuity rule.**

SHAWCROSS REPORT. The Report of the **Royal Commission on the Press, 1961-62** (Cmnd. 1811, September, 1962) under the chairmanship of Lord Shawcross. The report was notable for its criticisms of manning standards and demarcation in the national newspaper industry, based on a survey by Personnel Administration Ltd. The report appears to have had little direct affect, but it was the logical precursor of the **Joint Board for the National Newspaper Industry** (q.v.), a more thorough survey by the Economist Intelligence Unit (*The National Newspaper Industry,* 1966) and subsequent developments in Fleet Street.

SHEET MAKERS' CONFERENCE. An organisation in steel formerly made up of two separately constituted joint boards,

the **Sheet Trade Board** and the **Galvanising Conciliation Board** (q.v.). While these two boards still exist, the Sheet Makers' Conference disappeared after the nationalisation of iron and steel in 1967.

SHEET METAL WORKERS, COPPERSMITHS, HEATING AND DOMESTIC ENGINEERS, NATIONAL UNION OF (NUSMWC H AND DE). A trade union formed by the amalgamation of the National Union of Sheet Metal Workers and Braziers (NUSMW and B, 1920) and the National Society of Coppersmiths, Braziers and Metal Workers (NSCB and MW) to form the National Union of Sheet Metal Workers and Coppersmiths (NUSMW and C) in July 1959, to which was added, by a further amalgamation in April 1967, the Heating and Domestic Engineers' Union (HDEU) and in June 1973 the Birmingham and Midland Sheet Metal Workers' Society. For the history of sheet metal workers' societies, see A.T. Kidd, *History of the Tin-Plate Workers and Sheet Metal Workers and Braziers Societies,* NUSMW and B, 1949. *Address:* 75-77 West Heath Road, London NW3 7TL. *Tel:* 01-455 0053/5. *TUC Affiliated Membership, 1977:* 75,049.

SHEET METAL WORKERS' SOCIETY, BIRMINGHAM AND MIDLAND. A craft society catering for sheet metal workers in the Midlands. Until its amalgamation with the National Union of Sheet Metal Workers, Coppersmiths, Heating and Domestic Engineers in 1973 it appeared to be the last of the many local sheet metal workers' societies which grew up in the nineteenth century which had not become part of a national union. It seceded from the National Amalgamated Tinplate Workers of Great Britain in 1909, having previously been instrumental in bringing it about and found itself unable to become part of the National Union of Sheet Metal Workers and Braziers (1920).

SHEET TRADE BOARD. A joint board of operatives and employers constituted in 1926 to arbitrate on wages and conditions of workers in sheet steel and strip production. As a result of the nationalisation of the steel industry, the Board became part of the British Steel Corporation in 1968, but continues to function as an independent entity making agreements covering some 4,900 operatives represented by the ISTF. *Addresses:* Joint Secretaries; Employers' Secretary, British Steel Corporation, 33 Grosvenor Place, London SW1, Operatives' Secretary, Iron and Steel Trades Confederation, Swinton House, 324 Gray's Inn Road, London WC1. Together with the **Galvanising Conciliation Board**, the Sheet Trade Board formerly made up the **Sheet Makers' Con erence.**

SHEFFIELD OUTRAGES. A series of acts of violence, directed chiefly against **blacklegs,** occurring in Sheffield, especially in October 1866. The Outrages were the immediate cause of the establishment of the Royal Commission on Trade Unions of 1867, which was to inquire into '... any recent acts of intimidation, outrage or wrong alleged to have been promoted, encouraged or connived at by such Trade Union or other associations'; see Sidney and Beatrice Webb, *History of Trade Unionism, 1666-1920,* 1919, p. 259 *et seq.,* and *The Sheffield Outrages: Report Presented to the Trades Union Commission in 1867,* Adams and Dart, 1971.

SHEFFIELD SAWMAKERS' PROTECTION SOCIETY; see **Sawmakers' Protection Society, Sheffield.**

SHEFFIELD SHIFT AGREEMENT. A District Agreement on terms and conditions of work for manual workers in steel production and finishing arrived at between the Engineering Employers' Sheffield Association on the one side and the following unions on the other: Iron and Steel Trades Confederation, Transport and General Workers' Union, General and Municipal Workers' Union and the Amalgamated Society of Boilermakers, Shipwrights, Blacksmiths and Structural Workers (Blacksmiths' Section). The agreement applies to some fifty companies in the Sheffield area. It operates only in the private sector and is unusual in combining steel and engineering conditions.

SHEFFIELD WOOL SHEAR WORKERS' TRADE UNION; see **Wool, Shear Workers' Trade Union, Sheffield.**

SHIFT. A period of continuous work during a working day, denoted by length (e.g. an 8 hour shift) and/or by the time during any 24 hours in which it takes place, e.g. **day shift, afternoon shift, night shift;** also used to describe the group of workers involved e.g. 'the day shift' etc. Shift systems include **double day shift** and **three shift systems** of various types; see also **con**tinental shift system, continuous three shift system, discontinuous three shift system, fixed shift, rotating shift, twilight shift, graveyard or lobster shift, split shift, swing shift, relief shift.

SHIFT ALLOWANCE; see **shift differential.**

SHIFT BONUS; see **shift differential.**

SHIFT DIFFERENTIAL or **shift bonus, bonus hours, shift premium, shift allowance.** An additional payment for workers who work shifts other than dayshifts, in compensation for the inconvenience of the shift; see **differential.** Calculated either as a fixed supplement (e.g. of **gift hours** q.v.) or an extra percentage on the hourly rate. The following table shows the proportions of one method to another in agreements in 1969:

Type of shift	Fixed method %	Proportional method %	TOTAL %
Permanent night	28.5	71.5	100.0
Three shift	66.3	33.7	100.0
Double day	67.1	32.9	100.0
ALL TYPES	50.3	49.7	100.0

see Department of Employment, *Time Rates of Wages and Hours of Work,* HMSO (annual).

SHIFT PREMIUM; see **shift differential** and **gift hours.**

SHIFT RATE. A rate of payment for a shift worker which takes into account the **shift bonus** or **premium;** see also **shift differential.**

SHIFT SYSTEM. A pattern of **shift working;** see also **shifts.**

SHIFT WORKING. The working of multiple shifts, i.e. the situation involved in working a factory or establishment for more than a single shift, usually a day shift, and therefore involving **double day shift, night shift,** or **three shift** working. In the United Kingdom in one pay week in October 1964, 18 per cent of a group of 5½ million workers in manufacturing, mining and quarrying (except coal), gas, electricity, water, national and local government and miscellaneous services were working shifts, 41.2 per cent of them on three shift systems, 16.7 per cent on double day shifts, 23 per cent on alternating day and night shifts, 11.6 per cent on normal night shift and 6.8 per cent on evening employment for part-time workers (*Ministry of Labour Gazette,* April 1965, pp. 148-55 and June 1965, pp. 257-63). The economics of shift working are mainly involved with consideration of the balance between the falling costs implicit in greater capital utilisation and the rising costs of labour principally because of **shift differentials** (see R. Marris, *The Economics of Capital Utilisation; A Report on Multiple Shift Work,* CUP, 1964); the difficulties of introducing shift work during a period in which higher productivity was being pressed were examined by the National Joint Advisory Council in 1967 (Ministry of Labour, *Introduction of Shift Working,* HMSO, 1967), and the social consequences of shift work have attracted attention; see Central Committee of Study Groups, *Social and Industrial Implications of Shift Work,* Industrial Welfare Society, 1963; P.E. Mott, F.C. Mann, H. McLoughlin and D.P. Warwick, *Shift Work: The Social Psychological and Physical Consequences,* Ann Arbor, University of Michigan Press, 1965; P. and F. Pigors, *Human Aspects of Multiple Shift Operations,* Massachusetts Institute of Technology, 1944; see also **three shift system.** Shift working by women and young persons is limited by the **Factories Act 1961,** s. 97 (see **double day shift**).

'SHIP. Abbreviation for **companionship,** (q.v.).

SHIPBOARD HANDBOOK; see **shipboard liaison representatives.**

SHIPBOARD LIAISON REPRESENTATIVES or **liaison representatives;** trade union representatives on ships at sea introduced in the **Shipboard Liaison Scheme** in 1963 and recommended for general application by the Pearson Report (*Final Report of the Court of Inquiry concerning the Shipping Industry,* Cmnd. 3211) in 1967. The duties of Liaison Representatives are laid down in the National Union of Seamen's **Shipboard Handbook.** They are required to have service, trade union and age qualifications, to be voted for by secret ballot and have as their main duty the encouragement of the National Maritime Board **complaints procedure** (q.v.). Their powers differ formally from those of most **shop stewards;** their role is mainly informational

and advisory and they can only represent members at the express request of the Master or officers concerned and with the consent of the individual member or members involved in a complaint. D.H. Moreby, *Personnel Management in Merchant Ships,* Pergamon Press, 1968, pp. 108-15.

SHIPBOARD LIAISON SCHEME; see **shipboard liaison representatives.**

SHIPBUILDING AND ENGINEERING UNIONS, CONFEDERATION OF (CSEU). A federation of trade unions in the shipbuilding and engineering industry constituted in its present form in 1936, but having its origins in the Federation of Engineering and Shipbuilding Trades formed in 1891. In June 1977, the CSEU had 23 constituent organisations, with an affiliated membership of 2,416,576. After the second world war it became primarily a body making it possible for engineering unions to conduct common industry-wide negotiations with the **Engineering Employers' Federation** and with the Shipbuilders and Repairers National Association, to provide for exchange of views between them, and to act in a representative capacity in matters concerning national government. In such a role its success in promoting unity between engineering and shipbuilding unions was considerable. In part it was made possible by the affiliation to the CSEU in 1947 of the Amalgamated Engineering Union (now the Engineering Section of the **Amalgamated Union of Engineering Workers**), which had previously preferred to negotiate separately with the Engineering Employers, or to work with other unions on an *ad hoc* basis in the **Engineering Joint Trades Movement.** The AEU has remained affiliated since that time with a reduced, but dominating affiliated voting strength of 770,000 compared with the 500,000 of the **Transport and General Workers Union,** and its various engineering trade groups, the 180,000 of the **General and Municipal Workers' Union,** the 200,000 of the **Electrical, Electronic and Telecommunications Union-Plumbing Trades Union,** and the 120,000 of the **Amalgamated Society of Boilermakers, Shipwrights, Blacksmiths and Structural Workers.** The CSEU is also notable for its authorisation of **Joint Shop Stewards Works Committees** and for its promotion of **Minute 741** (q.v.); see A.I. Marsh, *Industrial Relations in Engineering,* Pergamon Press, 1965. *Address:* 140-142 Walworth Road, London SE17. *Tel:* 01-703 2215.

SHIPBUILDING INQUIRY COMMIT-TEE 1965-1966; see **Geddes Report.**

SHIPBUILDING TRADE JOINT COUNCIL (STJC); see **Whitleyism.**

SHIPPING FEDERATION LTD; see **General Council of British Shipping.**

SHOP CLUBS ACT 1902. An Act under which employers may not forbid their workmen to join a friendly society of their own choice, and may not compel them to join a 'shop club or thrift fund' unless it is registered with the Registrar of Friendly Societies and approved by three-quarters of the workmen concerned. Ian Fife and E.A. Machin, *Redgrave's Health and Safety in Factories,* Butterworths, 1976, p. 1754 *et seq.* The Act, which has intentions akin to those of the **Truck Acts** (q.v.) is substantially inoperative at the present time; see K.W. Wedderburn, *The Worker and the Law,* 2nd ed., 1971, p. 232 *et seq.* Certain pension schemes or arrangements are excluded from the definition of 'shop club or thrift fund' by the Coal Industry Nationalisation (Superannuation) Regulations 1950 (as amended) and the Dock Workers (Pensions) Act 1960.

SHOP, DISTRIBUTIVE AND ALLIED WORKERS, UNION OF (USDAW). An amalgamation of the National Union of Distributive and Allied Workers and the National Amalgamated Union of Shop Assistants, both unions having their origins in the 1880s, which took place in January 1947. The union has its base in the Co-operative Movement, has membership in private retail distribution and has extended over the years into many allied food trades. A high proportion of its members are women. In the early years of this century a major aim was the abolition of the **'living-in' system** (q.v.). Later union compaigns were directed against long working hours and in favour of, early closing and minimum standards of pay, and of the **Offices, Shops and Railway Premises Act 1963** under which, for the first time, employees in offices and shops were given welfare and safety provisions analogous to those applied to factory workers. P.C. Hoffman, *They Also Serve,* Porcupine Press, 1949. *Address:* Oakley, 188 Wilmslow Road, Manchester M14 6LJ. *Tel:* 061-224 2804. *TUC Affiliated Membership, 1977:* 412,627.

SHOPMAN. A name formerly applied to shop owners and later to shop assistants;

both usages now rare. Currently used *inter alia* of manual workers in railway workshops - hence **Railway Shopmen's National Council** - and of regular employees of market tenants at Smithfield Market, handling meat (see National Board for Prices and Incomes, *Smithfield Market,* Cmnd. 4171, October 1969).

SHOP RATE. Usually a **time rate** of pay, higher than the appropriate national or district time rate, applied to an establishment or part of an establishment, especially in the engineering industry; more loosely, the rate of earnings to be expected by a worker in a particular department or shop.

SHOP STATEMENT; see **statements.**

SHOP STEWARD. A representative accredited by a trade union who acts on behalf of trade union members in the establishment in which he is employed; thus defined, the term excludes **collecting stewards, sick stewards, money stewards, check stewards, card stewards** and other workplace officials of trade unions whose role does not require them to represent their members to management; it also excludes trade union members who act as representatives but have not been formally accredited by their unions, though this situation may not be uncommon; it includes workplace representatives bearing other titles than **shop steward** whose role may include representational functions - **fathers of the chapel, corresponding members,** members of **Local Departmental Committees** on the railways, staff and office representatives, and, in some circumstances, branch chairmen or secretaries, where these are based upon the place of work and act within it and where these are concerned with handling the grievances of members and negotiating and consulting with managements; see also **convener, senior shop steward, joint shop stewards' committee, combine committee** as examples of shop steward organisation, and **shop steward facilities.** The expression 'shop steward' appears to have originated and developed principally from the engineering industry. District committees of the Amalgamated Society of Engineers were first given discretionary authority to appoint such officials in 1896 (see G.D.H. Cole, A.I. Marsh (ed.), *Workshop Organisation,* Hutchinson, 1973, and Arthur Marsh, *Managers and Shop Stewards,* Institute of Personnel Management, 1973), but the function of workshop representatives is evidently much older and to be found, with some variations, in the late mediaeval father of the chapel in the printing industry and in **head shopmen** or **box stewards** of early nineteenth century textile unions (H.A. Turner, *Trade Union Growth, Structure and Policy,* Allen and Unwin, 1962, p. 85). The **Shop Stewards Movement** (q.v.) brought stewards into prominence during and after the first world war and it is then generally agreed that their functions declined, their modern growth in numbers (see A.I. Marsh and E.E. Coker, 'Shop Steward Organisation in the Engineering Industry', *British Journal of Industrial Relations,* June 1963) post-dating the Essential Work Order of 1941 (Arthur Marsh, op. cit., p. 7). Aggregate numbers of shop stewards have been variously estimated: 90,000 (H.A. Clegg, A.J. Killick and Rex Adams, *Trade Union Officers,* Basil Blackwell, 1961, p. 180), 100,000-120,000 (Marsh and Coker, op. cit., p. 189), 200,000 (TUC, *Report on Disputes and Workshop Representation,* TUC Report, 1960) and 175,000 (Donovan **Royal Commission on Trade Unions and Employers' Associations 1965-68,** Cmnd. 3623, June 1968, para. 99). The development of shop stewards has been associated with the growth of **workplace bargaining** and the activities of **work groups,** where, despite criticism of their work, inquiries have tended to show that it has been constructive in tone; see Clegg, Killick and Adams, op. cit., and Government Social Survey, *Workplace Industrial Relations, An Inquiry undertaken for the Royal Commission on Trade Unions and Employers' Associations in 1966,* SS 402, HMSO, March 1968. For general surveys; see also W.E.J. McCarthy, *The Role of Shop Stewards in British Industrial Relations,* Royal Commission on Trade Unions and Employers' Associations, Research Papers 1, 1966 and J.F.B. Goodman and T.G. Whittingham, *Shop Stewards in British Industry,* McGraw-Hill, 1969 and in engineering, A.I. Marsh, E.O. Evans and P. Garcia, *Workplace Industrial Relations in Engineering,* EEF and Kogan Page, 1971. The **Industrial Relations Code of Practice** 1972 contains paragraphs on the functions, appointment, status, co-ordination, facilities and training of shop stewards. On the legal liability of unions for the actions of their shop stewards before and since the **Industrial Relations Act 1971;** see Bob Hepple, 'Union Responsibility for Shop Stewards', *Industrial Law Journal,* Vol. I, No. 4, December 1972.

SHOP STEWARD FACILITIES; see **facilities for shop stewards.**

SHOP STEWARDS' MOVEMENT. A powerful workshop movement arising during the first world war as a challenge to the official leadership, and especially in the engineering industry, as a result of wartime changes, particularly **dilution** of labour and the **Treasury Agreement** (q.v.) whereby many unions agreed to **compulsory arbitration.** The Shop Stewards' Movement disintegrated in 1922 and was absorbed into the main movements in the country for **workers' control;** see G.D.H. Cole, *Trade Unionism and Munitions, Economic and Social History of the War,* OUP, 1923, and Branko Pribicevic, *The Shop Stewards' Movement and Workers' Control, 1910-1922,* Basil Blackwell, 1959. On the role of the Shop Stewards' Movement in developing the theory of struggle for Soviet power see J. Hinton, *The First Shop Stewards' Movement,* George Allen and Unwin, 1973.

SHOP STEWARDS AND WORKS COMMITTEE AGREEMENTS 1917-19. National agreements between the **Engineering Employers' Federation** and a number of trade unions in 1917 recognising and regulating for the first time the appointment and functions of **shop stewards** and in 1919 similarly recognising shop stewards of the Amalgamated Society of Engineers (later the **Amalgamated Engineering Union**) and the establishment of formal Works Committees consisting of seven representatives of management and seven shop stewards; the 1919 Agreement was in 1922 combined with the **York Memorandum** and additions made to form the Procedure - Manual Workers (see **Engineering Procedure Agreement**), from which the unions withdrew in 1971. Formal Works Committees constituted in the terms laid down in the 1919 Agreement have been rare in engineering, informal recognition of **Joint Shop Stewards' Committees** being thought preferable; see A.I. Marsh, *Industrial Relations in Engineering,* Pergamon Press, 1965, Appendices C4 and C5 for the texts of the 1917 and 1919 Agreements. With the trade union repudiation of the 1922 Procedure Agreement in 1971, the 1917 and 1919 agreements also lapsed. The 1976 Procedure Agreement for the industry makes similar, though not identical, provisions to replace them.

SHOPS ACT 1950. An Act primarily

designed to ensure that shop assistants are not worked for excessive hours and that they are allowed adequate leisure. Its main features are the obligatory weekly half-day holiday (words replaced in the Shops (Early Closing Days) Act 1965 by the words 'early closing day'), obligatory closing hours on other days of the week, provisions in respect of Sunday employment, and rules regarding the hours and conditions of work of shop assistants. It applies to retail shops, to wholesale shops, and to warehouses occupied by retail traders or wholesale dealers for the purposes of their trade.

SHORT-TIME WORKING. Defined by the Department of Employment as 'arrangements made by an employer for working less than normal hours', not including time lost through sickness, holidays and absenteeism. Time lost by short time working in Britain appears to be small overall. In most years less than one-half per cent of operators are affected, and these lose between one and two days each per year, representing on average less than one-tenth of an hour for all workers employed; see National Board for Prices and Incomes, *Hours of Work, Overtime and Shiftworking*, Report No. 161, Cmnd. 4554, December 1970; also **guaranteed week.** Under the **Redundancy Payments Act 1965**, s. 5, an employee is on short-time in any week in which, because of a diminution of work belonging to his job, he earns less than half a week's pay calculated according to Schedule 2 of the Act; he is entitled to a redundancy payment if after short-time lasting four consecutive weeks or a total of six weeks in any thirteen weeks, he leaves after giving proper notice, except in certain specified conditions (s. 6). For another type of **lost period** in the Act, see **lay-off.**

SHREWSBURY PICKETS. Flying pickets (q.v.) during the national building workers' strike of 1972, members of the 'Building Workers' Charter', who were subsequently arrested and found guilty at Shrewsbury on a number of offences concerned with the violence which broke out as the pickets moved from site to site, *inter alia*, in the case of three defendants, John Jones, Eric Tomlinson and Dennis Warren, with intimidation under s. 7 of the **Conspiracy and Protection of Property Act 1875.** Tomlinson and Warren, who received the longer prison sentences, became known as the 'Shrewsbury Two'; see **R. v. Jones**, and, for a view on the situa-

tion, J. Arnison, *The Shrewsbury Three*, Lawrence and Wishart, 1974.

SHUTTLEMAKERS, SOCIETY OF. A trade union founded in 1891 and changing from Amalgamated Society of Shuttlemakers to its present title in 1935. *Address:* 21 Buchan Towers, Manchester Road, Bradford, Yorks BD5 0Q5. *TUC Affiliated Membership, 1977:* 128.

SICKNESS ABSENCE; see also **absence.** The failure of workers to report for work because of sickness. **Certified sickness absence** rates in Great Britain (i.e. more than three-day absences on which national insurance payments were made) represented in the year ending June 1968, a total of 10 million spells and 328 million working days, 0.48 spells and 15.6 working days lost for every man at risk, and 0.52 spells and 18.5 working days lost for every woman at risk; there was also an upward trend in all rates in the later 1960s; see P.J. Taylor, 'Some International Trends in Sickness Absence, 1950-1968'. *British Medical Journal*, 4, 1969 and Office of Health Economics, *Off Sick*, January 1971.

SICKNESS AND ACCIDENT BENEFIT; see **sickness benefit.**

SICKNESS BENEFIT. Benefit payable to employed and self-employed persons under the **National Insurance Act 1965** or that payable to trade union members according to the relevant rules of their unions in the event of their sickness; also payments made by employers to their employees under **sick pay schemes** (q.v.). Under the National Insurance Scheme benefit is not payable for the first three days, exclusive of Sundays (known as **waiting days**), several periods of interruption of employment of three days or more within a period of thirteen weeks being linked together to form one period of interruption, and the 'waiting days rule' applying therefore to the first period only. An identical rule applies to **unemployment benefit.** From 6 October 1966 **earnings-related supplements** have been payable, subject to certain qualifications, to employees with 'reckonable earnings' of at least £650, providing that they are aged 18 and over and have not yet reached the minimum pensionable age (National Insurance *Leaflet* 155A, December 1977). In 1965, 100 registered trade unions with a total membership of 7 millions incurred expenditure on **sickness and accident benefits,**

some union schemes being concerned with sickness only, some with occupational accidents, and some with a combination of both; a relatively small number of unions also had non-occupational accident benefits; see Arthur Marsh and Peter Cope, 'The Anatomy of Trade Union Benefits in the 1960s', *Industrial Relations Journal*, Summer 1970.

SICK-OUT. A form of industrial action devised by West German air traffic controllers in 1973 in order to evade a statutory prohibition on striking arising from their classification in 1962 as *'Beamte'*, a category of civil servant to which this is denied by law. At one point 90 per cent of air traffic controllers were away from work with medical certificates in connection with a claim for increased pay which the authorities claimed would upset civil service differentials. The action seemed to have tapered off during the oil crisis towards the end of the year.

SICK PAY SCHEMES or **occupational sick pay schemes**. A form of **fringe benefit** (q.v.) in which employers, whether as a result of negotiation and agreement with a trade union or unilaterally, make arrangements for payment of employees during sickness. In 1961, virtually all workers in the public sector and most white collar workers and about one-third of manual workers in private industry were involved in such schemes. Since that time numbers appear to have grown rapidly. In 1970 a sample survey by the Department of Health and Social Security showed 73 per cent of males and females to be covered; four years later the percentages were 80 per cent of males and 78 per cent of females (DHSS, *Report of a Survey of Occupational Sick Pay Schemes*, HMSO, 1977). It is not known how many are the result of negotiation and how many of unilateral action by employers; negotiated schemes appear, however, to be spreading at industry level in the 1960s; see Ministry of Pensions and National Insurance, *Report on an Inquiry into the Incidence of Incapacity for Work: Part I: Scope and Characteristics of Employers' Sick Pay Schemes*, HMSO, 1964; Ministry of Labour, *Sick Pay Schemes*, HMSO, 1964; G.L. Reid and D.J. Robertson (eds), *Fringe Benefits; Labour Costs and Social Security*, George Allen and Unwin, 1965, Ch. 8; Industrial Society, *Sick Pay*, 1967 and Institute of Personnel Management, *Sick Pay Schemes*, Information Report 7, March 1971.

SICK STEWARD. A trade union branch official whose task it is to visit sick members and to report their condition to the branch.

SIGN AND DISPLAY TRADES UNION (SDTU). A trade union organising sign and glass sign writers, ticket writers, cinema and poster writers, etc., and now merged with the **National Society of Operative Printers, Graphical and Media Personnel** (q.v.). The union was founded in 1918; it adopted its present title in 1945, having been known before 1938 as the National Union of Sign, Glass and Ticket Writers and Kindred Trades, and after 1938 more simply as the National Union of Sign, Glass and Tickets Writers. The National Society of Glassworkers and the Northern Glassworkers' Employees' Association transferred their engagements to the SDTU in 1950.

SIMA. Steel Industry Management Association (q.v.).

SINGLE ARBITRATION or **one-man arbitration**; see **single arbitrator**.

SINGLE ARBITRATOR. A person appointed to be the sole arbitrator in an industrial dispute; also **single arbitration**. Single arbitrators (who may on rare occasions be assisted by **assessors** (q.v.)) are used in the arbitration arrangements of a number of industries and companies. Powers enabling the Secretary of State for Employment to appoint such arbitrators, on the application of both parties to a dispute or difference formerly existed under the Conciliation Act 1896 and the Industrial Courts Act 1919, the latter Act being most frequently used and the former being usually reserved for cases in which it was necessary to confer other powers, e.g. those as conciliator, as well as arbitrator; see K.W. Wedderburn and P.L. Davies, *Employment Grievances and Disputes Procedures in Britain*, University of California Press, 1969, p. 182 *et seq.* The **Employment Protection Act 1975** has now repealed the Conciliation Act and the relevant sections of the Industrial Courts Act, giving the powers previously exercised by the Secretary of State to the **Advisory, Conciliation and Arbitration Service** (q.v.). The informality and other features of single arbitrators have remained unchanged, but there has been a notable increase in the number of cases dealt with. There were 247 such cases in 1977; see ACAS, *Annual Report, 1977*, p. 65.

SINGLE-INDUSTRY UNION. A classification of trade unions preferred by H.A. Clegg, A.J. Killick and Rex Adams (*Trade Union Officers*, Basil Blackwell, 1961, p. 15) to **industrial union** (q.v.) on the grounds that there are no unions in Britain which include all the workers, or even all the manual workers, in a given industry, but many that have a predominant interest in a particular industry, which are not limited to skilled workers or white collar workers, and which are not **ex-craft unions** (q.v.), e.g. the **National Union of Railwaymen**, the **Iron and Steel Trades Confederation**, the **National Union of Seamen**, the former **Amalgamated Weavers' Association**, the **Union of Post Office Workers**, etc.; see also **typology of unions**.

SINGLE MANNING. The manning of a railway locomotive by a driver only, rather than by a driver and a fireman. The introduction of single manning became especially a question at issue between the (then) British Transport Commission and the railway unions on changes in the 1950s and 1960s from steam to diesel or electric power units. A relaxation of manning was agreed in 1957, and restrictions on manning at night were accepted as part of the Pay and Efficiency Agreement of 1968. Charles McLeod, *All Change: Railway Industrial Relations in the Sixties*, Gower Press, 1970.

SIT-DOWN STRIKE. A stoppage of work in which the workers concerned sit down at their machines or remain at their jobs or at their place of work, but do no work; sometimes a type of **token strike**; alternatively a strike designed to make it difficult for an employer to introduce **blacklegs**, to assert the rights of the workers concerned to their jobs, to force a speedier settlement of an issue, etc. and therefore taking on the character of a **sit-in strike** (q.v.). It has been claimed that one of the first sit-down strikes occurred at General Electric's Schenectady plant in New York in 1906, followed by that of women garment workers in the same city in 1910; Joel Seidman, *Sit-Down*, League for Industrial Democracy, March 1937; large scale sit-downs were a feature of the 'évènements' of May 1968 in France and of Italy throughout 1969; see also the General Motors' sit-down of 1936-37; Alfred Sloan, *The Story of the General Motors' Strike*, General Motors, April 1937 and Walter Linder, *The Great Flint Strike against GM*, Solidarity Pamphlet No. 31,

1969; see K.G.J.C. Knowles, *Strikes*, Basil Blackwell, 1952, p. 10.

SIT-IN; a **sit-in strike** (q.v.).

SIT-IN STRIKE. A form of industrial action in which workers stop work and arrange shifts to occupy their place of work around the clock, management remaining on the premises but having no authority over employees; a type of stoppage distinguished for various reasons from **work-ins, stay-ins** and **worker-occupations** (q.v.), though akin to them in that all involve some degree or type of factory occupation and that the object is frequently to resist **redundancy** or closure (hence **redundancy sit-in**), and to assert the **right to work**. Alternatively sit-ins may be concerned with attempts to secure trade union recognition, or to improve wages and conditions of work (**wage sit-ins** or collective bargaining sit-ins) and may in this sense be an alternative to withdrawal of labour and subsequent **picketing** or to other industrial actions such as overtime bans or working to rule. Wages sit-ins were, especially in Manchester, a feature of the events following the breakdown of national negotiations in the engineering industry in December 1971, some 33 such actions taking place in that area between March and August 1972; see Colin Beever and Brian Tritton, *An Analysis of Sit-ins*, Metra Consulting, 1972 and IPM, *Sit-ins and Work-ins*, Institute of Personnel Management, 1976.

SIZE-EFFECT. The proposition, often associated with theories of bureaucratisation (see **bureaucracy**) that the size of organisations has significant effects on the behaviour and attitudes of workers employed in them. The notion that conflict between labour and capital intensifies as the scale of industrial units grows is to be found in E. Durkheim, *The Division of Labour in Society*, Collier-Macmillan 1964. Empirical studies have related size with strike activity, with **absenteeism**, with **accidents**, with **labour turnover** and with **job satisfaction** as well as with the quality of industrial relations in general (see, *inter alia*, R.W. Revans, 'Industrial Morale and Size of Unit', *Political Quarterly*, Vol. 27, 1956 and Human Relations, Management and Size in E.M. Hugh Jones, (ed.), *Human Relations and Modern Management*, Amsterdam, 1958; Acton Society Trust, *Size and Morale*, I and II, 1953 and 1957; S. Cleland, *The Influence of Plant Size on Industrial Relations*, Princeton,

1955; D. Hewitt and J. Parfit, 'A Note on Working Morale and Size of Group', *Occupational Psychology*, Vol. 27, 1953 and S. Talacchi, 'Organisational Size, Individual Attitudes and Behaviour', *Administrative Science Quarterly*, Vol. 5, 1960). For a critical appraisal of propositions about size-effect; see G.K. Ingham, *Size of Industrial Organisation and Worker Behaviour*, CUP, 1970.

SJIC. Statutory Joint Industrial Council; see **Wages Councils.**

SKILLCENTRES; formerly **Government Training Centres.** Training centres operated by the government as part of a **Vocational Training Scheme** for adult workers operated under the **Employment and Training Act 1948.** The principal objects of the scheme are to help overcome persistent shortages of skilled labour by providing accelerated training courses, and to assist those adult workers in need of special help to fit themselves for suitable employment. In March 1977 it was reported that there were 63 Skillcentres in operation, 27 of these with one or more separate Annexe and in December 1977 that the Training Service Division of The Manpower Services Commission was planning to open 13 new Centres and one Annexe by 1981. In some areas the placing of Skillcentre trained workers is said to have been hampered by trade union fears of **dilution** (q.v.); see also **Training Opportunities Scheme.**

SKILL DIFFERENTIAL; see **differential.**

SKILLED RATE; see **craft rate.**

SKILLED UNION. A trade union catering for skilled workers; more precisely, according to the **typology of trade unions** used by H.A. Clegg, A.J. Killick and Rex Adams (*Trade Union Officers*, Basil Blackwell, 1961), unions which are wholly or mainly confined to skilled workers (or **craft unions**) as distinct from those which were formerly craft unions, but which have opened their ranks widely to semi-skilled and unskilled workers (**ex-craft unions**).

SKYLARKING. Indulging in sport or horse-play while at work, to the danger of oneself and of others; frequently quoted as the cause of **accidents**, e.g. from the firing of rivet and nail guns on building sites, from misuse of tools, or from practical jokes. The term seems to have originated as a nautical term to describe play about the rigging and later in any part of a ship (*Oxford English Dictionary*).

SLADE AND PW or SLADE. Society of Lithographic Artists, Designers, Engravers and Process Workers; see **Lithographic Artists, Designers, Engravers and Process Workers, Society of.**

SLADE Art Union (SAU). A section of the **Society of Lithographic Artists, Designers, Engravers and Process Workers** established from 1 January 1975 for members engaged in the preparation and production of art and photographic material. The constitution of the section leaves it formally free to determine its own rules and policy. It is aimed principally at the recruitment of art workers and photographers at studios and employed by advertising and other agencies whether directly or as freelances, and claimed at the end of 1977 a membership of 8,000.

SLATE SYSTEM. A system of displaying the earnings of weavers on a slate exhibited in a weaving shed which came into prominence in the early twentieth century. It was regarded by weavers as part of a system of **driving** by overlookers to obtain higher production. E. Hopwood, *A History of the Lancashire Cotton Industry and the Amalgamated Weavers' Association*, AWA, 1969, pp. 61-2.

SLATING. Standing or waiting for copy in the newspaper industry. Derived from the practice of compositors writing their names on a slate when out of copy (A.E. Musson, *The Typographical Association*, OUP, 1954, p. 175). Slating may be heavy when newspapers are small, and intermittent when the flow of work is irregular; Economist Intelligence Unit, *Survey of the National Newspaper Industry*, 1966, p. 112.

SLIDING SCALES; see **cost of living sliding scales, selling price sliding scales, indexation.**

SLOW-GEAR STRIKE; see **ca'canny.**

SMALL FIRMS EMPLOYMENT SUBSIDY. A subsidy of £20 per week paid to manufacturing firms employing fewer than 50 people in **Special Development Areas** (q.v. and **assisted areas**) for up to 26 weeks for every additional job they create. The scheme was started in July 1977. It has been claimed that over 2,500 jobs have been created by it between that date and 9 December 1977.

SMOKE-O. Tea break (merchant navy).

SMOOTING. Working in more than one office: John Child, *Industrial Relations in the British Printing Industry,* Allen and Unwin, 1967, p. 141; to do casual work in a house in which one is not regularly employed.

SNAP READING METHOD; see **activity sampling.**

SNAP TIME. Meal time or meal break (coal mining industry).

SOCIAL CONTRACT. An affirmation of the mutual social and economic objectives of the Labour Party and of the General Council of the Trades Union Congress originating in July 1972 during the Conservative government of Mr Heath and having as an important element at that time the undertaking of a future Labour government to repeal the **Industrial Relations Act 1971.** The original intention of the Contract was to halt a deterioration in relationships between the Labour Party and the trade union movement which had resulted from the statutory incomes policy of the previous Wilson government (see **National Board for Prices and Incomes)** and from its proposals to reform industrial relations (see 'In Place of Strife'). Later, with a Labour government again in office in February 1974, development of the Contract became concerned, *inter alia,* with problems of inflation. In its statement *Collective Bargaining and the Social Contract* (September 1974) the TUC General Council showed itself sympathetic to the development of a voluntary **incomes policy.** It produced recommendations on how bargaining should be conducted, subscribing in 1975-76 to a Stage 1 policy of £6 increases across the board and in 1976-77 to Stage 2 guidelines comprising an increase of 5 per cent on total earnings with a cash minimum of £2.50 and an upper cash maximum of £4 per week, while keeping in review the Labour government's side of the Contract, particularly where the relief of unemployment was concerned. The Social Contract in this form effectively came to an end with the failure of the two parties to agree acceptable Stage 3 pay guidelines for 1977-78 and the unilateral announcement by the govern-

ment of a voluntary 10 per cent norm as a stage in an orderly return to free collective bargaining in its White Paper *The Attack on Inflation after 31st July 1977* (Cmnd. 6882) July 1977, leaving only the **twelve month rule** (q.v.) for agreed application until existing collective agreements came to an end.

SOCIAL SCIENCE RESEARCH COUNCIL INDUSTRIAL RELATIONS RESEARCH UNIT. A research unit set up at the University of Warwick in 1970 with finance provided by the SSRC and an Advisory Committee consisting of four SSRC representatives, three from the University of Warwick and three assessors, one each from the **Trades Union Congress,** the **Confederation of British Industry** and the **Department of Employment.** The unit has undertaken major research projects into (1) piecework payment systems and wage drift in Coventry, (2) conceptions of fairness in wages, (3) organisational behaviours of trade unions, (4) union growth, (5) coloured immigrants in industry, (6) labour markets and (7) monitoring the **Industrial Relations Act 1971;** see *Industrial Relations Journal,* Vol. 2, No. 2, Register of Current Research and *Personnel Review,* Vol. 1, No. 1, Autumn 1971, Research in Progress.

SOCIAL SECURITY PENSIONS ACT 1975; see **occupational pensions.**

SOCIETY OF CIVIL AND PUBLIC SERVANTS (EXECUTIVE AND DIRECTING GRADES); see **Civil and Public Servants, Society of.**

SOCIETIES (MISCELLANEOUS PROVISIONS) ACT 1940; see **transfer of engagements.**

SOCIETY OF GRAPHICAL AND ALLIED TRADES (SOGAT); see **Graphical and Allied Trades, Society of.**

SOCIETY HOUSE; see **union house.**

SOGAT. Society of Graphical and Allied Trades; see **Graphical and Allied Trades, Society of.**

SOCIETY OF LITHOGRAPHIC ARTISTS, DESIGNERS, ENGRAVERS AND PROCESS WORKERS (SLADE and PW); see **Lithographic Artists, Designers, Engravers and Process Workers, Society of.**

SOCIETY OF MASTER PRINTERS OF SCOTLAND; see **British Printing Industries Federation.**

SOCIETY OF PRESSED GLASSMAKERS; see **Pressed Glassmakers, Society of.**

SOCIETY OF SHUTTLEMAKERS; see **Shuttlemakers, Society of.**

SOCIETY OF TECHNICAL CIVIL SERVANTS (STCS); see **Professional Civil Servants, Institution of.**

SOCIOLOGY. A journal published by the Oxford University Press, Press Road, Neasden, London NW10, and containing articles of interest to those engaged in industrial relations.

SOCIOLOGY REVIEW. A sociological journal published by the University of Keele and containing from time to time articles of interest to those engaged in industrial relations.

SOLDIERING. Idleness or deliberate reduction of output or time-wasting, usually by individual employees. Sometimes used in a more collective sense to describe **restrictive labour practices** q.v. (see Tom Lupton, 'Systematic Soldiering', *The Listener,* 20 March 1960), but generally distinguished from partial stoppages of work in the form of **ca'canny** or **go-slow.**

SOLE BARGAINING AGENT. Defined in s. 44(c) of the **Industrial Relations Act 1971** as 'the organisation of workers or joint negotiating panel having negotiating rights in relation to [a particular bargaining] unit to the exclusion of all other organisations of workers and joint negotiating panels, except in respect of matters which are dealt with under more extensive bargaining arrangements'; see **bargaining unit** and **sole bargaining rights.** With the repeal of the Act in 1974 the legal significance of the term has disappeared.

SOLE BARGAINING RIGHTS. Traditionally in Britain the right of a single trade union, or by extension of more than one trade union, to represent and negotiate as a result of custom or more explicit voluntary agreement, for workers in a particular **bargaining unit.** The **Industrial Relations Act 1971** (s. 45 to s. 50) established procedures whereby, if voluntary agreement could not be reached, either a registered trade union (or trade unions) or an employer (or employers), or the Secre-

tary of State for Employment, might ask the **National Industrial Relations Court** to refer to the **Commission on Industrial Relations** the questions whether a specified group of employees constituted a bargaining unit, whether a **sole bargaining agent** should be recognised by the employer or employees, and if so, which organisation of workers (a **registered trade union**) or which joint negotiating panel should be the sole bargaining agent for that bargaining unit. These procedures came to an end with the repeal of the Industrial Relations Act in 1974, claims for new recognitions being dealt with under s. 11 of the **Employment Protection Act 1975** (see **Section 11**) and other issues principally through the **Bridlington Agreement** (q.v.).

SPATIAL MOBILITY; see **geographical mobility.**

SPECIAL DEVELOPMENT AREAS; see **assisted areas;** at the beginning of 1978, South Wales, North West Wales, Merseyside, West Cumbria, North East, Girvan, West Central Scotland, Livingston New Town, Leven and Methil, Dundee and Arbroath and Glenrothes New Town.

SPECIAL REGISTER. A register of organisations, mainly of a professional character formerly maintained by the **Chief Registrar of Trade Unions and Employers' Associations,** under the terms of the **Industrial Relations Act 1971** (now repealed). These organisations were distinguished from **registered trade unions** in that the regulation of relations between workers and employers was recognised to be only one of their activities, e.g. in the case of the Royal College of Nursing or the **British Medical Association.**

SPECIALISED BARGAINING; see **fractional bargaining.**

SPECIFIC PERFORMANCE. An order compelling both parties to a contract to perform their obligation. The rule that the courts will not enforce specific performance of a contract for personal service appears to date from the first half of the nineteenth century (**Pickering v. The Bishop of Ely** (1843)), though cases may fall within some recognised exception (**Whitwood Chemical Co. v. Hardman** (1891) 2 Ch. 416). The refusal also applies to injunctions, and has been repeatedly affirmed (see Lord Reid in **Ridge v. Baldwin** (1964) HL, and K.W. Wedderburn,

Cases and Materials on Labour Law, CUP, 1967, pp. 34-40 for other instances), the argument probably originally centring on two well-established equity reasons, that the courts would not enforce bargains involving close personal relationships, and that in such cases specific performance could not be adequately supervised (O. Aikin and J. Reid, *Employment, Welfare and Safety at Work,* Labour Law 1, Penguin Education, 1971, p. 151 *et seq.*). **The Trade Union and Labour Relations Act 1974, s.** 16, prohibits the order of specific performance or an injunction restraining the breach of any contract of employment so as to compel any employee to do any work or to attend any place for the doing of any work. See **Hill v. C.A. Parsons and Co. Ltd** as an exceptional case.

SPEEDERS; see pacers.

SPEED-UP. A term used by workers to describe a situation in which they are required to do more work for the same pay (e.g. by speeding up the assembly line, or by an increase in work load), or without a corresponding proportionate increase in pay (e.g. in the operation of **premium bonus systems**) speed-up and **rate cutting** are analogous notions, especially where the latter involves unilateral reductions in **allowed times;** see also **stretch out.**

SPELLING; see welting.

SPENCER UNION; see company union.

SPENT CONVICTION; see Rehabilitation of Offenders Act 1974.

SPHERES OF INFLUENCE AGREEMENT. An agreement incorporating one method of avoiding inter-union competition (and **inter-union disputes**) by understanding between unions on the geographical, occupational or job basis on which they will recruit and represent members; such agreements may involve employers in that they may involve definitions of **bargaining units;** while they are strictly about membership, and therefore concerned with preventing **jurisdictional disputes,** they may sometimes involve **demarcation,** and are therefore sometimes (inaccurately) known as 'demarcation agreements'. Spheres of influence arrangements between unions were recommended by the **Trades Union Congress** in the Hull Main Principles of 1924 and continued in the **Bridlington Agreement;** see Trades Union Congress, *Trade Union Structure and Closer Unity,* TUC, 1947.

SPINNERS AND TWINERS, AMALGAMATED ASSOCIATION OF OPERATIVE COTTON. (AAOCST). A trade union formed in 1870 by amalgamation of some 40 district associations with a total of approximately 12,000 members, and more recently organised, with a much smaller membership, in six semi-autonomous associations, the occupation of mule-spinning, traditionally an important part of the union, having declined in recent years. Roger Dyson, *The Development of Collective Bargaining in Cotton Spinning,* PhD Thesis, University of Leeds, 1972, and H.A. Turner, *Trade Union Growth, Structure and Policy,* Allen and Unwin, 1962. The union transferred its engagement to the Amalgamated Textile Workers' Union in June 1976.

SPLINTER UNION; see breakaway union.

SPLIT SHIFT. (1) an arrangement in which the working day is not continuous but is split into two or more working periods with a substantial time interval in between. Usually found in industries in which peak demand varies at different times of the day, e.g. road passenger transport, catering, and cinemas and theatres, which operate **spreadovers** (q.v.); also in hospitals; also known as **broken time.** (2) a payment equal to the earnings of an absentee worker made to the individuals who have undertaken his duties in addition to their own work; often subject to a maximum extra payment, e.g. half a shift to any individual, and sometimes known as **dead man's money** (steel industry).

SPOE. Society of Post Office Executives; see **Post Office Executives, Society of.**

SPONSORED TRAINING SCHEME. A scheme whereby employers may sponsor their employees for training biased towards their particular needs at **Skillcentres.** It includes conversion training, training in additional skills, updating training and training for limited skills.

SPREADOVER. A situation or arrangement in which a worker has a split-duty, working, for instance, part of his working day on one shift or turn and part on another, with an interval of time in between; a **split shift.** Spreadovers tend to be inconvenient for workers and have caused controversy in particular in the omnibus industry (see NBPI *Reports* Nos. 16, 50 and 63), but they also exist in other industries in which peak demand tends to vary at different times of the day, e.g. in cinemas, catering establishments etc.

SPRING v. NATIONAL AMALGAMATED STEVEDORES AND DOCKERS (1956) 2 All ER 221.

A case in which it was ruled that Mr Spring, alleged by the **Transport and General Workers' Union** to have been poached by the **Blue Union** (National Amalgamated Stevedores and Dockers) and ordered to be returned to the TGWU along with other such members by the Disputes Committee of the Trades Union Congress under the **Bridlington Agreement** (q.v.), was not so bound to be returned, since the Bridlington Agreement was no more than 'a morally binding code of conduct made between persons of similar views'. The case had a worsening effect on the relations between the Blue Union (q.v.) and the TGWU in the docks, and together with that of **Andrew v. National Union of Public Employees** (q.v.) resulted in advice from the TUC to affiliated unions to amend their rules so as to include the Bridlington Agreement within their terms; K.W. Wedderburn, *Cases and Materials on Labour Law,* CUP, 1967, pp. 619-21.

SPRING TRAPMAKERS' SOCIETY.

A trade union formed in 1890 as the Wednesbury Spring Trapmakers' Society and changing to its present name in 1916. It has been associated with the **National Union of Lock and Metal Workers** since 1924. *Address:* Bellamy House, Wilkes Street, Willenhall, Staffs. *Tel:* 0902 66651. *TUC Affiliated Membership, 1977:* 90.

SR AND O No. 1367, 1936; see **double day shift.**

STA. Scottish Typographical Association (q.v.).

'STAB. A term applied to establishment printers, i.e. those paid a set weekly wage as distinct from piecework, hence **'stab hands, 'stab wages, 'stab rates, 'stab system** also 'to be on stab'; see, for example, A.E. Musson, *The Typographical Association,* OUP, 1954, *passim.*

'STAB HANDS; see **'stab.**

'STAB RATES; see **'stab.**

'STAB SYSTEM; see **'stab.**

'STAB WAGES; see **'stab.**

STABILISED BONUS. A fixed bonus payable irrespective of output, especially in the steel industry.

STABILISED PRODUCTION BONUS; see **production bonus.**

STAFF. Most usually **white collar workers,** as distinct from **manual** or **blue collar workers,** and hence enjoying **staff conditions; weekly staff,** staff workers enjoying staff conditions, but paid weekly; **monthly staff,** staff workers enjoying staff conditions and paid by the month. **Works staff** may, however, be manual workers, especially in the engineering industry, e.g. stores clerks, or booking clerks and other indirect non-manual workers associated with production. The word 'staff' may also be used to designate workers generally, e.g. teaching staff, hospital staff; or all workers who are not managerial, e.g. in British Railways. Also in the civil service, **staff side,** the opposite of the 'official side' in, for example, Whitley Councils. Sometimes, though relatively rarely in industry, used by companies in a para-military sense, e.g. 'headquarters staff'; see also **staff status, manual workers on staff conditions, mensualisation.**

STAFF APPRAISAL; see **performance appraisal.**

STAFF ASSESSMENT; see **performance appraisal.**

STAFF ASSOCIATION. In the non-industrial Civil Service, the expression used to describe independent trade unions, whether **recognised associations** (q.v.) or not, which cater, for the most part, for particular grades or classes of civil servants, and which are free to affiliate to the **Trades Union Congress** and any political party. In private employment, a term commonly applied to associations alleged by the trade union movement to be dominated by or sponsored by employers, and hence not **bona fide trade unions** (q.v.); see also **company union** and **freedom of association.** The complaint of the **National Union of Bank Employees** to the International Labour Organisation's Committee on Freedom of Association (*Report of the Inquiry by the Honourable Lord Cameron,* Cmnd. 2202, November 1963) raised the allegation that, in breach of the British government's acceptance of **International Labour Convention No. 98,** the union was being prevented by banking employers from exercising its proper and normal functions by their support and use of staff associations; the allegation was not upheld by the Inquiry. Staff associations in private industry are not debarred from seeking the status of **independent trade unions** under the **Trade Union and Labour Relations Act 1974,** and many have done so with success; see Certification Office of Trade Unions and Employers' Associations, *Annual Reports of the Certification Officer,* 1976 and 1977.

STAFF CONDITIONS. A generic expression used to describe the terms, conditions and fringe benefit which may be enjoyed by **white collar workers** compared with **manual,** or **blue collar workers.** They may include some or all of the following: shorter hours, longer holidays, pensions, improved sick pay schemes, absence of **clocking,** payment for *ad hoc* leave, differences in lavatory, dining room and other amenities etc. For the development of **manual workers on staff conditions,** see **mensualisation;** see also **staff status.**

STAFF SIDE; see **staff.**

STAFF STATUS. The status accorded by being employed on **staff conditions** (q.v.); hence **staff status agreements,** collective agreements which accord staff status, as defined in each instance, to manual workers, e.g. in the electricity supply industry (see **status agreement**), in Imperial Chemical Industries, etc. Staff status for all workers may form part of the philosophy of non-union companies, e.g. in the case of Texas Instruments and IBM, the former based upon the motivational theory of Maslow and Herzberg, and the latter upon that of its founder T.J. Watson; it may also be involved in federated engineering firms in the growth of **manual workers on staff conditions** (see **mensualisation**) H.J. Schotranger, *Staff Status for Manual Workers,* Industrial Society, 1967.

STAFF STATUS AGREEMENTS; see **staff status.**

STAGGER. Staggered hours, staggered holidays; working hours or annual holidays so arranged that they occur at different times of the day or year, thus reducing, for example, travel congestion. Electricity supply industry: **stagger allowances** (allowances for the inconvenience of staggered arrangements); **seven day stagger, six day stagger** (normal weekly work hours spread on an agreed rota over seven or six days); **winter/summer stagger** (transfer of an agreed number of working hours from winter to summer); **work load stagger** (agreed rotating of light and heavy loads); *NJIC Agreements,* April 1968 ed., pp. 17-18; arrangements devised to prevent systematic heavy overtime.

STAGGER ALLOWANCE; see **stagger.**

STAGGERED DAY WORK. A shift system in which employees are divided into groups starting and finishing at fixed intervals, e.g. three groups starting and finishing at intervals of one hour. A system found in some seasonal industries, such as food preserving, and is a means of avoiding excessive hours of work for individual employees, while at the same time giving a longer working period while the crop is in season and making use of the longer hours of daylight. F.P. Cook, *Shift Work,* Institute of Personnel Management, 1954.

STAGGERED HOLIDAYS; see **stagger;** also Board of Trade, *Staggered Holidays,* Cmnd. 2105, HMSO, 1963, which reviewed the situation and suggested that there might be some spreading of summer holidays within the months of July and August, some development of secondary holidays in spring and autumn and that avoidance of holidays starting at weekends might reduce congestion - limited gains which might be attained at the expense of some disruption of established holiday procedures.

STAGGERED HOURS; see **stagger.**

STAGGERED WORKING HOURS; see **stagger.**

STAGING. The award of improvements in wages, salaries or conditions of work by stages. Staging has become more common in Britain since the development of **productivity bargaining** and **fixed-term agreements** (q.v.). The staging of any increase over 7 per cent was an item of contention between Civil Service unions and the government in 1968; Civil Service Clerical Association, *Strike Policy,* Civil Service Clerical Association, 1969, pp. 13-14. It became associated with **prices and incomes policy;** see *Prices and Incomes Policy after 30th July 1967,* Cmnd. 3235, 1967, para. 24.

STAMP SECTION. The Supervisory, Technical, Administrative, Managerial and Professional Section of the **Union of Construction, Allied Trades and Technicians;** formerly the **Association of Building Technicians.** *Address:* UCATT House, 177 Abbeville Road, Clapham, SW4 9RL. *Tel:* 01-622 2442.

STANDARD CONSOLIDATED TIME RATE. An hourly rate for fully skilled craftsmen employed in the British Steel Corporation and operative from 6 March 1969. The standard consolidated time rate was made up of the following items; the previous standard hourly rate, cost of living payment, tonnage bonus of 65s. per week, efficiency payment of 10s. per week, service/educational qualification payments of 15s. per week, and an increase in the hourly rate itself, making a total consolidated rate at that time of 9s. 5.50d. per hour.

STANDARD HOUR SYSTEM. An incentive payment or payment by results system sometimes known as **time piecework,** in which the worker, if he finishes a job in less than the original time allowed, is still paid for the original time, thus giving him the advantage of the time saved.

STANDARD INDUSTRIAL CLASSIFICATION (SIC). A classification by industry (*not* occupations), first issued in 1948 to promote uniformity and comparability in official statistics in the United Kingdom. It was revised in 1958 and 1968. In the current (1968) SIC, industrial units (or **establishments,** q.v.) are grouped in 27 Orders (distinguished by roman numerals) according to kind of service provided, e.g. Mining and Quarrying (Order II), Vehicles (Order XI) and Distributive Trades (Order XXIII), and 181 **Minimum List Headings** (MLH) (distinguished by arabic numerals) giving a more detailed breakdown, e.g. Order II includes MLH 101, Coal Mining, Order XI, MLH 381, Motor Vehicle Manufacturing, and Order XXIII MLH 810, Wholesale Distribution of Food and Drink. In industrial relations, the SIC is principally used for statistics on employment and unemployment, wages and earnings, etc.; see Central Statistical Office, *Standard Industrial Classification,* HMSO, 1968, for short descriptions of Orders and MLHs; see also **Nomenclature Générale des Activités Économiques des Communautés Européennes (NACE).**

STANDARD PACE; see **standard performance.**

STANDARD PERFORMANCE. Defined by the British Standards Institution, *Glossary of Terms Used in Work Study,* BS 3138, 1969, No. 34001, as 'the rate of output which qualified workers will naturally achieve without over-exertion on the average over the working day or shift, provided that they know and adhere to the specified method and provided they are motivated to apply themselves to the work. This performance is denoted as 100 on the **standard rating** and performance scales'. **Standard performance** therefore depends on the maintenance by the worker of **standard pace,** or work at standard rating, i.e. the observer's view of a rate of working compared with some standard level which he is holding in his mind, most generally in the United States and Great Britain the speed of motion of the limbs of a man of average physique walking without a load in a straight line on level ground at 4 miles per hour. Examples of studies of the problems associated with the determination of standard rating and standard performance; see Institution of Production Engineers and Institute of Cost and Works Accountants, *Measurement of Productivity,* 1949; T.U. Matthew, 'The Accuracy and Use of Time Study', *Operational Research Quarterly,* 6, 1955; K.A. Lifson, 'Errors of Time-study Judgments of Industrial Work Pace'. *Psychological Monogs,* 67, No. 5, 1953, and W. Rodgers and J. Hammersley, 'The Consistency of Stopwatch Time-study Practitioners', *Occupational Psychology,* 28, 1954; see also **standard time learning curve.**

STANDARD RATE. Usually the negotiated or agreed hourly rate of pay for a job, grade or occupation; the **union rate.** This may sometimes imply a **minimum rate** or **basic rate** to which other payments may be added to make up total earnings, and sometimes a 'standard' rate in the sense of a fixed rate, or **upstanding wage.** The term may also be applied to weekly, monthly or annual rates of pay in some circumstances.

STANDARD RATING; see **standard performance.**

STANDARD TIME. The total time in which a job should be completed at **standard performance** i.e. work content, **contingency allowance** for delay, **unoccupied time** and **interference allowance,** where applicable: British Standards Institution, *Glossary of Terms Used in Work Study,* BS 3138, 1969, No. 35010; see also **allowed time.**

STAND-BY. Stand-by duty; stand-by crew; to be 'on stand-by' to be available for duty, either at, or away from the workplace, or **on call,** in case of emergency (as in medical services), because of irregular availability of work (as in the port transport industry), to replace crews which have failed to report for work (as in the bus industry) etc. Also **stand-by payment,** or **stand-by allowance:** a payment made for being on stand-by, usually at a lower rate than when the worker is actually at work.

STAND-BY ALLOWANCE or **on-call allowance.** An **allowance** paid to a worker who is required, particularly in emergency, to be immediately available for work, and paid whether that worker is recalled to work in such circumstances or not, especially among certain medical grades.

STAND-BY CREW; see **stand-by.**

STAND-BY DUTY; see **stand-by.**

STAND-BY PAYMENT; see **stand-by.**

STANDING; see **slating.**

STANDING ADVISORY COMMITTEE ON THE PAY OF THE HIGHER CIVIL SERVICE. A committee established in February 1957 following the report of the (Priestley) Royal Commission on the Civil Service, 1953-55, to undertake, either on its own initiative or on the government's request, reviews of the pay of the Higher Civil Service. The Committee ceased to function in May 1971; its role was transferred to the **Top Salaries Review Body** (q.v.).

STANDING TIME. Time spent by piece hands in the printing industry waiting for copy; known in most industries as **waiting time** (q.v.); also used in other industries (e.g. coalmining) when mechanical breakdown prevents work.

STARTING RATE; see **beginner's rate.**

STATEMENT OF PARTICULARS; see **Contracts of Employment Act 1972.**

STATEMENTS, shop statements; or **uni-form statements.** Piece-rate lists covering smaller or larger areas in the boot and shoe industry. Alan Fox, *A History of the National Union of Boot and Shoe Operatives,* Blackwell, 1958, p. 63; see **uniform list** for examples of similar arrangements in the cotton industry.

STATE SUBSIDY THEORY OF STRIKES. The proposition that social security benefits and income tax rebates during strikes either (a) reduce the incentive of workers to resist calls for strike action (b) result in short strikes developing into long ones or (c) reduce the incentive for strikers to come to a settlement with their employer; alternatively (d) that trade unions are relieved of some of the responsibility for supporting their members while on strike (e) that strikes during the later part of the PAYE tax year are made more attractive and (f) that a result of state benefits is to weaken the employer's resistance for fear of prolonged stoppages; see Conservative Political Centre, *Financing Strikers,* 1974. J. Durcan and W.E.J. McCarthy ('The State Subsidy Theory of Strikes', *British Journal of Industrial Relations,* Vol. XII, No. 1, March 1974) offer a model in rebuttal of the theory; L.C. Hunter ('The State Theory of Strikes a reconsideration', *British Journal of Industrial Relations,* Vol. XII, No. 3, November 1974) doubts whether sufficient information exists to reach a positive conclusion on the matter. J. Gennard (*Financing Strikers,* Macmillan, 1978) argues from interviews with strikers and other sources that their individual knowledge of supplementary benefit arrangements is small, that two-thirds of those eligible do not take the trouble to claim and that personal savings, wives' earnings and pay in hand from the employer are other important sources of finance, as well as union benefits; see also **strike.**

STATISTICAL DRIFT; see **wage drift.**

STATISTICS OF TRADE ACT 1947. An Act to enable government departments to obtain information for the appreciation of economic trends and for the provision of a statistical service for industry. Matters specified in the Act about which persons may be required to furnish returns include the nature of the undertaking, the persons employed, the nature of their employment, their remuneration and hours worked. It contains provisions restricting the disclosure of information obtained in the course of inquiries.

STATUS AGREEMENT. A collective agreement, usually a **productivity agreement,** which includes, in whole or in part, the granting of staff conditions of service to manual workers. The first industry-wide agreement of this kind is said to have been made in the electricity supply industry; see Sir Ronald Edwards, *An Experiment in Industrial Relations,* Electricity Council, 1967. The agreement made all full-time industrial employees annual salaried staff on conditions which included the elimination of all overtime payment wherever possible, the best utilisation of labour, and the acceptance of practices which improved individual and collective efficiency. Various companies have developed agreements on similar lines, including Imperial Chemical Industries; see **MUPS;** also **staff status** and **mensualisation.**

STATUS QUO. The condition pertaining in circumstances in which actions proposed by management cannot be implemented if disputed by workers until agreement has been reached or dispute procedure exhausted; the opposite of **managerial functions** i.e. the condition that workers are required to work on management terms until procedure has been exhausted; see **managerial functions clause.** Differences between trade unions and employers' associations on the principles involved in these distinctions have mainly arisen in the engineering industry; see A.I. Marsh, *Industrial Relations in Engineering,* Pergamon Press, 1965. In recent years it has also been raised by the **Trades Union Congress;** see TUC, *Report,* 1960 and *Programme for Action, 1969;* see also Confederation of British Industry, *Disputes Procedures,* 1970, p. 22 *et seq.* In 1971 manual worker unions in engineering withdrew from the 1922 **Engineering Procedure Agreement** after failing to secure the inclusion of a *status quo* provision satisfactory to them. Such a provision was finally accepted in 1976.

STATUTORY ACCIDENT BOOK; see **Accident Book.**

STATUTORY FAIR WAGES; see **Central Arbitration Committee** and **Road Haulage Wages Act.**

STATUTORY HOLIDAYS; see **Bank Holidays.**

STATUTORY JOINT INDUSTRIAL COUNCIL; see **Wages Councils.**

STATUTORY OVERTIME; see **overtime.**

STATUTORY RULE AND ORDER NO. 1367, 1936; see **double day shift.**

STAY-DOWN STRIKE; see **stay-in strike.**

STAY-IN STRIKE. A form of work stoppage in which workers remain at the workplace either doing no work (see **sit-down strike**) or restricting their output (see **ca'canny**). **Stay-down strike** is the equivalent in the coal mining industry. K.G.J.C. Knowles, *Strikes,* Blackwell, 1952, p. 10, suggests that its object, in addition to making it difficult for employers to introduce **blacklegs** (q.v.) may sometimes be to assert the notion of investment and property rights in jobs or to resist redundancy. Used in this sense, stay-in may be indistinguishable from **work-in, sit-in,** or **worker-occupation** (q.v.).

STCS. Society of Technical Civil Servants; see **Professional Civil Servants, Institution of.**

STEEL INDUSTRY MANAGEMENT ASSOCIATION (SIMA). A trade union for middle management staff recognised nationally by the British Steel Corporation and at Group, Division or individual Works by agreement with the appropriate management at each level (February 1969). SIMA began as an Association of Managerial Staff, principally on the North-East Coast in 1949, became active towards the end of 1950 and applied for recognition by the Iron and Steel corporation of Great Britain in October 1951 as the British Iron and Steel Management Association (BISMA), changing to its present title after the return of the industry to public ownership by the Iron and Steel Act 1967. *Address:* Rigby House, 34 The Parade, High Street, Watford WD1 7EA Herts. *Tel:* Watford 25909 and 27341. Current membership exceeds 12,000.

STEEP RATINGS; see **rating.**

STEPPED BONUS PLAN; see **differential piece-work plan.**

STEPPED INCENTIVE SCHEME. An incentive payment system bearing resemblance to some types of **differential piece-rate plans,** but more frequently associated with a variation on **measured daywork,** especially of the **Premium Pay Plan** type;

hence sometimes known as **stepped measured daywork**. The basic notion behind such a scheme is that workers on measured work shall be given the choice of a range of rates of payment for appropriate levels of effort, such rates and levels being specified in advance by agreement or otherwise, thus associating measured work and fixed rates with some incentive element, e.g.

Performance level	Hourly rate (p)
56	59.5
64	67.6
72	75.7
80	83.8
88	91.9
96	100.0

STEPPED INCREASE; see **across-the-board settlement**. A pay settlement involving pay increases in steps, e.g. some groups, grades or classes of worker receiving different increases from others, especially where the lower paid receive a greater proportionate increase than the higher paid.

STEPPED MEASURED DAYWORK; see **stepped incentive scheme** and **Premium Pay Plan**.

STEPPING SCHEME; see **Brown Booklet Agreement**.

STERLING ENGINEERING CO. v. PATCHETT (1955) AC 534; see **Patents Act 1977**.

STEVEDORES AND DOCKERS, NATIONAL AMALGAMATED (NASD); see **Blue Union**.

STEVENSON, JORDAN AND HARRISON LTD v. MACDONALD AND EVANS (1952) ITLR 107; see **contract of service**.

STICKER. A worker, who though eligible for promotion (see **promotion ladder**) opts not to accept it (steel industry). It was agreed in the 1969 **Green Book Agreement** between the British Steel Corporation and the **Iron and Steel Trades Confederation** (C1.11) that works managements and branches should review promotion lines to provide greater flexibility and alternative channels for men who chose to 'stick'.

STINKERS. Workshop slang for piecework jobs on which prices or times are tight, and on which it is therefore difficult to make money; the opposite of **gravy** jobs; see also **goldbricking**. Donald Roy, 'Quota Restrictions and Goldbricking in a Machine Shop,' *American Journal of Sociology,* Vol. 67, No. 2, 1952 (also reprinted in Tom Lupton (ed.), *Payment Systems,* Penguin Modern Management Read ngs, 1972).

STINT. An allotted **task,** either in amount of work to be done, or in time to be taken, or both. In coalmining, said originally to have been applied to a length of face allocated under the contract system; now applied to a length of face irrespective of method of payment, or generally to any given task. **Stint wage system;** a **job-and-finish** arrangement in which a daily task is assigned and in which the worker is free to go home when this is completed. **Stint system;** a method alleged to have been used in the shoe repairing trade to avoid the Trade Boards Act by setting a stint and bonus to produce a lower average rate per piece than the piece price fixed by the Trade Board; Denning, *New Survey of London Life and Labour,* P.S. King, 1931, pp. 179-80.

STINT SYSTEM; see **stint**.

STINT WAGE SYSTEM; see **stint**.

STOPPAGE or **stoppage of work.** Usually applied in instances where work ceases because of a **strike,** a **lock-out** or other industrial action (see *Engineering Industry, Terms of Settlement,* 1898, 6; 'there shall be no stoppage of work, either of a partial or general character, but work shall proceed meantime under the current conditions'); also used more generally to describe a cessation of work from causes unconnected with a strike, e.g. from air raids (**Sheet Trade Board,** *Minute No. 882,* 30 July 1941).

STOPPAGE OF WORK; see **stoppage**.

STRAIGHT PIECEWORK; see **piecework**.

STRAP. Credit; the payment of wages by building up credit (hence **strap book** and **strap system**), a further stage beyond the payment of wages in goods. Both practices were made illegal by the **Truck Acts** (q.v.) E. Hopwood, *A History of the Lancashire Cotton Industry and the Amalgamated Weavers' Association* AWA, 1969, p. 120.

STRAP BOOK; see **strap**.

STRAP SYSTEM; see **strap.**

STRATFORD AND SON v. LINDLEY (1965) AC 269. A leading case in which the Watermen's Union, having been denied recognition by BK Ltd, and this recognition having been given to the **Transport and General Workers' Union,** placed an embargo on a barge company which was a subsidiary of BK, and controlled by the same person, Mr J.C. Stratford. The House of Lords rejected the view that the defendants had acted in contemplation or furtherance of a **trade dispute,** on the grounds that there was no live 'dispute', that it was not about terms and conditions of employment, and the element of union rivalry in the case was so large as to cause it to fall outside the terms of s. 5(3) of the **Trade Disputes Act 1906;** see K.W. Wedderburn, *Cases and Materials on Labour Law,* CUP, 1967, p. 405 and p. 478. The case followed that of **Rookes v. Barnard** and was followed by **Morgan v. Fry,** all of which contributed to questioning about the courts' interpretation of the 1906 Act.

STRETCH OUT. A form of **speed up** in which workers are required to take on additional responsibilities, especially in minding more machines when these become more automatic in operation, e.g. in the textile or engineering industries, without a corresponding increase in rates or earnings.

STRIKE. A refusal of employees to continue working; a withdrawal of labour or **stoppage of work** when this is associated with such a withdrawal, action taking the form either of concerted non-attendance at work, of leaving the job or the workplace (**walk-out**), of workers remaining at their places but doing no work (**sit-down strike** or **stay-down strike**), or of other similar methods, the object usually being to secure an improvement, or to resist a worsening, in the terms and conditions of work of the workers concerned, or to achieve similar results for other workers, e.g. by **sympathetic strike;** a shortened form of to 'strike work' (by analogy with striking a mast or sail), or to 'strike off work' (presumably a variation on to 'knock off work') the former being first recorded in use in the late eighteenth century (*Annual Register* 107, 9 May 1768) and the latter in the early nineteenth century (*Home Office Papers,* 1819); see also **bumper strike, constitutional strike, general strike, irritation strike, lightning strike, official strike, pearl strike, propensity to strike, token**

strike, **unconstitutional strike, unofficial strike, wildcat strike;** also **right to strike.** The word 'strike' appears at first to have been understood to include **lock-outs** by employers as well as withdrawals of labour by employees, the two expressions becoming separated in the mid-nineteenth century (see K.C.J.C. Knowles, *Strikes,* Basil Blackwell, 1952, the principal historical study of British strikes). Current definitions of strikes fall into three broad categories, those reflecting general usage, those adopted for statistical purposes, and those relating to legal enactments. General usage tends to regard as a strike any wilful act of non-co-operation with authority, whether relating to terms or conditions of work or not, whether by individuals or groups, organised or unorganised, and whether or not involving a complete withdrawal of labour; hence, under the last point some forms of **ca'canny, working-to-rule,** and even **restrictive practices,** may be thought of as strikes, and under the first it is unlikely that 'industrial strikes' will be sharply distinguished from **political strikes** (q.v.). Statistical definitions vary, but normally emphasise the types of industrial action which are more easily enumerated, and their effects measured, in terms of workers involved, working days lost, etc. Hence they usually, but not invariably, record withdrawals of labour rather than **restrictions, ca'canny, working without enthusiasm** and other similar actions; frequently they attempt also to exclude political strikes. Data published by the **Department of Employment** are supplied by regional and local officials and seek only to record stoppages involving more than ten workers or those lasting more than one day, unless the aggregate number of working days lost exceeds 100, political disputes being excluded; it includes both strikes and lock-outs, though the latter are relatively few in number. The Department's statistics do not, therefore, include 'very small' strikes, **go-slows** or other restrictions (the latter no doubt because of lack of precise definition and therefore the possibility of measurement); nor, since there is no obligation on employers to report stoppages of work, is it certain how many of the total stoppages occurring in the country are in fact recorded in the statistics. For a commentary on this and other issues arising from stoppages of work; see R. Hyman, *Strikes,* Fontana-/Collins, 1972. The **Industrial Relations Act 1971,** (now repealed) defined a strike as 'a concerted stoppage of work by a group of workers in contemplation or furtherance of an **industrial dispute'** (now a **trade dispute**), and attempted to cast the net even wider by designating all other actions tantamount to striking but not actually involving a complete withdrawal of labour as **irregular industrial actions short of a strike**, as well as establishing **national emergency procedures** for a third class of strikes likely to injure the national economy, create serious risk of public disorder or endanger lives. These distinctions have lapsed with the repeal of the Act in 1974. To some extent they reflected anxieties about the strike proneness of British industry which grew up in the later 1950s and in the 1960s and which were one reason for the setting up of the Donovan **Royal Commission on Trade Unions and Employers' Associations, 1965-1968.** While it was widely asserted in the earlier of these periods that there had been a world-wide 'withering away of the strike' since the second world war (see, for example, Arthur M. Ross and Paul T. Hartman, *Changing Patterns of Industrial Conflict,* John Wiley, 1960) British experience showed a growth of short and usually unofficial and unconstitutional strike action of a kind not experienced elsewhere and this was continued into the 1960s, being attributed by some during the period of the cold war to systematic subversion (e.g. in Harry Welton, *The Third World War,* Pall Mall Press, 1959) at shop floor level, and by the **Donovan Commission** (para. 454) principally to the inadequacies of industrial relations practice at company and plant level; see also H.A. Turner, *Is Britain Really Strike Prone?,* CUP, 1959 and W.E.J. McCarthy, 'The Nature of Britain's Strike Problem', *British Journal of Industrial Relations,* Vol. 8, No. 2, July 1970 for discussion of international strike statistics and the situation in general; also A.I. Marsh, E.O. Evans and P. Garcia, *Workplace Industrial Relations in Engineering,* EEF and Kogan Page, 1971 and *Department of Employment Gazette,* November 1976 and January 1978, for evidence of the concentration of strikes in that industry in a small proportion of establishments. On the further growth of strikes both of a workplace and industry-wide character since 1968, and on the unpredictability of strike trends, see Michael Silver, 'Recent British Strike Trends: A Factual Analysis', *British Journal of Industrial Relations,* Vol. XI, No. 1, March 1973, pp. 66-104; see also E.W. Evans (ed.), *Industrial Conflict in Britain,* Frank Cass 1977; see also **sit-in** and **picketing** for recent developments in these prac-

tices and **state subsidy theory of strikes.**

STRIKE BALLOT. A ballot of members of a trade union to determine whether or not a strike should be called. Many British trade unions provide in their rules for strike ballots in certain circumstances, the best known, perhaps, being that of the **National Union of Mineworkers;** in most industries their use declined in the 1950s and 1960s, in part because of the prevalence of **unconstitutional** and **unofficial strikes.** To avoid this, and in the belief that trade union members would frequently vote against strike action if given the opportunity, proposals have sometimes been made to make secret ballots compulsory *before* strike action. The Donovan **Royal Commission on Trade Unions and Employers' Associations 1965-68** (Cmnd. 3623, June 1968, para. 426 *et seq.*) rejected this view on the grounds that a law to this effect could not be administered in the case of the prevalent small-scale unofficial stoppages, that there was nothing to suggest that workers would be less likely to vote for strike action than their leaders, and that they might make disputes harder to settle. The **Industrial Relations Act 1971** (now repealed) adopted strike ballots in national emergency disputes (see **national emergency procedures**). In the industrial relations climate of the later 1970s there has been some return to balloting habits among trade unions, but legislative proposals to enforce such procedures seem to have lost credibility. See also K.G.J.C. Knowles, *Strikes,* Basil Blackwell, 1952.

STRIKE BENEFIT. Dispute benefit (q.v.).

STRIKE PAY. Dispute benefit (q.v.).

STRIKE SOCIETY; see **trade protection society.**

STRIKEBREAKING. Attempts to defeat strike action by systematic intimidation, by the hiring of professional or organised strikebreakers, or by other methods not countenanced by normal collective bargaining, and usually having as their subject the destruction of trade union organisation. Strikebreaking organisations of **free labourers** were to be found in Britain before and after the first world war and during the period of the **General Strike;** see K.G.J.C. Knowles, *Strikes,* Basil Blackwell, 1952, pp. 125-31. The existence of **blacklegs** (q.v.) may sometimes suggest strikebreaking in a systematic sense, and sometimes not.

STRIKE-IN-DETAIL. A term used by Sidney and Beatrice Webb (*Industrial Democracy,* 1913 ed., p. 169) to describe the trade union technique of harassing unco-operative employers by continually withdrawing small groups of men, or individuals, and so increasing labour turnover and costs. J.E. Mortimer (*History of the AESD,* AESD, 1960, p. 40) uses the expression to mean 'arranging for the gradual withdrawal of labour, accompanied by posting the offending firm on the **vacancy list** (q.v.)'. K.G.J.C. Knowles (*Strikes,* Basil Blackwell, 1952, p. 12) thinks that the term is sometimes confused with **bumper strike** (q.v.).

STRUCTURAL UNEMPLOYMENT. Unemployment resulting from shifts in the relative supply and demand for labour in particular regions and industries, as distinct from unemployment of other kinds, e.g. **frictional unemployment, seasonal unemployment,** etc. Structural unemployment may be associated with a number of factors, e.g. falling demand for a product, coal and ships, for example, and hence with decline in the coalmining and shipbuilding industries; with the exhaustion of raw materials (for example, iron ore); with foreign competition (for example in cotton textiles); with taxation or other policies (for example, **Selective Employment Tax,** which is claimed to have reduced employment in the distributive trades by 9.4 per cent and in miscellaneous services by 17.7 per cent between June 1966 and June 1970), technological change (hence **technological unemployment**); see **automation;** see also **assisted areas.**

STUC. Scottish Trades Union Congress (q.v.).

STUDENT APPRENTICE; see **apprenticeship.**

SUBBING. An interim payment made to payment by results workers whose period of settlement is longer than one week. Subbing is usually done at time rate, payment being assessed against the final settlement of the job (engineering industry).

SUBSISTENCE THEORY OF WAGES. A supply theory of wages which asserted that the price of labour depended upon the cost to society of 'enabling labourers to subsist and perpetuate their race' (David Ricardo, 1772-1823). It relied for its validity upon the law of population propounded by Robert Malthus (1766-1834); see D.V. Glass (ed.), *Introduction to Malthus,* Watts and Co., 1953) which implied that labour supply would increase indefinitely if the price rose above subsistence level, increased supply then leading to a fall in price back to the same level. Attempts by labourers to improve their real wages could therefore only be temporary; they were therefore constrained by the **iron law of wages.** The iron law was to some extent modified in Ricardian thinking by the admission that the level of subsistence might change as a result of habit or custom, and that new 'subsistence' standards might therefore emerge in an 'improving society'; such an admission suggesting to economists, and particularly to John Stuart Mill (1806-1873) a somewhat more flexible **wages-fund theory** (q.v.); see Maurice Dobb, *Wages,* Nisbet, 1956, and **wage theories.**

SUBSTANTIVE AGREEMENT; see **substantive terms.**

SUBSTANTIVE TERMS. Terms of a collective agreement which refer to rates of pay or other matters of remuneration, or to the application of specific conditions of work (such as the duration of holidays and the payment to be made for them), or to the application of fringe benefits of a similar kind which, taken together, form a **substantive agreement;** usually contrasted with **procedural terms** (q.v.), i.e. terms of a collective agreement concerned with regulating conflict between the parties which make up a procedural or **procedure agreement.** Allan Flanders (*Industrial Relations: What is Wrong with the System?,* Institute of Personnel Management and Faber & Faber 1965, pp. 11-12) regards procedural terms (or rules) as regulating the behaviour of the parties to agreements and those who act on their behalf and substantive terms (or rules) as regulating jobs, i.e. the behaviour of employees as parties to individual contracts of employment, both types of rules being concerned with status. It is clear, however, that procedural terms may include substantive elements (such as those providing for **facilities** or payment **for shop stewards**), that substantive terms may be regarded as providing structures as well as individual job regulation (as where methods of payment are concerned), and that in the context of a single situation, the roles of both types of rules may be far from easy to disentangle (see **Royal Commission on Trade Unions and Employers Associations, 1965-68,** Cmnd. 3623, June 1968, p. 49; also J.T. Dunlop, *Industrial Relations Systems,* Henry Holt, 1958).

SUBSTITUTION ALLOWANCE. An allowance paid to an employee of one grade for performing temporarily the duties of a higher grade, e.g. when an employee of the higher grade is sick or on holiday, secondment etc., or **substitution pay** (e.g. United Kingdom Atomic Energy Authority, *Handbook of Rules and Agreements,* 1971, D. 19).

SUBSTITUTION PAY; see **substitution allowance.**

SUGGESTION SCHEME. A method of encouraging and rewarding employees for putting forward ideas for improving efficiency, devising new methods, reducing costs, eliminating waste, conserving time and materials and preventing accidents. Schemes are usually thought of as having two objectives, the one direct - increase in output or profits, reduction of costs and better quality, for example, and the other indirect - the improvement of worker-management relations; see The Industrial Society, *Successful Suggestion Schemes,* Eyre and Spottiswoode Ltd, 1971. Recent critics have argued that suggestion schemes may weaken organisational channels by encouraging the by-passing of foremen, and may have a potentially dangerous effect on relationships within the work group; see C.T. Young, 'Suggestion Schemes, Boon or Bane?', *Personnel Journal,* Vol. 42, 1963, p. 130 *et seq.* C.G. Gorfin, 'The Suggestion Scheme: A Contribution to Morale or an Economic Transaction?', *British Journal of Industrial Relations,* Vol. VII, No. 3, November 1969, pp. 368-84, argues that both critics and advocates may be right, depending on the success of management in designing schemes which express the type of worker participation desired and tailor rewards to expectations. The National Institute of Industrial Psychology (*Joint Consultation in British Industry,* Staples Press, 1952, Ch. 16) has suggested that the large number of failures with schemes is due less to insufficient awards than to such psychological factors as the involvement of workers in running them, the support given by middle management and foremen, lack of advice to overcome workers' hesitations on technical presentation, and so on.

SUMMARY DISMISSAL. Termination of a contract of employment without notice, or **instant dismissal.** Summary dismissal is ordinarily a breach of contract unless there are grounds which the law regards as sufficient to justify termination, and these are likely to include dishonesty and persistent misconduct. At common law an employer is not required to give any reason for dismissal, it being open for the person dismissed to take an action for **wrongful dismissal;** nor is the employer required to follow any particular procedure, or give any reference or testimonial. The **Industrial Relations Act 1971,** however, introduced the concept of **unfair dismissal** and this, the **Industrial Relations Code of Practice** (q.v.) and subsequent legislation have encouraged the giving of reasons and the development of **dismissal procedures;** see B.A. Hepple and P. O'Higgins, *Employment Law,* Sweet and Maxwell, 1976, p. 194 *et seq.,* for a summary of the situation. In the case of **apprentices,** a reason sufficient to justify summary dismissal of an ordinary worker does not suffice. In the absence of an express term permitting summary dismissal for misconduct, the employer's only remedy is to sue the apprentice for breach of contract, or terminate the contract if he is unable to perform his part of it (op. cit., p. 209-210); see also **industrial misconduct.**

SUPERANNUATION. A **retirement pension,** or scheme for providing for old age or retirement, provided by the state or by private or public industry (see **occupational pension schemes**), or by a trade union, making allowance for **superannuation benefit.** In 1965, 71 registered trade unions with a membership of 3.18 millions were spending money on superannuation benefits, though the importance of such schemes has over a long period declined as other forms of superannuation have grown; see Arthur Marsh and Peter Cope, 'The Anatomy of Trade Union Benefits in the 1960s', *Industrial Relations Journal,* Summer 1970. The **Industrial Relations Act 1971,** Sch. 5, Part III, following the recommendation of the **Donovan Commission,** provided that superannuation schemes of **registered trade unions** and **employers' associations** should be examined by a qualified actuary. This provision was retained for trade unions and employees' associations in the **Trade Union and Labour Relations Act 1974,** Sch. 2, Part 2, para. 23. The **Certification Officer** has power to exempt a scheme from actuarial examination if the number of members involved is too small, or for any other special reason, all the schemes must be reported to him and maintain for such a scheme a separate fund.

SUPERANNUATION BENEFIT; see **superannuation.**

SUPERCUT. An economy measure announced in July 1921 reducing the bonuses on all Civil Service salaries in excess of £500 by varying sums depending on the amount by which they exceeded that level. The cut, taken without consultation with the National Whitley Council, was confirmed by the Industrial Court in 1925 and was extended until consolidation of Civil Service salaries and bonuses in 1934; see L.D. White, *Whitley Councils in the British Civil Service,* Chicago University Press, 1933, pp. 126-30.

SUPERSTRUCTURE. Payments or bonuses made at plant level over and above those laid down in national agreement (chemical industry) Pramod Verma, 'The Chemical Industry', Ch. 3 in S.W. Lerner, J.R. Cable and S. Gupta (eds), *Workshop Wage Determination,* Pergamon Press, 1969.

SUPERVISOR. Defined by the Department of Employment (Ministry of Labour, *Glossary of Training Terms,* HMSO, 1967) as 'a person at the first or second level of the total managerial structure who is in charge, whether directly or indirectly, of a particular area of operations within the organisation, and who is regularly found in that area. He is normally responsible for making the most efficient use of the resources of men, materials and machines available to him'. The definitional problem is concerned principally with the meaning of the word 'supervise' and the limits to be set to it. At the lower end a **leading hand** or a **working chargehand** may have some supervisory responsibility, but is also an operative; at the upper end a 'manager' is usually distinguished from a supervisor (National Institute of Industrial Psychology, *The Foreman: a Study of Supervision in British Industry,* Staples Press, 1951, p. 16). There is general agreement that nearness to the working group or the shop floor, and more immediate and direct control of labour are characteristics of supervisors; see, for example, Ministry of Labour, *Report of the Committee on the Selection and Training of Supervisors,* HMSO 1962 and K.E. Thurley and A.C. Hamlin, *The Supervisor*

and His Job, Problems of Progress in Industry, No. 13, HMSO, 1963, p. 5. The latter distinguish three levels of supervision, **semi-supervisors** (leading toolsetters, senior process men, head girl, technical assistants), **first-line supervisors** (the working group's immediate boss; **chargehand** or **foreman**), and the **second-line supervisor** who directs the supervisory system and links it with higher management; supervisory foremen, shift engineer) distinguishing these from management in that they exercise control by 'actually overseeing' rather than by administrative methods. Other observers have doubts about limits. Joan Woodward (*Industrial Organisation and Practice,* OUP, 1965, pp. 26-7), notes that many clerical and technical staff supervise, and defines a first line supervisor for research purposes, as 'the first line of authority spending more than 50 per cent of the time on supervisory duties' and including usually the foreman, but, in some cases, the working chargehand or non-working chargehand. K. McCullough (*Department of Employment and Productivity Gazette,* October 1969, p. 504), regards the distinction between a manager and a supervisor as mainly one of social status and, despite technological implications, hierarchical considerations, and confusions of nomenclature on the workshop floor, superfluous. Supervisory styles have been much discussed in recent years, with some indication that 'democratic' supervision achieves better results than 'autocratic'; for consideration of this and other problems see A.F. Donovan, *Management of Supervisors,* Macmillan, 1971, also K. Thurley and H. Wirdenius, *Supervision: A Reappraisal,* Heinemann, 1973.

SUPERVISORY AND EXECUTIVE ENGINEERS, ASSOCIATION OF (ASEE). A trade union registered under the **Industrial Relations Act 1971** and recruiting engineers not belonging to one of the constituent organisations of the Council of Engineering Institutions, 'but who may hold positions of comparable responsibility'. The ASEE transferred its engagements to the January 1977 Electrical Power Engineers' Association in January 1977; see **Engineers and Managers' Association.**

SUPERVISORY MANAGEMENT, INSTITUTE OF (ISM). A professional institute for supervisors, formed in 1944 as the Institute of Industrial Supervisors, and taking its present title in March 1966.

The Institute awards membership in various grades - Student, Graduate, Associate Member, Member and Fellow, and is closely involved in job directed training and education, including courses in aspects of industrial relations. *Headquarters:* King Edward House, New Street, Birmingham 2. *Tel:* 021-643 7845.

SUPERVISORY STUDIES NATIONAL EXAMINATION BOARD IN (NEBSS).

An independent body established in June 1964 on the initiative of the Department of Education and Science to provide examinations in the field of foremanship and supervisory studies, including industrial relations. The Board encourages technical colleges and industrial and commercial undertakings to devise suitable courses and examinations to meet specific needs while establishing and maintaining national standards. Courses are approved by the Board for the award of the Certificate, Supplementary Certificate and Advanced Certificate in Supervisory Studies on the basis of internal examinations assessed by the Board; the Board formerly set its own external examinations for other colleges and undertakings but these were phased out in 1972. *Address:* 76 Portland Place, London W1N 4AA. *Tel:* 01-580 3050.

SURVIVAL CURVE.

A method of examining **labour turnover** (q.v.) by showing how many recruits to work in a given establishment survive after a given period of time - percentage leaving rates; see, for example, Hotel and Catering EDC, *Staff Turnover,* National Economic Development Office, 1969.

SUSPENSION.

The temporary lay-off of a worker, usually as a disciplinary measure, but sometimes also to allow time for consideration of a charge or incident in which he may have been involved, and which may result in penalty or dismissal. In the absence of express terms of contract (which may be set out in **works rules** or other documents), an employer has no right to suspend a worker without wages (**Hanley v. Pease and Partners** (1915) 1 KB 696), though the courts may regard an established practice of suspension in an establishment as of equivalent force (**Marshall v. English Electric Co. Ltd** (1945) 61 TLR 379; (1945) 1 All ER 653); see also **Bird v. British Celanese.** According to the **Employment Protection Act 1975** an employee with more than four weeks' service is entitled to be paid while suspended for a period not exceeding 26 weeks on medical grounds in a number of situations specified in Schedule 2 to the Act on any provision of a Code of Practice issued under the **Health and Safety at Work Act 1974.** It is not clear how wide a range of circumstances this provision covers.

SWAINE v. WILSON (1899) 24 QBD 252; see **benefits.**

SWEAR WORD DISPUTE.

Applied especially to a dispute at Deep Duffryn Colliery, South Wales in 1965. A swearing incident between a deputy and a young workman on 21 April led to a walk-out of colliers and later to a strike of under-officials. The difference was subject to an Inquiry by Mr J.G. Picton and a report published dated 12 August 1965.

SWEATING also **sweated labour, sweated trades, greeners** (q.v.), **sweating system, sweating masters, sweatshops.** Sweating was classically defined by the House of Lords Select Committee on the Sweating System (*Fifth report,* HL No. 62, 1890, p. xliii) as a combination of three evils - 'a rate of wages inadequate to the necessities of the workers or disproportionate to the work done, excessive hours of labour, and the insanitary state of the houses in which the work is carried on'. It was often associated with home work. Popular concern about the exploitation of workers by sweating grew in the 1880s and 1890s, partly as a result of public and private inquiries in the 1900s and partly because of the publicity attracted by the National **Anti-Sweating League** formed after the Sweated Industries Exhibition held in 1906. This resulted in the **Trade Boards Act** of 1909; **Wages Councils** (q.v.); see B.L. Hutchins, *Home Work and Sweating: the Causes and the Remedies,* 1907; F.J. Bayliss, *British Wages Councils,* Basil Blackwell, 1962, Chapter I, and for the USA, Thomas S. Adams and Helen L. Sumner, *Labor Problems;* New York, Macmillan, 1912; E. Cadbury and G. Shann, *Sweating,* Headley Bros, 1907.

SWING SHIFT.

A crew of workers, sometimes known as the fourth shift, on some types of continuous three shift systems; see **three shift system.** The name derives from the need to have at least one shift, and in some systems, all four shifts, rotating to different days and hours at specified intervals.

SYMPATHETIC STRIKES, also known

as **sympathy strikes** and **secondary strikes.** Stoppages of work or **boycotts** declared, not on account of a dispute in which the strikers are directly concerned, but in sympathy with other workers engaged in a dispute in which the secondary strikers may have no immediate interest or benefit. Sympathetic strikes may simply be an assertion of solidarity, but they may sometimes have political or economic motives; see K.G.J.C. Knowles, *Strikes,* Basil Blackwell, 1952, p. 17 *et seq.*

SYMPATHY STRIKE; see sympathetic strikes.

SYNDICALISM. A form of **workers' control** (q.v.). Syndicalist doctrine was first evolved in France at the end of the last century, and chiefly held that workers' emancipation could be achieved only by means of revolutionary industrial action, political and parliamentary methods being completely rejected. Syndicalism had a great impact in France, particularly through the General Confederation of Trade Unions. Tom Mann, formerly an advocate of **industrial unionism** (q.v.) became the principal advocate of British syndicalism after 1910, advocating 'a condition of society where industry will be controlled by those engaged therein on the basis of free societies, these to co-operate for the production of all the requirements of life in the most efficient manner, and the distribution of the same with the truest equity, a society in which Parliaments and Governments will have disappeared, having served their purpose with the capitalist system'; *From the Single Tax to Syndicalism,* p. xv. The doctrine was reflected particularly among railwaymen and in *The Miners' Next Step,* 1912 (Dent, 1973). In its purest form it was short lived and overtaken by more reformist movements such as **Guild Socialism** (q.v.), but it had its reflections in such developments as the Busmen's Unofficial Reform Movement in the late 1930s (see H.A. Clegg, *Labour Relations in London Transport,* Basil Blackwell, 1950); see Branko Pribićević, *The Shop Stewards' Movement and Workers' Control, 1910-1922,* Basil Blackwell, 1959.

SYNTHETIC DATA; see synthetic times.

SYNTHETIC TIMES. Times arrived at by statistical methods for basic human motions and used in **predetermined motion time systems** (q.v.); provided as **synthetic data,** i.e. as tables and formulae derived from the analysis of accumulated work measurement information, arranged in a form suitable for building up **standard times,** machine process times, synthetically.

SYSTEMATIC OVERTIME; see overtime.

T

TAFF VALE CASE. Taff Vale Railway Company v. Amalgamated Society of Railway Servants (1901) AC 426, in which the House of Lords held that the ASRS, a trade union registered under the **Trade Union Act 1871** could be sued in its registered name for the torts of its servants or agents. The action was brought against the union in its registered name and against two of its officials, for an injunction and damages in respect of picketing and persuasion of blacklegs engaged by the company in order to break a strike, to breach their contracts of employment and go home. The case was a blow to the trade union movement in that the provisions of the Trade Union Act 1871 were thought to be inconsistent with an intention to incorporate registered unions or to make their funds generally liable. The **Trade Disputes Act 1906** systematically reversed the Taff Vale decision and others (see **conspiracy**), restoring the general immunity of union funds, not only in respect of tortious acts during trade disputes, but against liability for any tort; K.W. Wedderburn, *Cases and Materials on Labour Law,* CUP, 1967, p. 541, *et seq.*

TAFT-HARTLEY ACT 1947. The **Labour-Management Relations Act** of 1947 in the United States of America. Taft-Hartley was the first major revision of the **Wagner Act 1935.** It attempted to equalise power between the parties by providing a number of union **unfair labor practices** to parallel those for which employers were liable under the Wagner Act, and limited **union security** provisions by outlawing the **closed shop** and the automatic **check-off,** substituting for them a form of **union shop** in certain circumstances. It also provided special machinery for dealing with national emergency disputes, including the use of an injunction for approximately 80 days during which time a Board of Inquiry would attempt to provide information on the basic issues of a dispute, and hold ballots on the employer's last offer, the so-called **cooling off period**; see Harold W. Davey, 'The Operational Impact of the Taft-Hartley Act upon Collective Bargaining Relationships', in H.W. Davey, H.S. Kaltenborn and S.H. Ruttenberg (eds), *New Dimensions in Collective Bargaining*, Harper, 1959; C.W. Summers, 'A Summary Evaluation of the Taft-Hartley Act', *Industrial and Labor Relations Review*, April 1958; L. Spielman, 'The Taft-Hartley Law: Its Effects on the Growth of the Labor Movement', *Labor Law Journal*, April 1962.

TAILORS AND GARMENT WORKERS, NATIONAL UNION OF (NUTGW). A trade union originating in the numerous organisations of tailors and tailoresses established in the nineteenth century. These gave rise to craft amalgamations and also to the Amalgamated Union of Clothing Operatives (1895), the first national organisation for all workers in the industry, which subsequently changed its name to the United Garment Workers in 1916, was joined by the Scottish Operative Tailors and Tailoresses Union four years later, and adopted its present title in 1931, when it was joined by the craft based Amalgamated Society of Tailors and Tailoresses. The growth of the union has been closely involved with the institution of statutory collective bargaining through **Trade Boards** and **Wages Councils** (q.v.). It now places emphasis on the establishment of voluntary collective bargaining in the clothing industry. It claims to have in membership approximately one-third of the labour force. In 1972 it amalgamated with the **Waterproof Garment Workers' Trade Union** which had at that time about 700 members. F.W. Galton, *Select Documents Illuminating the History of Trade Unionism; The Tailoring Trade*, 1896. Margaret Stewart and Leslie Hunter, *The Needle is Threaded*, Heinemann, 1964. *Address*: Radlett House, West Hill, Aspley Guise, Milton Keynes, MK17 8DT. *Tel*: 0908 583099. *TUC Affiliated Membership, 1977*: 112,783.

TAINTED GOODS. Goods used, manufactured, processed or carried by employers with whom a trade union or trade unions are in dispute, and which may therefore be subject to **blacking** (q.v.). William O'Brien (*Forth the Banners Go: Reminiscences of William O'Brien*, as told to Edward Maclysaght, The Three Candles Ltd, 1969, pp. 46-7)

recalls that during a strike of timber workers in 1911, business was carried on by blacklegs, 'when a consignment of timber was sent to the Kingsbridge railway station the railwaymen refused to touch it, describing it as "tainted goods". That was the first time, so far as I can remember, that that description was used'; see also **black goods, boycott.**

TAKE-HOME PAY. The amount of pay which a worker actually receives in his pay or salary check; gross earnings less tax deducted on Pay As You Earn, national insurance contribution, etc, and any other authorised **deductions** (see also **Truck** Acts).

TAKEOVERS; see **multi-establishment companies.**

TALKING MONEY. A pay increase demanded by a trade union as a preliminary to, or as a condition of, co-operation in negotiation, particularly in **productivity bargaining**; similar to, but not identical with, **payment on account** (q.v.).

TAPERED INCREASE; see **tapering.**

TAPERING. The application of increases in wages or salaries in such a way that those at lower levels of income receive greater proportionate advances than those at higher levels, in the interest of greater income equality; **tapered increases**; see Barbara Wootton, *The Social Foundations of Wage Policy*, George Allen and Unwin, 1962, p. 177 for a discussion of the use of tapering in **wage policy**, and National Board for Prices and Incomes, for recommendations as to methods for dealing with low pay in Report No. 27 (*Retail Drapery, Outfitting and Footwear Trades*, Cmnd. 3224, March 1967) and Report No. 10 (*Clothing Manufacturing Industries*, Cmnd. 4002, April 1969); see also **pro tanto settlement.**

TASK. An allotted, given or expected piece of work: a **stint**. A major element of work or a combination of elements of work by which a specific result is achieved (Ministry of Labour, *Glossary of Training Terms*, 1967). **Task analysis**, the analysis of tasks for the purpose of improving working methods, of developing vocational guidance and selection, and especially to break down jobs for the purposes of training (Department of Employment, *Task Analysis*, Training Information

Paper No. 6, HMSO, June 1971); see also **task bonus system, taskworker.**

TASK ANALYSIS; see **task.**

TASK BONUS SYSTEM. Any system of **payment by results**, or **incentive payment system**, in which bonus is paid on the basis of time saved, the task being set by work study methods; hence sometimes identified with **premium bonus plans** or **systems**. Also loosely applied to situations in which workers may be paid a bonus on completion of given tasks.

TASKWORKER. (1) A worker employed on a **task bonus system** (q.v.). (2) A worker who is paid to perform a specific task, e.g. formerly in the coal industry; '. . . a person whose normal work is assessed in other than units of time and who receives for performing a specific task per shift a fixed and predetermined sum of money which has been commuted by reference to piecework and to which a completion of task bonus may or may not be added'; *Daywage Structure Agreement,* Schedule, Part A, 3(iv)(b), 1955.

TASS. Sometime used as a further abbreviation of AUEW/TASS, the Technical and Supervisory Section of the **Amalgamated Union of Engineering Workers**, formerly known as the **Draughtsmen's and Allied Technicians' Association** (q.v.).

TAVISTOCK INSTITUTE OF HUMAN RELATIONS. An institute founded in 1946 and incorporated in 1947, to study human relations in the family, the work group and the larger organisation, with the general intention of contributing to the health and effectiveness of individuals, families and organisations by application of the social and psychological sciences. The Institute works through five units, three of which (the Centre for Applied Social Research, the Human Resources Centre and the Institute for Operational Research), do work of direct concern in industrial relations including **labour turnover**, selection, attitudes, and motivation, ecology of work, career and individual development, **industrial democracy** (q.v.), etc. *Address*: Tavistock Centre, Belsize Lane, London NW3. *Tel*: 01-435 7111.

TAYLOR DIFFERENTIAL PIECE-RATE PLAN; see **differential piece-rate plan.**

TAYLORISM. A philosophy of management, and particularly of motivation and incentives, associated with the name and practice of F.W. Taylor (1856-1915); another name for **scientific management** (q.v.).

TEACHERS, NATIONAL UNION OF (NUT). The largest teachers' union in Britain. The union functions both as a trade union and a professional organisation. It was founded at a meeting of 100 teachers at King's College, London, on 25 June 1870. Among its early successes were the ending of payment by results for teachers in 1895, the gaining of security of tenure and, after the foundation of the **Burnham Committee** (q.v.) in 1919, a national salary scale. The union was the first to reject the notion that it was necessary to segregate elementary and secondary teachers into separate organisations, and has campaigned for extension of educational opportunities both in relation to the Education Act 1944 and subsequently. It has also been in favour of **equal pay** for women, the lengthening of teacher training, raising of the school leaving age, and against the cutting of educational expenditure, with the ultimate object of an all-graduate profession, with a four-year course of training for teachers. At Easter 1970, after a militant campaign for higher salaries, the union took the decision to ask for affiliation to the **Trades Union Congress** and has more recently compaigned against education cuts and oversized classes; see Walter Roy, *The Teachers' Union,* Schoolmaster Publishing Co., 1968; Richard Bourne and Brian Macarthur, *A Struggle for Education,* Schoolmaster Publishing Company, 1970. *Address*: Hamilton House, Mabledon Place, London WC1H 9BD. *Tel*: 01-387 2442. *TUC Affiliated Membership, 1977*: 289,107.

TEACHERS IN TECHNICAL INSTITUTIONS, ASSOCIATION OF (ATTI). A trade union founded in 1906 to promote and safeguard the professional interests of teachers in technical institutions on such matters as tenure, pensions, registration, training and qualifications, and schemes of examination and inspection, and to lay their views before education authorities and the public. See D. Farnham, 'The Association of Teachers in Technical Institutions (1904-14)' *International Review of Social History,* Vol. XIX, 1974, Part 3. The Northern Union of Teachers in Technical Institutions was dissolved in 1969.

The union amalgamated in 1976 with the Association of Teachers in Colleges and Departments of Education to form the **National Association of Teachers in Further and Higher Education** (q.v.).

TECHNICIAN. Workers carrying out functions intermediate between scientists and technologists on the one hand and craftsmen and operatives on the other, whether in research or development, production, testing or maintenance (Ministry of Labour, *Glossary of Training Terms*, 1967). Functions and duties are defined by the Ministry (*The Metal Industries*, Manpower Studies No. 2, 1965) as including the application of proved techniques, the supervision of craftsmen, and the experience and knowledge to undertake engineering work and to work with qualified scientists, appropriate qualifications including Higher National Diploma, Higher National Certificate, Ordinary National Diploma, Ordinary National Certificate, City and Guilds Technician Certificates and General Certificate of Education at advanced level. For an extended discussion of 'technician' and of the attitudes of technicians, particularly to trade unionism; see B. C. Roberts, Ray Loveridge and John Gennard, *Reluctant Militants*, Heinemann, 1972.

TECHNOLOGICAL UNEMPLOYMENT. Unemployment which results from changes in techniques of production which reduce the amount of labour required to make a particular product or article. Discussion on technological unemployment has tended to centre around **automation** (q.v.) especially in the United States. In the long run, and in the labour force as a whole, there is no evidence that automation in itself raises the level of unemployment significantly, though it may do so in the short run; see E. Clague and L. Greenberg, 'Employment', in J.T. Dunlop (ed.) *Automation and Technological Change*, Prentice-Hall, 1962; W. Buckingham, *Automation, Its Impact on Business and People*, Harper and Row, 1963; C.E. Silberman, *The Myths of Automation*, Harper and Row, 1966; see also **redundancy.** Technological unemployment can be regarded as a form of **structural unemployment** (q.v.).

TEMPORARILY STOPPED. A category of 'registered unemployed persons who, on the date of the [unemployment] count, are suspended from work by their employers on the understanding that they will shortly resume work' (*Ministry of Labour Gazette*, Vol. 76, Jan. 1968, p. 98); i.e. those out of work as a result of temporary **lay-off** (q.v.); see also **registered unemployed** and **wholly unemployed.**

TEMPORARILY UNATTACHED REGISTER; see **Aldington-Jones Report.**

TEMPORARY EMPLOYMENT SUBSIDY (TES). A scheme introduced by the Wilson government on 18 August 1975 to alleviate unemployment in **Assisted Areas** (Development Areas, Special Development Areas and Intermediate Areas) in which firms in industry and commerce prepared to defer planned redundancies affecting fifty or more are paid a weekly subsidy for a maximum period of time for each full-time job maintained. The scheme is voluntary and was originally intended to last for one year. Successive time extensions have been given and the scheme broadened to cover the whole country. It is claimed to have saved 224,000 jobs between August 1975 and March 1977 at a cost of £212 millions and to be one of the government's most effective measures for tackling high unemployment.

TEMPORARY RATE. A rate of pay set tentatively or provisionally for a job until a permanent rate has been determined, especially in the operation of an **incentive payment system** in which times and prices cannot be satisfactorily established until the job has been running for some time; sometimes known as **trial rates, experimental rates, pre-production rates**, depending on the terminology used in the particular trade or industry. The levels at which temporary rates are fixed, and arrangements about retrospective payment also vary from one situation to another.

TEMPORARY STAFF CONTRACTOR; see **Employment Business.**

TERM AGREEMENTS. Short for **fixed-term agreements** (q.v.).

TERMINAL ARBITRATION. Arbitration agreed by both parties to a collective agreement as the final or terminal step in a negotiating or grievance procedure; built-in final and **voluntary arbitration**, as distinct from arbitration which takes place *ad hoc* or from **compulsory arbitration** (q.v.). The phrase is commonly used in the United States of America, and rarely in Britain, though such arbitration arrangements are a feature of many negotiating bodies, particularly **joint industrial councils**; see also **Ince Plan.**

TERMINATION OF EMPLOYMENT; see **termination with notice, discharge, dismissal, dismissal with notice, abusive dismissal, unfair dismissal, lay-off, redundancy, dismissal procedure.** The International Labour Organisation's Termination of Employment Recommendation 1963 (No. 119) provides that 'termination of employment should not take place unless there is a valid reason . . . connected with the capacity or conduct of the worker or based upon the operational requirements of the undertaking, establishment or service', and lists certain things which, among others, are not to be regarded as valid reasons; these include union membership or participation in union activities outside working hours, or with the consent of the employer, within working hours, seeking office or acting as a workers' representative, filing in good faith a complaint against an employer alleging violation of laws and regulations, race, colour, sex, marital status, religion, political opinion, national extraction or social origin. Subject to certain reservations the British government accepted the Recommendation in December 1964 (Cmnd. 2548). Some of its provisions were incorporated into the **Industrial Relations Act 1971** and now in subsequent legislation, especially **unfair dismissal** (q.v.).

TERMINATION WITH NOTICE; see **dismissal with notice.**

TERMS AND CONDITIONS OF EMPLOYMENT ACT 1959, SECTION 8 (now repealed); see **Schedule 11 Claims.**

TES. Temporary Employment Subsidy (q.v.).

TESTON INDEPENDENT SOCIETY OF CRICKET BALL MAKERS; see **Cricket Ball Makers, Teston Independent Society of.**

TEXTILE AND ALLIED WORKERS, NATIONAL UNION OF (NUTAW). An amalgamation of district unions in the cotton industry dating in its present form from 1886. Until 1969 it was known as the National Association of Card, Blowing and Ring Room Operatives, the change of name being related to an interest in recruiting more generally in the textile industry.

In 1971 the **Textile Officials' Association** affiliated to the National Union and formed its Staff Section; see H.A. Turner, *Trade Union Growth, Structure and Policy,* Allen and Unwin, 1962 and Amalgamated Association of Card, Blowing and Ring Room Operatives, *After 50 Years; Golden Jubilee Souvenir, 1886-1936,* AACB and RRO, 1936. Later the Amalgamated Association of Operative Cotton Spinners also joined and finally in January 1974 the Amalgamated Weavers' Association, the whole union then being renamed the **Amalgamated Textile Workers' Union** (q.v.). Before the AWA Amalgamation NUTAW had a membership of about 20,000.

TEXTILE CRAFTSMEN, YORKSHIRE SOCIETY OF. A trade union in the wool textile industry formed in 1952 by an amalgamation of four unions: the Yorkshire Warp Twisters' Society, the Bradford Warp Dressers' Society, the Halifax Warp Dressers' Society and the Huddersfield Worsted and Woollen Warpers' Association. In 1968 the Textile Daymen and Cloth Pattern Makers' Association transferred its engagements to the Society and the Leeds and District Warp Dressers, Twisters and Kindred Trades Associates in 1975. The union was suspended from membership of the TUC by decision of the 1972 Congress for failing to comply with Congress policy of non-registration under the **Industrial Relations Act 1971** and has not since reaffiliated. *Address:* Textile Hall, Westgate, Bradford BD1 2RG. *Tel:* 0274 27965. *Membership 1977:* 998.

TEXTILE OFFICIALS' ASSOCIATION. A trade union, formerly independent, which affiliated to the Association of Supervisory Staffs, Executives and Technicians (now the **Association of Scientific, Technical and Managerial Staffs**), in 1948 and broke away again in the following year. Following the breakaway it was refused affiliation to the **Trades Union Congress** but later accepted into the **General Federation of Trade Unions** (1958). In 1971 it amalgamated with the **National Union of Textile and Allied Workers,** and is now the staff section of the **Amalgamated Textile Workers' Union** (q.v.). *Membership, end 1976:* 1,133.

TEXTILE TECHNICIANS, BRITISH FEDERATION OF (BFTT). An alliance between the **General Union of Loom Overlookers** (q.v.), the **Yorkshire Association of Power Loom Overlookers** (q.v.), and the **Scottish Union of Power Loom Over-lookers** (q.v.) formed in February 1971. All three unions are independently affiliated to the Trades Union Congress. The Federation is responsible for the determination of overall policy in negotiations for other matters for textile technicians represented by the three organisations. *Address*: Textile Hall, Westgate, Bradford, Yorkshire BD1 2RG. *Tel*: 0274 27966.

TEXTILE WAREHOUSE OPERATIVES AMALGAMATED. A textile trade union founded in 1895 and consisting of a number of branches with autonomy to settle their own affairs under the amalgamation's rules. Now part of the **Amalgamated Textile Workers' Union** and known as the Amalgamated Textile Warehouse Operatives Association. *Address*: 80 St. George's Road, Bolton BL1 2DD. *Tel*: 0204 25398.

TEXTILE WORKERS AND KINDRED TRADES, AMALGAMATED SOCIETY OF (ASTWKT). A trade union organising workers in the silk and textile trades predominantly in Leek, Macclesfield and Congleton, but also other parts of the country. The Society developed from the Leek Textile Federation (1907), which had seven affiliated unions: The Amalgamated Society of Silk Twisters (1866), the Associated Trimming Weavers' Society (1871), the Amalgamated Society of Silk Pickers (1884), the Amalgamated Society of Braid Workers and Kindred Trades (1889), the Leek Amalgamated Society of Silk and Cotton Dyers (1897), the Amalgamated Society of Women Workers (1906), and The Leek Spinners, Throwsters and Reelers' Union (1907). Of these unions, all but the Silk Twisters joined the Amalgamated Society on its foundation in 1919, the six unions being joined by the Leek Spun Silk Dressers' Union (1907), and the National Silk Workers' and Textile Trades (founded in 1903 as the Macclesfield Power Loom Silk Weavers), in 1965. Frank Birchill and J. Sweeney, *A History of Trade Unionism in the North Staffordshire Textile Industry*, 1971, Department of Adult Education, University of Keele. *Address*: Foxlowe, The Market Place, Leek, Staffs ST13 6AD. *Tel*: 0538 382068. *TUC Affiliated Membership, 1977*: 5,517.

TEXTILE WORKERS' UNION, AMALGAMATED (ATWU). A union representing workers in the spinning and weaving sector of the textile industry in North West England and formed as a result of a merger in January 1974 of the **National Union of Textile and Allied Workers** (q.v.) and the **Amalgamated Weavers' Association** (q.v.). The **Amalgamated Textile Warehouse Operatives** (q.v.) joined the amalgamation in 1976. It has a Staff Section deriving from the **Textile Officials' Association** (q.v.). *Address*: Textile Union Centre, 5 Caton Street, Rochdale, Lancs OL16 1QJ. *Tel*: 0706 59551 and 58367. *TUC Affiliated Membership, 1977*: 44,102.

T GROUP. An abbreviation for 'training group', involving methods also referred to as **sensitivity training, group dynamics,** and **group relations training,** i.e. methods whereby a group of people, often in isolation from their everyday environment, discuss their own relationships with each other. T Groups differ from other participative training methods in that the material for learning is derived from the interplay of relationships between the trainees themselves, making them less 'structured' than business games, role playing exercises, case study discussion, etc., in which situations are externally provided and their purposes prearranged. Their advocates claim that, given a favourable environment, T Groups can make significant improvements in individual sensitivity to the reactions of others, in perceiving the state of relationships between other people, and in the skill of acting as the situation requires; see P.B. Smith, *Improving Skills in Working with People*, Department of Employment and Productivity, Training Information Paper 4, HMSO, 1969; C.L. Cooper and I.L. Mangham (eds,) *T Groups; A Survey of Research*, Wiley-Interscience, 1971, and, for a short summary of the current research situation, P.B. Smith, 'Why Successful Groups Succeed: The Implications of T-Group Research', in C.L. Cooper (ed.), *Developing Social Skills in Managers*, Macmillan, 1976.

TGWU. Transport and General Workers' Union (q.v.).

THEATRICAL, TELEVISION AND KINE EMPLOYEES, THE NATIONAL ASSOCIATION OF (NATTKE). A trade union established in 1890 and incorporating the Cinema, Film Studio, Television Operatives and Projectionists. It has in membership workers in theatres, exhibitions, circuses, ballrooms and other places of public entertainment, and also those in theatrical box offices and advertising agencies, theatrical, television and cinema workshops, and film studios. *Address*: 155 Kennington Park Road, London SE11 4JU. *Tel*: 01-735 9068. *TUC Affiliated Membership, 1977*: 16,070.

THREE SHIFT SYSTEM. A system of **shift working** (q.v.) under which three successive shifts or **turns**, usually of 8 hours, are worked by different teams of operatives during a period of 24 hours. Two types of three shift systems are usually to be found: in a **discontinuous (or non-continuous) three shift system** continuity is provided for five or six, but not seven days per week, usually with workers on some rotating shift arrangement; in a **continuous three shift system** continuity is provided for seven days a week, using either three crews, or four crews, also on a rotating shift arrangement, one of which may be the so-called **continental shift system**, or 3 x 2 x 2 system, in which a worker changes his shift in that order, e.g. 3 mornings, 2 afternoons, 2 nights, 3 rest days, etc.; see S. Wyatt and R. Marriott, 'Night Work and Shift Changes', *British Journal of Industrial Medicine*, July 1953; J. Walker, 'Shift Changes and Hours of Work', *Occupational Psychology*, Vol. 35, 1961 and 'Frequent Alterations of Shifts on Continuous Work', *Occupational Psychology*, Vol. 40, October 1966.

THREE-DAY WEEK. A measure introduced by the Heath Conservative government and applied to manufacturing industry from 20 December 1973 as a result of a state of emergency earlier declared because of an overtime ban followed by a national stoppage in the coal industry and because of problems of electricity supply due in part to shortages in the supply of fuel oil. The three-day week continued until 8 March 1974, following the return of a Labour government to office in the 28 February General Election and the subsequent settlement of the miners' strike.

'THREE ON THE HOOK AND THREE ON THE BOOK'. A former practice of Glasgow dockers whereby, as a result of the incidence of the **continuity rule** (q.v.) in conjunction with the Unemployment Insurance Scheme they could occasionally choose not to work more than three in six consecutive days, although employment was available to them, hence getting paid for three days' work and three on the dole; Ministry of Labour, *Port Labour in*

Aberdeen and Glasgow; Report of the Board of Inquiry, HMSO, 1937, p. 28.

THREE WISE MEN. The **Council on Prices, Productivity and Incomes** (q.v.) so called after its membership of three distinguished public figures.

THRESHOLD AGREEMENT. A provision in a collective agreement allowing for wage rates to rise by a predetermined amount in the event of cost-of-living proceeding beyond a 'threshold', usually a given number of points on an agreed index, or beyond a series of such thresholds; hence a form of **cost-of-living sliding scale** (q.v.). Interest in such agreements was revived in the early 1970s by the **Trades Union Congress** and investigation of their use as a means of controlling wage inflation was suggested in a report issued by the **National Economic Development Council** in November 1971. Provision for threshold agreements was made in Stage 3 of the Heath government's Prices and Incomes Policy (*Counter Inflation, Price and Pay Code*, No. 2, SI 1785, 1973). This made provision for a maximum of 40p per week for every one per cent rise in the Retail Price Index in excess of 7 per cent rise on the October 1973 figure, such arrangements to last for 12 months. See also **reopener clause**.

THRESHOLD LIMIT VALUES. Airborne concentrations of substances representing conditions under which it is believed that nearly all workers may be repeatedly exposed without adverse effects. Threshold limit values refer to time-weighted concentrations for a 7 or 8 hour workday and a forty-hour workweek, and are designed to be used as guides in the control of health hazards rather than as fine determining lines between safe and dangerous concentrations. Adopted values and notice of intended changes are given in Department of Employment, *Threshold Limit Values for 1971*, Technical Data Note 2/71, HM Factory Inspectorate.

TIE CUTTERS, LONDON SOCIETY OF. A society formed in 1911 by tie cutters in London which has remained independent of the **National Union of Tailors and Garment Workers** (q.v.). *Address*: 67 Wessex Drive, Erith, Kent DA8 3AE. *Tel*: Erith (032 24) 39810. *Membership 1977*: 84.

TIED COTTAGE. A house provided by

the employer for a worker, the right to occupation of which ends with the termination of the contract of employment. It has been estimated that some 750,000 houses in England and Wales are 'tied' in this way, among them 100,000 farm cottages, and calculated that over one-half of farm workers occupy such cottages. Objections to the tied cottage system have come principally from the **National Union of Agricultural and Allied Workers** which has advocated its abolition for more than 50 years. A number of attempts have been made to improve the security of tenure of the tied cottage occupant. The security of farm workers who have qualified by having worked whole-time in agriculture for two years has now been greatly strengthened by the **Rent (Agriculture) Act 1976**. This provides that qualified farm workers become statutorily protected occupiers of their cottages as soon as the contract of service is terminated by either party. The ex-employer of the occupier can then obtain possession of the cottage only when he can satisfy the Agricultural Dwelling House Advisory Committee that he has a *bona fide* agricultural need for the cottage to house an essential worker, in which case the Committee will so advise the Local Housing Authority which will use its best endeavours to rehouse the ex-worker. If no urgent agricultural need can be shown, the farmer can obtain possession of the cottage only by an order from the County Court within the usual provisions of the Rent Acts.

TIGHT RATING; see **rating.**

TIGHT TIMES; see **rating.**

TIME-AND-A-HALF or **Time-and-one-half. Premium payment** (q.v.) for work performed at one-and-a-half times the standard rate for the job, e.g. on **overtime, shiftworking** etc.

TIME-AND-A-THIRD or **Time-and-one-third. Premium payment** (q.v.) for work performed at one-and-a-third times the standard rate for the job, e.g. on **overtime, shiftworking,** etc.

TIME AND MOTION STUDY. A popular term for **work study** (q.v.).

TIME CARD or **clock card;** see **clocking.**

TIME CRIBBING. '... a practice used by a number of employers to increase production by starting the mill engine a number

of minutes before the official starting time and running beyond the usual finishing time' (later nineteenth century); E. Hopwood, *A History of the Lancashire Cotton Industry and the Amalgamated Weavers' Association*, AWA, 1969, p. 60.

TIMEKEEPING BONUS; see **clocking.**

TIME OFF FOR TRADE UNION DUTIES; see **facilities for trade unions, Codes of Practice.**

TIME PIECEWORK. An incentive payment, or payment by results system in which the worker, if he finishes a job in less than the original time allowed, is still paid for the original time, thus giving him the advantage of the time saved. R. Marriott (*Incentive Payment Systems*, Staples, 3rd (revised) ed., 1968, p. 34) regards this as a confusing use of the word **piecework** (q.v.) and prefers the expression **standard hour system.**

TIME RATE; see **minimum time rate.**

TIME-SAVED SYSTEM; see **task bonus system** and **premium bonus plan (system).**

TIME-SERVED MAN. A skilled worker or craftsman recognised as such because he has served the full term of an **apprenticeship,** as distinct from other workers who may be in receipt of a skilled rate of pay, but who are **dilutees** or, in some industries, have acquired a sufficient measure of skill by practice on the job.

TIME-SPAN or **time-span of discretion.** Defined by Elliott Jaques, its originator (*Time Span Handbook*, Heinemann, 1964, p. 17) as 'the maximum period during which the manager relies upon the discretion of his subordinate, and the subordinate works on his own account'. Jaques argues that time-span measures levels of responsibility, and therefore establishes job hierarchies. For each level of responsibility, he claims, **felt-fair pay** (q.v.) can be established intuitively; time-span is therefore the key to the setting-up of fair differentials and payment structures; see also Elliott Jaques, *Measurement of Responsibility*, Heinemann Education, 1972, and *Equitable Payment*, Heinemann, 2nd ed., 1970; R. Richardson, *Fair Pay and Work*, Heinemann, 1971. The **National Board for Prices and Incomes,** considering time-span as a form of **job evaluation** (q.v.) concluded that where white collar workers were concerned, time-span might form an important part of measurement, but was more doubtful about its application to manual workers (*Job Evaluation*, Report No. 83. Cmnd. 3772, September 1968, p. 8). For a critique of the theory; see Alan Fox, *The Time-Span of Discretion Theory: An Appraisal*, Institute of Personnel Management, 1966.

TIME SPAN OF DISCRETION; see **time-span.**

TIME STUDY. A **work measurement** technique for recording the times and rates of working for the elements of a specified job carried out under specified conditions, and for analysing the data so as to obtain the time necessary for carrying out the job at a defined level of performance; British Standards Institution, *Glossary of Terms Used in Work Study*, BS 3138, 1969, No. 31001.

TIME-WASTING. Defined by the Final Report of the *Committee of Inquiry under the Rt. Hon. Lord Devlin on certain matters concerning the Port Transport Industry*, Cmnd. 2734, August 1965, p. 11, as any practice which results in a man's time not being used to the best advantage, excluding those practices which are reasonably designed to secure safety. The Devlin Committee identified time-wasting arising out of inefficient management methods as well as labour practices, e.g. **continuity rule,** excess manning, bad time-keeping; see also **blow times, welting, spelling, work sharing.**

TIMEWORK STROKE. The speed or effort expected while working on timework or daywork, compared with the higher speed or effort to be expected in piecework; see **piecework stroke.**

TIMEWORKERS' BONUS; see **lieu rate.**

'TINA LEA' CLAUSE; see **disclaimer clause.**

TIP. A gratuity given by a customer or patron in recognition of satisfactory personal service or as a customary practice in certain trades; most frequently found in Britain where taxis, hairdressing and catering are concerned. In the latter case attempts have been made since the 1939-45 war by **Wage Councils** to discourage tipping, but without much success, the Licensed Residential Establishment and Licensed Restaurant Wages Council, for example, ultimately fixing lower minimum rates for 'tippable' than for other grades of workers in the industry; see Brian McCormick and H.A. Turner, 'The Legal Minimum Wage: an Experiment', *Manchester School*, Vol. XXV, No. 3, September 1957, p. 297 for attempts to deal with the problem during the period of the Catering Wages Commission (1947-1959); see also **tronc; service charge.**

TMA. Tobacco Mechanics' Association (q.v.).

TMR. True money rate (q.v.).

TOBACCO MECHANICS' ASSOCIATION (TMA). A trade union formed in the tobacco industry to cater for cigarette machine operators after the introduction of the Baron cigarette machine in 1897. Until 1975 it was known as the Cigarette Machine Operators' Society. The union has retained a small membership in the industry, the largest membership being in the **Tobacco Workers' Union** (q.v.). *Address*: 9 Wootton Crescent, St Anne's Park, Bristol BS4 4AN. *Tel*: 0272 773848. *TUC Affiliated Membership, 1977*: 357.

TOBACCO WORKERS' UNION (TWU). A trade union originating in the Friendly Society of Operative Tobacconists, a craft union formed in 1834 among tobacco spinners, membership being extended in 1836 to tobacco cutters, stovers and dryers and the name of the union changed to the United Tobacconists Society. Hand made cigarettes, introduced in 1851 brought new membership and a further change of name to the United Kingdom Operative Tobacconists throughout the Kingdom in 1881, which was again changed in 1910 to United Kingdom Operative Tobacconists Society, partly as a result of the growth of cigarette machine operatives, a new grade developing from the introduction of the Baron cigarette making machine (1897). In 1918, membership was extended to all tobacco workers, male or female, and the present title adopted in 1925, with the 1918 objective of becoming an industrial union, an aspiration which led to its withdrawal from the **Trades Union Congress** between 1926 and 1936. The TWU is the principal union and leads the employees' negotiations in the National Joint Negotiating Committee for the Tobacco Industry (1947). It absorbed the national Cigar and Tobacco Workers' Union in 1946. It now organises clerical and supervisory workers as well as manual workers in the tobacco industry. *Address*: 9 Station Parade, High Street, London E11 1QF. *Tel*: 01-989 1107. *TUC Affiliated Membership, 1977*: 21,070.

TOBYMAN. A cyclist who 'tops up' newsagents who are running short of copies of newspapers for current counter sales; national newspaper industry.

TOKEN STRIKE. A short stoppage of work intended to underline the threat of serious strike action. K.G.J.C. Knowles (*Strikes*, Blackwell, 1952, p. 11) notes that 'token strikes have naturally become common in recent years because of economic stringency and official trade union reluctance to undertake serious strikes'.

TOLPUDDLE MARTYRS. The six agricultural labourers of Tolpuddle in Dorset who were sentenced to transportation in 1834 for administering illegal oaths while founding a branch of the Friendly Society of Agricultural Labourers. The courthouse at Dorchester at which they were sentenced was purchased by the Trades Union Congress in 1956 and returned to the Rural District Council in 1967. Trades Union Congress, *The Book of the Martyrs of Tolpuddle*, 1934 and Joyce Marlow, *The Tolpuddle Martyrs*, André Deutsch, 1972.

TOMLIN FORMULA. A formula for comparison between classes in the Civil Service and outside occupations introduced by the Tomlin *Royal Commission on the Civil Service, 1930-1951*, Final Report, para. 308, based on the criterion that Civil Service remuneration should reflect the long term trend in the country in respect of wages and economic conditions. The formula governed the attitudes in negotiation of the Official Side until the Priestley *Royal Commission on the Civil Service, 1953-1955*; see **Priestley Formula**. B.V. Humphreys, *Clerical Unions in the Civil Service*, Blackwell and Mott, 1958, pp. 196-212.

TOMMY SHOP. A store, often run by an employer of labour, to supply 'tommy', i.e. food, household goods, and clothing, to workers in exchange for orders or vouchers given to them in lieu of money payment. The abuse of this system led to the passing of the **Truck Acts** (q.v.), Ian Fife and E.A. Machin, *Redgrave's Health and Safety in Factories*, Butterworths 1976, p. 1710 *et seq*.

TONNAGE PAYMENTS. A form of bonus related to tonnage produced, general in the iron and steel industry. Tonnage payments are said to have been introduced originally as a result of the decline of the **contract system** in the industry. The **Melters' Brown Book Agreement** which came into operation in 1930 was occasioned by the desire of the Steel Ingot Makers' Association to revise melting rates in the light of the increased capacity and output of melting furnaces during and after the first world war.

TOOL ALLOWANCE. A monetary allowance, usually weekly, paid to craftsmen who are required to provide and maintain their own tools. In **work study**, an allowance of time, which may be included in **standard time**, to cover adjustment and maintenance of tools.

TOOL BENEFIT. Compensation paid under some union rule books for loss of tools or damage to tools; sometimes referred to as **tool insurance**. Very few unions currently appear to provide for such benefit, seven main unions in 1965; see Arthur Marsh and Peter Cope, 'The Anatomy of Trade Union Benefits in the 1960s', *Industrial Relations Journal*, Summer 1970.

TOOL INSURANCE; see **tool benefit**.

TOOLPUSHER. A worker who keeps one or more drilling rigs supplied with the necessary materials to continue drilling, and who is responsible for the efficient operation of his rig or rigs (petroleum industry).

TOOLROOM AGREEMENT; see **Toolroom Operatives' Agreement**.

TOOLROOM AVERAGE; see **Toolroom Operatives' Agreement**.

TOOLROOM OPERATIVES' AGREEMENT. A national agreement between the Engineering Employers' Federation on the one hand and the Amalgamated Engineering Union and the National Society of Metal Mechanics on the other, and sometimes known as the **Bevin Award**, in which it was agreed that, for the purpose of ensuring a continuing supply of skilled toolroom workers in wartime, their earnings should not be less than the average earnings of skilled production workers in the same establishment for the same number of comparable hours worked (*Handbook of National Agreements*, 3.117, 1940, extended 1946 to skilled toolroom inspectors, 3.1171). The agreement has continued to operate in peacetime; see also **Coventry Toolroom Agreement.**

TOP HAT PENSIONS. Supplementary pensions for executives over and above basic pension arrangements, firms normally paying the whole of the premiums; see J. Gaselee, 'Points on Pensions', *The Manager*, September 1965.

TOP SALARIES REVIEW BODY. A committee appointed in May 1971 to advise the Prime Minister on the remuneration of the chairmen of the boards of nationalised industries, the higher judiciary, senior civil servants, senior officers in the armed forces and of other groups which may be referred to it. The Review Body now performs, *inter alia*, the functions formerly undertaken by the **Standing Advisory Committee on the Pay of the Higher Civil Service** (q.v.); see also **review bodies.** The Review Body issued its tenth report (*Second Report on Top Salaries*) in June 1978 (Cmnd. 7253). Its first salaries report was made in 1974.

TOPS. Training Opportunity Scheme (q.v.).

TORQUAY HOTELS LTD. v. COUSINS (1968) 3 WLR 506 (CA), (1969) 2 WLR 289. A leading case in which the High Court granted an injunction against union officials who interfered with **commercial contracts** by industrial action when seeking recognition of the union, even though no breach of the contracts was caused; see also **injunction** and **boycott.**

TOTTING. The practice of collecting saleable salvage. The expression is used both in the case of private 'rag-and-bonemen' collectors and of local authority dustmen who collect salvage as a supplement to their earnings. The right to continue totting was the issue in a strike of Lambeth dustmen early in 1969 the borough ultimately paying out £100,000 in compensation to bring the practice to an end.

TOUCH MONEY. Money paid for working for a title other than the one by whom the worker is employed (newspaper industry), i.e. for working for the *Sunday Express* when employed by the *Daily Express*; see also **dual working.**

TRADE BENEFITS. Trade union **benefits** distinguished from **provident** or **friendly benefits** in that they are made to trade union members in respect of direct industrial action, and therefore include **dispute benefit**, or **strike pay** or **victimisation benefit. Unemployment benefit** may be thought of as a provident benefit for some purposes and for others as a trade benefit in that it may contribute to industrial action; see Arthur Marsh and Peter Cope, 'The Anatomy of Trade Union Benefits in the 1960s', *Industrial Relations Journal*, Summer 1970.

TRADE BOARDS; see **Trade Boards Acts.**

TRADE BOARDS ACTS. Acts of Parliament in 1909 and 1918 designed to deal with the evils of **sweating** (q.v.). **Trade Boards** consisting of equal numbers of representatives of employers and workers, together with three **independent members** appointed by the Board of Trade (and after 1916 by the Ministry of Labour) were established to fix statutory minimum time rates of wages, at first in four trades only (1909 Act) and later in cases in which no adequate machinery existed for the regulation of such wages (1918 Act). Some 50 Trade Boards existed in 1938 and covered about 1½ million workers. Trade Boards were replaced by **Wages Councils** (q.v.) in 1945; see D.M. Sells, *The British Trade Board System*, P.S. King, 1923 and *British Wages Boards*, Brookings Institution, Washington DC 1939; also F.J. Bayliss, *British Wages Councils*, Basil Blackwell, 1962.

TRADE BOARDS ACTS 1909 and 1918; see **sweating** and **Wages Councils.**

TRADE DISPUTE. As defined in the **Trade Union and Labour Relations Act 1974** s. 29(1), a dispute between employers and workers, or between workers and workers (but *not* between employers and employers) 'connected with' terms and conditions of employment, working conditions, hiring and firing, work allocation, discipline, membership or non-membership of a trade union, facilities for trade union officials, negotiation, representation and consultation. The definition is a wide one, somewhat wider than that provided in the **Trade Disputes Act 1906** and (as an **industrial dispute**) by the more recent **Industrial Relations Act 1971** (now repealed). It applies to acts 'connected with' the above events, whether in process i.e. 'furtherance', or in prospect i.e. 'contemplation', in protecting the parties against actions for torts.

TRADE DISPUTES ACT 1906. An Act passed to reverse the decision in the **Taff Vale Case** and to reinstate the law on trade disputes as it had been understood to exist as a result of the **Conspiracy and Protection of Property Act 1875**. The Act defined a **trade dispute** (q.v.), and removed from such disputes the application of the doctrine of civil conspiracy (s. 1), of trade interference and actions for the tort of procuring breaches of contract (s. 3); it also (s. 4) conferred upon trade unions generally an immunity from actions for tort, and reinforced the legality of peaceful picketing done in contemplation or furtherance of a trade dispute (s. 2); see **picketing**. Aspects of the Act were increasingly questioned in the courts in the 1960s; see for example **Rookes v. Barnard**, and **intimidation**, resulting in the reinforcement of s. 3 by the **Trade Disputes Act 1965**. Both the Trade Disputes Act 1906 and the Trade Disputes Act 1965 were repealed by the **Industrial Relations Act 1971**; their provisions are now embodied in the **Trade Union and Labour Relations Act 1974**; see **trade dispute, conspiracy, injunction**. For a detailed analysis of the 1906 Act see M.A. Hickling, *Citrine's Trade Union Law*, 3rd ed., Stevens, 1967, Ch. 10.

TRADE DISPUTES ACT 1965. An Act occasioned by the case of **Rookes v. Barnard**; see also **intimidation**. Its object was to restore the law on **trade disputes** (see **trade dispute**) to what was generally believed to be the law before Rookes v. Barnard and arising from the **Trade Disputes Act 1906**. The Act was repealed by the **Industrial Relations Act 1971**; its provisions are now incorporated in the **Trade Union and Labour Relations Act 1974**.

TRADE DISPUTES AND TRADE UNIONS ACT 1927. An Act passed by the Baldwin administration after the **General Strike** of 1926 (q.v.), which made sympathetic strikes and strikes directly or indirectly against the government illegal, substituted contracting-in for contracting-out (see **political fund**), substantially prohibited **picketing**, restricted established civil servants from joining outside unions, and prohibited local and other public authorities from making it a condition of employment that any person should or should not be a member of a trade union. The Act was bitterly resented by the trade union move-

ment and was repealed in its entirety by the Attlee administration in the **Trade Disputes and Trade Unions Act 1946**.

TRADE DISPUTES AND TRADE UNIONS ACT 1946; see **Trade Disputes and Trade Union Act 1927**.

TRADE GILDS; see **craft gilds**.

TRADE JOINT COUNCILS; see **Whitleyism**.

TRADE MOVEMENT. A trade union bargaining strategy in which a favourable settlement in one particular firm or district is demanded in other firms and districts, or in which a common policy of demands is evolved and pursued by similar methods. Trade movements were a notable late nineteenth century trade union practice (see W. Mosses, *The History of the United Patternmakers' Association*, 1972, *passim*), and are still catered for in the rule book of the **Confederation of Shipbuilding and Engineering Unions**. Their use among manual workers in engineering has been progressively reduced by use of disputes procedures originating in 1898 (see **Engineering Procedure Agreement**), though common in a modified form among draughtsmen in the 1960s. The device is akin to **pattern bargaining** in the United States; see also **whipsawing, leapfrogging, wage rounds**.

TRADE PROTECTION SOCIETY, wage-protection association or **strike society**. A trade union making provision only for victimisation and strike pay, and for no **friendly** or **provident benefits**. The terms were applied particularly to late nineteenth and early twentieth century societies of this description; see, for example, J.H. Jones, *The Tinplate Industry*, P.S. King and Son, 1914, p. 183.

TRADE SHOP. A workshop, particularly in the engineering industry, which specialises in sub-contracting jobs from larger companies.

TRADE SOCIETY OF MACHINE CALICO PRINTERS; see **Machine Calico Printers, Trade Society of**.

TRADE UNION. The classic definition is that of Sidney and Beatrice Webb (*The History of Trade Unionism*, 2nd ed., 1920, p. 1): '. . . a continuous association of wage earners for the purpose of maintaining and improving the conditions of their working lives' ('. . . of their employment' in the 1st ed., 1894). The **Trade Union Act 1871**, which was amended in 1876 and in 1913, regulated the main legal position of trade unions of employees or of employers for a century, provided that the expression meant 'any combination, whether temporary or permanent, the principal objects of which are under its constitution the regulation of the relations between workmen and masters, or between workmen and workmen, or between masters and masters, or the imposing of restrictive conditions on the conduct of any trade or business, and also the provision of benefits to members, whether such combination would or would not, if the Trade Union Act 1871 had not been passed, have been deemed to have been an unlawful combination by reason of some one or more of its purposes being in restraint of trade' (see M.A. Hickling, *Citrine's Trade Union Law*, 3rd ed., 1967, p. 393 *et seq.*) This definition, and the concepts of **registered trade unions** and **certified trade unions** associated with the **Chief Registrar of Friendly Societies**, remained until the **Industrial Relations Act 1971**, which separated **organisations of employers** from **organisations of workers** and from friendly societies, placed them both under a **Chief Registrar of Trade Unions and Employers' Associations,** and employed the expression 'trade union' to mean *registered* trade union only, other organisations of workers being without the legal advantages which registration provided. The **Trade Union and Labour Relations Act 1974**, s. 28, in repealing the 1971 Act, abandoned these distinctions in favour of one nearer to that of 1871, though trade unions have to possess certificates of independence to obtain certain privileges from the Act (see **independent trade union**). The **Certification Officer** (q.v.) is, however, required to maintain a list (see **listed trade union**) of all organisations which appears to him to be a trade union within the meaning of the Act (i.e. conform to s. 28). This list is akin to that compiled for many years by the Department of Employment in its annual report in the *Department of Employment Gazette* on 'Membership of Trade Unions': '. . . all organisations of employees - including those of salaries and professional workers, as well as those of manual wage earners - which are known to include in their objects that of negotiating with employers with a view to regulating the wages and working conditions of their members' (*British Labour Statistics Yearbook, 1969*, 1971). The Certification Offi-

cer is the sole judge of the 'principal purposes' of the organisation concerned. Listed trade unions may therefore include **professional** or **staff associations** which would not be regarded by the trade union movement as **bona fide trade unions** (see also **breakaway union, company union, house union, Spencer unions, unionisation, unionateness, wrong union**). Numbers of British trade unions have diminished steadily over the past quarter of a century in particular, and at the end of 1977 there were 485 trade unions of employees on the Certification Officer's list, with a membership of about 12.1 millions. In 1976 115 trade unions were affiliated to the **Trades Union Congress** with an aggregate membership of 11.5 millions. There has also been an increasing concentration of membership into larger trade unions by **amalgamation** (including **transfer of engagements**), particularly since the middle 1960s, and a growth of **open unions** (see **typology of trade unions**) and **white collar unions** (q.v.). On the effects of trade unions on income distribution, see **share of wages**; on trade union functions in society, Allan Flanders, *Management and Unions, The Theory and Reform of Industrial Relations*, Faber & Faber, 1975; Martin Harrison, *Trade Unions and the Labour Party since 1945*, George Allen and Unwin, 1960; J.A. Banks, *Marxist Sociology in Action, A Sociological Critique of the Marxist Approach to Industrial Relations*, Faber & Faber, 1970; V.L. Allen, *Militant Trade Unionism*, Merlin Press, 1966 and *The Sociology of Industrial Relations*, Longman, 1971, and M. van de Vall, *Labor Organisations*, CUP, 1970: on trade unions and productivity; R. Harle, 'The Role of Trade Unions in Raising Productivity', *Political Quarterly*, January-March 1956; C. Kerr, 'Productivity and Labor Relations', in *Labor and Management in Industrial Society*, Doubleday-Anchor Books, 1964; J.E. Mortimer, *Trade Unions and Technological Change*, OUP, 1971 and see **restrictive labour practices**: on trade union government and democracy, J. Goldstein, *The Government of British Trade Unions*, Allen and Unwin, 1952; V.L. Allen, *Power in Trade Unions*, Longmans, 1954; B.C. Roberts, *Trade Union Government and Administration in Great Britain*, London School of Economics 1956; Graham Wootton, 'Parties in Union Government, the AESD', *Political Studies*, Vol. IX, No. 2, 1961; H.A. Clegg, A.J. Killick and Rex Adams, *Trade Union Officers*, Basil Blackwell, 1961; H.A. Turner, *Trade Union*

Growth, Structure and Policy, A Comparative Study of the Cotton Unions, George Allen and Unwin, 1962; J. Hughes, *Trade Unions Structure and Government,* Royal Commission on Trade Unions and Employers' Associations, Research Papers 5, Parts 1 and 2, 1967 and 1968; see also Trades Union Congress, *Trade Unionism,* Evidence to the Royal Commission on Trade Unions and Employers' Associations, 1966; H.A. Clegg, Alan Fox and A.F. Thompson, *A History of British Trade Unions since 1889,* Vol. 1, 1889-1910, OUP, 1964 and as general introductions, Allan Flanders, *Trade Unions,* 7th ed., Hutchinson, 1968 and N. Robertson and J.L. Thomas, *Trade Unions and Industrial Relations,* Business Books, 1968; see also **shop stewards.** There has been no full scale general history of British trade unions since the Webbs (see above); but see Henry Pelling, *A History of British Trade Unionism,* 3rd ed., Macmillan, 1976, A.E. Musson, *British Trade Unions, 1800-1875* and John Lovell, *British Trade Unions 1875-1933,* Macmillan 1977.

TRADE UNION ACT 1871. An Act, sometimes referred to as the Charter of Trade Unions, passed as a result of the recommendations, and particularly those of the Third Dissent or Minority Report, of the **Royal Commission on Trade Unions, 1867-69.** The Act had two main objects; first to relieve trade unions from some of the civil and criminal liabilities under which they laboured as a result of application to them of the common law doctrine of restraint of trade, and second to provide for a voluntary system of trade union registration. Its effect, therefore, was partially to legalise trade unions and to confer upon them, provided they registered with the **Chief Registrar of Friendly Societies,** a special legal status involving certain obligations and advantages (see **registered trade union**). The Act was subsequently amended by the **Trade Union Act Amendment Act 1876.** Both Acts were repealed by the **Industrial Relations Act 1971;** see M.A. Hickling, *Citrine's Trade Union Law,* 3rd ed., Stevens, 1967.

TRADE UNION ACT AMENDMENT ACT 1876. An Act amending the definition of a trade union and making a number of changes designed to remedy deficiencies in the **Trade Union Act 1871;** see M.A. Hickling, *Citrine's Trade Union Law,* 3rd ed., Stevens, 1967, p. 376 *et seq.* The whole Act was repealed by the **Indus-**trial Relations Act 1971; see also **nomination procedure.**

TRADE UNION ACT 1913. An Act enabling a trade union to pursue objects ·and to exercise powers of any lawful kind, provided its principal objects are 'statutory' as defined in the Act, and particularly to lay down conditions as to the expenditure of union funds on the political objects mentioned in it. These necessitate the holding of a ballot of members under rules approved by the **Chief Registrar of Friendly Societies** (now the **Certification Officer for Trade Unions and Employers' Associations** q.v.), and the adoption of rules approved by the Certification Officer providing for a separate **political fund** (q.v.); for the right of members to contract out (see **contracting-out**) of the fund; that a contracted-out member is not to be victimised; and that contribution to the fund is not to be a condition of admission to the union. Any member aggrieved by any alleged breach of the rules may complain to the Certification Officer who may make such order for remedying the breach as he thinks just in the circumstances, such an order being enforceable in the County Court. The purpose of the Act was to negative the decision of the House of Lords in **Osborne v. Amalgamated Society of Railway Servants** (q.v.); see M.A. Hickling, *Citrine's Trade Union Law,* 3rd ed., Stevens, 1967, Ch. 6. The terms of the Act have remained unchanged under the **Industrial Relations Act 1971** and subsequent legislation.

TRADE UNION, ADMISSION TO; see **membership of a trade union.**

TRADE UNION (AMALGAMATION) ACT 1917; see **amalgamation.**

TRADE UNION (AMALGAMATIONS ETC.) ACT 1964; see **amalgamation.**

TRADE UNION CONTRIBUTIONS or **dues.** Periodic payments, usually weekly, made by members of trade unions in order to defray the costs of their organisations. They consist in some cases of **all-in contributions** and in others of a basic contribution with additional payments for specific **benefits** (q.v.); see also **political fund.** Trade union contributions in Britain are notably low compared with those in most other countries and in 1957-58 were reckoned at 2.10 Swiss francs per month compared with 3.65 Swiss francs in the

German Federal Republic, 3.40 in Belgium, 9.45 in Denmark, 2.25 in France, 9.00 in Norway and 3.30 in Switzerland itself; G. Spyropoulos, *Les Finances des Syndicats Européens*, International Labour Office, 1958: in 1965 average weekly contributions as a percentage of average weekly earnings of adult male manual workers in Britain and Italy were 0.4 per cent compared with 1.8 per cent in Belgium, 0.8 per cent in the German Federal Republic, 1.0 per cent in the Netherlands and in the United States of America, and 1.3 per cent in Sweden. Since 1956 the average contribution per member in Britain for trade unions as a whole has only rarely exceeded average expenditure. It did not do so in 1975 though the latest data for 1976 show that, though many unions are still meeting deficits from contributions out of investment income, the overall position is now one of surplus, the average contribution being 10.7p per member for the year and expediture 10.3p; see A.I. Marsh and P. Cope, *Trade Union Benefits and Finance*, Royal Commission on Trade Unions and Employers' Associations, Research Paper, 1968, RC/P/238 and Arthur Marsh and Peter Cope, 'The Anatomy of Trade Union Benefits in the 1960s', *Industrial Relations Journal*, Summer 1970; see also **check-off**.

TRADE UNION FUNCTIONS or **union functions**. Functions claimed by trade unions as essential to the operation of trade unionism, contrasted with **managerial prerogatives**, i.e. functions considered by management to be essential for the operation and survival of management itself; sometimes expressed in terms of rights, e.g. **freedom of association**, freedom to organise, right to be consulted, **right to strike, right to work** etc., justifying a trade union's function in taking action to support these rights; see Carter L. Goodrich, *The Frontier of Control*, Dent/Pluto Press, 1975, and N.W. Chamberlain, *The Union Challenge to Management Control*, 1948, Archon Books, 1967.

TRADE UNION AND LABOUR RELATIONS ACT 1974. An Act principally concerned to repeal the **Industrial Relations Act 1971**, to re-establish the pre-1971 legal basis of trade unions and employers' associations and to maintain and extend the 1971 Act in respect principally of its provisions for **Codes of Practice** and for **unfair dismissal**. It was an early condition of the **Social Contract** between the General Council of the Trades Union Congress and the Labour Party in 1972 that, on the return of a Labour government to office, priority should be given to repeal of the Industrial Relations Act which the trade union movement had so solidly resisted and to this became attached two further stages in the reform of industrial relations law, the **Employment Protection Act 1975** and further legislation on **industrial democracy** (q.v.). The passage of the Act was effectively resisted by the Opposition on several points, notably on **union membership agreements** and on the redefinition of **trade disputes**, the government position being restored in an Amendment Act in 1976 (see also **Lever Amendments**). In general, the Act restored the law on industrial relations generally to its pre-1971 position, though with some strengthening of the **closed shop**, increase of immunities in relation to trade disputes and other matters reckoned by employers to be in favour of trade unions; see B.A. Hepple and P. O'Higgins, *Employment Law*, Sweet and Maxwell, 1976.

TRADE UNION LAW; see labour law.

TRADE UNION MEMBERS, DISCIPLINE OF; see membership of a trade union.

TRADE UNION, MEMBERSHIP OF; see **membership of a trade union.**

TRADE UNION RECOGNITION. The acceptance of a trade union by an employer for the purposes of representation of his employees on matters concerning their terms and conditions of work. Two types of recognition are sometimes distinguished: **procedural recognition**, i.e. acceptance that members of the union may have their individual grievances handled by workplace representatives and/or full-time officials as these grievances arise; and **negotiating recognition**, i.e. acceptance that, in addition to such recognition for procedural purposes, the union may also negotiate collectively with the employer on behalf of its members on pay and conditions. Such a distinction has historically seldom been made where manual workers are concerned. It dates particularly from the later 1960s, and coincides with the growth of white collar unions in the private sector of industry. After the second world war, however, it became increasingly common for the first formal stage in the recognition of a union of either kind to be signalled by the signing of a **procedure agreement** containing provisions for either or both of these situations. National or industry-wide procedure or negotiating agreements between trade unions and employers' associations, as distinct from those made at company or plant level, have rarely committed each and every member of those associations to comparable recognition within their establishments. 'Recognition' of a trade union, whether of a procedural or negotiating kind, has no precise content in terms of facilities to be afforded to unions, conditions of operation of representatives or other such considerations; nor, until the Industrial Relations Act 1971 were any statutory procedures available which trade unions could use to obtain recognition in particular cases (see **Commission on Industrial Relations**). Following the repeal of that Act, the **Employment Protection Act 1975** now provides for such a situation; see **Section 11 Procedure**. The same Act makes provision for independent trade unions recognised by an employer to be accorded disclosure of information and a number of other statutory advantages; see also **Health and Safety Representatives**.

TRADE UNION TYPOLOGY; see **typology of trade Unions.**

TRADE UNION UNIT TRUST. A Unit Trust formed in August 1961, following the Trustee Investment Act of that year, to enable trade unions to take advantage of the possibilities of more professional handling of their funds and of greater opportunities of capital gains. The Trust was subsequently opened to investment by individual trade unionists and their families both on an insurance-linked and non-linked basis. The Trades Union Congress withdrew from the Trust early in 1973 on the issue of investments in South Africa.

TRADES COUNCILS. Bodies composed of representatives of local trade union branches and acting as local agents of the **Trades Union Congress** in most towns and cities of England and Wales and numbering about 450. In a few cases the Trades Council is the industrial section of a Joint Trades Council and Labour Party (**Trades and Labour Council**). The continuous history of Trades Councils begins at about 1860 and they were originally recognised by the Trades Union Congress as of equal status with national unions. Direct representation at Congress was ended by a change of Standing Orders in 1895 (see B.C. Roberts, *The Trades Union Con-*

gress, 1868-1921, George Allen and Unwin, 1958, p. 143 *et seq.*), and this and other measures have been aimed at keeping them under Congress control, and particularly from pursuing political and other activities independently of national trade union leadership. Since 1924 a Trades Councils' Joint Consultative Committee of nine General Council representatives and nine Trades Council representatives have supervised their work, and a registration scheme provides that official recognition can be withdrawn from Councils whose actions are not approved. In 1935, Circular 16 of the General Council withdrew recognition from Councils with delegates who were Communists or Fascists (see **Black Circular**). The powers of Trades Councils are limited and their functions chiefly consist in presenting a trade union viewpoint on local affairs and in making nominations to local tribunals, advisory bodies, Hospital Boards etc. It is the policy of the TUC that there should be only one Trades Council in the area of each local government District Council. Each Trades Council affiliates to one of the 53 County Associations of Trades Councils in England and Wales and these are in turn grouped into eight Regional Advisory Committees. Some writers regard with regret the limited scope and financial resources of Trades Councils, and their chequered history of relationships with national trade union leadership; see, for example, Allan Flanders, *Trade Unions*, Hutchinson, 1968, pp. 66-9. The Trades Union Congress issues a *Trades Councils Guide*. Revised Ed., January 1976. For the position of Trades Councils in Scotland, see **Scottish Trades Union Congress;** see also **Wales Trade Union Council.**

TRADES AND LABOUR COUNCILS; see **Trades Councils.**

TRADES UNION CONGRESS (TUC). The principal national body representative of trade unions in the United Kingdom, formed in 1868 and meeting annually since that time, except for the years 1870 and 1914. In 1976 the TUC was representative of 115 trade unions with an affiliated membership of 11.5 millions. It originated from the needs of the nationwide amalgamated societies which emerged in Britain in the middle of the last century to work together in influencing governmental attitudes and policies. In general this has resulted in close relationships with the Labour Party without resort to direct political action, in non-involvement with strikes especially of a political nature (see **General Federation of Trade Unions**) and in policies of co-operation with whatever government might be in power. There are, however, exceptions. The TUC became involved in the **General Strike** of 1926 and defied the Heath government in laying down non-registration of its affiliates under the Industrial Relations Act 1971. Between 1974 and 1977, its co-operation with the Labour government of the day in incomes policy under the so-called **Social Contract** and its involvement in the repeal of the 1971 Act and its replacement by legislation in industrial relations including and following the **Trade Union and Labour Relations Act 1974** were of an unusually close variety. The TUC is not directly affiliated to the Labour Party, nor is this a condition of affiliation to the TUC, though most of its members are so affiliated. Nor is the TUC a federal body with powers over its member unions, though since 1921 it has had a General Council which acts as an executive committee of Congress and has the ultimate responsibility for carrying out the decisions made at the Congress's annual meeting held in the first full week of September. In addition to its pressure group functions and its role as a platform for trade union leaders, the TUC is concerned about disputes in which affiliated unions are involved (see **Rule 11**), disputes between affiliated organisatons (see **Bridlington Agreement** and **Rule 12**) and the conduct of unions (see **Rule 13**). Recent developments are increased involvement in training since the amalgamation of the interests of the **National Council of Labour Colleges** (NCLC) and the **Workers' Educational Trade Union Committee** (WETUC) under the TUC Education Committee in 1964 and the development of Industry Committees since a major decision taken in 1970. These Committees now number nine. They have in some cases (as in Printing) taken the place of defunct federations of unions or originally been set up for particular purposes (e.g. in Construction, the issue of **The Lump**). Some, like that for the Health Services, have been set up from scratch and one, the Steel Committee, has negotiating functions. To some degree the Industry Committees represent a break in the reluctance of affiliated unions to compromise their independence by too close a relationship on day-to-day matters with the TUC and there is no doubt that the TUC has tended to act with a greater sense of authority since enforcing its policy of non-registration under the

1971 Act which resulted in 32 unions, representing about 500,000 members, being suspended from membership. All but a handful of these have now returned; see also **trades councils**; see TUC *Annual Reports*; B.C. Roberts, *The Trades Union Congress, 1868-1921*, George Allen and Unwin, 1958; John Lovell and B.C. Roberts, *A Short History of the TUC*, Macmillan, 1968; TUC, *Trade Unionism, Evidence to the Royal Commission on Trade Unions and Employers' Associations*, 1966. *Address*: Congress House, Great Russell Street, London WC1. *Tel*: 01-636 4030; see also **Wales Trade Union Council**, **Scottish Trades Union Congress** and **Irish Congress of Trade Unions**.

TRADES UNION CONGRESS EDUCATIONAL TRUST. An educational trust to which the **Trades Union Congress** makes convenated grants, the objects of the Trust being to provide for trade unionists facilities for the study of history, economic history and the principles and administration of trade unions, to grant scholarships for study at adult colleges, and for British students to study abroad or foreign students to study in this country. *Address*: Congress House, Great Russell Street, London WC1. *Tel*: 01-636 4030.

TRAINEE RATE; see beginner's rate.

TRAINING CENTRES; see Government Training Centres.

TRAINING OPPORTUNITIES SCHEME (TOPS). A training scheme introduced by the Department of Employment on 7 August 1972 to replace the **Vocational Training Scheme** (q.v.) and intended to meet the training needs of individuals and offer to those who have failed to acquire skills immediately after the end of their full-time education, or have mistaken their first choice of career, a wider choice of free courses, with training allowances, than hitherto. Courses under TOPS are directly vocational, generally more than four weeks and less than one year in duration, and applicants are required to be at least 19 years of age and three years from full-time education. The scheme is operated by the **Manpower Services Commission** through its Training Services Division; 520,365 people entered training under the Scheme to 28 February 1978; see also **Sponsored Training Scheme**.

TRAINING SERVICES AGENCY; see Industrial Training Act 1964.

TRAINING WITHIN INDUSTRY (TWI).

A training scheme for supervisors introduced into Britain in 1945 and now provided by the Training Services Division of the Manpower Services Commission. TWI originated in the USA to meet a wartime problem of manpower by training workers within industry to make the best use of their skills, and courses had been attended by more than 2 million supervisors by 1945. The TWI scheme in Britain provides some 18 courses related to supervisory skills in **Job Instruction and Communication, Job Relations, Job Methods, Job Safety**, distribution and selling techniques, in short courses over a number of days, either within a firm or from several firms. In 1977 it was estimated that over 35,000 people from industry a year were passing through the scheme. *Information from:* MSC, Training Services Division, 1/2 Cambridge Gate, Regent's Park, London NW1 4LA. *Tel:* 01-935 7711.

TRAMPING, tramp (or tramping) system; tramping relief system; also travelling.

'. . . a characteristic feature of the old trade union organisation before the establishment of employment exchanges. It was a method of enabling unemployed craftsmen to go from town to town in search of work. It ensured the member on tramp of lodging for the night and money for food in every town through which he passed. It provided him with an address where he would find an officer of the society to examine his credentials, to give him information concerning prospects of employment in the town, to introduce him to the fellowship of the trade . . .', National Union of Vehicle Builders, *A Hundred Years of Vehicle Building, 1834-1934*, NUVB, 1934, pp. 57-8. Hence **tramping benefit** or **travelling benefit** (see Sir A. Pugh, *Men of Steel*, Iron and Steel Trades Confederation, 1951, p. 112), payment by trade unions to unemployed members when travelling the country in search of work, later abolished in favour of **out-of-work benefit** or **unemployment benefit**; see also E.J. Hobsbawm, 'The Tramping Artisan', *Economic History Review*, Vol. III, No. 3, 1951.

TRAMPING BENEFIT; see tramping.

TRAMPING RELIEF SYSTEM; see tramping.

TRAMPING SYSTEM; see tramping.

TRANSACTIONAL ANALYSIS.

In its widest sense, claimed to be a total system of concepts which offers a convenient explanation of all human behaviour and experience; as used in industrial relations, a technique for encouraging skill improvement in inter-personal behaviour. Transactional Analysis was largely developed by Eric Berne, a Californian psychiatrist, in part as a means of developing a language of psychiatry which should be generally comprehensible to the layman, and based upon the assumption that human personality is made up of three 'ego states' - Parent, Adult and Child - each with its behavioural characteristics, which are derived from experience and easily identified by the individual concerned. Each, it is claimed, can be manipulated to obtain particular results in 'transactions', i.e. encounters, verbal or non-verbal, with other individuals, thus producing a number of methods of structuring them, the most important of which from the industrial relations point of view may be thought of as 'games', i.e. as the unconscious use of ploys of one kind or another to achieve particular results to problems. Transactional Analysis can be seen as a tool which may improve the performance of managers by enabling them to analyse behaviour as well as a practical framework of references for the theories of McGregor (Theory X and Theory Y), Blake and Moulton (see **managerial grid**), Likert and Maslow; see Eric Berne, *The Games People Play, The Psychology of Human Relationships*, Deutsch, 1966, D. Jongeward, *Everybody Wins: Transactional Analysis applied to Organisations*, Addison Wesley, Reading, Mass., 1974 and, for a summary, K. Carby and M. Thakur, *Transactional Analysis at Work*, Institute of Personnel Management, 1976.

TRANSFER.

The movement of a worker from one job to another, or from one location to another or both; hence **transfer procedure**, a procedure laying down the conditions under which such transfers may be made, the rules of seniority to be observed, the arrangements to be followed about payment, maintenance of earnings in event of transfer, etc; see also **retain and transfer, labour mobility**.

TRANSFER OF ENGAGEMENTS.

A method of trade union merger, and an alternative to **amalgamation** (q.v.) first introduced by the **Societies (Miscellaneous Provisions) Act 1940** and now incorporated in the **Trade Unions (Amalgamations, etc.) Act 1964**. The intention of the former Act was to provide a simpler way of securing mergers than that provided for in the Trade Union (Amalgamation) Act 1917 by allowing this to take place with a two-thirds majority vote of the transferor union only. The 1964 Act has made this even simpler by allowing merger by transfer of engagements on a simple majority of votes of the transferor union only. The method is usually thought most appropriate where a small union is proposing to merge with a much larger union; see Cyril Grunfeld, *Modern Trade Union Law*, Sweet and Maxwell, 1970.

TRANSFER PROCEDURE; see trans-fer.

TRANSPORT AND GENERAL WORKERS' UNION (TGWU). The largest of British trade unions and the direct descendant of Ben Tillett's Dockers' Union which achieved fame in the dock strike of 1889. The union took its name and constitution as a result of an original amalgamation of fourteen unions which came into force on 1 January 1922, the unions being principally concerned with docks and transport, subsequent growth and amalgamations spreading the union's interests into almost every British industry. The scheme of national trade groups to prevent loss of identity is attributed to Ernest Bevin who was then Assistant General Secretary of the Dockers' Union, and may have been derived from the system of trade departments of the American Federation of Labour (AFL), amalgamations taking place as follows:
1922: Amalgamated Society of Watermen, Lightermen and Bargemen; Amalgamated Carters, Lorrymen and Motormen's Union; Amalgamated Association of Carters and Motormen; Associated Horsemen's Union; Dock, Wharf, Riverside and General Workers' Union; Labour Protection League; National Amalgamated Labourers' Union; National Union of Docks, Wharves and Shipping Staffs; National Union of Ships' Clerks, Grain Weighers and Coalmeters; National Union of Vehicle Workers; National Amalgamated Coal Workers' Union; National Union of Dock, Riverside and General Workers; National Union of British Fishermen; North of England Trimmers' and Teemers' Association; North of Scotland Horse and Motormen's Association; United Vehicle Workers; Belfast Breadservers' Association; Greenock Sugar Porters' Association.
1923: Dundee Jute and Flax Stowers'

Association; North Wales Craftsmen and General Workers' Union; North Wales Quarrymen's Union; Scottish Union of Dock Labourers.
1924: United Order of General Labourers.
1925: Association of Coastwise Masters, Mates and Engineers.
1926: Weaver Watermen's Association; Irish Mental Hospital Workers' Union; National Amalgamated Union of Enginemen, Firemen, Motormen; Mechanics and Electrical Workers.
1928: Cumberland Enginemen, Boilermen and Electrical Workers.
1929: Workers' Union.
1930: Belfast Operative Bakers' Union; Northern Ireland Textile Workers' Union.
1933: London Co-operative Mutuality Club Collectors' Association; National Union of Co-operative Insurance Society Employees; Portadown Textile Workers' Union; Scottish Farm Servants' Union.
1934: Altogether Builders' Labourers and Constructional Workers' Union; Scottish Busmen's Union.
1935: National Winding and General Engineers' Society.
1936: Electricity Supply Staff Association (Dublin); Halifax and District Carters' and Motormen's Association.
1937: Power Loom Tenters' Trade Union of Ireland; Belfast Journeymen Butchers' Association; Scottish Seafishers' Union.
1938: Humber Amalgamated Steam Trawlers' Engineers and Firemen's Union; Imperial War Graves Commission Staff Association.
1939: Port of London Deal Porters' Union; North of England Engineers' and Firemen's Amalgamation.
1940: National Glass Workers' Trade Protection Society; Radcliffe and District Enginemen and Boilermen's Provident Society; National Glass Bottle Makers' Society.
1942: Liverpool Pilots' Association.
1943: Manchester Ship Canal Pilots' Association.
1944: Grangemouth Pilots' Association.
1945: Leith and Granton Pilots; Dundee Pilots; Methil Pilots.
1946: Government Civil Employees' Association.
1947: Liverpool and District Carters' and Motormen's Union.
1951: Lurgan Hemmers', Veiners', and General Workers' Union; United Cut Nail Makers of Great Britain Protection Society.
1961: Scottish Textile Workers' Union.
1963: Gibraltar Confederation of Labour and the Gibraltar Apprentices and Ex-

Apprentices Union; Gibraltar Labour Trades Union.

1965: North of Ireland Operative Butchers' and Allied Workers' Association.

1966: United Fishermen's Union.

1968: Scottish Slaters', Tilers', Roofers' and Cement Workers' Society; National Association of Operative Plasterers.

1969: Process and General Workers' Union; Amalgamated Society of Foremen Lightermen of the River Thames.

1970: Sheffield Amalgamated Union of File Trades.

1971: Scottish Commercial Motormen's Union; Irish Union of Hairdressers and Allied Workers; Chemical Workers' Union; Watermen, Lightermen, Tugmen and Bargemen's Union.

1972: National Union of Vehicle Builders; Scottish Transport and General Workers' Union (Glasgow Dockers).

1973: Iron, Steel and Wood Barge Builders' and Helpers' Association.

1974: Union of Kodak Workers; Union of Bookmakers' Employees.

1975: File Grinders' Society.

1976: Grimsby Steam and Diesel Fishing Vessels Engineers' and Firemen's Union.

In Ireland the union is known as the **Amalgamated Transport and General Workers Union** (affiliated to the **Irish Congress of Trade Unions** on 60,000 members in 1977) and its clerical, supervisory and technical section as the **Association of Clerical, Technical and Supervisory Staffs** (ACTSS). The period of the general secretaryship of Ernest Bevin (1922-1945) was one of militancy, struggle, and consolidation by negotiation and, during his period at the Ministry of Labour, one of war (see Alan Bullock, *The Life and Times of Ernest Bevin*, Vol: 1: Trade Union Leader (1881-1940), and Vol. 2, Minister of Labour (1940-1945), Heinemann, 1967). His successor, Arthur Deakin from 1940 to 1955, identified himself with a moderate national wages policy without parliamentary intervention, with centralised authority and with anti-Communism, leading the move for secession from the **World Federation of Trade Unions** into the **International Confederation of Free Trade Unions** in 1949 (V.L. Allen, *Trade Union Leadership: Based on A Study of Arthur Deakin*, Longmans, 1957). A move towards militancy returned with the election of Frank Cousins as General Secretary in 1956 (Margaret Stewart, *Frank Cousins, A Case Study*, Hutchinson, 1968). Under his successor Jack Jones it became associated with opposition to the **Industrial Relations Act 1971**, with the

encouragement of shop-floor bargaining and of workers' participation and under the **social contract** (q.v.), with incomes policy; see also *Unity, Strength, Progress: The Story of the Transport and General Workers' Union*, TGWU, 1967. *Address*: Transport House, Smith Square, London SW1P 3JB. *Tel*: 01-828 7788. *TUC Affiliated Membership, 1977*: 1,929,834.

TRANSPORT AND GENERAL WORKERS' UNION, AMALGAMATED (ATGWU). The title used by the **Transport and General Workers' Union** in Ireland.

TRANSPORT AND GENERAL WORKERS UNION, IRISH (ITGWU); see **Irish Transport and General Workers' Union.**

TRANSPORT SALARIED STAFFS ASSOCIATION OF GREAT BRITAIN AND IRELAND (TSSA). A trade union founded in 1897 as the National Association of General Railway Clerks. A year later it became the Railway Clerks' Association, taking its present title in 1951. The Association represents the administrative, professional and supervisory staff of the British Railways Board, British Transport Hotels, London Transport, British Transport Docks Board, British Waterways Board, National Carriers Ltd, British Road Services, National Freight Corporation, Freightliners, London Country Bus Services, Scottish Transport Group, Estuarial Ports Authorities, the Manchester Ship Canal, Coras Iompair Eireann and transport undertakings in Northern Ireland. The scope of its membership in transport has widened since its original attempts to organise railway clerks; national recognition of the union as representative of clerks, stationmasters and supervisors was secured in 1919, further extensions taking place especially as a result of the nationalisation of public transport in 1948. Membership has declined from a peak of 91,000 in 1952, along with the reduction in numbers of British Railways staff. *Address*: Walkden House, Melton Street, London NW1 2EJ. *Tel*: 01-387 2101. *TUC Affiliated Membership, 1977*: 73,842.

TRANSPORT UNION, UNITED ROAD, (URTU). A trade union originally formed in Cheshire in 1890 as the United Carters' Association. In 1891 it changed its name to United Carters' Association of England, in 1912 to the United

Carters' and Motormen's Association of England. In 1926 it absorbed the National Motor Drivers' Association and became the United Road Transport Workers' Association of England, a title which it retained until 1964. *Address*: 76 High Lane, Chorlton-cum-Hardy, Manchester M21 1FD. *Tel*: 061-881 6245/6. *TUC Affiliated Membership, 1977*: 25,300.

TRAVELLING; see **tramping**.

TRAVELLING ALLOWANCE; see travelling time.

TRAVELLING BENEFIT; see tramping.

TRAVELLING EXPENSES; see travelling time.

TRAVELLING TIME. Time occupied in travelling to and from the job. Arrangements for payments related to travelling time vary from one industry to another and often from one situation to another. Time spent by a worker in travelling from his home to his accustomed place of work normally attracts no payment of any kind, payment for travelling time being confined to **outworking**, or similar circumstances and regulated by a formula; e.g., payment at plain time rates, but at overtime rates if the travelling time exceeds a given limit, say one hour, sometimes with no such payment if the travelling takes place within a given radius, as in the building industry, where each Local Joint Committee lays down a **free area** (National Joint Council for the Building Industry, *National Working Rules*). Where travelling time is concerned, **travelling allowances** are sometimes payable under given conditions, and at given rates, e.g. at so much per mile, or in some proportion to time spent in travelling, and also **travelling expenses**, i.e. refund of cost of conveyance by bus, train, taxi, car, as laid down.

TREASURY AGREEMENT. An agreement on **compulsory arbitration** between the Government and some thirty trade unions in March 1915, whereby the latter agreed to recommend to their members that stoppages of work on munitions should not take place for the duration of the war, and that all issues should be settled by arbitral means. The Agreement was given legislative effect in the Munitions of War Act of July 1915 and extended by Proclamation outside munitions proper. It caused much unrest among workers and was an important cause of the **Shop Stewards' Movement**; see Lord Amulree, *Industrial Arbitration*, OUP, 1929; G.D.H. Cole, *Trade Unionism and Munitions*, Economic and Social History of the War, OUP, 1923, p. 69 *et seq.*

TREASURY DEDUCTION SCHEME. A scheme for **check-off** (q.v.) agreed between the Treasury and the Staff Side of the National Whitley Council in July 1965 authorising facilities to any nationally or departmentally recognised association requesting them, on condition that individuals were free to opt out if they wished, that forms of authority should be completed by each assenting member, and that **political levy** (q.v.) should be returned *in advance* by those unions with **all-in contributions** (q.v.) in respect of contracting-out members. The scheme was authorised to start in January 1966, and greatly stimulated the growth of check-off in the public sector. *Establishments Circular* No. 27/65.

TRIAL RATE; see temporary rate.

TRIPLE ALLIANCE. A loose federation of miners, railwaymen and transport workers for mutual support in **trade movements** formed in 1914 and ratified by the unions concerned in the following year. It was regarded by some as a weapon of **syndicalism** and by others as a menace to the state. In fact its object of joint action was unambitious but was never achieved. It collapsed in April 1921 when the railwaymen and transport workers, on **Black Friday** (15 April 1921), refused to support the miners who had been locked out by the owners, leaving them to be forced to return to work in June. An attempt was made to revive the Triple Alliance in 1925 without success; see G.D.H. Cole, *A Short History of the British Working Class Movement, 1787-1947*, Allen and Unwin, 1948 ed.

TROLLOPE v. LONDON BUILDING TRADES' FEDERATION; see blacklisting.

TRONC. A pool of tips given to hotel staff and distributed by a **troncmaster**, usually a supervisor, on a points basis according to status established by custom and practice; from the French, a money or poor box; see also **tip, service charge**.

TRONCMASTER; see tronc.

TRUCK ACTS. Acts of 1831, 1887, 1896

and 1940 originally designed to prevent the abuse of employers paying their workers in kind, and not in cash, especially through 'tommy shops' run by them and providing inferior and highly priced goods as part of wages. The Acts apply to 'workmen' as defined by s. 10 of the **Employers and Workmen Act 1875** (q.v.), i.e. to all persons except domestic servants engaged in manual labour, and principally provide (1831 Act) that the entire amount of wages must be paid in current coin of the realm (s. 3), and not in kind (s. 1), without any restrictions as to how they shall be spent (s. 2). Ian Fife and E.A. Machin, *Redgrave's Health and Safety in Factories*, Butterworths, 1976, p. 1715 *et seq*. In modern conditions the Acts are somewhat difficult to interpret and apply. Two official attempts have been made to amend them, in 1909 and 1961, without result, though the **Payment of Wages Act 1960** (q.v.) has modified the notion of payment in coin of the realm, and **check-off** (q.v.) would no longer be thought of as precluded and an illegal deduction, subject to express or implied agreement between the worker and his employer; see also **Williams v. Butlers Ltd**. The proposals of the **Karmel Committee 1961** (q.v.) to repeal the Acts on grounds, *inter alia*, of irrelevance and ready observance by employers, were disapproved of by some lawyers; see 25 MLR, 1962 and K.W. Wedderburn, *The Worker and the Law*, Penguin, 2nd ed. 1971, pp. 231-234; also G.W. Hilton, *The Truck System*, Greenwood Press, 1976.

TRUE MONEY RATE (TMR). A term used by the Priestley *Royal Commission on the Civil Service 1953-1955*, Cmd. 9613, November 1955, paras. 171-4 and employed by the **Civil Service Pay Research Unit** to describe '... the rate of pay arrived at after adjusting the survey rate for **quantifiable emoluments** and also for any other adjustment that may need to be made, e.g. for location, hours etc.' Geoffrey Walker, *Pay Research in the Civil Service*, National Association of Local and Government Officers, TUE 6, 1968, p. 16.

TRUST RELATIONS. The basis of a form on analysis of industrial society adopted by Alan Fox (*Beyond Contract: Work, Power and Trust Relations*, Faber & Faber 1974). Fox argues that many aspects of modern industrial society engender low-trust relations and responses because of their emphasis on extreme differentiation and specialisation and on 'low-discretion' work for employees. Given that high-trust relations and 'high-discretion' work with its necessarily 'reciprocal diffuseness of obligations' may be qualitatively superior and desirable for its own sake what, he asks, would happen if there was a fundamental shift of preferences of employees in this direction? Fox is not certain, but believes that there are alternative social patterns towards which we could move, given sufficient resolve, and that theorising may establish standards not only for judging what at present exists, but also for deciding what to avoid in shaping a new social order.

TSA. Training Services Agency; see **Industrial Training Act 1964**.

TSSA. Transport Salaried Staffs Association (q.v.).

TUC. Trades Union Congress (q.v.).

TURN. A shift; hence **late turn, early turn**; to be hired as casual labour **for the turn**, or by the half day (docks industry before decasualisation): since decasualisation, one of the two four-hour periods into which the working day may be divided (sometimes also known as sessions; see **session money**).

TURN OFF; see **lock-out**.

TURNING-OUT MONEY. An allowance payable when a worker 'is given advance notice to work a shift at a sector, other than his own, and travels by his own means outside shift hours ... where it is necessary for a man to be transferred to a sector, other than his own, in normal shift time, no turning out money is payable'; *Productivity Agreement, Devlin Stage II*, concluded by the Enclosed Docks Employers with the Transport and General Workers' Union and the National Amalgamated Stevedores and Dockers, Schedule 5, 1 and 2.

TURN-OUT. A **strike**: a term commonly used in the early part of the nineteenth century.

TURNOVER. (1) An apprentice who for some reason is transferred or 'turned over' to another master to complete his apprenticeship; see A.E. Musson, *The Typographical Association*, OUP, 1954. (2) The rate at which workers move into and out of employment; **labour turnover** (q.v.).

TWELVE MONTH RULE. A statutory

requirement, or a voluntary understanding, that claims and agreements for the improvement of terms and conditions of work shall, in each instance, be made at no shorter interval than twelve months. Before the development of long-term agreements (see **fixed term agreements**) in the 1960s it was common practice in Britain for no termination dates to be placed on collective agreements. Both this habit and that of long-term agreements became eroded by the onset of inflation and the requirements of staged increases under the statutory incomes policies of the Wilson and Heath governments (see **National Board for Prices and Incomes** and **Pay Board**) and formed part of the voluntary policy conducted under the **Social Contract** from 1975 to 1977, when it became the sole element of that policy to survive into 1978.

24 HOUR RULE. A rule of procedure, said to have originated in the Ingersoll Milling Machine Tool company of Rockford, Illinois, USA, that a worker having a suggestion, problem or a complaint should be entitled to a definite answer from his immediate supervisor within 24 hours, and, failing satisfaction, an answer from each successive procedural step within 24 hours also. In the application of the Rule, also operated at one time at the former Herbert-Ingersoll Ltd factory at Daventry, it is a principle that the individual himself presents his own problem at each level.

TWI. Training Within Industry (q.v.).

TWICER. A worker in the printing industry who does work overlapping from one craft to another and who may, therefore, break demarcation lines; A.E. Musson, *The Typographical Association*, OUP, 1954.

TWILIGHT SHIFT. An evening shift, falling partly or wholly outside normal working hours on dayshift; see **part-time shift**.

TWO-SHIFT SYSTEM. Either **double day shift** (q.v.) or a system of alternative day and night shifts under which the same operatives alternate between day and night shifts. The latter may also include systems in which the number of workers employed on day and nights, or the numbers of weeks worked on days and nights are unequal (e.g. two weeks on days and one on nights); see **shift working**; Home Office, *Report on the Departmental Committee on the Employment of Women and Young Persons on the Two Shift System*, HMSO, 1935; Ministry of Labour and National Service, *Report of Committee on Double Day-Shift Working*, HMSO, 1947; 'Expansion of Double Day-Shift Working in Industry', *Ministry of Labour Gazette*, August 1953; Cotton Board Conference Proceedings: H.A. Clegg, *Single and Double Day-Shift Working in the Cotton Industry*, 1952; *Double Day-Shift Working in the Cotton Industry*, 1953; 'Two-shift Factory Operation', *Journal of the Institution of Works Managers*, June 1950; 'Two-shift Working: Procedure and Problems', *Journal of the Institute of Personnel Management*, May/June 1951 (corrected July/August 1951).

2X + Y; see Bullock Committee.

TWU. Tobacco Workers' Union (q.v.).

TYNAN v. BALMER; see picketing.

TYPOGRAPHICAL ASSOCIATION, SCOTTISH; see Scottish Typographical Association.

TYPOLOGY OF TRADE UNIONS. The distinguishing of trade unions by type. Traditionally, unions have been distinguished as **craft unions, industrial unions and general unions**, categories of increasingly little use for analytical purposes since, for example, very few pure craft unions still remain, industrial unions are seldom a clear category, and, in so far as 'type' is intended to suggest behaviour, the traditional three types only give partial indications; H.A. Clegg, A.J. Killick and Rex Adams (*Trade Union Officers*, Basil Blackwell, 1961) suggest **general, single-industry, skilled, ex-craft** and **white collar**. Other commentators have found it useful to categorise trade unions as **horizontal, vertical, occupational, sectoral, sectoral-general**. More recently it has become popular to think of unions as **open** or **closed** (see H.A. Turner, *Trade Union Growth, Structure and Policy*, George Allen and Unwin, 1962, p. 241 *et seq.*, and J. Hughes, *Trade Union Structure and Government*, Royal Commission on Trade Unions and Employer's Associations, Research Papers 5, Part 1, 1967), and the growth of white collar unions has brought consideration of the trade union status of **professional associations**, etc. (q.v.); see also **company union, house union, staff associa-**

tion, **bona fide trade unions, breakaway union, class unionism.**

U

UADW. Universal Alliance of Diamond Workers; see **International Trade Secretariats.**

UCATT. Union of Construction, Allied Trades and Technicians; see **Construction, Allied Trades and Technicians, Union of.**

UIP. Unfair industrial practice (q.v.).

UIS. Union of Insurance Staffs; see **Insurance Staffs, Union of.**

UJFKTO. Union of Jute, Flax and Kindred Textile Operatives; see **Jute, Flax and Kindred Textile Operatives, Union of.**

UKAPE. United Kingdom Association of Professional Engineers; see **Professional Engineers, United Kingdom Association of.**

UMPIRE. A synonym for **arbitrator** (see **arbitration**). Its use seems to have been more common in the nineteenth century in connection with **Boards of Conciliation and Arbitration** (see E.H. Phelps Brown, *The Growth of British Industrial Relations*, Macmillan, 1965, p. 126 *et seq.*, S. and B. Webb, *Industrial Democracy*, 1913 ed., p. 222). Specific instances of its use still remain, especially in the Pit Conciliation Scheme of the coalmining industry.

UNAUTHORISED ABSENCE. Being away from work without **leave of absence**, or without a sickness note or without compliance with a procedure laid down or agreed by which absence is authorised; see **absenteeism.**

UNCONSTITUTIONAL STRIKE. A strike which takes place in violation of a no-strike clause of a procedure agreement or procedure for the avoidance of disputes between a trade union and an employer or employers' association; the opposite of a **constitutional strike** which only takes place after such a procedure has been exhausted. Not identical with an **unofficial strike** (q.v.).

UNDEREMPLOYMENT. The under-utilisation or inefficient use of existing labour resources. In particular in the situation of manpower shortage of the 1960s, attention was drawn to higher manpower productivity in other developed countries than in Britain, where it was estimated that 10 per cent to 15 per cent more manpower was being employed than was necessary to maintain current output, in part because of management failures to organise work efficiently, and in part because of **restrictive labour practices** (q.v.). The idea was popularised by William Allen of Emerson Consultants ('Half-time Britain', *Sunday Times*, 1 March 1964). Remedies were associated with measures to lessen the impact of change upon individuals (**Contracts of Employment Act 1963, Redundancy Payments Act 1965, earnings related supplements,** etc.), joint manpower bodies in various industries (**Joint Board for the National Newspaper Industry,** etc.), with education and with **productivity bargaining** (q.v.). L.C. Hunter, G.L. Reid and D. Boddy (*Labour Problems of Technical Change*, George Allen and Unwin, 1970, Ch. 11), discuss **overmanning** in terms of surplus manning standards being built in to circumstances of technological change, as well as trade union job protection; see also **concealed unemployment.**

UNEMPLOYMENT. A situation in which a significant part of the **working population** is without jobs, or in which the fact that they have no jobs is concealed or disguised (see **concealed unemployment**); in the former sense measured by Department of Employment statistics of **registered unemployed** (q.v.). Some degree of unemployment is usually considered to be compatible with **full-employment** and, for analytical and policy making purposes, different types of unemployment are commonly distinguished, e.g. **frictional unemployment** (or **search unemployment**), **seasonal unemployment, technological unemployment, structural unemployment, cyclical unemployment.**

UNEMPLOYMENT BENEFIT. or **out-of-work benefit.** Benefit paid to workers while out of a job, first developed by trade unions in the nineteenth century as part of a system and trade union method of **mutual insurance** (q.v.). Governmental involvement in the provision of unemployment benefit dates from the **National Insurance Act 1911.** Benefit was at first confined to certain trades, engineering and shipbuilding in particular, coverage being extended to all those employed under a contract of service by the **Unemployment Insurance Act 1920**, the principal exception being agriculture, which was brought into the scheme in 1936. Under the **National Insurance Act 1965** and the Social Security Act 1975 benefit is now paid as flat-rate benefit plus additions for dependants and **earnings-related supplements**. The Acts provide for disqualifications from benefit in certain circumstances. *Inter alia* s. 22 (2) of the National Insurance Act provides that a person may be deprived of benefit for a period not exceeding six weeks if he loses his employment through his own misconduct or voluntarily leaves his employment without just cause. The Social Security Act, s. 19 (1) and (2) provides that benefit shall be stopped for any person put out of work by a stoppage of work due to a **trade dispute** (whether himself on strike or not), unless he can prove that he is not participating or directly interested in the dispute which caused the stoppage. The payment of benefit against production of National Insurance Cards went out of use from April 1975, Inland Revenue forms P45 from the previous employer being substituted; see B.A. Hepple and Paul O'Higgins, *Employment Law*, Sweet and Maxwell 1976, p. 245 *et seq.* and, on the dispute disqualification, the Donovan **Royal Commission on Trade Unions and Employers' Associations, 1965-1968,** Cmnd. 3623, June 1968, para. 953 *et seq.* Unemployment benefit has never been universal as a trade union provision, rather more than one-half making it available to members in 1893, and just under that proportion in 1965; state unemployment benefit has, however, eroded its functions in trade unions which paid out a little more than 40p per member in 1893, an average of 2½p between 1947 and 1966 and in 1976 8.2p; see Arthur Marsh and Peter Cope, 'The Anatomy of Trade Union Benefits in the 1960s', *Industrial Relations Journal*, Summer 1970; see also **tramping, waiting days.**

UNEMPLOYMENT   INSURANCE ACT 1920; see **unemployment benefit.**

UNFAIR DISMISSAL. Dismissal of an **employee** contrary to the terms of the First Schedule of the **Trade Union and Labour Relations Act 1974.** The concept was first introduced in the **Industrial Relations Act 1971**, ss. 22-26. Under the Act it was laid down that no employee was to be dismis-

sed from his job (with or without notice) unfairly and, if he is so dismissed the employer dismissing him might be required to pay **compensation** of an amount not exceeding 104 weeks' pay or £4,160, whichever was the less (s. 118). The primary remedy at that time was a recommendation by an **industrial tribunal** for re-engagement, with compensation awarded only if no such recommendation was made, or, if made, was not complied with. The onus was generally upon the employer to show a reason for the dismissal connected with the employee's capability, qualifications, conduct or redundancy or some other reason sufficiently substantial to justify his dismissal from the particular post he held, and the tribunal was required to be satisfied that the employer had acted reasonably in dismissing for the reason shown (s. 24). Since 1971, within the framework of provisions then laid down, a number of developments have taken place. The qualifying period of service is now 52 weeks, the time limit for complaints has been extended, '**constructive dismissal**' is now more carefully set out, and reinstatement is now the primary remedy. It is now automatically *unfair* to dismiss an employee with a spent conviction (see **Rehabilitation of Offenders Act 1974**), a woman because she is pregnant (see **maternity leave**) and on grounds of trade union membership and activity (Trade Union and Labour Relations Act 1974, Schedule 1). Compensation since 1 June 1976 consists of a *basic award* to a limit of £2,400 at a maximum weekly pay of £80 and with a minimum of two weeks' pay, and a *compensatory award*, e.g. for expenses, lost benefits and for future loss of benefits and pension rights. There were 35,389 unfair dismissal applications in 1977. Of these 9,932 were withdrawn without further action, 12,615 conciliated to settlement and the remainder heard by tribunals (12,842). Of the latter 9.2 per cent were dismissed and an award made in almost all the remaining cases. The concept of unfair dismissal has been developed from **International Labour Recommendations No. 119** on Termination of Employment (1963); reference to 'unjust dismissal' (as distinct from **wrongful dismissal**) featured in the Conservative Party's policy statement **Fair Deal at Work** (April 1968) and (as 'unfair dismissal') in the Report of the Donovan **Royal Commission on Trade Unions and Employers' Associations 1965-68** (Cmnd. 3623, June 1968) para. 545 *et seq*; see G. de N. Clark, *Remedies for Unjust Dismissal,*

PEP Broadsheet 518, June 1970; B.A. Hepple and P. O'Higgins, *Employment Law*, Sweet and Maxwell, 1976, Ch. 17, and S.D. Anderman, *Voluntary Dismissals Procedure and the Industrial Relations Act*, PEP Broadsheet 538, September 1972, D. Jackson, *Unfair Dismissals - Why and How the Law Works*, CUP, 1975, and J.E. McGlyne, *Unfair Dismissal Cases*, Butterworths, 1976. For dismissals law in Europe see M. Panayotopoulos, *Le Contrôle Judicaire du Liceniement dans le Droit des Pays Membres de la C.E.E. et celui de la Grèce*, Paris, 1969; see also **dismissal with notice, summary dismissal, redundancy, abusive dismissal.**

UNFAIR HOUSES also **unfair shops, unfair offices;** establishments paying less than the recognised rate or observing conditions unfavourable to the union, especially in the printing industry; workers employed in such establishments may be known as **rats;** A.E. Musson, *The Typographical Association*, OUP, 1954, *passim.*

UNFAIR INDUSTRIAL PRACTICE (UIP). Any action or failure to act which under the provisions of the **Industrial Relations Act 1971** (now repealed), rendered a trade union, other organisation of workers, employer, organisation of employers, or an individual liable to an action in the **National Industrial Relations Court** or before an **industrial tribunal** for orders either determining rights, restraining actions or awarding compensation. The term is no longer in use; it bore considerable resemblance to the American concept of **unfair labor practices** (q.v.).

UNFAIR LABOR PRACTICES (United State of America). Actions of employers or unions which are prohibited as unfair labor practices under federal or state labor relations statutes, those involving the former being first established under the **Wagner (National Labor Relations) Act 1935**, in order to uphold the union right to organise, and those involving the latter under the **Taft-Hartley** (Labor Management Relations) **Act 1947**, which attempted to equalise the bargaining power of the parties. Charges of unfair labor practices are adjudicated by the National Labor Relations Board, which may issue cease and desist orders which are enforceable in the federal courts of appeals; see H.A. Mills and E. Clark Brown, *From the Wagner Act to Taft-Hartley*, University of Chicago Press,

1950. A similar concept was introduced into British industrial relations in 1971 under the heading of **unfair industrial practices** (q.v.).

UNFAIR OFFICES; see unfair houses.

UNFAIR SHOPS; see unfair houses.

UNFILLED VACANCIES. Opportunities for employment; unfilled posts or jobs (see **vacancy**). Statistics published monthly in the *Department of Employment Gazette* give data on unfilled vacancies by region. A quarterly occupational analysis of vacancies for men and women is also published. The data relate to vacancies which are notified by employers to local **employment offices** and **careers offices** which, at the date of the count, remain unfilled. Since they exclude all the vacancies not notified to these offices, they do not purport to measure the extent to which the immediate manpower requirements of employers remain unsatisfied, though they do broadly indicate changes in the pressure of demand upon the labour market.

UNIFORM LIST. or Uniform Standard List. A standard list of piecework prices applying to districts or trades, especially in the cotton industry. Such lists are known to have existed from the latter part of the seventeenth century and became a highly sophisticated system among weavers, particularly after the Blackburn List of 1853, other trades adopting them more slowly. The effect of the **Cotton Manufacturing Industry (Temporary Provisions) Act 1934** (q.v.) was to legalise the main uniform lists by means of Statutory Orders on textile workers' wages and so to prevent employers from paying less than the list laid down. The **Legalised Uniform List** embodied in Order No. 298 of 1937 was continued until 1957, when the 1934 Act was allowed to lapse; see H.A. Turner, *Trade Union Growth, Structure and Policy*, George Allen and Unwin, 1962, and E. Hopwood, *A History of the Lancashire Cotton Industry and the Amalgamated Weavers' Association*, 1969; see also **statements** for similar lists in the boot and shoe industry. The cotton weavers' uniform list was renegotiated into the **CMC Wage System** (q.v.) in 1949.

UNIFORM STATEMENT; see statements.

UNILATERAL ACTION. Action by one

of the parties in a collective relationship without agreement, or, in some cases, without consultation, with the other; an action which is not agreed, or joint, in character. Hence **unilateral decision making,** the making of decisions by either party without reference to the other; **unilateral management decision,** a decision made by management alone. The issue of unilateral or joint action lies behind controversy about **managerial functions, status quo, joint consultation** etc.

UNILATERAL DECISION MAKING; see **unilateral action.**

UNILATERAL MANAGEMENT DECISION; see **unilateral action.**

UNION; see **trade union.**

UNIONATENESS. A concept used by R.M. Blackburn (*Union Character and Social Class*, Batsford, 1967) and described as the commitment of an organisation to the general principles and ideology of trade unionism. Blackburn regards the measurement of unionateness as consisting in the consideration of seven characteristics: acceptance of collective bargaining as a main function: independence of employers for negotiating purposes; willingness to be militant; declaration to be a trade union; registration as a trade union; affiliation to the **Trades Union Congress**, and affiliation to the Labour Party.

UNION OF CONSTRUCTION, ALLIED TRADES AND TECHNICIANS (UCATT); see **Construction, Allied Trades and Technicians, Union of.**

UNION DENSITY or **density of unionisation;** the proportion of potential members who are actually in membership of a trade union, or of trade unions generally. Union density in Britain grew steadily up to 1920, after which it fell and reached its lowest level (22.6 per cent) in 1933. Thereafter it grew to a further peak of 45.2 per cent in 1948, falling subsequently to 42 per cent in 1962. Since 1963 density has tended to rise, especially after 1969 and in 1976 stood at 52.5 per cent; see Keith Hindell, *Trade Union Membership,* Political and Economic Planning, 1962; George Sayers Bain, *The Growth of White Collar Unionism*, OUP, 1970, and Robert Price and George Sayers Bain, 'Union Growth Revisited', *British Journal of Industrial Relations,* Vol. XIV, No. 3, November

1976, pp. 339-55. R.M. Blackburn (*Union Character and Social Class*, Batsford, 1967) regards the expression as incorrect and prefers his own term **completeness.**

UNION DUES. Trade union dues (q.v.).

UNION FUNCTIONS; see **trade union functions.**

UNION HOUSE. A printing establishment in which only trade union members are employed; sometimes known as a **society house;** John Child, *Industrial Relations in the British Printing Industry*, George Allen and Unwin, 1967.

UNIONISATION. The process of forming a trade union; the growth of trade union membership; or a measure of **union density** (q.v.). R.M. Blackburn (*Union Character and Social Class*, Batsford, 1967) favours a wider definition of unionisation than numbers of members as a proportion of total employees eligible to join, arguing that 'union character' ought to be taken into account so as to include organisations, e.g. the **British Medical Association**, which have different characters from trade unions, but perform union functions: hence in his view unionisation = **unionateness** (q.v.) x **completeness** (q.v.), and is 'the measure of the social significance of unionism' in a particular field, regardless of union structure.

UNION OF INSURANCE STAFFS (UIS); see **Insurance Staffs, Union of.**

UNION OF JUTE, FLAX AND KINDRED TEXTILE OPERATIVES (UJFKTO); see **Jute, Flax and Kindred Textile Operatives, Union of.**

UNION LABEL. A form of **boycott**, more commonly used in the USA than in Britain, designed to give preference in making purchases to articles made by trade union labour. In 1928, the General Council reported to the **Trades Union Congress** on union labels and **fair lists** (q.v.) and took no action, the former being considered impractical because of varying degrees of trade union organisation and the processing of articles by different firms. The union label is said to have been introduced into Britain by the **Amalgamated Society of Journeyman Felt Hatters** (q.v.); see S.J. Chapman, *Work and Wages,* Part II, Longmans Green, 1908, p. 152 *et seq.*

UNION MEMBERSHIP AGREE-

MENT. An agreement for a **closed shop** (q.v.); defined in the **Trade Union and Labour Relations Act 1974**, s. 30, as amended by the **Trade Union and Labour Relations Act 1976**, s. 3(3), as an agreement or arrangement entered into or *de facto* between an employer and an **independent trade union** (q.v.) under which the employees concerned are required to be or to become members of the signatory union or of another specified union. Where such an agreement exists, it is fair for the employer to dismiss any employee if he is not, or refuses to become, a member of one of the unions concerned, unless he genuinely objects on grounds of religious belief to joining any trade union whatsoever (see **unfair dismissal** and **Saggers v. British Railways Board**); Schedule 1, para. 6(5), Trade Union and Labour Relations Act 1974, as amended by the Trade Union and Labour Relations (Amendment) Act 1976, s. 1(c); in effect, therefore, a union membership agreement makes trade union membership a compulsory part of the contract of employment; see also **Ferrybridge Six.**

UNION OF POST OFFICE WORKERS (UPW); see **Post Office Workers, Union of.**

UNION OF SHOP, DISTRIBUTIVE AND ALLIED WORKERS (USDAW); see **Shop, Distributive and Allied Workers, Union of.**

UNION RATE. A negotiated rate of pay, by the hour, week, month or other time interval, which is regarded as the **standard rate**, or the **minimum rate**, for a particular craft, grade or occupation; it may sometimes refer to a national or industry-wide rate, sometimes to a district rate, and sometimes to a rate set at company or plant level; originally the rate set by a trade union as the terms on which its members should or would accept employment, and later extended to mean a negotiated or agreed rate.

UNION REFERENCE. A question or issue taken up by a trade union in a **grievance procedure** or **disputes procedure** as contrasted with a question or issue referred to such a procedure by an employer, e.g. an **employer reference**. The majority of issues so processed are union references; see, for the engineering industry, A.I. Marsh and R.S. Jones, 'Engineering Procedure and Central Conference at York in 1959', *British Journal of Industrial Relations*, June 1964.

UNION SECURITY CLAUSES. A term used, especially in the United States and Canada, to describe conditions in collective agreements which are designed to protect the institutional life of the union against various types of situations such as anti-union action by employers, non-union employees, **poaching** by other unions, etc. Such provisions may include various devices associated with the **closed shop (preferential hiring, union shop, maintenance of membership, agency shop** etc.); see Orme W. Phelps, *Union Security*, Institute of Industrial Relations, University of California, Los Angeles, 1953; US Department of Labor, *Union Security and Check-off Provisions in Major Union Contracts, 1958-1959*, BLS Bulletin, No. 1272, 1960; Michael Dudra, 'Union Security in Canada', *Labor Law Journal*, July 1961; see also **check-off** and **right to work**. The phrase 'union security' is being increasingly used in Britain.

UNION SHOP. A form of **closed shop** (q.v.) in which a worker is required to join the union *after* he is accepted for work by an employer, sometimes within a specified period. In the United States this period is usually thirty days. The union shop is regarded by some as a less stringent form of **closed shop** where this is regarded as requiring trade union membership *before* hiring. The same expression is sometimes used to describe a situation in which a shop is closed by one method or another, but in which trade union membership is not confined to a single union; see also **post-entry closed shop.**

UNIT FOR MANPOWER STUDIES; see **qualified manpower.**

UNITARY SYSTEM. A system which has one source of authority and one focus of loyalty; the opposite of a **pluralistic system**, i.e. one which has many sources of authority and many foci of loyalty. On the use of these concepts in industrial relations; see **plural society.**

UNITED KINGDOM ASSOCIATION OF PROFESSIONAL ENGINEERS (UKAPE); see **Professional Engineers, United Kingdom Association of.**

UNITED KINGDOM ASSOCIATION OF PROFESSIONAL ENGINEERS v. ADVISORY, CONCILIATION AND

ARBITRATION SERVICE. Times Law Report, 30 June 1978. A case in which it was held that in a **Section 11 reference** involving an independent trade union, the United Kingdom Association of Professional Engineers, the decision by the Advisory, Conciliation and Arbitration Service that no recommendation as to recognition should be made was a nullity in that it failed sufficiently to give effect to the statutory duty of ACAS contained in s.1 of the Employment Protection Act 1975 to encourage the extension of collective bargaining and, where necessary, to reform collective bargaining machinery. UKAPE obtained 79 per cent of those in the relevant grades who answered the ACAS questionnaire at W.H. Allen, Sons and Co. Ltd, Bedford. The ACAS decision was taken on the grounds that recognition would proliferate bargaining units and might well lead to industrial strife.

UNITED PATTERNMAKERS' ASSOCIATION (UPA); see **Patternmakers and Allied Craftsmen, Association of.**

UNITED ROAD TRANSPORT UNION (URTU); see **Transport Union, United Road.**

UNITED RUBBER WORKERS OF GREAT BRITAIN (URWGB), Rubber Workers of Great Britain, United; later **Rubber, Plastic and Allied Workers.**

UNIVERSAL ALLIANCE OF DIAMOND WORKERS (UADW); see **International Trade Secretariats.**

UNIVERSAL STANDARD DATA. A **predetermined motion time system** developed from **Methods Time Measurement** (q.v.). It consists of seven tables of data of time standards which can, it is claimed, be applied to any type of manual activity with a high degree of accuracy on any but short cycle operations.

UNIVERSITY TEACHERS, ASSOCIATION OF (AUT). A federation of local associations of university teachers and related administrative, library and research staff in the United Kingdom recognised as speaking for university academic staff on matters of salary and related conditions. The AUT was formed nationally in 1919, and had its origins in discontents among non-professorial staffs before the first world war. A parallel Scottish Association was formed nationally in 1922, and the two organisations merged into a single union in 1949. National negotiating machinery involving the AUT, university authorities and the government was established for the first time in May 1970, awards previously being made unilaterally by the government after consultation, except for the years 1963-64, when settlement was referred to the **National Incomes Commission,** and after November 1967 when the pay of university teachers became for a time subject to a Standing Reference of the **National Board for Prices and Incomes.** Harold Perkin, *Key Profession: The History of the Association of University Teachers,* Routledge and Kegan Paul, 1969. The union affiliated to the Trades Union Congress in May 1976. *Address:* United House, 1 Pembridge Road, London W11 3HJ. *Tel:* 01-221 4370. *TUC Affiliated Membership, 1977:* 28,149.

UNJUST DISMISSAL; see **unfair dismissal.**

UNOCCUPIED TIME ALLOWANCE (work study); see **allowances.** 'An allowance made to the worker when there is unoccupied time during machine or process controlled time. This may also apply to team work'; British Standards Institution, *Glossary of Terms Used in Work Study,* BS 3138, 1969, A 1020; to be distinguished from **waiting time, down time** and **idle time** (q.v.).

UNOFFICIAL STRIKE. A strike which takes place without the official approval of the union according to the provisions of its rule book. Sometimes identified as a **wildcat strike** (q.v.) though in Britain this term may not necessarily be an exact parallel; often confused with an **unconstitutional strike** (q.v.).

UNRECOGNISED ASSOCIATION; see **recognised association.**

UNRESTRICTED WORK. Work to which **work study** has been applied, and in which the output of the worker is restricted only by factors within his control; International Labour Office, *Introduction to Work Study,* Geneva, 1969, p. 309.

UNSOCIAL HOURS. The description given in Stage Three of the Heath government's Price and Pay Code effective from 1 November 1973 (see **incomes policy** and **Pay Board**) to describe hours worked on shifts between 8 p.m. and 6 a.m. on any day including Saturday and Sunday.

Under the Code premium payments for such hours could be increased over and above the pay limit of 7 per cent, provided that the average hourly rate of such payment did not exceed the equivalent of one-fifth of the appropriate basic time rate for daytime hours of the workers concerned. It was believed at the time that the 'unsocial hours' provision was inserted into the Code to ease the problem of a pay settlement in the coalmining industry. The phrase was already known in the industry; see, for example *The Clerk*, January-February 1950.

UPA. United Patternmakers' Association; see **Patternmakers and Allied Craftsmen, Association of.**

UPGRADING. The practice of raising workers to a higher grade of wages and/or status, especially where white collar workers and professional workers are concerned; e.g. to upgrade from junior lecturer to lecturer, etc; promotion. Among manual workers, upgrading is usually less systematic, except where a **seniority ladder** operates, or where wage structures permit; it may, when employed from time to time take the form of **dilution**, especially when the labour situation is tight, e.g. the upgrading of experienced semi-skilled workers to skilled rates of pay, and has been common in **productivity agreements**, where mates have been upgraded to craftsmen, on the grounds that they have been only partly occupied in their previous grade; see Allan Flanders, *The Fawley Productivity Agreements*, Faber & Faber, 1964.

UPLIFT UNIONISM or **welfare unionism.** Trade Unionism primarily concerned with improving the workers' standard of living and conditions of employment, whether by collective bargaining or by protection against unemployment, sickness, accidents, etc., or by improvements in the behaviour and techniques of government; an expression primarily used in the United States of America; see Carroll R. Daugherty, *Labor Problems in American Industry*, Houghton Mifflin, 1933.

UPPER CLYDE SHIPBUILDERS. A merger of shipbuilding companies on the Upper Clyde consisting of Yarrow's, Stephen's of Linthouse, Connell's of Scotstoun, John Brown's and Fairfield's; (see **Fairfields Experiment**) in February 1968 following the proposals of the **Geddes Report**. It was the scene of the Clyde ship-building workers' **work-in** (q.v.) of 1971-72; see also F. Herron, *Labour Market in Crisis; Redundancy at Upper Clyde Shipbuilders*, Macmillan, 1976.

UPSTANDING WAGE. An all-in weekly wage paid regardless of hours worked, i.e. with no payment for overtime; sometimes, in current usage, applied to any fixed weekly wage, whether subject to overtime additions or not, but including all 'extras'.

UPW. Union of Post Office Workers; see **Post Office Workers, Union of.**

URTU. United Road Transport Union; see **Transport Union, United Road.**

URWGB. United Rubber Workers of Great Britain; later **Rubber, Plastic and Allied Workers** (q.v.).

USDAW. Union of Shop, Distributive and Allied Workers; see **Shop, Distributive and Allied Workers, Union of.**

V

VA. Value analysis (q.v.).

VACANCY. An employment opportunity; a job or post unfilled; hence Department of Employment statistics on **unfilled vacancies** (q.v.); see also **vacancy list, vacant book.**

VACANCY LIST. A type of **fair list** (q.v.) employed by the Association of Engineering and Shipbuilding Draughtsmen (later the **Draughtsmen's and Allied Technicians' Association** and now the Technical and Supervisory Section (TASS) of the **Amalgamated Union of Engineering Workers**). The practice of listing vacancies for members and the salaries offered began early in the life of the union, and also of 'posting' those firms which refused to recognise it, or where conditions were particularly bad in order to discourage draughtsmen from taking jobs there. In 1920 the policy was begun of refusing to accept advertisements from employers paying below minimum rates set by the union; see J.E. Mortimer, *A History of the Association of Engineering and Shipbuilding Draughtsmen*, AESD, 1960. The

DATA Vacancy List ceased to be published in 1963.

VACANT BOOK. A branch book required in the rules of some unions in which members out of employment in receipt of trade union unemployment benefit can, at specified intervals, write their names and the numbers of their contribution cards (e.g. Amalgamated Union of Engineering Workers, Engineering Section, Rule 12); **vacant book-keeper,** an officer appointed to keep a vacant book. The vacant book is designed to act both as a means of claiming unemployment benefit, and as a method of informing members of available jobs; see also **tramping.**

VACANT BOOK-KEEPER; see **vacant book.**

VALUE ADDED; see **added value.**

VALUE ADMINISTRATION; see **value analysis.**

VALUE ANALYSIS (VA). One of a cluster of techniques aimed at providing better 'value for money' in various aspects of industry e.g. **value analysis** (or **value improvement),** the more economic production of manufactured items by the use of alternative materials or simplified or improved design; **value engineering** (or **value assurance)** the application of similar techniques and approaches to items in course of development; **value administration,** the examination of systems, e.g. of paperwork, with similar objects in mind, and **value management,** the analysis of organisations, with the object of cost saving and increased efficiency. The concept of value analysis is said to have originated with H. Erlicher, a Vice-President of the General Electric Company of America as a result of the use of substitute materials during the second world war and was subsequently developed by an employee of the company, L.D. Miles. As a rule-of-thumb guide towards cost saving it seems to have advatages where engineering tools, or equipment or bureaucratic software or procedures are concerned; application to the management or organisation of people seems to be more questionable. There may be no necessary relationship between cost savings and better value in organisation; nor does the technique necessarily help in the production of change. See L.D. Miles, *Techniques of Value Analysis and Engineering,* McGraw-Hill, 1961; W.L. George, *Value Analysis,* McGraw-Hill,

1967; J.C.H. Roberts, *ABC of Value Analysis,* Modern Management Techniques, 1967; J.F.A. Gibson, *Value Analysis,* Pergamon, 1968; A.D. Raven, *Profit Improvement by Value Analysis, Value Engineering and Purchase Price Analysis,* Cassell, 1971; and D.E. Williams, 'Value Engineering - The Human Aspect', *Value Engineering,* 1969.

VALUE ASSURANCE; see **value analysis.**

VALUE ENGINEERING; see **value analysis.**

VALUE IMPROVEMENT; see **value analysis.**

VALUE MANAGEMENT; see **value analysis.**

VARIABLE FACTOR PROGRAMMING (VFP). A technique for improving the ultilisation of labour in offices, other white collar and indirect areas introduced into England by the Wofac Corporation of the United States in 1962. VFP provides a means of determining how long it should take to do a given volume of work, enabling supervision to plan and control the number of staff required and to balance man hours with the work load. It involves, in consultation with workers, the identification of work on daily work activity sheets, the development of target times, and the organisation of subsequent manning arrangements and controls; see British Institute of Management, *Variable Factor Programming and Control of Indirect Labour,* Information Note 37, 1967, and J.E. Bayhylle, *Productivity Improvement in the Office,* Engineering Employers' Federation, Research Paper 2, December 1968, pp. 16-22; also **Clerical Work Improvement Programme** (CWIP), **Group Capacity Assessment** (GCA) and **Clerical Work Evaluation** (CWE).

VARIABLE WORKING HOURS. A practice according to which each employee is given complete freedom of choice of working times, subject to his responsibility for completing his contractual hours and for ensuring that during the normal period of the working day there is a deputy to carry out essential work in his absence; said to have been introduced into a garment factory in Berlin and a waterworks in Kassel; see J. Harvey Bolton, *Flexible Working Hours,* Anbar Publications Ltd, 1971; see also **fixed working**

hours, staggered working hours, flexible working hours, rational working hours.

VEHICLE BUILDERS, NATIONAL UNION OF (NUVB). A union formed in 1919 from the amalgamation of the United Kingdom Society of Coachmakers, the London and Provincial Coachmakers, the Operative Coachmakers' Federal Union and the Coachsmiths' and Vicemen's Trade Society, to which were added the Amalgamated Wheelwrights', Smiths' and Kindred Trades Union (1925) and the Wheelwrights' and Coachmakers' Operatives Union (1948). Between the two world wars the union was mainly representative of craftsmen in shops operating under national agreements made with employers in membership of the United Kingdom Joint Wages Board of Employers for the Vehicle Building Industry. After 1945 it was more concerned with workers, both skilled and semi-skilled, employed by the main mass production vehicle manufacturers, especially Rover, Vauxhall, and British Leyland. The union merged with the Transport and General Workers' Union in 1972. National Union of Vehicle Builders, *A Hundred Years of Vehicle Building, 1834-1934,* NUVB, 1934, and *NUVB: 1834-1959, One Hundred and Twenty-Fifth Anniversary,* 1959.

VERSATILITY GRADES. New grades of railwaymen introduced as part of a pay and efficiency agreement between the British Railways Board and the National Union of Railwaymen subsequent to the **Penzance Agreement** of 5 July 1968. Four new designations of Railman, Leading Railman, Senior Railman and Chargeman replaced fourteen pay groups with 109 separate job titles and allowed for greater flexibility in the performance of duties between them. Charles McLeod, *All Change: Railway Industrial Relations in the Sixties,* Gower Press, 1970, pp. 140-65.

VERTICAL DEMARCATION. Defined by Kate Liepmann (*Apprenticeship,* Routledge and Kegan Paul, 1960, p. 158) as a device to defend craftsmen's jobs against unapprenticed workers, i.e. as a protection against **dilution** (q.v.). The writer distinguishes **vertical demarcation** from **demarcation** (q.v.).

VERTICAL UNION; see **industrial unionism.**

VERTRAUENSMANN   (plural VERTRAUENSLEUTE). A trade union shop floor representative in the Federal Republic of Germany. Such representatives are not the equivalent of British **shop stewards.** They have no role in formal relationships between workers and employers, since this is the province of **betriebsräte** or Works Councils. On the difficulties of translating German and British industrial relations terms, see G.R. Gegen, *Shop Stewards,* Schriftenreibe die Otto Brenner Stiftung, No. 6, Frankfurt, 1976, pp. 20-23.

VFP. Variable Factor Programming (q.v.).

VICARIOUS LIABILITY; see **employers' liability.**

VICTIM PAY; see **victimisation benefit.**

VICTIMISATION; see **discrimination.**

VICTIMISATION BENEFIT or **victim pay.** A **trade benefit** paid to a trade union member in the event of **victimisation** or **lock-out** by an employer, and sometimes known by other names, e.g. **lock-out pay, sacrifice,** etc. Benefits of this kind are commonly provided for by manual worker, and sometimes by non-manual worker unions in Britain; see Arthur Marsh and P.J. Cope, 'The Anatomy of Trade Union Benefits in the 1960s', *Industrial Relations Journal,* Summer 1970.

VICTUALLING ALLOWANCE. A daily allowance made to a seafarer who provides his own food (**National Maritime Board** (q.v.) **Agreements**). Such an allowance is made in addition to the higher pay rates made in such circumstances. The majority of merchant seamen are provided with food and accommodation by the shipping company employing them.

VIGILANCE COMMITTEES; see **vigilance men.**

VIGILANCE MEN sometimes **vigilantes;** also **vigilance committees.** Individuals or committees, sometimes official and sometimes not, operating at workplace level to protect the interests of groups of organised workers and to report to their unions workplace developments and grievances. The title remains in a few unions (e.g. Card Setting Machine Tenters' Society, *Rules,* 1948, Rule 14) but has mostly been overtaken by that of **shop stewards** (q.v.). **Vigilance committees** were commonly associated with **workers' control** movements (q.v.) during and after the first world war.

VIGILANTES. Vigilance men (q.v.).

VOCATIONAL GUIDANCE. Defined in **International Labour Recommendation No. 87** as 'assistance given to an individual in solving problems related to occupational choice and progress with due regard for the individual's characteristics and their relation to occupational opportunity'; sometimes used as synonymous with **employment counselling** (or simply **counselling**), though vocational guidance is often thought of as applying to young persons, including those in school, while **employment counselling** is a term applied to adults. In Britain the former was, until 1974, officially supplied by the **Youth Employment Service** (q.v.), though there was evidence that most school-leavers and parents thought that this had a 'placement' rather than 'counselling' function; **occupational guidance** is preferred by the Department of Employment to describe counselling for workers of all ages over the age-limit of the Youth Employment Service (see LEC, Memorandum 29, *Occupational Guidance Service*). In September 1970, the Department provided a free service through 30 occupational guidance units and 10 permanent outstations; see also **Seven Point Plan** and B. Hopson and J. Hayes, *The Theory and Practice of Vocational Guidance*, Pergamon Press, 1968, Part II, for readings in recent literature on the subject; also **Employment Service** for changes proposed in December 1971.

VOCATIONAL TRAINING SCHEME (VTS). A government scheme for provision of accelerated training courses for adults to overcome labour shortages and to assist workers with special needs to fit themselves for suitable jobs. The Scheme originated in the 'instructional factories' first set up in 1917 to train disabled ex-servicemen, and was associated with the **Government Training Centres** (now known as **Skillcentres**), first set up in 1925 as a means of dealing with the problem of unemployment. After the second world war the Centres were concerned particularly with resettlement and reconstruction especially in relation to housing, and after 1950 to training for regular ex-servicemen. In 1963 the emphasis moved to meeting shortages of skilled labour. A consultative document *Training for the Future* in February 1972 drew attention to the small scale of the Scheme, to the limited range of courses offered and to delays in obtaining training, and proposed that it should be replaced by an enlarged **Training Opportunities Scheme (TOPS)** (q.v.).

VOLUNTARISM. The doctrine that voluntary action, individually and collectively, in social affairs, is preferable to action by the state; in industrial relations, frequently used to refer to this doctrine as held by trade unions and to the trade union belief 'that workers could best achieve their goals by relying on their own voluntary associations' (Michael Rogin, 'Voluntarism: The Political Functions of an Antipolitical Doctrine', *Industrial and Labor Relations Review*, July 1962). In the United States voluntarism was the policy of Samuel Gompers and of the American Federation of Labor (see Samuel Gompers, *Seventy Years of Life and Labor; An Autobiography*, Merlin/Kelley, 1970) and has now given way to the acceptance of government intervention and support in addition to the maintenance of collective bargaining. In Britain, the doctrine of voluntarism has not been confined to trade unions only, but has traditionally reflected the preference of both trade unions and employers; hence the characterisation of industrial relations as a **voluntary system** i.e. a system of industrial relations operating without a legal framework of regulation provided by the State. The voluntary basis of the system was commended by the Donovan **Royal Commission on Trade Unions and Employers' Associations, 1965-1968** (Cmnd. 3623, HMSO, June 1968), with some proposals for change, which were broadly accepted by the Wilson government of the time; the policy of the Heath government which succeeded it broke to some extent with the principle of voluntarism by providing a legal framework for industrial relations through the **Industrial Relations Act 1971**. The **Trade Union and Labour Relations Act 1974** and **Employment Protection Act 1975**, the current basis of industrial relations law, go some way to restoring voluntarism, but contain more of the spirit of legal intervention than would have been thought acceptable a decade ago. On the characteristics of the British voluntary tradition; see Allan Flanders, *Collective Bargaining; Prescription for Change*, Faber & Faber, 1967, and *Management and Unions: The Theory and Reform of Industrial Relations*, Faber & Faber, 1975, 'The tradition of

voluntarism', *British Journal of Industrial Relations*, Vol. XII, No. 3, November 1974, pp. 352-70, and A.I. Marsh, *Disputes Procedures in British Industry*, Research Papers 2 (Part I), Royal Commission in Trade Unions and Employers' Associations, HMSO, 1966; see also Kevin Hawkins, 'The Decline of Voluntarism', *Industrial Relations Journal*, Summer 1971, and on the conditions of its interwar development, Rodger Charles, *The Development of Industrial Relations in Britain, 1911-1939*, Hutchinson, 1973.

VOLUNTARY ARBITRATION. An **arbitration** procedure in which the parties to a **difference** or **dispute** mutually agree to submit the issue to arbitration, either *ad hoc*, or as part of an agreement to do so, and are thereby morally, but not legally, bound by the award of the arbitrator; the opposite of **compulsory arbitration** (q.v.).

VOLUNTARY SYSTEM; see voluntarism.

VTS. Vocational Training Scheme (q.v.).

W

WAGE or **wages.** The **earnings** or **take-home pay** of a **wage earner**, as distinct from the **salary** of a grade of worker not regarded as a workman or servant. The distinction, while having an historical significance, is to some extent arbitrary, not all workers of a similar kind being regarded as wage earners or salary earners in different industries or situations. A list of occupations regarded by the Office of Censuses and Surveys as wage earners (see, for example, *Sample Census 1966 (Great Britain)*, Economic Activity Tables, Part III, p. xlii) includes **operatives** and other **manual workers** together with some, such as shop assistants, in occupations classified as non-manual. It is a nice point whether the concept of wages should be broadened to include other **compensation**, such as pensions and **fringe benefits** generally. The word 'wage', though less often the word 'wages', is sometimes used more narrowly to mean **wage rate** (q.v.).

WAGE DEDUCTIONS; see deductions, Truck Acts, check-off.

WAGE DETERMINATION; see wage theories.

WAGE DIFFERENTIALS. Variations between **wage rates** due to a number of factors; skill, job content, location, industry, sex, etc.; see **differentials, labour markets.** Sometimes used loosely to describe differentials between **earnings** rather than **wage rates.**

WAGE DISPARITY. A concept used by W. Baldamus, *Efficiency and Effort*, Tavistock, 1967, p. 104 *et seq.;* contrasted with **wage parity.** Baldamus defines wage parity as 'a hypothetical equilibrium between effort and pay on a given level of expectations' and hence wage disparity as arising from 'non-parallel movements of the components of effort value', the most usual case of disparity arising where 'both effort intensity and wages move to a higher level but effort more than wages'. He regards such a disparity as 'the very centre of industrial conflict'. The concept is taken up in Dan Gowler, 'Determinants of the Supply of Labour to the Firm', *Journal of Management Studies,* Vol. 6, No. 1, February 1969, p. 80.

WAGE DRIFT. A concept originating in Scandinavia, and particularly in Sweden, where the term 'löneglidning' ('wages-glide' or 'wages-slip') was used in the early 1950s to describe the persistent excess of the total wage bill over that envisaged in central agreements. 'Löneglidning' was adapted into British use as **wage drift** by H.A. Turner ('Wages: Industry Rates, Workplace Rates and the Wage Drift', *Manchester School,* May 1956, pp. 95-123). The concept has been important in influencing thought about **incomes policy** and on the operation of **payment by results** (q.v.), the latter being thought of as an important element in drift (National Board for Prices and Incomes, *Payment by Results Systems,* Report No. 65, December 1968). Discussion of the concept of wage drift has centred around its possible consequences, its measurement, and its causes. Consequences are usually analysed in terms of effects on labour costs (often by implication their increase over and above rises in productivity), and in terms of institutional control: hence the well-known definition: 'The essence of drift is that the effective rate of pay per unit of labour input is raised by arrangements outside the control of recognised procedures for scheduling rates' (E.H. Phelps Brown, 'Wage Drift', *Economica,*

1962, pp. 339-56), a concept sometimes known as **pure drift** (S.W. Lerner, J.R. Cable and S. Gupta, *Workshop Wage Determination,* Pergamon Press, 1969, pp. 20-21). Other definitions may vary according to emphasis, or to availability of measurable data. In Sweden drift has commonly been defined as the actual national wage bill *less* estimated wage bill ÷ wage bill before the central agreement x 100, and this has correspondence with the calculations of the NBPI (op. cit.). In Britain, an early shortage of data led to the definition of drift as the difference between increases in indices of earnings and indices of increases in wage rates (sometimes called **statistical drift**), a formula later refined by making allowances for various facttrs such as hours worked, and therefore also of overtime payment (Ministry of Labour, *Statistics on Incomes, Prices, Employment and Production,* No. 16, p. 42). Such a calculation is sometimes thought of as measuring **earnings drift,** and has been followed, with variations, by a number of writers, e.g. S.W. Lerner and J. Marquand ('Workshop Bargaining, Wage Drift and Productivity in the British Engineering Industry', *Manchester School,* January 1962, pp. 15-50), and L.A. Dicks-Mireaux and J.R. Shepherd ('The Wage Structure and Some Implications for Incomes Policy', *National Institute Economic Review,* November 1962, pp. 38-48). Calculations of drift may vary according to the precise definition adopted and this in turn may be affected by assumptions about the relationship between the various factors making for drift. Movements of earnings may, for example, be in part independent of and in part related to, changes in basic rates, and the role of each is difficult to separate; upgrading, as well as other factors, may lead to increased aggregate earnings, and its effects may also be difficult to distinguish. It is partly for this reason that, for practical purposes of policy, attention has tended to shift from conceptual analysis and attempts at precise measurement, towards the importance of appreciating the components of increases in earnings, whether these arise from national agreements, from payment by results, from overtime and changes in working hours, from changes in the composition of the labour force and so on (NBPI, op. cit.); see also **piecework wage drift, wage rounds, grade creep, earnings gap.** Less has been heard of wage drift in publii discussion and policy since the 1960s, in part because higher rates of unemployment may have relieved some pressures, but also because of a franker acknowledgement of the primacy of **workplace bargaining** in the economic system.

WAGE EARNER; see **wage.**

WAGE EXPLOSION. A popular description of a period of time, usually dated from large scale stoppages of local authority workers and miners in the autumn of 1969, in which percentage claims for wage and salary increases were exceptionally high, and in which rapidly increasing levels of earnings were accompanied by rising unemployment, thus questioning the operation of the **Phillips Curve** (q.v.). H.A. Clegg (*How to Run an Incomes Policy and Why We Made Such a Mess of the Last One,* Heinemann, 1971) argues that the wage explosion cannot be attributed to any specific cause, but was rather the culmination of a process at work over a number of years, beginning at workshop level, to raise earnings, relativities playing an important part in the process. H.A. Turner and Frank Wilkinson ('Real Net Incomes and the Wage Explosion', *New Society,* 25 February 1971 and D. Jackson, H.A. Turner and F. Wilkinson, *Do Trade Unions Cause Inflation?,* CUP, 2nd ed., 1975) attribute the explosion principally to the movement of post-tax real wages. From June 1970, the Heath government attempted to 'de-escalate' wage claims to progressively lower levels but later reverted to a more orthodox approach to a **prices and incomes policy** under the heading of a programme for controlling inflation (*A Programme for Controlling Inflation,* the First Stage, Cmnd. 5125. November 1972).

WAGE-FOR-AGE SCALE. An arrangement by which wage rates or salaries of various amounts are paid to workers according to their age, older workers receiving more than younger workers. In the engineering industry the Women's National Schedule of Rates has incorporated a minimum wage-for-age scale since 1939; apprentices have a wage-for-age scale based on percentages of the skilled rate and a national minimum scale on the same principle has existed for draughtsmen and tracers since 1968; see *Handbook of National Agreements;* the wage-for-age scale is a special type of **incremental scale** (q.v.).

WAGE INDEXATION; see **cost of living sliding scale.**

WAGE PARITY. A state of equilibrium between effort and pay on a given level of expectations; a concept used by W. Balda-mus, *Efficiency and Effort,* Tavistock, 1967, pp. 104 *et seq.*; see also **wage dispar-ity.**

WAGE POLICY or **wages policy.** (1) The factors, theories and considerations which affect or determine the attitudes and prac-tices of a trade union in collective bargain-ing about wages, e.g. as in A.M. Ross, *Trade Union Wage Policy,* University of California, Berkeley, 1948 (see also **coer-cive comparison**); (2) the formal practices of an industry, a company or plant in rela-tion to wages, e.g. levels, systems of pay-ment, **differentials** etc.; (3) in the sense of **national wages policy,** tangible objectives or criteria for influencing, in the national interest, the outcome of wage bargaining, e.g. in relation to differentials affecting the distribution of labour, or to the aggregate growth of wage incomes in order to secure **wage restraint** to moderate or remove infla-tion, etc.; usually distinguished from **incomes policy** in that it relates to wages and salaries as they affect incomes, while incomes policy includes also **non-wage incomes.** Earlier writings on this theme in Britain usually employed the term 'wage policy', e.g. in Allan Flanders, *A Policy for Wages,* Fabian Tract 281, July 1950. 'Incomes policy' or 'prices and incomes policy' became more usual in the 1960s, particularly because of trade union sup-port at that time for 'an incomes policy to include salaries, wages, dividends and pro-fis and social security benefits' (Frank Cou-sins, General Secretary of the Transport and General Workers' Union, Labour Party Conference 1963) and the control of prices. For a discussion of the broad social issues involved in wage policy see Barbara Wootton, *The Social Foundations of Wages Policy,* Allen and Unwin, 1962.

WAGE PROTECTION ASSOCIA-TION; see **trade protection society.**

WAGE RATE. The amount of money paid to a **wage earner** for a period of time worked or for a unit of output produced on a particular job; it may therefore, for a **timeworker,** be his hourly, daily (**datal rate**) or weekly rate, exclusive of **premium payments,** and other payments in addition to the **basic rate,** or it may be his **piece rate,** i.e. the amount paid to him per piece pro-duced, or other form of incentive rate (see **incentive payment systems**); see also **wage.**

WAGE RESTRAINT. An expression syn-onymous with **wage policy** and **incomes policy** in so far as these have been designed to restrain the gowth of wage incomes in order to control the rate of inflation, as in the title of the book by Lloyd Ulman and Robert J. Flanagan, *Wage Restraint: A Study of Incomes Policy in Western Europe,* University of California Press, 1971; more specifically, used to describe particular attempts at a wage policy, espe-cially that connected with the name of Sir Stafford Cripps and with the Attlee gov-ernment in Britain between 1948 and 1950. The policy was initiated by a White Paper on Personal Incomes, Costs and Prices (Cmd. 7321, February 1948), and laid down no particular criteria for wage increases, but only that each claim should be voluntarily considered 'on its national merits'. It was effectively brought to an end by an adverse vote at the Trades Union Congress of 1950. There is evidence that it had the effect of restraining claims and settlements for a short period (see A.T. Peacock and W.J.L. Ryan, 'Wage Claims and the Pace of Inflation', *Econ-omic Journal,* June 1953). The rising price of raw materials beween 1949 and 1952 may have contributed to the breakdown of the policy (Allan Flanders, 'Wage Move-ments and Wage Policy in Post-war Bri-tain', *Annals of the American Academy,* March, 1957); differential movements of earnings were also involved (see John Corina, 'The British Experiment in Wage Restraint with Special Reference to 1948-60', unpublished D.Phil. thesis, Oxford, 1961, quoted in H.A. Clegg, *The System of Industrial Relations in Great Britain,* Basil Blackwell, 1970, 3rd ed., 1976).

WAGE REVIEW. A periodic review of the performance of individuals to deter-mine those whom the management consid-ers to be eligible for increases or for promotion to higher rated jobs; see also **merit rating scheme.** Also sometimes used to designate a periodic general review of wage rates paid in accordance with a collec-tive agreement or unilaterally.

WAGE ROUNDS. A term which became current after the second world war to describe cycles of wage demands and settle-ments within national economies. Its use generally declined in the 1960s. Such cycles, although referred to by official bod-ies (see, for example, Cohen Council, 2nd Report, August 1958, p. 30) may well have been more apparent than real; at the very least they were more complex than popular report suggested (K.G.J.C. Knowles and E.M.F. Thorne, 'Wage Rounds, 1948-1959', *Oxford University Institute of Statistics Bulletin*, Vol. 23, No. 1, February 1961 and K.G.J.C. Knowles and D. Robinson, 'Wage Rounds and Wage Policy', *Oxford University Institute of Statistics Bulletin*, Vol. 34, No. 2, 1962). The analysis of **wage drift** (q.v.) tended in the 1960s to move away from wage round theory. In the Republic of Ireland a discernible pattern of wage rounds existed in the 1960s (David O'Mahony, *Economic Aspects of Industrial Relations*, The Economic Research Institute, Paper No. 24, February 1965); see Hilde Behrend, Ann Knowles and Jean Davies, *Views on Pay Increases, Fringe Benefits and Low Pay*, Economic and Social Research Institute, Dublin, Paper No. 56, August 1970; see also **whipsawing, pattern bargaining, comparability, trade movements.**

WAGE SIT-IN; see **sit-in.**

WAGE STRUCTURE. An expression used to describe one or more, or a combination of all the following in an establishment, company, industry or community, and usually distinguished from, though associated with, a wage or **payment system** (q.v.): (1) The components of a wage or pay packet, e.g. in the heavy steel industry traditionally for production workers, a time rate expressed as a rate per shift or hour, a tonnage bonus, a cost of living payment, and shift and week-end premium payments, or iommonly in engineering, for pieceworkers, a minimum time rate, plus a piecework supplement, plus a merit or other supplementary rate, plus payment by results earnings, plus overtime or shift premium, etc.; (2) Differentials in rates between different groups of workers by occupation, e.g. labourers, welders, fitters, tool-setters, electricians, etc.; (3) Differentials in rates between different groups of workers by grade or status, e.g. by levels of skill, by distinguishing between manual, clerical, supervisory, managerial and other grades, male and female, young persons, apprentices, etc.; (4) Differentials implied in distributions of earnings under (2) and (3). The United States Department of Labour, and other observers, may define 'wage structure' even more widely to include such factors as provisions for meal breaks and rest, and **fringe benefits.** Attention to plant wage structures in Britain in recent years has been directed particularly at the consequences of poorly understood, and poorly conceived, structures leading to conflict between working groups and to **earnings drift;** see Derek Robinson (ed.), *Local Labour Markets and Wage Structures,* Gower Press, 1970; D.J. Robertson, *Factory Wage Structures and National Agreements,* CUP, 1960, and Harold Lydall, *The Structure of Earnings,* OUP, 1968; see also **job evaluation.**

WAGE THEORIES. Models, or statements of principles or laws, developed by economists and others to explain **wage determination,** i.e. general levels of wages and their movement, the distribution of wages, or the spread of wages, and the functions and relationships of wages in **labour markets.** Older theories include the **wages-fund,** and the **subsistence theory** (or **iron law of wages);** more recently the **marginal productivity theory of wages** and the **bargaining theory of wages;** see also **share of wages, Phillips Curve, prices and incomes policy, wage policy.** For a summary of research see: Melvin W. Reder, Wage Determination in Theory and Practice, in N.W. Chamberlain, Frank C. Pierson and Theresa Wolfson (eds), *A Decade of Industrial Relations Research, 1946-1956,* Industrial Relations Research Association Publication No. 19, Harper, New York, 1958, and E. Robert Livernash, 'Wages and Benefits', in *A Review of Industrial Relations Research,* Vol. I, Industrial Relations Research Association, 1970 and D.J. Robertson, *The Economics of Wages,* Macmillan, 1961.

WAGES; see **wage.**

WAGES COUNCILS. Statutory bodies with powers to make orders fixing minimum remuneration, holidays, holiday pay and other terms of employment for workers within their scope. Wages Councils originated as Trade Boards under the **Trade Boards Acts 1909 and 1918** (q.v.); see also **sweating.** These were converted into Wages Councils by the Wages Councils Act 1945 (see Alan Bullock, *Ernest Bevin,* Vol. 2, Minister of Labour 1940-1945, Heinemann, 1967, pp. 351-4). In 1948 the Wages Councils Act of that year turned the Road Haulage Central Wages Board set up under the Road Haulage Wages Act 1938 into a Wages Council and in 1959 the Terms and Conditions of Employment Act similarly converted the Wages Boards established by the Catering Wages Act 1943. Councils now operate under the Wages Councils Act 1959 and the Employment Protection Act 1975, the provisions of these Acts being administered by the Secretary of State for Employment. Wages Councils operate as 'assisted' collective bargaining institutions, being made up of representatives of employers and of workers, together with **independent members** (q.v.), one of whom is appointed Chairman. The role of the independants is to act as conciliators and obtain, if possible, voluntary agreement; failing this they act in a decisive voting capacity to resolve disagreements. Wages Orders made by Wages Councils have statutory force in the industries or trades concerned, employers who fail to comply being liable to a fine for each offence. Enforcement is in the hands of Wages Inspectors of the Department of Employment who may examine wages records and interview workers in the establishments concerned. A standard proportion of establishments is examined annually, in 1977, $7\frac{1}{2}$ per cent. There were 42 Wages Councils in January 1978 covering 3 million workers and in addition two Agricultural Wages Boards operating on similar lines (see Agricultural Wages Act 1948 and Agricultural Wages (Scotland) Act 1949). Wages Councils have been subject to criticism principally on the grounds that they have seemed to do little to extend voluntary collective bargaining or effectively to raise the pay of lower paid workers; see Donovan, **Royal Commission on Trade Unions and Employers' Associations, 1965-1968,** Cmnd. 3623, June 1968, paras 234, 259, and 260 and comments by the four trade unions principally concerned, the Transport and General Workers' Union, the General and Municipal Workers' Union, the Union of Shop, Distributive and Allied Workers and the National Union of Tailors and Garment Workers. In consequence a number of changes have been made in their operation in the **Industrial Relations Act 1971** (now repealed) and the **Employment Protection Act 1975,** ss. 89-98. **Schedule 11 Claims** (q.v.), can now be made in Wages Council trades and industries. Wages Orders no longer need ministerial confirmation, and may have effect from a date earlier than that of the Order and the **Advisory, Conciliation and Arbitration Service** (q.v.) now performs the role formerly assigned to Commissions of Inquiry and under the 1971 Act to the Commission on Industrial Relations to recommend on the abolition of a Council by the Secretary of State for Employment. In particular the Employment Protection Act now authorises the Secretary of State, after an application from an employers' association or trade union concerned, separately or jointly, and after an inquiry by the Advisory, Conciliation and Arbitration Service, to convert a Wages Council into a **Statutory Joint Industrial Council,** the principal effect of the change being to remove the independent members and their role in breaking deadlocks and to leave the two sides, in case of disagreement, to conciliation and, if necessary, arbitration by ACAS, any finding being subject to statutory application as in normal Wages Council procedures. No such Orders have so far been made; see C.W. Guillebaud, *The Wages Council System in Great Britain,* Nisbet, 1962, F.J. Bayliss, *British Wages Councils,* Basil Blackwell, 1962, E.A.G. Armstrong, 'Minimum Wages in a Fully Employed City', *British Journal of Industrial Relations,* March 1966 and 'Wages Councils, Retail Distribution and the Concept of Cut-off', *Industrial Relations Journal,* Vol. 2, No. 3, Autumn 1971; also the various publications of the **Low Pay Unit** (q.v.). The Wages Councils' Secretariat is at 12 St. James's Square, London SW1Y 4LL. *Tel:* 01-214 6274.

WAGES COUNCILS ACT 1959; see **Wages Councils.**

WAGES-FUND THEORY. A theory of wages developed from the **subsistence theory** of Ricardo, especially by John Stuart Mill (1806-73). It rejected the subsistence notion which implied that there was a single equilibrium (subsistence) level to which wages must inevitably return, and allowed for a natural rate of wages depending upon the changing ratio of capital to population, capital being regarded as a 'wages-fund' out of which workers were paid. It followed from this that 'wages not only depend upon the relative amount of capital and population, but cannot, under the rule of competition, be affected by anything else'; hence trade union action was impotent to alter the wage-level as a whole, and any measure hampering the accumulation of capital (e.g. progressive taxation) was bound to lower wages by depleting the wages-fund; see Maurice Dobb, *Wages,* Nisbet, 1956; also **wage theories,** and **share of wages.**

WAGES INSPECTORS. Officials of the **Department of Employment** appointed to enforce the minimum remuneration, holidays, holiday remuneration and other terms and conditions specified in Orders made by **Wages Councils** (q.v.).

WAGES ORDERS; see **Wages Councils.**

WAGES POLICY; see **wage policy.**

WAGE-WORK BARGAINING. A type of collective bargaining in which the performance of work is taken into account in resolving terms and conditions of employment, as contrasted with collective bargaining in which wage rates, etc., are varied according to considerations not directly related to such performance, e.g. to the cost of living, to relativities, etc. **Wage-work bargaining** may be defined to include **effort bargaining, productivity bargaining** (q.v.) and other types of bargaining in which work is done in relation to payment (Royal Commission on Trade Unions and Employers' Associations, Research Paper 4, 1, *Productivity Bargaining,* p. 1), see also W.W. Daniel, *Beyond the Wage-work Bargain,* Political and Economic Planning Broadsheet 519, July 1970.

WAGNER ACT; also known as the Wagner-Connery Act; the **National Labor Relations Act** passed in July 1935 in the United States of America. The Act established the right of employees to organise; also the machinery for holding elections to establish which unions shall have exclusive bargaining rights in particular circumstances. It set out **unfair labor practices** by employers, i.e. practices considered harmful to the rights of workers to organise, and attempted generally to redress collective bargaining power in favour of employees. Major amendments were made to the Act by the **Taft-Hartley Act 1947** (q.v.). H.A. Mills and E.C. Brown, *From the Wagner Act to Taft-Hartley,* University of Chicago Press, 1950.

WAITING DAYS; see **sickness benefit, unemployment benefit.**

WAITING TIME. Time spent by a payment by results worker unproductively outside unoccupied time allowed for in standard time (see **unoccupied time allowance**), due to causes beyond his control, especially shortage of materials or breakdown of machinery (see **idle time** and **down time**). Payment varies from workshop to workshop; workers seldom receive less than time rate in such circumstances and higher levels of payment for waiting

time, such as average earnings, are not uncommon. Known in the printing industry as **standing time.** In the coal mining industry, time taken in preparing for work at the pit (putting on clothes, collecting lamp, walking to cage) and time spent at the end of the shift returning lamp and gear, bathing etc.

WALES TRADE UNION COUNCIL (Wales TUC). An organisation representing trade unions with membership in Wales which held its first conference at Llandrindod Wells in February 1973. The rules of the Wales TUC provide that subsequent conferences shall be held annually on the fourth Friday in April and for the following Saturday and Sunday, and that it shall have a General Council of 45 members on the basis of 16 industrial trade groups together with representatives of County Associations of Trade Councils. Representation at Annual Conference is on the basis of one delegate per 2,500 members (or part thereof) in Wales in respect of trade unions, two delegates from each trades council, one or two delegates from each County Association of Trades Councils. The General Secretary is elected annually. The Congress is the result of efforts to establish a TUC in Wales lasting for 30 years or more. In 1977 its affiliated membership was 634,625 in 74 trade unions, all affiliated to the British Trades Union Congress with members in Wales. The Wales TUC forms part of the TUC's regional structure and its normal expenses are met by that body. *Address:* 42 Charles Street, Cardiff CF1 4SN. *Tel:* Cardiff 30211.

WALK-OUT; see **strike.**

WALLCOVERINGS, DECORATIVE AND ALLIED TRADES, NATIONAL UNION OF. A trade union formed in 1919 as the Wallpaper Workers' Union by the amalgamation of a number of small unions totalling about 2,000 members and organising mainly in wall-paper manufacturing, irrespective of occupation. In January 1969 the Print, Block, Roller and Stamp Cutters' Association transferred its engagements to the WPWU, and in 1971 a new union, the **Wallcoverings Staff Association** was formed, with a common General Secretary, to represent staff employees. This was reabsorbed in July 1975 and the united organisation given its present title. It is represented on the Wall Paper Makers' Industrial Council. *Address:* 233 Bury New Road, Whitefield, Nr.

Manchester. *Tel:* 061-766 3645/6. *TUC Affiliated Membership, 1977:* 4,227.

WALLCOVERINGS STAFF ASSOCIATION (WSA). See **Wallcoverings, Decorative and Allied Trades, National Union of.**

WAR BONUS; see **piecework supplement.**

WASH-UP PERIOD; see **wash-up time** and **clean-up period.**

WASH-UP TIME. A period allowed before meal breaks or at the end of the shift for workers to wash, change their clothes etc.; see also **clean-up period.**

WASTAGE. Loss of manpower by death, retirements, resignations or individual dismissals; **separation** (see **labour turnover**). **Natural wastage;** to run down a labour force by wastage without recourse to **redundancy** (q.v.) and therefore in some cases used to avoid declaring workers redundant where the labour force of an establishment or company has to be run down; an expression which came into use especially with the development of mergers and productivity bargaining in the 1960s.

WATCHING AND BESETTING; see **Conspiracy and Protection of Property Act 1875** and **picketing.**

WATERMEN, LIGHTERMEN, TUGMEN AND BARGEMEN'S UNION (WLTBU). A trade union catering for watermen, lightermen and tugmen in the port transport industry. It merged with the **Transport and General Workers' Union** in 1971.

WATERPROOF GARMENT WORKERS' TRADE UNION. A trade union founded in 1907 as the Waterproof Garment Makers' and Machinists' Trade Union and taking its present name in 1914. The union joined with the United Garment Workers in 1915 and seceded in the following year; it was also for a time amalgamated with the United Garment Workers (Tailors), but broke away in 1921, and was much concerned in internal strife during the years of bad trade in the 1930s. In 1972 the union amalgamated with the **National Union of Tailors and Garment Workers.**

WAYZGOOSE. The name sometimes given to a printers' annual outing; according to OED a corruption of 'waygoose', conjectured by Bailey (1831) to be connected with 'wayz goose' or 'stubble goose'. Harvey (*Oxford Companion to English Literature*) prefers the derivation from 'wake-goose' - an entertainment given by a master printer to his workmen 'about Bartholomewtide', marking the beginning of the season of working by candlelight.

WCL. World Confederation of Labour; see **International Labour Movement.**

WEAVERS' ASSOCIATION, AMALGAMATED (AWA). An organisation of district associations of weavers originally formed in 1884 as the Northern Counties Amalgamated Association of Weavers, with the object of establishing and maintaining a uniform and fair rate of wages. It is affiliated to the Northern Counties Textile Federation (formed in 1906) and the United Textile Factory Workers' Association. The history of the Weavers' Association is connected in particular with the development of a **uniform list** (q.v.) of weaving prices. It reached the peak of its membership in 1921 (224,219) and has declined since in numbers as the cotton industry has contracted, leaving some of its district associations so tiny as to bring into question its long standing principle of local autonomy within a federal system; see E. Hopwood, *A History of the Lancashire Cotton Industry and the Amalgamated Weavers' Association,* AWA, 1969. In January 1974 it merged with the **National Union of Textile and Allied Workers,** to form the **Amalgamated Textile Workers' Union** (q.v.). At the time of the merger it had about 26,000 members.

WEAKLEY v. AMALGAMATED UNION OF ENGINEERING WORKERS (ENGINEERING SECTION) (1975), *The Times,* 12 June 1975. A case in which it was ruled that a decision to exclude the votes on the National Committee of properly elected delegates from South Wales on a resolution on postal voting was invalid and that the President, since he was not a delegate himself, had no casting vote; see **membership of a trade union.**

WEEK-END EXTRAS. Steel industry: **gift hours** payable over and above **clocked hours** for work performed at weekends, e.g. plus 50 per cent for time worked between 6 a.m. Saturday and 10 p.m. Sunday and between 10 p.m. Sunday and 6 a.m. Monday and plus 100 per cent for time worked between 10 p.m. Saturday and 10 p.m. Sunday.

WEEKLY REST; see **International Labour Convention No. 14.**

WEEKLY STAFF; see **staff.**

WEEKLY STAFF AGREEMENT (WSA). A type of **productivity agreement** made between Imperial Chemical Industries Ltd and its trade unions in 1969. The agreement involved greater shopfloor participation than its less successful predecessor, the **Manpower Utilisation and Payment Structure Agreement** (MUPS) (q.v.); see J. Roeber, *Steps to a New Social Contract*, Duckworth, 1974.

WEIGHTING. A statistical technique for arriving at the mean of a data distribution by giving greater emphasis, or weight, to some items than to others because of their greater importance; e.g. in a **cost of living index**, in which food items, constituting a larger part of total expenditure than other groups of items, such as expenditure on clothing, rent etc., may be given proportionately greater weight; or in **job evaluation** (q.v.) in which **points rating** (q.v.) involves similar weighting. The term weighting may also be applied to **differential** payments made to workers on various grounds, including residence in locations where living costs are reckoned to be higher than normal; see **London weighting,** for example.

WEIR SYSTEM; see **Halsey Premium Bonus System.**

WELFARE UNIONISM; see **uplift unionism.**

WELSH PLATE AND SHEET MANUFACTURERS' ASSOCIATION; see **Welsh Tinplate Board.**

WELSH TINPLATE BOARD. A joint negotiating body formed in January 1972 between the British Steel Corporation and trade unions representing workers in the sheet and tinplate trade in South Wales. The Board replaced the **Welsh Tinplate and Sheet Trades Joint Industrial Council** formed in 1924 and consisting of representatives of the Welsh Plate and Sheet Manufacturers' Association (formed in 1899) and the Transport and General Workers' Union, the Iron and Steel Trades Confed-

eration, the Amalgamated Union of Engineering Workers and the Electrical, Electronic, Telecommunication and Plumbing Union.

WELSH TINPLATE AND SHEET TRADES JOINT INDUSTRIAL COUNCIL; see **Welsh Tinplate Board.**

WELTING. The practice in Liverpool docks (known in Glasgow as **spelling**), whereby only half of a gang is working at any particular time, each half having one hour off and one hour on. The Devlin Committee (*Final Report of the Committee of Inquiry under the Rt. Hon. Lord Devlin into certain matters concerning the Port Transport Industry*, Cmnd. 2734, HMSO, August 1965) considered that welting and spelling bred indiscipline and resulted in a slower turn-round of ships and an underutilisation of capital equipment; see **restrictive practices,** also **blow system.**

WESTERN EXCAVATING (ECC) LTD v. SHARP. *The Times*, 15 November 1977; see **constructive dismissal.**

WET MONEY. An **allowance** or extra payment made when workers are required to work in water (coal mining).

WET TIME. Time during which work is interrupted by wet weather and during which men are required to remain on the site to resume work when circumstances permit, e.g. in Outside Steelwork Erection (*Engineering Handbook of National Agreements*, 6.2 (16)) where wet time is paid at one-half normal time rates where time is lost from this cause in any one day.

WETUC. Workers' Educational Trade Union Committee (q.v.).

WFTU. World Federation of Trade Unions (q.v.).

WGGB. Writers' Guild of Great Britain (q.v.).

WHIMSEYING. Working at the trade without being a member of the union; *Rules of the Amalgamated Society of Journeymen Felt Hatters and Allied Workers of Great Britain*, 1948.

WHIPPING; see **whips.**

WHIPS. Pacesetters introduced by managements to workshops to speed up jobs; John Child, *Industrial Relations in the British Printing Industry*, Allen and Unwin, 1967, p. 140); hence **whipping** as one possible element in **driving**; also **pacers** and **ratebusters**.

WHIPSAWING. Described by Harold S. Roberts (*Dictionary of Industrial Relations*, Bureau of National Affairs, 1966) as 'a union stratagem seeking to obtain benefits from a number or group of employers by applying pressure to one, the object being to win favourable terms from this one employer and then use this as a pattern, or perhaps a base, to obtain the same or greater benefits from the other employers, under the same threat of pressure (including a strike) used against the first one'. Whipsawing would therefore seem to be a tactic of **pattern bargaining** (q.v.) in the United States, and the term imported into Britain (see E.H. Phelps Brown, 'The Importance of Works Agreements', *Personnel Management*, March 1960, and A.W. Gottschalk in B. Towers and T.G. Whittingham (eds), *The New Bargainers*, Department of Adult Education, University of Nottingham, 1970, p. 118), to describe **leapfrogging**, or wage and condition demands based on **comparability**, or the tactics involved in **trade movements** (q.v.); see also **coercive comparison** and **wage rounds**.

WHITE COLLAR UNION. A trade union which caters exclusively or principally for **white collar workers;** a non-manual worker union, as distinct from a union designed to represent, wholly or principally, **manual workers**, e.g. the **National and Local Government Officers' Association**, the **Association of Professional, Executive, Clerical and Computer Staff**, the **Transport Salaried Staffs Association**, the **Civil and Public Services Association** and similar organisations. White collar workers are also to be found in membership of clerical and staff sections of manual worker unions, e.g. in the Technical and Supervisory Section of the **Amalgamated Union of Engineering Workers** (AUEW/TASS), in the **Association of Clerical, Technical and Supervisory Staffs** (a section of the **Transport and General Workers' Union**) etc., and where separately differentiated, these sections may have something of the character of white collar unions; see also **professional association**. No official data exists distinguishing membership of white collar organisations of both these types from manual worker trade union membership; private estimates show the rapid rise in white collar membership in Britain since the second world war from almost 2 millions in 1949 to rather more than 3.5 millions in 1970, an increase of 79 per cent, manual worker trade union membership (7.4 millions in 1948 and 7.5 millions in 1970) remaining substantially unchanged during the same period. From 1948 to 1964, the growth of white collar membership barely kept pace with the growth of the white collar labour force; since that time **union density** among white collar workers is calculated to have increased from 29.6 per cent in 1964 to 39.4 per cent in 1974. (George Sayers Bain, *The Growth of White Collar Unionism*, OUP, 1970 and George Sayers Bain and Robert Price, *Union Growth and Employment Trends in the United Kingdom, 1964-1970*, Industrial Relations Research Unit, University of Warwick Discussion Paper, March 1972 and Robert Price and George Sayers Bain, 'Union Growth Revisited', *British Journal of Industrial Relations*, Vol. XIV, No. 3, November 1976, pp. 339-55). David Lockwood (*The Blackcoated Worker*, Allen and Unwin, 1966) regards the unionisation of white collar workers as 'very closely associated with what may be called "bureaucratisation"'; George Bain (*op. cit.*) considers three strategic variables - employment concentration, union recognition and government action - as a more adequate explanation; in rebuttal of theories of white collar union growth supposedly based upon union character, Bain also prefers the proposition that this may be a function of union participation in job regulation; see George Bain, David Coates and Valerie Ellis, *Social Stratification and Trade Unionism*, Heinemann, 1973; see also A. Sturmthal (ed.), *White Collar Trade Unions*, University of Illinois Press, 1966.

WHITE COLLAR WORKER. A non-**manual worker**, or a **blackcoated worker**, as distinct from a **manual worker** or a **blue collar worker**; a worker who earns his living with his head rather than his hands (Emil Lederer, *Die Privatangestellten in der modernen Wirtschaftsentwicklung*, JCB Mohr/P. Siebeck, Tübingen, 1912 and, in an American example, Edwin F. Beal and Edward D. Wickersham, *The Practice of Collective Bargaining*, Richard D. Irwin, 1963, p. 228); hence also a **salaried employee**, a category which may be said to include 'persons employed in commerce and industry who are entrusted by an employer with labour which is mental rather than physical' ('The Problem of

Defining a Salaried Employee', *International Labour Review*, XXXVII, June 1938, p. 767). These and other definitions based on functions or job content (F. Croner, *Tjänstemannakåren i det moderna samhället*, H. Gebers, Stockholm, 1951), and on work milieu and the object and function of the work done (R. Girod, *Études Sociologiques sur les Couches Salariées: Ouvriers et Employés*, Marcel Rivière, Paris, 1961), are discussed by George Sayers Bain and Robert Price (*Who is a White Collar Employee?*, Industrial Relations Research Unit, University of Warwick, Discussion Paper, January 1972), who find that all definitions have their limitations of logic and consistency. For statistical purposes **administrative technical and clerical staff** (q.v.), is the most usual official definition; this, applied to Censuses of Production, shows an increase in white collar employment as a proportion of the total United Kingdom manufacturing labour force from 8 per cent in 1907 to 25.1 per cent in 1968, and, applied to Department of Employment data for Great Britain, from 16 per cent in 1948 to 27.1 per cent in 1971; George Sayers Bain and Robert Price, *Union Growth and Employment Trends in the United Kingdom, 1964-1970*, Industrial Relations Research Unit, University of Warwick, Discussion Paper, March 1972, and Albert A. Blum, *et al., White Collar Workers*, New York, Random House, 1972.

WHITE COLLAR WORKERS' CHARTER. The **Offices, Shops and Railway Premises Act 1963** (q.v.).

WHITLEY COMMITTEE; see Whitleyism.

WHITLEY COUNCIL; see Whitleyism.

WHITLEYISM. A system of industrial relations based on **Joint Industrial Councils** advocated by the **Whitley Committee** (1916-18); a term often applied specifically to the Whitley Committee recommendations as applied to the Civil Service; sometime also used to describe a form of **workers' participation** involving **self-government in industry.** Whitleyism has been regarded as the most formative single influence on the shape of British industrial relations between the first and second world wars. The **Committee on Relations between Employers and Employed** (usually known as the Whitley Committee after its Chairman, Mr J.H. Whitley, then Chairman of the Committees of the House of Commons and later its Speaker) originated in a sub-committee of the Cabinet Committee on Reconstruction set up in March 1916, which in the following year became a committee of the Ministry of Reconstruction, with terms of reference involving suggestions for securing a permanent improvement in the relations between employers and workmen, and the recommending of means for securing a systematic review of industrial conditions affecting these relations to ensure future improvements. The Committee issued five reports in 1917 and 1918. Its most important contribution to the structure of British industrial relations was its advocacy of 'a triple form of organisation, representative of employers and employed, consisting of **joint industrial councils,** joint district councils and works committees, each of the three forms of organisation being linked up with the others so as to constitute an organisation covering the whole of the trade'. While industries with firmly rooted machinery (e.g. engineering and steel) remained unaffected, and while the joint district councils and works committees proposed by the Whitley Committee failed to develop as anticipated, JICs (sometimes known as **Whitley Councils**), confirmed and extended the industry-wide bargaining pattern established during the first world war in many others, and provided the model for an industrial relations system in Britain which remained formally unchallenged until the Donovan **Royal Commission of Trade Unions and Employers' Associations, 1965-68.** Some 200 Joint Industrial Councils continue to provide standing machinery for negotiation at industry-wide level at the present time. Whitleyism has provided a basis for staff relations in the Civil Service since 1919, non-industrial staff being covered by a **National Whitley Council,** and by Whitley Councils or Committees at departmental and local levels, with arrangements for arbitration through the **Civil Service Arbitration Tribunal** and, since 1956, the services of the **Civil Service Pay Research Unit** (q.v.) in applying the principle of comparability; see H.M. Treasury, *Staff Relations inn he Civil Service*, HMSO 1965; Richard Hayward, *Whitley Councils in the United Kingdom Civil Service*, Civil Service National Whitley Council (Staff Side), 1963; J. Callaghan, *Whitleyism*, Fabian Society Research Series, No. 159, 1953 and the Fulton Report (**Committee on the Civil Service, 1966-68**, Cmnd. 3638, 1968, pp. 88-90), which criticised the management of the Civil Service for allowing the Whitley system to operate in ways hampering effective management. The industrial Civil Service, unlike the non-industrial, has no single National Council, though there is a **Joint Co-ordinating Committee for Government Industrial Establishments** which performs a similar function. There are also Departmental Councils in Departments which employ substantial numbers of industrial staff, and three **Trade Joint Councils**, covering Government industrials in all Departments in the trades in which they are respectively concerned - the **Engineering Trades Joint Council**, the **Shipbuilding Trade Joint Council**, and the **Miscellaneous Trades Joint Council**; see National Board for Prices and Incomes, *Pay of Industrial Civil Servants,* Report No. 18, Cmnd. 3034, June 1966. The principles underlying the Whitley Reports included that of adequate organisation by both employers and work-people, of voluntary collective bargaining, and self-government in industry in the sense of the provision of a greater opportunity for participation and discussion by workers in matters concerning their daily working lives - working conditions, methods of payment and a share in industrial prosperity, security, piecework systems, education and training, and other subjects. Perhaps because some of these subjects were, during the second world war, separated from collective bargaining, Whitleyism is sometimes considered to be a form of **joint consultation** (q.v.), though the imputation appears to be incorrect, since the Whitley Committee made no such distinction. In some contexts, however, comment on Whitleyism in the Civil Service seems to regard the whole of the system as 'consultation' e.g. Fulton Report (op. cit.) paras 270, 272 and 273. There are very few up-to-date studies of Whitleyism; see I.G. Sharp, *Industrial Conciliation and Arbitration in Great Britain,* Allen and Unwin 1950; Allan Flanders and H.A. Clegg, *The System of Industrial Relations* in Great Britain, Basil Blackwell, 1954; L.D. White, *Whitley Councils in the British Civil Service,* Chicago University Press 1933; E.N. Gladden, *Civil Service Staff Relationships,* William Hodge, 1943; B.V. Humphreys, *Clerical Unions in the Civil Service,* Basil Blackwell, 1958; see also R. Charles, *The Development of Industrial Relations in Britain 1911-1939,* Hutchinson, 1973, and more recently, H. Parris, *Staff Relations in the Civil Service,* George Allen and Unwin, 1973. The Whitley Committee also made recommendations resulting in the **Industrial Courts Act 1919** and in the further development of **Trade Boards** (q.v.).

WHITWOOD CHEMICAL CO. v. HARDMAN (1891) 2 Ch. 416; see **specific performance.**

WHOLLY UNEMPLOYED. Registered unemployed (q.v.), including **casual workers,** excluding those who are **temporarily stopped,** as recorded in Department of Employment monthly unemployment statistics.

WILBERFORCE REPORT. The name given especially to one of two reports of Courts of Inquiry under the chairmanship of the Rt Hon. Lord Wilberforce; that into a *Dispute between the Parties Represented on the National Joint Industrial Council for the Electricity Supply Industry,* Cmnd. 4594, February 1971, and into the *Dispute between the National Coal Board and members of the National Union of Mineworkers,* Cmnd. 4903, February 1972. The first of these inquiries brought to an end a ban on overtime and work to rule in the electricity supply industry, and the second provided the basic terms of settlement for a national coal strike starting on 9 January 1972 and ending seven weeks later, in both of which stoppages the government declared a State of Emergency; see also **Saltley Depot Incident.**

WILDCAT STRIKE. A phrase, originally American, used to describe a work stoppage, generally spontaneous in character, by a group of trade union members without union authorisation or approval. First used in Britain in the late 1950s and usually equated with **unofficial strike** (q.v.). It is doubtful whether the American and British usages are identical. In the USA it is usually (though not always) a strike against the contract and a challenge to the formal leadership (A.W. Gouldner, *Wildcat Strike,* Antioch Press and Harper and Row 1965) with a 'sense of alienation from the established union' (J.E.T. Eldridge, *Industrial Disputes,* Routledge and Kegan Paul 1968, p. 79); in Britain the agreement situation is different, and neither the challenge to the leadership nor the sense of alienation from the union may be present; but see Tony Lane and Kenneth Roberts, *Strike at Pilkingtons,* Collins/Fontana, 1971, for a recent classic in which both were involved.

WILLIAMS v. BUTLERS LTD (1975), *The Times*, 28 February, QBD. A case in which it was ruled that, where a tripartite agreement on **check-off** existed between the union, the company and the employee, a legal request to cease deduction of union dues in the case of a particular individual could only be made by the union, the refusal of the company to cease on the instructions of the employee not being a breach of the **Truck Act 1831**, s. 3.

WILLINK COMMISSION. The **Royal Commission on the Police, 1960-62**, (*Interim Report*, Cmnd. 1222, November 1960, *Final Report*, Cmnd. 1728, May 1962), under the chairmanship of Sir Henry Willink. The Commission had broad terms of reference on the constitution and functions of local police authorities, the relationships of police and public and the principle which should govern the remuneration of constables. It rejected **fair comparisons** as a method of settling police pay, but recommended that the pay of constables should be related to wages rates in selected skilled occupations.

WILSON v. AMALGAMATED SOCIETY OF ENGINEERS; see **Osborne v. Amalgamated Society of Railway Servants.**

WILSON v. SCOTTISH TYPOGRAPHICAL ASSOCIATION; see **Osborne v. Amalgamated Society of Railway Servants.**

WINDEYER REPORT. The *Report of Committee under the Chairmanship of Sir Brian Windeyer appointed to inquire into Lead Poisonings at the Rio Tinto Zinc Smelter at Avonmouth* (Command No. 5042, July 1972). The Committee found that the number of cases was disquieting, but that only mild symptoms of lead poisoning were recorded and that there was no evidence of serious or lasting damage to health. It recommended greater attention to industrial hygiene, more research and more information and education for workers about health hazards.

WINDING TIME. Coal mining industry; the time spent in the cage being wound down the shaft from pit top to pit bottom.

WINGMEN. Members of a **Board of Arbitration**, a **Court of Inquiry** or other arbitral or inquiry body or tribunal (including the **industrial tribunals**) who sit on either side of the Chairman, usually appointed from panels of employers and employees not involved in the issue in question, or *ad hoc* for the hearing of a particular case. One object of the introduction of **wingmen** may be to broaden the basis of authority of a court or tribunal by extending it from a neutral chairman only to a body indirectly representative of the parties to a dispute; another may be to avoid an appearance of legalism by introducing laymen into the situation (as in German and Swedish **labour courts** and in British industrial tribunals); a third motive may be to have available expertise in the practical concerns of industrial situations which a neutral chairman may lack, making the wingmen akin to assessors. No study appears to exist of the functions or philosophy of wingmen, though some issues involved in their use are raised by K.W. Wedderburn in Benjamin Aaron (ed.), *Dispute Settlement Procedures in Five Western European Countries*, University of California, 1969.

WIRE DRAWERS AND KINDRED TRADES, AMALGAMATED SOCIETY OF. A trade union dating its history from 1840. In 1890 it was known as the Amalgamated Wire Drawers Society of Great Britain, a name which was changed in 1924. The union was federated to the **Iron and Steel Trades Confederation** from February 1921 to March 1924 when it ceased as a result of differences between the two organisations. *Address:* Prospect House, Alma Street, Sheffield S3 8SA. *Tel:* 0742 21674. *TUC Affiliated Membership, 1977:* 10,858.

WITHOUT PREJUDICE BARGAINING; see **without prejudice offer.**

WITHOUT PREJUDICE OFFER also **without prejudice bargaining.** Civil Service: an offer made by the Official Side in settlement of a trade union claim without prejudice to what the **Civil Service Arbitration Tribunal** might award; hence a without prejudice offer cannot be quoted to the Tribunal by the Staff Side, the formal position being that arrived at when the Official Side made its last 'open offer' (Civil Service Clerical Association, *CSCA, Strike Policy*, February 1969, p. 11). In other industries the implication of a without prejudice offer is similar, i.e. that of offering a solution to a claim or issue, on the understanding that it does not rule out the possibility of an alternative solution.

WLTBU. **Watermen, Lightermen, Tugmen and Bargemen's Union** (q.v.).

WOBBLIES. The popular name given to the **Industrial Workers of the World,** or IWW, an organisation established by the American Industrial Unionists in 1905 and dedicated to **workers' control** through the establishment of **industrial unionism** (q.v.). A similar organisation, the British Advocates of Industrial Unionism, was established in Britain, though it failed to make comparable progress to the IWW in the United States. Both the IWW and the BAIU split into anarchist and political factions in 1908, the former in Britain forming the Industrial League, claiming to represent 'pure' industrial unionism and warfare against both employers, trade unions and any kind of political involvement, sabotage and other forms of violence being advocated. In 1910, the BAIU became the Industrial Workers of Great Britain; neither organisation made any impact on the British Labour Movement; see Paul F. Brissenden, *The IWW, A Study in American Syndicalism,* Columbia University Press, 1920; F. Thompson (ed.), *The IWW - Its First Fifty Years, (1905-1955),* IWW, 1955; Branko Pribićević, *The Shop Stewards' Movement and Workers' Control, 1910-1922,* Basil Blackwell, 1959; Patrick Renshaw, *The Wobblies,* Eyre and Spottiswoode, 1967. The present address of the IWW is: Industrial Worker, 752 West Webster Avenue, Chicago, Illinois, 60614, USA; see also **general strike.**

WOFAC CORPORATION. An American firm of management consultants responsible for the development of **Variable Factor Programming** (VFP) for the measurement and control of work in indirect areas. It introduced VFP into England in 1962.

WOMEN'S CONSULTATIVE COMMITTEE; see **Women's Employment, Advisory Committee on.**

WOMEN'S EMPLOYMENT, ADVISORY COMMITTEE ON. A committee of members appointed in a personal capacity and established in May 1970, 'to advise the Secretary of State for Employment on problems of employment policy relating to women'. It was formerly known as the **Women's Consultative Committee,** which was originally set up in 1941.

WOMEN'S TRADE UNION LEAGUE. Founded in 1874 by Emma Paterson to promote trade unionism among working women. The League deprecated strike, advocated arbitration and was by no means hostile to employers. In twelve years it established in England and Scotland some forty women's societies, including one for bookbinding (Emma Paterson's original trade), eight for dressmakers and milliners and one for general labour in Oxford which survived until 1913. They were almost all short lived. After Mrs Paterson's death in 1886, the League continued to establish women's organisations and local women's trade union councils as well as promoting factory legislation and encouraging men's unions to open their ranks to women. In 1906 it founded the National Federation of Women Workers as a federation of tiny bodies sponsored by the League, which claimed 80,000 members by the end of the first world war and which in 1921 amalgamated with the National Union of General Workers (see **General and Municipal Workers' Union).** The League's secretary, Mary Macarthur, became secretary of the NFWW in 1908. The League itself continued in existence until after the 1914-18 war; see Barbara Drake, *Women in Trade Unions,* 1921.

WOOD REPORT. Name given to a number of inquiries and arbitrations carried out under the chairmanship of Professor John C. Wood, especially that into the *Standard-Triumph Dispute* (1969), the **Pilkington Strike** (1970) (q.v.) and on the *Pay of Teachers in Establishments of Further Education under the Remuneration of Teachers Act, 1965* (see **Burnham Committees)** in 1971. Professor Wood is now chairman of the **Central Arbitration Committee** (q.v.).

WOODCUTTING MACHINISTS, AMALGAMATED SOCIETY OF (ASWM). A trade union catering for sawyers and woodcutting machinists founded by amalgamation in 1866. No detail is available on the previous history of the unions involved in the amalgamation, though these may have included a sawyers' union in Scotland, a woodcutting machinists' union in Ireland, and a similar union in England. The union, which had some 23,000 members in 1970, transferred its engagements in September 1971 to the **Furniture, Timber and Allied Trades Union** (q.v.).

WOODWORKERS, **AMALGA-**

MATED SOCIETY OF (ASW); see Construction and Allied Trades and Technicians, Union of.

WOOL SHEAR WORKERS' TRADE UNION, SHEFFIELD. A trade union founded in 1890 and originally known as the Sheffield Wool Shear Grinders Makers Finishers, Benders' Union. It adopted its present title in 1914 after being known as the Wool Shear Grinders and Benders' Society (Sheffield) (1912), and the Wool Shear Makers, Grinders, Finishers and Benders' Society (1913). Membership of the union has declined steadily since 1937, when it had 114 members. It is now the smallest union affiliated to the Trades Union Congress. Amalgamation talks with the **General and Municipal Workers' Union** in 1966 fell through. *Address:* 19 Rivelin Park Drive, Malin Bridge, Sheffield S6 5GC. *TUC Affiliated Membership, 1977:* 27.

WOOL SORTERS' SOCIETY, NATIONAL. A textile trade union founded in 1921, which has declined considerably in recent years. *Address:* 40 Little Horton Lane, Bradford BD5 0AL. *Tel:* 0274 20392. *TUC Affiliated Membership, 1977:* 747.

WORK EXPERIENCE PROGRAMME. A scheme, administered by the Manpower Services Commission, to give unemployed young people aged 16 to 18 a realistic introduction to working life. The Scheme started in September 1976 and is being merged into a **Youth Opportunities Programme** (q.v.).

WORK FACTOR SYSTEM; see predetermined motion time system.

WORK GROUPS. Sometimes known as **primary work groups;** groups of workers having, because of one, or a combination of characteristics, common interests, especially in relation to their management, and patterns of behaviour, influence and authority in the workplace, particularly in **workplace bargaining.** L.R. Sayles (*The Behaviour of Industrial Work Groups,* John Wiley, 1958) distinguishes 'subordinate groups', defined by having a common superior or supervisor, 'friendship cliques', 'functional' or 'task groups' of people who must co-operate in work tasks, and 'interest groups', those who share a common economic interest, many of these types overlapping from one person to another, arguing that membership

in the small group contributes directly to the shaping of attitudes and behaviour to the entire work situation, and classifying groups in terms of their behaviour as 'apathetic', 'erratic', 'strategic' and 'conservative'. It seems now to be generally agreed that **workers' participation** is likely to be greatest where the work group is involved (see, for example, Roger Sawtell, *Sharing Our Industrial Future?,* Industrial Society, 1968, p. 5) and that **shop stewards** may be 'work group leaders' rather than 'leaders of work groups' (J.W. Kuhn, *Bargaining in Grievance Settlement,* Columbia University Press, 1961), though primary group theory may be insufficiently developed to have settled such issues beyond a peradventure (see J.F.C. Goodman and T.G. Whittingham, *Shop Stewards in British Industry,* McGraw-Hill, 1969, Ch. 4). In Britain, the growth of more formal approaches to **workplace bargaining,** and especially **productivity bargaining,** has underlined the need to evaluate work group reactions (Allan Flanders, *The Fawley Productivity Agreements,* Faber & Faber, 1964, p. 140); see also **work group bargaining.**

WORK GROUP BARGAINING; see **fractional bargaining** and **fragmented bargaining.**

WORK LOAD. The amount of work performed, or expected to be performed, during a given period of time, e.g. in the hour, day or week. In **work study,** the proportion of the overall cycle time required by a worker by carry out the necessary work at **standard performance** during a machine or process controlled cycle; British Standards Institution, *Glossary of Terms Used in Work Study,* BS 3138, 1969, No. 36001; also known as **load factor.**

WORK LOAD STAGGER; see **stagger.**

WORK MEASUREMENT. Defined in the *British Standard Glossary of Terms Used in Work Study,* BS 3138, British Standards Institution, 1969, No. 10003, as 'the application of techniques designed to establish the time for a qualified worker to carry out a specified job at a defined level of performance'. Work measurement is usually described as the second stage in **work study,** that of determining how long it should take to carry out a job after the best way of performing that job has been determined by **method study;** see **Interna-**

tional Labour Office, *Introduction to Work Study,* Geneva, 1969, Ch. 3.

WORK PERMIT. A permit issued by the Department of Employment to an overseas worker to enable him to be employed in the United Kingdom. Permits are not required by EEC nationals or by Commonwealth citizens of the UK ancestry or by a number of other categories, e.g. ministers of religion, doctors etc., visitors who take employment during their stay, or students (see Daniel Duysens, 'Work Permits - Department of Employment Control', *Industrial Law Journal,* Vol. 6, No. 2, June 1977, p. 92). Procedures for issuing permits are determined solely by the Department. Applications are made by the employer and issued in the first instance for a maximum of 12 months. Rules applying to the Department are made under the overall authority of the Immigration Act 1971 (as from 1 January 1973) and are subject to approval by Parliament, see I. Macdonald, *The New Immigration Law,* Butterworths, 1972 and J.M. Evans, *Immigration Law,* Sweet and Maxwell, 1976.

WORK PRACTICES; see **workshop practices.**

WORK RESEARCH UNIT. A unit formed by the Department of Employment in 1974 to provide information and advice to firms, and to act as consultants, on taking practical steps to improve the quality of working life in British industry to the mutual advantage of employees and employers by improving the design of jobs and the organisation of work. Its establishment was recommended by a Steering Group on Job Satisfaction set up by the Department in 1973 at the time of the Wilson Report (N.A.B. Wilson, *On the Quality of Working Life,* DE Manpower Paper No. 7, June 1973). Among the long term objectives of the unit are those of obtaining more precise knowledge of what makes jobs satisfying and of improving methods of introducing change in different types of work. It has initiated a number of action research projects to be carried out by research institutes and universities, and takes part in this work itself. It has published a number of reports. *Address:* Steel House, 11 Tothill Street, London SW1H 9LN. *Tel:* 01-799 7777; see also **expectancy theory, job enlargement, job enrichment, job rotation, job satisfaction, work-structuring.**

WORK SAMPLING; see **activity sampling.**

WORK SATISFACTION or **job satisfaction** (q.v.).

WORK SHARING. The spreading of available work among the workers in a factory or the members of a working group in order to avoid **redundancy** or **lay-off,** or in order to equalise the distribution of income between them. In the United States the Department of Labor (*Analysis of Lay-off, Recall and Work Sharing Procedures in Union Contracts,* Washington DC: GPO Bulletin 1209, 1957), in a study of 400 contracts, found 20 per cent with some form of work-sharing procedure as an alternative to lay-offs and a further 20 per cent with no fixed procedure, but with an understanding that, in the event of redundancy, consultation would take place and some form of work-sharing be introduced. Such formal undertakings are much more uncommon in British redundancy agreements, though informal understandings no doubt exist in greater numbers, work sharing being commonly thought of as a unilateral demand by the trade union to avoid redundancy, or even more generally as a **restrictive practice** (q.v.) to maintain artificially high manning levels or to control overtime; see also **ca'canny, continuity rule, blow times, welting, spelling, time-wasting** etc.; for social problems in work sharing; see S. Cunnison, *Wages and Work Allocation,* Tavistock, 1966. Rising unemployment in Britain in the 1970s has stimulated the notion of work sharing on a national scale, e.g. by a lowering of the retirement age, reduction of the normal working week, increased holiday entitlements and reduction of overtime working (see *Department of Employment Gazette* March and April 1978). The possibilities of this approach to unemployment are at the present time speculative.

WORK-STRUCTURING. The organisation of work, the work situation and the conditions of labour in such a way that, while maintaining our improving efficiency, job-content accords as nearly as possible with the capacities and ambitions of the individual employee. The behavioural theory underlying work-structuring (see Frederick Herzberg, *Work and the Nature of Man,* Crosby-Lockwood, Staples, 1974) is that insufficient attention to conditions of work, including job security and consultation, leads to dissatisfactions and frustrations and that such techniques as **job enlargement** and **job rotation** (q.v.) may lead to higher productivity. Herzberg also believes that 'positive motivators' exist which may be stimulated by **job enrichment** (q.v.); see also **expectancy theory.** For a summary of current thinking see Lise Klein, *New Forms of Work Organisation,* CUP, 1976 and for a practical example at Volvo, Sweden, Pehr Gyllenhammar, *People at Work,* Addison-Wesley, 1977.

WORK STUDY. Defined in the *British Standard Glossary of Terms Used in Work Study* (BS 3138, 1969, No. 10001) as 'a generic term for those techniques, particularly **method study** and **work measurement**, which are used in the examination of human work in all its contexts, and which lead systematically to the investigation of all the factors which affect the efficiency and economy of the situation being reviewed, in order to effect improvement'. The term work study is said to have entered the language only after the second world war, an earlier term being **motion and time study,** a term still used in the United States (see R.M. Barnes, *Motion and Time Study,* J. Wiley, 5th ed. 1963), where **industrial engineering** is also common. The growing international adoption of the term work study is said to be due largely to the work of R.M. Currie (*Work Study,* Pitman, 4th ed. 1977), the former head of the Work Study Department of Imperial Chemical Industries Ltd. Current approaches to work study emphasise its role in raising productivity and the importance of the human factor, as well as discussing techniques of method study, and work measurement; see International Labour Office, *Introduction to Work Study,* Geneva, 1969 (revised ed.); see Department of Employment, *Training for Work Study Practice,* HMSO, 1971.

WORKER or in earlier usage in some circumstances, a **workman.** In general usage, one who works, usually with his hands, as distinguished from an employer, or **supervisor,** or one whose work is not manual in character; but also, either in special forms or otherwise, used to describe those who do work of any kind; hence **white-collar worker, black-coated worker,** 'clerical worker', or 'worker-by-hand-or-brain', etc. In law the term appears to lack precise definition. 'Workman' in late nineteenth century Acts excluded domestic servants and interpreted 'manual labour' narrowly; the Industrial Courts Act 1919, s. 8 (see arbitration) employed a wider definition, *viz.* 'any person who has entered into or works under a contract with an employer whether the contract be by way of manual labour, clerical work or otherwise, be expressed or implied, oral or in writing, and whether it be a contract of service or of apprenticeship or a contract personally to execute any work or labour'. The last named, e.g., the self-employed, are excluded from a similar definition in the **Contracts of Employment Act 1972,** s. 8(1): registered dock workers, certain seamen, close relatives, etc. are also excluded, and more exceptions are included in the **Redundancy Payments Act 1965,** ss. 16, 19 and 25. The **Trade Union and Labour Relations Act 1974** distinguishes between an '**employee**' (q.v.) and a 'worker', the latter being a wider term than the former, and including (s. 30) not only those employed, but also those temporarily unemployed, and not only those with contracts of employment but also those 'under any other contract ... whereby he undertakes personally to perform any work or services'. See B.A. Hepple and Paul O'Higgins, *Employment Law,* Sweet and Maxwell, 1976, p. 53 *et seq.,* for a discussion of the distinction.

WORKER DIRECTORS. A form of **workers' participation** in which workers form a part of boards of management in industry. One such form is that of **Mitbestimmung** or **co-determination** (q.v.) in the Federal Republic of Germany. Another is the **employee director** scheme instituted by the British Steel Corporation, in which nominees of the unions appointed by the Chairman of the Corporation sit on local boards in a personal capacity without representative functions and on a part-time basis; see Lord Melchett, 'Shop Floor Directors', *The Spectator,* 26 April 1968, P. Brannen, E. Batstone, D. Fatchett and P. White, *The Worker Directors,* Hutchinson, 1976 and, for a view of the employee directors themselves, John Bank and Ken Jones, *Worker Directors Speak,* Gower Press, 1977. The view of the British trade union movement on the worker director form of participation has varied from time to time. In 1932, after several years of debate, it came down against such a policy where nationalised boards were concerned; the opposite view was taken in 1935, and in 1944 the 1932 view restored, leaving direct trade union representation on consultative bodies only (see **joint consultation**). In 1966, the Trades Union Congress gave evidence to the Donovan **Royal**

Commission on Trade Unions and Employers' Associations 1965-68 that it would favour legislation giving discretion to allow companies generally to make provision for trade union representatives on boards of directors (*Trade Unionism,* 1966, para. 290, p. 107), *Industrial Democracy,* Report of a Labour Party Working Party, June 1967, approved experiments with worker directors in the public sector (para. 101, p. 59), but expressed greater caution in the private sector on the grounds that it would be dangerous to abstract the question of worker representation on boards from the more fundamental question of the strengthening and co-ordination of collective bargaining within a company. In a policy statement of 1974 (*Industrial Democracy,* July 1974) the TUC came down in favour of 50 per cent representation of trade union on supervisory boards in a two-tier company structure. In subsequent Congresses affiliated trade unions have shown themselves to be deeply divided on the issue and on the rather different proposals made in the **Bullock Report** (q.v.); see also F.E. Emery and Einar Thorsrud, *Form and Content in Industrial Democracy,* Tavistock, 1974, for experience of worker directors in Norway and elsewhere and the Callaghan Labour government's White Paper, *Industrial Democracy,* Cmnd. 7231, May 1978.

WORKER OCCUPATION. A form of **sit-in** (q.v.) in which workers not only occupy the workplace round the clock, but also expel the management; British examples are the occupation of Fisher Bendix Ltd, Liverpool, on 5 January 1972, and for the following 28 days, a similar occupation at the same factory in July 1973, and others at firms later involving **Workers' Co-operatives** (q.v.).

WORKERS' CONTROL. A term loosely used to describe any form of **workers' participation** in industry (q.v.), but more precisely the theory underlying or policies to achieve, the replacement of the capitalist industrial system by a new industrial order in which industries are controlled, partly or completely, by associations of workers employed in them. Proponents of workers' control are usually opposed to the notion of an all-embracing role of the state common to Marxism and other forms of socialism, and usually consider that industry ought to be the basis of a new society. Some theories and programmes of workers' control have been primarily revolutionary in character (e.g. **industrial**

unionism, syndicalism (q.v.); others have been more reformist (e.g. guild socialism, q.v.). Workers' control movements have usually been related to a shift of emphasis in trade unions from political to industrial action and from collective bargaining to social change, especially during the period from about 1910 to the General Strike of 1926, and required some basis for spontaneous action among dissatisfied workers: see Branko Pribićević, *The Shop Stewards' Movement and Workers' Control, 1910-1922,* Basil Blackwell, 1959. The output of publications and articles on the subject increased in the 1960s, as well as in the more general area of **industrial democracy** (q.v.).

WORKERS' CO-OPERATIVES. A term used to describe three producer co-operatives run by employees which resulted from workers' takeovers in 1973 and 1974 and which received financial assistance from the Wilson Labour government. In each case the takeovers followed threatened closures - by Norton-Villiers-Triumph at the Triumph factory at Meriden, Coventry, by International Property Development of the former Fisher-Bendix works at Kirkby, Liverpool and by the Beaverbrook Press of the *Scottish Daily Express* in Glasgow. The *Scottish Daily News* co-operative ceased publication in November 1975. Triumph Motorcycles Meriden and Kirkby Manufacturing and Engineering continue into 1978.

WORKERS' EDUCATIONAL TRADE UNION COMMITTEE (WETUC). A body formed in 1919, originally as a partnership between the Workers' Educational Association and the **Iron and Steel Trades Confederation,** and ultimately between the WEA and some 39 trade unions, to administer funds for the education of trade union members, especially in the form of day schools, week-end schools and summer schools. The foundation of the WETUC stimulated the rivalry of the **National Council of Labour Colleges** (q.v.) and attempts to reconcile their interests failed until 1964 when these were taken over by the TUC Education Committee; see Mary Stocks, *The Workers' Educational Association, The First Fifty Years,* George Allen and Unwin, 1953.

WORKERS' PARTICIPATION. An expression commonly applied to forms of **industrial democracy** short of **workers' control** (q.v.) as strictly defined, i.e. falling short of the taking over and running of industry by workers. Hence it may be applied to **Whitleyism, co-ownership, co-partnership, co-determination, joint consultation,** to **collective bargaining** (see H.A. Clegg, *A New Approach to Industrial Democracy,* Basil Blackwell, 1960), or to any scheme in which workers have a share or stake in industrial decision-making and in which an attempt is made to create a feeling of joint responsibility. May also be extended to **craft control** (q.v.) i.e. to the attempt by craft societies, particularly in the later nineteenth century to secure the recognition by employers of their right to interfere with or even to veto certain managerial decisions directly affecting the interests of their members (see Carter Goodrich, *The Frontier of Control,* Dent/Pluto Press 1975, and Branko Pribićević, *The Shop Stewards' Movement and Workers' Control, 1910-1922,* Basil Blackwell, 1959, p. 62).

WORKERS RECALLED TO WORK; see **call out.**

WORKERS' SELF-MANAGEMENT. An alternative expression to describe more thoroughgoing forms of **workers' control** (q.v.) e.g. the system of 'Work Collectives' in Yugoslavia. J.Y. Tabb and A. Goldfarb, *Workers' Participation in Management,* Pergamon Press, 1970, p. 14.

WORKERS' UNION OF IRELAND (WUI). An Irish trade union formed by James Larkin in 1924 as a rival organisation to the **Irish Transport and General Workers' Union** which he had also founded as the Irish Transport Workers' Union in 1909. It is the second largest union in the Republic. *Address:* 29 Parnall Square, Dublin 1. *Tel:* Dublin 748711. *ICTU Affiliated Membership, 1977:* 35,000.

WORK-IN. A form of industrial action in which workers occupy the workplace and attempt to continue the operation of the establishment under their own control, e.g. at **Upper Clyde Shipbuilders** where they resisted redundancy and the break-up of the company by remaining in the yard and working without payment until the proposals of the Heath administration for the yards were changed and further unemployment averted; an assertion of the **right to work.** The UCS work-in was announced by shop stewards on 30 July 1971 and substantially continued until the

formation of Govan Shipbuilders and arrangements with a US company for the development of the Clydebank yard in the spring of 1972. Its effectiveness resulted in part from the response of the Clydebank community, partly from the nature of shipbuilding planning and production, partly from general political pressures and partly from the practical possibilities of co-operation with the liquidator. It seems unlikely that such a combination of circumstances would often be found though work-ins have been attempted in other circumstances e.g. at Briant Colour Printers in 1972; see Alasdair Buchan, *The Right to Work; the Story of the Upper Clyde Confrontation,* Calder and Boyars, 1972, A.J. Mills, 'Factory Work-ins', *New Society,* 22 August 1974, p. 489. Work-ins have features which distinguish them from **sit-ins, stay-in strikes** and **worker occupations** (q.v.).

WORKING CHARGEHAND; see **chargehand** and **supervisor.**

WORKING DAY. In general usage, the length of time spent by a worker at work, or at his place of employment, during the course of a day; more specifically, the 'standard' **working day,** i.e. the basic number of daily hours of work allowed for by collective agreement, by statute or by order, excluding **overtime** hours worked; see **hours of work.**

WORKING HOURS; see **hours of work.**

WORKING POPULATION. Employees for national insurance purposes, together with employers and self-employed persons and members of HM Forces, both at home and overseas. Thus defined, working population includes registered unemployed and full-time students above minimum school leaving age if, in national insurance records, they have worked in their spare time. For a detailed discussion of the statistical problems involved see *Department of Employment and Productivity Gazette,* May 1966, p. 207. The size of the working population varies according to pressure of demand for labour, marginal groups being employed when demand is high (see **activity rates).** 'The fall in the working population since 1966' *DEP Gazette,* June 1970, pp. 492-5. The working population of Great Britain in 1971 was estimated as 25,153,000; this has been projected to increase to 26,804,000 in 1986, *Department of Employment Gazette,* 'Projections of the Working Population, 1971-

1986', August 1971, pp. 717-721. More recent projections have tended to use the concept 'labour force', omitting from the working population full-time students, even though some may take jobs in vacations. The latest of these estimates a labour force of 25,868,000 to increase to 27,781,000 in 1986; see *Department of Employment Gazette*, June 1977, pp. 587-92. Workers in **civil employment** are defined by the Department as those members of the working population who are not in HM Forces and who are not registered as wholly unemployed, i.e. employees in employment *plus* employers and self-employed persons. **Civilian labour force** is defined as working population *less* HM Forces.

WORKING ROUND. A system of **work sharing** in the steel industry whereby surplus labour in slack shops was spread over other departments. Sir Arthur Pugh, *Men Of Steel,* Iron and Steel Trades Confederation, 1951, p. 105.

WORKING RULES. Rules governing terms and conditions of employment, especially of craftsmen. Working rules may be agreed between trade unions and employers, e.g. in the National Working Rule Agreements in the Building Industry; at the level of the workplace, they may rest on **custom-and-practice,** or they may be unilateral in character, emanating from the **work group** or from rules laid down in trade union rule books, or in decisions of conferences or meetings.

WORKING TO RULE; see work-to-rule.

WORKING WEEK. In general usage, the length of time spent by a worker at work, or at his place of employment, during the course of a week; more specifically, the 'standard' or 'basic' **working week,** i.e. the number of hours of work allowed for by collective agreement, by statute or by order, excluding **overtime** hours worked; see **hours of work.**

WORKING WITHOUT ENTHU-SIASM. A form of **ca'canny** or **work-to-rule** practised by draughtsmen, especially as a protest against the government's **incomes policy** in 1967; 'the banning of overtime and performance of a minimum amount of work compatible with contracts of employment' (*DATA Journal;* October 1966).

WORKMAN; see worker.

WORKMEN'S COMPENSATION. A system of compensation for industrial injuries introduced by statute in 1897 and made general in 1906. Under the system the employer was made liable to compensate the employee for loss of earnings attributable to accident and industrial disease arising out of, or in the course of, employment, indemnification of the worker according to fault on the employer's part being replaced by a division of loss between employer and employee in which, subject to a maximum, the employee's earnings were taken into account. The system was criticised by the Beveridge Report and replaced by a new scheme in the National Insurance (Industrial Injuries) Act 1946 (see **Industrial Injuries Acts** and **employers' liability**).

WORKPLACE BARGAINING; see domestic bargaining; workplace bargaining is sometimes preferred to **workshop bargaining** where the latter is thought to be too narrowly associated with engineering, or other workshop conditions, and where it is considered desirable to extend the notion to warehouse, office, etc.; but it may also be used synonymously, e.g. in A.I. Marsh, E.O. Evans and P. Garcia, *Workplace Industrial Relations in Engineering,* Engineering Employers' Federation and Kogan Page, 1971, for a study of the effects of workplace bargaining on trade union organisation; see I. Boraston, H. Clegg and M. Rimmer, *Workplace and Union,* Heinemann, 1975.

WORKS AGREEMENT; see works bargaining.

WORKS BARGAINING. As generally used, collective bargaining at, or within, the works or factory as distinct from collective bargaining at district or national level; therefore including the possibility of bargaining at works level, and the making of **works agreements,** or **plant agreements** i.e. formal agreements applying to all workers in a works or plant, or to substantial proportions of them, as well as **domestic bargaining** within the works itself; see **plant bargaining.**

WORKS COMMITTEES; see works councils.

WORKS COUNCILS. In the Federal Republic of Germany, councils of managers and workers currently established under the Federal Works Constitution Acts (Betriebsverfassungsgesetz), 1952 and 1972 (see **Betriebsräte**). In Britain an expression with no specific meaning other than to describe a variety of committees at workplace level, some consisting of trade unionists only, others joint committees between workers and managers or trade union representatives and managers, set up for a variety of purposes from welfare and recreation to collective bargaining and grievance handling. Such councils or committees, particularly of a unilateral trade union kind, but also in some cases joint union-management committees, became numerous during the 1914-18 war (see Ministry of Labour, *Report of an Enquiry into Works Committees,* HMSO, 1918), and their growth and problems formed the background to the proposals of the Whitley Committee (see **Whitleyism**) and its notions of self-government in industry. Some joint union-management committees survived the decline of trade union workshop organisation between the wars (see, for example, Sir Charles Renold, *Joint Consultation over 30 Years,* George Allen and Unwin, 1950); others of a different type appeared, consisting of managers and directly elected workers' representatives and having mainly welfare functions. This concept of a works council (see Industrial Welfare Society, *Works Councils and Committees* (various editions, 1941-52) has declined with the growth of shop steward organisation in British industry since the 1939-45 war, and the expression is now often used to describe a **joint shop stewards' committee,** or a joint management-steward committee whose central functions may be collective bargaining and grievance handling, though other varieties remain. For Works Committees in federated engineering establishments; see **Shop Stewards and Works Committee Agreements, 1917-1919.**

WORKS RULES. Rules drawn up by the employer to regulate the behaviour of workers in the establishment and regarded by the courts as **express terms** of contract of employment between a worker and the employer, even without his express agreement to them; see **Carus v. Eastwood** (1875) 32 LT 855, and B.A. Hepple and P. O'Higgins, *Employment Law,* Sweet and Maxwell, 1976, p. 93 *et seq.* An inquiry into works rules in the engineering industry (E.O. Evans, 'Works Rules in Engineering', *Industrial Relations Journal,* Vol. 2, No. 1, Spring 1971, pp. 54-65) suggests that written rules commonly exist, that workers are frequently given a copy of them on engagement, that they are rarely discussed or agreed with workers' representatives, and that they are frequently regarded by managements as being primarily informational in character, despite the emphasis which they place on managerial rights. Kenneth Hudson (*Working to Rule: Railway Workshop Rules: A Study in Industrial Discipline,* Adams and Dart, 1970) supposes works rules to have originated in detailed codes of behaviour laid down by late eighteenth century industrialists (Josiah Wedgwood, 1780, the Soho Foundry rules of 1796, etc.), principally for disciplinary purposes, and now to have taken on a more popularised and persuasive character, especially since the 1950s.

WORKS STAFF; see **staff.**

WORKS UNIONISM. A phrase formerly used by trade unions to describe **workplace bargaining** (q.v.). Its meaning was pejorative. '"Works Unionism" was the worst enemy of trade unionism, since it might become the instrument by means of which the employer would evade the recognition of the uniform conditions established by collective bargaining for all workers in the trade and in the district concerned'; G.D.H. Cole, *Workshop Organisation,* ed. A.I. Marsh, Hutchinson, 1973, p. 7; OUP, 1923.

WORKSHOP AGREEMENT. A **collective agreement** arrived at for a workshop, department, or other portion of a factory or establishment; sometimes, when the establishment is small, for the whole establishment. The term carries no particular connotation of **formality,** some workshop agreements being written in character, others unwritten and others being thought of as arising out of **custom-and-practice.**

WORKSHOP BARGAINING; see **domestic bargaining.**

WORKSHOP PRACTICES; or sometimes **work practices.** Informal **custom and practice** regulating or affecting the behaviour of workers at work, in relation to pay, production, etc. These need not necessarily be **restrictive practices,** though they are often regarded as such; see, for example, A.F. Young, *Social Services in British Industry,* Routledge and Kegan Paul, 1968, p. 177, on the workshop practice of job **demarcation,** control of apprenticeship numbers, etc.

WORK-TO-CONTRACT; see **work-to-rule.**

WORK-TO-RULE or WORKING TO RULE. A **stoppage of work** taking the form of retarding or interrupting a service or process by the literal carrying out of orders, or rules, or the mass observation of safety regulations which are normally honoured in the breach; an expression said to have originated in the railway industry; see Kenneth Hudson, *Working to Rule,* Adams and Dart, 1970, p. 13. Public services, particularly transport, where detailed and formal written working rules are common, are particularly liable to stoppages of this kind; in some industries in which regulation is less formal, work-to-rule may be difficult to separate from **ca'canny** or **go-slow** (q.v.). Legal opinion has usually held that, where work-to-rule involved the performance of the employment contract in all its detail, and where all orders are obeyed, no breach of contract can occur, whereas deliberate **go-slow** tactics are open to action for such a breach (O.L. Aikin, 'Go-slow or Work-to-Rule', *British Journal of Industrial Relations,* Vol. 1, No. 2, June 1963, pp. 260-1). But see the judgement of Lord Denning MR in the case of **Secretary of State for Employment v. ASLEF and others.** Court of Appeal, Times Law Report, 19 May 1972 and (1972) 2 WLR 1370, 1403 (CA), that working to rule involves a breach of contract of employment if it involves wilful disruption of the employer's business; see Brian Napier, 'Working to Rule - A Breach of the Contract of Employment?', *Industrial Law Journal,* Vol. 1, No. 3, September 1972, pp. 125-34. It now seems that a work-to-rule in certain of its forms may be construed by the courts as an 'unreasonable' interpretation of the rules which are being observed.

WORLD CONFEDERATION OF LABOUR (WCL); see **International Labour Movement.**

WORLD FEDERATION OF TRADE UNIONS (WFTU). An international trade union organisation created at the Paris Conference of September-October 1945 which involved a structural merger of existing international organisations on a world-wide basis. The WFTU failed to obtain recognition at the United Nations, and attempted to replace the **International Trade Secretariats** (q.v.) with international trade departments directly under its control. This, the increasing tendency of WFTU leaders to lean in the direction of Soviet policies, and differences over the acceptance of Marshall Aid, led to a withdrawal of non-communist trade union organisations, and the formation of the rival **International Confederation of Free Trade Unions** (q.v.) in 1949. The Soviet Union accounts for a substantial part of the 155 million members in 62 countries claimed by the WFTU; outside communist countries, WFTU affiliates with substantial numbers exist in France and India. The Bureau of International Labor Affairs of the United States Department of Labor publishes a *Directory of World Federations of Trade Unions. Address:* Namesti Curieovych 1, 11688 Prague 1, Czechoslovakia.

WORTHINGTON PUMPING ENGINE CO. v. MOORE (1903) 20, RPC 41; see **Patents Act 1977.**

WPWU. Wall Paper Workers' Union; see **Wallcoverings, Decorative and Allied Trades, National Union of.**

WRITERS' GUILD OF GREAT BRITAIN (WGGB). A trade union representing writers' interests in film, television, radio and publishing, originally formed as the Screenwriters' Guild in 1959; book authors and stage authors became eligible to join in 1974. *Address:* 430 Edgware Road, London W2 1EH. *Tel:* 01-723 8074/5/6. *TUC Affiliated Membership, 1977:* 1,334.

WRONGFUL DISMISSAL. Dismissal, or termination of a contract of employment, in breach of that contract of employment. Where an employer wrongfully dismisses an employee, the employee has the right to recover from him damages for loss of earnings, these damages being sufficient to compensate the injured party but not to punish the wrongdoer and normally depending on the length of notice to which he was entitled, e.g. a person entitled to six months' notice and wrongfully dismissed could claim six months' salary. This the court might vary if tips or commission were involved, or if it seemed that deductions might be required on account of money received by the employee after his dismissal, or on account of sums which would have been deducted had his salary been paid by his employer; see B.A. Hepple and P. O'Higgins, *Employment Law,* Sweet and Maxwell, 1976, Chs. 15 and 16; see also **summary dismissal, unfair dismissal, dismissal with notice.** Notice also that the **Contracts of Employment Act 1972** provides that in the case of wrongful dismissal by the employer the rights to a guaranteed minimum income given for the period of notice shall be taken into account in assessing his liability for breach of contract.

WRONG UNIONS. An expression used by Shirley W. Lerner, *Breakaway Unions and the Small Trade Unions,* George Allen and Unwin, 1961, p. 194 *et seq.,* to describe trade unions which are not approved by established trade unions. This may be because they are **breakaway unions** (q.v.) or because they are minority organisations which might be regarded as potential rivals for membership and influence, or for other reasons. Such unions may be denied membership of national negotiating bodies by established unions and/or membership of representative trade union bodies such as the **Trades Union Congress.** Dr Lerner gives as examples of 'wrong' minority unions the **Chemical Workers' Union** (excluded from national negotiating rights in the chemical industry), and the Aeronautical Engineers' Association, denied representation on the National Joint Council for Civil Air Transport. On her definition, some unions may be 'wrong' in some situations and not in others. For example, the Association of Scientific, Technical and Managerial Staffs and the Association of Professional, Executive, Clerical and Computer Staff are nationally recognised and accepted by manual worker unions as representative bodies in engineering, but have been denied a similar status in the steel industry; see also **bona-fide trade union.**

WSA. Wallcoverings Staff Association; see **Wallcoverings, Decorative and Allied Trades, National Union of,** also **Weekly Staff Agreement** (q.v.).

WUI. Workers' Union of Ireland (q.v.).

WYNES v. SOUTHREPPS HALL BROILER FARM LTD (1968) ITR 407; see **Redundancy Payments Act 1965.**

Y

YELLOW DOG CONTRACT; see **the document.**

YORK MEMORANDUM. (1) A temporary agreement on national provisions for avoiding disputes between the Engineering Employers' Federation and the Amalgamated Society of Engineers at York in April 1914. The Memorandum followed the repudiation by the ASE of an earlier procedure agreement (the Carlisle Agreement of 1907), to which the union objected, and was subsequently incorporated in the 1922 Procedure Agreement-Manual Workers (II(2)); see **Engineering Procedure Agreement.** The York memorandum ceased to operate in 1971. The expression is sometimes, wrongly, used to describe the whole of the 1922 Agreement. A.I. Marsh, *Industrial Relations in Engineering,* Pergamon Press, 1965. (2) (or York Agreement) A joint statement signed by the Iron and Steel Employers' Association and the Iron and Steel Trades Confederation on 28 May 1926 in which the latter agreed that it had acted unconstitutionally in being involved in the **General Strike** and in which both parties reaffirmed existing procedures and agreements and agreed to set up a joint committee to deal with outstanding questions at issue between them. Similar statements were subscribed to by other unions in the iron and steel industry.

YORKSHIRE ASSOCIATION OF POWER LOOM OVERLOOKERS; see **Power Loom Overlookers, Yorkshire Association of.**

YORKSHIRE SOCIETY OF TEXTILE CRAFTSMEN; see **Textile Craftsmen, Yorkshire Society of.**

YOUNG PERSONS; see **children and young persons.**

YOUTH EMPLOYMENT BUREAUX; see **Youth Employment Service.**

YOUTH EMPLOYMENT SERVICE. A service operating in England, Wales and Scotland under the **Employment and training Act 1948** to give vocational advice and guidance to young people up to the age of 18. The service was run jointly by the Local Education Authorities and the Department of Employment under the direction of the Secretary of State for

Employment, in consultation with the Secretary of State for Education and Science and his counterpart in Scotland, some 85 per cent of young people beig covered by the LEAs and the remainder by the DE, 132 LEAs out of 163 in England and Wales and 11 out of 35 in Scotland providing a service. The Service dated from powers given to LEAs in 1906 to provide free meals and welfare services, including the finding of employment, for necessitous children, reinforced in 1910 by the **Education (Choice of Employment) Act** which empowered them to set up **Youth Employment Bureaux** to give advice on choice of employment to young people under 17 (raised to 18 under the Fisher **Education Act 1918)**. By 1939 the shape of the Service was established, and this was reinforced and enlarged as a result of the *Report of the Committee on the Juvenile Employment Service*)**ince Report**) of 1945, which led to the 1948 Act. The Youth Employment Service was reorganised in 1974 following the passing of the Employment and Training Act 1973; see **Careers Service**. Also see H. Heginbotham, *Youth Employment Service*, Methuen, 1951; A.F. Young, *Social Services in British Industry*, Routledge and Kegan Paul 1968, Ch. 2; also **employment service, Carr Report, apprenticeship.**

YOUTH EMPLOYMENT SUBSIDY. A subsidy introduced on 1 October 1976 offering employers £10 per week for each young person under 20 years of age and out of work for six months or more who was given a job. The scheme was ended on 31 March 1978, with the introduction of the **Youth Opportunities Programme** (q.v.). The subsidy is officially claimed to have had some useful effects (see *Department of Employment Gazette*, April 1978).

YOUTH OPPORTUNITIES PROGRAMME. A scheme announced in June 1977 and fully operational by September 1978 whereby young people registered as unemployed for six weeks or longer are offered courses of preparation for work or work experience for up to a year with a weekly allowance of £18 in order to increase their chances of finding a satisfactory permanent job. It is operated by the **Manpower Services Commission** through local boards representing appropriate local interests, funded by central government, and has absorbed the **Job Creation Programme** and the **Work Experience Programme** already operating.

Bibliography

In this Bibliography are listed all the books and articles referred to in the text of the Encyclopedia, together with a note of the particular entries under which they are to be found. Government publications have generally been excluded except where they can be attributed to a particular author or authors.

It is not the object of the Bibliography to give guidance on a comprehensive reading list of works and learned contributions in industrial relations. Each reference in the Encyclopedia arises from its relevance in illustrating, describing or contributing to the discussion of, some particular term or subject. For the same reason, it is not our intention to suggest that the sources quoted are the only sources available; only that they came most readily to mind, and were most readily available to us, as the process of compilation proceeded. Books and periodical articles are listed separately.

AIM.

BOOKS

Aaron, Benjamin. (ed.), *Labor Courts and Grievance Settlement in Western Europe*, University of California Press, 1971.

Labour Courts.

Acton Society Trust, *Size and Morale, I and II*, 1953 and 1957.

Size-effect.

Acton Society Trust, *Redundancy*, A Survey of Problems and Practices, 1958.

Redundancy.

Acton Society Trust, *Three Studies on Redundant Workers*, 1959.

Redundancy.

Acton Society Trust and Naylor, Guy, *Sharing the Profits*, Garnstone Press, 1968.

Co-partnership, Profit Sharing.

Adams, James F., *Problems in Counselling: A Case Study Approach*, Collier Macmillan, 1962.

Counselling.

Adams, Thomas S., and Sumner, Helen L., *Labour Problems*, New York, Macmillan, 1912.

Sweating.

Addison, M.E., *Essentials of Organisation and Methods*, Heinemann, 1971.

Organisation and Methods (O and M).

Aikin, Olga, and Reid, Judith, *Labour Law 1, Employment, Welfare and Safety at Work*, Penguin Education, 1971.

Apprenticeship, Industrial Misconduct, Specific Performance.

Alcock, G.W., *Fifty Years of Railway Trade Unionism*, Co-operative Printing Society Ltd, 1922.

Railwaymen, National Union of.

Aldridge, A., *Power, Authority and Restrictive Practices*, Blackwell, 1978.

Restrictive Practices.

Alexander, K.J.W., *Fairfields: A study in Industrial Change*, Allen Lane, The Penguin Press, 1970.

Fairfields Experiment.

356

Allen, E. *et al.*, *The North-East Engineers' Strike of 1871*, Frank Graham, 1971.
Nine Hours Movement.

Allen, S., *The Trade Union Movement and Discrimination, Collected Essays*, Runnymede Trust, 1971.
Race Relations Acts.

Allen, V.L., *Power in Trade Unions*, Longmans Green, 1954.
Compulsory Trade Unionism, Closed Shop, Trade Union.

Allen, V.L., *Trade Union Leadership: Based on A Study of Arthur Deakin*, Longmans, 1957.
Transport and General Workers' Union.

Allen, V.L., *Militant Trade Unionism*, Merlin Press, 1966.
Militancy, Trade Union.

Allen, V.L., *International Bibliography of Trade Unionism*, Merlin Press, 1968.
Bibliographies and Sources on Industrial Relations.

Allen, V.L., *The Sociology of Industrial Relations*, Longmans, 1971.
Industrial Relations, Trade Union.

Allport, Gordon W., *Handbook of Social Psychology*, ed. G. Lindzey, Addison-Wesley, 1968, Vol. 1.
Attitude.

Amalgamated Association of Card Blowing and Ring Room Operatives, *After 50 Years; Golden Jubilee Souvenir, 1886-1936*, AACB and RRO, 1936.
Textile and Allied Workers, National Union of.

Amalgamated Society of Lithographic Printers, *History and Progress of the Amalgamated Society of Lithographic Printers, 1880-1930*, ASLP, 1930.
Graphical Association, National.

Amulree, Lord, *Industrial Arbitration*, OUP, 1929.
Arbitration, Devonshire Commission, Difference, Industrial Arbitration Board, Industrial Council, Industrial Courts Act 1919, Treasury Agreement.

Anderman, S.D., *Voluntary Dismissals Procedure and the Industrial Relations Act*, Political and Economic Planning Broadsheet 538, September 1972.
Disciplinary Procedure, Unfair Dismissal.

Anstey, E., *Staff Reporting and Staff Development*, Allen and Unwin, 1969.
Performance Appraisal.

Anstey, E., Fletcher, C. and Walker, J., *Staff Appraisal and Development*, Allen and Unwin, 1976.
Employee Appraisal.

Anthony, Peter, and Crichton, Anne, *Industrial Relations and the Personnel Specialists*, Batsford, 1969.
Parallel Unionism.

Argyle, Michael, *The Scientific Study of Social Behaviour*, Methuen, 1957.
Action Research.

Argyris, C., *Integrating the Individual and the Organisation*, Wiley, 1964.
Human Relations.

Argyris, C., *Personality and Organisation*, Harper, 1957.
Organisational Behaviour.

Armstrong, Sir William, 'The Civil Service Department and its Tasks', Chapter 23 in Chapman, R.A., and Dunsire, A. (eds), *Style in Administration; Readings in British Public Administration,* George Allen and Unwin, 1971.
Civil Service Department.

Arnison, J., *The Shrewsbury Three,* Lawrence and Wishart, 1974.
Shrewsbury Pickets.

Ashdown, R.T., and Baker, K.H., *In Working Order, A Study of Industrial Discipline,* Department of Employment, Manpower Papers No. 6, HMSO, 1973.
Disciplinary Procedure.

Ashley, W.J., *The Adjustment of Wages,* Longmans, 1903.
Selling-price Sliding Scales.

Bagwell, Philip S., *The Railwaymen, A History of the National Union of Railwaymen,* Allen and Unwin, 1963.
Railwaymen, National Union of.

Bain, G.S., *Trade Union Growth and Recognition,* Royal Commission on Trade Unions and Employers' Assocations, Research Papers, 6, 1967.
Donovan Commission.

Bain, G.S., *The Growth of White-Collar Unionism,* OUP, 1970.
Bureaucracy, Professional, Executive, Clerical and Computer Staff, Association of, Scientific, Technical and Managerial Staffs, Association of, Union Density, White Collar Union.

Bain, G.S., Coates, D. and Ellis, N., *Social Stratification and Trade Unionism,* Heinemann, 1973.
White Collar Union.

Bain, G.S. and Price, Robert, *Union Growth and Employment Trends in the United Kingdom, 1964-1970,* Industrial Relations Research Unit, University of Warwick Discussion Paper, March 1972.
Union Density, White Collar Union, White Collar Worker.

Baker, Arthur, *The Employers' Federation of Papermakers and Boardmakers, A Brief History,* March 1953.
British Paper and Board Industries Federation.

Baldamus, W., *Efficiency and Effort,* Tavistock, 1967.
Goldbricking, Incentive Payment System, Quota Restriction, Wage Disparity, Wage Parity.

Baldwin, George B., *Beyond Nationalisation,* Harvard University Press, 1955.
Bull Weeks, Butty, Concessionary Coal, Conciliation, District Referee, Dual Membership Agreement.

Balfour, Campbell, *Incomes Policy and the Public Sector,* Routledge and Kegan Paul, 1972.
Incomes Policy.

Balke, Siegfried, *Expansion of Co-determination in the Federal Republic of Germany* Bundesvereinigung der Deutschen Arbeitgeberbände, Köln, 1970.
Co-determination.

Bank, J. and Jones, K., *Worker Directors Speak,* Gower Press, 1977.
Worker Directors.

Banks, J.A., *Marxist Sociology in Action, A Sociological Critique of the Marxist Approach to Industrial Relations,* Faber & Faber, 1970.
Trade Union.

Barbash, Jack, *Labor Unions in Action,* Harper, New York, 1948.
International Union.

Barber, R., *Picketing: The Law of Violence,* Bow Group, 1972.
Picketing.

Barnes, G.N., *History of the International Labour Office,* Williams and Norgate, 1926.
International Labour Organisation.

Barnes, R.M., *Motion and Time Study,* John Wiley and Sons, 5th ed. 1968.
Scientific Management, Work Study.

Barou, Noah, *British Trade Unions,* Gollancz, 1947.
Closed Shop, Industrial Union.

Barrett, P.F., *The Human Implications of Mergers and Takeovers,* IPM, 1973.
Multi-establishment Company.

Bartholomew, J.D. and Forbes, A.F., *Statistical Techniques of Manpower Planning,* Wiley, 1978.
Manpower Planning.

Bateson, Walter, *The Way We Came, History of the Dyers, Bleachers and Textile Workers,* Thornton and Pearsons, Bradford, 1928.
Dyers, Bleachers and Textile Workers, National Union of.

Bayhylle, J.E., *Productivity Improvement in the Office,* Engineering Employers' Federation, Research Paper 2, December 1968.
Clerical Work Improvement Programme, Group Capacity Assessment, Variable Factor Programming.

Bayliss, F.J., *British Wages Councils,* Blackwell, 1962.
Independent Members, Sweating, Trade Boards Act, Wages Councils.

Beal, Edwin F. and Wickersham, Edward D., *The Practice of Collective Bargaining,* Richard D. Irwin, 1963.
White Collar Worker.

Bealey, F., *The Post Office Engineering Union,* Bachman and Turner, 1976.
Post Office Engineering Union.

Beaumont, P.B., 'Experience under the Fair Wages Resolution of 1946', *Industrial Relations Journal,* Vol. 8, No. 3, Autumn 1977.
Fair Wages Principle.

Beckhard, R., *Organisation Development; Strategies and Models,* Addison-Wesley, 1969.
Organisation Development.

Beer, Stafford, *The Theory of Operational Research,* SIGMA Paper, 1964.
Operational Research.

Beever, R.C. and Tritton, B., *An Analysis of Sit-ins,* Metra Consulting, 1972.
Sit-in Strike.

Behrend, Hilde, *Absence under Full Employment,* University of Birmingham, 1951.
Absence, Blue Monday.

Behrend, Hilde, Lynch, Harriet, Thomas, Howard and Davies, Jean, *Incomes Policy and the Individual,* Oliver and Boyd, 1967.
Prices and Incomes Policy.

Behrend, Hilde, Knowles, Ann and Davies, Jean, *Views on Pay Increases, Fringe Benefits and Low Pay*, Economic and Social Research Institute, Dublin, Paper No. 56, August 1970.
Wage-rounds.

Behrens, B. Beddington, *The International Labour Office*, Leonard Parsons, 1924.
International Labour Organisation.

Bell, J.D.M., *Industrial Unionism, a Critical Analysis*, Department of Economic and Social Research, University of Glasgow, 1948.
Industrial Union.

Bell, J.D.M., 'Trade Unions'; Chapter III in Flanders, Allan and Clegg, H.A. (eds), *The System of Industrial Relations in Great Britain*, Blackwell, 3rd ed. 1976.
Autonomous Regulation.

Bennett, M.G., 'Operational Research in Industry'; in Welford, A.T. (ed.), *Society: Problems and Methods of Study*, Routledge and Kegan Paul, 1967.
Operational Research.

Bennis, W., *Changing Organisations*, McGraw-Hill, 1966.
Human Relations, Organisation Development.

Bennis, W.G. and Stater, P.E., *The Temporary Society*, Harper and Row, 1968.
Organisational Behaviour.

Benson, Sir Henry and Brown, Sir Sam, *Report on the Formation of a National Industrial Organisation*, April 1964.
British Employers' Confederation.

Bentley, F.R., *People, Productivity and Progress*, Business Publications Ltd, 1964.
Rucker Plan.

Bercusson, B., *Fair Wages Resolutions*, Mansell, 1978.
Fair Wages Principle.

Bergman, J., Jacobi, O. and Muller-Jentsch, W., *Gewerkschaften in der Bundesrepublik*, Frankfurt am Main, 1975.
Adversary Trade Unions.

Berne, E., *The Games People Play; the Psychology of Human Relationships*, Deutsch, 1966.
Transactional Analysis.

Bernstein, Irving, 'Arbitration'; in Kornhauser, Arthur, Dubin, Robert and Ross, Arthur M. (eds), *Industrial Conflict*, McGraw-Hill, 1954.
Contract Arbitration.

Beveridge, Andrew, *Apprenticeship Now*, Chapman and Hall, 1963.
Indentured Apprentice.

Beveridge, W.H., *Full Employment in a Free Society*, Allen and Unwin, 1960.
Cyclical Unemployment.

Birchill, Frank and Sweeney, J., *A History of Trade Unionism in the North Staffordshire Textile Industry*, Department of Adult Education, University of Keele, 1971.
Textile Workers and Kindred Trades.

Bittel, L.R., *Management by Exception: Systematizing and simplifying the mangerial job*, McGraw-Hill, 1965.
Management By Exception.

Blackburn, R.M., *Union Character and Social Class*, Batsford, 1967.
Bank Employees, National Union of, Completeness, Militancy, Professional Association, Unionateness, Unionisation, Union Density.

Blackman, J.L., *Presidential Seizure in Labor Disputes*, Harvard UP, 1967.
Presidential Seizure.

Blain, A.N.J., *Pilots and Management; Industrial Relations in the U.K. Airlines*, Allen and Unwin, 1972.
British Airline Pilots Association.

Blake, Robert and Moulton, Jane, *The Managerial Grid: Key orientations for achieving production through people*, Gulf Publishing Company, Houston, Texas, 1977.
Managerial Grid.

Blanc-Jouvan, Xavier, 'The Settlement of Labor Disputes in France', in Aaron, Benjamin (ed.), *Labor Courts and Grievance Settlement in Western Europe*, University of California Press, 1971.
Conseils de Prud'hommes.

Blandford, Oliver and Jenkins, C.L., *The Fairfields Experiment*, Industrial Society, 1969.
Fairfields Experiment.

Blauner, R., *Alienation and Freedom*, University of Chicago Press, 1964.
Alienation, Blue-collar Workers, Human Relations, Organisational Behaviour.

Blauner, R., 'Work Satisfaction and Industrial Trends in Modern Society', in Bendix, R. and Lipset, S.M. (eds), *Class, Status and Power*, Routledge and Kegan Paul, 1967.
Job Satisfaction.

Blum, Albert A., *et al.*, *White Collar Workers*, New York, Random House, 1972.
White Collar Worker.

Blum, Fred H., *Work and Community; The Scott Bader Commonwealth and the Quest for a New Social Order*, Routledge and Kegan Paul, 1969.
Scott Bader Commonwealth Ltd.

Blumenthal, W.M., *Co-determination in the German Steel Industry*, Princeton, 1956.
Co-determination.

Blyth, D., *Remuneration and Incentives*, Editype, 1969.
Measured Daywork.

Bolton, J. Harvey, *Flexible Working Hours*, Anbar Publications Ltd, 1971.
Fixed Working Hours, Flexible Working Hours, Rational Working Hours, Variable Working Hours.

Boraston, I., Clegg, H. and Rimmer, M., *Workplace and Union*, Heinemann, 1975.
Workplace Bargaining.

Bourne, Richard and Macarthur, Brian, *A Struggle for Education*, Schoolmaster Publishing Company, 1970.
Teachers, National Union of.

Bowey, Angela M., *A Guide to Manpower Planning*, Macmillan, 1974.
Induction Crisis.

Bramham, J., *Practical Manpower Planning*, IPM, 1975.
Manpower Planning.

Brannen, P., Batstone, E., Fatchett, D. and White, P., *The Worker Directors*, Hutchinson, 1976.
Worker Directors.

Brentano, L., *The History and Development of Gilds and the Origins of Trades Unions*, Trübner, 1870.
Craft Gilds

Brissenden, P.F., *The IWW, A Study in American Syndicalism,* Columbia University Press, 1920.
Wobblies.

Brissenden, P.F. and Frankel, E., *Labour Turnover in Industry,* Macmillan, New York, 1922.
Induction Crisis.

British Airline Pilots Association, *History of Balpa,* ᴅALPA, 1957.
British Airline Pilots Association.

British Institute of Management, *Merit Rating: A Practical Guide*, Personnel Management Series, 1954.
Merit Rating.

British Institute of Management, *Absence from Work,* BIM, 1955.
Absence, Lateness.

British Institute of Management, *Abolition of Time Clocks,* BIM Information Note 11, January 1961.
Clocking.

British Institute of Management, *Company Redundancy Policies,* 1969.
Redundancy.

British Institute of Management, *Job Evaluation,* A Practical Guide, 1970.
Job Evaluation.

British Institute of Management, *Some notes on Company-wide incentive schemes,* BIM Information Note 26, 1964.
Rucker Plan, Scanlon Plan.

British Institute of Management, *The Measurement of Work,* BIM, 1965.
Analytical Estimating.

British Institute of Management, *Leave of absence for other reasons than sickness or annual vacation,* Information Summary 118, October 1965.
Leave of Absence, Sabbatical Leave.

British Institute of Management, *Fringe Benefits for Executives,* Information Summary 120, December 1965.
Fringe Benefits.

British Institute of Management, *Company Redundancy Policies,* Information Summary, 137, March 1969.
Redundancy.

British Printing Industries Federation, *The Printing Industries'* (formerly the *Master Printers') Annual,* BPIF.
British Printing Industries' Federation.

British Standards Institution, *Glossary of Terms used in Work Study,* BS 3138, 1969.
Activity Sampling, Allowances, Analytical Estimating, Bonus Increment, Changeover Allowance, Contingency Allowance, Excess Work Allowance, Idle Time, Interference Allowance, Job, Learner Allowance, Method Study, Policy Allowance, Predetermined Motion Time Systems, Relaxation Allowance, Standard Performance, Standard Time, Time Study, Unoccupied Time Allowance, Work Load, Work Measurement, Work Study.

Brooks, D. and Smith, R., *Mergers: the impact on the shopfloor,* Acton Society Trust, 1966.
Multi-establishment Company.

Brown, Wilfred, *Exploration in Management.* Heinemann, 1960.
Appeals Procedure, Glacier Project.

Brown, Wilfred, *Piecework Abandoned,* Heinemann, 1962.
Clocking, Glacier Project, Lateness.

Brown, Wilfred, *Organisation,* Heinemann, 1971.
Appeals Procedure, Glacier Project.

Brown, Wilfred and Jaques, Elliott, *Product Analysis Pricing,* Heinemann, 1964.
Glacier Project.

Brown, Wilfred and Jaques, Elliot, *Glacier Project Papers,* Heinemann, 1965.
Glacier Project.

Buchan, Alasdair, *The Right to Work; the Story of the Upper Clyde Confrontation,* Calder and Boyars, 1972.
Work-in.

Buckingham, W., *Automation, Its Impact on Business and People,* Harper and Row, 1963.
Technological Unemployment.

Bullock, Alan, *The Life and Times of Ernest Bevin,* Volume 1, Trade Union Leader, 1881-1940, and Volume 2, Minister of Labour, 1940-1945, Heinemann, 1967.
Transport and General Workers' Union, Wages Councils.

Bundock, C.J., *The National Union of Journalists,* 1907-1957. OUP, 1957.
Journalists, National Union of.

Bundock, C.J., *The National Union of Printing, Bookbinding and Paper Workers,* OUP, 1959.
Graphical and Allied Trades, Society of.

Burns, T. and Stalker, G.M., *The Management of Innovation,* Tavistock, 1966.
Human Relations.

Cadbury, E. and Shann, G., *Sweating,* Headley Bros., 1907.
Sweating.

Calvez, J-Y. and Perrin, J., *The Church and Social Justice,* Burns Oates, 1961.
Catholic Industrial Relations Teaching, Just Wage.

Callaghan, J., *Whitleyism,* Fabian Society Research Series, No. 159, 1953.
Whitleyism.

Cameron, G.C., 'The Growth of Holidays with Pay in Britain', in Reid, G.L. and Robertson, D.J. (eds), *Fringe Benefits, Labour Costs and Social Security,* Allen and Unwin, 1965.
Amulree Report, Holidays with Pay.

Carby, K. and Thakur, M., *Transactional Analysis at Work,* IPM, 1976.
Transactional Analysis.

Carnegie, D., *The Promotion of Industrial Harmony,* 1919.
Garton Memorandum.

Carpenter, W.H. Jr. and Handler, E., *Small Business and Pattern Bargaining,* Babson Institute Press, 1961.
Pattern Bargaining.

Carr-Saunders, A.M., Caradog Jones, D. and Moser, C.A., *A Survey of Social Conditions in England and Wales*, OUP, 1958.
Profession.

Carr-Saunders, A.M. and Wilson, P.A., *The Professions*, Frank Cass, 1964.
Profession.

Cartter, A.M., *Theory of Wages and Employment*, Irwin Inc., 1959.
Share of Wages.

Cemach, Harry, *Work Study in the Office*, Anbar Pubns, 4th ed. 1969.
Organisation and Methods (O and M).

Central Committee of Study Groups, *Some Social and Industrial Implications of Shift Work*, Industrial Welfare Society, 1963.
Shift Working.

Challinor, R., *The Lancashire and Cheshire Miners*, Frank Graham, 1972.
Mineworkers, National Union of.

Chamberlain, Neil W., *The Union Challenge to Management Control*, Harper and Row, 1948, and Archon Books, 1967.
Fractional Bargaining, Managerial Prerogatives, Trade Union Functions.

Chamberlain, Neil W. and Kuhn, J.W., *Collective Bargaining*, McGraw-Hill, 2nd ed. 1965.
Collective Bargaining, Conjunctive Bargaining, Co-operative Bargaining.

Chamberlain, Waldo, *Industrial Relations in Wartime: Great Britain 1914-1918*, Stanford University Press, 1940.
Bibliographies and Sources on Industrial Relations.

Chandler, Margaret, *Management Rights and Union Interests*, McGraw-Hill, 1964.
Managerial Prerogatives.

Chapman, S.J., *Work and Wages*, Part II, Longmans Green, 1908.
Union Label.

Charles, R., *The Development of Industrial Relations in Britain 1911-1939*, Hutchinson, 1973.
Building Industry, National Joint Council for, Industrial Council, National Industrial Conference, Voluntarism, Whitleyism.

Chernish, William N., *Coalition Bargaining: A Study of Union Tactics and Public Policy*, University of Pennsylvania Press, and OUP, 1969.
Coalition Bargaining.

Child, John, *Industrial Relations in the British Printing Industry*, Allen and Unwin, 1967.
Certification, Darg, Relaxation Agreements, Mixed Office, Smooting, Union House, Whips.

Chisholm, Cecil (ed.), *Communications in Industry*, Business Publications, in collaboration with B.T. Batsford Ltd, 1955.
Communications.

Citrine, Lord, *Men and Work*, Greenwood Press, 1976.
General Strike, Mond Turner Conferences.

Civil Service Clerical Association, *Memorandum*, December 1965.
Horizontal Unionism.

Civil Service Clerical Association, *CSCA Strike Policy*, Civil Service Clerical Association, 1969.
Staging, Without Prejudice Offer.

Clack, G., *Industrial Relations in a British Car Factory,* CUP, 1967.
Downer, Participant Observation.

Clague, E. and Greenberg, L., 'Employment', in Dunlop, J.T. (ed.), *Automation and Technological Change,* Prentice-Hall, 1962.
Technological Unemployment.

Clark, G. de N., *Remedies for Unjust Dismissal,* Political and Economic Planning Broadsheet 518, June 1970.
Unfair Dismissal.

Clarke, R.O., Fatchett, D.J. and Roberts, B.C., *Workers' Participation in Management in Britain,* Heinemann, 1972.
Industrial Democracy.

Clarke, R.O., Fatchett, D.J. and Rothwell, S.G., *Workers' Participation and Industrial Democracy, A Bibliography,* 1969.
Industrial Democracy.

Clegg, H.A., *Labour Relations in London Transport,* Blackwell, 1950.
Coronation Strike, Syndicalism.

Clegg, H.A., *Single and Double Day-shift Working in the Cotton Industry,* Cotton Board Conference Proceedings, 1952.
Two-shift System.

Clegg, H.A., *Double Day-shift Working in the Cotton Industry,* Cotton Board Conference Proceedings, 1953.
Two-shift System.

Clegg, H.A., *General Union,* Blackwell, 1954.
Better Conditions Clause, General and Municipal Workers' Union.

Clegg, H.A., *A New Approach to Industrial Democracy,* Blackwell, 1960.
Collective Contract, Cross-booking, Guild Socialism, Industrial Democracy, Joint Consultation, Workers' Participation.

Clegg, H.A., *General Union in a Changing Society,* Blackwell, 1964.
General and Municipal Workers' Union.

Clegg, H.A., *The System of Industrial Relations in Great Britain,* Blackwell, 1970, 3rd ed., 1976.
Comparability, Donovan Commission, Formalisation, Wage Restraint, Whitleyism.

Clegg, H.A., *How to run an Incomes Policy and why we made such a mess of the last one,* Heinemann, 1971.
Incomes Policy, National Board for Prices and Incomes, Prices and Incomes Policy, Wage Explosion.

Clegg, H.A. and Adams, Rex. *The Employers' Challenge,* Blackwell, 1957.
Jack Report, Price Plateau.

Clegg, H.A. and Chester, T.E., 'Joint Consultation'; in Flanders, Allan, and Clegg, H.A., *The System of Industrial Relations in Great Britain,* Blackwell, 1954.
Joint Consultation, Mond Turner Conferences.

Clegg, H.A., Fox, A. and Thompson, P., *A History of British Trade Unions Since 1889,* Vol. I, OUP, 1964.
The Document, National Bargaining, Trade Union.

Clegg, H.A., Killick, A.J. and Adams, Rex, *Trade Union Officers,* Blackwell, 1961.
Convener or Convenor, Craft Union, Ex-craft Union, General Union, Industrial Union, Shop Steward, Single-Industry Union, Skilled Union, Trade Union, Typology of Trade Unions.

Cleland, S., *The Influence of Plant Size on Industrial Relations*, Princeton, 1955.
Size-effect.

Cliff, Tony, *The Employers' Offensive, Productivity Deals and How to Fight Them*, Pluto Press, 1970.
Productivity Bargaining.

Coates, Ken (ed.), *Can the Workers Run Industry?* Bertrand Russell House, 1976.
Industrial Democracy.

Coates, Ken, Topham, Tony and Brown, M. Barratt, *Trade Union Register*, Merlin Press, 1969.
Engineering Package Deal Agreements.

Coates, Ken and Topham, Tony (eds), *Industrial Democracy in Great Britain*, Bertrand Russell House, 1974.
Guild Socialism, Industrial Democracy.

Cole, G.D.H., *Self-Government in Industry*, 1917, Hutchinson, Introduction by J. Corina, 1972.
Guild Socialism.

Cole, G.D.H., *Guild Socialism Re-stated*, Leonard Parsons Ltd, 1920.
Guild Socialism.

Cole, G.D.H., *Trade Unionism and Munitions*, Economic and Social History of the War, OUP, 1923.
Shop Stewards' Movement, Treasury Agreement.

Cole, G.D.H., *Workshop Organisation*, OUP, 1923, Introduction by A. I. Marsh, Hutchinson, 1973.
Collective Contract, Dilution, Rate Cutting, Shop Steward, Works Unionism.

Cole, G.D.H., *A Short History of the British Working Class Movement, 1787-1947*, Allen and Unwin, 1948 ed.
Contract System, Craft Gilds, New Unionism, Triple Alliance.

Cole, G.D.H. and Page Arnot, R., *Trade Unionism on the Railways*, Labour Research Department, 1917.
Railwaymen, National Union of.

Cole, G.D.H. and Postgate, R., *The Common People, 1746-1946*, Methuen, 4th ed., 1949.
Luddites.

Coleman, Terry, *The Railway Navvies*, Hutchinson, 1965.
Navvy.

Confederation of British Industry, *Communication and Consultation, Report of a Working Party*, CBI, 1965.
Communications, Joint Consultation.

Confederation of British Industry, *Absenteeism*, CBI, 1966.
Absence, Attendance Money.

Confederation of British Industry, *Disputes Procedures*, 1970.
Status Quo.

Connelly, T.J., *The Woodworkers, 1860-1960*, Amalgamated Society of Woodworkers, 1960.
Construction, Allied Trades and Technicians, Union of.

Connolly, J., *Labour, Nationality and Religion*, Dublin 1910.
General Strike.

366

Conservative Central Office, *Fair Deal at Work*, April 1968.
Closed Shop, Cooling-off Period.

Conservative Political Centre, *Financing Strikes*, 1974.
State Subsidy Theory of Strikes.

Cook, F.P., *Shift Work*, Institute of Personnel Management, 1954.
Inconvenience Payment, Staggered Day Work.

Cooper, C.L. and Mangham, I.L. (eds), *T Groups; a Survey of Research*, Wiley-Interscience, 1971.
T Groups.

Copeman, George, *The Challenge of Employee Shareholding*, Business Publications, 1958.
Co-partnership.

Corina, John, *The British Experiment in Wage Restraint with Special Reference to 1948-1960*, Unpublished DPhil thesis, Oxford, 1961.
Wage Restraint.

Corina, John, *The Development of Incomes Policy*, Institute of Personnel Management, 1966.
Incomes Policy, Prices and Incomes Policy.

Corina, John, *Forms of Wage Payment for High Productivity*, Organisation for Economic Co-operation and Development, 1970.
Organisation for Economic Co-operation and Development.

Corina, John, *Labour Market Economics*, Heinemann, 1972.
Labour Market.

Cotgrove, S., Dunham, J. and Vamplew, C., *The Nylon Spinners*, Allen and Unwin, 1971.
Job Enlargement, Productivity Bargaining.

Coventry and District Engineering Employers' Association, *Wage Drift, Work Measurement and Systems of Payment*, 1967.
Mutuality, Piecework Wage Drift.

Crabtree, Cyril, *The Industrial Relations Act*, Charles Knight and Co., 1971.
Collective Agreement, Unfair Industrial Practice.

Craigen, J.M., *The Scottish TUC, 1897-1973*, MLitt Thesis, Heriot-Watt, 1974.
Scottish Trade Union Congress.

Craik, W.W., *Bryn Roberts and the National Union of Public Employees*, Allen and Unwin, 1955.
Public Employees, National Union of.

Cresswell, W.L. and Froggatt, P., *The Causation of Bus Driver Accidents*, OUP, 1963.
Accident.

Crichton, Anne, *Personnel Management in Context*, Batsford, 1968.
Counselling, Indulgency Pattern, Personnel Management.

Crompton, Henry, *Industrial Conciliation*, London, 1876.
Conciliation.

Croner, F., *Tjänstemannakaren i det moderna sämhället*, H. Gebers, Stockholm, 1951.
White Collar Worker.

Crook, W.H., *The General Strike*, University of North Carolina Press, 1931.
General Strike.

Crossan, R.M. and Nance, H.W., *Master Standard Data*, McGraw-Hill, 1972 revised ed.
Master Standard Data.

Cummings, D.C., *An Historical Survey of the Boiler Makers' and Iron and Steel Ship Builders' Society*, R. Robinson, Newcastle-on-Tyne, 1905.
Boilermakers, Shipwrights, Blacksmiths and Structural Workers, Amalgamated Society of.

Cunnison, Sheila, *Wages and Work Allocation*, Tavistock, 1966.
Work Sharing.

Currie, R.M., *Work Study*, Pitman 4th ed., 1977.
Analytical Estimating, Rated Time Study, Scientific Management, Work Study.

Currie, R.M., *Simplified PMTS*, British Institute of Management, 1963.
Predetermined Motion Time Systems.

Currie, R.M., *The Measurement of Work*, British Institute of Management, 1965.
Analytical Estimating.

Cuthbert, N.H., *The Lace Makers' Society*, Amalgamated Society of Operative Lace Makers and Auxiliary Workers, 1960.
Lace Makers and Textile Workers, Amalgamated Society of Operative.

Dalton, Melville, 'The Industrial "Rate-buster"; a Characterisation', in Lupton, Tom (ed.), *Payment Systems*, Penguin Modern Management Readings, 1972.
Ratebuster.

Daly, G.F., *Industrial Relations, Comparative Aspects*, The Mercier Press, 1968.
Negotiating Licence.

Daniel, W.W., *Beyond the Wage-Work Bargain*, Political and Economic Planning Broadsheet 519, July 1970.
Job-and-finish, Productivity Bargaining, Restrictive Practices, Wage-work Bargaining.

Dankert, Clyde E., Mann, Floyd C. and Northrup, Herbert R. (eds), *Hours of Work*, Harper and Row, Industrial Relations Research Association, Publication No. 32, 1965.
Hours of Work.

Darragh, John, *The Closed Shop*, 1959.
Closed Shop.

Daugherty, Carroll R., *Labor Problems in American Industry*, Houghton Mifflin, 1933.
Uplift Unionism.

Davey, D. Mackenzie, Gill, D. Rockingham and McDonnell, P., *Attitude Surveys in Industry*, IPM, 1970.
Attitude.

Davey, Harold, 'The Operational Impact of the Taft-Hartley Act upon Collective Bargaining Relationships'; in Davey, H.W., Kaltenborn, H.S. and Ruttenberg, S.H. (eds), *New Dimensions in Collective Bargaining*, Harper, 1959.
Taft-Hartley Act 1947.

Davison, J., *Northumberland Miners 1919-39*, NUM, 1973.
Mineworkers, National Union of.

De Jong, J.R.; in *Time and Motion Study*, September 1964.
Learning Curve.

Delamotte, Yves, *The Social Partners Face the Problems of Productivity and Employment,* OECD, Paris, 1971.
Productivity Bargaining.

Denning, *New Survey of London Life and Labour,* P.S. King, 1931.
Stint.

Department of Employment, *Women at Work,* Manpower Paper No. 11, 1975. Department of Employment, *Women at Work; Overseas Practice,* Manpower Paper No. 12, 1975.
Sex Discrimination Act 1975.

Department of Employment, *An Introduction to Predetermined Motion Time Systems,* HMSO, 1976.
Predetermined Motion Time Systems.

Derber, Milton, *Labor-Management Relations at the Plant Level under Industry-wide Bargaining, A Study of the Engineering Industry in Birmingham, England,* University of Illinois, 1955.
Industry-wide Bargaining.

Derrick P. and Phipps, J-F., *Co-ownership, Co-operation and Control,* Longmans, 1969.
Co-partnership.

de Schweinitz, D., *How Workers find Jobs,* University of Pennsylvania Press, 1932.
Labour Market.

Dickens, Linda, *What future for the Professional Union?,* Industrial Relations Research Unit, University of Warwick, Discussion Paper, March 1972.
Professional Engineers, United Kingdom Association of.

Dictionary of Printing Terms, Print Buyer Magazine Ltd revised, 1976.
Journeyman.

Diebold, John, *Automation. The Advent of the Automatic Factory,* 1952.
Automation.

Dix, Waddy D. Knight, *Dix on Contracts of Employment,* 5th ed., 1976.
Contracts of Employment Act 1963.

Dobb, Maurice, *Wages,* Nisbit, 1956
Subsistence Theory of Wages, Wages-Fund Theory.

Doewenberg, J.J. *et al., Compulsory Arbitration,* Lexington Books, 1976.
Compulsory Arbitration.

Donovan, A.F., *Management of Supervisors,* Macmillan, 1971.
Supervisors.

Drake, Barbara, *Women in Trade Unions,* 1921.
Women's Trade Union League.

Drake, C.D., *Labour Law,* Sweet and Maxwell, 2nd ed., 1973.
Abusive Dismissal, Disablement Benefit, Industrial Injuries Acts.

Dubin, Robert, 'Constructive Aspects of Industrial Conflict'; in Kornhauser, Arthur, Dubin, Robert and Ross, Arthur M., (eds), *Industrial Conflict,* McGraw-Hill, 1954.
Industrial Conflict.

Duckworth, E., *A Guide to Operational Research,* Methuen, 3rd ed., 1976.
Operational Research.

Dunkerley, D., *The Foreman,* Routledge and Kegan Paul, 1975.
Foreman.

Dunkerley, D., *Occupations and Society,* Routledge and Kegan Paul, 1975.
Occupation.

Dunlop, J.T., *Industrial Relations Systems,* Holt-Dryden, 1958.
Industrial Relations, Procedural Terms, Substantive Terms.

Dunlop, J.T. (ed.), *The Theory of Wage Determination,* Macmillan, 1964.
Bargaining Theory of Wages.

Dunlop, J.T., *Wage Determination Under Trade Unions,* A.M. Kelly Inc., 1970.
Share of Wages.

Dunlop, J.T. and Neil W. Chamberlain, *Frontiers of Collective Bargaining,* Harper and Row, 1968.
Cost-reduction Plans.

Dunning, John H. (ed.), *The Multi-National Enterprise,* Allen and Unwin, 1971.
Multi-national Corporation.

Durkheim, E., *The Division of Labour in Society,* Collier Macmillan, 1964.
Size-effect.

Dyson, Roger, *The Development of Collective Bargaining in Cotton Spinning,* PhD Thesis, University of Leeds, 1972.
Spinners and Twiners, Amalgamated Association of Operative Cotton.

Economist Intelligence Unit, *Survey of the National Newspaper Industry,* 1966.
Blow, Chapel, Fat, Progress Payment Scheme, Seniority Premiums, Shawcross Report, Slating.

Edmonds, J. and Radice, G., *Low Pay,* Fabian Research Series 270, July 1972.
Low Pay.

Edwards, Ness, *History of the South Wales Miners' Federation,* Vol. 1, Lawrence and Wishart, 1938.
Mineworkers, National Union of.

Edwards, Sir Ronald, *An Experiment in Industrial Relations,* Electricity Council, 1967.
Status Agreement.

Egan, Bowes, *Dismissals,* Commercial Publishing Co., 1977.
Unfair Dismissal.

Eldridge, J.E.T., *Industrial Disputes,* Routledge and Kegan Paul, 1968.
Demarcation, Wildcat Strike.

Electrical Trades Union, *Fifty Years of the Electrical Trades Union,* ETU, 1939.
Electrical, Electronic, Telecommunication and Plumbing Union.

Electrical Trades Union, *The Story of the ETU,* ETU, 1952.
Electrical, Electronic, Telecommunication and Plumbing Union.

Emery, F.E. and Thorsrud, Einar, *Form and Content in Industrial Democracy,* Tavistock, 1974.
Worker Directors.

Engineering and Allied Employers' National Federation, *Thirty Years of Industrial Conciliation,* Engineering and Allied Employers' National Federation, December 1927.
Mackenzie Report.

Engineer Surveyors' Assocation, *ESA Jubilee 1914-1964,* ESA Manchester, 1964.
Engineer Surveyors' Association.

Erdmann, Ernst-Gerhard, *The Myth of Co-determination,* Bundesvereinigung der Deutschen Arbeitgeberverbände, Köln 1970.
Co-determination.

Esher, Lord, *Journals and Letters,* (ed.) M. V. Brett, 1934-1938, vol. 4.
Garton Memorandum.

Etzioni, A., *Modern Organisations,* Prentice-Hall, 1964.
Human Relations.

Etzioni, A. (ed.), *A Sociological Reader on Complex Organisations,* 2nd ed., Holt, 1969.
Job Satisfaction.

European Productivity Agency, *Glossary of Work Study Terms,* European Productivity Agency.
Alternate Standard, Geared Incentive Scheme, High Task Rating Method, Low Task Rating Method.

Evans, E.W. (ed.), *Industrial Conflict in Britain,* Cass, 1977.
Strikes.

Evans, Wyn, *Miners of South Wales,* University of Wales Press, 1961.
Mineworkers, National Union of.

Evans, J.M., *Immigration Law,* Sweet and Maxwell, 1976.
Work Permit.

Fabian Society, *Management by Consent,* A Report by a research group appointed jointly by ASSET and the Fabian Society, Fabian Research Series No. 125, 1948.
Management by Consent.

Farman, Christopher, *The General Strike, May 1926.* Panther, 1974.
General Strike.

Faubert, Carole, *Personnel Management, A Bibliography,* Institute of Personnel Management, 1968.
Bibliographies and Sources on Industrial Relations.

Federated Employers' Press, *Building by Direct Labour,* Federated Employers' Press, 1960.
Direct Labour.

Fels, Allan, *The British Prices and Incomes Board,* Department of Applied Economics Occasional Paper 29, CUP, 1972.
National Board for Prices and Incomes, National Incomes Commission.

Fiedler, F., *A Theory of Leadership Effectiveness,* McGraw-Hill, 1967.
Job Satisfaction.

Fife, Ian and Machin, E.A., *Redgrave's Health and Safety in Factories,* Butterworths, 1976.
Checkweigher, Children and Young Persons, Deductions, Double Day Shift, Employment of Women, Extended Hours, Factories Act 1961, Health and Safety at Work Act 1974, Payment of Wages Act 1960, Shop Clubs Act 1902, Tommy Shop, Truck Acts, Young Persons and Children Act 1920.

Fire Brigades Union, *Fifty Years of Service,* 1918-1968.
Fire Brigades Union.

Fisher, Alan and Dix, Bernard, *Low Pay and How to End it,* Pitman, 1974.
Low Pay Unit.

Flanders, Allan, *A Policy for Wages,* Fabian Tract 281, July 1950.
Wage Policy.

Flanders, Allan, *Industrial Relations, the Nature of the Subject,* Ruskin College, January 1960.
Industrial Relations.

Flanders, Allan, *The Fawley Productivity Agreements,* Faber & Faber, 1964.
Blue-book, Upgrading, Productivity Bargaining, Work Groups.

Flanders, Allan, *Industrial Relations - What is Wrong with the System?,* Faber & Faber, 1965.
Industrial Relations, Substantive Terms, Job Regulation.

Flanders, Allan, *Collective Bargaining: Prescription for Change,* Faber & Faber, 1967.
Custom and Practice, Procedural Terms, Voluntarism.

Flanders, Allan, *Trade Unions,* 7th ed., Hutchinson, 1968.
Trade Union, Trades Councils.

Flanders, Allan, (ed.), *Collective Bargaining,* Penguin Modern Management Readings, 1969.
Collective Bargaining.

Flanders, Allan, *Management and Unions,* Faber & Faber, 1975.
Collective Bargaining, Custom and Practice, Individual Bargaining, Mutual Insurance, Trade Union, Voluntarism.

Flanders, Allan, Pomeranz, Ruth and Woodward, Joan, *Experiment in Industrial Democracy, A Study of the John Lewis Partnership,* Faber & Faber, 1968.
John Lewis Partnership.

Fletcher, J. (ed.), *The Uses of Economics Literature,* Butterworths, 1971.
Bibliographies and Sources on Industrial Relations, British Journal of Industrial Relations, Industrial and Labor Relations Review, Industrial Relations, Industrial Relations Journal, Industrial Relations Research Bulletin, Management Studies, Journal of, Manchester School of Economic and Social Studies, Oxford Economic Papers, Oxford University Institute of Economics and Statistics Bulletin, Personnel Management, Personnel Review, Scottish Journal of Political Economy.

Florence, P.S., *Labour,* Hutchinson University Library, 1950.
Piecework.

Fogarty, M.P., *The Just Wage,* Greenwood Press, 1976.
Just Wage.

Follett, Mary Parker, *Dynamic Administration,* ed. H. C. Metcalf and L. Urwick, Pitman, 1973.
Constructive Conflict, Joint Consultation.

Fowler, W.H. *A Dictionary of Modern English Usage,* 2nd ed., revised by Sir Ernest Gowers, OUP, 1965.
Federation.

Fox, Alan, *History of the National Union of Boot and Shoe Operatives,* Blackwell, 1958.
Boot and Shoe Operatives, National Union of, Greener, Guarantee Fund, National Minority Movement, Statements.

Fox, Alan, *The Milton Plan: An Exercise in Manpower Planning and Transfer of Production,* Institute of Personnel Management, 1965.
Milton Plan.

Fox, Alan, *The Time-Span of Discretion Theory: An Appraisal,* Institute of Personnel Management, 1966.

Time-span

Fox, Alan, *Industrial Sociology and Industrial Relations,* Royal Commission on Trade Unions and Employers' Associations, Research Papers 3, HMSO, 1966.

Donovan Commission, Plural Society.

Fox, Alan, *A Sociology of Work in Industry,* Collier-Macmillan, 1971.

Industrial Conflict, Job Satisfaction.

Fox, A., *Beyond Contract: Work, Power and Trust Relations,* Faber & Faber, 1974.

Trust Relations.

Frank, H., *Kybernetik und Philosophie,* Dunker and Humbolt, 1966.

Cybernetics.

Freedland, Mark, *Attachment of Earnings,* Jordan and Sons, 1971.

Attachment of Earnings Order.

Free Journeymen Printers, *The Case and Proposal of the Free Journeymen Printers in and about London,* 1666.

Foreigners.

Freedland, M., *The Contract of Employment,* OUP, 1976.

Contracts of Employment Act 1972.

French, Wendell L. and Bell, Cecil H., *Organisation Development,* Prentice Hall, 1973.

Action Research, Organisation Development.

Friedrichs, J. and Lüdtke, H., *Participant Observation; Theory and Practice,* Saxon House, 1975.

Participant Observation.

Frost, G.F., Wakeley, J.H. and Ruh, R.A., *The Scanlon Plan for Organisational Development,* Michigan State UP, 1974.

Scanlon Plan.

Frow, R. and E. and Katanka, M., *The History of British Trade Unionism: A Select Bibliography,* Historical Association, London, 1969.

Bibliographies and Sources on Industrial Relations.

Fyrth, H.J. and Collins, Henry, *The Foundry Workers: A Trade Union History,* AUFW, 1959.

Foundry Workers, Amalgamated Union of, Hagman System.

Galenson, Walter, *Rival Unionism in the US,* American Council on Public Affairs, 1940.

Dual Unionism, Rival Unionism.

Galenson, Walter, *Comparative Labour Movements,* Prentice-Hall, 1952.

Mediation.

Galton, F.W., *Select Documents Illuminating the History of Trade Unionism; The Tailoring Trade, 1896*

Tailors and Garment Workers, National Union of.

Garside, W.R., *Durham Miners, 1919-1960,* Allen and Unwin, 1972.

Mineworkers, National Union of.

Gaudet, Frederick J., *Solving the Problems of Employees Absence,* American Management Association Research Study 57, 1963.

Absence.

Gegan, G.R., *Shop Stewards*, Schriftenreibe die Otto Brenner Stiftung, No. 6, Frankfurt, 1976.
Vertrauensmann.

Geldart, W.M., *The Osborne Judgement and After*, Manchester Guardian Ltd, 1911.
Osborne v. Amalgamated Society of Railway Servants.

Gennard, J., *Financing Strikers*, Macmillan, 1978.
State Subsidy Theory of Strikes.

Gennard, J., *Multinationals: Industrial Relations and the Trade Union Response*, Occasional Papers in Industrial Relations 1, IPM, 1976.
Multinational Corporation.

George, W.L., *Value Analysis*, McGraw-Hill, 1967.
Value Analysis.

Gibson, J.F.A., *Value Analysis*, Pergamon, 1968.
Value Analysis.

Giles, W.J. and Robinson, D., *Human Asset Accounting*, IPM, 1972.
Human Resource Accounting.

Gillespie, Sarah C., *A Hundred Years of Progress: The Record of the Scottish Typographical Association*, Robert Maclehose and Co., Glasgow, 1953.
Scottish Typographical Association.

Gilpin, Alan, *Dictionary of Economic Terms*, Butterworths, 4th ed., 1977.
Dead Horse.

Girod, R., *Études Sociologiques sur les Couches Salariées; Ouvriers et Employés*, Marcel Rivière, Paris, 1961.
White Collar Worker.

Gladden, E.N., *Civil Service Staff Relationships*, William Hodge, 1943.
Whitleyism.

Glass, D.V. (ed.), *Introduction to Malthus*, Watts and Co., 1953.
Subsistence Theory of Wages.

Goldberg, A.J., *AFL-CIO; Labor United*, McGraw-Hill, 1956.
American Federation of Labor-Congress of Industrial Organisations.

Golden, Clinton S. and Ruttenberg, Harold J., *The Dynamics of Industrial Democracy*, New York, Harper and Bros, 1942.
Paternalism.

Goldstein, J., *The Government of British Trade Unions*, Allen and Unwin, 1952.
Trade Union.

Goldthorpe, J.H. and Hope, K., *The Social Grading of Occupations*, OUP, 1974.
Occupation.

Goldthorpe, J.H., Lockwood, D., Bechofer, F. and Platt, J. *The Affluent Worker: Industrial Attitudes and Behaviour*, CUP, 1968.
Embourgeoisement.

Gompers, Samuel, *Seventy Years of Life and Labor; An Autobiography*, Merlin/Kelley, 1970.
Voluntarism.

Goodman, J.F.B. and Whittingham, T.G., *Shop Stewards in British Industry*, McGraw-Hill, 1969.
Convener or Convenor, Fixed-term Agreements, Shop Steward, Work Groups.

Goodrich, Carter L., *The Frontier of Control*, Harcourt, Brace and Howe, 1920. Dent / Pluto Press, 1975.
Managerial Prerogatives, Trade Union Functions, Workers' Participation.

Gottschalk, A.W. *et al.*, *British Industrial Relations, An Annotated Bibliography*, University of Nottingham, Department of Adult Education, 1969.
Bibliographies and Sources on Industrial Relations.

Gottschalk, A.W., Towers, B. and Whittingham, T.G. (eds), *The New Bargainers*, Department of Adult Education, University of Nottingham, 1970.
Whipsawing.

Gouldner, A.W., *Wildcat Strike*, Antioch Press and Harper and Row, 1965.
Indulgency Pattern, Wildcat Strike.

Gouldner, A.W., *Patterns of Industrial Bureaucracy*, The Free Press: Collier-Macmillan, 1964.
Indulgency Pattern.

Goyder, C., *Sabbaticals for All*, Fabian Society, 1977.
Sabbatical Leave.

Gracie, J.J., *A Fair Day's Pay*, Management Publications Trust, 1949.
Fair Day's Work.

Gray, J.L., *The Glacier Project, Concepts and Critiques*, Heinemann, 1976.
Glacier Project.

Gregory, D.L. and Smyth, R.L., *The Worker and the Pottery Industry*, Department of Economics, University of Keele, 1971.
Ceramics and Allied Trades Union.

Griffin, A.R., *The Miners of Nottinghamshire; a History of the Nottinghamshire Miners' Association*, Vol. 1, 1881-1914, Nottingham Printers Ltd, 1957, Vol. 2, 1914-1944, Allen and Unwin, 1962.
Mineworkers, National Union of.

Gross, B.M., *The Managing of Organisations*, Collier-Macmillan, 1964, 2 vols.
Scientific Management.

Groves, Reg., *Sharpen the Sickle*, The Porcupine Press, 1949.
Agricultural and Allied Workers, National Union of.

Grunfeld, Cyril, *Modern Trade Union Law*, Sweet and Maxwell, 1970.
Amalgamation, Blacklisting, Check-off, Injunction, Labour Law, Political Fund, Transfer of Engagements.

Grunfeld, Cyril, *The Law of Redundancy*, Sweet and Maxwell, 1971.
Constructive Dismissals, Redundancy Payments Act 1965, Seniority.

Guillebaud, C.W., *The Works Council: A German Experiment in Democracy*, CUP, 1922.
Betriebsräte.

Guillebaud, C.W., *The Wages Council System of Great Britain*, Nisbet, 1962.
Independent Members, Wages Councils.

Günter, Hans (ed.), *Transcontinental Industrial Relations*, Macmillan, 1971.
Multi-national Corporation.

Gyllenhammar, P., *People at Work*, Addison-Wesley, 1977.
Work-structuring.

Hale, A.R. and Hale, M., *A Review of the Industrial Accident Research Literature*, Committee on Safety and Health at Work, Research Paper, HMSO, 1972.
Accident, Robens Report.

Hamlin, A., Thurley, K. and Voon, D., *Essential Facts on the British Foreman*, Institute of Industrial Supervisors, 1965.
Foreman.

Hand, Michael, *Staff Status for Manual Workers*, Productivity Progress, Pergamon Press, 1968.
Mensualisation.

Hannington, Wal, *The Rights of Engineers*, Gollancz, 1944.
Joint Consultation.

Hannington, Wal, *Never on Our Knees*, Lawrence and Wishart, 1967.
Donation, National Minority Movement, National Unemployed Workers' Movement.

Hansen, B.L., *Work Sampling for Modern Management*, Prentice-Hall, 1960.
Activity Sampling.

Hare, A.E.C., *Industrial Relations in New Zealand*, London 1946.
Co-operative Contracting.

Harris, A.I. and Clausen, R., *Labour Mobility in Britain, 1953-1963*, SS333, HMSO, March 1966.
Geographical Mobility, Labour Mobility.

Harrison, F.H., 'Collective Bargaining and American Capitalism'; in Kornhauser, Arthur, Dubin, Robert and Ross, Arthur M. (eds), *Industrial Conflict*, McGraw-Hill, 1954.
Industrial Conflict.

Harrison, F.H., *Goals and Strategy in Collective Bargaining*, Harper, 1951.
Collective Bargaining.

Harrison, J.F.C., *Learning and Living, 1790-1960*, Routledge and Kegan Paul, 1961.
National Council of Labour Colleges.

Harrison, Martin, *Trade Unions and the Labour Party*, Allen and Unwin, 1960.
Block Vote, Hastings Agreement, Political Fund, Trade Union.

Harvey, Sir Paul, *Oxford Companion to English Literature*, 4th ed., OUP, 1967.
Wayzgoose.

Havelock Wilson, J., *My Stormy Passage Through Life*, Vol. I (Vol. II not published), Co-operative Press, 1925.
Seamen, National Union of.

Hayward, Richard, *Whitley Councils in the United Kingdom Civil Service*, Civil Service National Whitley Council, (Staff Side), 1963.
Whitleyism.

Heath, C.G., *A Guide to the Industrial Relations Act 1971*, Sweet and Maxwell, 1971.
Registered Trade Union.

Heginbotham, H., *Youth Employment Service,* Methuen, 1951.
Youth Employment Service.

Hepple, B.A., *Race, Jobs and the Law in Britain,* Harmonsworth, 2nd ed. 1970.
Discrimination, Implied Terms.

Hepple, B.A. and O'Higgins, Paul, *Encyclopaedia of Labour Relations Law,* Sweet and Maxwell, 1972.
Industrial Relations Act 1971.

Hepple, B.A. and O'Higgins P., *Employment Law,* Sweet and Maxwell, 2nd ed., 1976.
Discrimination.

Herron, F., *Labour Market in Crisis; Redundancy at Upper Clyde Shipbuilders,* Macmillan, 1976.
Redundancy, Upper Clyde Shipbuilders.

Herzberg, Frederick, *Work and the Nature of Man,* Crosby, Lockwood, Staples, 1974.
Hygiene Factors, Incentive Payment System, Job Enrichment, Work Structuring.

Herzberg, F., Mausner, B. and Snyderman, B., *The Motivation to Work,* John Wiley and Sons, 1968.
Hygiene Factors.

Hickling, M.A., *Citrine's Trade Union Law,* Stevens, 1967.
All-in Contribution, Amalgamation, Labour Law, Trade Disputes Act 1906, Trade Union, Trade Union Act 1871, Trade Union Act (Amendment) Act 1876, Trade Union Act 1913.

Hicks, J.R., *The Theory of Wages,* Macmillan, 1963.
Labour Market, Marginal Productivity Theory of Wages.

Higenbottam, S., *Our Society's History,* ASW, 1939.
Construction, Allied Trades and Technicians, Union of.

Hill, J.M., *Special Leave Allowances,* IPM, Information Report 15, 1974.
Sabbatical Leave.

Hill, S., *The Dockers,* Heinemann, 1976.
Dock Labour Scheme.

Hilton, G.W., *The Truck System,* Heffer, 1961, Greenwood Press, 1976.
Truck Acts.

Hilton, John (ed.), *Are Trade Unions Obstructive?* Gollancz, 1935.
Demarcation.

Hilton, W.S., *Foes to Tyranny,* AUBTW, 1963.
Building Trade Workers of Great Britain and Ireland, Amalgamated Union of.

Hilton, W.S., *Industrial Relations in Construction,* Pergamon Press, 1968.
Building Industry, National Joint Council for the; Civil Engineering Construction Board for Great Britain; Construction Unions, National Federation of.

Hindell, Keith, *Trade Union Membership,* Political and Economic Planning, 1962.
Union Density.

Hineman, H. Jr, Fox, H. and Goder, D., *Patterns of Labor Mobility,* Minneapolis, 1948.
Labour Market.

Hinton, J., *The First Shop Stewards' Movement,* George Allen and Unwin, 1973.
Craft Control, Shop Stewards' Movement.

Hobson, J.A., *The Economics of Unemployment,* Macmillan, 1931.
Cyclical Unemployment.

Hoffman, P.C., *They Also Serve: The Story of the Shop Workers,* Porcupine Press, 1949.
Living-in; Shop, Distributive and Allied Workers, Union of.

Hopson, B. and Hayes, J., *The Theory and Practice of Vocational Guidance,* Pergamon Press, 1968.
Vocational Guidance.

Hopwood, E., *A History of the Lancashire Cotton Industry and the Amalgamated Weavers' Association,* AWA 1969.
Driving, Half-time System, Protection Societies, Slate System, Strap, Time Cribbing Uniform List, Weavers' Association, Amalgamated.

Howe, Ellic (ed.), *The London Compositor, 1875-1900,* OUP, 1947.
Graphical Association, National.

Howe, Ellic, *The British Federation of Master Printers, 1900-1950,* BFMP, 1950.
British Printing Industries' Federation.

Howe, Ellic and Waite, Harold E., *The London Society of Compositors,* Cassell and Co., 1948.
Chapel, Grass-hands, Graphical Association, National.

Howells, R. and Barnet, B., *The Health and Safety at Work Act: A Guide for Managers,* IPM, 1975.
Health and Safety at Work Act 1974.

Hoxie, R.F. *Scientific Management and Labor,* Merlin Kelley, 1970.
Scientific Management.

Hudson, Kenneth, *Working to Rule; Railway Workshop Rules, A Study of Industrial Discipline,* Adams and Dart, 1970.
Footings, Works Rules, Work to Rule.

Hughes, Fred, *By Hand and Brain, The Story of the Clerical and Administrative Workers' Union,* Lawrence and Wishart, 1953.
Professional, Executive, Clerical and Computer Staff, Association of.

Hughes, John, *Trade Union Structure and Government,* Royal Commission on Trade Unions and Employers' Associations, Research Papers 5 (Parts 1 and 2), 1967 and 1968.
Bridlington Agreement, Craft Union, Donovan Commission, Federation, Industrial Union, Occupational Union, Open Union, Sectoral Union, Trade Union, Typology of Trade Unions.

Humble, John W. (ed.), *Management by Objectives in Action,* McGraw-Hill, 1970.
Management by Objectives.

Humphreys, B.V., *Clerical Unions in the Civil Service;* Blackwell and Mott, 1958.
Civil and Public Services Association, Civil Service Alliance, Priestley Formula, Tomlin Formula, Whitleyism.

Hunt, N.C., *Methods of Wage Payment in British Industry,* Pitman, 1951.
Bedeaux System, Contract Piecework, Differential Piece-rate Plan, Emerson Wage Payment Plan, Group Incentive Schemes, Grouppiece Work, Halsey Premium Bonus System, Point Premium System, Premium Bonus Plan (System), Priestman Plan, Rowan System.

Hunter, L.C., Reid, G. L. and Boddy, D., *Labour Problems of Technological Change,* Allen and Unwin, 1970.
Industrial Relations, Promotion Ladder, Seniority, Underemployment.

378

Hutchins, B.L., *Home Work and Sweating: the Causes and the Remedies,* 1907.
Sweating.

Hutchins, B.L. and Harrison, A., *A History of Factory Legislation,* F. Cass 1966.
Factories Act 1961.

Hutchinson, John, *The Constitution and Government of the AFL-CIO,* University of California, Berkeley, 1959.
American Federation of Labor-Congress of Industrial Organisations.

Hutt, Allen, *Post-War History of the British Working Class,* EP Publishing 1974.
National Minority Movement.

Hyman, R., *Strikes,* Fontana/Collins, 1972.
Strike.

Hyman, R., *Industrial Relations: A Marxist Interpretation,* Macmillan, 1975.
Industrial Relations.

Hyman, R. and Brough, I., *Social Values and Industrial Relations,* Blackwell, 1975.
Fair Day's Work, Industrial Relations.

Ince, Sir Godfrey, *The Ministry of Labour and National Service,* Allen and Unwin, 1960.
Employment, Department of.

Industrial Society, *Sick Pay,* 1967.
Sick Pay Schemes.

The Industrial Society, *Successful Suggestion Schemes,* Industrial Society 1971.
Suggestion Scheme.

Industrial Welfare Society, *Works Councils and Committees,* (various editions, 1941-52).
Works Councils.

Ingham, G.K., *Size of Industrial Organisation and Worker Behaviour,* CUP, 1970.
Size-effect.

Inman, P., *Labour in the Munitions Industries,* HMSO and Longmans, 1957.
Relaxation Agreements.

Inns of Court Conservative and Unionist Society. *A Giant's Strength,* Christopher Johnson, 1958.
Industrial Relations Act 1971.

Institute of Personnel Management, *Company Day Nurseries,* IPM Information Note, April 1970.
Day Nurseries.

Institute of Personnel Management, *Sit-ins and Work-ins,* IPM, 1976.
Sit-in Strike.

Institute of Personnel Management, *Sick Pay Schemes,* Information Report 7, March 1971.
Sick Pay Schemes.

Institute of Personnel Management, *Flexible Working Hours,* Information Report 12, October 1972.
Flexible Working Hours.

Institution of Production Engineers and Institute of Cost and Works Accountants, *Measurement of Productivity,* 1949.
Standard Performance.

International Confederation of Free Trade Unions, *Report of the Ninth World Congress,* July 1969.
International Confederation of Free Trade Unions.

International Confederation of Free Trade Unions, *Trade Union Handbook.*
Open Shop.

International Encyclopaedia of the Social Sciences, Vol. 11; Macmillan and Free Press, 1968.
Norm.

International Labour Office, *Freedom of Association, A Workers' Educational Manual,* ILO, Geneva, 1972.
Freedom of Association.

International Labour Office, *Job Evaluation* 1969.
Job Evaluation.

International Labour Office, *Examination of Grievances and Communications within the Undertaking,* ILO, Geneva, 1965.
Communications, Formalisation, Grievance.

International Labour Office, *The ILO in the Service of Social Progress,* ILO, 1969.
Philadelphia, Declaration of.

International Labour Office, *Introduction to Work Study,* ILO, 1969 ed.
Activity Sampling, Allowances, Analytical Estimating, Basic Time, Method Study, Predetermined Motion Time Systems, Rating, Rating Scale, Unrestricted Work, Work Measurement, Work Study.

International Labour Office, *Encyclopaedia of Occupational Health and Safety,* ILO, Geneva, 2 Vols, 1972.
Accident.

Irish Transport and General Workers' Union, *Fifty Years of Liberty Hall 1909-1959,* 1959.
Irish Transport and General Workers' Union.

Jackson, D., *Unfair Dismissals - Why and How the Law Works,* CUP, 1975.
Unfair Dismissal.

Jackson, D., Turner, H.A. and Wilkinson, F., *Do Trade Unions Cause Inflation?,* CUP, 1975, 2nd ed.
Wage Explosion.

Jacobs, Paul, *Dead Horse and the Featherbird; the Specter of Useless Work,* University of California, Berkeley, Reprint 190, 1962.
Dead Horse, Featherbedding.

Jaques Elliott, *The Changing Culture of a Factory,* Routledge and Kegan Paul, 1951.
Glacier Project, Induction Crisis.

Jaques, Elliott, *Time Span Handbook,* Heinemann, 1964.
Time-span.

Jaques, Elliott, *Equitable Payment,* Heinemann, 1970 2nd ed.
Felt-fair Pay, Glacier Project, Time-span.

Jaques, Elliott, *Measurement of Responsibility,* Heinemann Education, 1972.
Glacier Project, Time-span.

Jaques, Elliott, *Bureaucracy,* Heinemann, 1976.
Bureaucracy.

Jefferys, J.B., *The Story of the Engineers,* EP Publishing 1971.
Amalgamated Engineering Union, Machine Question.

Jefferys, M., *Mobility in the Labour Market, Employment Changes in Battersea and Dagenham,* Routledge and Kegan Paul, 1954.
Labour Mobility.

Jenkins, C.L. and Alexander, K.J.W., *Fairfields: A Study in Industrial Change,* Allen Lane, The Penguin Press, 1970.
Fairfields Experiment.

Jenkins, Peter, *The Battle of Downing Street,* Charles Knight, 1970.
Donovan Commission.

Jenks, C. Wilfred, *The International Protection of Trade Union Freedom,* Stevens, 1957.
Freedom of Association, International Labour Organisation.

Jenks, C. Wilfred, *Human Rights and International Labour Standards,* Stevens, 1960.
Freedom of Association, International Labour Organisation.

Jenks, C. Wilfred, *Social Justice in the Law of the Nations,* OUP, 1970.
Freedom of Association.

Johnson, Frank (ed.), *Alienation; Concept, Term and Meanings,* Seminar Press, 1973.
Alienation.

Johnston, T.L. *Collective Bargaining in Sweden,* Allen and Unwin, 1962.
Interest Disputes, Rights Disputes.

Johnston, T.L., 'Public Sector and White Collar Bargaining'; in Robertson, D.J. and Hunter, L.C. (eds), *Labour Market Issues in the 1970s,* Oliver and Boyd, 1970.
Grade Creep.

Jones, J.H., *The Tinplate Industry,* P.S. King and Son, 1914.
Trade Protection Society.

Jones, Ken and Golding, John, *Productivity Bargaining,* Fabian Research Series, 257, November 1966.
Conventional Bargaining.

Jones, R.M., *Absenteeism in Britain,* Manpower Papers No. 4, HMSO, 1971.
Absence.

Jongeward, D., *Everybody Wins; Transactional Analysis applied to Organisations,* Addison-Wesley, 1974.
Transactional Analysis.

Kahn, Hilda R., *Repercussions of Redundancy,* Allen and Unwin, 1965.
Redundancy.

Kahn, Hilda R., *Salaries in the Public Services in England and Wales,* Allen and Unwin, 1962.
Incremental Scale.

Kahn-Freund, O. (ed.), *Labour Relations and the Law,* Stevens 1965.
Collective Agreement, Right to Strike.

Kaplan, A.D.H., *The Guarantee of Annual Wages,* Brookings Institution, 1947.
Constant Wage Plan, Guaranteed Annual Wage.

Kaun, D.E. *Economics of The Minimum Wage: the Effects of the Fair Labour Standards Act, 1945-1960,* PhD Thesis, Stanford University, 1963.
National Minimum Wage.

Kaye, Barrington, *The Development of the Architectural Profession in Britain*, Allen and Unwin, 1960.
Profession.

Keenan, D.J. and Crabtree, L., *Essentials of Industrial Law*, Pitman, 1972.
Labour Law, Contract of Service.

Kelly, J., *Is Scientific Management Possible?* Faber & Faber, 1968.
Glacier Project.

Kerr, Clark, *Labour and Management in Industrial Society*, Doubleday-Anchor, New York, 1964.
Industrial Conflict, Trade Union.

Kerr, Clark, *Migration to the Seattle Labor Market Area 1940-42*, University of Washington, 1942.
Labour Market.

Kerr, Clark and Siegel, Abraham, 'The Inter-Industry Propensity to Strike'; Chapter 13 in Kornhauser, Arthur, Dubin, Robert, and Ross, Arthur M. (eds), *Industrial Conflict*, McGraw-Hill, 1954.
Industrial Conflict, Propensity to Strike.

Keynes, J.M., *The General Theory of Employment, Interest and Money*, Macmillan, 1974.
Cyclical Unemployment.

Keyte, P.S., *The Customs and Excise Federation 1917-1967*, Customs and Excise Federation, 1967.
Customs and Excise Federation.

Kidd, A.T., *History of the Tin-plate Workers and Sheet Metal Workers and Braziers Societies*, National Union of Sheet Metal Workers and Braziers, 1949.
Rat, Sheet Metal Workers, Coppersmiths, Heating and Domestic Engineers, National Union of.

Kiddier, William, *The Old Trade Unions - from unprinted records of the Brushmakers*, London, 1930.
Brushmakers and General Workers, National Society of.

Killingsworth, C., 'Automation, Jobs and Manpower'; in *Exploring the Dimensions of the Management Revolution*, Government Printing Office, Washington, 1964.
Automation.

Kingsley, Roger and Mary, *An Industrial Day Nursery: The Personnel Manager's Guide*, Institute of Personnel Management, 1969.
Day Nurseries.

Klein, L., *New Forms of Work Organisation*, CUP, 1976.
Work-structuring.

Kley, Gisbert, *Co-determination in Coal and Steel, Replies to the DGB's Demands*, Bundesvereinigung der Deutschen Arbeitgeberverbande, Koln, and CDU-Wirtschaftsrat-Series 'Zum Dialog', 1970.
Co-determination.

Knowles, K.G.J.C., *Strikes*, Blackwell, 1952.
Blacking, Blacklisting, Bumper Strike, Company Union, Fair List, General Strike, Indemnity Fund, Irritation Strike, Lock-out, Political Strike, Red Friday, Sit-down Strike, Stay-in Strike, Strike, Strike Ballot, Strike-breaking, Strike-in-detail, Sympathetic Strikes, Token Strike.

382

Kolvenbach, W., *Workers' Participation in Europe*, Kluwer/Metzner, 1977.
Co-determination.

Kornhauser, Arthur, Dubin, Robert and Ross, Arthur M. (eds), *Industrial Conflict*, McGraw-Hill, 1954.
Industrial Conflict, Propensity to Strike.

Kuhn, James W., *Bargaining in Grievance Settlement*, Columbia University Press, 1961.
Fractional Bargaining, Work Groups.

The Labour Party, *Industrial Democracy, A Working Party Report*, June 1967.
Industrial Democracy, Management By Consent, Worker Directors.

Landsberger, H.A., *Hawthorne Revisited*, New York State School of Industrial Relations, Cornell University Press, 1958.
Hawthorne Experiment, Human Relations.

Lane, Tony and Roberts, Kenneth, *Strike at Pilkingtons*, Collins/Fontana, 1971.
Pilkington Strike, Wildcat Strike.

Langenfelt, Gösta, *The Historic Origin of the Eight Hours Day*, Stockholm, 1954.
Eight Hours Day Movement.

Lawrence, P.R. and Lorsch, J.W., *Organisation and Environment*, Addison-Wesley, 1969.
Organisation Development.

Lazarus, R.S., 'Environmental Planning in Stress and Adaptation'; in Levi, L. (ed.), *Society, Stress and Disease*, OUP, 1971.
Occupational Stress.

Leavitt, H., *Managerial Psychology*, University of Chicago Press, 1958.
Organisational Behaviour.

Lederer, Emil, *Die Privatangestellten in der modernen Wirtschaftsentwicklung*, JCB Mohr/P. Siebeck, Tübingen, 1912.
White Collar Worker.

Lees, D. and Shaw, S. (eds), *Impairment, Disability and Handicap*, Heinemann, 1974.
Disabled Persons.

Leiserson, W.M., *Constitutional Government in American Industries*, American Economic Review, Supplement, 1922.
Collective Bargaining.

Leiserson, W.M., 'Wage Decisions and Wage Structure in the United States'; in Hugh-Jones, E.M., *Wage Structure in Theory and Practice*, North-Holland Publishing Co., 1966.
Incentive Payment System.

Leisner, T. and King, M. (eds), *Indexing for Inflation*, Heinemann, 1975.
Cost-of-living Sliding Scale.

Lerner, S.W., *Breakaway Unions and the Small Trade Union*, Allen and Unwin, 1961.
Breakaway Unions, Bridlington Agreement, Chemical Workers' Union, Dual Unionism, Inter-union Disputes, Jurisdictional Dispute, Poaching, Post Office Engineering Union, Wrong Unions.

Lerner, S.W., Cable J.R. and Gupta, S. (eds), *Workshop Wage Determination*, Pergamon Press, 1969.
Bargaining Theory of Wages, Ex Gratia Payment, Lieu Rate, Merit Rate, Service Increments, Wage Drift.

Lesieur, Frederick G. (ed.), *The Scanlon Plan: A Frontier in Labor-Management Co-operation*, The Massachusetts Institute of Technology Press, 1969.
Scanlon Plan.

Lester, Richard A., *Manpower Planning in a Free Society*, Princeton University Press, 1966.
Employment Service.

Levinson, Charles, *Capital, Inflation and the Multi-Nationals*, Allen and Unwin, 1971.
Multi-national Corporation.

Levinson, Charles, *International Trade Unionism*, Allen and Unwin, 1972.
Multi-national Corporation, International Labour Movement.

Lewis, R. and Maude, A., *Professional People*, Phoenix House Ltd, 1952.
Profession.

Lewis, Spedan, *Partnership for All*, Kerr-Cross Publishing, 1948.
John Lewis Partnership.

Lewis, Spedan, *Fairer Shares*, Staples Press, 1954.
John Lewis Partnership.

Liepmann, Kate, *Apprenticeship*, Routledge and Kegan Paul, 1960.
Apprenticeship, Demarcation, Vertical Demarcation.

Likert, Rensis, *The Human Organisation*, McGraw-Hill, 1971.
Human Relations.

Likert, Rensis, *New Patterns of Management*, McGraw-Hill, 1961.
Organisational Behaviour.

Linder, W., *The Great Flint Strike Against GM*, Solidarity Pamphlet No. 11, 1969.
Sit-down Strike.

Livernash, E. Robert, 'Wages and Benefits'; in *A Review of Industrial Relations Research*, Volume 1, Industrial Relations Research Association, 1970.
Wage Theories.

Livy, B., *Job Evaluation: A Critical Review*, Allen and Unwin, 1975.
Job Evaluation.

Lockwood, David, *The Blackcoated Worker*, Allen and Unwin, 1966.
Blackcoated Worker, Bureaucracy, White Collar Union.

Lockyer, K.G., *An Introduction to Critical Path Analysis*, Pitman, 1969, 3rd ed.
Network Analysis.

London School of Economics and Political Science, *A London Bibliography of the Social Sciences*, London School of Economics and Political Science, (1931—).
Bibliographies and Sources on Industrial Relations.

Lorwin, L.L., *The American Federation of Labor*, Brookings Institution, Washington, 1933.
American Federation of Labor.

Lovell, John, *Stevedores and Dockers, A Study of Trade Unionism in the Port of London 1870-1914*, Macmillan, 1969.
Blue Union.

Lovell, J., *British Trade Unions 1875-1933*, Macmillan, 1977.
Trade Union.

384

Lovell, John and Roberts, B.C. *A Short History of the TUC,* Macmillan, 1968.
Trades Union Congress.

Lucas, Harry, *Pensions and Industrial Relations,* Pergamon, 1977.
Occupational Pension Schemes.

Lupton, Tom, *Money for Effort,* HMSO, 1961.
Incentive Payment System.

Lupton, Tom, *On the Shop Floor,* Pergamon, 1963.
Participant Observation.

Lupton, Tom, *Industrial Behaviour and Personnel Management,* Institute of Personnel Management, 1964.
Industrial Relations.

Lupton, Tom (ed.), *Payment Systems,* Penguin Modern Management Readings, 1972.
Stinkers.

Lydall, Harold, *The Structure of Earnings,* OUP, 1968.
Differentials, Goldbricking, Gravy Jobs, Low Pay, Quota Restriction, Wage Structure.

Lyon, Hugh, *The History of the Scottish Horse and Motormen's Association, 1898-1919,* Civic Press Ltd, Glasgow, 1919.
Commercial Motormen's Union, Scottish.

Macamhaigh, Donall, *An Irish Navvy,* Routledge and Kegan Paul, 1976.
Navvy.

Macbeath, Innis., *The Times Guide to the Industrial Relations Act, 1971.*
Cowboy, High Flier.

McBeath, G. and Rands, D.N. *Salary Administration,* Business Books Ltd, 3rd ed. 1976.
Employee Appraisal, Job Analysis, Maturity Curves, Salary Administration.

McCarthy, C., *The Decade of Upheaval, Irish & Trade Unions in the Nineteen Sixties,* Institute of Public Administration,
Irish Congress of Trade Unions.

McCarthy, C., *Trade Unions in Ireland 1894-1960,* Institute of Public Administration,
Irish Congress of Trade Unions.

McCarthy, W.E.J., *The Closed Shop in Britain,* Blackwell, 1964.
Closed Shop, Compulsory Trade Unionism.

McCarthy, W.E.J., *The Role of Shop Stewards in British Industrial Relations,* Royal Commission on Trade Unions and Employers' Associations, Research Papers 1, 1966.
Convener or Convenor, Donovan Commission, Joint Consultation, Shop Steward.

McCarthy, W.E.J., *Compulsory Arbitration in Britain; the Work of the Industrial Disputes Tribunal,* Report of the Royal Commission on Trade Unions and Employers' Associations. Research Papers No. 8, 1968.
Compulsory Arbitration, Donovan Commission, Industrial Disputes Tribunal.

McCarthy, W.E.J. and Ellis, N.D., *Management by Agreement,* Hutchinson, 1973.
Industrial Relations Act 1971.

McConville, J., *The Shipping Industry in the United Kingdom,* International Institute for Labour Studies, 1977.
Established Service Scheme, Logging, National Maritime Board.

McCormick, E.J. and Tiffin, J., *Industrial Psychology,* Allen and Unwin, 1975, 6th ed.
Job Requirements.

McCullough, K. *Department of Employment and Productivity Gazette*, October 1969.
Supervisor.

Macdonald, I., *The New Immigration Law*, Butterworths, 1972. **Work Permit.**

McDougall, I. (ed.), *An Interim Bibliography of the Scottish Working Class Movement*, Scottish Committee for the Study of Labour History, 1965.
Bibliographies and Sources on Industrial Relations.

McGlyne, *Unfair Dismissal Cases*, Butterworths, 1976. **Unfair Dismissal.**

McGregor, D., *The Human Side of Enterprise*, McGraw-Hill, 1960.
Incentive Payment System, Organisational Behaviour.

McGowan, John F. and Schmidt, Lyle D., *Counseling: Readings in Theory and Practice*, Holt, Rinehart and Winston, 1962. **Counselling.**

Machin, Frank, *The Yorkshire Miners: A History*, Vol. 1, NUM, 1958.
Mineworkers, National Union of.

Mackay, D.I. *et al.*, *Labour Markets under Different Employment Conditions*, Allen and Unwin, 1971.
Anti-pirating Agreements, Labour Market, Labour Mobility, Labour Turnover, Manpower Planning.

Mackenzie, Sir William, (Lord Amulree) *The Industrial Court, Practices and Procedures*, 1923.
Industrial Arbitration Board.

McKersie, Robert B., 'Changing Methods of Wage Payment'; in Dunlop, John T. and Chamberlain, Neil W. (eds), *Frontiers of Collective Bargaining*, Harper and Row, 1967.
Cost-reduction Plans.

McKillop, Norman, *The Lighted Flame: A History of the Associated Society of Locomotive Engineers and Firemen*, Thomas Nelson and Sons, 1950.
Locomotive Engineers and Firemen, Associated Society of.

McLean, A. (ed.), *Occupational Stress*, Charles C. Thomas, Illinois, 1974.
Occupational Stress.

McLeod, Charles, *All Change; Railway Industrial Relations in the Sixties*, Gower Press, 1970.
Conciliation Grades, Guillebaud Report, Local Departmental Committees, Penzance Agreement, Railway Shopmen's National Council, Railway Staff Joint Council, Single Manning, Versatility Grades.

McPherson, W.H. and Myers, F., *The French Labor Courts: Judgment by Peers*, University of Illinois, 1966.
Conseils de Prud'hommes.

Mace, C.A., *Incentives, Some Experimental Studies*, Industrial Health Research Board Report, HMSO 1935.
Differential Piece-rate Plan.

Maher, John R. (ed.), *New Perspectives in Job Enrichment*, Van Nostrand Reinhold, 1971.
Job Enrichment.

Mandell, M.M., *The Selection Process*, American Management Association, 1964.
Job Engineering.

Mann, Tom, *From the Single Tax to Syndicalism,* 1910.
                                                    Syndicalism.

Mann, Tom, *What a Compulsory Eight Hours Working Day means to the Workers,* Dent Pluto Press 1972.
                                       Eight Hours Day Movement.

Mansfield, F.J., *Gentlemen - the Press!, The Official History of the National Union of Journalists,* W. H. Allen and Co., 1943.
                      Blacking, Journalists, National Union of.

Marks, W.R., *Induction - acclimatizing people to work,* Institute of Personnel Management, Practical Handbook No. 3, April 1970.
                                                         Induction.

Marlow, Joyce, *The Tolpuddle Martyrs,* André Deutsch, 1972.
                                               Tolpuddle Martyrs.

Marriott, R., *Incentive Payment Systems,* 3rd (revised) ed. Staples Press, 1968.
Allowances, Bedeaux System, Differential Piece-rate Plan, Emerson Wage Payment Plan, Gain Sharing Plans, Halsey Premium Bonus System, Incentive Payment System, Merit Rating, Piecework, Premium Bonus Plan (System), Payment by Results, Rowan System, Time Piecework.

Marris, R., *The Economics of Capital Utilisation; A Report on Multiple Shift Work,* CUP, 1964.
                                                      Shift Working.

Marsh, A.I., *Managers and Shop Stewards,* Institute of Personnel Management, 1973.
                                                      Shop Steward.

Marsh, A.I., *Industrial Relations in Engineering,* Pergamon Press, 1965.
Carlisle Agreement, Clause (j), Consolidated Time Rate, Constitutional Strike, Coventry Toolroom Strike, Craft Control, Demonstration, Domestic Bargaining, Employer Reference, Engineering Employers' Federation, Engineering Joint Trades Movement, Engineering Package Deal Agreements, Engineering Procedure Agreement, Enticement of Labour, Federated Firm, Indemnity Fund, Joint Consultation, Joint Shop Stewards Works Committees, Loosing Rate, Manchester Piecework Regulations, Minimum Piecework Standard, Minute 741, Mutuality, Non-federated Firm, Piecework Supplement, Provisions for Avoiding Disputes, Railway Shopmen's National Council, Relaxation Agreements, Shipbuilding and Engineering Unions, Confederation of, Shop Stewards and Works Committee Agreements 1917-1919, Status Quo, Wage-for-age Scales, York Memorandum.

Marsh, A.I., *Industrial Relations in Engineering, A Collection of Teaching Documents and Case Studies,* Pergamon Press, 1966.
                         Managerial Prerogatives, Minute 741.

Marsh, A.I., *Disputes Procedures in Britain,* Research Papers 2 (Part 1), Royal Commission on Trade Unions and Employers' Associations, HMSO, 1966.
                   Dispute Procedure, Donovan Commission, Voluntarism.

Marsh, A.I. and Cope, P., *Trade Union Benefits and Finance,* Royal Commission on Trade Unions and Employers' Associations, Research Paper, 1968.
                                        Trade Union Contributions.

Marsh, A.I., Evans, E.O. and Garcia, P., *Workplace Industrial Relations in Engineering,* Engineering Employers' Federation and Kogan Page, November 1971.
Collective Agreement, Combine Committee, Company Bargaining, Convener or Convenor, Facilities for Shop Stewards, Indulgency Pattern, Joint Shop Stewards Works Committees, Multi-establishment Company, Plant Bargaining, Shop Steward, Strike, Workplace Bargaining.

Marsh, A.I. and McCarthy, W.E.J. *Disputes Procedures in Britain,* Royal Commission on Trade Unions and Employers' Associations, Research Papers, 2 (Part 2), 1968.
Chemical Industries Association Limited, Donovan Commission, Employer Conciliation, Engineering Procedure Agreement, Green Book Procedure, Joint Conciliation, Labour-only Sub-contracting, Papermakers and Boardmakers, Employers Federation of, Power Loading Agreements, Referable Dispute.

Marsh, A.I. and Staples, J.W., *Check-off Agreements in Britain,* Royal Commission on Trade Unions and Employers' Associations, Research Papers 8, 1968.
Check-off, Donovan Commission.

Marsh, A.I., 'The Contribution of Employers' Associations'; in Towers, B., Whittingham, T.G. and Gottschalk, A.W., *Bargaining for Change: Productivity Bargaining and Industrial Relations,* Allen and Unwin, 1972.
Employers' Association, Productivity Bargaining.

Marshall, A., *Principles of Economics,* Macmillan, 8th ed., 1920, and 3rd ed., 1895.
Division of Labour, Higgling of the Market.

Martin, Roderick, *Communism and the British Trade Unions, 1924-1933,* Clarendon Press, Oxford, 1969.
National Minority Movement.

Marx, Karl, *Selected Writings in Sociology and Social Philosophy,* ed. Bottomore and Rubel, Penguin 1970.
Alienation.

Mason, Anthony, *The General Strike in the North East,* University of Hull, Occasional Paper in Economic and Social History, 1970.
General Strike.

Maynard, H.B., Stegemerten, G.J. and Schwab, J.L., *Methods-Time Measurement,* McGraw-Hill, 1940.
Predetermined Motion Time Systems.

Mayo, Elton, *The Human Problems of an Industrial Civilisation,* Macmillan, 1933.
Hawthorne Experiment, Industrial Conflict.

Mayo, Elton, *The Social Problems of an Industrial Civilisation,* Routledge and Kegan Paul, 1975.
Industrial Conflict.

Meeks, G., *Disappointing Marriage: A Study of Gains from Mergers,* CUP, 1977.
Multi-establishment Companies.

Mellish, M., *The Docks after Devlin,* Heinemann, 1972.
National Modernisation Committee.

Melman, S., *Decision-making and Productivity,* Blackwell, 1958.
Group Piece-work.

Mepham, G.J., *Problems of Equal Pay,* Institute of Personnel Management, 1969.
Equal Pay.

Merton, R.K., *Social Theory and Social Structure,* Collier-Macmillan 1968.
Anomie.

Messner, J., *Social Ethics,* Herder, 1965.
Catholic Industrial Relations Teaching.

Meyers, F., *'Right to Work' in Practice,* New York; The Fund for the Republic, 1959.
Closed Shop, Right to Work.

Meyers, F., *Ownership of Jobs,* Institute of Industrial Relations, University of California, Los Angeles, 1964.
Right to Work.

Michels, Robert, *Political Parties,* New York, International Library, Collier-Macmillan 1966.
Iron Law of Oligarchy.

Miles, L.D., *Techniques of Value Analysis and Engineering,* McGraw-Hill, 1961.
Value Analysis.

Millerson, G., *The Qualifying Associations,* Routledge and Kegan Paul, 1964.
Profession, Professional Association.

Mills, C.W., *White Collar: The American Middle Classes,* Galaxy, 1956.
Occupational Community.

Mills, H.A. and Brown, E. Clark, *From the Wagner Act to Taft-Hartley,* University of Chicago Press, 1950.
Unfair Labour Practices, Wagner Act.

Milne-Bailey, W., *Trade Union Documents,* G. Bell and Sons, 1929.
The Document, New Unionism.

Milward, G.E. (ed.), *Organisation and Methods: A Service to Management,* Macmillan, 1967.
Organisation and Methods (O and M).

Mitchell, G. Duncan, *A Dictionary of Sociology,* Routledge and Kegan Paul, 1968.
Action Research, Attitude.

Mitrofanov, S.P., *The Scientific Principles of Group Technology,* USSR, 1959.
Group Technology (GT).

Moonman, Jane, *The Effectiveness of Fringe Benefits in Industry,* Gower Press, 1973.
Fringe Benefits.

De Montgomery, B.G., *British and Continental Labour Policy,* 1912.
Garton Memorandum.

Moran, James, *NATSOPA, 75 Years,* OUP, 1964.
Operative Printers, Graphical and Media Personnel, National Society of.

Moran, M., *The Origin, Life and Death of the 1971 Industrial Relations Act,* Macmillan Press, 1977.
Industrial Relations Act 1971.

Moran, M., *The Union of Post Office Workers,* Macmillan, 1974.
Post Office Workers, Union of.

Moreby, D.H., *Personnel Management in Merchant Ships,* Pergamon Press, 1968.
Complaints Procedure, Dual-purpose Manning, Established Service Scheme, General Council of British Shipping, General Purpose Manning, Logging, Merchant Navy and Airline Officers' Association, National Maritime Board, Shipboard Liaison Representatives.

Morris, J.O., 'The Conflict within the AFL; A Study of Craft versus Industrial Unionism 1891-1938', *Cornell University Studies in Industrial and Labor Relations,* Vol. X, 1958.
American Federation of Labor.

Morris, Margaret, *The General Strike,* Penguin, 1976.
General Strike.

Morse, David. A., *The Origin and Evolution of the ILO and its Role in the World Community,* New York State School of Industrial and Labor Relations, Cornell University, Ithaca, New York, 1969.
International Labour Organisation.

Morse, Dean, *The Peripheral Worker,* Columbia University Press, 1969.
Peripheral Worker.

Mortimer, J.E., *A History of the Association of Engineering and Shipbuilding Draughtsmen,* AESD, 1960.
Corresponding Member, Draughtsmen's and Allied Technicians' Association, Strike-in-detail, Vacancy List.

Mortimer, J.E., *Trade Unions and Technological Change,* OUP, 1971.
Trade Union.

Mortimer, J.E., *A History of the Boilermakers' Society,* Allen and Unwin, 1973.
Boilermakers, Shipwrights and Structural Workers, Amalgamated Society of.

Morton, Bernard (ed.), *Action, 1919-1969,* Educare, 1969.
Schoolmasters and Union of Women Teachers, National Association of.

Mosses, W., *The History of the United Patternmakers' Association,* UPA, 1922.
Patternmakers and Allied Craftsmen, Association of, Trade Movement.

Mosses, W., *UPA: Seventy-Five Years Progress, 1872-1947,* UPA, 1947.
Patternmakers and Allied Craftsmen, Association of.

Motor Industry Joint Labour Council, *First Report,* December 1966, and *Second Report,* March 1968.
Motor Industry Joint Labour Council.

Mott, P.E. *et al., Shift Work: The Social Psychological and Physical Consequencies,* Ann Arbor, University of Michigan Press, 1965.
Moonlighting, Shift Working.

Moxon, G.R., *The Growth of Personnel Management in Great Britain during the War,* IPM, 1946.
Personnel Management, Institute of.

Moxon, Joseph, *Mechanick Exercises,* 1683, Martin Robertson, 3rd ed., 1970.
Chapel.

Mumford, Enid, *Job Satisfaction,* Longmans, 1972.
Job Satisfaction.

Mumford, Enid and Banks, Olive, *The Computer and the Clerk,* Routledge and Kegan Paul, 1967.
Automation.

Mundella, A.J., *Arbitration as a Means of Preventing Strikes,* Bradford, 1868.
Arbitration, Conciliation.

Munkman, J., *Employers' Liability at Common Law,* Butterworths, 8th ed., 1975.
Employers' Liability, Law Reform (Contributory Negligence) Act 1945.

Munns, V.G. and McCarthy, W.E.J., *Employers' Associations,* Royal Commission on Trade Unions and Employers' Associations, Research Papers 7, HMSO, 1967.
Employers' Association, Engineering Employers' Federation.

Murlis, H., *Employee Benefits Today,* Management Survey Report No. 19, BIM, 1974.
Fringe Benefits.

Murray, J.G., *The General Strike of 1926*, Lawrence and Wishart, 1951.
General Strike.

Murrell, K.F.H., *Ergonomics: Man in His Working Environment*, Chapman and Hall, 1971.
Ergonomics.

Musson, A.E., *The Typographical Association*, OUP, 1954.
Fat, Graphical Association, Illegal Men, National, Mixed Office, Open Shop, Slating, Stab, Turnover, Twicer, Unfair Houses.

Musson, A.E., *British Trade Unions, 1800-1875*, Macmillan, 1972.
Trade Union.

Myers, G. and Schultz, G.P., *The Dynamics of a Labor Market*, Prentice Hall, 1951.
Labour Market.

Nash, M., *The Sex Discrimination Act 1975: A Guide for Managers*, IPM, 1975.
Sex Discrimination Act, 1975.

National Institute of Industrial Psychology, *The Foreman: a Study of Supervision in British Industry*, Staples Press, 1951.
Supervisor.

National Institute of Industrial Psychology, *Joint Consultation in British Industry*, Staples Press, 1952.
Constructive Conflict, Joint Consultation, Negotiation, Paternalism, Suggestion Scheme.

National Union of Seamen, *The Story of the Seamen*, NUS, 1964.
Seamen, National Union of.

National Union of Boot and Shoe Operatives, *Fifty Years, the History of the National Union of Boot and Shoe Operatives 1874-1924*, NUBSO, 1924.
Boot and Shoe Operatives, National Union of.

National Union of Vehicle Builders, *A Hundred Years of Vehicle Building, 1834-1934*, NUVB, 1934.
Tramping, Vehicle Builders, National Union of.

National Union of Vehicle Builders, *NUVB: 1834-1959, One Hundred and Twenty Fifth Anniversary*, NUVB, 1959.
Vehicle Builders, National Union of.

Neumann-Duesberg, H., *Betriebsverfassungsrecht*, Berlin, 1960.
Betriebsräte.

Newman, A.D. and Rowbottom, R.W., *Organisation Analysis*, Heinemann, 1968.
Glacier Project.

Newman, Bernard, *Yours for Action*, Civil Service Clerical Association, 1953.
Civil and Public Services Association.

Newspaper Society, *The Provincial Newspaper Society*, 1886.
Newspaper Society.

Newspaper Society, *The Newspaper Society, 1836-1936*
Newspaper Society.

Newspaper Society, *Newspaper Society's 125 Years of Progress*, 1961.
Newspaper Society.

Niven, M.M., *Personnel Management, 1913-1963*, IPM, 1967.
Personnel Management, Institute of.

Norgren, Paul H., *The Swedish Collective Bargaining System*, 1941.
Fractional Bargaining.

North, D.T.B. and Buckingham, G.L., *Productivity Agreements and Wage Systems*, Gower Press, 1969.
Grievance, Negotiating Procedure.

Northrup, R., *Boulwarism*, University of Michigan, Ann Arbor, Michigan, 1964.
Boulwarism.

O'Brien, William, *Forth the Banners Go: Reminiscences of William O'Brien*, as told to Maclysaght, Edward, The Three Candles Ltd, 1969.
Tainted Goods.

Office of Health Economics, *Off Sick*, January, 1971.
Sickness Absence.

Office of Manpower Economics, *Equal Pay; First Report on the Implementation of the Equal Pay Act, 1970*, 1972.
Equal Pay.

Office of Manpower Economics, *Measured Daywork*, HMSO, 1972.
Measured Daywork.

Office of Manpower Economics, *Wage Drift*, HMSO, 1973.
Wage Drift.

Office of Manpower Economics, *Incremental Pay Systems*, HMSO, 1973.
Incremental Pay System.

Oldfield, F.E., *New Look Industrial Relations*, Mason Reed, 1966.
Blue Book, Productivity Bargaining.

O'Mahony, D., *Industrial Relations in Ireland; The Background*, The Economic Research Institute, Paper No. 19, May 1964.
Labour Court, Registered Agreement.

O'Mahony, David, *Economic Aspects of Industrial Relations*, The Economic Research Institute, Paper No. 24, February 1965.
Wage Rounds.

Oppenheim, A.N., *Questionnarie Design and Attitude Measurement*, Heinemann, 1968.
Attitude.

Page Arnot, R., *The Miners: A History of the Miners Federation of Great Britain*, Allen and Unwin, 1949.
Checkweigher, Miners, National Union of.

Page Arnot, R., *The Miners: The Years of Struggle*, Allen and Unwin, 1953.
Mineworkers, National Union of.

Page Arnot, R., *A History of the Scottish Miners from the Earliest Times*, Allen and Unwin, 1955.
Mineworkers, National Union of.

Page Arnot, R., *The Miners in Crisis and War*, Allen and Unwin, 1961.
Mineworkers, National Union of.

Page Arnot, R., *South Wales Miners, 1893-1914*, Allen and Unwin, 1967.
Mineworkers, National Union of.

Panayotopoulos, M., *Le Contrôle Judicaire du Liceniement dans le Droit des Pays Membres de la CEE et celui de la Grèce*, Paris, 1969.
Unfair Dismissal.

Parker, H.M.D., *Manpower*, HMSO, 1957.
Guaranteed Wage.

Parker, L.D., *The Reporting of Company Financial Results*, Institute of Chartered Accountants of England and Wales, 1977.
Employee Reports.

Parker, P.A.L., Hawes, W.R. and Lumb, A.L., *The Reform of Collective Bargaining at Plant and Company Level*, Department of Employment, Manpower Papers No. 5, HMSO, 1971.
Collective Agreement, Company Bargaining, One-step Agreement, Plant Bargaining.

Parker, S.R. *et al, Effects of the Redundancy Payments Act*, HMSO, 1971.
Redundancy Payments Act 1965.

Parnes, H.S., *Research on Labor Mobility*, American SSRC, 1954.
Labour Market, Labour Mobility.

Parris, H., *Staff Relations in the Civil Service*, Allen and Unwin, 1973.
Civil Service Arbitration Tribunal, Civil Sevice Pay Research Unit, Incomes Policies, Whitleyism.

Paterson, T.T., *Job Evaluation - Vol. 1, A New Method*, Business Books, 1972.
Castellion Method, Guide Chart Profile Method, Paterson Method.

Paterson, T.T., *A Manual for the Paterson Method*, Business Books, 1972.
Paterson Method.

Patterson, Sheila, *Immigrants in Industry*, OUP, 1968.
Race Relations Acts.

Paul, W.J. and Robertson, K.B., *Job Enrichment and Employee Motivation*, Gower Press, 1970.
Hygiene Factors, Job Enrichment.

Paulden, Sydney and Hawkins, Bill, *Whatever happened at Fairfields?* Gower Press, 1969.
Fairfields Experiment.

Pay Board, *Relativities*, Report No. 2, Cmnd. 5535, January 1974.
Pay Club, Relativities.

Payne, S.L., *The Art of Asking Questions*, Princeton University Press, 1951.
Attitude.

Pearson, N. Stewart, *The Offices, Shops and Railway Premises Act 1963* (2nd ed.), Charles Knight and Co., 1971.
Offices, Shops and Railway Premises Act 1963.

Perlman, R. (ed.), *Wage Determination, Market or Power Forces?* D.C. Heath and Co., 1964.
Bargaining Theory of Wages.

Pellegrini, J., *The Effects of the SET on British Manufacturing Industry*, Unpuelished PhD Thesis, University of London, 1972.
Sele ive Employment Tax.

Pelling, H., *A History of British Trade Unionism*, 3rd ed., Macmillan, 1976.
Trade Union.

Pelzer, Martin and Boer, Ralf, *Betriebsverfassungsgesetz (Labour Management Relations Act),* Fritz Knapp Verlag, Frankfurt am Main, 1977, 2nd ed. (in German and English).
Betriebungsräte.

Perkin, Harold, *Key Profession: The History of the Association of University Teachers,* Routledge and Kegan Paul, 1969.
University Treachers, Association of.

Peterson, Florence, *American Labor Unions,* New York; Harper, 1963.
Rival Unionism.

Pettman, B.O. (ed.), *Labour Turnover and Retention,* Gower Press, 1975.
Labour Turnover.

Phelps, Orme, W., *Union Security,* Institute of Industrial Relations, University of California, Los Angeles, 1953.
Union Security Clauses.

Phelps, Orme W., *Discipline and Discharge in the Unionised Firm,* University of California Press, 1959.
Disciplinary Procedure.

Phelps Brown, E.H., *The Growth of British Industrial Relations,* Macmillan, 1965.
Bedstead Alliance, Boards of Conciliaion and Arbitration, Con, General Federation of Trade Unions, Selling Price Sliding Scale, Umpire.

Phelps Brown, E.H. and Browne, Margaret H., *A Century of Pay: The Course of Pay and Production in France, Germany, Sweden, the United Kingdom and the United States of America,* Macmillan, 1968.
Differentials.

Pickstock, F.V., *British Railways. The Human Problem,* Fabian Research Series 142, 1950.
Local Departmental Committees.

Pigors, P. and F., *Human Aspects of Multiple Shift Operations,* Massachusetts Institute of Technology, 1944.
Shift Working.

Pigou, A.C., *The Theory of Unemployment,* Franc Caes 1968.
Cyclical Unemployment.

Pollock, F., *The Economic and Social Consequences of Automation,* Blackwell, 1957.
Automation.

Poor, Riva (ed.), *4 Days, 40 Hours,* Pan Books, 1972.
Four Day Week.

Pope Leo XIII, *Rerum Novarum,* 1891.
Catholic Industrial Relations Teaching.

Pope John XXIII, *Mater et Magistra,* 1961.
Catholic Industrial Relations Teaching.

Pope Paul VI, *Populorum Progressio,* 1967.
Catholic Industrial Relations Teaching.

Pope Pius XI, *Quadragesimo Anno,* 1931.
Catholic Industrial Relations Teaching.

Pope Pius XII, *La Solennita della Pentecoste,* 1941.
Catholic Industrial Relations Teaching.

Pornschlegel, H. and Birkwald, R., *Handbuch der Erholungszeitermittlung,* Cologne, Bund-Verlag, 1968.
Allowances.

Postgate, R., *The Builders' History,* 1923.
Building Industry, National Joint Council for the.

Post Office Engineering Union, *75 Years: A Short History of the Post Office Engineering Union,* 1962.
Post Office Engineering Union.

Potter, Beatrice, *The Co-operative Movement of Great Britain,* 1891.
Collective Bargaining.

Powell, L.H., *The Shipping Federation; A History of the First Sixty Years, 1890-1950,* Shipping Federation, 1950.
General Council of British Shipping.

Prandy, K., *Professional Employees,* Faber & Faber, 1965.
Profession, Professional Association.

Pribićević, B., *The Shop Stewards Movement and Workers' Control, 1910-1922,* Blackwell, 1959.
Engineering Employers' Federation, Guild Socialism, Industrial Unionism, Managerial Prerogatives, Post Office Workers, Union of, Shop Stewards Movement, Syndicalism, Wobblies, Workers' Control, Workers' Participation.

Pugh, Sir Arthur, *Men of Steel,* Iron and Steel Trades Confederation, 1951.
Brown Booklet Agreement, Contract System, Iron and Steel Trade Confederation, Melters' Sliding Scale, Selling-price Sliding Scales, Working Round.

Radford, Frederick, *Fetch the Engine,* Fire Brigades Union, 1950.
Fire Brigades Union.

Ralph, Chris, *The Picket and the Law;* Fabian Research Series 331, April 1977.
Picketing, Mass Picketing.

Randell, G.A., 'Job Analysis' in *Industrial Training Handbook,* ed. John W. Barber, Iliffe Books, 1968.
Job Analysis.

Randell, G.A., Packard, P.M.A., Shaw, R.L. and Slater, A.J., *Staff Appraisal,* Institute of Personnel Management (revised ed.) 1974.
Performance Appraisal.

Rankin, M.T., *Arbitration Principles and the Industrial Court,* P.S. King and Son, 1931.
Arbitration, Industrial Arbitration Board, Industrial Courts Act 1919.

Raven, A.D., *Profit Improvement by Value Analysis, Value Engineering and Purchase Price Analysis,* Cassell, 1971.
Value Analysis.

Reader, W.J., *The Weir Group, A Centenary History,* Weidenfeld and Nicolson, 1971.
Halsey Premium Bonus System.

Reder, Melvin W., Wage Determination in Theory and Practice; in Chamberlain, N.W., Pierson, Frank C. and Wolfson, Theresa (eds), *A Decade of Industrial Relations Research, 1946-1956,* Industrial Relations Research Association Publication No. 19, Harper, New York, 1958.
Wage Theories.

Reddaway, W.B. and Associates, *Effects of the Selective Employment Tax, Final Report*, CUP, 1973.
Selective Employment Tax.

Redgrave's *Factories Acts;* see Fife and Machin.

Reid, G.L. and Bates, J., 'The Cost of Fringe Benefits in British Industry'; in Reid, G.L. and Robertson, D.J. (eds), *Fringe Benefits, Labour Costs and Social Security*, Allen and Unwin, 1965.
Amulree Report, Fringe Benefits, Sick Pay Schemes.

Reid, G.L. and Robertson, D.J., *Fringe Benefits, Labour Costs and Social Security*, Allen and Unwin, 1965.
Fringe Benefits, Holidays with Pay.

Renold, Sir Charles, *Joint Consultation over 30 Years*, Allen and Unwin, 1950.
Works Councils.

Renshaw, Patrick, *The Wobblies*, Eyre and Spottiswoode, 1967.
Wobblies.

Revans, R.W., 'Human Relations, Management and Size'; in Hugh Jones, E.M. (ed.), *Human Relations and Modern Management*, Amsterdam, 1958.
Size-effect.

Reynolds, L., *The Structure of Labour Markets*, Harper, 1951.
Labour Market.

Reynolds, L.G. and Taft, G.H., *The Evolution of Wages Structure*, Yale University Press, 1956.
Share of Wages.

Rhee, H.A., *Office Automation in Social Perspective*, Blackwell and Mott, 1968.
Automation.

Rhenman, E., Strömberg, L. and Westerlund, G., *Conflict and Co-operation in Business Organisations*, Wiley-Interscience, 1970.
Line-staff Doctrine.

Richardson, J.H., *Industrial Relations in Great Britain*, Allen and Unwin, 1938.
Indemnity Fund.

Richardson, J.H., *Introduction to the Study of Industrial Relations*, Allen and Unwin, 1954.
Compulsory Arbitration.

Richardson, R., *Fair Pay and Work*, Heinemann, 1971.
Time-span.

Rideout, Roger W., *Principles of Labour Law*, 2nd ed. 1976.
Membership of a Trade Union.

Rideout, R.W., *The Right to Membership of a Trade Union*, University of London, the Athlone Press, 1963.
Right to Work.

Rideout, R.W., *The Practice and Procedure of the National Industrial Relations Court*, Sweet & Maxwell, 1973.
National Industrial Relations Court.

396

Rivett, P. and Ackoff, R.L., *A Manager's Guide to Operational Research,* Wiley, 1963.
Operational Research.

Roberts, B.C., *Trade Union Government and Administration in Great Britain,* London School of Economics 1956.
Trade Union.

Roberts, B.C., *The Trades Union Congress, 1868-1921,* Allen and Unwin, 1958.
Trades Councils, Trades Union Congress.

Roberts, B.C., Loveridge, Ray and Gennard, John, *Reluctant Militants,* Heinemann, 1972.
Professional Engineers, United Kingdom Association of, Technician.

Roberts, Bryn, *At the TUC,* National Union of Public Employees, 1947.
Public Employees, National Union of.

Roberts, Bryn, *The Price of TUC Leadership,* Allen and Unwin, 1961.
Public Employees, National Union of.

Roberts, Harold S., *Dictionary of Industrial Relations,* Bureau of National Affairs, 1966.
Blue Sky Bargaining, Gain Sharing Plans, Grievance, Lock-out, Manual Worker, Preferential Hiring, Presidential Seizure, Whipsawing.

Roberts, J.C.H., *ABC of Value Analysis,* Modern Management Techniques, 1967.
Value Analysis.

Robertson, D.J., *Factory Wage Structures and National Agreements,* CUP, 1960.
Bargaining Theory of Wages, Wage Structure.

Robertson, D.J., *The Economics of Wages and the Distribution of Income,* Macmillan, 1961.
Share of Wages, Wage Theories.

Robertson, D.J. and Hunter, L.C. (eds), *Labour Market Issues of the 1970s,* Oliver and Boyd, 1970.
Grade Creep, Productivity Bargaining.

Robertson, N. and Thomas, J.L., *Trade Unions and Industrial Relations,* Business Books, 1968.
Trade Union.

Robinson, Derek, *Incomes Policy and Capital Sharing in Europe,* Croom Helm, 1973.
Capital-sharing Schemes.

Robinson, D., *Non-Wage Incomes and Prices Policy, Report of a Trade Union Seminar,* Organisation for Economic Co-operation and Development, 1966.
Non-wage Incomes, Organisation for Economic Co-operation and Development.

Robinson, D., *Wage Drift, Fringe Benefits and Manpower Distribution,* Organisation for Economic Co-operation and Development, 1968.
Fringe Benefits, Organisation for Economic Co-operation and Development.

Robinson, D. (ed.), *Local Labour Markets and Wage Structures,* Gower Press, 1970.
Going Rate, Labour Market, Wage Structure.

Rodger, Alec, *The Seven Point Plan,* National Institute of Industrial Psychology, Paper No. 1, 3rd ed., 1970.
Seven Point Plan.

Roeber, J., *Steps to a New Social Contract*, Duckworth, 1974.
Manpower Utilisation and Payment Structure Agreement, Weekly Staff Agreement.

Roethlisberger, F.J. and Dickson, W.J., *Management and the Worker*, Harvard University Press, 1939.
Hawthorne Experiment.

Rogaly, Joe, *Grunwick*, Penguin Special, 1977.
Grunwick Dispute.

Rolph, C.H., *All Those in Favour? The ETU Trial*, André Deutsch, 1962.
Ballot Rigging.

Ross, A.M., *Trade Union Wage Policy*, University of California Press, 1948.
Bargaining Theory of Wages, Coercive Comparison, Marginal Productivity, Theory of, Labour Market, Wage Policy.

Ross, A.M. and Hartman, P.T., *Changing Patterns of Industrial Conflict*, John Wiley, 1960.
Strike.

Ross, N., 'Organised Labour and Management, The United Kingdom'; Chapter 5 n Hugh Jones, E.M. (ed.), *Human Relations and Modern Management*, North Holland Publishing Co., 1958.
Plural Society.

Routh, Guy, *Occupation and Pay in Great Britain, 1906-1960*, CUP, 1965.
Differentials, Felt-fair Pay.

Rowe, J.W.F., *Wages in Theory and Practice*, Routledge, 1928.
Marginal Productivity Theory of Wages.

Roy, Donald, 'Quota Restriction and Goldbricking in a Machine Shop'; in Lupton, Tom (ed.), *Payment Systems*, Penguin Modern Management Readings, 1972.
Goldbricking, Gravy Jobs, Quota Restriction.

Roy, Walter, *The Teachers' Union*, Schoolmaster Publishing Co., 1968.
Teachers, National Union of.

Rubin, J.Z. and Brown, B.R., *The Social Psychology of Bargaining and Negotiation*, Academic Press, 1975.
Negotiation.

Rubner, A., *Fringe Benefits: The Golden Chains*, Putnam, 1962.
Perks.

Sadler, P., *Social Research on Automation*, A Social Science Research Council Review, Heinemann, 1968.
Automation.

SAF, *The Condemned Piecework*, Svenska Arbetsgivareföreningen, 1970.
Incentive Payment Systems, Measured Daywork.

Salaman, Graeme, *Community and Occupation*, CUP, 1974.
Occupational Community.

Salz, Arthur, in *Man, Work and Society. A Reader in the Sociology of Occupations*, Form, W.H. and Nosow, S. (eds), Basic Books, 1962.
Occupation.

Samuel, P.J., *Labour Turnover? Towards a Solution*, Institute of Personnel Management, 1969.
Induction, Labour Turnover.

Samuels, H. and Stewart Pearson, N., *The Offices, Shops and Railway Premises Act, 1963*, 2nd ed., Charles Knight and Co., 1971.
Offices, Shops and Railway Premises Act 1963.

Sargeaunt, M.J., *Operational Research for Management*, Heinemann, 1965.
Organisation Behaviour.

Saunders, C.T., *Seasonal Variations in Employment*, Longmans, Green and Co., 1936.
Seasonal Unemployment.

Sawtell, R., *Sharing our Industrial Future*, Industrial Society, 1968.
Work Groups.

Sayles, L. and Chandler, M.K., *Managing Large Systems*, Harper and Row, 1971.
Organisational Behaviour.

Sayles, L.R. and Strauss, G., *The Local Union: Its Place in the Industrial Plant*, Harper, New York, 1953.
Local.

Sayles, L.R. and Strauss, G., *Human Behaviour in Organisations*, Prentice-Hall, 1966.
Grapevine.

Schaffer, Gordon, *Light and Liberty: Sixty Years with the Electrical Trades Union*, Electrical Trades Union, 1949.
Electrical, Electronic, Telecommunication and Plumbing Union.

Schein, E.H., *Process Consultation: Its Role in Organisation Development*, Addison-Wesley, 1969.
Organisation Development.

Schevenels, Walter, *Forty-Five Years, 1901-1945; International Federation of Trade Unions*, Brussels, Board of Trustees, 1956.
International Federation of Trade Unions.

Schotranger, H.J., *Staff Status for Manual Workers*, Industrial Society, 1967.
Mensualisation, Staff Status.

Scientific and Industrial Research, Department of, *Automation*, HMSO, 1956.
Automation.

Scopes, Frederick, *The Development of the Corby Works*, Stewarts and Lloyds Ltd, 1968.
Change of Practice Principle.

Scott, W.H., *Industrial Democracy; a Revaluation*, Liverpool University Press, 1955.
Industrial Democracy, Joint Consultation.

Scott, W.H., *Office Automation*, OECD, July 1965.
Organisation for Economic Co-operation and Development.

Scottish Trades Union Congress, *Submission to the Royal Commission on Trade Unions and Employers' Associations*, May, 1966.
Scottish Trades Union Congress.

Segur, A.B., *Manufacturing Industry*, 1927.
Predetermined Motion Time Systems.

Seidman, J., *Sit-Down*, League for Industrial Democracy, 1937.
Sit-down Strike.

Sellitz, C. *et al.*, *Research Methods in Social Relations*, Methuen, 1959. **Attitude.**

Sells, D.M., *The British Trade Board System*, P. S. King, 1923.
Trade Board Acts.

Sells, D.M., *British Wages Boards*, Brookings Institution, Washington DC, 1939.
Trade Board Acts.

Sessions, Mary, *The BFMP: How It Began*, William Sessions Ltd, 1950.
British Printing Industries' Federation.

Shadwell, A., *The Engineering Industry and the Crisis of 1922*, John Murray, 1922.
Engineering Employers' Federation, Managerial Prerogative.

Sharp, I.G., *Industrial Conciliation and Arbitration in Great Britain*, Allen and Unwin, 1950.
Building Industry, National Joint Council for the, Whitleyism.

Sherman, T.P., *O and M in Local Government*, Pergamon Press, 1969.
Organisation and Methods (O and M).

Shils, E.A., *Torment of Secrecy*, Heinemann, 1957. **Plural Society.**

Shimmin, Sylvia, *Payment by Results*, Staples Press, 1959.
Incentive Payment System.

Shimmin, Sylvia, 'Postscript - A 1968 Survey of Recent Literature'; Chapter X in Marriott, R., *Incentive Payment Systems*, Staples Press, 3rd ed. 1968.
Group Incentive Schemes.

Shipp, P.J. and Sutton, A.S., *A Study of the Statistics relating to Safety and Health at Work*, Committee on Safety and Health at Work Research Paper, 1972.
Accident, Robens Report.

Shuchman, Abraham, *Co-determination*, Public Affairs Press, Washington DC, 1957.
Co-determination.

Sidney, Elizabeth, *The Industrial Society*, 1918-1968.
The Industrial Society.

Silberman, C.E., *The Myths of Automation*, Harper and Row, 1966.
Technological Unemployment.

Simey, T.S. (ed.), *The Dockworker*, Liverpool University Press, 1954.
Floater.

Simmel, G., *Conflict*, Free Press, Glencoe, 1955.
Industrial Conflict.

Simmel, G., *The Sociology of Georg Simmel*, ed. K. H. Wolff, Collier-Macmillan, 1964.
Completeness.

Singleton, N., *Industrial Relations Procedures*, Department of Employment Manpower Paper No. 14, 1976.
Disputes Procedures.

Sisson, K., *Industrial Relations in Fleet Street*, Blackwell, 1975.
Newspaper Publishers' Association.

Slichter, S.H., *Union Policies and Industrial Management*, Brookings Institution, 1941.
Industrial Jurisprudence.

Slichter, S.H., Healy, J.J. and Livernash, E.R., *The Impact of Collective Bargaining on Management*, The Brookings Institution, Washington, 1960.
Measured Daywork.

Sloan, A., *The Story of the General Motors' Stike*, General Motors, April 1937.
Sit-down Strike.

Sloane, P.J., *Changing Patterns of Working Hours*, Department of Employment Manpower Paper No. 13, 1975.
Flexible Working Hours, Hours of Work.

Smith, Adam, *Wealth of Nations, 1776*, Everyman ed. 1910.
Division of Labour, Labour Market.

Smith, A.D., *Redundancy Practices in Four Countries*, OECD, October 1966.
Organisation for Economic Co-operation and Development.

Smith, E.J., *The New Trades Combination Movement*, 1899.
Bedstead Alliance.

Smith, J.H., *The University Teaching of Social Sciences: Industrial Sociology*, UNESCO, 1961.
Industrial Relations.

Smith, P., 'The Engineering Settlement'; in Coates, K., Topham, T. and Barratt Brown, *Trade Union Register*, Merlin Press, 1969.
Engineering Package Deal Agreement.

Smith, P.B., *Improving Skills in Working with People*, Department of Employment and Productivity, Training Information Paper 4, HMSO, 1969.
T Group.

Smith, P.B., 'Why Successful Groups Succeed: The Implications of T-Group Research'; in Cooper, C.L. (ed.), *Developing Social Skills in Management*, Macmillan, 1976.
T Group.

Snow, C.P., *The Two Cultures and the Scientific Revolution*, CUP, 1959.
Scientific Management.

Society of Labour Lawyers, *Occupational Accidents and the Law*, Fabian Research Series 280, Jan. 1970.
Robens Report.

Sorel, G., *Reflections on Violence*, Collier-Macmillan, 1961.
Industrial Conflict.

Speirs, M., *One Hundred Years of a Small Trade Union; A History of the Card Setting Machine Tenters' Society*, CSMTS, 1972.
Card Setting Machine Tenters' Society.

Spoor, Alec, *White Collar Union; Sixty Years of NALGO*, Heinemann, 1967.
Industrial Disputes Tribunal, National and Local Government Officers' Association.

Spyropoulos, G., *Les Finances des Syndicats Européens*, ILO, 1958.
Trade Union Contributions.

Stagner, Ross and Rosen, Hjalmar, *The Psychology of Union Management Relations*, Tavistock, 1965.
Mediation.

Stainer, Gareth, *Manpower Planning,* Heinemann, 1971.
Manpower Planning.

Stamford, J.M., *Pay-Day Simplified,* Productivity Progress, Pergamon Press, March 1968.
Pay-day Simplification.

Statistical Office of the European Communities, *NACE: General Industrial Classification of Economic Activities within the European Communities,* Luxembourg, January 1970.
Nomenclature Générale des Activités des Communautés Européennes.

Stern, J.L., Rehmus, C.M., Loewenberg, J.J., Kasper, H. and Dennes, B.D., *Final Offer Arbitration,* Lexington Books, 1975.
Final Offer Arbitration.

Stewart, Margaret, *Frank Cousins, A Case Study,* Hutchinson, 1968.
Transport and General Workers' Union.

Stewart, Margaret and Hunter, Leslie, *The Needle is Threaded,* Heinemann, 1964.
Tailors and Garment Workers, National Union of.

Stocks, Mary, *The Workers' Educational Association, The First Fifty Years,* Allen and Unwin, 1953.
Workers' Educational Trade Union Committee.

Sturmthal, A. (ed.), *White Collar Trade Unions,* Urbana, University of Illinois Press, 1968.
Bureaucracy, White Collar Union.

Suchman, E.A., On Accident Behaviour; in *Behavioural Approaches to Accident Research,* Association for the Aid of Crippled Children, New York, 1961.
Accident.

Suthers, R.B., *The Story of NATSOPA,* NATSOPA, 1929.
Printers, Graphical and Media Personnel, National Society of Operative.

Symons, J., *The General Strike,* Cresset Press, 1957.
General Strike.

Tabb, J.Y. and Goldfarb, A., *Workers' Participation in Management,* Pergamon Press, 1970.
Workers' Self-management.

Taft, Philip, *The AF of L from the Death of Compers to the Merger,* Harper, 1959.
American Federation of Labor.

Taylor, Eric, *The Better Temper, a commemorative history of the Midland Iron and Steel Wages Board 1876-1976,* ISTC, 1976.
Midland Iron and Steel Wages Board.

Taylor, F.W., *The Principles of Scientific Management,* Harper, 1911.
Scientific Management.

Taylor, J.K.L., *Attitudes and Methods of Communication and Consultation between Employers and Workers at Individual Firm Level,* Organisation for Economic Co-operation and Development, 1962.
Communications.

Temperley, R., *Merchant Shipping Acts,* Stevens, 3rd ed. 1976.
List System, Merchant Shipping Act 1894.

Thakur, M., *O.D.: The Search for Identity*, Information Report 16, IPM, 1974.
                                                    Organisation Development.

Thomas, G., *Labour Mobility in Britain, 1945-1949*, Social Survey Report 134.
                                                    Labour Mobility.

Thomas G., Bowen, *Manpower Problems in the Service Sector*, Organisation for Economic Co-operation and Development, 1967.
                    Organisation for Economic Co-operation and Development.

Thomas, R., *An Exercise in Redeployment*, Pergamon Press, 1969.
                                                    Redeployment.

Thomason, G., *A Textbook of Personnel Management*, IPM, 1975.
                                                    Personnel Management.

Thompson, F. (ed.), *The IWW - Its First Fifty Years, 1905-1955*, IWW. 1955.
                                                    Wobblies.

Thomson, A.W.J. and Engleman, S.R., *The Industrial Relations Act*, Martin Robertson, 1975.
                        Industrial Relations Act 1971, Level Amendments.

Thurley, K.E. and Hamlin, A.C., *The Supervisor and His Job*, Problems of Progress in Industry, No. 13, HMSO, 1963.
                                                    Supervisor.

Thurley, K.E. and Wirdenius, H., *Supervision: A Reappraisal*, Heinemann, 1973.
                                                    Supervisor.

Totten, Malcolm, *Founded in Brass: The First Hundred Years of the National Society of Metal Mechanics*, NSMM, 1972.
                            Metal Mechanics, National Society of.

Towers, B., Whittingham, T.G. and Gottschalk, A., *Bargaining for Change*, Allen and Unwin, 1972.
                                            Employers' Association.

Trades Union Congress, *The Book of the Martyrs of Tolpuddle*, 1934.
                                            Tolpuddle Martyrs.

Trades Union Congress, *Report*, TUC, 1946.
                                                    Closed Shop.

Trades Union Congress, *Trade Union Structure and Closer Unity*, TUC, Final Report, 1947.
Amalgamation, Class Unionism, Federation, Recognition of Cards, Spheres of Influence Agreement.

Trades Union Congress, *The Share of, Production Plan*, 1959.
                                        Share of Production Plan.

Trades Union Congress, *Report on Disputes and Workshop Representation*, TUC Report, 1960.
                    Combine Committee, Shop Steward, Status Quo.

Trades Union Congress, *TUC Report*, 1961.
                                                    Ballot Rigging.

Trades Union Congress, *An Outline of Job Evaluation and Merit Rating*, 1964.
                                                    Job Evaluation.

Trades Union Congress, *Relations Between Unions*, TUC, 1964.
Bridlington Agreement.

Trades Union Congress, *Trade Unionism*, Evidence to the Royal Commission on Trade Unions and Employers' Associations, 1966.
Amalgamation, Trade Union, Inter-union Disputes, Trades Union Congress.

Trades Union Congress, *Programme for Action*, 1969.
Status Quo.

Trades Union Congress, *Post Donovan Conference: Private Sector*, March 1969.
Exclusive Jurisdiction Agreement.

Trades Union Congress, *International Companies*, TUC, 1970.
Multinational Corporation.

Trades Union Congress, *The Chequers and Downing Street Talks*, TUC, November 1972.
Chequers and Downing Street Talks.

Trades Union Congress, *Industrial Democracy*, 1974.
Worker Directors.

Trades Union Congress, *Trades Councils Guide*, (rev. ed.) January 1976.
Trades Councils.

Trades Union Congress, *Homeworking*, 1978.
Homeworking.

Transport and General Workers' Union, *Unity, Strength, Progress, The Story of the Transport and General Workers' Union*, TGWU, 1967.
Transport and General Workers' Union.

Trow, Martin A. and Coleman, James S., *Union Democracy: The Internal Politics of the International Typographical Association*, Glencoe, The Free Press, 1956.
Iron Law of Oligarchy.

Tuckett, Angela, *The Scottish Carter*, Allen and Unwin, 1967.
Commercial Motormen's Union, Scottish.

Turner, Ben, *A Short History of the General Union of Textile Workers*, General Union of Textile Workers, 1920.
Dyers, Bleachers and Textile Workers, National Union of.

Turner, H.A., *Arbitration: A Study in Industrial Experience*, Fabian Research Series 153, 1952.
Arbitration, Conciliation, Industrial Courts Act 1919.

Turner, H.A., *Trade Union Growth, Structure and Policy*, Allen and Unwin, 1962.
Inter-union Disputes, Shop Steward, Open Union, Spinners and Twiners, Amalgamated Association of Operative Cotton; Textile and Allied Workers, National Union of, Trade Union, Typology of Trade Unions, Uniform List.

Turner, H.A., *Is Britain Really Strike Prone?*, CUP, 1969.
Industrial Dispute, Presidential Seizure, Strike.

Turner, H.A., Clack, Garfield and Roberts, Geoffrey. *Labour Relations in the Motor Industry*, Allen and Unwin, 1967.
Bellringer Dispute, Industrial Relations, McHugh Dispute.

Ulman, Lloyd and Flanagan, Robert J., *Wage Restraint: A Study of Incomes Policy in*

404

Western Europe, University of California Press, 1971.

Incomes Policy, Wage Restraint.

Union of Post Office Workers, *How We Began: Postal Trade Unionism, 1870-1920,* UPW, 1920.

Post Office Workers, Union of.

Union of Post Office Workers, *Official Recognition - How it was Gained,* UPW, n.d.

Post Office Workers, Union of.

United States Department of Labor, *Directory of World Federations of Trade Unions,* 1955.

World Federation of Trade Unions.

United States Department of Labor, *Analysis of Lay-off. Recall and Work Sharing Procedures in Union Contracts,* Washington DC; GPO Bulletin 1209, 1957.

Work Sharing.

United States Department of Labor, *Union Security and Check-off Provisions in Major Union Contracts, 1958-1959,* BLS Bulletin, No. 1272, 1960.

Union Security Clauses.

Unofficial Reform Committee of the South Wales Miners' Federation, *The Miners' Next Step,* Dent 1973.

Syndicalism.

Vall, M. van de, *Labour Organisations,* CUP, 1970.

Trade Union.

Verma, Pramod, 'The Chemical Industry'; in Lerner, S.W., Cable, J.R. and Gupta, S. (eds), *Workshop Wage Determination,* Pergamon Press, 1969.

Superstructure.

Vroom, V.H., *Work Motivation,* John Wiley and Sons, 1964.

Job Satisfaction.

Wabe, J. Stuart (ed.), *Problems in Manpower Forecasting,* Saxon House, 1974.

Manpower Planning.

Wall, Ernest, *Progressive Co-partnership,* Nisbet, 1921.

Co-partnership.

Walker, Geoffrey, *Pay Research in the Civil Service,* National and Local Government Officers' Association, TUE 6, 1968.

Analogue, True Money Rate, Quantifiable Emoluments.

Walton, R.D., *Interpersonal Peacemaking: Confrontation and Third Party Consultation,* Addison-Wesley, 1969.

Organisation Development.

Walton, Richard E. and McKersie, Robert B., *A Behavioral Theory of Labor Negotiations,* McGraw-Hill, 1965.

Attitudinal Structuring, Collective Bargaining, Distributive Bargaining, Integrative Bargaining, Intraorganisational Bargaining, Negotiation.

Warburton, W.H., *History of Trade Union Organisations in the Potteries,* Unwin Brothers Ltd, 1931.

Ceramic and Allied Trades Union.

Ward, George, *Fort Grunwick,* Maurice Temple Smith, December 1977.

Grunwick Dispute.

Ware, Norman J., *Labor in Modern Industrial Society*, D. C. Heath and Co., Boston, 1935.
Paternalism.

Watson, Tony J., *The Personnel Managers*, Routledge and Kegan Paul, 1977.
Personnel Management.

Webb, Sidney J., *The Story of the Durham Miners, 1662-1921*, Fabian Society, 1921.
Mineworkers, National Union of.

Webb, Sidney and Beatrice, *Industrial Democracy*, 1898.
Autonomous Regulation, Collective Bargaining, Common Rule, Conciliation, Federation, Higgling of the Market, Individual Bargaining, Industrial Democracy, Legal Enactment, Strike-in-detail, Umpire.

Webb, Sidney and Beatrice, *History of Trade Unionism, 1666-1920*, 1920 ed.
Amalgamation, Craft Gilds, The Document, Dunedin Commission, Employmental Unionism, Ephemeral Unions, Erle Commission, Illegal Men, New Unionism, Rattening, Sheffield Outrages.

Webb, Sidney and Cox, Harold, *The Eight Hours Day*, Walter Scott, 1891.
Eight Hours Day Movement.

Wedderburn, D., *Redundancy and the Railwaymen*, CUP, 1965.
Redundancy.

Wedderburn, D., *Enterprise Planning for Change*, April 1968.
Organisation for Economic Co-operation and Development.

Wedderburn, K.W., *Cases and Materials on Labour Law*, CUP, 1967.
Bird v. British Celanese Ltd, Bonsor v. Musicians' Union, Contract of Service, Emerald Construction Co, Ltd v. Lowthian, Employers Liability, Faramus v. Film Artistes Association, Hanley v. Pease and Partners Ltd, Hornby v. Close, Ilford Agreement, Lee v. Showmen's Guild of Great Britain, Marshall v. English Electric Co. Ltd, Martin v. Scotish Transport and General Workers' Union, Nagle v. Fielding, Quinn v. Leatham, R. v. Bunn, Recognised Terms and Conditions, Schedule 11, Specific Performance, Spring v. National Amalgamated Stevedores and Dockers, Stratford and Son v. Lindley, Taff Vale Case.

Wedderburn, K.W., *The Worker and the Law*, 2nd ed., Pelican, 1971.
Ex Parte Injunction, Industrial Tribunals, Labour Law, Redundancy Payments Act 1965, Right to Work, Shop Clubs Act 1902, Truck Acts.

Wedderburn, K.W., Conflicts of Rights and Conflicts of Interest in Labor Disputes'; in Aaron, Benjamin (ed.), *Dispute Settlement Procedures in Five Western European Countries*, Institute of Industrial Relations, University of California, Los Angeles, 1969.
Rights Disputes, Wingmen.

Wedderburn, K.W. and Davies, P.L., *Employment Grievances and Disputes Procedures in Britain*, University of California Press, 1969.
Arbitration, Committee of Inquiry, Committee of Investigation, Conciliation, Conciliation Act 1896, Court of Inquiry, Disciplinary Procedure, Industrial Arbitration Board, Industrial Courts Act 1919, Industrial Tribunals, Injunction, Single Arbitrator.

Weekes, B., Mellish, M., Dickens, L. and Lloyd, J., *Industrial Relations and the Limits of Law*, Blackwell, 1975.
Closed Shop, Industrial Relations Act 1971.

Weiner, N., *Cybernetics or Control and Communication in the Animal and the Machine*, MIT Press, 1961.
Cybernetics.

Weinstein, Paul A. (ed.), *Featherbedding and Technological Change*, D. C. Heath & Co., Boston, 1965.
Featherbedding.

Weir, Mary (ed.), *Job Satisfaction*, Fontana, 1976.
Job Satisfaction.

Welbourne, E., *The Miners' Unions of Northumberland and Durham*, CUP, 1923.
Mineworkers, National Union of.

Wellens, John, *The Training Revolution*, Evans Bros, 1963.
Apprenticeship.

Wells, H.G., *Kipps*, 1905.
Living-in.

Welton, H., *The Third World War*, Pall Mall Press, 1959.
Strike.

White, L.D., *Whitley Councils in the British Civil Service*, Chicago University Press, 1933.
Supercut, Whiteleyism.

Whiteside, K., and Hank, G., *Industrial Tribunals*, Sweet and Maxwell, 1975.
Industrial Tribunals.

Whybrew, E.G., *Overtime Working in Britain*, Royal Commission on Trade Unions and Employers' Associations, Research Papers 9, 1968.
Donovan Commission, Overtime.

Whyte, W.F., *Money and Motivation*, Harper, 1955.
Incentive Payment System, Organisational Behaviour, Scientific Management.

Wigham, Eric, *The Power to Manage: A History of the Engineering Employers' Federation*, Macmillan, 1972.
Engineering Employers' Federation.

Williams, Gertrude, *Recruitment to Skilled Trades*, Routledge and Kegan Paul, 1957.
Apprenticeship, Improver.

Williams, Gertrude, *Apprenticeship in Europe*, Chapman and Hall, 1963.
Apprenticeship.

Williams, J.E., *The Derbyshire Miners*, Allen and Unwin, 1962.
Mineworkers, National Union of.

Williams, M.R., *Performance Appraisal in Management*, Heinemann, 1972.
Performance Appraisal

Williams, Raymond, *Communications*, Chatto and Windus, 1966, Penguin Books, 1968.
Communications.

Williamson and Harris, *Trends in Collective Bargaining*, New York, 1945.
Lock-out.

Wilson, David F., *Dockers*, Fontana/Collins, 1972.
Dock Labour Scheme, National Modernisation Committee.

Wilson, J. Havelock, *My Stormy Passage through Life*, Vol. I, Co-operative Press, 1925.
Seamen, National Union of.

Wilson, J.A., *A History of the Durham Miners' Association 1870-1904*, Veitch and Sons, Durham, 1907.
Mineworkers, National Union of.

Wilson, N.A.B., *On the Quality of Working Life*, Department of Employment Manpower Paper No. 7, June 1973.
Work Research Unit.

Wilson, P.A., *The Professions*, OUP, 1933.
Profession.

Wiseman, J., 'Occupational Pension Schemes'; in Reid, G.L. and Robertson, D.J. (eds), *Fringe Benefits, Labour Costs and Social Security*, Allen and Unwin, 1965.
Occupational Pension Schemes.

Wolff, A.D., *The Time Barrier to Personal Injuries Claims*, Butterworth, 1969.
Cartledge and others v. E. Jopling and Sons Ltd.

Woodward, J., *Industrial Organisation*, OUP, 1965.
Human Relations, Supervisor, Line-staff Doctrine, Organisational Behaviour.

Wootton, Barbara, *The Social Foundations of Wage Policy*, Allen and Unwin, 1962.
Marginal Productivity Theory of Wages, Tapering, Wage Policy.

Wright, P.L., *The Coloured Worker in British Industry*, OUP, 1968.
Race Relations Act.

Yates, M.L., *Wages and Labour Conditions in British Engineering*, Macdonald and Evans, 1937.
Lieu Rate.

Young, A.F., *Social Services in British Industry*, Routledge and Kegan Paul, 1968.
Workshop Practices, Youth Employment Service.

Young, K., *Personality and Problems of Adjustment*, Appleton-Century-Crofts, New York, 1952.
Anomie.

ARTICLES

Aikin, O.L., 'Go-slow or Work to Rule', *British Journal of Industrial Relations*, Vol. 1, No. 2, June 1963.

Work to Rule.

Alden, J., 'The Extent and Nature of Double-jobbing in Great Britain', *Industrial Relations Journal*, Vol. 8, No. 3, Autumn 1977.

Moonlighting.

Allen, V.L., 'Some Economic Aspects of Comuplsory Trade Unionism', *Oxford Economic Papers*, Vol. 6, No. 1, February 1954.

Closed Shop, Compulsory Trade Unionism.

Allen, William, 'Half-time Britain', *Sunday Times*, March 1st, 1964.

Under-employment.

Arbous, A.G. and Kerrich, J.E. 'Accident Statistics and the Concept of Accident Proneness', *Biometrics*, Vol. 7, No. 4, 1951.

Accident.

Armstrong, E.A.G., 'Minimum Wages in a Fully Employed City', *British Journal of Industrial Relations*, March 1966.

Wages Councils.

Armstrong, E.A.G., 'Wages Councils, Retail Distribution and the Concept of the "Cut-off"', *Industrial Relations Journal*, Vol. 2, No. 3, Autumn 1971.

Wages Councils.

Armstrong, E.A.G., 'Birmingham and some of its low-paid workers', *Manchester School*, December 1968.

Low Pay.

Backman, Jules, 'Red Circle Rates', *Labor Law Journal*, June 1961.

Personal Rate.

Bain, G.S. and Woolven, G.B., 'The Literature of Labour Economics and Industrial Relations, A guide to its Sources', *Industrial Relations Journal*, Summer 1970.
Bibliographies and Sources on Industrial Relations, British Journal of Industrial Relations, Industrial and Labor Relations Review, Industrial Relations, Industrial Relations Journal, Industrial Relations Research Bulletin, Management Studies, Journal of, Manchester School of Economic and Social Studies, Oxford Economic Papers, Oxford University Institute of Economics and Statistics Bulletin, Personnel Management, Personnel Review, Scottish Journal of Political Economy.

Bain, G.S. and Woolven, G.B., 'The Primary Materials of British Industrial Relations', *British Journal of Industrial Relations*, Vol. IX, No. 3, November 1971.
Bibliographies and Sources on Industrial Relations.

Baldwin, George B., 'Structural Reform in the British Miners' Union', *Quarterly Journal of Economics*, November 1953.

Mineworkers, National Union of.

Bancroft, G. and Garfinkle, S., 'Job Mobility in 1961', *Monthly Labor Review*, Vol. 86, 1963.

Occupational Mobility.

Banks, R.F. 'Long Term Agreements and Package Deals', *Industrial Welfare*, Vol. XLVII, October 1965.

Fixed-term Agreements.

Bayliss, F.J., *Industrial and Labor Relations Review*, Vol. 12, No. 1, October 1958.
National Minimum Wage.

Beaumont, P.B., 'Experience under The Fair Wages Resolution of 1946', *Industrial Relations Journal*, Vol. 8, No. 3, Autumn 1977.
Fair Wages Principle.

Bedolis, Robert A., 'The Steel Labor Agreem. , 1903', *Business Management Record*, December 1963.
Sabbatical Leave.

Behrend, Hilde, 'Absence and Labour Turnover in a Changing Economic Climate', *Occupational Psychology*, 1953.
Labour Turnover.

Behrend, Hilde, 'The Effort Bargain', *Industrial and Labor Relations Review*, July 1957.
Effort Bargain (Effort Bargaining).

Behrend, Hilde, 'Financial Incentives as a System Beliefs', *British Journal of Sociology*, June 1959.
Incentive Payment System.

Behrend, Hilde, 'A Fair Day's Work', *Scottish Journal of Political Economy*, Volume VIII, June 1961.
Fair Day's Work.

Behrend, Hilde, 'The Field of Industrial Relations', *British Journal of Industrial Relations*, Vol. 1, No. 3, October 1963.
Industrial Relations.

Behrend, Hilde, 'An Assessment of the Current Status of Incentive Schemes', *Journal of Industrial Relations*, October 1963.
Incentive Payment System.

Blackburn, R.M. and Prandy, K., 'White-Collar Unionism: A Conceptual Framework', *British Journal of Sociology*, XVI, June 1965.
Bureaucracy.

Blain, A.N.J. and Gennard, John, 'Industrial Relations Theory; A Critical Analysis', *British Journal of Industrial Relations*, Vol. VIII, No. 3, November 1970.
Industrial Relations.

Bosanquet, N. and Stephens, R.J., 'Another Look at Low Pay', *Journal of Social Policy*, January-July 1972.
Low Pay.

Bourne, Richard M., 'Wage Guarantees - a Re-examination', *Labor Law Journal*, February 1960.
Guaranteed Annual Wage.

Bowlby, R.L., 'Union Policy Toward Minimum Wage Legislation in Post-War Britain', *Industrial and Labor Relations Review*, Vol. 11, No. 11, October 1957.
National Minimum Wage.

Bragan, F.A. and Hamel, H.R., 'Multiple Job Holders in May 1963', *Monthly Labor Review*, March 1964.
Moonlighting.

Brown, A.J., 'Further Analysis of the Supply of Labour to the Firm', *Journal of Management Studies*, Vol. 8, No. 3, October 1971.
Labour Market.

Brown, William, 'A Consideration of Custom and Practice', *British Journal of Industrial Relations,* Vol. X, No. 1, March 1972.

Custom and Practice.

Buzzard, R.B., 'Attendance and Absence in Industry; the Nature of the Evidence', *British Journal of Sociology,* Vol. 5, No. 3, 1954.

Absence.

Campbell, C. and R., 'State' Minimum Wage Laws as a Cause of Unemployment', *Southern Economic Journal,* 1969.

National Minimum Wage.

Cemach, H.P., 'Nos Nod Needed Now', *Office Management,* March 1957.

Nos Nod.

Clarke, R.O., 'The Dispute in the British Engineering Industry 1897-1898, An Evaluation', *Economica,* May, 1957.

Craft Control, Engineering Employers' Federation, Managerial Prerogatives.

Clegg, H.A., 'Come Consequences of the General Strike', *Manchester Statistical Society,* January 1954.

General Strike.

Clegg, H.A., 'The End of the IDT', *Personnel Management,* March 1959.

Industrial Disputes Tribunal.

Clegg, H.A., 'Pluralism in Industrial Relations', *British Journal of Industrial Relations,* Vol. XIII, No. 3, November 1975.

Plural Society.

Cohany, H.P. and Neary, J., 'Unaffiliated Local and Single-employer Unions in the United States', *Monthly Labor Review,* September 1962.

Independent Union.

Cooke, P.J.D., 'Learning Curves', *Management Today,* November 1967.

Learning Curves.

Crichton, Anne, 'Changes in the Status of the Personnel Officer since 1939', *Personnel Management,* December 1952.

Personnel Management, Institute of.

Crichton, Anne, 'The IPM in 1950 and 1960', *Personnel Management,* December 1961.

Personnel Management, Institute of.

Crichton, Anne and Collins, R.G., 'Personnel Specialists - A Count by Employers', *British Journal of Industrial Relations,* Vol. IV, No. 2, July 1966.

Personnel Management.

Dalton, Melville, 'The Industrial "Rate-buster"; a Characterisation', *Applied Anthropology,* Winter 1948.

Rate-buster.

Davies, Norah M., 'A Study of a Merit Rating Scheme', *Occupational Psychology,* 27, 1953.

Merit Rating.

Davies, P.L. and Anderman, S.D., 'Injunction Proceedings in Labour Disputes', *Industrial Law Journal,* Vol. 2, No. 1, December 1973.

Injunction.

Davies, P.L. 'Heaton Transport v. TGWU (1972)'; Casenote, *36 Modern Law Review,* 78, 1973.

Heaton Transport v. TGWU (1972).

Davis, L., 'The Design of Jobs', *Industrial Relations*, Vol. 6, 1966.

Job Design.

Deiter, J.C., 'Moonlighting and the Short Work Week', *South Western Social Science Quarterly*, December 1966.

Moonlighting.

Department of Employment and Productivity, 'Cost of Equal Pay', *Employment and Productivity Gazette*, Vol. LXXVIII, No. 1, January 1970.

Equal Pay.

Dickens, Linda, 'UKAPE: A Study of a Professional Union', *Industrial Relations Journal*, Vol. 3, No. 3, Autumn 1972.

Professional Engineers, United Kingdom Association of.

Dicks-Mireaux, L.A. and Shepherd, J.R., 'The Wage Structure and Some Implications for Incomes Policy', *National Institute Economic Review*, November 1962.

Wage Drift.

Donoughue, Bernard, 'Wages Policies in the Public Sector', *Planning*, PEP, Vol. XXVIII, No. 467, November 1962.

Pay Pause.

Drake, C.A., 'Accident Proneness: a hypothesis', *Character and Personality*, Vol. 8, 1942.

Accident.

Drake, Charles D., The Right to Picket Peacefully', *Industrial Law Journal*, Vol. I, No. 4, December 1972.

Picketing.

Dudra, Michael, 'Union Security in Canada', *Labor Law Journal*, July 1961.

Union Security Clauses.

Duffy, A.E.P., 'The Eight Hours Day Movement in Britain', *Manchester School*, September 1968.

Eight Hours Day Movement.

Durcan, J.W. and McCarthy, W.E.J., 'The State Subsidy Theory of Strikes', *British Journal of Industrial Relations*, Vol. XII, No. 1, March 1974.

State Subsidy Theory of Strikes.

Duysens, D., 'Work Permits - Department of Employment Control', *Industrial Law Journal*, Vol. 6, No. 2, June 1977.

Work Permit.

Eaton, J., Gill, C.R. and Morris, R.S., 'The Staffing of Industrial Relations Management in the Chemical Industry', *Chemistry and Industry*, 17, September 1977.

Personnel Management.

Engles, F., 'A fair day's wages for a fair day's work, the old time-honoured watch-word', *Labour Standard*, 7 May 1881.

Fair Day's Work.

Evans, E.O., 'Works Rules in Engineering', *Industrial Relations Journal*, Vol. 2, No. 1, Spring 1971.

Works Rules.

Fallick, J.L., 'The Growth of Top Salaries in the Post-war period', *Industrial Relations Journal*, Vol. 8, No. 3, Autumn 1977.

Review Bodies.

Farnham, D., 'The Association of Teachers in Technical Institutions (1904-14)', *International Review of Social History,* Vol. XIX, 1974, Part 3.
Teachers in Technical Institutions, Association of.

Flamholtz, Eric, 'Human Resource Accounting: A Review of Theory and Research', *Journal of Management Studies,* Vol. 11, No. 1, February 1974.
Human Resource Accounting.

Flanders, Allan, 'Measured Daywork and Collective Bargaining', *British Journal of Industrial Relations,* Vol. XI, No. 3, November 1973.
Measured Daywork.

Flanders, Allan, 'Wage Movements and Wage Policy in Postwar Britain', *Annals of the American Academy,* March 1957.
Ince Plan, Wage Restraint.

Flanders, Allan, 'How Dangerous is Productivity Bargaining?', *British Industry,* 18 March 1966.
Productivity Bargaining.

Flanders, Allan, 'Collective Bargaining: A Theoretical Analysis', *British Journal of Industrial Relations,* March 1968.
Collective Bargaining, Higgling of the Market, Individual Bargaining, Mutual Insurance.

Flanders, Allan, 'The Tradition of Voluntarism', *British Journal of Industrial Relations,* Vol. XII, No. 3, November 1974.
Voluntarism.

Fletcher, J., 'The Primary Materials of British Industrial Relations', *British Journal of Industrial Relations,* Vol. IX, No. 3, November 1971.
Bibliographies and Sources on Industrial Relations.

Fox, Alan and Flanders, Allan, 'The Reform of Industrial Relations, Donovan to Durkheim', *British Journal of Industrial Relations,* Vol. III, No. 2, July 1969.
Anomie, Norm.

Frankel, S.J., 'Arbitration in the British Civil Service', *Public Administration,* Vol. XXXVIII, 1960.
Civil Service Arbitration Tribunal, Civil Service Pay Research Unit, Incomes Policies.

Fryer, R.H., 'The Myths of the Redundancy Payments Act', *Industrial Law Journal,* March 1973.
Redundancy Payments Act 1965.

Fürstenberg, F., 'Workers' Participation in Management in the Federal Republic of Germany', *International Institute for Labour Studies Bulletin,* 6, June 1969.
Betriebsräte, Co-determination.

Gaselee, J., 'Points on Pensions', *The Manager,* September 1965.
Top Hat Pensions.

Gerstl, J., 'Determination of Occupational Community in High Status Occupations; *Sociological Quarterly,* 1961.
Occupational Community.

Gill, C., Morris, R.S. and Eaton, J., 'APST: the rise of a professional union', *Industrial Relations Journal,* Vol. 8, No. 1, Spring 1977.
Professional Scientists and Technologists, Association of.

Giuigni, G., 'Recent developments in collective bargaining in Italy', *International Labour Review,* Vol. 91, No. 4, April 1965.
Articulated Bargaining.

Goldstone, E., 'Executive Sabbaticals; about to take off?', *Harvard Business Review*, Sept./Oct. 1973.
Sabbatical Leave.

Goldthorpe, J.H. and Lockwood, D., 'Affluence and the British Class Structure', *Sociological Review*, Vol. II, No. 2, July 1963.
Embourgeoisement.

Goodman, J.F.B. and Krislov, J., 'Conciliation in industrial disputes in Great Britain: A survey of the attitudes of the parties', *British Journal of Industrial Relations*, Vol. XII, No. 3, November 1974.
Conciliation.

Goodman, J.F.R. and Thomson, G.M., 'Cost of Living Indexation Agreements in Post-War Collective Bargaining', *British Journal of Industrial Relations*, Vol. XI, No. 2, July 1973.
Cost-of-living Sliding Scale.

Gorfin, C.G., 'The Suggestion Scheme: A Contribution to Morale or an Economic Transaction?', *British Journal of Industrial Relations*, Vol. VII, No. 3, November 1969.
Suggestion Scheme.

Gowler, Dan, 'Determinants of the Supply of Labour to the Firm', *Journal of Management Studies*, Vol. 6, No. 1, February 1969.
Labour Market, Wage Disparity.

Gray, R.B., 'The Scanlon Plan - A Case Study', *British Journal of Industrial Relations*, Vol. IX, No. 3, November 1971.
Linwood Plan, Scanlon Plan.

Greenwood, E., 'Attributes of a Profession', *Social Work*, Vol. 2, July 1957.
Profession.

Hackman, J.R. and Lawler, E.E., 'Employee relations to job characteristics', *Journal of Applied Psychology*, Vol. 5, No. 3, 1971.
Expectancy Theory.

Hall, K. and Miller, I., 'Industrial Attitudes to Skills Dilution', *British Journal of Industrial Relations*, Vol. IX, No. 1, March 1971.
Dilution.

Handy, L.J., 'Absenteeism and Attendance in the British Coalmining Industry', *British Journal of Industrial Relations*, Vol. 6, No. 1, March 1968, pp. 27-50.
Absence.

Hanson, C.G., 'Profit Sharing Schemes in Great Britain', *Journal of Management Studies*, October 1965.
Profit Sharing.

Harbison, Frederick H., 'The General Motors-United Auto Workers Agreement of 1950', *Journal of Political Economy*, October 1950.
Annual Improvement Factor.

Harle, R., 'The Role of Trade Unions in Raising Productivity', *Political Quarterly*, January-March 1956.
Trade Union.

Harris, D.J., 'The European Social Charter', 13 *International and Comparative Law Quarterly*, 1964.
European Social Charter.

414

Hawkins, Kevin, 'The Decline of Voluntarism', *Industrial Relations Journal*, Summer 1971.
Voluntarism.

Hawkins, Kevin, 'Brewer-Licensee Relations: A Case Study in the Growth of Collective Bargaining and White Collar Militancy', *Industrial Relations Journal*, Spring 1972.
Licensed House Managers, National Association of.

Hay, E.N. and Purves, D., 'A New Method of Job Evaluation - the Guide Chart Profile Method', *Personnel*, Vol. 28, 1951.
Guide Chart Profile Method.

Hepple, Bob, 'Union Responsibility for Shop Stewards', *Industrial Law Journal*, Vol. 1, No. 4, December 1972.
Heaton Transport (St Helens) Ltd v. Transport and General Workers' Union, Shop Steward.

Herberg, Will, 'Bureaucracy and Democracy in Labor Unions', *Antioch Review*, III Fall 1943.
Iron Law of Oligarchy.

Herzberg, Frederick, 'One More Time: How do you Motivate Employees?', *Harvard Business Review*, January-February 1968.
Job Enrichment.

Hewitt, D. and Parfit, J., 'A Note on Working Morale and Size of Group', *Occupational Psychology*, Vol. 27, 1953.
Size-effect.

Hill, J.C., 'Stabilisation of Fringe Benefits', *Industrial and Labor Relations Review*, 7, 2.
Fringe Benefits.

Hill, T.P. and Knowles, K.G.J.C., 'The Variability of Engineering Earnings', *Bulletin of the Oxford University Institute of Statistics*, Vol. 18, No. 2, May 1956.
Pro Tanto Settlement.

Hirsch, Jr. John S., 'Strike Insurance and Collective Bargaining', *Industrial and Labor Relations Review*, Vol. 22, No. 3, April 1969.
Mutual Strike Aid.

Hobsbawn, E.J., 'General Labour Unions in Britain, 1889-1914', *Economic History Review* (2), 1, 2 and 3, 1948-1949.
New Unionism.

Hobsbawn, E.J., 'The Tramping Artisans', *Economic History Review*, Vol. III, No. 3, 1951.
Tramping.

Howells, R.W.L., 'The Robens Report', *Industrial Law Journal*, Vol. 1, No. 4, December 1972.
Robens Report.

Hughes, J.P.W., 'Sickness Absence Recording in Industry', *British Journal of Industrial Medicine*, Vol. 9, No. 4, 1952.
Absence.

Hunt, N.C., *The Director*, 1950.
Group Incentive Schemes.

Hunter, L.C., 'The State Subsidy Theory of Strikes; a reconsideration', *British Journal of Industrial Relations*, Vol. XII, No. 3, November 1974.
State Subsidy Theory of Strikes.

Hutchinson, John, 'The Constitution and Government of the AFL-CIO', *California Law Review,* December 1968.
American Federation of Labor - Congress of Industrial Organisations.

Hyman, R., 'Economic Motivation and Labour Stability', *British Journal of Industrial Relations,* Vol. VIII, No. 2, July 1970.
Labour Turnover.

International Labour Office, 'The Problem of Defining a Salaried Employee', *International Labour Review,* XXXVII, June 1938.
White Collar Worker.

International Labour Office, *Official Bulletin,* Vol. XXXVII, No. 4, 30 November 1954.
Freedom of Association.

Jenkins, Clive, 'Tiger in a White Collar?', *Penguin Survey of Business and Industry,* 1965.
Scientific, Technical and Managerial Staffs, Association of.

Jones, Aubrey, 'The Price of Prosperity', *The Observer, 1 November 1970.*
National Board for Prices and Incomes.

Kalis, P.J., 'The Bridlington Agreement and Awards of the TUC Disputes Committee', *Industrial Law Journal,* Vol. 5, No. 4, December 1976.
Rothwell v. APEX and Trades Union Congress (1976).

Karsh, Bernard and London, Jack, 'The Coal Miners: a Study in Union Control', *Quarterly Journal of Economics,* LXVIII, August 1954.
Iron Law of Oligarchy.

Kerr, Clark, 'Trade Unionism and Distributive Shares', *American Economic Review,* May 1954.
Share of Wages.

Knauft, E.B., 'A Classification and Evaluation of Personnel Rating Methods', *Journal of Applied Psychology,* 31, 1947.
Merit Rating.

Knowles, K.G.J.C. and Robinson, D., 'Wage Rounds and Wage Policy', *Oxford University Institute of Statistics Bulletin,* Vol. 24, No. 2, 1962.
Wage-rounds.

Knowles, K.G.J.C. and Thorne, E.M.F., 'Wage Rounds, 1948-1959', *Oxford University Institute of Statistics Bulletin,* Vol. 23, No. 1, February 1961.
Wage-rounds.

Laffer, Kingsley, 'Industrial Relations, Its Teaching and Scope; an Australian Experience', *International Institute for Labour Studies Bulletin,* November 1968.
Industrial Relations.

Lawler, Edward E., 'The Mythology of Management Compensation', *California Management Review,* 1966.
Cafeteria Wage Plan.

Lerner, S.W., 'The TUC Jurisdictional Dispute Settlement, 1924-1957', *Manchester School,* September 1968.
Bridlington Agreement.

Lerner, S.W. and Bescoby, J., 'Shop Steward Committees in the British Engineering Industry', *British Journal of Industrial Relations,* July 1966.
Combine Committee.

416

Lerner, S.W. and Marquand, J., 'Workshop Bargaining, Wage Drift and Productivity in the British Engineering Industry', *Manchester School,* January 1962.

Wage Drift.

Lerner, S.W. and Marquand, J., 'Regional Variations in Earnings, Demand for Labour and Shop Stewards Combine Committees in the British Engineering Industry', *Manchester School,* 1963.

Combine Committee.

Levinson, H., 'Pattern Bargaining; A Case Study of the Automobile Workers', *Quarterly Journal of Economics,* 1960.

Pattern Bargaining.

Lewis, Roy, 'The Legal Enforceability of Collective Agreements', *British Journal of Industrial Relations,* Vol. VIII, No. 3, November 1970.

Ford v. Amalgamated Engineering and Foundry Workers Union and others, Penalty Clauses.

Liddle, R.J. and McCarthy, W.E.J. 'The Impact of the Prices and Incomes Board on the Reform of Collective Bargaining', *British Journal of Industrial Relations,* Vol. X, No. 3, November 1972.

National Board for Prices and Incomes.

Lifson, K.A., 'Errors of Time-study Judgments of Industrial Work Pace', *Psychological Monogs',* 67, No. 5, 1953.

Standard Performance.

Likert, Rensis and Bowers, David G., 'Organisation Theory and Human Resource Accounting', *American Psychologist,* September 1968.

Human Resource Accounting.

Lipsey, R.G., 'The Relation between Unemployment and the Rate of Change of Money Wage Rates in the United Kingdom 1861-1957: A Further Analysis', *Economica,* Vol. 27, February 1960.

Phillips Curve.

Lipsey, R.G. and Parkin, J.M. 'Incomes Policy: A Reappraisal', Economica, May 1970.

Prices and Incomes Policy.

Loftus, P.J., 'Labour's Share in Manufacturing', *Lloyds Bank Review,* No. 92, April 1969.

Share of Wages.

Lupton, Tom, 'Systematic Soldiering', *The Listener,* 20 March 1960.

Soldiering.

Lupton, Tom, 'Methods of Wage Payment, Organisational Change and Motivation', *Work Study and Management,* December 1964.

Measured Daywork.

McCarthy, W.E.J., 'The Nature of Britain's Strike Problem', *British Journal of Industrial Relations,* Vol. VIII, No. 2, July 1970.

Industrial Dispute, Strike.

McCarthy, W.E.J. and Clifford, B.A., 'The Work of Industrial Courts of Inquiry', *British Journal of Industrial Relations,* Vol. IV, March 1966.

Court of Inquiry.

McCormick, Brian and Turner, H.A., 'The Legal Minimum Wage: an Experiment', *Manchester School,* Vol. XXV, No. 3, September 1957.

Tip.

McCormick, C.E., 'The Redundancy Payments Act in the Practice of the Industrial Tribunals', *British Journal of Industrial Relations*, Vol. VIII, No. 3, November 1970.
Industrial Tribunals.

McKersie, R.B., 'Productivity Bargaining: Deliverance or Delusion?', *Personnel Management*, Supplement, 1966.
One-shot Agreement.

Mackay, D.I., 'Redundancy and Re-engagement: A Study of Car Workers', *Manchester School*, Vol. 40, September 1972.
Shake-out.

Mangum, G.L., 'Are Wage Incentives Becoming Obsolete?', *Industrial Relations*, October 1962.
Incentive Payment System.

Margerison, C.J., 'What do we mean by Industrial Relations?', *British Journal of Industrial Relations*, Vol. VII, No. 2, July 1969.
Industrial Relations.

Marriott, R., 'An Exploratory Study of Merit Rating Systems in Three Factories', *Occupational Psychology*, 36, 1962.
Merit Rating.

Marsh, A.I., 'The Staffing of Industrial Relations Management in Engineering', *Industrial Relations Journal*, Summer 1971.
Engineering Procedure Agreement, Multi-establishment Company, Personnel Management.

Marsh, A.I. and Coker, E.E., 'Shop Steward Organisation in the Engineering Industry', *British Journal of Industrial Relations*, June 1963.
Shop Steward.

Marsh, Arthur and Cope, Peter, 'The Anatomy of Trade Union Benefits in the 1960's', *Industrial Relations Journal*, Summer 1970.
Death Benefit, Dowry Grant, Friendly Benefits, Mutual Insurance, Retirement Benefits, Sickness Benefits, Superannuation, Tool Benefit, Trade Benefits, Unemployment Benefit, Victimisation Benefit, Trade Union Contributions.

Marsh, A.I. and Jones, R.S., 'Engineering Procedure and Central Conference at York in 1959', *British Journal of Industrial Relations*, June 1964.
Employer Conciliation, Engineering Procedure Agreement, Union Reference.

Marsh, A.I. and Rosewell, R., 'A Question of Disclosure', *Industrial Relations Journal*, Vol. 7, No. 2, Summer 1976.
Disclosure of Information.

Marsh, A.I. and Speirs, M., 'The General Federation of Trade Unions, 1945-1970', *Industrial Relations Journal*, Vol. 2, No. 3, Autumn 1971.
General Federation of Trade Unions.

Matthew, T.U., 'The Accuracy and Use of Time Study', *Operational Research Quarterly*, 6, 1955.
Standard Performance.

Melchett, Lord, 'Shop Floor Directors', *The Spectator*, 26 April 1968.
Worker Directors.

Metcalf, David and Richardson, Ray, 'The Nature and Measurement of Unemployment in the U.K.', *Three Banks Review*, No. 93, March 1972.
Concealed Unemployment.

Miller, R.L., '"Right-to-work" laws and compulsory union membership in the United States', *British Journal of Industrial Relations*, Vol. XIV, No. 2, July 1976.
Right to Work.

Mills, A.J., 'Factory Work-ins', *New Society*, 22 August 1974.
Work-in.

Milward, N. and McQueeney, J., 'The industrial effects of mergers and takeovers', *Department of Employment Gazette*, September 1977.
Multi-establishment Company.

Mogeridge, Basil, 'Militancy and Inter-Union Rivalries in British Shipping, 1911-1929', *International Review of Social Science*, Vol. 6, No. 3, 1961.
Seamen, National Union of.

Mortished, R.J.P., 'The Industrial Relations Act, 1946', *Public Administration in Ireland*, Vol. 11.
Labour Court.

Mumford, Enid, 'Job Satisfaction - A New Approach Derived from an Old Theory', *Sociological Review*, Vol. 18, No. 1, March 1970.
Job Satisfaction.

Napier, B., 'Working to Rule - A Breach of the Contract of Employment?', *Industrial Law Journal*, Vol. I, No.3, September 1972.
Work-to-rule.

Peacock, A.T. and Ryan, W.J.L., 'Wage Claims and the Pace of Inflation', *Economic Journal*, June 1953.
Wage Restraint.

Pelling, Henry, 'The Knights of Labor in Britain, 1880-1901', *Economic History Review*, 2nd Series, Vol. 9, No. 2, December 1956.
Knights of Labor.

Pencavel, J.H., 'A Note on the Comparative Predictive Performance of Wage Inflation Models in the British Economy', *Economic Journal*, March 1971.
Phillips Curve.

Phelps Brown, E.H., 'The Importance of Works Agreements', *Personnel Management*, March 1960.
Whipsawing.

Phelps Brown, E.H., 'Wage Drift', *Economica*, 1962.
Wage Drift.

Phelps Brown, E.H. and Hart, P.E., 'The Share of Wages in National Income', *Economic Journal*, June 1952.
Share of Wages.

Phillips, A.W., 'The Relation Between Unemployment and the Rate of Change of Money Wage Rates in the United Kingdom 1861-1957', *Economica*, Vol. 25, November 1968.
Phillips Curve.

Price, James L., 'The Meaning of Turnover', *Industrial Relations Journal*, Vol. 6, No. 2, Winter 1975/6.
Labour turnover.

Price, R. and Bain, G.J., 'Union Growth Revisited', *British Journal of Industrial Relations*, Vol. XIV, No. 3, November 1976.
Union Density, White Collar Union.

Pym, D., 'Is There a Future for Wage Incentive Systems?', *British Journal of Industrial Relations,* November 1964.
Incentive Payment System.

Ramsey, J.C., 'Negotiating in a Multi-Plant Company', *Industrial Relations Journal,* Vol. 2, No. 2, Summer 1971.
Multi-establishment Company.

Reid, G.L., 'The Concept of Fringe Benefits', *Scottish Journal of Political Economy,* Vol. IX, 1962.
Fringe Benefits.

Revans, R.W., 'Industrial Morale and Size of Unit', *Political Quarterly,* Vol. 27, 1956.
Size-effect.

Rice, A.K., Hill, J.M.M. and Trist, E.L. 'The Representation of Labour Turnover as a Social Process', *Human Relations,* Vol. 3, No. 4, 1950.
Induction Crisis, Labour Turnover.

Rideout, R.W., 'The Content of Trade Union Disciplinary Rules', *British Journal of Industrial Relations,* Vol. 3, July 1965.
Membership of a Trade Union.

Rideout, R.W., 'The Content of Trade Union Rules Regulating Admission', *British Journal of Industrial Relations,* Vol. 4, March 1966.
Membership of a Trade Union.

Rideout, R.W., 'Admission to Non-Statutory Associations Controlling Employment', 30 *Modern Law Review,* 1967.
Membership of a Trade Union.

Rideout, R.W., 'The Industrial Tribunals', *Current Legal Problems,* 1968.
Industrial Tribunals.

Rideout, R.W. 'Edwards v. Sogat', *Federation News,* Vol. 20, No. 4, October 1970.
Edwards v. Society of Graphical and Allied Trades.

Roberts, B.C., 'Multinational Collective Bargaining: A European Prospect', *British Journal of Industrial Relations,* March 1973.
Multinational Corporation.

Roberts, B.C. and Gennard, John, 'Trends in Plant and Company Bargaining', *Scottish Journal of Political Economy,* Vol. XVII, No. 2, June 1970.
Company Bargaining, Plant Bargaining, Productivity Bargaining.

Roberts, B.C. and May, J., 'The Response of Multinational Enterprises to International Trade Union Pressure', *British Journal of Industrial Relations,* November 1974.
Multinational Corporation.

Robinson, D., 'Myths of the Local Labour Market', *Personnel,* Vol. 1, No. 1, 1967.
Labour Market.

Robinson, D., 'Low Paid Workers and Incomes Policy', *Bulletin of the Oxford University Institute of Statistics,* Vol. 29, No. 1, February 1967.
National Minimum Wage.

Rodgers, W. and Hammersley, J., 'The Consistency of Stop-Watch Time-Study Practitioners', *Occupational Psychology,* 28, 1954.
Standard Performance.

Rogin, Michael, 'Voluntarism: The Political Functions of an Antipolitical Doctrine', *Industrial and Labor Relations Review,* July 1962.
Voluntarism.

Roy, Donald, 'Quota Restriction and Goldbricking in a Machine Shop', *American Journal of Sociology*, Vol. 67, No. 2, 1952.

Goldbricking, Gravy Jobs, Quota Restriction, Stinkers.

Rubner, A., 'A Working Definition of Fringe Wages', *Journal of Industrial Relations*, Sidney, Australia, November 1965.

Fringe Benefits.

Sales, W.H. and Davies, J.L., 'Introducing a new wage structure into coalmining', *Bulletin of the Oxford University Institute of Statistics*, August, 1957.

Grading, Personal Rate.

Sallis, H., 'Joint Consultation and Meetings of Primary Working Groups in Power Stations', *British Journal of Industrial Relations*, Vol. III.

Local Advisory Committee.

Scanlon, J.N., 'Profit Sharing under Collective Bargaining: Three Case Studies', *Industrial and Labor Relations Review*, October 1948.

Profit Sharing.

Seastone, Don A., 'The History of Guaranteed Wages and Employment', *Journal of Economic History*, Vol. 15, No. 2, 1955.

Guaranteed Annual Wage.

Seidman, Joel, London, Jack and Karsh, Bernard, 'Leadership in the Local Union', *American Journal of Sociology*, November 1950.

Local.

Shaw, Anne, 'Measured Daywork - a step towards a Salaried Workforce', *The Manager*, 32, 1964.

Measured Daywork.

Shimmin, Sylvia, 'Case Studies in Measured Daywork', *Personnel Magazine*, October 1966.

Measured Daywork.

Shulzinger, M.S., 'A Closer Look at Accident Proneness', *National Safety News*, Vol. 69, No. 6, 1954.

Accidents.

Silcock, H., 'The Phenomenon of Labour Turnover', *Journal of the Royal Statistical Society*, A. 117, 1954.

Labour Turnover.

Silcock, H., 'The recording and measurement of labour turnover', *Journal of the Institute of Personnel Management*, Vol. 37, No. 3, 1955.

Induction Crisis.

Silver, M., 'Recent British Strike Trends', *British Journal of Industrial Relations*, Vol. XI, No. 1, March 1973.

Strikes.

Sloane, Peter, J., 'The Labour Market in Professional Football', *British Journal of Industrial Realtions*, Vol. VII, No. 2, July 1969.

Retain and Transfer.

Sloane, P.J. and Chiplin, B., 'The Economic Consequences of the Equal Pay Act, 1970', *Industrial Relations Journal*, December 1970.

Equal Pay.

Speirs, M., 'The G.F.T.U. and the Future', *Federation News*, Vol. 22, No. 1, January 1972.

General Federation of Trade Unions.

Spielman, L., 'The Taft-Hartley Law. Its Effects on the Growth of the Labor Movement', *Labor Law Journal,* April 1962.
Taft-Hartley Act 1947.

Suchman, E.A. 'A Conceptual Analysis of the Accident Phenomenon', *Social Problems,* Vol. 8, No. 3, 1961.
Accident.

Summers, C.W., 'A Summary Evaluation of the Taft-Hartley Act', *Industrial and Labor Relations Review,* April 1958.
Taft-Hartley Act 1947.

Sykes, A.J.M., 'The Ideological Basis of Industrial Relations in Great Britain', *Management International,* 1965, Vol. 5, No. 6.
Right to Work.

Sykes, A.J.M., 'Trade Union Workshop Organisation in the Printing Industry - the Chapel', *Human Relations,* Vol. 13, No. 1, 1960.
Chapel.

Sykes, A.J.M., 'Navvies; their work attitudes', *Sociology* 3: 21-35.
Navvy.

Sykes, A.J.M., Navvies: their social relations', *Sociology* 3: 157-172.
Navvy.

Taft, Philip, 'On the Origins of Business Unionism', *Industrial and Labor Relations Review,* October 1963.
Business Unionism.

Talacchi, S., 'Organisational Size, Individual Attitudes and Behaviour', *Administrative Science Quarterly,* Vol. 5, 1960.
Size-effect.

Tannenbaum, Robert, 'Some Current Issues in Human Relations', *California Management Review,* Vol. II, No. 1, Fall 1959.
Human Relations.

Taylor, P.J., 'Some International Trends in Sickness Absence, 1950-1968', *British Medical Journal,* 4, 1969.
Sickness Absence.

Taylor, R., 'Pickets and the Law', *New Society,* 21 November 1974.
Picketing, Flying Pickets.

Theale, E.S., 'The Story of the Amalgamated Musicians' Union', *Musicians' Journal,* April 1929.
Musicians' Union.

Trade Union Research Unit, 'The Guaranteed Week', *Federation News,* October 1972.
Guaranteed Week.

Tripp, L. Reed, 'The Industrial Relations Discipline in American Universities', *Industrial and Labor Relations Review,* Vol. 17, No. 4, July 1964.
Industrial Relations.

Troy, Leo, 'Local Independent Unions and the American Labor Movement', *Industrial and Labor Relations Review,* April 1961.
Independent Union.

Tuerkheimer, Frank M., 'Strike Insurance and the Legality of Inter-Employer Economic

Aid under the Present Federal Legislation', *New York University Law Review*, Vol. 38, No. 126, January 1963.

Mutual Strike Aid.

Turner, H.A., 'Wages: Industry Rates, Workplace Rates and Wage Drift', *Manchester School*, May 1965.

Wage Drift.

Turner, H.A. and Wilkinson, Frank, 'Real Net Incomes and the Wage Explosion', *New Society*, 25 February 1971.

Wage Explosion.

Volker, D., 'NALGO's Affiliation to the TUC', *British Journal of Industrial Relations*, Vol. IV, No. 1, March 1966.

National and Local Government Officers' Association.

Walker, J., 'Shift Changes and Hours of Work', *Occupational Psychology*, Vol. 35, 1961.

Three Shift System.

Walker, J., 'Frequent Alterations of Shifts on Continuous Work', *Occupational Psychology*, Vol. 40, October 1966.

Three Shift System.

Wallington, P.T., 'Criminal Conspiracy and Industrial Conflict', *Industrial Law Journal*, June 1977.

Picketing.

Wallington, P.T., 'The Criminal Law Act 1977', *Industrial Law Journal*, March 1978.

Criminal Law Act 1977.

Warner, Malcolm, 'The Big Trade Unions: Militancy or Maturity?', *New Society*, 11 December 1969.

Iron Law of Oligarchy.

Warner, Malcolm, 'Towards Transcontinental Unions', *New Society*, 15 October 1970.

Multi-national Corporation.

Warner, Malcolm, 'An Organisation Profile of the Small Trade Union', *Industrial Relations Journal*, Winter 1972.

Occupational Interest Associations.

Warner, Malcolm and Donaldson, Lex, 'Dimensions of Organisation in Occupational Interest Associations', *Third Joint Conference on Industrial Relations and Manpower Organisation*, London, 21 December 1971.

Occupational Interest Associations.

Warren, Edgar L., 'The Role of Public Opinion in Relation to the Mediator', *Proceedings of the Fifth Annual Meeting, Industrial Relations Research Association.*

Mediation.

Weekes, B., 'Law and the Practice of the Closed Shop', *Industrial Law Journal*, Vol. 5, No. 4, December 1976.

Closed Shop, Compulsory Trade Unionism, Independent Review Committee.

Weisbard, S., 'Industrial Tribunals', *New Law Journal*, 1969.

Industrial Tribunals.

Weller, M.F., 'Seventy Years On - Inaugural Lecture at the Annual Conference of 1966', *International Journal of Nursing Studies*, Vol. 4, 1967.

Health Visitors Association.

Whybrew, E.G. 'Qualified Manpower: Statistical Sources', *Statistical News*, HMSO, May 1972.
Qualified Manpower.

Wilding, R.W.L., 'The Post-Fulton Programme, Strategy and Tactics', *Public Administration*, Vol. 48, Winter 1970.
Civil Service Department.

Wilensky, H.A., 'The Moonlighter: A Product of Relative Deprivation', *Industrial Relations*, Vol. 3, No. 1, October 1963.
Moonlighting.

Williams, D.E., 'Value Engineering - The Human Aspect', *Value Engineering*, 1969.
Value Engineering.

Wootton, Graham, 'Parties in Union Government: the AESD', *Political Studies*, Vol. IX, No. 2, June 1961.
Draughtsmen's and Allied Technicians' Association, Iron Law of Oligarchy, Trade Union.

Worthington, F., 'The Hatters', *Federation News*, Vol. 1, No. 2, 1951.
Felt Hatters and Allied Workers, Amalgamated Society of Journeymen.

Wyatt, S. and Marriott, R., 'Night Work and Shift Changes', *British Journal of Industrial Medicine*, July 1953.
Three Shift System.

Young, C.T., 'Suggestion Schemes, Boon or Bane?', *Personnel Journal*, Vol. 42, 1963.
Suggestion Scheme.